Encyclopedia
of the Environment
in American Literature

REFERENCE
ONLY

Encyclopedia of the Environment in American Literature

Edited by GEOFF HAMILTON
and BRIAN JONES

McFarland & Company, Inc., Publishers
Jefferson, North Carolina, and London

With thanks to Patricia Bostian for help in preparing this index.

LIBRARY OF CONGRESS CATALOGUING-IN-PUBLICATION DATA

Encyclopedia of the environment in American literature / edited by
Geoff Hamilton and Brian Jones.
p.   cm.
Includes bibliographical references and index.

ISBN 978-0-7864-6541-5
softcover : acid free paper ∞

1. American literature — History and criticism — Encyclopedias.
2. Environmental literature — United States — History and criticism —
Encyclopedias.   3. American literature — Bio-bibliography.
4. Environmental protection in literature.
5. Environmentalism in literature.   6. Nature in literature.
I. Hamilton, Geoff, editor of compilation.
II. Jones, Brian, 1959– editor of compilation.
PS169.E25E53 2013   810.9'3603—dc23   [B]   2012050318

BRITISH LIBRARY CATALOGUING DATA ARE AVAILABLE

Front cover image © 2013 Shutterstock

Manufactured in the United States of America

*McFarland & Company, Inc., Publishers
Box 611, Jefferson, North Carolina 28640
www.mcfarlandpub.com*

Table of Contents

Preface

The present work offers a sketch of the essential landscape of the American environmental imagination as conveyed through literature, from Native American creation myths, to works reflecting the early European encounters with this new environment and shifting frontier, to contemporary American writing. It is arranged by persons and topics in one sequence, with the authors' key works following the author entries. There are entries for special subjects of particular import, as well as for works the authorship of which is ill-defined or of less import than the work itself (e.g., the Bible).

Taken as a whole, this encyclopedia demonstrates the evolution of a complex dialogue between humankind and the American environment, as each has defined and redefined the other over time. As with any overview, it seeks to strike a balance between overinclusiveness and neglect, by focusing on the nodal points and essential relationships that define the most characteristic contours of the American landscape. This is intended to allow readers to navigate this landscape with some facility, sense its overall shape, and pursue any interests that lead away from the entries with the help of the book's machinery (of cross-references, further readings, bibliographical material, and so on).

The encyclopedia's focus is not on "environmental literature" *per se*, however that be defined, but rather on works that have unquestionably reflected and shaped the environmental imagination of Americans, from the most exploitative and rapacious plunderers selling nature for whatever it will fetch, to the most reverent, eco-sensitive admirers determined to protect nature from whoever would ill serve it. (Surely, there are few who think it does not need protection.) This is an encyclopedia of the *environment*, imagined and revealed in literature, not of *literature* on or about the environment.

Beyond these general aims, the choice of authors was governed by two principal criteria: that their work constituted one of the key points in the American environmental imagination (thus including a host of regional authors whose works may otherwise rest at the margins of the American canon), or that their work was so significant to the American imagination in general that it could not fail to shape that landscape, even indirectly, in the universal manner of great art.

Though the work's focus is literary, that term is understood to include oral accounts, poetry, fiction, and literary nonfiction — anything that has fundamentally shaped the American environmental imagination. The necessity of exclusions (for example, much of the science and mathematics of the environment) was reluctantly accepted by the editors, so that the work may serve its function as a map of this vast landscape.

Introduction

America stands in a peculiar, if not unique, relation to its natural surroundings. No nation on earth, perhaps, has defined itself so profoundly, for so long, or so intimately, in terms of its environment. This long, rich and complex process of self-definition (or rather mutual definition, of nature by humans, and humans by nature), begun even before the Pilgrim landing — in the thoughts and writings of European merchants, ideologues, adventurers and poets (think of Donne's "Oh my America!" in Elegy XIX) — continues today, and with even greater significance in the face of the urgent environmental issues confronting America in our time.

The authors and works represented within show the progression of the American environmental imagination, from the earliest (effectively *European*) voices in this environmental interaction, with the seminal "shapers" of America (and "the American") from Jefferson to Hemingway, to the most recent (to some, *un*–American) voices of environmental awareness. The overall sense one gets, when viewing the topic as a whole, is of a people, largely undefined at the outset, boundless in energy and potential, *unlearning* a series of ill-fated and often fatal assumptions regarding nature — from radical Calvinism and capitalism, through the rugged (and doomed, yet eternal) frontiersman, transcendentalism, and utopianism, to the modern dichotomies of alienation and embrace, mastery and subservience; yet, unlearning these in a strikingly interesting, imaginative, fruitful, and ultimately even *wise* manner.

The authors and works discussed here have been selected, then, not for their special sensitivity to or sympathy with the environment, but for their importance to America's historical conception of that environment, and of itself. Thus, the early exploitive, anthropocentric colonial agents such as Thomas Harriot or John Smith, selling the New World to the Old for as many shillings as it would fetch, or the social "managers" in Harry Harrison's dystopian fantasy *Make Room, Make Room,* speak beside and *to* America's ecocentric, sympathetic voices such as Barry Lopez, Gary Snyder or Richard Wright.

Just as some of nature's greatest wonders are the least noticed, as in the teeming microcosms of Pacific tidal-pools described by Ed Ricketts, or E.O. Wilson's ant colonies, so too some of the most important voices, voices of the land in all its local specificity and color, have been heard by few: *Susan* Fenimore Cooper, Mary Austin, Eliza Farnham, Caroline Stansbury Kirkland, Elizabeth Madox Roberts — the gender is not coincidental, since much of the hard-won wisdom aforementioned has come from women. Long after the European ego had first confronted the vast unknown of a new environment, had fought or feared it, had tried (and failed) in the transcendentalists to encompass and be one with it, had then slowly and grudgingly learned simply to *respect* it and to recognize itself, that lofty ego, as but one modest (though potentially destructive) *part* of it — at the very summit of this European wisdom, so hard won and tenuous even now, we find what the American Indians had always known:

that there is no earth without us (being wise), and no us without the earth.

Here, the poetry of Emily Dickinson and Mary Oliver, or the philosophy of Emerson and Thoreau, has more affinity with Ricketts' (or Robinson Jeffers') tidal-pools or Steinbeck's *Log from the Sea of Cortez* than with other poets, philosophers and travel authors. It is these lines of force and affinity that we seek to trace, and thus the encyclopedia might be used in two complementary ways: "spatially," following one theme or concern through the works of disparate authors from different periods (for this, the index); and temporally, tracing the evolution of that peculiarly American dialogue between people and the environment, from the instant of its inception to the present day.

THE ENCYCLOPEDIA

Abbey, Edward (1927–1989)

Author of 25 books of fiction and non-fiction mostly about the desert Southwest, Edward Abbey is best known as the author of *Desert Solitaire* (1968), alternately compared to *Walden* by Henry David Thoreau and *A Sand County Almanac* by Aldo Leopold. Abbey saw his second book *The Brave Cowboy* (1956) made into a movie in which he played a bit part as a Sheriff's deputy, and earned both fame and infamy as the author of *The Monkey Wrench Gang* (1975).

Edward Abbey was born to Paul and Mildred Abbey in Indiana, Pennsylvania, but grew up on what Abbey called a "sub-marginal farm" in Home, Pennsylvania. He first encountered the Southwest hitchhiking from coast to coast before being drafted into the Army near the end of World War II. Spared combat, he served in post-war Italy and patrolled the streets on a motorcycle named "Crash." After returning to the United States, he intermittently studied at the University of New Mexico in Albuquerque, and eventually earned a Master's degree in Philosophy. His thesis, "Anarchy and the Morality of Violence," was a harbinger of the themes that would pervade much of his work and philosophy: resisting the powerful, the greedy, and the forces of uncontrolled technology and consumerism that were, in his eyes, equally endangering the country, freedom, and the wilderness. By the time he graduated from the University of New Mexico he had published his first novel, the largely autobiographical *Jonathon Troy* (1954), and was at work on *The Brave Cowboy*. He attended graduate school at Yale University, but left after only one term, homesick for the Southwest.

Edward Abbey's landmark work is *Desert Solitaire: A Season in the Wilderness* (1968). Written over three seasons as a ranger in then Arches National Monument (now National Park), the work is a polemical memoir of a solitary ranger in an undeveloped park in Southwest Utah in the late 1950's, and intertwines fiction, non-fiction, philosophy and natural history in a passionate plea for the protection of the wilderness from developers, the government, and what he calls "industrial tourism." Abbey claims that people should enjoy wild places without the aid of cars and motorboats; visitors to the wilderness should walk or boat in ways that place them in direct contact with the natural world and all of the beauty and terror therein. Just a few years before *Desert Solitaire* was published, the Wilderness Act was signed into law, and protected vast tracts of wilderness from development. Although Abbey may have protested federal management of wilderness areas, the philosophy behind the Wilderness Act changed the way people viewed barren or unusable land. *Desert Solitaire* likewise changed the way people viewed the desert, and contains some of the most eloquent language ever written about the area that is now Arches and Canyonlands National Parks. It is also an impassioned plea for humans to reshape their relationship to the land and all of it inhabitants, in the spirit of *Walden* and *A Sand County Almanac*.

Abbey intensely disliked the anthropocentric attitudes prevalent in modern society, which viewed wilderness and wild creatures as intrinsically worthless or subservient, and he was one of the first to encourage direct action to defend them. In 1975 he published *The Monkey Wrench Gang*, a story about four friends who carry out a surreptitious campaign of "eco-sabotage" around the desert Southwest, disabling construction and logging machinery and damaging bridges. The novel popularized the idea of direct action to save wild places from development and destruction, and to protest the unchecked growth and power of giant corporations and bureaucracies. Partly in response to Abbey's work, groups such as EarthFirst! and the Earth Liberation Front emerged (The Conservation Movement), and carried out acts of industrial sabotage in direct defense of wild places in danger of development, logging, or mining. The book and its depicted acts of intentionally disabling equipment spawned the word "monkeywrenching," and Abbey himself was known to occasionally engage in his own acts of monkeywrenching, cutting down billboards and removing road surveying tape with friends.

Irascible, eloquent, uncompromising, and contradictory, Abbey was nonetheless so able and committed that "even when he was wrong he was almost right," as the poet GARY SNYDER once put it. Abbey disliked being called an environmentalist, a nature writer, or even a professional writer, insisting that he merely lived a life centered on writing and freedom. Over the course of his very active life, he embraced many issues that seemed to put him at odds with his environmentally conscious audience, harshly criticizing environmental groups, liberal movements, and tourism, while supporting gun rights, hunting, and restricted immigration. Still others took issue with his tendency to litter the roadside with beer cans, and Abbey defended this practice by stating that the road was more of a nuisance than beer cans. His work is easily misunderstood, with its often-sardonic tone, its tendency to embrace conflicting subjects, and its deft and often perplexing mixture of fact and fiction. But viewed as a whole, it may be seen as arguing, ultimately, for one simple and consistent claim: that anything which separates or distances us from the basic freedoms of life, as they play out in the wild world, deserves scorn and ridicule.

Most of his finest work may be found in his collections of literary non-fiction, *Abbey's Road* (1979), *Down the River* (1982), *Beyond the Wall* (1984), and *One Life at a Time, Please* (1988), which established Abbey as a major essayist and allowed him to collaborate with some of the finest nature photographers and environmental philosophers working in the field. Despite his notoriety, Abbey always held to his core beliefs, and in the background of even his finest, most unpolemical nature writing, lies an insistence on the active preservation of wild places as sites for rejuvenation and renewal in the face of an indifferent government and society.

To the end of his life, Edward Abbey maintained his stand to live and die as he wished, free from the intrusions of technology and bureaucracy. Suffering from an uncontrollable bleeding disorder, he had himself removed from the hospital and taken to the desert by his friends and family to die beside a campfire. Not passing in the night, he was moved to the writing cabin behind his house, where he died on March 14, 1989. After his death, he was placed in his sleeping bag and carried by friends and family many miles, over rugged terrain, to his final resting place hidden deep in the Sonoran Desert of Southern Arizona.—Michael Sims

BIBLIOGRAPHY

Abbey, Edward. *Confessions of a Barbarian: Selections from the Journals of Edward Abbey 1951–1989*. David Peterson, ed. New York: Little, Brown, 1994.
_____. *Desert Solitaire: A Season in the Wilderness*. New York: Ballantine, 1968.
_____. *The Monkey Wrench Gang*. New York: Avon, 1975.
_____. *Slumgullion Stew: An Edward Abbey Reader*. New York: E.P. Dutton, 1984.
Bishop, James, Jr. *Epitaph for a Desert Anarchist*. New York: Atheneum, 1994.
Hepworth, James, and Gregory McNamee, eds. *Resist Much, Obey Little: Some Notes on Edward Abbey*. Tuscon: Harbinger House, 1989.
Loeffler, Jack. *Adventures with Ed: A Portrait of Abbey*. Albuquerque: University of New Mexico Press, 2002.

Desert Solitaire: A Season in the Wilderness, Edward Abbey (1968)

Edward Abbey's *Desert Solitaire* is a work of nonfiction describing the author's three seasons as a Park Ranger in Arches National Monument (now National Park) near Moab, Utah. It was Abbey's first full-length work of non-fiction and, along with the novel THE MONKEY WRENCH GANG (1975), made him a cult hero for wilderness advocates and defenders in the Southwestern United States. The work is often compared to WALDEN by HENRY DAVID THOREAU, because it records the reflections of a solitary individual (in voluntary isolation) on the natural world and local culture, and is shaped by an overarching sense that people have lost the capacity to appreciate properly the completeness and wonder of the natural world under the constrictive influence of modern society. *Desert Solitaire* was one of many works of natural history and environmental writing that appeared in the late 1950's and 1960's, which ultimately resulted in a wave of environmental protection legislation such as the Wilderness Act in 1964, and the creation of the United States Environmental Protection Administration in 1970 (THE CONSERVATION MOVEMENT).

As a work of natural history, *Desert Solitaire* evokes the rugged and vast canyon landscape that many at the time thought an inappropriate place to visit or explore. Abbey, on the contrary, argues that the very ruggedness and harshness of the land generate a unique form of life, both tenacious and valuable, whether plant, animal, or human. In "Cliffrose and Bayonets," Abbey explains his preference for the desert landscape, "the strangeness and wonder of existence here, in the desert, [with] the comparative sparsity of the flora and fauna: life not crowded upon life as in other places but scattered abroad in spareness and simplicity, so that the living organism stands out bold and brave and vivid against the lifeless sand and barren rock. The extreme clarity of the desert light is equaled by the extreme individuation of desert life forms. Love flowers best in openness and freedom" (29). And here we can see, in outline, the central thematic core of all Abbey's work. As in the protagonists of his novels that preceded *Desert Solitaire*— Jonathon Troy in *Jonathon Troy* and Jack Burns in *The Brave Cowboy*— Abbey celebrates individuals whose character is hard, shaped by the winds of life, seeking freedom in lands and ideas far distant from city life. Many of the landscape and character sketches, adventure stories and musings in *Desert Solitaire* are centered on these ideas.

Abbey employs observations of the natural world as means not only to capture the wonders of the desert landscape, but to support his claim that the desert, with its limited resources, should not be developed. "There is no shortage of water in the desert, but exactly the right amount, a perfect ratio of water to rock, of water to sand, insuring that wide, free, open generous spacing among plants and animals, homes and towns and cities…. There is no lack of water here, unless you try to establish a city where no city should be" (145). The development of resources intensively consumed by humans but lacking in the desert results in wanton destruction of the landscape, habitat, and lifestyle of those who enjoy the relative isolation and sparseness of the desert. The alteration of the landscape to supply water to cities was first appearing around the time that Abbey began his work in Arches National Monument; in 1956, for example, construction began on the Glen Canyon Dam, which by 1966 would result in the inundation of the Glen Canyon on the Colorado River. Abbey's dim views of the construction of Glen Canyon Dam are detailed in the chapter "Down the River."

Despite the fact that Abbey was an employee of the National Parks System at the Arches, he reserved some of his most pointed criticism for the national parks administration, especially for its approach to the promotion of visitation. Wilderness and undeveloped parks such as Arches National Monument in the 1950's, offered urban dwellers the chance to experience the natural world on its own terms. The attitude of the National Parks System was different, however, and Arches, as well as many other Monuments and Parks in the Southwest, was under development pressure to improve visitor and vehicle access, with paved roads, modern campgrounds with restrooms, and visitors' centers. Abbey called this "Industrial Tourism" because it centered on the automobile and brought with it the same deleterious developmental pressures on the natural world that cities did. He faulted the Park Service for favoring this type of "accessible" development over its mission of preserving natural landscapes. He regarded the automobile as a "bloody tyrant," dictating the direction of park development, which "almost succeeded in strangling our cities"; and he worried that it will "also destroy our national parks" (59).

Beyond its obvious threat to the landscape, such "Industrial Tourism" was inherently destructive for Abbey, as it cheated the visitor of any real encounter with the natural world. The ideal vacation, he argued, is "out in the open…following the quiet trail through forest and mountains, bedding down at evening under the stars, when and where they feel like it" (59). The real work of the National Park Service should be to free visitors from automobiles, roads, and the trappings of civilization that alienate people from the wilderness. Not to do this, he claimed, runs counter to the original mission of the National Park Service, to preserve, unimpaired, the landscape for the enjoyment of future generations. "They are being robbed and robbing themselves," he wrote. "So long as they are unwilling to crawl out of their cars, they will not discover the treasures of the national parks and will never escape the turmoil of the urban-suburban complexes which they had hoped, presumably, to leave behind for awhile" (59). This type of experience, inside an automobile, cut off from the very thing that visitors had traveled to see, is not the kind of interaction that can yield the feeling of "loveliness and a quiet exultation" (15) which Abbey identifies with a true experience of nature.

Ultimately, *Desert Solitaire* is a kind of polemical memoir in which the authorial persona, the characters, and the landscape intertwine to reveal the paradoxical hardness and fragility of the desert, and the adaptation that must occur in order to thrive in such a harsh environment. Through this interaction, all of the participants are enriched in some way. The people in the landscape are transformed through a variety of experiences, some pleasant, some tragic. The landscape, as a catalyst of these experiences, becomes alive and immediate; the sky, land, plants, and animals acquire added value as critical elements in the human experience. And when this relationship is severed, whether in an automobile or through building a dam to inundate a landscape to provide water to a city, the alienation that occurs will often lead to environmental destruction. Once separated from the natural world, people are still more vulnerable to the exploitive practices and persuasions of self-serving developers. Recognizing and repairing the rift between people and the wilderness is the central message of *Desert Solitaire,* and the main reason that it continues to be a seminal touchstone and common starting point for studies of humanity's complex relationship to the natural world.— Michael Sims

BIBLIOGRAPHY

Abbey, Edward. *Confessions of a Barbarian: Selections from the Journals of Edward Abbey, 1951–1989.* David Peterson, ed. New York: Little, Brown, 1994.
_____. *Desert Solitaire: A Season in the Wilderness.* New York: McGraw-Hill, 1968.
_____. *Postcards from Ed: Dispatches and Salvos from an American Iconoclast.* David Peterson, ed. Minneapolis: Milkweed Editions, 2006.

The Monkey Wrench Gang, Edward Abbey (1975)

Edward Abbey's imaginatively compelling and socially influential *The Monkey Wrench Gang* focuses on four people from disparate backgrounds who band together to prevent or disrupt environmentally incursive operations by dismantling and destroying equipment and structures; in the words of the author, "Four little humans against the Glittering Tower of the Power Complex, Mega-Machine." The story is mostly set in Abbey's beloved "Four Corners" region of Arizona and Utah, and it popularized the notion of "monkeywrenching," imagining direct action in general, and ecological sabotage in particular, as viable and defensible means of environmental protection.

The book follows the exploits of four like-minded individuals brought together on a river trip, who decide to disable or destroy symbols of development such as power lines, railroads, construction equipment, and bridges. The four protagonists are separately and skilfully introduced, to represent a wide and sympathetic spectrum of American society. Seldom Seen Smith, an outfitter and owner of Back of Beyond Expeditions, provides in-depth knowledge of the area in which the group operates; George Washington Hayduke, a Vietnam veteran with a Special Forces background, coordinates operations and is the main protagonist of the group; Doc Sarvis, a physician with a successful practice in Albuquerque, New Mexico tends to be the eponymous gang's voice of reason, and also provides funding for its operations; Doc and his partner, Bonnie Abbzug, serve as lookouts for most of the operations.

The group meets during a river trip guided by Smith, during which they collectively bemoan the pace of development in the desert southwest, particularly the damming of the Colorado River by the Glen Canyon Dam. They decide to target machinery and infrastructure, but emphatically agree that no harm should be done to people. Though they are often, humanly, unsure about the absolute rightness of their intent (their internal debates are an important part of the novel's fabric and appeal), fateful actions nevertheless ensue. The first target is a road construction operation where the group disables machinery by cutting wires and cables, pouring syrup into fuel tanks, and sand into engines. Each subsequent operation is slightly more ambitious, and the group eventually attracts the attention of the law. The story's climax comes when the group attempts to destroy the White Canyon Bridge, but fails; a chase ensues and all the members of the gang are captured except for Hayduke, who becomes trapped on a cliff and appears to perish in a gunfight with local and state law enforcement.

Although not the first work to envision sabotage as a form of environmental activism, *The Monkey Wrench Gang* captured an increasingly eco-conscious public's imagination, and its imagined activism was soon emulated in reality. The notion of direct action, such as road blockades or tree sitting, in an effort to thwart developmental progress, or indeed, to protest against any dominant-culture's practice, may be traced at least as far back as THOREAU in America, and Gandhi in India. A satirical work about ecological sabotage, called *Ecotage!* was published in 1972, three years before the *The Monkey Wrench Gang*; and soon after, DAVE FOREMAN published *Ecodefense* (1985), while *Zodiac: An Ecological Thriller* (1988) by Neal Stephenson, more loosely inscribes a similar thematic.

After *The Monkey Wrench Gang* was published, in 1975, Abbey wrote in his journal, "Doubtless I'll be accused of a rash of crimes now. Every time some Boy Scout sugars a bulldozer, or shellacs an earthmover, they'll come looking for me. The men in blue, with their tiresome questions"; and indeed, Abbey's previous stature as the author of *DESERT SOLITAIRE* (1968) garnered ecological sabotage widespread attention it may not otherwise have received, ultimately inspiring a new generation of far-flung but singularly focused wilderness defenders who sought to prevent or disrupt logging, development, and other encroachments on the natural world.

In 1979, inspired by Abbey's work, a group of three friends, Dave Foreman, Howie Wolke, and Mike Roselle, formed a group whose slogan was, "No compromise in defense of Mother Earth"; and this group became the nucleus of the first direct-action environmental group, EARTHFIRST! (*see* THE CONSERVATION MOVEMENT). Originally envisaged as a non-violent direct action group, EarthFirst! initially drew attention to the pace and effects of environmental destruction by advancing a "no compromise" attitude to current scientific research; but soon became involved in monkeywrench activity in the burgeoning environmental civil disobedience movement, by organizing the first tree-sits in the Pacific Northwest, blocking logging roads, and engaging in large scale publicity stunts that highlighted environmental destruction in the name of profit or progress.

Along with the rise of EarthFirst! came Foreman's direct-action and ecotage manual, *Ecodefense: A Field Guide to Monkeywrenching*, a compilation of letters written to the *EarthFirst! Journal* concerning the mechanics of monkeywrenching. Much of the book's content is straight out of *The Monkey Wrench Gang*, and what is not directly traceable to Abbey's work, is clearly rooted in it. There are articles on the mainstays of direct-action environmental defense: tree-spiking, dismantling machinery, fence-cutting, ad-billboard trashing and revision; while other sections of the book discuss methods of *urban* monkeywrenching, such as condo-trashing, daylight actions against corporate offices, attacks on residences and automobiles, and computer sabotage.

A more nuanced and tangential, but no less significant outcome of the publication of *The Monkey Wrench Gang* was the popularization of the philosophy of "deep ecology." Developed by the Swiss philosopher Arne Naess about the same time Abbey was writing his book, this concept forms one of the key pillars in the philosophical foundations of the EarthFirst! movement. Deep ecology maintains that all elements of the natural world have inherent worth that deserves to be considered, appreciated, and defended; as such, it provided many environmental groups, otherwise widely varying in their character and aims, with a single, resonant and compelling motif, both for intellectual integration and political inspiration. While not a direct result of *The Monkey Wrench Gang*, it reflects both the informing animus of the work, and the shared conviction of its protagonists, that everything under the sun deserves the same consideration and respect that we properly accord to one another.

Ultimately, *The Monkey Wrench Gang* illustrates and inspires reverence for the natural world, articulated in the philosophy of deep ecology, and issues a clear and stirring call to defend that world with passion, courage and resourcefulness.—Michael Sims

BIBLIOGRAPHY

Abbey, Edward. *Confessions of a Barbarian: Selections from the Journals of Edward Abbey, 1951–1989*. David Peterson, ed. New York: Little, Brown, 1994.
_____. *The Monkey Wrench Gang*. New York: Lippencott, Williams, and Wilkins, 1975.
_____. *Postcards from Ed: Dispatches and Salvos from an American Iconoclast*. David Peterson, ed. Minneapolis: Milkweed Editions, 2006.
Foreman, Dave. *Confessions of an EcoWarrior*. New York: Harmony Books, 1991.
_____, and Bill Haywood, eds. *Ecodefense: A Field Guide to Monkeywrenching*. Tucson: Nedd Ludd Books, 1985.

The American Dream *see* Ideologies

American Gothic and the Environment

The attempt to create a truly American Gothic is as old as American literature itself. In 1799, Charles Brockden Brown, considered to be America's first professional author, wrote in the preface to his novel *Edgar Huntly* how he hoped to create a distinctly American form of the Gothic tale, one that differed from the European version of "puerile superstition and exploded manners, Gothic castles and chimeras." This new, American version would include "incidents of Indian hostility, and the perils of the Western wilderness." Implicit in Brown's words is the idea that this new Gothic would be rooted in the inseparable worlds of human society and the natural environment — ultimately, in the unstable but fecund borderline *between* them.

Despite Brown's efforts to create a distinctively *American* Gothic, there is no question that, 200 years after its genesis, similarities abound with its European counterpart; both versions of the Gothic trade in the shock of the profane and the sublimity of terror; both seek to explore the burdens of the past while fluctuating between conservative and liberal values toward revolution and change. In the European (especially British) Gothic, however, locations and plots were largely chosen based on their distance from the contemporary reader: Anglicans read about medieval Spanish monasteries with Satanic monks or banditti chasing lost aristocrats through the mountains of Italy. Even when works had a more contemporary setting, the presence of a malicious supernatural element created exotic distance from the British reader.

From the outset of the American Gothic, however, the pathologies explored were anchored to the American experiment and the American environment. In both of Brown's most widely read novels, *Wieland* and *Edgar Huntly*, a European stranger introduces chaotic and dangerous intellectual and religious elements into the lives of Americans in a frontier community. Isolated, with only their own judgment to guide them in matters of truth and morality, characters descend into anxiety and trauma; the revolutionary impulse finds its dark side in alienation and lack of authority. Brown, understanding that the American Gothic was inherently political, sent a copy of *Wieland* to President Jefferson as a warning of what could happen to the United States.

The expression of this particularly American anxiety is consistently found in the depiction of the natural landscape, thus fusing the political (including slavery), cultural, and environmental foundations of the country within the fabric of an American Gothic. In *Wieland* and *Edgar Huntly,* the characteristics of the frontier — the physical isolation, the ignorance of what lies beyond, and the threat of natives and animals alike — express the anxieties of the community. In the British Gothic an isolated woman wanders the halls of a medieval castle where she is trapped by a social usurper; in *Edgar Huntly* the titular character wanders the caves of the Pennsylvania frontier, trapped by Delaware Indians and marauding panthers.

Later Gothic authors such as WASHINGTON IRVING, NATHANIEL HAWTHORNE and HERMAN MELVILLE continued what Brown began. Irving's "The Legend of Sleepy Hollow," for instance, is centered on a haunting that emerges from the American soil: the dead settlers of Sleepy Hollow groan against the country's expansion, the Headless Horseman is the ghost of a German soldier of fortune from the Revolution, and the spot where Ichabod Crane flees the Horseman is also the spot where Major Andre, who assisted Benedict Arnold's betrayal, was hanged. The ghosts the environment emanates are particular to the American experience. When Hawthorne reimagines the Puritan communities of his heritage (*THE SCARLET LETTER,* "The Maypole of Merry-Mount," "YOUNG GOODMAN BROWN," etc.), the untamed wilderness becomes the expression of the Puritans' most profane desires and paralyzing fears. It is in the wilderness where Goodman Brown meets Satan, but it is also where Hester Prynne and Arthur Dimmesdale meet for the first time since the former's punishment. What repentance Dimmesdale completes on the gallows, he begins in the uncultured wilderness of early America. Melville too uses the environment to explore the anxiety inherent in the American experiment, though he looks toward the sea rather than the land. In *MOBY-DICK* Ishmael opens the novel by articulating Americans' desire to descend on the battery and look into the sea like a modern Narcissus, and the cabin boy Pip plunges into the sea where he finds the workings of God (an arguably American, Calvinist one) that drives him mad; he spends the rest of his short life wandering the *Pequod* an idiot, serving as a warning to the rest of the crew. Melville's great work on American slavery, "Benito Cereno," uses not just the sea but the ship itself to externalize the fear and anxiety inherent in the country's "peculiar institution."

Although EDGAR ALLAN POE's writings are often set in Europe or a non-descript location, the anxieties manifested in the environment are often distinctly American. This is perhaps best seen in Poe's only finished novel, *The Narrative of Arthur Gordon Pym,* where the titular hero sails to the South Pole to be confronted by "black skin warriors" who are horrified by anything white. When Pym eventually escapes the natives, he sails into a mysterious cataract of whiteness. Other shorter tales such as "The Gold-Bug" and "The Black Cat" suggest that some of Poe's tales use the environment as an exploration of the pathological effects of slavery.

In the twentieth century, the Gothic became nearly synonymous with Southern writers. Authors such as WILLIAM FAULKNER, Flannery O'Connor, and Walker Percy seem to have little in common with British Gothic writers, and even early American authors such as Irving and Hawthorne. What connects them all, however, is their profound relationship to America's environment and history. Gothic works express the struggle between the conservatism of the past and the revolutionary spirit of the present. In the United States, the revolution has occurred, yet the old order remains with us. In Brown the ghost of this order is the European ideal, in Hawthorne and Melville a Puritan God, and in Faulkner an antebellum Mississippi. The struggle to negotiate identity in the midst of what is often self-imposed change is essential to the American Gothic, and consistently expressed through the natural environment, which witnessed, framed, and in many ways informed the nation's political, cultural and religious upheaval. — Brent Cline

BIBLIOGRAPHY

Fielder, Leslie. *Love and Death in the American Novel.* 2nd edition. New York: Doubleday, 1992.
Goddu, Teresa. *Gothic America: Narrative, History, and Nation.* New York: Columbia University Press, 1997.
Levin, Harry. *The Power of Blackness: Hawthorne, Poe, Melville.* Athens: University of Ohio Press, 1980.
Martin, Robert K., and Eric Savoy, eds. *American Gothic: New Interventions in a National Narrative.* Iowa City: University of Iowa Press.
Punter, David. *The Literature of Terror: A History of Gothic Fictions from 1765 to the Present Day.* New York: Longmans, 1980.

American Naturalism and Environment

Naturalism was a dominant literary movement in the United States from roughly 1885 to 1925, bridging the American Renaissance of THOREAU,

EMERSON, WHITMAN and MELVILLE, and the Modernist era of ELIOT, POUND, FAULKNER and HEMINGWAY. Naturalistic authors in America often began with the assumption that the physical environment itself—whether urban, natural, or somewhere in between—was a powerful force in shaping and determining the fates of their characters. Drawing upon the work of French author Emile Zola, American authors such as STEPHEN CRANE, JACK LONDON, Frank Norris, and Theodore Dreiser sought to explore, within the context of their fictional worlds, exactly *how* these forces in the physical environment operate, and operate on humankind.

As much a philosophic experiment as a literary project, American naturalism was defined by two primary goals: first, it aimed at a detached, objective, and scientific treatment of human life in order to test the ways in which characters relate to their environments; and second, it either adhered to or experimented with the philosophy of determinism, an outlook rooted in the theories of Charles Darwin. Determinism holds that in the "natural" world around us a particular set of factors and circumstances lead to a specific outcome. The naturalistic author investigates how these factors—including heredity, socioeconomic conditions, and the historical moment—operate and converge to shape a character's experience in a world controlled by indifferent natural law. At the core of all these forces, however, is the physical environment; the specific setting in which each story takes place provides a unique convergence of circumstances that could not occur elsewhere.

Environment, then, is extremely important to American naturalism, providing not only the backdrop for action but functioning as a central force that shapes and limits characters. Authors such as Stephen Crane and Jack London focus on the overwhelming power of natural environment; in works such as Crane's "The Open Boat" and London's "To Build a Fire," for example, characters struggle to survive in environments largely indifferent to their survival. Crane's omniscient narrator in "The Open Boat" describes this feminized and careless nature while his characters are stranded at sea in a raft: "She did not seem cruel to him, nor beneficent, nor treacherous, nor wise. But she was indifferent, flatly indifferent." Similarly, nature's lack of regard for the existence of London's nameless main character in "To Build a Fire" is vividly apparent in the "flat" and declarative description of the extreme conditions of the Yukon environment, highlighting man's limitations in the face of the extreme cold.

In naturalistic texts with urban environments as their primary setting, the city environment acts with a similar apathy toward human will. Authors such as Upton Sinclair, Theodore Dreiser, and Frank Norris explore the forces at work in their fictionalized representations of real American cities such as Chicago, New York, Philadelphia, and San Francisco. While critics often characterize the urban environments in these authors' work as harsh, limiting, and monolithically deterministic, natural environments in these texts often offer characters a sense of relief by contrast, introducing a curious and fundamental paradox into the determinist thematic: the very "nature" that in human, volitional society radically undermines any substantive notion of "freedom," in *nature* liberates and relieves. In Upton Sinclair's *The Jungle*, for example, Jurgis escapes Chicago's meatpacking district and ventures into the country, where he "felt like a bird lifted up and borne away upon a gale" (211); his health returns and he feels more in touch with his rural Lithuanian roots. Similarly, the presence of nature within the city of San Francisco in Frank Norris's novel *McTeague* offers the eponymous protagonist a sense of liberation; Norris presents a detailed description of San Francisco's streets and neighborhoods, and the city itself is a source of restriction and discomfort, but McTeague feels free as he walks along the shore of the bay. Norris writes, "He liked the solitude of the tremendous, tumbling ocean; the fresh, windy downs; he liked to feel the gusty Trades flogging his face, and he would remain for hours watching the roll and plunge of the breakers with the silent, unreasoned enjoyment of a child" (187).

Thus, while naturalistic authors often seem to present the environment as restrictive and deterministic, naturalism's environments are never quite that simple or consistent. Collectively, the movement can be seen as an apparent rebellion against romantic predecessors such as Emerson and Thoreau, who celebrate the environment as a source of potential liberation of the self; but a closer look at naturalism's environments reveals a far subtler and more paradoxical relationship between the human and nonhuman, as if, by reducing traditional, egocentric human "free will" (which proved so destructive to both humanity and nature alike) to the same forces governing the plant and animal world, these authors in a sense liberated that will on a deeper and more profound level, more in keeping with the Native Americans' circle of life.—Annette R. Dolph

BIBLIOGRAPHY

Crane, Stephen. "The Open Boat." *The Norton Anthology of American Literature*. Ed. Nina Baym et al. 7th ed. Vol. C. New York: Norton, 2007. 1000–1016.

Lawlor, Mary. *Recalling the Wild: Naturalism and the Closing of the American West*. New Brunswick, NJ: Rutgers University Press, 2000.

Link, Eric Carl. *The Vast and Terrible Drama: American Literary Naturalism in the Late Nineteenth Century.* Tuscaloosa: University of Alabama Press, 2004.

London, Jack. "To Build a Fire." *The Norton Anthology of American Literature.* Ed. Nina Baym et al. 7th ed. Vol. C. New York: Norton, 2007. 1057–1067.

Norris, Frank. *McTeague.* Ed. Donald Pizer. New York: Norton, 1977.

Sinclair, Upton. *The Jungle.* New York: Signet, 1960.

American Pastoral

The pastoral in literature is nearly as old as literature itself, recognizable both as a landscape and as a type of relationship between characters and society, and between characters and nature — the ultimate liminal space. As a landscape, pastoral calls forth the rural world, the *locus amoenus*, or place of delight, a middle place of balance and harmony that is neither civilized nor totally wild. As a representation of the lives of people, pastoral evokes a life of ease separated from the distractions and corruption of the urban world, yet not overtaken by the hardships of wilderness survival. In the pastoral world, nature supplies man's needs, and man's impact on the land is minimal. The pastoral figure, originally a shepherd but later expanded to include all kinds of country people, is one dedicated to simple rustic pleasures, not competition or private accumulation. And owing to his special relation to nature, he or she has a privileged relationship to the creator. In praising the independent farmer, THOMAS JEFFERSON called upon two thousand years of pastoral tradition when he proclaimed, "Those who labour in the earth are the chosen people of God, if ever he had a chosen people, whose breasts he has made his peculiar deposit of substantial and genuine virtue" (164–165).

Alongside and complementing the mythopoeic influence of THE BIBLE, the pastoral ideal has played a critical role in the evolution of American literature and environmental thought. European explorers' first encounters with the New World were filtered through a lens of pastoral imagery. In the colonial and early national period, the virtuous shepherd/yeoman farmer and the generous landscape were deemed ideal images for the new American republic. Beginning in the Romantic period, writers used pastoral and anti-pastoral images to explore forces ranging from slavery to Indian relocation, to the forces of industrialism that threatened the ideal American garden. In the present day environmental writers have reclaimed the pastoral as a means for examining and redefining the human relationship to the non-human world, and for calling attention to threats civilization poses to the ecological order.

LEO MARX, in *THE MACHINE IN THE GARDEN*, draws a useful distinction between two kinds of pastoral: the simple and the complex. Marx characterizes the simple, or sentimental, pastoral as primitivism, nostalgia, "an urge to withdraw from civilization's growing power and complexity" (9). An example of sentimental pastoral can be found in the paintings of Thomas Kincaide. Marx contrasts the "puerile fantasies" (9) of the sentimental pastoral with the more realistic and far-reaching aims of the "complex" pastoral, in which writers employ pastoral images as a way of engaging with, not escaping from, culture's conflicts and meanings (10). The complex pastoral is often employed in political and cultural critique. Even in its earliest versions the complex pastoral is built upon contrasts, what Harold Toliver calls dialectical pairings, contrasting the forces of nature and society, nature and art, the material and the spiritual (3). That such pairings can be ambiguous (pastoral nature may be associated with freedom, democracy, simplicity, health, and moral purity; but also with chaos, violence, temporality, and death) speaks to the challenges of reading the pastoral.

While pastoral imagery of the *locus amoenus* may remain fairly consistent, the meaning of the pastoral varies widely. As William Empson put it, there are many versions of the pastoral. Pastoralism is not an ideology *per se*; it is rather, to use LAWRENCE BUELL's term, an "ideological grammar." As Buell points out, the pastoral is "multivalent"; it has been put to many ideological uses: some democratic and progressive, some conservative and regressive (36).

The roots of the American pastoral tradition reach back to the classical era, to the poetry of Theocritus and Virgil, whose *Idylls* and *Eclogues*, respectively, depict the lives of shepherds indulging in singing contests and romantic engagements against the backdrop of an Arcadian landscape, all harkening back to a Golden Age when men were free from "the curse of work" (Toliver 6). Even in its earliest examples, however, the pastoral is a foil against which larger social conflict is addressed. Virgil's first Eclogue opens with the pastoral figure, Tityrus, playing his reed pipe and praising his god while his sheep and cattle graze. His friend, Meliboeus, drives his flock into forced exile, having lost his farm. In their ensuing conversation we learn that Tityrus, a former slave, gained his farm from the state after petitioning for his freedom, while Meliboeus had his farm confiscated by the state and given to a foreign soldier, a veteran of one of Rome's many wars. The pastoral world here, then, is one threatened with exclusion and eviction.

The pastoral was revived and in a sense reinvented during the Renaissance. As it was translated from Italian to French to English, it was also translated from a literary ideal to a *topos* for property and politics. English poets in the employ of landowners re-located the pastoral setting from the mythical Arcadia to country-house estates of a newly rising gentry. In the visual arts, Italian and French painters, such as Giorgione and Titian, Claude and Poussin, devel-oped and perfected realistic landscape paintings, which they populated with figures from classical pas-toral poetry, establishing a recognizable and contem-porary visual vocabulary for the *locus amoenus*. Young men of the gentry, returning to England from their grand tours of Europe with copies of paintings by Claude and other landscapists, laid the groundwork for England's great contribution to the pastoral re-vival: the landscape garden. These perspective views of imaginary scenes were adopted by England's newly emerging landed class as the ideal way of seeing the real rural world. The Arcadian landscapes in pastoral painting became models for the gardens and pleasure parks the new gentry designed around their estates, funded by the rents they collected from the sur-rounding farmers. The visual language of the pastoral thus idealized and naturalized private property and the new economic order. This landscape "way of see-ing," as geographer Denis Cosgrove puts it, enhanced and endorsed by the pastoral, was also, importantly, the landlord's way of seeing (189–205).

The interest in landscape gardens led to a corre-sponding interest in tourism of more uncultivated scenery in nature, and a new aesthetic philosophy of the picturesque. Picturesque viewing favored scenery that had a "wild" aspect to it, yet could be aestheti-cized like a painting. Unlike true wilderness, which filled viewers with a sense of horror or dread, the pic-turesque scenery was untamed yet unthreatening, and lent itself to tasteful religious or patriotic asso-ciations. Picturesque tourism enabled those who did not possess land, but did possess the taste and value system of the landed class, to assert their place in so-ciety. Cowper's oft-repeated lines, "I am Monarch of all I *survey,/* My right there is none to dispute," reinforced the ideological connection between pas-toral landscape and the rights of property. Raymond Williams notes that the rise of picturesque tourism and the appreciation of uncultivated nature occurred just as much of England was lost to agriculture and the cities were giving themselves over to manufac-turing — and with this came a powerful sense of fear and anxiety (128). However, the pastoral was not employed merely to celebrate the power of the landed and wealthy. In the hands of the Romantics it ex-pressed respect for the larger human community through the idealization of common men. If older pastoral conventions deployed the simple rustic figures as stand-ins for the rich and powerful (Emp-son 17), Romantic pastoralism celebrated the rustic

laborer's independence from a cruel and abusive social order. Using what Raymond Williams calls "green language," the pastoral figure became no longer a literary type but an actual laborer in an actual landscape, "in which the affirmation of Nature is intended as the essential affirmation of Men" (132). And this English view of the landscape, with all its ambiguities, was one of the most significant cultural exports that helped to define America as pastoral, and define the "pastoral" for America.

Numerous critics, including Perry Miller, Henry Nash Smith, Leo Marx, and Annette Kolodny have observed that, from its first discovery, the American landscape was experienced through a pastoral frame-work. For early explorers, the lush, city-less land-scapes, populated by indigenous peoples who lived in harmony with nature, seemed a literal manifesta-tion of the literary ideal. The American landscape was the *locus amoenus* on which settlers' pastoral fan-tasies could be realized, first as a "lubberland" of ease and effortless comfort, then as a place to establish one's hereditary estate, as England's common lands had been gobbled up; and finally as the site for a pas-toral republic of freeholders who would expand American democracy and American virtue ever west-ward, most famously illustrated in Crevecoeur's *Letters from an American Farmer*.

After the Revolution, through the first half of the 19th century, the progress of American civilization was justified in essentially pastoral terms. The less savory effects of utilitarian advances and material wealth were mitigated by the fact that Americans possessed such majestic scenery and were always somehow "close" to Nature's powers. Indeed, a new pastoral "American Adam," independent of the Old World's corrupting forces, thrived because he was the sovereign inhabitant of "Nature's Nation" (Lewis 5–8; Miller 209).

But as Leo Marx notes, the pastoral American re-public was fraught with anxiety over the changes that progress was bringing with it; not merely the indus-trial "machine in the garden," but the threat of ex-ploding commerce, guilt over the Indian "removal," and the implacable contradiction of slavery in a democracy — all of which, and more, threatened to undermine the self-flattering blandishments of the American pastoral. Just as early American national-ism found its endorsement in pastoral discourse, crit-ics of the emerging society found in *anti*-pastoral discourse an appropriate rhetoric of dissent. Thomas Cole and artists of the Hudson River School praised nature for its spiritual balm while frantically painting the New York landscape in an effort to preserve it from annihilation by the axe. James Fenimore Coop-er's famous scene in *The Pioneers* (The Leather-

STOCKING NOVELS), describing the slaughter of pigeons, upbraided the thoughtless "wastey ways" of early townlife; and his hero Natty Bumppo chooses to remain in the wilderness with the native Chingachgook rather than be saddled with the hypocrisy and materialism of the settlements. THOREAU used his pastoral retreat on the shore of Walden Pond as a base to rhetorically dismantle American capitalism, charging that the true flavor of nature is lost once it is carted to market. In *Uncle Tom's Cabin*, Stowe attacks slavery by withdrawing the screen of the Southern plantation's "Arcadia" to reveal the tragedy of separated families and the sadistic hell of Simon Legree's forced labor camp. Yet behind the anti-pastoral critique lies the belief that a pastoral reality can be attained, whether in the well-ordered estate of Cooper's Littlepages, in the mornings on Walden Pond, or in the matriarchal utopia of Stowe's Quaker Settlement.

Other critics have noted that the pastoral is freighted with more than anxiety over technological and social change. Annette Kolodny and Louise Westling observe how in the pens of male writers pastoral landscapes have been constructed as female, and that gendered vocabulary profoundly shaped early American responses to the land. This "gendered landscape" is nurturing and seductive, fertile and chaotic, requiring a masculine hand to control it, and thus works hand in hand with the project of colonial expansion. Consequently, the sexual dominance that controls and exploits nature also threatens it with sexual violence. Kolodny notes a consistent tone of sexual anxiety and guilt in early American pastoral writing. Yet in the hands of female writers, this same gendered pastoral landscape serves as the site, and provides the model, for building communities based on "ecological" mutual support.

The pastoral has also served as a touchstone for pointedly environmental writing. In writers ranging from Thoreau to SUSAN FENIMORE COOPER, MARY AUSTIN and Jonathan Schell, Buell sees a pastoral pattern in American nature writing, wherein the writer withdraws from society into nature, in order to save both. Thoreau withdraws from Boston society in order to reveal its flaws, and serve as a pioneer in the search for a path to its recovery. RACHEL CARSON introduces her readers to an idealized rural village only to destroy it in order to highlight the threat of pesticides to humans and nature. The two faces of the ancient pastoral — the happy co-opted Tityrus and the alienated exiled Meliboeus — are the ambiguous face of the modern pastoral as well: accommodation or radical change. Buell sees in the future of the American pastoral the potential to form a bridge "from anthropocentric to more specifically ecocentric concerns," and suggests that the ancient

dream of man harmonized with nature may help to advance nature's claim on human society (52). — Roger W. Hecht

BIBLIOGRAPHY

Buell, Lawrence. *The Environmental Imagination: Thoreau, Nature Writing, and the Formation of American Culture.* Cambridge: Belknap-Harvard University Press, 1995.

Cosgrove, Denis E. *Social Formation and Symbolic Landscape.* 1984. Madison: University of Wisconsin Press, 1998.

Empson, William. *Some Versions of Pastoral.* 1935. Hammondsworth, Middlesex: Peregrin-Penguin, 1966.

Jefferson, Thomas. *Notes on the State of Virginia.* 1787. Ed. William Peden. New York: Norton, 1982.

Kolodny, Annette. *The Lay of the Land: Metaphor as Experience and History in American Life and Letters.* Chapel Hill: University of North Carolina Press, 1975.

Lewis, R. W. B. *The American Adam: Innocence, Tragedy, and Tradition in the Nineteenth Century.* Chicago: University of Chicago Press, 1955.

Marx, Leo. *The Machine in the Garden: Technology and the Pastoral Ideal in America.* New York: Oxford University Press, 1964.

Miller, Perry. *Errand into the Wilderness.* Cambridge: Harvard University Press, 1956.

Tolliver, Harold E. *Pastoral Forms and Attitudes.* Berkeley: University of California Press, 1971.

Virgil. *The Eclogues and the Georgics.* Trans. C. Day Lewis. New York: Oxford University Press, 1983.

Westling, Louise H. *Green Breast of the New World: Landscape, Gender, and American Fiction.* Athens: University of Georgia Press, 1976.

Williams, Raymond. *The Country and the City.* New York: Oxford University Press, 1973.

Apocalyptic Fiction: A Brief History of American Apocalyptic Literature

From its beginnings in the colonial era up to the present day, American literature has been characterized by apocalyptic imaginings. The expectation of destructive events such as storms and earthquakes, pollution of air and water, fires and plagues, harmful enough to end the world, originate mainly in the Holy Scriptures (THE BIBLE), especially the Book of Revelation, also known as the Revelation to John (Apocalypse). In the Book of Revelation, the apocalyptic events usher in the Second Coming of Jesus Christ and, after his millennial reign and final defeat of the Devil, God's Last Judgment of all humanity. After the Judgment, "the first things," including the earth and sea are "no more," instead, the faithful reside in a new spiritual and non-material world of eternal salvation (Revelation 21:4 ff.).

(It is important to note that although the Bible has exercised an unparalleled influence on the American imagination, anticipations of the apocalypse are not exclusive to Christianity, but figure in the narratives of many world religions, including Judaism, Zoroastrianism, Hinduism, and Islam. When not particularly focused on the apocalypse, they yet share the expectation of the savior-figure, moral decay of the society toward the end of the time-cycle, and the judgment of sinners.)

In seventeenth- and eighteenth-century America, the Biblical view of the apocalypse was dominant. Puritan sermons and other literature contemplated the arrival of the Kingdom of God, preceded by the apocalypse. Writers and preachers such as COTTON MATHER (1663–1728) and JONATHAN EDWARDS (1703–1758) anticipated the entrance into the heavenly world for those worthy of God's salvation and, more often, admonished the insufficiently pious members of the community to mend their ways before the disaster struck. In the imminent destruction of the world, the wayward Christians were sure to suffer at the hands of "an angry God," to use Edwards' famous phrase.

Although they used the language of war and battle (against the Devil), and referred to God's anger and punishment, colonial American writers continued to imagine and represent the apocalypse in terms of natural disasters such as earthquakes, floods, and storms. A prominent metaphor in colonial texts, the "natural" disaster served Puritan writers in heralding the approaching Armageddon and a new type of existence in its aftermath.

In nineteenth-century American literature, the focus changed from the religious to a more secular view of the apocalypse. By including apocalyptic events in their novels and stories, writers such as NATHANIEL HAWTHORNE, EDGAR ALLAN POE, HERMAN MELVILLE, and MARK TWAIN sought to examine the rapidly industrializing American society, often criticizing its materialism and violence, as well as its unbounded optimism toward progress and the widespread belief that industrialization would lead to a better future. Nineteenth-century apocalyptic literature also explored questions of the history and destiny of the nation, and the (in)ability of individual human beings to achieve the moral excellence required for salvation.

For nineteenth-century American writers, imagining the apocalypse became a tool of social critique, with varied degrees of focus on the dangers posed to the natural world. Hawthorne's story *The New Adam and Eve* (1843) imagines the "Day of Doom" in which all humanity is wiped out, but nature recovers itself, leaving the "beauty of earth, sea, and sky" untouched, "for beauty's sake." Hawthorne criticizes the "artificial" world created by human beings as well as artificial behaviors, implying that our practices go against Nature literally and metaphorically, leading

to our extinction. In Twain's novel *A Connecticut Yankee in King Arthur's Court* (1889), a time-traveling American Hank Morgan brings about the demise of the medieval society that he seeks to reconstruct and rule through the use of technology and weapons. Hawthorne and Twain both warn against the overwhelming might of industrial civilization, and its threat to nature and human life (for example, through the development of increasingly sophisticated weapons).

Nineteenth-century narratives also presented the apocalypse as a spectacle of destruction, focusing on the emotional and aesthetic effect of the end of the world. This approach is evident in works of Edgar Allan Poe, especially in his story *The Fall of the House of Usher* (1839), where the disturbing disappearance of the Usher family line is completed with the death of its two last members and their crumbling, falling house. Similarly, in his poems "The Conqueror Worm" (1843) and "The City in the Sea" (1845), Poe focuses on the (suggestive) *anatomy* of the apocalypse rather than on its explicit social or political implications.

Fictional apocalypses proliferated in twentieth-century literature to include a variety of newly emerging causes and their moral implications. With growing knowledge about the cosmos and the growing audience for pulp fiction magazines — popular American genre magazines in the 1920s, '30s and '40s — the cosmic cataclysm story, describing asteroid impacts and planetary collisions, came to prominence, beginning with Frank L. Pollack's 1906 story *Finis*. The increased knowledge and threat of viral disasters in mid–twentieth century itself inspired a sub-genre of stories with virus-related apocalypse themes. George R. Stewart's 1949 novel, *Earth Abides*, is a well-known early example of this sub-genre, based on the nineteenth-century apocalyptic stories wherein the destruction is caused by plagues. Also in the mid–twentieth century, nuclear apocalypse stories reflected the contemporary political sentiments and fears, in America and the world, marked by cold war realities and anxieties. A host of nuclear holocaust novels and stories, such as Andre Norton's *Daybreak 2250 AD* (originally *Star Man's Son*, 1952) and Pat Frank's *Alas Babylon* (1959), warned against the horrors of nuclear war.

Literary imaginings of apocalyptic devastation evolved dramatically in the mid–twentieth century, along with growing fears of environmental catastrophy caused by human neglect; and such environmental disasters are often portrayed without any sense of renewal or hope afterwards. For example, classic mid-century novels, Walter Miller, Jr.'s *A Canticle for Leibowitz* (1960) and Philip K. Dick's

Do Androids Dream of Electric Sheep? (1968) locate their characters on a dying Earth, ruined and depleted by nuclear warfare. *A Canticle for Leibowitz* focuses on the painstaking development of the post-apocalyptic human race and its final demise in a further nuclear catastrophe. In *Do Androids Dream*, the Earth is replete with degeneration and death due to nuclear fallout. Animal species are almost extinct, and so valuable that owning them indicates an elite social status; the desolate Earth cannot renew itself.

The apocalyptic fiction of the 1970s reflected yet another development in American society: the struggle for civil rights. Female writers such as Alice/Raccoona Sheldon (writing under the pseudonym James Triptree, Jr.) used the apocalyptic scenario to address issues both of gender relations and biotechnology in her classic story "The Screwfly Solution" (1977). African American writers such as Ralph Ellison in *Invisible Man* (1952) and TONI MORRISON in *Sula* (1973) assailed their racially prejudiced society and its mores by representing the apocalypse as a call to end such discrimination, and usher in a racially just world. In this sense, African American writers return to an almost Biblical understanding of apocalypse as a form of sheer destruction that nonetheless renews hope.

Today, novels such as Octavia Butler's *Parable of the Sower* (1993) combine concerns with global warming, pollution, and racial and gender tensions, while works such as CORMAC MCCARTHY's award-winning novel *THE ROAD* (2006) continue to ponder the nature of existence in the face of total destruction. Both Butler's and McCarthy's novels illustrate a larger trend in the American literature of the twentieth- and early twenty-first-century: the literature of *post*-apocalyptic narratives — stories dealing with the aftermath of the apocalypse — rather than the apocalypse itself.

In Jeff Goldberg's apocalyptic short story, *These Zombies Are Not a Metaphor* (2006), the narrator remarks, "let's be very clear. These zombies are not a metaphorical scourge upon the Earth. These zombies are an actual scourge upon the Earth." The characters in the story reflect a more general literary pattern, the inability to accept or imagine the total destruction of our race and habitat, replaced instead with a tendency to ponder survival, despite the mass-scale of destruction. Goldberg's story illustrates another modern twist on the apocalypse narrative — the zombie sub-genre — the literal representation of the walking dead, prophesied centuries ago in the Book of Revelation and presented as a spectacle of horror in modern literature and media.

In the long tradition of apocalyptic thought, evident in American religion and literature, the apoca-

lypse is understood as either a final and total destruction, involving the environmental downfall of humanity and the planet, or as a hopeful event that brings rebirth. Environmental novels typically employ apocalyptic and post-apocalyptic language to explore environmental crises; however, some critics see these "eco-doom" fictional accounts as overly alarmist. Other critics, like Zbigniew Lewicki and Frederick Buell, rather chillingly argue that apocalyptic views in environmental fiction may be increasingly describing not the apocalypse, but the (perhaps even more frightening) intrinsic apathy and entropy of the universe — a portrayal of the imagined world, and of our attitudes, that ends not with a bang, but with a whimper.—Lejla Kucukalic

BIBLIOGRAPHY

Kermode, Frank. *The Sense of an Ending*. New York: Oxford University Press, 1967.
Lehigh, David. *Apocalyptic Patterns in Twentieth-Century Fiction*. Notre Dame: University of Notre Dame Press, 2008.
Lewicki, Zbignev. *The Bang and the Whimper*. Westport: Greenwood Press, 1984.
May, John R. *Toward a New Earth: Apocalypse in the American Novel*. Notre Dame: University of Notre Dame Press, 1972.
Montgomery, Maxine Levon. *The Apocalypse in African-American Fiction*. Gainesville: University Press of Florida, 1996.
Taylor, Justin. *The Apocalypse Reader*. New York: Thunder's Mouth Press, 2007.

Audubon, John James (1785–1851)

John James Audubon, illegitimate son of French Lieutenant Jean Audubon and Jeanne Rabin, a servant girl, was a born naturalist, an indefatigable artist and a pioneer of conservation. Soon after his birth, his mother died, and until he was six he lived on his father's sugar plantation in Haiti. Volatile uprisings in the plantation caused his father to send him to Nantes, France, where his second wife, Anne Moynet, raised him as her own. Under her tutelage, he developed his love for birds. He narrates that Anne Moynet had several pet parrots, and a pet monkey who one day killed a parrot because it had been uppity. This killing so upset Audubon that he begged for the monkey to be killed; however, the monkey was restrained and the parrot given an appropriate burial. This incident triggered Audubon's passion for birds, which turned into an obsession to revivify dead birds through the art of bird imaging. His father was his first ecology teacher, taking him on long nature walks, pointing out to him the variety, beauty and cyclical nature of the natural environment.

At 18 Audubon was sent to America to escape

conscription in Napoleon's army, and at 21 he became an American citizen. In Mill Grove, Philadelphia, he lived on his father's farm and spent his time walking in the woods, hunting, fishing, and drawing. Even then he felt a nascent mission to investigate the natural world, observing, collecting and drawing birds with fastidious accuracy. Armed with La Fontaine's *Fables* as guide, and William Turton's translation of Linnaeus as his companion, he taught himself ornithology. At Mill Grove, Audubon met his wife, Lucy, who sympathized with his passion for the outdoors and especially for birds. She was his best friend and greatest supporter, and made an independent living raising their children, while Audubon continued his peripatetic life looking for bird specimens and drawing them for posterity.

Eventually supporting himself through his art, within 15 years Audubon had created a comprehensive, illustrated book of North American birds called *Birds of America*. The first edition of the book, ironically published in England, was a four-volume, leather-bound, double-elephant portfolio of bird illustrations drawn on 26" by 39" sheets. It contained 435 individual plates of 497 species of birds, and featured 1,065 hand-sketched and colored images of life-sized birds. So devoted was Audubon to his task that he not only drew and illustrated the birds, but raised money to finance the book's printing and was involved in every stage of its publication. A subsequent edition of *Birds of America,* called the royal octavo edition, was later published in America in 1840. This edition was much less expensive, as it used the new lithography technique of reproduction and reduced the size of the sheets to 6.5" by 10". Although this seven-volume edition of 650 hand-colored prints was one-eighth the size of the first edition, it had a longer (and definitively nationalistic) title: *The Birds of America from Drawings made in the United States and their Territories.*

To accompany his avian illustrations, Audubon produced the five-volume *Ornithological Biography,* containing bird biographies, and occasional sketches of American frontiersmen. These sketches, influenced by the idealized pastoralism of his time (AMERICAN PASTORAL), depict frontier living and the pristine condition of the American wilderness before it was settled. Audubon's frontier-living experience, in fact, caused him to sound the first alarm concerning the large-scale slaughter of birds, and the destruction of habitat, as settlers penetrated into the American wilderness. Although he himself hunted game for consumption and drawing, it was measured and pragmatic, and he bemoaned the indiscriminate slaughter of birds, and the wasted carnage that was left to rot, when flocks of migratory birds were rapidly and sys-

tematically shot down. Moreover, when Audubon first started sketching birds he did so without killing and stuffing them, as was the practice then, but his attempt to save the lives of the birds was not successful, and he was forced to resort to killing the very birds he loved so much, in order to immortalize them for posterity.

Audubon lived the hard life of a frontiersman, walked the forests, and drifted down rivers to observe, gather and draw birds, unafraid and largely unaware of potential dangers. To understand bird behavior he entered the dark hollows of trees, once falling into quicksand and almost dying as he pursued his specimens. He was the first to band birds, tying a silver thread to the leg of the fly-catching Phoebe. He also kept and raised birds, including hawks, turkeys and swans, and tracked birds through their droppings. Although his main focus was birds, he also spent time observing other animals in the wild, which he recorded in *The Viviparous Quadrupeds of North America,* later completed by his sons and longtime friend John Bachman.

Audubon's principal contribution to the empirical understanding and preservation of the American environment was threefold: his masterpiece, *Birds of America,* popularized the field of ornithology in America and made bird watching a serious pastime for subsequent generations; his bird illustrations led to the identification, cataloguing and understanding of bird species and their immense variety; and his rudimentary bird banding led to the understanding of avian migration, population and habitat. His contribution to America's imaginative environment is incalculable.—Sukanya B. Senapati

BIBLIOGRAPHY

Ford, Alice, ed. *Audubon, By Himself.* Garden City, NY: Natural History Press. 1969.
Rhodes, Richard. *John James Audubon.* New York: Alfred A. Knopf, 2004.

Birds of America, J. J. Audubon (1827–39)

During the early decades of the nineteenth century, when photography had not yet been invented, bird images were made through drawings and paintings. Alexander Wilson pioneered the painting of North American birds, but J. J Audubon set the standard for avifauna images and their reproductions with his *Birds of America,* a portfolio of realistic, dynamic and life-sized bird images. Audubon, a born naturalist and superb artist, painstakingly drew and painted 1,065 different bird images, in their habitats, with absolute detail and accuracy, while at the same time letting his artistry seep through in the lines, contours and compositions of the paintings.

The 435 color plates in *Birds of America* represent 45 bird families. Of the approximately 700 species of birds that exist in North America, Audubon painted close to 500, and his paintings are still used both by experts and amateurs to verify and authenticate species identity. Identification is made possible by Audubon's drawing of pairs of male and female birds, in dynamic motion, in their natural habitats, amidst botanicals of twigs, leaves, and flowers. Since the birds are often drawn in motion, both the top and underside plumage are visible. In each pair, one bird is painted perched with wings closed and the other with wings wide open, giving viewers a 3D image of the species. The spread wings reveal details and arrangements of both long and short feathers, and the overlapping folding and fanning of feathers. Audubon's intensely observant scientific eye, and adherence to detail in drawing both bird and habitat, not only made the identification and cataloguing of birds possible, but also gave viewers glimpses of specific habitats and a holistic image of birds in the wilderness.

The backgrounds against which the birds are painted, especially if they are water birds, show distant horizons of mountains, landscapes or vast, infinite skies. The birds and their backgrounds together show how well camouflaged the birds are in their natural habitats, for the colors in the backgrounds are just shades darker or lighter than the birds themselves, and viewers sometimes have to pause and look hard to discern the birds at all. Often the birds are shown chasing prey, caught in the dynamic motion of the hunt, with the prey painted with as much detail and care as the birds themselves. Details of the prey reveal bird eating habits, as is indicated in Plate 333 showing the Green Heron feeding on the Luna moth, its favorite food. Similarly, in Plate 34, showing the Worm-eating Warbler eating pokeberries, the birds are painted foraging in dead leaves, which is a characteristic of this species. These images, along with the bird biographies in Audubon's *Ornithological Biography*, provided the first scientific compendium of avian life and culture, and greatly enhanced our understanding of birds and their habitats.

When Audubon first began drawing birds, he tried to do so without killing and stuffing the birds as was common practice then; however, he soon discovered that it was impossible to do so with any degree of veracity or dynamism, so he resorted to killing the very birds he loved so much. His exacting approach also resulted in him killing many birds in his search for the perfect specimen. However, he never killed merely for sport, and tried to dissuade woodsmen

from slaughtering migratory birds, such as American Golden Plovers which he described as "innocent fugitives from a winter storm"; and he wrote with great sorrow and compassion about the manner in which they were lured and systematically butchered (Rhodes 184). One infamous day he recorded the death of 63 dozen plovers at the hands of a single hunter, and estimated that 48,000 plovers had died on that single day. After observing frontiersmen shooting down far more birds than they could consume, he urged them to shoot fewer birds in the following season. It was then that he wrote in his journal that if such slaughter continued there would be a serious dip in population, and bemoaned the unthinking carnage and waste of wild game. He similarly wrote of the death of 40,000 crows one season, and could not understand why the crow was so hated by mankind when it helped farmers by consuming crop pests. Hence Audubon reveals an awareness of unnecessary carnage at a time when sheer plenitude eclipsed the possibility, it seemed, of future scarcity and extinction.

Audubon was also the first to band birds, which he did by tying pieces of silver strings to the birds' legs and awaiting their return the following season. He began banding the first season he was in America, in order to check the homing instincts of the Phoebes that nested in the caves of Perkiomen Creek. Banding not only affords scientists data about population and migration, but also creates a sense of anticipation in bird watchers and a desire for their survival and return. Audubon's reverent fascination with birds energized his family and friends alike, and fostered both the serious pastime of bird watching and the desire for avifauna survival in subsequent generations.

Even a cursory consideration of any plate in *Birds of America*, provides viewers with an illustration of Audubon's perfect balancing of scientific veracity and mixed-media artistry. For example, Plate 431, showing the American Flamingo, is a breathtakingly beautiful image of a gorgeous scarlet flamingo bent over with its beak close to the ground, almost parallel to its feet, doubled over to give viewers an indication of its size. It stands on a darkened embankment, with its scarlet plumage magnificently contrasted against the blue of the water and sky. Not all the plates, however, are so picturesque; some, for example, show the violence of predatory birds, such as Plate 16, which depicts a pair of Great-Footed Hawks tearing open, with surgical precision, a duck that lies dead on the ground with its entrails spilling out. Nonetheless, each bird image shows Audubon's perfect balance of science and art, through which he inspired America's imagination and informed its collective consciousness, teaching us to look carefully at birds, and admire their beauty, and in this way urging us to protect and preserve them in the wild.

Although Audubon harvested felts, furs and birds to make a living and draw them, he did so with prudence, never slaughtering for sport. Through his bird images he immortalized the very birds he had killed, and through his artistry he introduced us to the art of bird-watching, inducing us to pay attention to minute details of the natural world. With little formal education, and through sheer will power and hard work, he singlehandedly composed a seminal, comprehensive encyclopedia of American avifauna that was as scientific as it was artistic. In loving birds and in passing on this love and desire to know everything about them, he taught us to love and thereby save one part of our natural environment; for as the Senegalese conservationist Baba Doom says: "In the end we will conserve only what we love, [and] we will love only what we understand" (Wilson 320). Long before THOREAU became America's iconic woodsman walker, Audubon had set out on his peripatetic journey into the American wilderness, doggedly seeking out and drawing every species of bird. And while the frontiersmen were carving out a nation with little cognizance of its effects on the wilderness, Audubon was unobtrusively observing nature and imaging it for posterity.— Sukanya B. Senapati

BIBLIOGRAPHY

Digital Research Library & University Library System. *Audubon's Birds of America.* University of Pittsburgh. 2008. Available online. URL http://digital.library. pitt.edu/a/audubon. 19 May 2011.

Ford, Alice, ed. *Audubon, by Himself.* Garden City, NY: Natural History Press, 1969.

Rhodes, Richard. *John James Audubon: The Making of an American.* New York: Alfred A. Knopf, 2004.

Wilson, Edward O. *The Diversity of Life.* New York: Norton, 1992.

Austin, Mary Hunter (1868–1934)

Born in 1868 in Carlinsville, Illinois, Mary Hunter (Austin) was in a sense reborn in 1888 when she and her family moved to California to join a brother who had settled there. This move transformed Austin's life in two interconnected ways. First, she fell in love with the desert landscape and its people; she had always wanted to be a writer, and this move gave her a subject and a motivation. Second, because these largely unsettled areas were still quite free and lawless, Austin could escape the conventional storyline expected of women in her time. We know from her autobiographical novel *Earth Horizon* (1932) that Austin's lifelong ambition was to describe and protect this fragile region, and that she sought ways to combine this career with a successful family life.

Austin began by publishing a number of short pieces, but her first and best known full-length work is THE LAND OF LITTLE RAIN (1903). This short, beautiful book consists of 14 sketches, some of them consisting of traditional nature writing (as in her description of how the balance of species is affected by a flood), while others provide narrative accounts of the life and adventures of Mexicans, Indians or settlers. All of them share a hauntingly archaic yet lyrical prose style. For example, she writes that the "rainbow hills, the tender bluish mists, the luminous radiance of the spring have a lotus charm. They trick the sense of time, so that once inhabiting there you always mean to go away without quite realizing that you have not done it" ((8). Yet, neither the language nor the narrator are obtrusive; Austin keeps careful focus on the *place*, giving her descriptions a timeless, liquid, folkloric feel that imitates the region she portrays.

After *The Land of Little Rain*, Austin's oeuvre shows a gradual shift in focus. Whereas in her early work she had described precious places in hopes of increasing interest in them and thus generating a will to rescue them from development, she later comes to focus on the people who support themselves by working communally with the land. Like JOHN MUIR she sought to protect her beloved landscape from overuse and destruction, but she believed the land was a place to live and work; and in books like *The Flock* (1906) and *The Ford* (1917) she pleads the cause of sustainable rural communities. Like Muir, she wanted to preserve nature from ravaging hoards, but he defined these as farmers and their sheep, while she "feared the unquenchable urban thirst for water and recreation" (Nelson 233). Austin returns to this theme throughout her career, arguing that nature is not something to look at or pass through, but rather something that supports life in a cycle of work and renewal.

Austin's distaste for tourists and urbanites was heightened by her admiration for indigenous cultures, and especially for the more liberating gender norms and sustainable environmental practices they offered. She recorded many indigenous traditions, which she feared were evaporating under the direct control of the Bureau of Indian Affairs, and the indirect pull of capitalism and urban encroachment. *The Land of Journey's Ending* (1924) records many of these customs and legends. Throughout, her focus on landscape, animals, and nature remains, as does her heightened language, giving this book of essays an almost Biblical feel. By this time Austin had settled permanently in New Mexico, and she reflects, "I was Indian enough, I hope, not to miss the birds that are place marks" (305).

Austin's 1912 novel *A Woman of Genius* explores

(and decries) the challenges faced by independent, artistic women of this time. Like Austin its heroine is married and has a child, but leaves her family in order to pursue her professional ambitions. When Austin left her husband initially, she took their daughter with her, but she soon chose to institutionalize the mentally disabled child. Though sounding at times like a rebellious character, Austin was also very attracted to domesticity and traditional feminine roles, and she regretted her inability to sustain them. One factor that attracts her to indigenous and Mexican culture is that both genders have active and useful roles. Starting with the basket weavers she describes in *The Land of Little Rain,* Austin sees women as closer to the land. Anticipating modern eco-feminists, she identifies "the ways in which Western patriarchal culture subjects women even as it exploits nature" (Blend 73). In Austin's view, indigenous and local peoples, like the shepherds she describes in *The Flock,* had found ways to live in and fully appreciate nature without harming it. Her insights as a feminist, an anthropologist, and an environmentalist come together in her rejection of "the strange passion of the touring American, not so much to see notable places as to prove to other people that one has seen them" (*Land of Journey's Ending* 230); and her oeuvre substitutes for this urge to mark, claim, and possess, a desire to see and know how landscape, plants, and animals — including humans — can best coexist.— Anne Balay

BIBLIOGRAPHY

Austin, Mary Hunter. *Land of Journey's Ending*. New York: Century, 1924.
_____. *Land of Little Rain*. 1903. New York: Modern Library, 2003.
_____. *A Woman of Genius*. 1912. Old Westbury: Feminist Press, 1985.
Blend, Benay. "Building a 'House of Earth': Mary Austin, Environmental Activist and Writer." *Critical Matrix* 10.1–2 (1996): 73.
Nelson, Barney. "The Flock: An Ecocritical Look at Mary Austin's Sheep and John Muir's Hoofed Locusts" in *Exploring Lost Borders: Critical Essays on Mary Austin*, ed. Melody Graulich and Elizabeth Klimasmith (Reno: University of Nevada Press, 1999), 221.

The Land of Little Rain, Mary Austin (1903)

Mary Austin's *The Land of Little Rain,* her first book-length publication, is widely recognized as a classic of American nature writing. A collection of 14 prose sketches about the desert and mountain region of eastern California, a landscape that spans the Mojave Desert and the Owens Valley east of the Sierra Nevadas, the book is ostensibly a tribute to the American Southwest. Each vignette documents with ample detail a distinct aspect of the biocultural landscape of the California desert, as Austin variously describes the flora and fauna of the place, explains the unique aesthetic qualities of the desert, and chronicles the cultural mythologies of the people who have inhabited the land, most notably the Paiute and Shoshone. Austin makes explicit in the opening chapter one of the primary themes of the book as a whole: "Not the law, but the land sets the limit" (3); and she celebrates those features of the desert that reflect this dialectical engagement between human culture and nonhuman nature. As Vera Norwood notes in an essay commemorating Austin as one of the "heroines of nature," *The Land of Little Rain* demonstrates how "human culture is affected by the landscape as well as effecting change on it" and "teaches [our] culture how best to respond in an interactive rather than an hierarchical mode" (334).

In reading the arid landscape and the rhythms of its plant and animal inhabitants, Austin uncovers what she takes to be the principal lesson of the desert, one of accommodation: a process of attuning oneself to the nature of the place one inhabits, of appreciating the land's limitations as well as its transcendent mysteries. The flora and fauna of the California deserts offer models of this accommodation. In "The Scavengers," for example, Austin chronicles the routines and habits of desert-dwelling animals that survive and even thrive in the austerity of the arid lands. She celebrates especially those species — the vultures, buzzards, coyotes, and ravens — who feed on carrion, the detritus of the desert's cycle of life. While these creatures embody violence, inherent in the harsh landscape, that from an aesthetic standpoint is difficult to admire, Austin honors their role within "the economy of nature" because they thrive most at times when the rest of desert life suffers most (19).

Death in the desert, of course, is linked to the defining feature of the biome: scarcity of water. While the bottom feeders provide an extreme example of how to survive in the face of this limitation, *The Land of Little Rain* is replete with other, more sophisticated models of animal and human inhabitants who have successfully accommodated themselves to the contours of desert life. Striking a theme to be found in many of her other works — including *The American Rhythm* (1923), her autobiography *Earth Horizon* (1932), and her most popular play *The Arrow Maker* (1915) — Austin holds up the indigenous people of the California deserts, the Paiutes and Shoshone, as the best example of what it means to adhere to the dictates of the land. In chapters like "Shoshone Land" and "The Basket Maker" she provides sketches of both individual characters, like

Winnenap' and Seyavi, and whole Native communities whose customs and manners of living seem to spring from the land itself: "The manner of the country makes the usage of life there, and the land will not be lived in except in its own fashion. The Shoshones live like their trees, with great spaces between, and in pairs and in family groups they set up wattled huts by the infrequent ponds" (26).

Such statements reiterate Austin's emphasis on the desert's demand for accommodation, but also reflect her tendency to romanticize the Indian as an inseparable (even indistinguishable) part of a primitive and diminishing landscape. Her portraits of Winnenap' and Seyavi, who embody a fledgling connection to a waning way of life, are often tinged with romantic nostalgia. At such times Austin employs the worn, and from a postcolonial point of view deeply problematic, stereotypes of the Vanishing American and the Ecological Indian. In her study of Austin's representations of Native Americans, Martha Viehmann argues that throughout her oeuvre, "Native people […] become a source of inspiration, a form of food to nourish hungry spirits, but unnecessary as living, acting, and writing members of contemporary society. […] Indians are virtually interchangeable with wild grapes" (28).

Problematic as they may be, however, Austin's representation of and admiration for the Native communities of the desert are consistent with her theory of regionalism, which is perhaps her most enduring legacy. This theory, while focused on the Hispanic and Native communities she chronicles in *The Land of Little Rain,* is ultimately applicable across cultures. Thus, although Austin is generally disdainful and wary of the surge of Euroamerican industry and conquest that accompanies the influx of miners and land developers to eastern California, she makes it clear that the potential of achieving harmony with the landscape is open to all. As she ruefully notes in the "Jimville" chapter, specters of boom-to-bust mining towns litter the landscape and record the ruin and waste that attend Euro-american attempts to impose one's will on the desert; yet she contrasts the story of Jimville with the narrative of "The Pocket Hunter," a solitary pick-and-pan miner who, as the result of his vocation and general openness to the rhythms of the desert, acquires a deep sense of place, coming to "[depend] for the necessary sense of home and companionship on the beasts and trees, meeting and finding them in their wonted places" (22). "The Pocket Hunter" illustrates the profound and inevitable influence that regional experience has on human culture and the individual psyche; an influence that Austin describes most explicitly in her essay "Regionalism in American Fiction" (1932):

"[The regional environment] orders and determines all the direct, practical ways of [one's] getting up and lying down, of staying in and going out, of housing and clothing and food-getting; it arranges by its progressions of seed times and harvests, its rain and wind and burning suns, the rhythms of his works and amusements" (130)

Like that of the Pocket Hunter, Austin's connection to the California desert she writes about is that of an outsider-turned-convert, someone who, after moving to the region with her family in 1888, accommodated herself to the place, only to emerge as one of the primary Muses of the American Southwest. Both as an expression of this accommodation and as an articulation of the unique beauty of the desert itself, *The Land of Little Rain* stands as a compelling testament to the power of the particular places we inhabit. — Matthew Cella

BIBLIOGRAPHY

Austin, Mary. *The Land of Little Rain.* 1903. New York: Dover, 1996.
_____. "Regionalism in American Fiction." 1932. *Beyond Borders: The Selected Essays of Mary Austin.* Ed. Reuben J. Ellis. Carbondale: Southern Illinois University Press, 1996. 130–40.
Blend, Benay. "Building a 'House of Earth': Mary Austin, Environmental Activist and Writer." *Critical Matrix* 10.1–2 (1996): 73–89.
Graulich, Melody, and Elizabeth Klimasmith, eds. *Exploring Lost Borders: Critical Essays on Mary Austin.* Reno: University of Nevada Press, 1999.
Norwood, Vera L. "Heroines of Nature: Four Women Respond to the American Landscape." *The Ecocriticism Reader: Landmarks in Literary Ecology.* Ed. Cheryl Glotfelty and Harold Fromm. Athens: University of Georgia Press, 1996. 323–50.
Schaefer, Heike. *Mary Austin's Regionalism: Reflections on Gender, Genre, and Geography.* Charlottesville: University of Virginia Press, 2004.
Viehmann, Martha L. "A Rain Song for America: Mary Austin, American Indians, and American Literature and Culture." *Western American Literature* 39.1 (2004): 5–35.

Bass, Rick (1958–)

The prominent contemporary environmental writer and activist Rick Bass was born in Fort Worth, Texas in 1958, to C. R. Bass, a petroleum geologist, and Mary Lucy Robson Bass, a teacher. During his childhood and adolescence, Bass explored "the tiny de facto wilderness between outlying subdivisions" near his parents' home on the western edge of Houston ("On Willow Creek" 214), and spent short but equally formative periods of time on the wild tract of land leased by his family in the Texas Hill Country, where he also learned to hunt with his father and other male relatives. As a student at Utah State

University in the late 1970s, Bass became entranced by the wilderness of the mountainous American West, encountered the work of influential environmental(ist) writers such as EDWARD ABBEY, and took the first tentative steps toward his later literary career in a composition class taught by Thomas J. Lyon. After completing his B.Sc. in geology in 1979, he worked as a petroleum geologist in Mississippi for the next eight years. As several critics have noted, Bass's first two book-length publications dating from this period, the short story collections *The Deer Pasture* (1985) and *Wild to the Heart* (1987), not only reflect the distinctive and apparently indelible Texan and South(west)ern sensibility discernible in his broader corpus, but also frequently betray his strong desire to return to the West. Bass finally took a leap of faith, and in the summer of 1987 he and his partner and later wife, the visual artist Elizabeth Hughes, moved to the Yaak Valley in northwestern Montana, where they have raised their two children, Mary Katherine and Lowry Elizabeth, and have lived and worked ever since.

As Bass has repeatedly explained in interviews and in his non-fiction writings about the Yaak, the move to this remote, unprotected part of the Rocky Mountain West dramatically affected his subsequent development and career as a writer. Witnessing the unchecked economic exploitation and ongoing environmental destruction of his beloved, beautiful and wild valley, primarily due to the unsustainable logging and business practices of international timber companies, Bass felt compelled to forego the idealized existence of a reclusive author producing only supposedly non-political works of literary art such as novels or poems. Gradually adapting to the Yaak, and somewhat reluctantly accepting the time-consuming and often exhausting responsibilities of a writer and activist for the place he quickly came to call home, Bass began, from the early 1990s onwards, to write prolifically, passionately and persuasively about the wilderness, and the threats to this wilderness, in northwestern Montana in particular and the American West in general. In numerous "'Yaaktivist" publications (Michael T. Branch's term) that bridge and blur the gap between art and activism, for instance *The Book of Yaak* (1996), *Fiber* (1998), or *Brown Dog of the Yaak: Essays on Art and Activism* (1999), Bass has vividly portrayed the endangered ecosystems and wild animals of the region, and presented pragmatic proposals that seek to balance permanent wilderness protection and ecologically responsible, locally controlled economic development. For almost 25 years now, Bass has worked tirelessly according to the moral and ethical principles that he, as critic Terrell F. Dixon suggests, first articulated in

an essay included in *Wild to the Heart*, and that are at the core of his work: "'If it's wild to your own heart, protect it. Preserve it. Love it. And fight for it, and dedicate yourself to it'" (Bass qtd. in Dixon 76).—Micha Edlich

BIBLIOGRAPHY

Bass, Rick. *The Book of Yaak*. Boston: Mariner-Houghton Mifflin, 1996. Print.
_____. *Brown Dog of the Yaak: Essays on Art and Activism*. Minneapolis: Milkweed Editions, 1999. Print. Credo Ser.
_____. *Fiber*. Athens: University of Georgia Press, 1998. Print.
_____. "On Willow Creek." *At Home on the Earth: Becoming Native to Our Place*. Ed. David Landis Barnhill. Berkeley: University of California Press, 1999. 211–26. Print.
_____. *Why I Came West*. Boston: Houghton Mifflin, 2008. Print.
Dixon, Terrell F. "Rick Bass." *American Nature Writers*. Ed. John Elder. Vol. 2. New York: Scribner's, 1996. 75–88. Print.
Hunt, Richard. "Rick Bass." *Twentieth-Century American Nature Writers: Prose*. Ed. Roger Thompson and J. Scott Bryson. Detroit: Thomson-Gale, 2003. 29–38. Print. Dictionary of Literary Biography 275.
Weltzien, O. Alan, ed. *The Literary Art and Activism of Rick Bass*. Salt Lake City: University of Utah Press, 2001. Print.
_____. "Rick Bass." *Contemporary Authors Online*. Gale-Cengage Learning, 2009. Web. 25 Jan. 2010.

The Book of Yaak, Rick Bass (1996)

Rick Bass's collection of essays, *The Book of Yaak*, is a closely observed and deeply felt description of a remote wilderness valley in Montana. Praised by Scott Slovic for his "furiously intense imagination" and called "a born-and-bred raconteur" (Slovic 124), Bass writes not only to educate readers about the flora and fauna of this area, not only to delight and inspire them with deftly told tales of hunting dogs and homesteaders, grizzly bears and berry picking, but also to compel readers to take political action. Bass hopes that the power of an informed citizenry can change ill-conceived public policy, that seemingly disparate groups, such as artists and loggers, can reach consensus on issues affecting their daily lives. The written word remains Bass's primary weapon in the defense of the Yaak Valley's roadless wilderness, though he admits that activism is risky for a literary writer: "it's a sin, to ask something of the reader, rather than to give; and to know the end, to know your agenda, from the very start" (xiii). This approach betrays the sanctuary, mystery, and peace Bass finds writing fiction. Yet he takes this risk and urges his readers to act: "I know you're not going to travel this far to catch an eight-inch rainbow. But maybe you can travel over to your desk and pick up a pen" (130).

Because Bass conceived of *The Book of Yaak* as a means of persuading readers to take grass-roots action to defend a particular ecosystem from irrevocable damage, the book exemplifies what Karla Armbruster terms "literary environmental advocacy: the practice of using literary writing to speak for nature in opposition to prevailing cultural ideologies that sanction the domination, manipulation, and destruction of the nonhuman world" (Armbruster 197). Similarly O. Alan Weltzien insists that "we read [Bass] not only to experience the joys, infinitely varied, of being in place in the natural world. We also read him as a test case: as one eager to close the gap [...] between art and activism" (Weltzien 10).

Rick Bass moved to Yaak Valley in 1987, a wilderness area located in the extreme northwest corner of Montana, where the flora and fauna of two major ecosystems (the Pacific Northwest and the northern Rockies) overlap and intermingle. Inaccessible forests of cedars and lodgepole pines harbor some of the last wild remnants of the American frontier's mythic animals — wolves, badgers, and grizzlies; the meadows and riverbanks are resplendent with glacier lilies, lupine, and paintbrush; and bullhead trout and sturgeon swim in the rivers and ponds.

Weltzien claims *The Book of Yaak* identifies Bass as both "psalmist and prophet" (Weltzien 13). In it, Bass speaks directly to the reader, as if in conversation, sometimes earnest, sometimes jocular, always sincere, alternating meditative and lyrical passages with discursive reportage and polemic. Bass's lyrical descriptions, such as this on the approach of autumn, reveal the Yaak Valley's attraction: "ash trees stunned with gold, blue skies, and the huckleberry fields burnt red, blood red, and geese flying south, south with the music of their leaving" (47). In reporting changes in the valley, Bass notes that the Forest Service has used public funds to build 500,000 miles of roads on public lands, to benefit the "corporate timber industry" (69). In the 1960s the Yaak Valley had only one road; in 1996 "there are over a thousand miles (126). Such reportage becomes the documentary foundation for his plea to protect the wilderness from further incursions.

Protection, Bass believes, will only be attained when Congress prohibits all road-building on Yaak Valley's public lands. He seeks to protect the roadless wildness of the valley from clear-cut logging operations and their inevitable environmental degradation, resulting in a denuded landscape he compares to the desolate bleakness of the moon. Moreover, as Bass carefully explains, roads and clear-cutting fragment the territorial homes of grizzlies and other large mammals, and this isolates the individuals and small groups into finite breeding populations, making them more vulnerable to population stresses. In addition, runoff from clear-cut areas, even those replanted by the timber companies, leads to silting in pristine rivers and lakes. Ultimately Bass warns that we risk losing something that humans cannot fix or replace; not simply precious megafauna like the grizzly, but "entire interwoven systems" (Slovic 125). Furthermore, he asserts, "as order and logic become increasingly lost to our societies, I'm certain that these things — art, and the wilderness — are critical to stabilizing the troubling tilt, the world's uneasiness, that we can all feel with every nerve of our senses" (11).

Thus, in the end, the plea to protect Yaak Valley becomes a plea to protect all remaining wilderness, and the Valley itself a symbol of fragile environments worldwide. The book's final pages contain addresses of members of Congress, Forest Service officials, and wildlife protection groups; and Bass notes that he has given a copy of the book to every member of Congress and to the Clinton administration, insisting "I was willing, and am, to work at it forever" (104).

The Book of Yaak, according to Bass, is finally not a book at all, but "an artifact of the woods, like a chunk of rhyolite, a shed deer antler, a bear skull, a heron feather" (xiv). Yet it is also a "sourcebook, a handbook, a weapon of the heart" (xiii). And these two passages illustrate an internal conflict so deep that, in Bass' own account, it disturbs him even as he sleeps, and makes his heart pound "so hard in anger" that it hurts inside his chest when he awakens (66); namely, his simultaneous desire to live the life of a poet, the life of beauty, magic, and spirit, and yet to protect the Yaak Valley, his family's home, through political advocacy.— Diane Warner

BIBLIOGRAPHY

Armbruster, Karla. "Can a Book Protect a Valley?: Rick Bass and the Dilemmas of Literary Environmental Advocacy." In *The Literary Art and Activism of Rick Bass*, edited by O. Alan Weltzien. Salt Lake City: University of Utah Press, 2001.

Bass, Rick. *The Book of Yaak*. Boston: Houghton Mifflin, 1996.

Slovic, Scott. "Rick Bass: A Portrait." In *Brown Dog of the Yaak: Essays on Art and Activism,* by Rick Bass. Minneapolis: Milkweed, 1999.

Weltzien, O. Alan. "Introduction." In *The Literary Art and Activism of Rick Bass*, edited by O. Alan Weltzien. Salt Lake City: University of Utah Press, 2001.

Beaty, Richard Edward (1867–1941)

Born in the northern section of the Shenandoah area of Warren County, Virginia in 1867, Richard

Edward Beaty revelled both in the natural richness of the area, and in the personal and spiritual growth that accompanied his enjoyment of it — experiences figuring prominently in his literary work. He married in 1900 and lived for over 20 years in Mount Vernon, Washington, where he wrote THE MOUNTAIN ANGELS. He later returned to Virginia and resided again in the Warren County area. His gravestone in Prospect Hill Cemetery in Front Royal, Virginia, bears the inscription "The plant improver and mountain author."

Beaty positions himself outside the modernist perspective of his era, with its emphasis on the individual's struggle for identity and happiness in a confrontation with an impersonal, industrialized world; he returns to a pre-industrial time in a mode reminiscent of the New England TRANSCENDENTALISTS. Aspects of EMERSON's "NATURE" and "SELF-RELIANCE" appear in both the fictional and personal accounts: daily observation and interaction with nature consistently provide spiritual consolation and inspiration. Similarly, the insights and character-defining elements of the simple life that THOREAU explores in WALDEN are echoed in Beaty's treatment of an individual's interactions with the Shenandoah wilderness. However, he also respects the dangers inherent in this environment, and, like JACK LONDON in his tales of the Yukon, emphasizes the pragmatic truth that a sympathetic understanding of nature ensures a better chance of survival.

Beaty wrote and personally published *The Mountain Angels: Trials of the Mountaineers of the Blue Ridge and Shenandoah Valley* (1928). Building upon a tradition of Romantic writers both in England and America, he notes in the "Preface" that his intent is to write a story that "is made up of facts, fiction and unwritten history, is largely romantic, and I hope, inspirational." Similar to W. H. Hudson's response in *Green Mansions*, Beaty counters violent political turmoil with the rejuvenating powers of Nature. Loosely based on the details of his father's Civil War experiences when a band "of thieves and cutthroats ... tried to drive the stock from my father's farm," Beaty's story recounts the hardships, endurance, and eventual success of two young men, Oscar Asplund and Frank Owen, and their adaptation to the Shenandoah wilderness in order to survive. After the war, the young men make their fortunes in the larger world, Oscar going into land development west of Chicago and Frank into the mercantile business in New Jersey and New York State. Still dissatisfied after attaining financial success, the two return in 1882 to the peaceful and benignant tranquility they originally discovered in the natural simplicity of the Shenandoah region.

As a companion piece to *The Mountain Angels,*

Beaty later wrote and published *Blue Ridge Boys: Narrations of Early, Actual Mountain Experiences and Humorous Anecdotes of the Shenandoah National Park Section* (1938). Based on personal and recounted experiences in the park, Beaty's compilation of stories elaborates his defining belief in the personal and spiritual fulfillment possible through open and appreciative interaction with nature. — Thomas P. Fair

BIBLIOGRAPHY

Beaty, Richard Edward. *Blue Ridge Boys: Narrations of Early, Actual Mountain Experiences and Humorous Anecdotes of the Shenandoah National Park Section.* Front Royal, VA: R. E. Beaty, 1938.
_____. *The Mountain Angels: Trials of the Mountaineers of the Blue Ridge and Shenandoah Valley.* Front Royal, VA: R. E. Beaty, 1928.

The Mountain Angels: Trials of the Mountaineers of the Blue Ridge and Shenandoah Valley, Richard Edward Beaty (1928)

Reminiscent of William Henry Hudson's romances, *Green Mansions* and *The Purple Land*, Richard Beaty's boys' adventure story, *The Mountain Angels: Trials of the Mountaineers of the Blue Ridge and Shenandoah Valley*, details the hardships, endurance, and eventual success of two young men who must adapt to the wilderness in order to survive. Although contemporary readers may find the work racially offensive, the novel vividly evokes the spirit and attitudes of its time, as well as the natural environment and inherent beauty of the Blue Ridge Mountains and Shenandoah Valley. The central experiences of the two protagonists, Oscar Asplund and Frank Owen, portray the region as a refuge from the harshness of the world and the cruelties of the Civil War. The novel concludes several decades after the war, with the two, now successful young men's disappointment with the impersonal and artificial world of society and business, and their return to the truth and goodness they originally discovered in the rustic simplicity of the mountains and valley.

After readers come to terms with the racism embedded in the characterization of the freed slave Jane Carter, they can appreciate the novel's celebration of Nature's power and beauty. Although in the "Preface" Beaty implies a desire to provide a favorable portrait of "the colored race" (3), his portrayal of 'Aunt Jane' frequently undermines her ennobling actions. Often described in pejorative terms, Jane tends to be self-deprecating and self-effacing as she privileges European Americans over African Americans, including herself. However, she fully understands the prevalent social dangers engendered by the war, and despite the rude and racist responses to her offers of assistance, she remains willing to aid the Asplund family. She embodies patience, endurance and forgiveness at a time when bigotry, hatred and violence were the norm; and provides not merely a compelling racial analogue to the equally misconstrued and maltreated native peoples of America, but a human analogue to the environment that was equally in bondage to Euro-American ambition. Thus, while Beaty's presentation of a compliant and diffident black woman conforms to 1920s conventions, it is not surprising that Jane ultimately figures as one of the novel's most significant characters, in her recognition and address of the social and moral disruptions in the protagonists' lives, in her rescue of the Asplunds' infant daughter from probable death, and above all, in her revelation of the truth in the novel's dénouement.

Like W. H. Hudson's *Green Mansions*, Beaty's *The Mountain Angels* counters violent political turmoil with the rejuvenating powers of Nature. The nurturing and supportive animus of the Blue Ridge Mountains and Shenandoah Valley stands in stark contrast to what seems an arbitrary and often soulless outer world, morally eviscerated by the deadly social chaos of the Civil War. The 12-year-old Oscar Asplund witnesses a Rebel mob burn his home and murder his parents, forcing him to escape to the safety of the woods. Oscar quickly adapts to the wilderness, and even thrives, after he discovers protected shelter and supplies in an abandoned moonshine distillery. Similarly, 12-year-old Frank Owen must fend for himself when, after being orphaned and adopted by a kind neighbor, his adopted father is conscripted into the Confederate army and killed in battle. Frank must survive with the few supplies they were able to cache in the forest before his guardian left for war. Acclimated to the forest, both boys "grew strong and learned to love the mountain more and more" (71). The orphaning of Oscar and Frank, and the war's brutal violence, reinforces one of Beaty's major themes — life's inherent and inexplicable cruelty — and establishes human society as unforgiving, violent, and often merciless. The beneficent side of Nature, however, provides invaluable life lessons for the young men, and establishes a positive alternative to society's hostility and pitfalls.

Oscar and Frank's experiences parallel each other, as each boy encounters characteristic challenges in the forest and learns to use its many resources in developing self-reliance, confidence, and independence. Both boys become expert hunters and woodsmen, and achieve self-sufficiency. After a brief, initial confrontation, the two quickly recognize their mutual connection to Nature and proclaim their brotherhood. Buoyed by their successful encounters with Nature, Oscar and Frank negotiate a trade, of work and wild game for milk, meals, and other necessities, with the Fitzgeralds, a mountain farming family. Recognizing their need for a formal education, the boys barter their hunting skill and part of Frank's leather supply to a teacher, for instruction and board during the winter terms. However, even the sheltering Nature is not always benign, and presents predictable dangers such as a treacherous snow pack and ice storm that Oscar encounters while hunting. Despite the threat, he recognizes that Nature also provides the means to *endure* such difficulties, and sensibly exercises his accumulated knowledge and skill to survive. Ultimately, both boys emerge as capable young men, and after the war achieve considerable success: Oscar as a land speculator in the West and Frank as a businessman in the East. However, despite their accomplishments, the young men's spirits are ultimately under-nourished by "civilized" life, and they return to the Shenandoah region to recover, on a higher and more complex level, the benignancy of their youthful environment.

A second thematic focus, centering on Oscar's sister Lenea and her adoptive sister Sarah Jones, relies on traditional and idealized sexual stereotypes for the young women's characterization. Their innocence and goodness personify Nature's virtues: "The girls themselves were as beautiful as the natural scenery around them [...] they loved so much the independent life and the beautiful surroundings around them" (37–38). They too, however, demonstrate self-reliance and an independent spirit through their management of a small farm and their sale of honey from the wild bees they track through the forest; and in a sense, the manifestation of the region's animus in the girls themselves, marks them as appropriate mates for the boys: "Frank and Oscar became very much interested in those tanned faces and sunburned hands that had formed themselves to fit the surrounding beauty as a first touch of evolution to a more sane and higher life of woman" (115).

After the young people meet, the narrative soon ends, assisted by Aunt Jane's revelation of Lenea's true identity as Oscar's sister; and Frank concludes, "We have found two mountain angels who live a life of beauty and purity, and not like the city life I have been trying to live" (118). Although financial success may be found in business and westward development, Beaty asserts, with the simple but enduring wisdom of the folk artist, that real happiness and contentment reside in Nature — in a simple life, such as that found in the Blue Ridge Mountains and the Shenandoah Valley.— Thomas P. Fair

BIBLIOGRAPHY

Beaty, Richard Edward. *The Mountain Angels: Trials of the Mountaineers of the Blue Ridge and Shenandoah Valley.* Front Royal, VA: R. E. Beaty, 1928.

Berry, Wendell (1934–   )

As a writer Wendell Berry has, in his own words, chosen to belong to his farm, "not just as a circumstance, but as a part of the informing ambience of my mind and imagination" (*Way of Ignorance* 48). In each of his many public roles — as farmer, essayist, novelist, poet, and activist — he draws on his patiently and locally gained perceptions about the way the natural world functions, and the analogous ways in which humans should relate to the land and to each other.

Berry was born near Port Royal, Kentucky, and grew up on the land tended by his parents, grandparents, and great-grandparents (*The Long-Legged House* 170–71). He left his family farmland to go to the University of Kentucky and then, after marrying, studied writing as a Wallace Stegner Fellow at Stanford University with other young writers, including Ken Kesey and Ernest Gaines. After traveling to Europe and landing a job at New York University, Berry writes, his "hopes and plans [...] turned [...] back toward Kentucky" (*The Long-Legged House* 153). So in 1964 Wendell Berry left the cultural center of the East coast to farm a marginal Kentucky hillside and teach occasionally at the University of Kentucky. Since then he has remained faithful to his "marriage with the place," providing a marginal and yet increasingly influential defense of local, sustainable communities against an economy that values global, mass consumption (*The Long-Legged House* 166).

From his farm Berry has written prolifically in three genres, grappling with diverse cultural, economic, political, moral, and religious issues. In his seminal book of essays, *The Unsettling of America*, he identifies two opposing American values: exploitation and nurture. While historically Americans more often relate to other people and the land in exploitative ways — robbing the Indians of their land and the land of its health — there have also been Americans who care for the order of the earth and its communities (6–8). Berry challenges readers to consider their ways of life and imagine how they might be able to nurture their exploited communities — the land and its human and non-human life — back to health. Politically, as Jason Peters notes, Berry "supports decentralization and the proliferation of as many small landholders as are possible" (8). His hope, however, lies not in political solutions: "Our environmental problems ... are not, at root, political;

they are cultural.... [O]ur country is not being destroyed by bad politics; it is being destroyed by a bad way of life" (*What Are People For?* 37).

Berry's belief in the need for a cultural shift generates and is reflected in poetry that imagines new ways of relating to the land and community. One group of poems is written in the voice of the "Mad Farmer" who articulates the life Berry embraces, a life counter to the consumerist, industrial political economy. As Berry's farmer commands in "Manifesto: The Mad Farmer Liberation Front,"

> Friends, every day do something
> that won't compute. Love the Lord.
> Love the world. Work for nothing.
> Take all that you have and be poor.
> Love someone who does not deserve it [*Collected Poems* 151].

Perhaps the most searching and comprehensive expression of his stand against the hurry and noise of the profit economy is found in his long series of "Sabbath poems" in A TIMBERED CHOIR (1998), written on Sunday afternoon walks on his farm. In these poems he explores what it means to belong to and be at rest in a place, in his place:

> I, through woods and fields, through fallen days
> Am passing to where I belong:
> At home, at ease, and well,
> In Sabbaths of this place
> Almost invisible,
> Toward which I go from song to song [*A Timbered Choir* 28].

His fiction, in eight novels and numerous short stories, provides another imagined instantiation of this nurturing culture. Port William, the fictional location in which his stories take place, offers Berry a chance to portray the way of life he knew as a boy, and which is now in decline. As Berry puts it, "I have made the imagined place of Port William, its neighborhood and membership, in an attempt to honor the actual place where I have lived" (*Way of Ignorance* 50). Set during World War II and the subsequent decades during which American farmland was largely depopulated, Berry's novels and stories vividly evoke a community that cares for the health of its land and all its members. While Berry's fiction can be seen as nostalgic, his characters embody values that he believes contemporary America desperately needs to regain, in order to sustain its land, communities, and citizens.

Berry turns to the past to find cultural values for the future because he sees an analogous pattern in the way fertile land makes the old new, turning the deaths of plants and animals into new life (*A Continuous Harmony* 150). As he states in his book of essays, *Life Is a Miracle*, positive change regarding our "use of the living world [...] is imaginable only if we are willing to risk an unfashionable recourse to our cultural tradition. Human hope may always have resided in our ability, in time of need, to return to our cultural landmarks and reorient ourselves" (3). Kimberly Smith summarizes Berry's "stance toward tradition" as "conservative but critical": "His goal, then, is to *revive and renew* the intellectual traditions he has inherited" (*Wendell Berry and the Agrarian Tradition* 6). And just as Berry works to rehabilitate the exploited and worn-out farm he has inherited, so he writes to nurture and reinvigorate the cultural traditions he has inherited.

While Berry expressed deep skepticism about the Christian church early in his life, his stance toward tradition has more recently led him to seek a revitalization of American religion. In a 2007 interview Berry articulates the way in which the Christian gospel has become increasingly important to his understanding of how to care for his place: "The gospels are exhilarating because ... essentially the invitation that Christ was giving [is,] Do you want to live free, do you want to live in a great world that includes all the works of God, that includes all you can imagine and more, or do you want to live in some little capsule defined by politicians or scientists or philosophers or denominational bosses?" (231). Through living in this larger world, while faithfully caring for a particular part of it, Berry sustains the hope that humans can adequately care for their home — the land and all its inhabitants. — Jeffrey Bilbro

BIBLIOGRAPHY

Berry, Wendell. *Collected Poems: 1957–1982*. New York: North Point Press, 1999.
_____. *A Continuous Harmony: Essays Cultural and Agricultural*. San Diego: A Harvest Book, 1972.
_____. "Hunting for Reasons to Hope: A Conversation with Wendell Berry." Interview with Harold K. Bush. *Christianity and Literature* 56.2 (2007): 215–234.
_____. *Life Is a Miracle: An Essay Against Modern Superstition*. New York: Counterpoint, 2001.
_____. *The Long-Legged House*. Washington D.C.: Shoemaker & Hoard, 2004.
_____. *A Timbered Choir: The Sabbath Poems 1979–1997*. New York: Counterpoint, 1998.
_____. *The Unsettling of America: Culture and Agriculture*. San Francisco: Sierra Club Books, 1996.
_____. *The Way of Ignorance*. Washington D.C.: Shoemaker and Hoard, 2005.
Cornell, Daniel. "The Country of Marriage: Wendell Berry's Personal Political Vision." *The Southern Literary Journal* 16.1 (Fall 1983): 59–70.
Peters, Jason. Introduction. *Wendell Berry: Life and Work*. Ed. Jason Peters. Culture of the Land: A Ser. in the New Agrarianism. Lexington: University Press of Kentucky, 2007.
Smith, Kimberly K. *Wendell Berry and the Agrarian Tradition: A Common Grace*. Lawrence: University Press of Kansas, 2003.

A Timbered Choir:
The Sabbath Poems 1979–1997,
Wendell Berry (1998)

In *A Timbered Choir*, a collection that reprints and supplements poems originally published as *Sabbaths* (1987), Wendell Berry attempts to reveal and revitalize the intrinsic vitality of traditional forms. The book relies on traditional poetic forms — particularly rhyme schemes — while exploring the typical forms of agrarian life on Berry's Kentucky farm. These latter forms, the often subtle but telling shapes of a family farm's interdependent community, are in a sense also traditional: "The field finds its source / in the old forest" (46). Frequently likened to field work, Berry's poetic work interrogates any sort of progress that hastily denudes life forms that are, the poet insists, "not raw sources [...] but fellow presences" (51). Imagining the fallout from such so-called progress, another poem declares, "The only new thing could be pain" (8). Yet the forms of small-farm life, Berry recognizes, continue a tradition gapingly removed from the experiences of most contemporary Americans. That JEFFERSONIAN heritage — the established life of farming in which one must "live like a tree / That does not grow beyond / The power of its place" (142) — has become so exceptional as to be radical. In this sense, the agrarianism of the book, as of most of Berry's oeuvre, resists rather than reinforces tradition. It speaks against that dominant tradition for which forests are spaces in need of clearing. Modern rapacity provokes two images depicted, and also lamented, in several poems: first, the sight of a carelessly "cleared field" as "[a] place no human made," indeed "a place unmade / By human greed" (16); and second,

> the sound of cars [...] passing
> on the road, that simplest form
> going only two ways,
> both ways away [101].

The poet suggests that human greed can do ecological harm precisely because inhumane technologies so easily dislocate. Along a straight line that always leads elsewhere, they shuttle people away from the site and the pain of "unmaking." Berry has written that "To farm," by contrast, "is to be placed absolutely" ("Imagination" 46). *A Timbered Choir* also attempts the work of placing, of locating its readers within its received forms, if only temporarily.

Berry did not always turn to formal rhyme schemes to realize his — to borrow LAWRENCE BUELL's term — "intensely lococentric" ambitions (Buell 230). Rather, as Jeffery Alan Triggs explains, prior to *Sabbaths* the poet often wrote in "free verse forms" reflecting a "colloquial" style (Triggs 192–193). Triggs suspects "a latent contradiction" between Berry's informality in those earlier works and his austere "philosophical positions" (Triggs 193). If so, *Sabbaths* and, later, *A Timbered Choir* smooth out the contradiction by tapping into traditional poetic resources. In the essay "The Specialization of Poetry" (1974), a useful supplement to these poems, Berry questions contemporary poetry's fondness for formlessness, which he finds "neither civilized nor natural" ("Specialization" 12). He claims that the formed poem or song

> rises [...] in reference to daily and seasonal — and surely even longer — rhythms in the life of the poet and in the life that surrounds him. The rhythm of a poem resonates with these larger rhythms that surround it; it fills its environment with sympathetic vibrations. Rhyme, which is a function of rhythm, may suggest this sort of resonance; it marks the coincidences of smaller structures with larger ones, as when the day, the month, and the year all end at the same moment. Song [....] is the testimony of the singer's inescapable relation to the world, to the human community, and also to tradition ["Specialization" 17].

For Berry the Sabbath inscribes these coinciding endings, offering a space of rest between the fall and rise of rhythms that coordinate the civilized with the natural. Written on Sundays, the Sabbath poems in *A Timbered Choir* are divided by year, each year's entries further identified by Roman numerals. (Some poems also carry specific titles, and a few appear below dedications or other epigraphs.) The characteristic tenor of the series is itself highly rhythmical. Poems mark Sabbath days, and those days mark the weeks they complete as well as those they inaugurate, weeks that accumulate to form years, each such year nonetheless ending with a single day. In this collection, as in Berry's "Specialization" essay, rhyme heightens the way in which a line's ending, a small "native" element like a word or syllable, lends coherence to a larger, more complex structure such as a stanza or poem. Rhyme's economy suggests the temporal patterning of moments in days and seasons, but also evokes the biological ideal of the farm's constituents flourishing together in diversified harmony; that is, the economy of rhyme in *A Timbered Choir* is itself also an ecology. Thus, in the seventh 1982 poem, the speaker hopes and labors to see a vision in which "field and woods at last agree / In an economy / Of widest worth" [49].

Rhyme furnishes both the manner and the matter for much of the text, and Berry deploys a variety of rhyme schemes. Quatrains in *abab* patterns appear frequently, but the collection also incorporates *terza rima*, eight-line stanzas of couplets, sophisticated classical patterns (see the ten-line stanzas of 1979's fourth poem), and the English-sonnet structure (see the fourth work of 1983). Amid this variety of rhyming poems appear many that do not rhyme. And Berry often takes liberties with end-rhyming words, as in "dark"/"work" (68), "air"/"choir" (83), "invisible"/"still" (121). Such variants seem to signal that poetry's "artistry" (47), like that of the rhyming natural world, can operate in patterns that are discernible but not deafening. Numerous entries consider rhyme itself as a topic, using it to interpret the earth and earthly labor. An early poem notes, for instance, "When field and woods agree, they make a rhyme / That stirs in distant memory the whole" (15). Later, the poet captures the end of his work, his farming and his poetry, with rhyme's space and time:

> I stop the mower blade,
> And so conspire with time
> In the return of shade,
> Completion of this rhyme [120].

S.T. Coleridge wrote that a poem should "convert a *series* into a *Whole*," transforming apparent linearity into the circular image of "the snake with its Tail in its Mouth" (Coleridge 123). For Berry, who elsewhere laments our loss of "the ideal of a whole or complete life" ("Quantity" 82), poetic rhythm intimates such wholeness. He finds structures in poetry for hewing an imaginative whole from lived fragments — the resources of what one poem terms "the given life" (178). The culmination of a rhyme, then, evokes the fulfillment of a formed life. Rhyme thus understood enacts a well-prepared death, another topic that figures prominently in *A Timbered Choir*. Asserting that "[r]uin is in place here" (11), the work tries to account for "the way of death: loss of what might / Have been in what must come to be" (19). Accounting for death could mean answering critic Timothy Morton's call to "accept [...] the fact of mortality among species and ecosystems" (Morton 205). Yet deaths, like rhymes, are always particular, and Berry's highly situated poems ultimately consider how a way of life aware of death might be "not a way but a place" (216). In their sensitivity to the particular beings upon which, on a particularly shared plot, they depend, the poems try to renew forms of living whose ends are consonant with the facts of dying. — Dustin D. Stewart

BIBLIOGRAPHY

Berry, Wendell. "Imagination in Place." *The Way of Ignorance, and Other Essays.* Berkeley: Counterpoint, 2005. 39–51.

_____. *A Timbered Choir: The Sabbath Poems 1979–1997.* Washington, DC: Counterpoint, 1988.

_____. "Quantity vs. Form." *The Way of Ignorance, and Other Essays.* Berkeley: Counterpoint, 2005. 81–9.

_____. "The Specialization of Poetry." *Standing by Words.* San Francisco: North Point, 1983. 3–23.

Buell, Lawrence. "Religion and the Environmental Imagination in American Literature." *There Before Us: Religion, Literature, and Culture from Emerson to Wendell Berry.* Ed. Roger Lundin. Grand Rapids, MI: Eerdmans, 2007. 216–38.

Coleridge, Samuel Taylor. *Coleridge's Poetry and Prose.* Ed. Nicholas Halmi, Paul Magnuson, and Raimonda Modiano. New York: Norton, 2004.

Morton, Timothy. *Ecology Without Nature: Rethinking Environmental Aesthetics.* Cambridge, MA: Harvard University Press, 2007.

Triggs, Jeffery Alan. "Farm as Form: Wendell Berry's *Sabbaths.*" *Wendell Berry.* Ed. Paul Merchant. Lewiston, ID: Confluence, 1991. 191–203.

The Bible and the American Environmental Imaginary

"The Bible ... is our national text — whether we really read it or not," declares Vincent Wimbush in *The Bible and the American Myth*; "no other society in the world is so imbued both with the aura and the aroma of the Bible, while simultaneously subjecting it to such parasitic cultural captivity" (vii–viii).

Over the last 400 years, many Americans, both in religious and secular activities, have tended to assume the position of an exemplar, a "chosen people" among the world's cultures (consider the typical inaugural address of its presidents, for example). Inherited from the Puritan settlers of the 1600's, this pervasive conviction combines the imperialist notions of the Biblical Old Testament with the evangelistic philosophy of the New Testament (most notably analyzed in R.S. Sugirtharajah's *The Bible and Empire*; see also Daniell 417); and central to the story has been the American wilderness, a motif which early American literary authors leaned heavily on, as did the nation's scholars, painters, politicians, and others. Harvard's authority on the Puritans, and author of *Errand into the Wilderness*, Perry Miller focuses on the Calvinist assumption that permeated the nation's mindset during its first 200 years: our land is a reward, proof of God's approval, but it is also dangerous and needs human control (*Nature's Nation* 201). This ambiguous attitude has encouraged both intense appreciation of — and even subjugation to — nature, and its often simultaneous exploitation.

In sustaining the myth, early Americans looked to the Bible (selectively) as a guide, though with as much ambivalence as the Bible itself regarding the human use of the natural environment and its "value" to God. However, owing partly to the work of Eco-Criticism, Feminism, Marxism, and Post-Colonial studies, a growing "green theology" or "eco-theol-ogy" has (re)discovered the neglected side of the Puritan ambiguity, providing a new lens with which to perceive a *pro*-environment Bible; notable works here include *The Green Bible*, Carroll *et al.*'s *The Greening of Faith*, Habel and Balabanski's *The Earth Story in the New Testament*, and Ortiz's *Concordance of Over 1000 Environment-Friendly Scriptures in the King James and New KJV*.

One of the earliest, and certainly the most popular and influential, of the Bibles in English was the 1611 *King James Version* (KJV); however, at the time of the Revolutionary War it was not legal to print Bibles in English in North America because of England's Crown Copyright, and so the first Bible printed on American soil was actually Christopher Saur's 1743 Lutheran translation into German, in Pennsylvania (Daniell 630).

By the 1800's, however, the new nation's patriotic assurance resulted in the first American attempts to translate the Bible, rather than rely solely on the British KJV; and 1816 saw the establishment of the influential American Bible Society (ABS), which issued over 32 million bibles in the U.S. and abroad over a 60-year span (1818–1880), and continues today (Gutjahr 188). Yet the 1611 KJV proved "unassailable," according to Bible historian David Daniell: "It is ... as if God had said that in America His Word has always to be in the version of early British imperialism" (632), a view amply illustrated in the writings of early colonial authors such as THOMAS HARRIOT and JOHN SMITH. The American preference for the KJV is now gaining ground again in what some call the "KJV Only" stance, leading to a total of 1,500 new KJV editions in the 20th century alone (Daniell 765; Hills; Gutjahr). Two of the best-known Bibles to appear in the last half-century have been the "conservative" NIV (*New International Version*) and the "liberal" RSV (*Revised Standard Version*), both repeatedly and currently in revision due to ceaseless controversy, chronicled in P. Thuesen's *In Discordance with the Scriptures, American Protestant Battles Over Translating the Bible*. However, most *nature-oriented* scriptures differ little from one translation to another, as is evident in a perusal of comparative concordances such as the online *Bible Gateway*.

The religious text that most strikingly roots its claims in the American terrain is the *Book of Mormon* (1830), one of the best-selling "Life of Christ" accounts of the 19th century, which sold thousands of copies in 37 American and British editions (Gutjahr 151–160). This novel-influenced story in the King James style was intended as a KJV companion, and presented the prophecies of Joseph Smith, locating the Garden of Eden in the pre-colonized United States and depicting an ancient visit by Jesus to

America, linking America with the Holy Land and making her divinely favored in the scheme of world history.

The recent American-published *Green Bible* (2008) highlights, in green ink, over 1,000 pro-environment scriptures. Printed in earth colors with soy-based ink on recycled paper, this New Revised Standard Version (NRSV) is considered a "liberal" translation, supported by leaders of The Sierra Club, The National Wildlife Federation, and the Animals and Religion Program of The Humane Society of the United States.

Mostly owing to its greater length, the *Old* Testament, the original source of the devastating "dominion" myth, actually contains more green verses than the New, mostly concentrated in Genesis, Leviticus, Job, Psalms, Isaiah, and Ezekiel (Nash, Ortiz). But in John's Gospel alone, the Greek word *kosmos* occurs a full 78 times, providing an important "semantic range" for its interpretation, according to B. Balabanski in Habel and Balabanski's *The Earth Story in the New Testament* (89; see also Trainor's chapter in this text), a source which lists 600 pro-environment verses in the New Testament (Balabanski 89).

Especially fascinating is the Bible's tendency to interweave environmental conditions with social justice. A less explicit, but nonetheless profound concern for the environment may be extrapolated from the *ethical* perspective present in the Bible's care for the outsider or "other" in Jewish society. Examples abound in the British Bible Society's *Poverty and Justice Bible,* released in the U.S. in 2010, and highlighting over 2,000 social justice scriptures. The sheer number and variety of the Bible's dictums against the exploitively wealthy and *for* the unprivileged, is daunting; and significantly, the Bible defines the outsider not simply as the hungry and landless, but also as immigrants, widows, orphans, the sick, even the sad — all those vulnerable to exploitive power regimes — and tends to class them *together* with the land, waters, and wild animals (Robb; Ortiz).

As in the work of many American environmental authors, the "pro-environment" scriptures usually do not deploy broad, abstract terms like "nature," but rather specific descriptions of animals, trees, etc. In fact, ancient Hebrew contains no equivalents for the modern concepts of "environment" or "wilderness" (DeWitt 95; Kay 1). Thus translation has proven a complicated and often ambiguous enterprise, beginning with the Bible's first and most famous book (see esp. Habel & Balabanski, Thuesen). Until the 1980's, almost all commentary and interpretations in English have taken as their directive the "Genesis Mandate," the single most troublesome and debated scripture on the subject for environmentally minded biblical scholars:

> Then God said, "Let us make humankind in our image, according to our likeness; and let them have **dominion** over the fish of the sea, and over the birds of the air, and over the cattle, and over all the wild animals of the earth, and over every creeping thing that creeps upon the earth..." [Genesis 1:26–28, New KJV, emphasis added].

While the Hebrew words for "dominion" are *kabash* ("subdue") and *radah* ("to rule," Geisler 305), many liberal Bible commentators and some American conservatives now understand the passage in a whole-Bible context which implies care-taking or stewardship rather than domination (for example, Carroll *et al.* in *The Greening of Faith*; DeWitt; EEN).

Causing similar controversy among scholars is the Bible's use of the word "wilderness," described as one of the most powerful words in all of Judeo-Christianity by Harvard Divinity School's David Williams, who finds over 250 references to wilderness in both Bible testaments (24–5). Environmental historian Roderick Nash interprets most of the 300 wilderness references that he counts as synonymous with "desert" or "waste." In fact, the Puritans made "howling wilderness" a common American saying, after the Deuteronomy 32:10 passage wherein God finds Jacob "in the waste howling wilderness" (KJV) (Johnston, Nash). Environmental and religious scholars now generally agree that in America the idea of "wilderness" as a vacant wasteland and locus of evil began with WILLIAM BRADFORD's Puritan pilgrims, as first described in his 1620 work, *OF PLYMOUTH PLANTATION:*

> ...[W]hat could they see but a hidious and desolate wilderness, full of wild beasts & wild men? ...Yea, let them which have been redeemed of the Lord, show how he has delivered them from the hand of the oppressor. When they wandered in the desert wilderness out of the way, and found no city to dwell in, both hungry, and thirsty, their soul was overwhelmed... [Bradford 60–1; Daniell 423].

Yet, foreshadowing America's paradoxical perspective is the fact that Bradford's opinions about the wilderness were not the only views among the first white settlers. A constant thorn in Bradford's side, the pro-nature, pro–Indian businessman THOMAS MORTON described his more positive experiences in his *NEW ENGLISH CANAAN* (1637), leading to his eventual deportation through Bradford's machinations. Post-Colonial scholars like Callicot and Ybarra of the *Encyclopedia of Earth National Humanities Center* believe Morton subscribed to the "Noble Savage" view of North American Indians in contrast to Bradford's more primitivist view. They argue that the wilderness idea was, from the beginning, "a conceptual tool for colonialism," yet in typically ambiguous American style, this concept may still be at work today in helping *preserve* what wilderness remains (Callicot & Ybarra).

Miller and Nash (Nash, *Wilderness and the American Mind* and *The Rights of Nature, A History of Environmental Ethics*) extensively investigate how the landscape shaped the American identity amidst the influences of Romanticism, Sentimentalism, Utilitarianism, Materialism, and TRANSCENDENTALISM. The Puritans came to view their arrival in America as an "errand into the wilderness," referencing the Biblical Israelites' exodus from Egypt into the desert for 40 years, before entering (that is, invading) the "Promised Land," as told in the Book of Exodus. The "errand" refers to the Puritans' belief in their mission to serve God by evangelizing the North American continent (both land and inhabitants) and the world; and the "wilderness" symbolized the wild, untamed world that needed civilization and religion, that needed *saving*. To achieve this, the Puritans dreamed of creating the Bible's "city upon the hill" (Matthew 5:14, later used by JOHN WINTHROP as the title of his seminal 1630 sermon), a utopian community serving as a beacon for the rest of the world, a model of how to organize and live under the religious ideals that they believed a corrupted and crowded Europe had left far behind (Miller, *Errand...*).

But literary critic Paul Johnston offers a contrary view, arguing that JAMES FENIMORE COOPER's *The Pioneers* (1823), for example, "valorizes" the wilderness in American literature — a valorization explicitly based on Puritan biblical ideas, and one supported by his *The Wept of Wish-ton-Wish* (1829) about a pro-wilderness Puritan seeking escape from his corrupted civilization. The Biblical wilderness had therefore come to symbolize both sanctuary and punishment (Nash 15–16). Williams' Jungian approach in *Wilderness Lost, The Religious Origins of the American Mind* recapitulates this contradiction: "There has always been within English Calvinism a tension between those who saw themselves as sinners in need of wilderness trials and those who believe themselves safe and secure in the promised land of Canaan" (47). Williams concludes that what characterizes the best American writing is "not a serene acceptance but the frantic alienation of wanting to break free from false identity and idolatry ... even at the risk of madness if that is what it takes to reach the Promised Land" (252).

The work of NATHANIEL HAWTHORNE provides perhaps the best example of the age-old portrayal of the "howling wilderness" as dangerous and demonic (Nash 39). Yet eventually, "...the Romantic heart against the Enlightenment head flowered in a veneration of Nature," especially in 19th-century literary and art works considered to be at the root of American environmentalism (Miller, *Nature's Nation* 200). In that same century, the rise of Deism, Romanticism, and Enlightenment-inspired scientific explorations of the landscape, again allied nature and religion in the minds of many. European writers such as Burke, Kant, and Rousseau indirectly encouraged respect for nature's awesome beauty by introducing the concept of the "sublime," an idea many associated with God, while Alexis de Tocqueville and Lord Byron quite directly made the connection after they visited America (Nash 44–5). Meanwhile, American Transcendentalists such as HENRY DAVID THOREAU and RALPH WALDO EMERSON continued to marry nature with religion (Miller, Nash).

Other authors whose work notably engaged Biblical concerns or attitudes to the environment, sometimes equating it with Eden, include JONATHAN EDWARDS, WASHINGTON IRVING, WILLIAM CULLEN BRYANT, EMILY DICKINSON, and HERMAN MELVILLE. — Denise Ortiz

BIBLIOGRAPHY

The Bible Gateway (online concordance). BibleGateway. com. Nov. 2009.

Bradford, William. *Of Plymouth Plantation, 1620–1647*. Boston: Little, Brown, 1856. Ed. Harvey Wish. New York: Capricorn Books, 1962.

Callicot, Baird, and Priscilla Ybarra. "Puritan Origins of the American Wilderness Movement." Encyclopedia of Earth National Humanities Center, and TeacherServe. 19 June 2009. http://www/eoearth.org/article/Puritan_origins_of_the_American_wilderness_movement.

Carroll, John E., Paul Brockelman, and Mary Westfall, eds. *The Greening of Faith — God, the Environment, and the Good Life*. Hanover, NH: University Press of New England & University of New Hampshire, 1997.

The (CEV) Poverty & Justice Bible. Swindon, UK: The Bible Society, 2009.

Daniell, David. *The Bible in English, Its History and Influence*. New Haven and London: Yale University Press, 2003.

Geisler, Norman L. "Ecology" (Ch. 16). *Christian Ethics*. Grand Rapids, MI: Baker Book House, 1989. 293–310.

The Green Bible. NRSV Version. New York: HarperCollins/HarperOne, 2008.

Gutjahr, Paul C. *An American Bible, A History of the Good Book in the United States 1777–1880*. Stanford, CA: Stanford University Press, 1999.

Habel, Norman C., and Vicky Balabanski, eds. *The Earth Story in the New Testament*. Vol. 5. Earth Bible Series. London: Sheffield Academic Press, 2002.

Johnston, Paul K. "A Puritan in the Wilderness: Natty Bumppo's Language & America's Nature Today." 11th Cooper Seminar, *James Fenimore Cooper: His Country and His Art* at the State University of New York College at Oneonta, July 1997.

Kay, Jeanne. "Attitudes Toward Wilderness in the Hebrew Bible: A Geographical Reappraisal." *Proceedings, Association of American Geographers*, Portland, OR, April 21–26, 1987.

Miller, Perry. *Errand into the Wilderness*. (1956). Cambridge: Belknap Press of Harvard University Press, 1984.
_____. *Nature's Nation*. Cambridge: The Belknap Press of Harvard University Press, 1967.
Morton, Thomas. *New English Canaan, or New Canaan: Containing an Abstract of New England, Composed in Three Books...* Amsterdam: J.F. Stam, 1637.
Nash, Roderick. *Wilderness and the American Mind*. New Haven and London: Yale University Press, 1967.
Ortiz, Denise S. "Caring for Creation: The Greening of Faith, Part II." *Proceedings of the 1997 Borah Symposium on Peace and the Environment*, University of Idaho, Moscow, ID: 1997, in *The Electronic Green Journal #9* (University of Idaho Library, Moscow, ID).
_____. (Unpublished). *A Concordance of Over 1000 Environment-Friendly Scriptures in the King James and New King James Bible*. University of Idaho, Moscow, ID. 1997. dortiz@gonzaga.edu.
Robb, Carol. "Sabbath and Jubilee in Leviticus." *Whole Earth, Access to Tools, Ideas, and Practices*, Special Issue 91 (Winter 1997).
Sugirtharajah, R.S. *The Bible and Empire, Postcolonial Explorations*. Cambridge: Cambridge University Press, 2005.
Thuesen, Peter J. *In Discordance with the Scriptures, American Protestant Battles Over Translating the Bible*. New York: Oxford University Press, 1999.
Williams, David R. *Wilderness Lost, The Religious Origins of the American Mind*. London and Toronto: Associated University Presses, 1987.
Wimbush, Vincent L., ed. *The Bible and the American Myth, A Symposium on the Bible and Constructions of Meaning*. Studies in American Biblical Hermeneutics 16. Macon, GA: Mercer University Press, 1999.

Bishop, Elizabeth (1911–1979)

Elizabeth Bishop, eminent American poet and short-story writer, was born in 1911 in Worcester, Massachusetts. Her father, a builder, died when she was an infant. Her mother became mentally ill and was institutionalized in 1916, after which Bishop lived with her maternal relatives in Great Village, Nova Scotia, where she began to develop her extraordinary talent for observing the natural world in all its complex detail. This period of her life, suffused by the warmth of her maternal family and the beauty of the land, had a profound effect on her writing. She sought to recreate Nova Scotia in both prose and poems, some of which were not published until near the end of her life. "The Moose" (1976), a poem she composed over two decades, revisits a bus trip from Nova Scotia to New England after the funeral of her aunt. The bus stops when a moose steps into the road, "towering, antlerless, / high as a church, homely as a house (or, safe as houses)" (Bishop 173). To the poem's observer, the moose is "otherworldly" (173) and comes out of an "impenetrable wood" (172), exemplifying the natural world's power to interrupt human analysis and recollection just as it interrupts the bus ride. This interruption is a source of joy for

the passengers; for a moment, nature's inscrutability relieves the pressures of memory and loss. One of Bishop's lifelong concerns was the human tendency to see the nonhuman world in terms of its own structures — high churches, safe houses — and to seek in natural objects a reflection of subjective experience. Sometimes, her poems "us[e] natural encounters and landscape to sift and clarify individual memory and pain" (Kalstone 96), but almost always, the domesticating impulse of the human observer is seen as problematic.

In "Brazil, January 1, 1502" (1965), for example, the contemporary traveler is compared to European colonists of the sixteenth century who "ripped away into the hanging fabric" of nature's tapestry, behind which its native inhabitants are "always retreating" (Bishop 91–92). Here, as in many of Bishop's poems, a journey to a strange land is also a journey into the self, and an opportunity to explore the unsettling relationship of description to mastery. For Bishop, the representation of nature always raises questions about the nature of representation. Like the partially obscuring fog that emanates from the forest in "The Moose," the analogy between writing and conquest signals Bishop's investment in indirect ways of seeing, and raises the possibility of less invasive types of travel.

Bishop made her own journey to Brazil in 1951, where she settled with Brazilian architect Lota de Macedo Soares, who would be her partner until Macedo Soares's death in 1967. Until that point, Bishop rarely spent more than a year in one place. When she was seven, her paternal grandparents gained custody of her and moved her back to Worcester, where she received her first formal schooling. John Wilson Bishop was a successful building contractor, and the Bishop family was, by her account, distressed to find their granddaughter living so close to the earth in Great Village, a town without electricity or plumbing, "running about the village in bare feet" (Kalstone 27). After moving to Worcester, Bishop was often homesick for Nova Scotia and chronically ill. Out of the disruptions of her childhood evolved many of the recurrent themes in her work, among them homesickness, dislocation, and divided selfhood.

After graduating from Vassar College in 1934, she lived briefly in New York City and then traveled to Brittany, Paris, London, North Africa, Spain, Provence, and Italy, among other places. In 1938, she bought a house in Key West with Louise Crane, a college friend, but remained a restless traveler, taking trips to Nova Scotia, North Carolina, and Mexico. Although she was a lifelong itinerant, "travel in her poems largely remains the idea of travel," as Lorrie

Goldensohn puts it, and her poems speak mainly of places where she settled (Goldensohn 102).

Among those places, Florida is evoked brilliantly in her writing. She loved Florida for its ramshackle beauty as well as its ugliness, and described it as a place that was "about to become wild again" (Kalstone 63). Her letters from the period are full of descriptions of the natural wonders she found there; she often sent her friend the poet Marianne Moore, who lived in New York, bits of shell and specimens she collected from the sea. She wrote a series of celebrated landscape poems including "Florida," "Cape Breton," and "At the Fishhouses," which look outward at specific places in order to gaze inward at imagination and memory. The language of these poems is sharply attuned to organic growth and decay, and Bishop often discovers frailty and flux in the landscapes she studies, a dilapidation that seems tentatively to reflect human states and spaces. In "The Fish," similar patterns of deterioration are observed on the eponymous creature and in domestic space: "Here and there / his brown skin hung in strips / like ancient wallpaper, / and its pattern of darker brown / was like wallpaper: / shapes like full-blown roses / stained and lost through age" (Bishop 42). These poems often pit the scale of nature against the scale of human life. As David Kalstone writes, "her Florida is itself an organism, living and dying on a scale beyond human memory. It has its own geological and biological economy" (73). In "Cape Breton," the speaker remarks, "Whatever the landscape had of meaning appears to have been / abandoned" (Bishop 67). Thus, travel challenges the imagination's totalizing tendency.

Because of her minute attention to the details of the natural world, Bishop is often considered one of the major pioneers of descriptive poetry in the twentieth century. But her work is also interested in the psychological possibilities of observation, and critics have often noted her tendency to "interiorize" physical descriptions (Kalstone 46–7). Her work asks repeatedly what relationship the physical world has to the spirit. More often than not, the possibility of harmony between nature and mind or of epiphany through natural observation is foiled, emphasizing the distance between human knowledge or vanity, and nature. Bonnie Costello observes that for Bishop, "modernity's Nature ... doesn't have a human face or voice, does not confirm our personhood" (Costello 349–50). Though Bishop once wryly referred to herself as a "minor female Wordsworth" (*Letters* 222), her sketches of the natural world often implicitly reject the Romantic tendency to personify or subjectivize nature (Costello 349). As her Robinson Crusoe says in "Crusoe in England," the waterspouts on his

island are "beautiful, yes, but not much company" (Bishop 163). Not only does nature resist personification, its sublimity was for Bishop — unlike Wordsworth — "most powerful not when the natural object is vast but when it is small, when it appears that the observer can own or possess it, hold it in her hand" (Rosenbaum 82). She wrote that nature's power to ignite the imagination was in its minutiae: "Reading Darwin one admires the beautiful and solid case being built up out of his endless, heroic observations ... and then comes a sudden relaxation, a forgetful phrase, and one feels that strangeness of his undertaking, sees the lonely young man, his eyes fixed on facts and minute details, sinking or sliding giddily off into the unknown" (83). Her interest lay at the juncture of observable detail and the unfathomable.

Brazil, where Bishop spent most of her adult life, also provided a wealth of material for her work, including a number of translations of Portuguese poetry. She took a memorable trip down the Amazon River in 1960, which is partly described in the poem "Santarem." In the Brazil poems published in her penultimate collection, *Questions of Travel* (1965), tropical geography offers a lens on her childhood in Nova Scotia. "What I'm really up to," she wrote, "is recreating a sort of deluxe Nova Scotia all over again in Brazil" (Kalstone 152). The strangeness of Brazil enables her to return imaginatively to her equally strange childhood, as geographic scale shifts into temporal scale and globe-travel gives way to time-travel. — Katie Van Wert

BIBLIOGRAPHY

Bishop, Elizabeth. *The Complete Poems, 1927–1979.* New York: Farrar, Straus and Giroux, 1979.
_____. *One Art: Letters.* Ed. Robert Giroux. New York: Farrar, Straus and Giroux, 1994.
Costello, Bonnie. "Elizabeth Bishop's Personal Impersonal." *American Literary History* 15.2 (2003): 334–366.
Goldensohn, Lorrie. *Elizabeth Bishop: The Biography of a Poetry.* New York: Columbia University Press, 1992.
Kalstone, David. *Becoming a Poet: Elizabeth Bishop with Marianne Moore and Robert Lowell.* Ed. Robert Hemenway. New York: Farrar, Straus and Giroux, 1989.
Rosenbaum, Susan. "Elizabeth Bishop and the Miniature Museum." *Journal of Modern Literature* 28.2 (2005): 61–99.

Boyle, Thomas Coraghessan (1948–)

T. C. Boyle is something of a rarity among environmentally significant authors in America, for his distinctive fusion of passionate concern for the natural world on the one hand, and biting, often insouciant satire of America's attitude toward it on the other. He is the author of 12 novels and more than

150 short stories, having published regularly in all of the most prominent magazines and journals for fiction in the United States, including *The Paris Review*, *Antaeus*, *The New Yorker*, *Harper's*, *Playboy*, and *Atlantic Monthly*. Among his many honors, in 1988 his novel *World's End* won the PEN/Faulkner Award; many of his stories have been selected for the *Best American Short Stories* and *O. Henry* collections; he has received two fellowships from the National Endowment for the Arts, and in 1988 received a Guggenheim Fellowship.

At the age of 17, Thomas John Boyle of Peekskill, New York invented his first character — himself — by taking on the new middle name, Coraghessan. His working-class parents, a school custodian and a secretary, struggled to give him every advantage as a child, stressing the importance of education. After high school he enrolled at SUNY Potsdam to study music, but soon switched to studying English and history, and it was there in his junior year that he "walked into a class ... of all the weirdoes on campus" — his first creative writing class — and experienced his first success as a writer. He earned an MFA from the Iowa Writer's Workshop in 1974, and a PhD in Nineteenth Century British literature from Iowa in 1977. Since 1978 he has taught creative writing at the University of Southern California.

On the surface, Boyle's attitude toward the environment may be summed up as concerned but pessimistic. Beneath this pessimism, however, is a dogged and durable pragmatism about the very limited but real possibilities of human and environmental reform. Driven by the notion that human beings are above all else animals, he has — in novels such as *The Tortilla Curtain* (1995), *A Friend of the Earth* (2000), and *Drop City* (2003), and short story collections such as *After the Plague* (2001) and *Tooth and Claw* (2005) — rigorously interrogated what it means to be the top predator on the planet, living in close proximity with one another and in ever increasing proximity to the rest of the planet's wild animals, with intrinsic biological drives to reproduce and control territory. Unfortunately, according to Boyle, "We are doomed as a species, imminently. I was utterly depressed by the research I did for *A Friend of the Earth*. There is no hope whatsoever. It's over. Forget it. Kiss it goodbye, folks. It's done." And yet, he "certainly wouldn't want to discourage people ... from pursuing a greener world" (Farley).

Thus a common tension in Boyle's work involves a protagonist who has good environmental intentions but who is thwarted by other characters or by nature itself. For example, in his satirical story "Whales Weep" (1979), the narrator, Roger, is a fashion photographer who is inspired first to join and photo-graph a Greenpeace mission to stop a whaling fleet, and then an international project on right whales mating off the Patagonian coast. Both end in disaster; a frozen grapefruit hurled from a whaler sinks the Greenpeace raft, and watching the mating whales whips Roger and one of the married researchers into a frenzy of their own, destroying the ability of the research team to finish the job.

Thus, according to Boyle, it is often when human beings give in to their animal natures that their better judgment is overridden and the environment suffers. In *The Tortilla Curtain*, Boyle explores this idea through two pairs of protagonists, the nature writer Delaney and his real estate agent wife, Kyra, and the migrant worker Candido and his pregnant wife, America. Delaney begins with the best of intentions, arguing passionately in his community for open, unfenced spaces, but when his pet dogs are taken by coyotes, and it appears that illegal immigrants have ransacked a neighbor's house, he becomes as territorial as the others, fencing off his yard and eventually supporting a gate for the development.

Even the most tough-minded and dedicated environmentalists suffer similarly depressing fates, cursed ultimately by the same fallible human nature. In *A Friend of the Earth*, Boyle foresees a virtually uninhabitable future for humans, one where torrential rains alternate with killer droughts, disrupting food production cycles and turning the land itself into an impassable mess. The protagonist here is Ty Tierwater, who in the year 2025 zookeeps for an eccentric megastar musician who is trying to keep a few of the species left on the planet alive. Ty came around to his Boyle-like point of view on the environment after several failed attempts at ecotage in the 1990s with a parody of EarthFirst! called "Earth Forever!," the most tragic involving the death of his daughter after a Julia Hill Butterfly–esque extended tree sitting. Relinquishing the notion that ecotage, or really any single environmental act, can make the substantial cultural difference necessary to change the planet's fate, Ty cares for the animals for their own sake.

This too is reminiscent of Boyle's own self-professed "tremendous love for animals" (Adams), something he explores in stories such as "Descent of Man" (1974) and "The Ape Lady in Retirement" (1988), where a Jane Smiley–like character finds herself more at ease with her ape companion Konrad than with other humans. Just how easy (or difficult, depending on your point of view) it would be for a human to actually go feral is the subject of his story "Dogology" (2004), in which a woman researching the habits of a pack of neighborhood dogs eventually joins them. — Charles Waugh

BIBLIOGRAPHY

Adams, Elizabeth. "An interview with T. Coraghessan Boyle." *Chicago Review* 37 (1991): 51.

Birnbaum, Robert. "Author of Drop City talks with Robert Birnbaum." March 19, 2003. Identity Theory.com. Available online. URL: http://www.identitytheory.com/interviews/birnbaum94.html. Accessed June 8, 2009.

Boyle, T. C. Author website. Available online. URL: http://www.tcboyle.com. Accessed June 10, 2009.

Encyclopedia of World Biography. "T. C. Boyle Biography." Available online. URL: http://www.notablebiographies.com/newsmakers2/2007-A-Co/Boyle-T-C.html. Accessed June 16, 2009.

Farley, C. P. "Tune In, Turn On, and Drop Out with T. C. Boyle." March 26, 2003. Powells.com. Available online. URL: http://www.powells.com/authors/boyle.html. Accessed June 9, 2009.

Utley, Sandy. "All About T. Coraghessan Boyle Resource Center." May 2004. Available online. URL: http://www.tcboyle.net/sandye.html. Accessed June 10, 2009.

Bradford, William (1590–1657)

William Bradford's OF PLYMOUTH PLANTATION 1620–1647, documenting the Mayflower and her passengers' settlement in America, suggests how both the physical and spiritual survival of the individual are dependent on controlling the environment, and as such has a canonical place in the environmental debate.

Bradford was born in England, in 1590, to a middle-class farmer and his wife, both of whom died when William was only seven years old. His relatives raised him and taught him the skills of farming, which provided Bradford with the opportunity to witness the strong relationship between land and people. By his late teens, to the dismay of his family, Bradford became intrigued by a "radical" preacher and joined a community of people who wanted to separate from the Church of England. After years of trying to avoid the eyes of the Church, a group of these "Separatists," among them the 30-year-old William Bradford and his wife, left for America aboard the Mayflower to begin a new life.

The ship was supposed to land in northern Virginia, but encountered harsh winds and storms that drove it off course, causing it to land instead in Massachusetts. The passengers of the Mayflower found themselves in the middle of a cold, harsh New England winter in November of 1620. But although the hardships were daunting, they did not discourage the separatists from establishing a new settlement and building a life for themselves. In Bradford's journal, which would later be published as *Of Plymouth Plantation*, he documents the brutal conditions faced by the new society, which lead to the death of many people, including his wife and the governor. The in-habitants remained steadfast in their decision to stay in America, however, and elected Bradford the new governor, a position he held until his death in 1657.

Throughout his journal, Bradford's agricultural background provides him with an environmental perspective opposite to the Native Americans who were living in nearby settlements. As a farmer — and one plunged into harsh conditions — Bradford felt that man needed to master and control the environment in order to survive, perceiving the land as a negative force needing to be controlled; whereas the Native Americans saw the land as a positive force that was a natural and sacred provider. Indeed, in several of his entries Bradford conceives of the harshness of the environment as a religious test, comparing the brutality of the "desolate wilderness" to the evil and temptation that man must constantly struggle with and overcome.

The environmental historian Roderick Nash characterizes Bradford's description of the land as the start of a "tradition of repugnance" for nature (24), anchored in Bradford's belief that this "new land" was given to them by God, and that it is the people's right and responsibility to tame and control it; an idea explicitly articulated in Genesis and echoed constantly in the frontier literature that would follow — and in many ways spring from — Bradford's account. — Candace A. Henry

BIBLIOGRAPHY

Bradford, William. *Of Plymouth Plantation, 1620–1647.* New York: Random House, 1981.

Honiss Kelso, Dorothy. "William Bradford." Pilgram Hall Museum. Available online. URL: www.pilgramhall.org. Accessed 19 March 2009.

Nash, Roderick. *Wilderness and the American Mind*, 4th ed. New Haven: Yale University Press, 2001.

Of Plymouth Plantation, William Bradford (1856)

Bradford's *Of Plymouth Plantation* relates the first decades of the Plymouth colony's existence, but differs from the majority of colonial accounts of the Americas in that it does not represent the environment as bountiful in order to attract investors (called Adventurers in the seventeenth century) to exploit the natural resources of the discovered land. Though Adventurers were involved in the voyage and the colony, exploiting the land for profit was not Bradford's and his fellow Pilgrims' purpose. Their concern was, primarily, the physical and spiritual survival of the colony — to find a place that was both "fruitful and fit for habitation" (Bradford 25) and at a safe remove from other English colonies so that there would be no interference in the practice of their religion.

Of Plymouth Plantation is divided into two books

and Bradford's approach is significantly different in each. The first is a straightforward narrative account that quickly moves through the religious persecution the congregation faced in England, their move to the Netherlands in search of a place to practice their religion freely, the eventual decision to emigrate to America, and their arrival at Plymouth. There is a self-assured quality to the first book, as the author firmly locates the migration within a providential design. The migration to the Netherlands, for example, is a mini-exodus that foreshadows the more significant exodus to America. All of this occurs within the appropriately cosmic dimensions of seventeenth-century religious conflict (THE BIBLE):

> What wars and oppositions ever since, Satan hath raised, maintained and continued against the Saints, from time to time, in one sort or other. Sometimes by bloody death and cruel torments; other whiles imprisonments, banishments and other hard usages; as being loath his kingdom should go down, the truth prevail and the churches of God revert to their ancient purity and recover their primitive order, liberty and beauty [3].

The first book concludes, however, with a lengthy and foreboding description of the harsh New World landscape:

> what could they see but a hideous and desolate wilderness, full of wild beasts and wild men — and what multitudes there might be of them they knew not. Neither could they, as it were, go up to the top of Pisgah to view from this wilderness a more goodly country to feed their hopes; for which way soever they turned their eyes (save upward to the heavens) they could have little solace or content in respect of any outward objects [62].

While their exodus has not led them to a promised land, the passage signals a turning inward — away from "any outward objects" to the sublimity of the spirit. David Laurence, for example, argues that the environment described by Bradford is:

> No mere backdrop to the event, the setting functions as the crucial figure that reveals the Pilgrims' relation to spirit. More a poetic image than a historical reality, the landscape is described not in and for itself but for the sake of the insupportable idea it has been made to represent and over which the passage gains sublime triumph: the dreaded possibility that the Pilgrims have mistaken their call and that, far from being an advance of the community toward its goal, the migration may have been an error, a profane wandering that forebodes the subversion of everything Bradford holds most dear [56–7].

The quoted passage clearly suggests this, and Bradford ends the first book with the comment: "What could now sustain them but the Spirit of God and His grace?" (62–3). Physical survival in this "desolate wilderness," then, will reassure the Saints of God's providence.

Bradford's description of the landscape also serves another significant purpose, because he "deliberately uses the New World background to accent their plight. As he describes it, the country's "weather-beaten face" and "savage hue," reminiscent of the "barbarous shores that the Apostles reached," becomes an emblem of our fallen state" (Bercovitch 45). Hence, the "desolate" environment is often in fact empowering in Bradford's account, testing the spiritual strength of the Pilgrims as they withstand events like storms, droughts, and crop failure. As for the "wild men," while there was some conflict with the native people, others taught the Pilgrims how to plant and tend corn, which was essential for their physical survival in unfamiliar surroundings. Bradford regularly scans the landscape for evidence of providence, which must be read for signs of grace or divine displeasure with the colony. For example, during a drought in 1623 he writes,

> I may not here omit how, notwithstanding all their great pains and industry, and the great hopes of a large crop, the Lord seemed to blast, and take away the same, and to threaten further and more sore famine unto them.... Upon which they set apart a solemn day of humiliation, to seek the Lord by humble and fervent prayer, in this great distress. And He was pleased to give them a gracious and speedy answer [131].

However, as Wiliam J. Scheick states, Bradford gradually comes to realize "that the colony was in decline, its mission unfulfilled, its purpose apparently abandoned by divine providence" (11).

The Pilgrims' interaction with the environment, then, could also point to their all too human nature: if the environment leads Bradford to the transcendent heights of the spirit at the end of Book One, the second book confronts (and often broods on) the fallen state of humanity, and in a much less hopeful tone. Indeed, the hope to "revert" and "recover" the primitive purity of the early Christian church becomes a story of gradual decline into a temporal, fallen world. Originally Bradford, who served as governor after the first governor died (shortly after landing), wanted the colony to function as a tightly knit agricultural community in the spirit of early Christian communalism. Samuel Eliot Morison notes that "This endeavour to keep the Colony one compact settlement is discernible throughout the *History*. Bradford's object was not merely defense against

Indians, but to enable everyone to attend divine service, to maintain a vigorous community life, and to keep strict watch over sinners" (188). However, by 1623 these hopes were unraveling. Bradford decided to permit individual families to cultivate private land: "This action violated the Pilgrim ideal of early Christian communalism ... but it was taken as a practical means to motivate people who balked at working only for the collective benefit of the group" (Scheick 10). In 1632 Bradford recorded his bittersweet realization that,

> the people of the Plantation began to grow in outward estates, by reason of the flowing of many people into the country, especially into the Bay of Massachusetts. By which means corn and cattle rose to a great price, by which many were much enriched and commodities grew plentiful. And yet in other regards this benefit turned into their hurt, and this accession of strength to their weakness.... And if this had been all, it had been less, though too much; but the church must also be divided, and those that had lived so long together in Christian and comfortable fellowship must now part and suffer many divisions [252–3].

Ultimately, *Of Plymouth Plantation* imbues the untouched American environment with an effectively Biblical narrative of faith and weakness in the face of providential adversity; but ends without affirmation, or indeed conclusion, as if the sacred had yielded at last and irrevocably to the profane. — Jim Daems

Bibliography

Bercovitch, Sacvan. *The Puritan Origins of the American Self.* New Haven: Yale University Press, 1975.
Bradford, William. *Of Plymouth Plantation, 1620–1647.* Ed. Samuel Eliot Morison. New York: Alfred A. Knopf, 1975.
Laurence, David. "William Bradford's American Sublime." *PMLA.* Vol. 102, No. 1 (Jan. 1987). 55–65.
Scheick, William J. *Design in Puritan American Literature.* Lexington: University Press of Kentucky, 1992.

Bradstreet, Anne (1612–1672)

On April 13, 1645, John Winthrop, governor of the Massachusetts Bay Colony, noted in his journal that a friend's wife had grown sick, losing her "understanding and reason." He attributed the woman's sickness to her "giving herself wholly to reading and writing," and he alleged that "If she had attended her household affairs and such things as belong to women," then she might have "kept her wits and ... improved them usefully and honorably in the place God had set her." Although not referring to Anne Bradstreet specifically, Winthrop's defensive aggression might have been equally directed at her, for in

both her roles, as poet and wife in colonial North America, Bradstreet exhibited what many critics describe as a revolutionary spirit, with some even characterizing her as one of America's first feminists. The extent of Bradstreet's activism may be debated, but her ability to portray the harsh life of the Puritans with vivacity and sensitivity has ensured her a place of significance in the American literary canon.

Bradstreet was one of six children born to Thomas and Dorothy Dudley in Northampton, England. Her father served as a steward (an estate manager) for the Earl of Lincoln, and he was unusually liberal with his daughter's education while she was under his care in England. Bradstreet was given access to the Earl of Lincoln's library where she gained a solid Elizabethan education. She even reported learning the Scriptures at age six, and was exposed to the work of Edmund Spenser, Francis Bacon, and Michael Drayton among others during her formative years. At 16 Anne married her father's assistant, Simon Bradstreet. As her father and husband were both ardent Puritans, Anne's entire family uprooted their lives and joined John Winthrop on his famous voyage to America's new "wilderness" in June 1630. Winthrop's goal was to establish a model Christian community for the world to acknowledge, respect, and ultimately emulate.

Life in colonial America was not nearly as comfortable for Anne as she perhaps had expected or was accustomed to in England. Her heart "rose" against the "new World and new Manners" she encountered in the distant, harsh environment. She was plagued by constant sickness, succumbing to daily fevers and fainting spells, while others died around her, unable to withstand the hardships inherent in colonial existence. She wrote, however, that through constant prayer, she finally did become "convinced" her new life "was the way of God," so she "submitted to it and joined to the church at Boston."

Bradstreet was never completely comfortable, however, with Boston's city mindset, and in 1635 her family moved to Ipswitch, a relatively secluded Bay Colony settlement, which "abounded with fish, and flesh of fowls and beasts, [...] plowing grounds, many good rivers and harbours and no rattle snakes." It was in Ipswitch that Bradstreet turned to writing poetry, partly for relief and consolation in the face of the increasingly difficult wilderness conditions afflicting the isolated colonists. In her *Meditations Divine and Moral* she notes, "If we had no winter, the spring would not be so pleasant; if we did not sometimes taste of adversity, prosperity would not be so welcome." Because Bradstreet viewed nature as dangerous yet still divinely inspired, her poetry attempts to find reason (and love) behind what she views as God's direct manifestation in her everyday life. Her strict Puritan faith was tested by the harsh environment of colonial North America, and some of her most eloquent poetry, such as her masterpiece CONTEMPLATIONS, springs from her personal insights about the interconnectivity she perceived among God, nature, and man.

In 1645, Bradstreet moved again, this time to an even more remote woodland community in the Bay Colony named Andover. Five years after this last move of her life, Bradstreet's first book, *The Tenth Muse Lately Sprung Up in America*, was published. Though she claimed her brother-in-law took her poems to a printer without her knowledge (and purportedly was embarrassed by what she viewed as the collection's roughness) the book catapulted her to fame both in the colonies and abroad in England.

While some modern critics attempt to divorce Bradstreet from her Puritan roots, her lifelong struggle to understand the harshness of the world around her was always finally framed and explained by God. Like most Puritans, her writing consistently viewed nature, in all its forms, as indicative of God's glory and will, and she often employed natural imagery to convey her ongoing mission to achieve God's grace; for it is "His hand alone that guides nature and fate." — LuElla D'Amico

BIBLIOGRAPHY

Bradstreet, Anne *The Works of Anne Bradstreet*. Ed. Jeannine Hensley. Cambridge, MA: Harvard University Press, 2000.

Harvey, Tamara. "'Now Sisters ... Impart Your Usefulness and Force': Anne Bradstreet's Feminist Functionalism in the Tenth Muse (1650)." *Early American Literature* 35.1 (2000): 5–28.

Richardson, Robert D., Jr. "The Puritan Poetry of Anne Bradstreet." *Critical Essays on Anne Bradstreet*. Ed. Pattie Cowell and Ann Stanford. Boston: G. K. Hall, 1983.

Stanford, Ann. *Anne Bradstreet, the Worldly Puritan: An Introduction to Her Poetry*. New York: Franklin, 1974.

Winthrop, John. *The Journal of John Winthrop, 1630–1649*. Ed. Richard Dunn, James Savage, and Laetitia Yaendle. Cambridge, MA: Harvard University Press. 1996.

"Contemplations," Anne Bradstreet (1650)

Like all of Puritan Anne Bradstreet's poetry, "Contemplations" is deeply religious, an exploration of the interrelationship of nature, humanity, and the divine. The community of which she was a part, typically looked to nature as an indirect and dependent source of moral instruction. A constant state of introspection characterized those who followed the Puritan faith; its members perpetually sought for outward signs that they were living in God's favor. As Adrienne Rich notes in her introductory essay to

Bradstreet's volume of poems, "Seventeenth-century Puritan life was perhaps the most self-conscious ever lived in its requirements of the individual understanding: no event so trivial that it could not speak a divine message, no disappointment so heavy that it could not serve as a 'correction,' a disguised blessing" (x). Events that occurred in the natural world — thunderstorms, good (or bad) crop years, communicable diseases, a beautiful sunset — were visual evidence of Divine intervention, according to Puritan theology. Thus, much of "Contemplations" focuses on the natural world as an inspiration and starting point for Bradstreet's ruminations on the nature of the divine, and the tensions between doubt and faith, earth and heaven, the natural and the supernatural. In nature, even plants, birds, bugs, and animals pay tribute to God, a task that fallen humans all too often fail in.

The first stanza of the poem provides both form and matter for those that follow. Though inspired by English styles of the day, Bradstreet's poetic form here is unique. She employs an eight-line stanza, the first seven in iambic pentameter and the eighth a longer, alexandrine line, with the rhyme scheme *ababccc*. Charlotte Gordon claims that Bradstreet's aim was to find a middle ground between "fancy or overwrought" poetry and "a tedious sermon" (267). The poet typically describes a scene in nature in minute detail, and her sensory reaction to it: "Their leaves and fruits seem'd painted but was true/ Of green, of red, of yellow, mixed hew,/ Rapt were my senses at this delectable view." The poet is so taken with the vivid colors of the natural world that she first suspects they are false — that they are "painted" — and she stops in her tracks to focus all her attention on the physical beauty in front of her. A few lines later, she contemplates the meaning of what she sees, in a religious context, in order to offer a moral or spiritual lesson: "How excellent is He that dwells on high,/ Whose power and beauty by his works we know?" She gives credit to God as author of this beautiful scene in words that are deeply meditative and reverential, an expression of her Puritan belief that God created, and still directs, all things earthly.

In the fourth stanza the poet likens the sun to a bridegroom leaving his chamber every morning, giving life to the earth, insects, animals, and vegetation. She portrays "him" as creator of the seasons, and once again, muses reverently on the fact that the greatness of the sun is merely another indication and extension of the greatness of the Creator: "How full of glory then must thy Creator be!/ Who gave this bright luster unto thee."

Like the other Puritan poets, Bradstreet uses poetry to describe an ultimately fabular journey from earthly to spiritual knowledge. She may rely on her senses to appreciate the sun's role and greatness on Earth, but she must rely on her faith to comprehend the greatness of God, the sun's creator, whose glory is infinitely greater than that of the sun. The natural world thus provided, in a (rather Platonic) sense, the "raw material" to serve as inspiration for, and be shaped and ultimately transcended by, the Puritans, who engaged in constant meditation on the state of their mortal souls and the infinite power of their creator. The work as a whole, then, explores the anatomy and significance of the intersection of the divine and the mundane, but the poet's journey is a solitary one; there is no dialogue, or dialectic — only reflection and monologue. Through her spiritual ruminations, the poet continually discovers signs of God in the natural beauty around her, rejoicing in the fullness of the earth, but always turning her attention to the eternity that would follow her time on earth.

Nonetheless, it is a distinctive and characteristic feature of Bradstreet's poetry that it tends, as if from a sensual imperative in the author, to find heaven on earth, despite the Puritan call to reject all things earthly. For her, heaven promises the prolongation of earthly joy, rather than a renunciation of those pleasures she enjoys in life; and "Contemplations" — wittingly or not — suggests that Bradstreet at least partly committed herself to the religious concept of salvation because she so loved life on earth. Other poets of the day, notably Edward Taylor and Michael Wigglesworth, were more conventional in their equating of the natural world with sin, death, and destruction. Wendy Martin thus refers to Bradstreet's poetic themes as ruminations on "earth's pull and heaven's promise" (73), and Adrienne Rich calls "Contemplations" "the most skilled and appealing of [Bradstreet's] poems," partly because of this complex and delicate balance between a fervent embrace of life on earth and a deep-seated respect for the Puritan imperative to throw off all things earthly (xviii). True to her roots and milieu, however, Bradstreet ultimately confirms that any greatness or pleasure that nature brings is transitory, unlike the reward that the elect will experience in heaven. Nature's grandeur does not mean that heaven may be found on earth; the supervenient authority and grandeur lie elsewhere. The ultimate search in "Contemplations" is for "earth in heaven," a truism that EMILY DICKINSON would reverse two hundred years later (76). — Jacqueline Megow

BIBLIOGRAPHY

Gordon, Charlotte. *Mistress Bradstreet: The Untold Life of America's First Poet.* New York: Little, Brown, 2005.

Martin, Wendy. *An American Triptych: Anne Bradstreet, Emily Dickinson, Adrienne Rich.* Chapel Hill: University of North Carolina Press, 1984.

Rich, Adrienne. "Anne Bradstreet and Her Poetry." *The Works of Anne Bradstreet.* Ed. Jeannine Hensley. Cambridge: The Belknap Press of Harvard University Press, 1967. Ix–xx.

Showalter, Elaine. *A Jury of Her Peers: American Women Writers from Anne Bradstreet to Annie Proulx.* New York: Alfred A. Knopf, 2009.

Brand, Stewart (1938–)

Best known for his creation of the counterculture, appropriate-technology publication THE WHOLE EARTH CATALOG, Stewart Brand was born in Rockford, Illinois in 1938. After graduating from Stanford in 1960 with a degree in biology, Brand became involved with California's counterculture. He joined Ken Kesey's Merry Pranksters, and Tom Wolfe described him as "a thin blond guy with a blazing disk on his forehead too, and a whole necktie made of Indian beads" (2). After organizing the Trips Festival in San Francisco in 1966, a multimedia event organized similarly to Kesey's previous acid tests, Brand began a public campaign, lobbying NASA to release the rumored satellite image of the whole Earth. Fueled by 100 micrograms of LSD, Brand noticed the curvature of the earth, and recalled "that Buckminster Fuller had been harping on this at a recent lecture — that people perceived the earth as flat and infinite, and that that was the root of all their misbehavior" ("Why Haven't We…" 168).

With Brand's involvement in the counterculture came his awareness of ecological issues and their intersection with technology. *The Whole Earth Catalog* (*WEC*) was the culmination of his pragmatic optimism, the belief that individual lifestyle choice and consumption habits could lead to responsible and sustainable environmental interaction. His answer to the anti-technology side of the countercultural environmental movement was labeled "appropriate technology," and through all its inceptions, *WEC* included objective and apolitical reviews of a huge range of books and products. From books on communal living to tools for organic farming, from wilderness survival manuals to high-tech synthesizers, *WEC*, along with its successors and multiple supplements, offered readers the opportunity to examine their personal values and review products that would support them in their pursuit of responsible environmental stewardship as members of "Whole Systems." Andrew Kirk claims, "Brand's creation perfectly captured the post–Vietnam counterculture movement of the mid–1970s with its emphasis on lifestyle and pragmatic activism over utopian idealism and politics" (363).

Although Brand only published *WEC* from 1968 until 1972 (with its supplements published intermittently after that), he continued to remain involved with and explore the environmental movement, technological advancement, and alternative lifestyles. Besides co-founding the Whole Earth 'Lectronic Link (WELL), an early online community, in 1985, and The Long Now Foundation in 1996, whose purpose is "to provide counterpoint to today's 'faster/cheaper' mind set and promote 'slower/better' thinking," Brand has published many books on the subject of environmental pragmatism and futurism ("About Long Now"). Amongst these books is *Whole Earth Discipline*, published in 2009, which argues that the solutions to climate change lie in nuclear energy, urbanization, and the genetic engineering of crops.— Jill E. Anderson

BIBLIOGRAPHY

"About Long Now." *The Long Now Foundation*. The Long Now Foundation, n.d. Web. 16 Dec. 2010.

Brand, Stewart. "Why Haven't We Seen the Whole Earth?" *The Sixties: The Decade Remembered Now, By the People Who Lived It Then*. Ed. Lynda Rosen Obst. New York: Random, 1977. 168–70.

Kirk, Andrew. "'Machines of Loving Grace': Alternative Technology, Environment, and the Counterculture." *Imagine Nation: The American Counterculture of the 1960s and 70s*. Ed. Peter Braunstein and Michael William Doyle. New York: Routledge, 2002. 353–78.

Markoff, John. *What the Dormouse Said: How the Sixties Counterculture Shaped the Personal Computer Industry*. New York: Viking Penguin, 2005.

Turner, Fred. *From Counterculture to Cyberculture: Stewart Brand, the Whole Earth Network, and the Rise of Digital Utopianism*. Chicago: University of Chicago Press, 2006.

Wolfe, Tom. *The Electric Kool-Aid Acid Test*. New York: Farrar, Straus and Giroux, 1968.

Whole Earth Catalog, Steward Brand (1968–1998)

Published intermittently between 1968 and 1972 (the year the catalog won the National Book Award), with sporadic updates until 1998, the *Whole Earth Catalog* (*WEC*) was a publication begun and edited by one-time biology student at Stanford and member of Ken Kesey's Merry Pranksters, Stewart Brand. The catalog's title and central idea were born in 1966. Inspired by Barbara Ward's 1966 book *Spaceship Earth*, and BUCKMINSTER FULLER's philosophy of spheres and integrated systems (as well as 100 micrograms of LSD), Brand launched a public campaign to have the rumored NASA satellite image of the entire earth released to the public. Brand believed the image would make the American public realize the finiteness and fragility of Earth's resources, and cause a change in personal consumption habits. The *WEC*'s inception was The Whole Earth Truck Store, a mo-

bile supply mart, educational tour, and lending library that Brand brought to the communes of New Mexico and the West. The Truck Store was run by Brand and his then-wife, Lois Jennings, out of the back of their 1963 Dodge pick-up. Situated between the counterculture's back-to-land and commune movements, and the emerging technologies that later became part of the personal computer revolution, the *WEC* embraced the notion of "appropriate technology" (also known as "soft technology"). The catalog's subtitle, "Access to Tools," illustrates the publication's main mission — to provide objective and apolitical information on tools and ideas for individuals interested in sustainability and environmental awareness. Put simply: "*Whole Earth* provided moral support to young optimists working to map a brighter future free from the flaws of technocratic thinking but not free from technology. These appropriate technologists believed a survivable future was still a possibility if technological development could be wedded to insights emerging from ecology and environmentalism while avoiding the political entanglements of Right/Left ideologies" (Kirk 9).

Believing that individuals had the power and ability to fight against mainstream American industrialization and its attendant environmental destruction, Brand began the catalog as a critical information service (often and interestingly described as a precursor to the internet). The idea was to combat the technocracy that had not only destroyed and paved over much of the American landscape during the boom after the Second World War, but had also unleashed the atom bombs in Japan and was currently waging an unpopular war in (and on the environment of) Vietnam. In his seminal study on the counterculture, Theodore Roszak notes that in the struggle against technocracy, American youth "have been somewhat quicker to sense that the conventional tactics of political resistance have only a marginal place, largely limited to meeting immediate life-and-death crises" (4). Roszak observes that the key is "altering the total cultural context within which our daily politics takes place" (5). The philosophy of the *WEC* fits neatly into this call for an alteration of "daily politics."

Brand's declaration that "We are as gods," startlingly reminiscent of the intoxicating claims of EMERSONIAN TRANSCENDENTALISM, emphasizes the catalog's belief and confidence in individual action. The statement is culled from the 1968 edition of the catalog, in which Brand declares: "So far, remotely done power and glory — as via government, big business, formal education, church — has succeeded to the point where gross obscure actual gains. In response to this dilemma and to these gains a realm of intimate, personal power is developing — power of the individual to conduct his own education, find his own inspiration, shape his own environment, and share his adventure with whoever is interested. Tools that aid this process are sought and promoted by *Whole Earth Catalog*" (www.wholeearth.com). At a time when environmental movements typically relied on group action and conservation of pristine natural spaces, Brand's vision was individualized, optimistic and pragmatic — he believed each person had the ability to choose technologies that would help him/her live sustainably and responsibly. Lifestyle and personal consumption habits became the most important political expression for those who embraced appropriate technology.

Thus, the catalog included reviews, usually affirmative and often not particularly authoritative, of a massive range of products (mostly books) and ideas to help consumers make better choices about appropriate technology: books and magazines about gardening and composting, breastfeeding and women's health, foraging and wilderness survival, and manuals on how to build your own computer; power tools and tractors; musical instruments from banjos to Moog synthesizers; sourdough starters and cookbooks; looms for weaving, spinning wheels for making fiber, and kilns for firing ceramics. Each product review was designed to be easily accessed by the catalog's readers, and emphasized the utility of each item, which was selected according to the following criteria: "1) Useful as a tool, 2) Relevant to independent education, 3) High quality or low cost, 4) Easily available by mail" (www.wholeearth.com). Interspersed with product reviews and articles were poems and short vignettes, recipes, random illustrations and asides. The catalog also included articles by other well-known environmentalists such as Fuller, Murray Bookchin, WENDELL BERRY, GARY SNYDER, Gurney Norman, Peter Warshall, Donella Meadows, and Barry Commoner. J. Baldwin, a designer, served as Brand's main editor.

WEC's pages and reviews were divided into seven major and consistent sections: "Whole Systems," "Shelter and Land Use," "Industry and Craft," "Communications," "Community," "Nomadics," and "Learning." Each section highlighted an important aspect of the catalog's emphasis on appropriate technology. Perhaps most essential to the publication's vision, the "Whole Systems" section was based on the idea of integrated systems and the whole earth itself. In his study about consumption habits in the 1970s, Sam Binkley explains that the symbolism and actuality of the realized whole earth image provided "a deepened understanding of the inner meaning of lifestyle as a global responsibility, enfolding the personal needs and the place of goods in an integrated planetary system tied directly to the larger moral obligation of a terrestrial steward" (150). From articles about Native Americans and space colonies, through bird and flower field guides, to guides about home economics, the "Whole Systems" section emphasized the interconnectedness of all humans and each aspect of the natural and nonhuman worlds. "Shelter and Land Use" provided reviews about how to live sustainably within those whole systems, while the subjects of "Industry and Craft" ranged from architecture to sheep shearing and woodworking. Brand labeled "Learning" and "Community" "catch-all sections," although they were grounded in two complementary principles: "one is that living well and living free bear a lot of relation to living cheap. The second is that living cheap and living happily are all wrapped up with the complex life of neighborhood, family, friends, lovers, co-workers, community" (*The Next Whole Earth Catalog* 288).

Brand's own shift from emphasizing individualism in favor of community is evident in *WEC*'s later publications. The egalitarian and community perspective became an important part not merely of the catalog's written material but of its finances as well. *The Last Whole Earth Catalog*, the publication's June 1971 version, includes the following instruction for suggesting products and reviewing: "We are a bunch of amateurs. Our reviewers — seldom experts, never critics — got $10 and credit for their review" (2). Reviews are "wholly sincere," "often biased, very often wishful," and editors warn to "not rely on them too far" (2). This egalitarianism and "think for yourself" attitude are indicative of the counterculture's influence over the publication. Additionally, originally funded by the Portola Institute, Richard Raymond's research institution in Menlo Park, California, *WEC*'s first edition was created using basic typesetting and binding skills. Later funded by Brand's Point Foundation, the *WEC* fully disclosed its operating budget to its readers in every issue. Throughout its publication life, the *WEC* also included a host of eclectic and sometimes prophetic supplements, the most famous of which was the *CoEvolution Quarterly*. — Jill E. Anderson

BIBLIOGRAPHY

Binkley, Sam. *Getting Loose: Lifestyle Consumption in the 1970s*. Durham, NC: Duke University Press, 2007.

Kirk, Andrew G. *Counterculture Green: The* Whole Earth Catalog *and American Environmentalism*. Lawrence: University Press of Kansas, 2007.

The Last Whole Earth Catalog: Access to Tools. Ed. Stewart Brand. New York: Random, 1971.

The Next Whole Earth Catalog: Access to Tools. Ed. Stewart Brand. New York: Random, 1980.

Roszak, Theodore. *The Making of a Counterculture: Reflec-*

tions on the Technocratic Society and Its Youthful Opposition. Garden City, NY: Doubleday, 1969.

Whole Earth Catalog: Access to Tools and Ideas. New Whole Earth, LLC. Web. 17 Dec. 2010. http://www. whole earth.com/index.php

Brown, Sterling (1901–1989)

Critic Houston Baker, Jr., argues that the blues contain an "ecological testimony" (Ruffin 137). The blues-laced rhythms and lyrics of African-American poets such as Sterling A. Brown, provide testimony of a people for whom the environment has often been theirs to suffer, occasionally to shape, and seldom to own. Using folk and blues traditions, Brown's poetry and essays explore the relationship of African Americans to nature.

Brown is best known for SOUTHERN ROAD, a collection of poetry published in 1932, and a second volume, *The Last Ride of Wild Bill and Eleven Narrative Poems* (1975). Another highly acclaimed anthology, *Hiding Place*, was not released until the *Collected Poetry of Sterling A. Brown* was published in 1980. Several collections of essays on African American literature were also published.

Born to middle class parents in 1901, Brown attended Howard University. His father was a professor of Religion, and Brown followed in his father's footsteps, teaching at a number of schools before he settled at Howard, where he taught for 40 years. He was able to bridge the divide between highly educated friends and mentors and the everyday people that inspired his poetry. Brown was influenced by the folk vernacular employed by ROBERT FROST and Carl Sandburg, and sought to revivify the dialect tradition of such poets as Paul Laurence Dunbar, without the stereotyping and minstrelsy he often found there. It is his devotion to the folk tradition, its characters, stories, and language, married to the rhythms of blues, worksongs, and spirituals, that principally shaped his poetry.

Folk traditions, culled from years of travel in the rural areas of the South, informed Brown's ecological perspective. The argument is often made that there is no black THOREAU, no African-American equivalent of WALDEN. Recent critical efforts have tried to fill in the ecological "gaps" in African-American literature. What is the relationship of African Americans to an environment that provided such harsh obstacles for their ancestors? What environmental critiques have African-American authors made, either explicitly or by their silences on the subject of nature?

Environmental thought generally concerns the relationship between humans and the natural environment. But Kimberly S. Smith argues that 250 years of slavery "permanently alienated [black Americans] from the American landscape" (1). It is this alienation that Brown examines and addresses in his writings. As Editor of Negro Affairs for the Works Progress Administration (WPA) Federal Writers' Project from 1936 to 1940, he worked tirelessly to combat stereotypes and mis-representations of black Americans. In his critical essays, including *The Negro in Virginia* (1940), he explored the alienation of the African American from a landscape that was for too many years his enemy. Brown's examination of the ambivalent and often negative African-American attitude toward nature appears especially in his poems about workers who struggle for access to any but the harshest environments, who struggle to clear a wilderness for others while eking out a meager existence from that same wilderness, or who simply struggle to survive in city streets that offer no hope of fresh greenness.—Patricia Kennedy Bostian

BIBLIOGRAPHY

Ruffin, Kimberly N. *Black on Earth: African American Eco-literary Traditions*. Athens: University of Georgia Press, 2002. 137–138.

Smith, Kimberly K. *African American Environmental Thought: Foundations*. Lawrence: University Press of Kansas, 2007. 1.

Tidwell, John Edgar, and Steven S. Tracy, eds. *After Winter: The Life and Art of Sterling A. Brown*. Oxford: Oxford University Press, 2009.

Southern Road, Sterling Brown (1932)

Environmental writing typically explores the effect of people on nature. Sterling Brown's concern is centered more the effect of nature on people, specifically economically disadvantaged African Americans. Jean Wagner writes in *Black Poets of the United States*, that Brown "depicted the black man as [...] alone and powerless, confronting a universe all of whose elements are in league against him" (481–82). One of the most central and important of these elements, explored with sensitivity, skill and a subtle sense of optimism in Brown's 1932 collection of poetry, *Southern Road*, is the African American's natural environment.

Although born in Washington, D.C., Brown was drawn to the South—its people, language, and music. His poems are often narrated by characters based on real people he had met during his travels through the South. These narrators speak in a folk language that avoids the minstrelsy and stereotypical patois in which many poets, black and white, render the southern dialect. His characters' speech patterns are overlaid with the rhythms of the blues and jazz songs that he first encountered in Harlem, but which originated in the south of Tennessee and Mississippi.

Southern Road is organized into four parts. Part One, titled "Road so Rocky," contains the eponymous poem, "Southern Road," a perfect illustration of why the African-American attitude toward the environment is not couched in the rapturous tones of JOHN MUIR. The narrator is shackled in a chain gang. He has no cares for the environment in which he toils. What is the road under his feet to him with his many human concerns: his son is on the streets, as is one daughter, and his wife is at a clinic in labor with another child. The landscape is something in the background, not noticed except when weather is bad and the work hard. Nature is noticed in "the Dark of the Moon," but is seen as overtly evil, thwarting the farmer's best efforts to improve his land. Anything undertaken during that time of the month will "plant fo' nothin'" (31).

Part Two, "On Restless River," contains several of Brown's best known poems, including the Slim Greer poems, "Ma Rainey," and "Memphis Blues." It also offers some of his more direct comments on the human/nature relationship, such as the alienated cry of "Old King Cotton":

> Cotton, cotton,
> All we know;
> Plant cotton, hoe it,
> Baig it to grow;
> What good it do to us
> Gawd only know! [*Southern Road* 65–66]

Even after slavery's end, poor blacks still felt themselves chained to the land of their ancestors, begging the crops to grow, although precious little of its growth will line their own pockets. The anger the workers feel towards the farmer is mistakenly but naturally directed toward the land they are cultivating.

Along with the vagaries of the weather that determine the crops' outcome each year, the African-American tenant farmers and sharecroppers of Brown's poems face natural disasters. Tornados and floods punctuate his poems, illustrating the hostile face of nature that many faced. In "Tornado Blues," part of the poem "New St. Louis Blues," the destructive winds take out some "ofays"—white people—but mostly devastate the property of African Americans. The wind comes off of the plains "like a flock of giant aeroplanes," doing "its dirty work" and moving on (68).

"Children of the Mississippi" is one of the collection's flood poems. Again and again Brown's narrators describe the futility of living in the low areas alongside great rivers like the Mississippi and the Missouri. The river sweeps away their homes, their possessions, their livelihood, even their lives, and leaves behind wasteland, unable to be cultivated. In "Foreclosure," Uncle Dan shakes his fist impotently at Father Missouri for ruining his gardens, flooding his pigsties, and carrying off his prize hens: "Ain't got no right to act dat way at all!" (70). But the river is heedless to the cries of Uncle Dan and the thousands of other African Americans who Brown represents in his poems.

However, though sinister when coupled with the *human* environment of oppressive slavery and its aftermath, nature also shows a gentler, sheltering side, the root of Brown's subtle optimism (as of much southern gospel music). In "Riverbanks Blues," the water holds man trapped in its mild lapping, lulling him into hazy dreamy reflection:

> Lazy sun shinin' on a little cabin,
> Lazy moon glistenin' over river trees;
> Ole river whisperin', lappin' 'gainst de long roots:
> "Plenty of rest and peace in these...." [100]

The narrator explains that "A man git his feet set in a sticky mudbank," and he gets the river water in his blood. He becomes trapped by the water just as surely as the endless fields of cotton trap him in his poverty. "Muddy streams keep him fixed for good." The lushness of the environment feels almost edenic, harkening back to that blissful time in the garden before the fall of man (THE BIBLE). Yet, the narrator acknowledges that behind the beauty is a price. If one listens to the river's whispering, he loses his will to be a productive member of society. In the end, he sees the river as a "sulky Ole Man" with "creepy ways" and "evil ways," which, if one is not careful, will become the ways of anyone who lingers too long on its shores.

Milder still, almost pastoral in tone, is "After Winter," a beautiful descriptive poem illustrating the benignant, symbiotic relationship possible between man and nature (AMERICAN PASTORAL). An old man tours his garden after the chill of winter has passed. He digs his fingers in the rich black earth and quietly plans his spring planting: "Butter beans fo' Clara, / Sugar corn fo' Grace" (74). This is the well-spring of Brown's more hopeful message, and the reason why Brown critic Jean Wagner considers him a poet of the soil (477). The farmer endures the often trying cycle of the seasons, but is glad "the lean months are done with / the fat to come."—Patricia Kennedy Bostian

BIBLIOGRAPHY

Brown, Sterling A., and Michael S. Harper. *The Collected Poems of Sterling A. Brown.* New York: Harper & Row, 1980.

Tidwell, John Edgar, and Steven S. Tracy, eds. *After Winter: The Life and Art of Sterling A. Brown.* Oxford: Oxford University Press, 2009.

Wagner, Jean. *Black Poets of the United States: From Paul*

Laurence Dunbar to Langston Hughes. Urbana: University of Illinois Press, 1973.

Bryant, William Cullen (1794–1878)

William Cullen Bryant, whom WALT WHITMAN called the "bard of the river and wood, ever conveying a taste of open air, with scents as from hayfields, grapes, birch-borders" (267), worked to develop a uniquely American poetic style focusing on the country's raw, vital landscape.

Bryant was born in 1794 in Cumington, Massachusetts, the second son of Peter Bryant and Sarah Snell. Bryant was educated at Williams College, chose law as his career, and was admitted to the bar in 1815. He married Frances Fairchild in 1821. He struggled as a lawyer until his career as a poet and journalist took off in the mid–1820s.

Bryant's father cultivated his son's interest in poetry, training him in the Neo-Classical style current in the late eighteenth- and early-nineteenth centuries. However, while Bryant was never a revolutionary in his use of form, he quickly shed his Neo-Classical thematic concerns in favor of Romantic ones when he developed an interest in nature. This is apparent in the early "Thanatopsis" ("Death-vision"), perhaps his most famous work. In this blank-verse poem, the poet advises an unidentified listener concerned with death to "Go forth, under the open sky, and list / To Nature's teachings" (122), and thus learn, from the cyclical character of nature itself, that all must die, and that much wisdom flows there from. The poem's veneration for nature as instructor, and its fascination with death, indicate Bryant's growing Romanticism and attraction toward the natural world.

Bryant published the first edition of his *Poems* in the early 1820s. While this edition was important, the expanded 1832 edition, published under WASHINGTON IRVING's editorship, secured Bryant lasting fame. The collection contains Bryant's most famous compositions, in which he explores many themes central to his time's environmental thinking, among them, nationalism as it relates to the American landscape (MANIFEST DESTINY); a cyclical view of human history; and the Native American's place in the expanding United States.

Bryant's interest in developing an American poetic incorporates into his Romanticism JEFFERSONIAN ideals of pastoral virtue (AMERICAN PASTORAL). As Charles Sanford explains, the nationalism of Bryant's day contrasted "America's simple rural virtues with the supposed decadence of urban Europe. Celebrating the grandeur of native scenery especially

fulfilled the psychological needs of a nation bent upon greatness" (434). Working from this context in his "To an American Painter Departing for Europe," Bryant develops the idea that the proper subject for American cultural nationalism was America's landscape. Bryant addresses this sonnet to the nationalist landscape painter Thomas Cole. After exhorting Cole to remember American scenery when he arrives in Europe, Bryant ascends into an ekphrastic description of a Cole painting: "Lone lakes — savannahs where the bison roves —/ Rocks rich with summer garlands — solemn streams —/ Skies, where the desert eagle wheels and screams —/ Spring bloom and autumn blasé of boundless grove" (160–61). The poem is no mere flag-waving, however; Bryant's ekphrasis here also indicates his intense sense of the complex relation between man and nature. Glossing the lines, Robert Kern claims that "the speaker ... slip[s] ... into ... an inward mode of contemplation or visualization, in which he loses himself in what he evokes ... [the lines are,] I want to suggest, ecocentric" (439).

Bryant concludes the poem by exhorting Cole to remember America by reemphasizing the contrast between civilized, urban Europe and the pristine wildness of America. Bryant's description of the Plains in "The Prairies" further reflects his belief that wild, vital landscapes distinguish the United States; however, as in the poem to Cole, we should not read such descriptions as mere patriotic clichés. In a manner useful for understanding Bryant, Kern glosses LAWRENCE BUELL's concept of eco-criticism, claiming that it "may or should lead to ... the sense that we share our place with all that is other-than-human" (426).

Bryant provides such an outlook in "The Prairies." In the poem's opening simile, the poet loses himself in a vision of the ocean that the view of the Plains inspires in him: "Lo! they stretch / In airy undulations, far away, / As if the ocean, in his gentlest swell, / Stood still, with all his rounded billows fixed, / And motionless for ever" (102). In this sublime reverie, the poet loses his sense of self in a powerful transcendental epiphany. While the poet's return to his senses at the poem's close —"All at once / A fresher wind sweeps by, and breaks my dream, / And I am in the wilderness alone" (165)— suggests that for Bryant an ecocentric state can only persist momentarily, that Bryant even imagined such a state of perception attests to an interest in and approach to the environment unique in his time.

In his "The Ages," Bryant develops a stadialist historical narrative. He presented this long poem, which consists of 35 Spenserian stanzas, to the Harvard 1821 graduating class. Stadialism was a prominent contemporary philosophy of history positing that human history conforms to four states: the savage, the barbarian, the agrarian, and the civilized. These states are grounded in four modes of subsistence: hunting and gathering, herding, farming, and commerce. In a sense, then, this philosophy of history is rooted in a naturalistic worldview, because for stadialists history follows necessary, natural changes, much like the seasons. Unsurprisingly, therefore, the prospect of death and Bryant's meditation upon it prompt the historical discourse that comprises "The Ages," as death serves for Bryant as a reminder of humanity's subjection to cycle and nature. The poem owes much to stadialist thought in its conception of history as a set of progressive movements toward civilization. Bryant begins by exploring the savage state, when "he who felt the wrong, and had the might, / His own avenger, girt himself to slay" (135–36); then shifts to the rise of states when "The weak, against the sons of spoil and wrong, / Banded, and watched their hamlets, and grew strong" (136). As one can see from these lines, Bryant's historical narrativization tends to be normative as well as descriptive. While these earlier stages — as well as those of the Greeks, Romans, the Catholics of the European Dark Ages, and others — are necessary steps toward civilization, their foibles are regrettable for the poet. Those unfortunate characteristics, as one might expect from the nationalist Bryant, nonetheless yielded at last to the lofty (relative) merits that Bryant finds in his contemporary America. While many stadialists warned U.S. citizens that they must guard themselves against civilization's vices, to avoid the fate of prior great civilizations such as Rome, Bryant claims in "The Ages" that the United States will not fall victim to history: "But thou, my country, thou shalt never fall" (143). In other poems, however, Bryant could be less sanguine on this topic, which suggests that his statements here may partly reflect the rhetorical exigencies of motivating the young Harvard graduates.

Further evidencing Bryant's stadialist perspective is his belief in the necessity of Indian removal. In "The Ages," the United States effectively *subsumes* Native America, an example of the savage state giving way before a later, higher order. "The Prairies" also takes up this theme. After describing the Plains' grasslands, Bryant makes a characteristic *ubi sunt* gesture, asking what has happened to the glorious, idyllic race of mound builders that once inhabited the area. Answering this question, he claims that they fell to waves of marauding Indians. These mutabilities as well as the later removal of these Indians by Europeans, for Bryant, occur naturally: "Thus change the forms of being. Thus arise / Races of living things, glorious in strength, / And perish... The red man too —/ Has left the blooming wilds he

ranged so long, / And, nearer to the Rocky Mountains, sought / A wider hunting-ground" (164). While Bryant naturalizes the horrors and injustices of the Indian removal, he often mourns the loss of Indian culture; and this ethical dialectic has much to do with the poet's sense of the environment, as Bryant, like many in his time, sees Native Americans as an integral part of the New World landscape. While the move dehumanizes Native Americans, Bryant's lament over removal in this sense attests to his belief that U.S. expansion, while necessary, entails a tragic loss for the natural order. This poem, then, as well as others focused on Native America such as "An Indian at the Burying-Place of His Fathers," reflects his concern for man's ethical relation to nature. The tragedy of the native's fate, moreover, resides not only in the dispossession of the natives but also in the possibility that European Americans may one day suffer the same fate at history's hands.

At his death in 1878, Bryant was considered among the preeminent American poets of his time. Since then, his more radical contemporaries, Whitman and EMILY DICKINSON, have attained a higher place in the canon. In a time of growing environmental consciousness, however, Bryant's insights into the cultural and ethical dimensions of man's relation to nature still warrant attention. — John C. Havard

BIBLIOGRAPHY

Bryant, William Cullen. "The Ages." *American Poetry: The Nineteenth Century.* Vol. 1. Ed. John Hollander. New York: Library of America, 1993. 133–43. Print.

_____. "An Indian at the Burying-Place of His Fathers." *American Poetry: The Nineteenth Century.* Vol. 1. Ed. John Hollander. New York: Library of America, 1993. 147. Print.

_____. "The Prairies." *American Poetry: The Nineteenth Century.* Vol. 1. Ed. John Hollander. New York: Library of America, 1993. 162–65. Print.

_____. "Thanatopsis." *American Poetry: The Nineteenth Century.* Vol. 1. Ed. John Hollander. New York: Library of America, 1993. 122–24. Print.

_____. "To an American Painter Departing for Europe." *American Poetry: The Nineteenth Century.* Vol. 1. Ed. John Hollander. New York: Library of America, 1993. 160–61. Print.

Kern, Robert. "Fabricating Ecocentric Discourse in the American Poem (and Elsewhere)." *New Literary History* 37 (2006): 425–45. Print.

Muller, Gilbert H. *William Cullen Bryant: Author of America.* Albany: State University of New York Press, 2008. Print.

Sanford, Charles L. "The Concept of the Sublime in the Works of Thomas Cole and William Cullen Bryant." *American Literature* 28.4 (1957): 434–48. Print.

Whitman, Walt. *Specimen Days.* Ed. Floyd Stovall. New York: New York University Press, 1963. Print.

Buell, Lawrence (1939–)

Lawrence Buell is one of the first scholars to explain the project of environmental criticism and the characteristics of environmental literature, in his seminal 1995 work, THE ENVIRONMENTAL IMAGINATION, which helped to establish the legitimacy of the then-fledgling theory of "ecocriticism."

Buell received his B.A. in literature from Princeton and his Ph.D. in literature from Cornell. After teaching literature for 20 years at Oberlin College, he moved to Harvard University, where he is now the Powell M. Cabot Professor of American Literature. Buell has received numerous awards for both his commitment to undergraduate teaching and his contributions to literary scholarship, and has twice been nominated for the Pulitzer Prize.

In addition to his teaching and writing, Buell has some expertise as a natural historian (Buell 2). He shares this characteristic with HENRY DAVID THOREAU, whose work inspired Buell to focus his studies on American TRANSCENDENTALISM and the American Renaissance (Buell 23). However, in the mid–1980s Buell's scholarly interests took a turn when the Environmental Studies Department at Oberlin College asked him to teach a humanities course for their science-policy program (Winkler, "Literary"). This opportunity became a turning point for Buell: "In environmental studies, I liked the fact that I could talk about the real world and how human beings affected it" (qtd. in Winkler, "Literary"). At the time, literary theories largely ignored any connection between literature and the "real world," focusing instead on the text (or texts) alone, or questioning the ability of language to accurately reflect reality. For Buell environmental criticism is both a "recoil" from this separation of text and world and a response to the environmental challenges that face us (Winkler). As Buell explains, "Ecocriticism assumes that there is an extratextual reality that impacts human beings and their artifacts — and vice versa" (qtd. in Winkler, "Scholars").

Buell's continued interest in Thoreau's work, and the lessons learned from his experiences with environmental studies, produced *The Environmental Imagination,* which takes Thoreau's work as its focal point and is the first book in Buell's trilogy on environmental literature. The trilogy, which has become essential reading within the field of environmental criticism, also includes *Writing for an Endangered World* (2001) and *Shades of the Planet* (2007).

In *The Environmental Imagination* Buell responds to environmental philosophers who argue that the only way to address environmental problems is by revising "western metaphysics and ethics" (Buell 2).

Based on this premise Buell concludes that "environmental crisis involves a crisis of the imagination the amelioration of which depends on finding better ways of imaging nature and humanity's relation to it" (Buell 2). For Buell the purpose of environmental criticism is to "look searchingly at the most searching works of environmental reflection" in order both to identify the problems caused by our current images of the environment and to find images that will be less devastating for the environment (qtd. in Marx 2). — Lauren Mitchell Nadas

BIBLIOGRAPHY

Buell, Lawrence. *The Environmental Imagination: Thoreau, Nature Writing, and the Formation of American Culture.* Cambridge, MA: Belknap Press of Harvard University Press, 1995.
"Hubbell Winner Lawrence Buell." Modern Language Association. Available online. URL: http://als-mla.org/HMBuell.htm. Accessed March 4, 2009.
Marx, Steven. "The Environmental Imagination by Lawrence Buell." *Review essay: Buell's The Environmental Imagination.* Available online. URL: http://cla.calpoly.edu/~smarx/Nature/Buell.html. Accessed February 10, 2009.
Winkler, Karen J. "Literary Scholars Take Diversity of Approaches to Ecocriticism." *The Chronicle of Higher Education* (1996). Available online. URL: http://chronicle.com.ezproxy.lib.utexas.edu/che-data/articles.dir/art-42.dir/issue-48.dir/48a01401.htm. Accessed March 10, 2009.
_____. "Scholars Embark on Study of Literature About the Environment." *The Chronicle of Higher Education* A8+ (1996). Available online. URL: http://chronicle.com.ezproxy.lib.utexas.edu/che-data/articles.dir/art-42.dir/issue-48.dir/48a00101.htm. Accessed February 25, 2009.

The Environmental Imagination: Thoreau, Nature Writing, and the Formation of American Culture, Lawrence Buell (1995)

Universally considered a watershed in ecocriticism, Buell's book develops an approach to literary study that he believes will shed light on the environmental features of literary texts, and in so doing help to rehabilitate our culture's unhealthy ideas about the environment.

Our environmental crisis, Buell insists, is first and foremost a crisis of the imagination (2). Our ideas about and representations of nature are dangerously anthropocentric. We cause environmental harm, in other words, because we place humanity at the center of nature (or above it). To address the environmental crisis, we need to work towards an "ecocentric" perspective, in which we consider the interests and well-being of nonhumans (plants, animals, and so on) alongside those of humans (426).

Literature shoulders some of the blame for this

crisis of the imagination. Buell admits that many of the great works reinforce a human-centered worldview — including works traditionally classified as "nature writing." For example, Buell faults Keats's "Ode to a Nightingale" for "self-absorption" and anthropocentrism (7). In Buell's reading, the poem is more concerned with what the nightingale inspires in the human observer than it is with the nightingale itself. This sort of hidden anthropocentrism is a fault that Buell finds in many so-called nature poets and writers, including luminaries like Wordsworth and EMERSON.

However, if literature is complicit in the environmental crisis of the imagination, it also presents an opportunity for positive change. Indeed, Buell's book is an attempt to address this crisis through environmentally oriented reading and criticism. He hopes to call attention to environmental texts outside the canon, and to re-read canonical works to unearth their (previously neglected) environmental significance. His book, in short, aims to "to imagine how the voices of environmentalist dissent within western culture might help reinvision [that culture] and how they themselves must be critically reinvisioned in order to enlist them to this end" (22).

In his introduction, Buell constructs a rubric for evaluating the environmentality — that is, the environmental merit or worth — of literary texts. An "environmental text" according to Buell must have the following "four ingredients" (7). First, "the nonhuman environment is present not merely as a framing device but as a presence that begins to suggest that human history is implicated in natural history" (7). The environment, in other words, cannot be a simple setting or backdrop for the human characters, designed to set a certain mood or to double the characters' emotions — such as when a rainstorm doubles a character's low spirits. The environment must have its own "presence," it must operate independently of the human characters, or at least mold the characters as much as they mold it.

Secondly, the "human interest" in an environmental text must not be "understood to be the only legitimate interest" (7). This is the criterion that disqualifies Keats's "Ode to a Nightingale" from true environmentality. Though he dismisses Keats's bird poem, Buell endorses WHITMAN's bird poem, "Out of the Cradle Endlessly Rocking." While Keats' bird is deployed only to inspire human thought and emotion, Whitman's bird is "endowed with a habitat, a history, a story of its own" (7). Whitman's poem is environmental because it recognizes not only the interest of humans, but nonhumans as well.

The third ingredient of environmentality involves a "text's ethical orientation" (7): it must portray "human accountability to the environment" as a matter for ethical concern. Whether explicitly or implicitly, the text must applaud environmental care and/or condemn environmental harm. William Wordsworth's "Nutting" possesses this kind of environmentality, according to Buell: its narrator relates the sense of pain he felt as a boy after ravaging a virginal grove of hazel trees. The narrator's self-incrimination, Buell implies, reveals the text's praiseworthy ethical orientation towards the environment.

Finally, Buell also demands that "some sense of the environment as a process rather than as a constant or a given" be "at least implicit" in the environmental text (8).

Even if we can identify environmental texts within or outside the canon, however, we still need a mode of "environmental interpretation" — a new way to read literary texts that will reveal their full environmentality (2). According the Buell, the primary obstacle lying in the path of environmental interpretation is literary scholars' dogmatic insistence on a separation between the text and the real world. He contends that all the schools of literary theory prominent in the last century have relied, to some extent, on the (overstated) premise that "a text is obviously one thing and the world another" (82). Mid-century's "formalism," for example, approached writing as a self-contained artifact whose connections to any historical, biographical, or cultural — not to mention environmental — contexts were negligible (85). Today's prevailing theory of writing-as-discourse, inspired by thinkers like Michel Foucault, sees texts as conglomerations of larger ideologies or linguistic structures — abstract, webbed entities that refer less to the world than to each another.

Literary theories like these, Buell argues, ring hollow to most readers because they marginalize literature's "referential dimension," its ability to represent "factical" reality (86). He proposes that, for the sake of environmental interpretation, we recoup the concept of *mimesis*, that is, literature's ability to faithfully represent the real world. This means attending to a text's ability to communicate "the rich, complex texture, the credibility, of something that takes place 'out there'" (BARRY LOPEZ, qtd. in Buell 96). The most environmental of literary texts, Buell suggests, is one that pushes writer and reader towards a fuller eco-consciousness through the faithful rendering of actual, natural environments. The environmentality of such a text cannot be appreciated if we do not recognize literature's ability to achieve mimesis.

At the center of Buell's book is HENRY DAVID THOREAU and his masterpiece *WALDEN* (1854). However, *Walden* is an extraordinary environmental text not because Thoreau is perfectly ecocentric but rather, counterintuitively, because he is not. *Walden*, in Buell's reading, documents Thoreau's struggle to *overcome* "Eurocentric, androcentric, and homocentric culture" and "arrive at an environmentally responsive vision" (23). Therefore, the Thoreau of *Walden* can serve as a compelling "model" for how we — as individuals, and as a culture — might address our present crisis of imagination.

The Environmental Imagination is still considered a foundational work of ecocriticism; however, certain of Buell's arguments and assumptions have met challenges from fellow ecocritics, particularly in recent years. Dana Phillips in *The Truth of Ecology* (2004), for example, attacks Buell's "fundamentalist fixation on literal representation," that is, mimesis (7). Phillips disagrees with the idea that literature can, or should, capture the reality of nature, observing that "realistic depiction of the world [...] is one of literature's more pedestrian, least artful aspects" (8). Other scholars more sympathetic to *The Environmental Imagination* have nonetheless argued that ecocriticism needs to expand its sphere of concern to include environments beyond the wild and pastoral. The anthologies *Beyond Nature Writing* (2001), *The Environmental Justice Reader* (2002), and *Coming Into Contact* (2007) survey ecocritical work under this expanded charter.

In *The Future of Environmental Criticism* (2005) Buell responds to these and other criticisms, while in the process modifying some of the arguments and theoretical positions sketched out above. However, even though many (including Buell himself) have found flaws in *The Environmental Imagination*, all entrants into the field have found it necessary to acknowledge — whether admiringly or disparagingly — the contributions of what is perhaps the most provocative and enduring work of ecocriticism to date. — Erich Werner

BIBLIOGRAPHY

Beyond Nature Writing: Expanding the Boundaries of Ecocriticism. Karla Armbruster and Kathleen R. Wallace, eds. Charlottesville; London: University Press of Virginia, 2001.
Buell, Lawrence. *The Environmental Imagination: Thoreau, Nature Writing, and the Formation of American Culture.* Cambridge, MA; London: Harvard University Press, 1995.
_____. *The Future of Environmental Criticism: Environmental Crisis and Literary Imagination.* Malden, MA: Blackwell, 2005.
Coming Into Contact: Explorations in Ecocritical Theory and Practice. Annie Merrill Ingram, Ian Marshall, Daniel J. Phillipon, and Adam W. Sweeting, eds. Athens; London: University of Georgia Press, 2007.
The Environmental Justice Reader: Politics, Poetics, and Pedagogy. Joni Adamson, Mei Mei Evans, and Rachel Stein, eds. Tucson: University of Arizona Press, 2002.
Phillips, Dana. *The Truth of Ecology: Nature, Culture, and Literature in America.* New York: Oxford University Press, 2003.

Burroughs, Edgar Rice (1875–1950)

Edgar Rice Burroughs was a prolific writer of adventure and science fiction, but is most famous for his creation of Tarzan, the son of English aristocrats Lord and Lady Greystoke, who is stranded in a remote jungle following a mutiny aboard the ship carrying them to West Africa to settle colonial unrest. After the death of his parents Tarzan is raised by anthropoid apes and grows up completely at home in his untamed environment and among savage African animals. In the Tarzan saga Burroughs displays a fascination with untamed wilderness and expresses dissatisfaction with what he saw as the cruelty and corruption of western civilization, themes that were to occupy him throughout his writing career.

Burroughs was born in Chicago, in 1875, to Major George Tyler Burroughs, a Civil War veteran and successful businessman in Chicago's burgeoning distilling industry, and his wife Mary Evaline Burroughs. The youngest of five sons, one of whom died in infancy, Burroughs attended a number of schools before graduating from Michigan Military Academy in 1895. Until he began writing in his thirties, Burroughs life was peripatetic, beset by disappointment and often poverty. Among the careers he drifted into, and quickly out of, were instructor at the Michigan Academy, private with the Seventh United States Cavalry, railroad policeman in Salt Lake City, accountant, construction worker and door-to-door salesman. He had stints with his father's American Battery Company and on the family ranch in Idaho, and by 1911 he was married to Emma Centennia Hulbert, with two young children, working as the sales director of a failing pencil sharpener business and facing an uncertain future.

Inspired by the stories he chanced upon while monitoring the advertisements in pulp fiction magazines as part of his sales work, at the age of 35 Burroughs began work on his first novel. *Dejah Thoris, Martian Princess* (re-titled as *Under the Moons of Mars* and later *A Princess on Mars*) appeared in *All-Story Magazine* and is the first of ten novels in the Barsoom series dealing with the Martian adventures of John Carter, an American soldier and prospector. Burroughs' interest in the fantastic and often savage fauna of this planetary outpost, and his enthusiasm for a tough, frontiersman sensibility, are developed and refined in the environmental ideology inscribed in the 24 Tarzan stories.

Introduced in *Tarzan of the Apes* in 1912, Burroughs' hero vividly reflects a long tradition of British imperial writing, most notably that of Rudyard Kipling and H. Rider Haggard (in homage to whom Burroughs named a 1918 historical novel *H.R.H. The Rider*). The "natural man" living in harmony with exotic beasts recalls Mowgli from Kipling's 1894 *Jungle Books*, and illustrates the supposed value to human well-being, and specifically male well-being, of life lived in the wilds. As Burroughs wrote in a 1914 letter to the publisher M.N. Bunker, "Because Tarzan led a clean, active outdoor life he was able to accomplish ... feats that are ... beyond the average man" (cited in Porges, 1975, 212). Burroughs' colonial inheritance is also reflected in disparaging and paternalistic racial attitudes, particularly towards Africans, and he has been criticised for both a lack of zoological accuracy in his depictions of animals and a frequent tendency towards the anthropomorphic.

Nonetheless, the Tarzan books went from strength to strength with the feral hero appearing in a variety of settings and a range of media, with films in particular bringing Burroughs widespread fame. Tarzan's ongoing adventures included a visit to America with his wife-to-be Jane Porter, a trip to Britain where he regains his hereditary title, various scrapes involving lost treasure and civilizations in inaccessible African jungles, a spell in the R. A. F., and numerous victorious battles with assorted villains. Although Burroughs' work often reflected contemporary geopolitical events, with Germans and communists recurrently cast as the bad guys, an atavistic interest in an evolutionary past is the most striking feature of the series, along with violent engagements with animals that sit uncomfortably with many strands of twenty-first-century environmentalism. Burroughs' interest in lost worlds was developed in his "Pellucidar" series, in which a primitive culture is discovered at the centre of the earth, and in *THE LAND THAT TIME FORGOT* trilogy, a precursor of *Jurassic Park*, in which dinosaurs are discovered on a distant island. Burroughs continued, meanwhile, in a succession of failed business ventures, many involving the Californian estate he named Tarzana. He worked as a war correspondent in the South Pacific during the Second World War, and died from a heart attack in1950.—John Miller

BIBLIOGRAPHY

Holtsmark, Erling B. *Edgar Rice Burroughs*. Boston: Twayne, 1986.

Porges, Irwin. *Edgar Rice Burroughs: The Man Who Created Tarzan*. Provo, UT: Brigham Young University Press, 1975.

Vernon, Alex. *On Tarzan*. Athens: University of Georgia Press, 2008.

The Land That Time Forgot, Edgar Rice Burroughs (1918)

Part war story, part love story, part prehistoric fantasy, Edgar Rice Burroughs's *The Land That Time Forgot* is the first in his Caspak trilogy of novels, set in a mysterious island in the South Pacific, inhabited by dinosaurs and an assortment of anthropoid apes and primitive peoples. Published initially in 1918 in *Blue Book Magazine* and then in 1924 in book form (with its two sequels), it forms part of Burroughs' remarkably prolific output in the first years of his writing career. The discovery of a wild world beyond the reaches of western civilization is a recurrent theme in his writing and demonstrates the imaginative importance of wilderness in an age of rapid urbanisation and technological advancement. But while the humanoid fauna Burroughs' heroes encounter on the island exemplify the evolutionary relation of humans to their simian ancestors, and question human separateness from the natural world, the novel's environmental politics are uncomfortably colonial. Burroughs' savage, secret island is the scene most prominently of heroic testing for the stranded protagonists and, notwithstanding a sense of ecological wonder, affirms a dominatory agenda common in imperialist writing of the period.

The Land That Time Forgot begins with a teasing paragraph from Bowen Tyler, the central character and main narrator, who whets the reader's appetite with the revelation of a "lost pocket of the earth whither fate has borne me and where my doom is sealed" (7). Tyler's story is quickly interrupted, however, by the voice of the unnamed figure who provides the framing narrative. Spending the summer in Greenland for the benefit of his health, he discovers a manuscript in a thermos bottle floating in the surf and promptly retires from the text to allow Tyler to take center stage. The use of this narrative device and the setting in the freezing far north both recall the opening of Mary Shelley's *Frankenstein* (1818), a reference that Burroughs makes much of, particularly in the first half of the novel. Tyler, we discover, is a junior member of a Californian firm of shipbuilders specializing in the manufacture of submarines. Having obtained an appointment with the American ambulance service, he is en route to the First World War in France when his ship is attacked by a German U-Boat. Tyler's realisation that this submarine was built by his own company allows Burroughs to offer his first explicit allusion to Shelley's work as Tyler bitterly reflects how "this creature of my brain and hand had turned *Frankenstein*, bent upon pursuing me to my death" (11). After his ship is sunk Tyler finds himself in the water with his dog

Nobs until they are able to clamber aboard a lifeboat. Before long they rescue the novel's love interest, Lys La Rue, and man, woman and dog are soon picked up by an English tug. The reappearance of the U-Boat seems to herald further disaster but although the tug is also sunk, Tyler and the English crew are able to take control of the submarine, commanded, it turns out, by one Baron Friedrich von Schoenvorts, Lys's former fiancée. Despite raising a British flag, the U-Boat meets with a hostile reception from friendly vessels and the crew's intentions are further troubled by a series of acts of sabotage that Tyler mistakenly attributes to Lys. The Germans once again take charge of the submarine, only for the Allies to win it back, but with the navigation systems damaged, fuel running low and the water supply poisoned by the treacherous English sailor Benson, the outlook is grim.

Shortly after Benson is uncovered, shot and killed, Tyler and his crew chance upon a land mass, supposed to be the long-forgotten island of Caprona, and at this point the novel shifts dramatically from a patriotic narrative of war-time action to a stranger tale of weird beasts and evolutionary mysteries. Entering the interior of the island by a subterranean river they are astonished by the "strange and wonderful" fauna they come across; as Tyler explains, "there were all sorts and conditions of horrible things — huge, hideous, grotesque, monstrous — a veritable Mesozoic nightmare" (72).

Burroughs' depiction of the continued existence of long-extinct species in an isolated ecological enclave owes much to Arthur Conan-Doyle's 1912 novel *The Lost World*, in which dinosaurs are discovered on a remote Amazonian plateau; and there are clear echoes also of Jules Verne's *The Mysterious Island* (1874). Furthermore, as Tyler and crew set about the task of survival in this inhospitable environment, Burroughs leans notably toward the rhetoric of imperial hunting narratives in his portrayal of the bloody battles between man and dinosaur, and the submariners' search for game.

Lines like "I let him have it" (122) as a deer is shot for food, or "I let it have a bullet right between the eyes" (73) as a dinosaur is vanquished, are stock phrases of hunting tales that express a relish for violent confrontation and hint at colonialist aspirations for conquest.

At first the Germans and Allies co-operate in their residence on Caprona, building a fort to protect themselves from the island's pervasive hazards, among which is a large population of aggressive apes. Things appear to further improve as the Germans discover oil, raising the possibility of a return to civilization, and Tyler and Lys discover their mutual love. Catas-trophe, however, obtrudes on Tyler's happiness as the Germans escape with the sub and Lys is abducted. As Tyler leaves the camp in quest of his lover, he meets with a series of increasingly evolved primates, the Bo-Lu (club men), Sto-lu (hatchet men), Band-lu (spear men) and Kro-lu (bow men), each more sophisticated than the last in its language and use of tools. These species are able, in Burroughs world, to graduate up the evolutionary hierarchy through a mysterious ritual known as "Ata," in which females of each tribe bathe each day in a "large pool of warm water covered with a green scum and filled with billions of tadpoles" (120). Tyler is re-united with Lys only to be separated from her once more, and the novel ends with a final reunion as Tyler saves Lys from the clasps of a Neanderthal, and the manuscript is completed and tossed into the sea sealed in a thermos.

Burroughs revisited Caspak (the real name of Caprona) twice more in quick succession, with *The People That Time Forgot* and *Out of Time's Abyss*, both published in *Blue Book Magazine* later in 1918; and the novel was brought into the limelight once again in 1975 with the success of the film version, scripted by Michael Moorcock and directed by Kevin Connor. Fantasies of lost worlds and evolutionary anomalies continue to occupy a prominent place in the popular imagination (as the monumental success of *The Jurassic Park* films indicates), preserving Burroughs' enthusiasm for the possibility of environments still existing beyond the reach of human industrial culture.— John Miller

BIBLIOGRAPHY

Burroughs Edgar Rice. *The Land That Time Forgot.* London: Tandem, 1975 [1918].

Conan-Doyle, Arthur. *The Lost World.* Oxford: Oxford World's Classics, 1998 [1912].

Holtsmark, Erling B. *Edgar Rice Burroughs.* Boston: Twayne, 1986.

Porges, Irwin. *Edgar Rice Burroughs: The Man Who Created Tarzan.* Provo, UT: Brigham Young University Press, 1975.

Shelley, Mary. Frankenstein. London: Penguin, 2004 [1818].

Verne, Jules. *The Mysterious Island.* Tr. W. H. G. Kingston. London: Sampson and Low, 1875.

Burroughs, John (1837–1921)

John Burroughs was born and raised on a dairy farm in New York's Catskill Mountain region. After his father turned down his son's request for funds for higher education in 1854, Burroughs left home to become a teacher in the town of Olive, New York, where he also took courses at Cooperstown Seminary. It was there that Burroughs first read the works

of RALPH WALDO EMERSON and William Wordsworth, who profoundly inspired his own later writing.

In 1857, Burroughs took a teaching position in
Illinois, but was soon drawn back to New York, longing for the woman who would become his wife, Ursula North (1836–1917). While continuing to teach,
Burroughs began submitting essays for publication,
landing his first essay in *Atlantic Monthly* in 1860.
He stopped teaching in 1863, and began work as a
clerk and bank examiner, where he would remain
through the 1880s while continuing to write and
publish.

During the Civil War, Burroughs met poet WALT
WHITMAN, and the two became fast friends. Burroughs admired Whitman's work, and wrote a critical
biography, *Notes on Walt Whitman as Poet and Person*
(1867) which Whitman himself edited. Burroughs
published another tome on Whitman, in 1896, that
is credited for helping to establish the poet's literary
merit. Whitman, on his part, encouraged Burroughs'
writing efforts, and the latter soon found his essays
published, under pseudonyms "Philomel" and "All
Souls," in several periodicals.

It was not until his first collection of nature essays
appeared, however, that Burroughs found his niche
as a writer. *Wake-Robin* (1871) revealed Burroughs'
astute observations of nature, rooted in a deep yet
far-reaching sense of place, with essays focusing on
hiking the Catskill Mountains, rafting the Delaware
River, and fly fishing in New York's waters.

As a literary critic, Burroughs also wrote about
Emerson and HENRY DAVID THOREAU, with the latter of whom he was often compared. Burroughs re-
sented such comparisons, however, for he sought to
eschew the moralistic strain so central to (and prized
in) Thoreau's style. The "Thoreau charge" haunted
Burroughs throughout his career; he insisted he described nature only, and did not use it for teaching
morality. He rejected the "Book of Nature" metaphor
that many American writers used to assert that studying the natural world brought one closer to knowing
God; instead claiming that his nature writing
reflected only a greater feeling of spirituality, rather
than any substantive, let alone systemic, religiosity.

In 1874, Burroughs moved onto a nine-acre farm
called Riverby in what is now Esopus, NY. (He
would purchase additional land, and built a home
known as Slabsides, in 1895.) Here he learned that
his unadorned nature writing was also a valuable educational tool, and published essays specifically for
school readers. Two collections intended for younger
audiences, *Birds and Bees* (1887) and *Sharp Eyes*
(1888), sold over 200,000 copies. Burroughs also
personally tutored young people in ways to look at

nature, and hosted students from nearby Vassar College at Slabsides.

Though Burroughs was not involved in direct political action, as the CONSERVATION MOVEMENT accelerated, he became known as the "Grand Old Man
of Nature"; and what might be termed the pragmatic
reverence so prominent in his writings influenced
many of the movement's leaders. He published
several essays in *Century*, one of the leading conservation periodicals of the day, and as a respected literary naturalist, Burroughs was invited to accompany
an exploratory expedition to Alaska in 1899. Though
the Harriman Expedition was composed primarily
of scientists, two other writers, JOHN MUIR and the
poet Charles Keeler, as well as editor George Bird
Grinnell, were also included.

In April 1903, Burroughs accompanied President
THEODORE ROOSEVELT on a trip through Yellowstone National Park. They were both astute observers, and Burroughs tolerated Roosevelt's penchant
for hunting because the latter also found joy in spot-
ting birds of new species and had an understanding
of nature akin to his own. Roosevelt and Burroughs
found their strongest sympathy in their distaste for
writers who imbued nature with anthropomorphic
qualities. Burroughs, at Roosevelt's urging, published
an article in *Atlantic Monthly*, "Real and Sham Natural History," in which he assaulted the works of
Ernest Thompson Seton and William J. Long, arguing that their brand of "naturalistic" animal stories
were deleterious to people's understanding of nature
and, by extension, nature itself.

The "nature faker" debate, as it became known,
forced Burroughs to re-examine his own portrayals
of wildlife, and his later work reflects both a cautious
and empirical attitude toward animal psychology,
and a prudent reluctance to project human emotions
upon the animal world. He teased out his thoughts
on animal experiences in the essay, "Human Traits
in the Animals" and "The Reasonable but Unrea-
soning Animals" in *Leaf and Tendril* (1908)

In 1909, John Muir took Burroughs to see the
North Sigillaria Petrified Forest in Arizona, and the
Grand Canyon and Yosemite Valley. From California, Burroughs sailed to Hawaii. Muir encouraged
Burroughs to think about geology and the expansive
sublimity of nature. Burroughs read Darwin as well,
and his reflections on these journeys reveal the same
kind of "scientific imagination" that would later become such a dominant trait of environmental writing
in America. In Burrough's case this imagination had
a peculiarly apophatic character, finding spiritual inspiration precisely in the human *inability* to comprehend geologic time and evolutionary processes.
Echoing the ancient philosopher and mystic, Hera-

clitus, Burroughs wrote, in *Accepting the Universe* (1920), that "all is fixed, yet all is in motion," concluding that humans cannot "penetrate the final mystery of things, because behind every mystery is another mystery."

In 1901, Burroughs had met a young psychiatrist, Clara Barrus (1864–1931), who admired his work and became a close companion. When his wife, Ursula, died in 1917, Barrus moved in with Burroughs. Shortly after the removal of an abscess from his chest, Burroughs himself died on a train passing through Ohio in 1921.

Almost immediately upon his death, admirers formed the John Burroughs Association. After his death, Barrus published Burroughs' unpublished work and letters, and wrote her own biography of her companion. Altogether, Burroughs published 29 books, 23 of which were essay collections published together as the Riverby Editions. His work has been immensely influential in the field of nature writing, through its celebration — and demonstration — of the critical role of empirical observation, its rugged yet reverential poetry, and its pervasive but non-sectarian spirituality. Deeply rooted in place, Burroughs brought the nature of the Hudson Valley to life during an era increasingly focused on spectacular and monumental landscapes. Biographer James Perrin Warren also sees Burroughs as an ecocritic, citing his skilful interweaving of the human and nonhuman. Burroughs himself sums up his role as a literary naturalist in an era when scientific fields were becoming more specialized: "I know our birds well, but not as the professional ornithologist know them. I know them through my heart more than through my head" (*Life and Letters* 1:16).—Kelly Enright

BIBLIOGRAPHY

Bergon, Frank. "Burroughs, Literature, and Science in the Hudson Valley" in *The John Burroughs Review* 1:1 (3 April 1987).
Black, Ralph W. "The Imperative of Seeing: John Burroughs and the Poetics of Natural History." *The CEA Critic* 55:2 (Spring 1993).
Renehan, Edward J., Jr. *John Burroughs: An American Naturalist.* Post Mills, VT: Chelsea Green, 1992.
Warren, James Perrin, *John Burroughs and the Place of Nature.* Athens: University of Georgia Press, 2006.

Ways of Nature, John Burroughs (1905)

John Burroughs' *Ways of Nature*, his sixteenth book, collects a number of his short writings focusing on the literary treatment of nature. Burroughs explores what it is to "see straight" in observing nature, and to write carefully and truthfully about animal life and behavior in a way that creates an emotional or aesthetic understanding of nature in the reader, while respecting the truth of nature as it exists independent of man. The essays collected in *Ways of Nature* grew out of the "nature fakers" debate, a controversy between nature writers, which Burroughs had begun with his 1903 publication of "Real and Sham Natural History" in *The Atlantic Monthly* (Warren 197–98).

In that article, Burroughs had called out several popular nature writers of his day, including Ernest Thompson Seton and William J. Long, for over-humanizing their animal characters. In the attempt to make animal characters relatable to the increasingly wide audience for books of nature-writing, sentimental writers were giving the public a false impression of animal intellect and action, implying, for instance, that animals learn most of their behavior through direct parental instruction (304). The debate thus sparked involved prominent authors and naturalists, including THEODORE ROOSEVELT and JACK LONDON. By publishing *Ways of Nature*, Burroughs hoped to end his involvement with what had become a heated back-and-forth, though the debate continued for some time afterwards (Lutts 88).

Fortuitously, however, his attempt to close the debate, opened new and fruitful "ways" of approaching and understanding the nonhuman world. As Carol Dickson notes, Burroughs responded to the controversy by examining his own practice, becoming "more self-conscious about his own representations of animals" (228). Burroughs frames the book by recounting having been asked by a group of Californian schoolchildren to answer the question "whether or not birds have sense" (1). Throughout the essays in the book, he returns to this question, comparing animals to very young children: like them, animals have "simple perception and memory and association of memories"; but "the power of reflection and of generalization" is "a stage of mentality that the animal never attains to" (210). While allowing for a capacity of memory and imitation, Burroughs argues that inherited instinct accounts for most apparent animal wisdom. He notes, however, that "A large part of our own lives is instinctive and void of thought," and that "conscious reason" in man, when compared to the value of instinct, may be "a feeble matter after all" (212). Though *Ways of Nature* presents a more overtly analytical Burroughs than his previous books, he always returns to vivid and lovingly-rendered natural anecdote and observation to support his readings, and to encouraging re-readings or corrections of past attempts to characterize the natural world.

Showing his roots as a devoted reader of EMERSON and disciple of WALT WHITMAN, Burroughs echoes their belief in the importance of direct personal experience, and their concern with the problems of human perception, implying that what is needed is not "sugar-coated" versions of natural history that add artificial wonders, but a reform of perception, taste, and desire to see the wonders that are always there. "The reality always suffices," Burroughs argues, "If you have eyes to see it and ears to hear it" (15). Burroughs' scientific desire to know the thing in itself, to "see straight," "uncolored or unmodified by your own sentiments or prepossessions" (237), often appears at odds with his claim that experiential context, associated memories, and human sentiment are what provide us with our most profound subjective experience of nature; yet these two "ways," often seen as incompatible, even in our time, are intermingled at the deeper level of "seeing straight." He echoes Emerson's assertion in "Each and All" that experiencing the beauties of nature in their original environment and with regard to human experiential context is important. He notes that he does not enjoy the songs of caged birds for instance: "We have separated them from that which gives quality and meaning to their songs" (32). Likewise, Burroughs uses the example of an old man unexpectedly hearing the song of a bird native to his homeland; that man heard more in the song than Burroughs could: he "heard the bird through the vista of the years, the song touched with the magic of youthful memories" (33).

Curiosity and love, finally, make perception possible. We may go wrong, of course; but Burroughs stresses that we see little without love, "when our eyes are ... blunted by want or interest"—when we see nature as a means to an end. Most people see "more when we read the lives of the wild creatures about us in the light of our human experience and impute to the birds and beasts human motives and methods," but then we see with a reflected self-love, and see only ourselves (108). Burroughs, like Whitman, has a final purpose in inspiring his audience to reject vicarious or artificial experience, and seek out "Unadulterated, unsweetened observations": not to remake nature in the image of what you already love, but to come to love and recognize in yourself what is there in nature (15). This is the deeper sense of seeing straight, and one aspired to in much of the later literature on the environment, such as the prose of BARRY LOPEZ, the marine biology of ED RICKETTS and the poetry of MARY OLIVER. In *Ways of Nature*, Burroughs not only teaches the appreciation and observation of nature through literature, then, but as Dickson argues, recognizes "the limits and subjectivity of such teachings" (231).— Steve Marsden

BIBLIOGRAPHY

Burroughs, John. "Real and Sham Natural History." *The Atlantic Monthly* 91.545 (1903): 298–309.
_____. *Ways of Nature*. Vol. 11 of *The Complete Writings of John Burroughs: Wake-Robin Edition*. New York: Wm. H. Wise, 1924.
Dickson, Carol E. "Sense, Nonsense, and Sensibility: Teaching the 'Truth' of Nature in John Burroughs and Mary Austin." *Sharp Eyes: John Burroughs and American Nature Writing*. Ed. Charlotte Zoë Walker. Syracuse: Syracuse University Press, 2000. 220–231.
Lutts, Ralph H. *The Nature Fakers: Wildlife, Science & Sentiment*. Golden, CO: Fulcrum, 1990.
Renehan, Edward. *John Burroughs: An American Naturalist*. Post Mills, VT: Chelsea Green, 1992.
Walker, Zoë. "Reading the 'Fine Print' in the Catskills. John Burroughs Reinterprets the Book of Nature." *The Book of Nature in Early Modern and Modern History*. Ed. Klaas van Berkel and Arjo Vanderjagt. Leuven: Peeters, 2006. 209–226.
Warren, James Perrin. *John Burroughs and the Place of Nature*. Athens: University of Georgia Press, 2006.

Cabeza de Vaca, Álvar Núñez (ca. 1488/1490–ca. 1557/1559)

Cabeza de Vaca was a Spanish explorer of the New World. He was born in Jerez de la Frontera, a town near the port at San Lúcar de Barramed to a noble but impoverished family. His family is credited with an illustrious history of loyal service to the King, the highpoint of which occurred when a maternal ancestor used the "head of cow" to guide the Spanish forces to victory; thus, the honorary moniker "cabeza de vaca" was bestowed on future descendants. The teenaged Cabeza de Vaca followed in these footsteps when he began a career in the military. The year 1527 saw his designation to military leadership: treasurer and second in command to Pámfilo de Narváez, in an expedition to conquer the recently discovered land of Florida. Tragically, Cabeza de Vaca was one of the few to survive this foray into the Gulf Coast. According to his account of this ill-fated adventure [first published in 1542 as *LA RELACIÓN* (The Report), and later known as *Naufragios* (Shipwrecks)] he managed to survive only after learning to navigate the treacherous landscape. However, the Cabeza de Vaca that reached Mexico City after eight years of wandering around the future U.S. state of Texas, as well as the northeastern Mexican states of Tamaulipas, Nuevo León and Coahuila, and possibly smaller portions of New Mexico and Arizona, was not the man he was when first embarking upon a voyage to the Americas. Forced adaptation to a hostile wilderness filled with unknown peoples and unfamiliar flora and fauna transformed Cabeza de Vaca from a would-be conquistador to a proto-anthropologist/ecologist.

For this reason, the *Relación* reads like a pseudoscientific study of the region encountered by de Vaca, complete with detailed species descriptions and insightful cultural commentary, all addressed to the Spanish Crown in the hope that it would garner a subsequent position of leadership for its explorer turned author. Cabeza de Vaca's endeavor to write the story of the landscape and inhabitants of the frontier encountered during those eight years eventually bore fruit because it led to the lieutenant turned author's being named governor of Río de la Plata in South America, a province roughly comparable to present-day Paraguay. In this position, Cabeza de Vaca would continue to explore, analyze and write about the natural world that surrounded him, including the world-famous Iguazu Falls, which he is credited as being the first European explorer to see. Unfortunately, his respect for the American environment and the indigenous peoples that inhabited it would in due course force Cabeza de Vaca to return to Spain, penniless, in chains, and under a cloud of suspicion until his death (most likely in the year 1558) in Valladolid, Spain. Yet his fall from grace has not lasted into perpetuity; rather, the same absorption into *terra incognita* that brought about disgrace in life, resulted in fame after his death. — Christine Cloud

BIBLIOGRAPHY

Andrés Reséndez. A Land So Strange: The Epic Journey of Cabeza de Vaca. New York: Perseus Basic Books, 2007.
Cabeza de Vaca, Álvar Núñez. *The Narrative of Cabeza De Vaca.* Translation of *La Relacion*, Rolena Adorno and Patrick Charles Pautz. Lincoln: University of Nebraska Press, 2003.
Howard, David A. *Conquistador in Chains: Cabeza de Vaca and the Indians of the Americas.* Tuscaloosa: University of Alabama Press, 1996.
Schneider, Paul. *Brutal Journey, Cabeza de Vaca and the Epic First Crossing of North America.* New York: Henry Holt, 2007.

The Relation of Alvar Nunez Cabeza de Vacas, Alvar Cabeza de Vacas (1542)

Cabeza de Vaca secured a place in the annals of American history when tragedy struck the Pamfilo de Narváez–led mission to Florida and cast him unsuspectingly into the role of the first European to set foot in the future states of Florida, Texas, New Mexico, and Arizona. The narrative that he wrote upon his return to Spain as a report for king Carlos I of Spain, later published in 1542 under the title *La Relación* ("The Report," and later *Naufragios* or "Shipwrecks"), ensured that he remained a key part of American history in perpetuity. While not regarded as among the greatest literary chronicles of Spanish exploration and conquest in the New World, with its sympathetic portrayal of native peoples and subtle yet penetrating condemnation of Spanish cruelty and exploitation, this unique narrative has since become a primary source for historians and anthropologists focusing on pre–Columbian American life and customs. Moreover, as the first work by a European to discuss in detail the flora and fauna of North America, or to harrowingly describe the havoc wreaked by a Caribbean hurricane, Cabeza de Vaca's *Relación* stands as an enduring testament to survival in the early Southern-American wilderness environment.

Cabeza de Vaca's compelling first-person testimony to his harrowing adventures as treasurer and second-in-command of a voyage to what were for him uncharted territories begins with a description of the group's departure from Spain in June 1527. It would not be long, however, before the hierarchies of military leadership would be thrown by the wayside in the face of the disasters that would eventually doom the expedition to complete and utter failure. The desertion or death of 100 men that occurred in Cuba — before the journey even reached its desired destination — perhaps should have served as a warning of the calamitous events that would later doom the expedition. If it had, the lives of the 500 men that perished while on it might have been saved, and Cabeza de Vaca and the three others that lived to tell of their suffering in a strange land, would have been spared the eight years of wandering through treacherous terrain that transformed them from swashbuckling conquistadors to dispirited vagrants with nothing to show for their adventures — not even the clothes on their back. According to Cabeza de Vaca's biased recollection of events, the expedition's catastrophic ending could also have been avoided if Pámfilo de Narváez had taken his trusted treasurer's advice and refrained from separating the men on foot from their supply ships, causing them to fall victim to starvation, tropical diseases and the attacks by the coastal Indian tribes that most certainly did not welcome the aimlessly wandering Spaniards to their hitherto pristine shores. The 250 men that somehow managed to survive these dreadful consequences of Narváez's failure to heed his second-in-command's reputed warnings, were forced to fashion five crude rafts from the materials that they found on land and use them to sail west toward what they believed was New Spain. Unfortunately, several of these boats sank when they were pushed far out to sea as they passed the area where the Mississippi River empties into the Gulf of Mexico. However, Cabeza de Vaca's raft with several dozen men stayed afloat and eventually found itself washed ashore on the eastern coast of a land that is now called Texas. From here it would not be long before only four of the 500 men participating in the expedition remained alive: Cabeza de Vaca, Alonso Castillo, Andrés Dorantes, and Dorantes' African slave, Estevanico.

The book's remaining chapters, which make up the majority of its pages, describe the trauma faced by these four marooned Spaniards as they fought their way back to what they considered to be civilization. This part begins with a vexing description of how Cabeza de Vaca and his companions were first captured and then enslaved by Indians. These Indians were the indigenous peoples that greeted them when they landed on Galveston, a barrier island off the present-day Texas coast. It continues with a gripping account of the captives' continual attempts to escape, before turning to a retelling of how the prisoners came to be seen as healers and then heroes in the eyes of their captors. As the book recalls these events, it traces the men's long march across Texas, New Mexico, and Arizona, down through Sonora, Mexico, and concludes with a summary of Cabeza de Vaca and his comrades' heroes' welcome by the Spanish viceroy in Mexico City in 1536.

Cabeza de Vaca's reports of his travels and suffering in strange new lands had enough popular appeal to be regularly reprinted in Spanish and translated in 1556 into Italian. It subsequently inspired further quests for riches in the American interior, two of the most famous of which were led by De Soto and Coronado. Yet somehow the account itself did not garner much attention in the rest of Europe or North America until the middle of the nineteenth century, when it was translated into French, German, and English. Later on, several English translations in the twentieth century made the *Relación* available for historians and anthropologists in the United States, who found in the accounts of the author's long overland trek across the South-western U.S. desert valuable descriptions of flora, fauna, and Native American customs. Since then, the episodic tale of suffering, privation, and spiritual awakening in the Southwest has acquired a central place in American's understanding of its earliest selfhood and environment. In addition, Cabeza de Vaca's narrative may be seen as the prototype of much of modern American literature with its preoccupation with literal or figurative voyages of self-exploration. Because the journey it relates is inseparable from the landscape in which it takes place, Cabeza de Vaca's story of survival functions as an ecological tour de force, testifying powerfully to humankind's intimate and unending connection with the natural world that encompasses it, and shapes its life and death.— Christine Cloud

BIBLIOGRAPHY

Cabeza de Vaca, Álvar Núñez. *The Narrative of Cabeza De Vaca.* Translation of *La Relacion*, Rolena Adorno and Patrick Charles Pautz. Lincoln: University of Nebraska Press, 2003.

Howard, David A. *Conquistador in Chains: Cabeza de Vaca and the Indians of the Americas.* Tuscaloosa: University of Alabama Press, 1996.

Reséndez, Andrés. *A Land So Strange: The Epic Journey of Cabeza de Vaca.* New York: Perseus Basic Books, 2007.

Schneider, Paul. *Brutal Journey, Cabeza de Vaca and the Epic First Crossing of North America.* New York: Henry Holt, 2007.

Carson, Rachel (1907–1964)

The literary work of scientist and writer Rachel Carson had an enormous impact on the development of an environmental consciousness in the American public. Her life's work was devoted to making scientific concepts and natural phenomena understandable and interesting to the general public. Through her books, Carson introduced the public to the "biocentric" perspective, which holds that all living creatures (including humans) are interdependent, and that natural processes and phenomena should not be tampered with carelessly. According to biographer Mark Lytle, Carson's unique "capacity for broad synthesis and clear exposition shaped [her] world's understanding of nature in ways most scientists seldom could" (70).

Born in 1907 on a small farm outside of Springdale, Pennsylvania, Carson's love of nature and inquisitive mind was fostered by her mother. As a child, she explored the fields and forests surrounding their home, and her mother taught her to observe carefully, remember what she saw, and be respectful to the creatures that she encountered (Lytle 18). Her mother also encouraged Carson's interest in writing, and she began winning writing contests and publishing essays in children's magazines at the age of 11. These two early interests shaped the rest of her working life.

After graduating with a degree in Biology from Pennsylvania Women's College in 1929, Carson began her graduate studies at John's Hopkins Marine Biology Laboratory. She achieved some success with her research, but under pressure to provide more financial support to her family, she left the program at the master's level in 1932. She soon landed a job at the Bureau of Fisheries Division of Scientific Inquiries analyzing data, writing reports, and writing pamphlets that informed the public about the bureau's work. She remained in this position until she was able to support herself and her family with writing, but the experience and connections that she gained at the bureau would have a profound effect on her later work.

After the sudden deaths of both her father and sister, Carson became the sole bread-winner of the household, and began trying to supplement her salary by publishing some of her writing. Her first essay, "Undersea" which was published in the *Atlantic* in 1937 was so successful that it was expanded into Carson's first book *Under the Sea-Wind* (1941). Through *Under*, and her next two books *The Sea Around Us* (1951) and *The Edge of the Sea* (1951), Carson explained the mysteries of the sea to a general public that was largely unaware of what went on beneath the surface of the ocean. In addition, these texts introduced the public to new understandings of ecology and the natural world, including the balance of nature, the food chain, and the interdependence of species and environment in an ecology. But Carson's goals were not merely educational; she hoped that her writing would change the "human-centered view of nature that most Americans held" (Lytle 62).

To achieve this, *Under the Sea-Wind* was written entirely from the perspective of sea creatures that functioned as characters. As she followed each creature's journey, Carson illustrated how their life-cycles preserved the balance of nature: the death of one creature was the life of another. As a natural history of the ocean, *The Sea Around Us* took on a much more ambitious task. Here Carson's focus was to explain human dependence on the ocean and the interdependence of various species and environmental factors. This text was also "a celebration of science," informing the public about new discoveries, the methods used to make those discoveries, and "why some explanations remain contested and some mysteries remain unsolved" (Lytle 87).

In *The Sea Edge*, a field guide for the Atlantic coast, Carson's topic narrowed considerably. *Edge* is a much more intimate work, focusing on Carson's personal observations of the shoreline, often written in the first-person. This focus on personal observation illustrated Carson's belief in the importance of field research. In the mid-50s the laboratory had superseded the outdoors as the proper location for scientific research. However, Carson was part of a new movement in science which held that to properly understand any natural phenomenon, a scientist had to be intimately familiar with the interactions between it and its environment (Lytle 111). Thus, in her own quiet way, Carson was challenging the status quo in each of these works. In her own words, Carson's overall goal in these works was to "provide 'an imaginative searching out of what is significant in the life history of the earth's ocean,' while at the same time addressing 'questions thus raised in the light of the best scientific knowledge'" (qtd in Lytle 71).

These first three books were well-received, winning several prestigious awards and critical acclaim. The success of *The Sea Around Us,* which was a bestseller, allowed Carson to leave her position at the Bureau of Fisheries to write full-time. However, it is her last book for which Carson is most, and most justly famous. In *Silent Spring* she argues that the unrestricted use of pesticides such as DDT and dieldrin have detrimental effects on the environment because they poison not only the pests that are their targets, but other insects, the water system, wildlife, domestic animals, and ultimately humans.

Although Carson had been concerned about the over-use of DDT since 1945, she could not find a publisher interested in the topic until 1957. By then, concern over the effects of pesticides had taken root in the public consciousness after the controversial aerial spraying of pesticides over large portions of the southern and northeastern states. These sprayings ultimately resulted in the large-scale deaths of fish, birds, and livestock, with one agricultural official describing the affected areas in Alabama as "wasteland that 'reeked of the odor of decaying [wildlife]'" (Lytle 123). The sprayings also resulted in several major lawsuits, which pitted private citizens and local governments against pesticide companies and the U.S. Department of Agriculture (USDA). Given these events, Carson and her publisher knew that the book would be highly controversial, so special care was taken with her research. She worked on *Silent Spring* for four years, collecting expert testimony and research from a wide range of scientists.

Although *Silent Spring* was vehemently attacked by both the pesticide companies and the USDA, its message struck a chord with the public. It became a bestseller in both the U.S. and England, was serialized in *The New Yorker*, and won numerous and prestigious awards. However, *Silent Spring* is most valuable for its contributions to the then-fledgling environmental movement. In the decade after its publication, the Environmental Protection Agency was formed, DDT was banned for use as a pesticide, the Clean Water Act was passed, and Earth Day was established; and *Silent Spring* was the spark that ignited such environmental activism and legislation in the United States.

In addition, *Silent Spring* introduced the concept of environmental justice, that all citizens have a right to a clean environment — a revolutionary concept in Cold-War America. Carson explains this idea by comparing it to the Bill of Rights:

> We have subjected enormous numbers of people to contact with these poisons, without their consent and often without their knowledge. If the Bill of Rights contains no guarantee that a citizen shall be secure against lethal poisons distributed

either by private individuals or public officials, it is surely only because our forefathers, despite their considerable wisdom and foresight, could conceive of no such problem [22].

In passages like these, Carson reframed and altered forever the way that Americans think about the environment and their place within it. — Lauren Mitchell Nahas

BIBLIOGRAPHY

Carson, Rachel. *Silent Spring*. Greenwich, CT: Fawcett, 1962.
Lear, Linda. "Books Written by Rachel Carson." *Rachel-Carson.org: The Life and Legacy of Rachel Carson*. http://www.rachelcarson.org/BooksBy.aspx.
Lytle, Mark H. *The Gentle Subversive: Rachel Carson, Silent Spring, and the Rise of the Environmental Movement*. New York: Oxford University Press, 2007.

Silent Spring, Rachel Carson (1962)

Rachel Carson's epochal bestseller, *Silent Spring*, the result of three years of extensive research, first appeared in serialized and abridged form in *The New Yorker* in June 1962, and was published later that year by Houghton Mifflin. While Carson's earlier work had established her as a highly-regarded nature writer, *Silent Spring* was her first foray into environmentalist writing, if that term is to be understood as carrying a social message of activist engagement. Even the earliest sections of the book provoked a highly controversial debate, which saw an alarmed public confront the chemical industry. The book played a crucial role in the creation of the United States Environmental Protection Agency, and also contributed substantially to the public debate that led to legislation to ban DDT in the USA. Given its subject, it is not surprising that it continues to be maligned by critics who see in it an unnecessary stumbling block on the road to a future of chemically produced health and happiness (see Lytle 217–28). In spite of her detractors, however, Carson created, with *Silent Spring*, a work that not only inspired generations of readers with a profound love of nature but ultimately provoked actual policy changes that positively impacted the environment. For this alone, she unquestionably belongs among the most influential nature writers of the twentieth century (see Matthiessen).

Silent Spring famously opens with "A Fable for Tomorrow," in which Carson evokes the dystopian scenario of living in an environment so badly polluted by overuse of pesticides that not only all birds have disappeared but many other species show severe signs of physiological damage: cows, pigs, and fish have died, and even children would mysteriously fall ill and perish within days. Carson lyrically evokes "a shadow of death" and "a strange stillness." The closing lines of this short chapter admit to the poetic license taken, pointing out that while each horrific effect of aerial DDT dusting described has occurred somewhere, the cumulative effect has never been witnessed. And yet, by invoking "A grim specter," even in the muted conclusion to this chapter, Carson makes a strong case against both the lethal effect of pesticide overuse and the lack of knowledge that most people have about this practice. The section subtly evokes a nostalgic desire for the peace and harmony of small town life, but quickly passes from this literary *topos* to a post-apocalyptic indictment of the chemical industry, which is blamed for unleashing widespread suffering and death, in terms that summon images of the nuclear fallout from atomic bombs. It thus forms part of the literary tradition that sketches "a long-standing mythography of betrayed Edens" (BUELL 37).

The rest of the book is far less lyrical, and follows a much more rigorous pattern of science writing and philosophical argument. Unheard of at the time for a book aimed at a general readership (Murphy 9), Carson even included a long list of principal sources keyed to individual passages in the book. The second chapter outlines Carson's claim that the public has a right to know what kinds of chemicals the government and scientists have decided to use on humans, sometimes without even informing the people affected. Carson states unambiguously that her book is not in favor of a complete ban on DDT, but of more restricted use, informed by more extensive research into the effects that various pesticides have on human and nonhuman life. Subsequent chapters discuss the exact chemical properties of DDT and similar insecticides; show how the global ecosystem passes on these chemicals through surface and underground water; and explain how, for example, the deadly impact of DDT on all kinds of living organisms severely impedes the complex bio-organisms at work in the soil. Her frequently ironic tone is directed, in Chapter 7, against the common hubris that believes any problem can be solved with a technological "fix." To counter this, Carson elaborates on some telling historical case studies. She contrasts, for example, the strikingly different responses to foreign beetle infestations on the East coast (at a time when powerful chemicals were not yet available) and in the Midwest: while the coastal region suffered through the exposure, it fairly quickly recovered; but in the Midwest repeated pesticide sprayings not only led to substantial loss of wildlife, but failed even to deal a serious blow to the beetle population. In the chapter entitled "Beyond the Dreams of the Borgias," Carson points out that chemical residue is found in all kinds of food and in human tissue, often at levels far beyond what is permitted by law. Going even further, she questions to what extent officially sanctioned levels of toleration are merely concessions to agribusiness and the chemical industry; and here *Silent Spring* raises the crucial question of whose interest government agencies should put first. Carson also explores the deep systemic concern that all too often government decisions are not merely influenced by industry lobbying, but are supported by industry-financed research at supposedly independent universities; a connection that galled her during the public debate that followed the publication of her book, when scientists spoke out without revealing who financed their research (see Murphy 48).

The final four chapters offer an initially gloomy, but ultimately positive outlook. Carson first discusses the relationship between cancer and toxic chemicals (following a prolonged fight against the illness, Carson would eventually die of breast cancer just short of two years after the publication of *Silent Spring*). She then points out that nature often adapts to being exposed to particular chemicals, sometimes resulting in the development of resistance in the very species targeted by pesticides. The penultimate chapter envisions a future when public health, both in the West and particularly in tropical developing countries, may be threatened by an "avalanche" of species barely controllable by chemical spraying or dusting. The whole four-part section provides a close scientific counterpoint to the fable that opens the book.

In her final chapter, she suggests an alternative course, one in closer harmony with nature. Rather than disseminate chemicals indiscriminately from the air, biological intervention targets individual insects. In one such case, the screw-worm was eradicated from Florida by releasing 3.5 billion sterilized male flies, which quickly led to infertile screw-worm eggs, and soon after to the complete disappearance of the screw-worm. Other strategies revolve around the isolation of sex attractants to lure males into traps, or bacterial warfare that exclusively targets particular insects. The introduction of predator species also holds promise, and here Carson perspicaciously discusses the complex interconnections of any ecosystem, and hence the need to study in great detail the effect on the whole system, of introducing even one new species. She closes her book by once more denigrating chemical area-spraying as the equivalent of "the cave man's club," describing its underlying rationale as rooted in the scientistic faith in the power of technology, and the highly anthropocentric human conviction "that nature exists for the conven-ience of man"; her own ethical outlook being clearly more eco-centric.

Carson was a bold and eloquent forerunner of the environmentalist movement in its modern sense; that is, at a historical moment when preservation and conservation had developed as separate attitudes toward nature. She clearly had "a touch of the rebellious spirit of Henry David Thoreau and John Muir" (Lytle 199), and it served her well in writing an environmentalist book which was to become "a watershed event that catapulted the issue into the view of a previously ignorant general public" (Murphy 14). Indeed, with *Silent Spring* Carson "parted company with conservationists" (Lytle 200) precisely because of their ethical prioritizing of human needs. For Carson, the environment carries intrinsic value that deserves and even demands proper respect, and as a consequence, human stewardship and a sense of responsibility.

The kind of activism and public involvement encouraged by *Silent Spring* struck a chord with the reading public for other historical reasons, not all of which were directly connected to the environmentalist movement. The book, for instance, resonated deeply with the anxiety of a Cold War public painfully aware that technological innovations like nuclear weapons might usher in a grand finale to the human chapter of global history. The rise of agribusiness had also already created situations wherein the use of insufficiently tested and certified chemicals, in particular in the hands of people lacking proper training in their use, led to public health warnings. The resulting consumer panic brought with it a sense of unease in the general population, and nurtured a growing feeling that government needs to become involved in the monitoring and supervision of hazardous substances. However, given that at least some government agencies were amongst those in favor of aerial spraying, Carson's *Silent Spring* also made a substantial contribution to environmentalism by simply making people realize that public debate was needed in order to convince legislators that public health and the well-being of the natural world are entitled to more substantial protection.— Gerd Bayer

BIBLIOGRAPHY

Buell, Lawrence. *Writing for an Endangered World: Literature, Culture, and Environment in the U.S. and Beyond.* Cambridge: Harvard University Press, 2001.

Carson, Rachel. *Silent Spring.* Boston: Houghton Mifflin, 1962.

Lytle, Mark Hamilton. *The Gentle Subversive: Rachel Carson, Silent Spring, and the Rise of the Environmental Movement.* New York: Oxford University Press, 2007.

Matthiessen, Peter, ed. *Courage for the Earth: Writers, Scientists, and Activists Celebrate the Life and Writing of Rachel Carson.* Boston: Houghton Mifflin, 2007.

Murphy, Priscilla Coit. *What a Book Can Do: The Publication and Reception of* Silent Spring. Amherst: University of Massachusetts Press, 2005.

Cather, Willa Sibert (1873–1947)

Born in 1873 to a prosperous farming family in Virginia's Back Creek Valley, Willa Cather spent her earliest years in Virginia before her family moved to a farm in Webster County, Nebraska, in 1883. For the rest of her life she would publicly define herself in terms of that move. "I would not know," Cather later told an interviewer, "how much a child's life is bound up in the woods and hills and meadows around it if I had not been jerked away from all these and thrown out into a country as bare as a piece of sheet iron" (Slote 448). Upon arriving in Nebraska Cather was transfixed by the prairie stretching out before her, feeling alternately awed and a little frightened by its vast difference from the land to which she was accustomed. She quickly developed a place-sensitive devotion to the prairie and its inhabitants, however. "When I strike the open plains, something happens. I'm home," she confided to a *Lincoln State Journal* reporter many years later in 1921: "That love of great spaces, of rolling open country like the sea — it's the grand passion of my life" (O'Brien 68). It would become the grand passion animating her literary expression as well, which often represents natural environments as sites of wonder and comprehension.

After graduating from the University of Nebraska in 1895 Cather wrote for various newspapers and magazines while living first in Lincoln and then in Pittsburgh. In 1906 she was offered work as an editor at *McClure's* and moved to New York City where she maintained a residence for the rest of her life. Two years later, in 1908, Sarah Orne Jewett gave Cather advice that profoundly influenced the direction of her mature writing. Jewett admonished the younger writer to "find your own quiet centre of life, and write from that to the world" (Woodress 203). Cather understood her personal "center" to be the rural and wild landscapes in which she had grown up, and as she turned her attention to the environment of her childhood she threw herself into writing the characteristic prairie fiction for which she would become best known, publishing *O Pioneers!* in 1913, *The Song of the Lark* in 1915, and My ANTONIA in 1918.

The "love of great spaces" manifested itself anew in 1915 when Cather first visited the American Southwest, where she spent a month in New Mexico, saw Mesa Verde, and began to gather material for what would eventually become her major southwestern novels, *The Professor's House*, published in 1925, and *Death Comes for the Archbishop* in 1927.

Cather died in 1947 at the age of 73. She is buried in Jaffrey, New Hampshire, where her headstone is engraved with an excerpt from one of her most celebrated environmental passages, in which *My Antonia*'s Jim Burden exults in the sensation of sun-warmed earth between his fingers, realizing "...that is happiness; to be dissolved into something complete and great." — Rachel Collins

BIBLIOGRAPHY

O'Brien, Sharon. *Willa Cather: The Emerging Voice.* New York: Oxford University Press, 1987.

Slote, Bernice, ed. *The Kingdom of Art: Willa Cather's First Principles and Critical Statements, 1893–1896.* Lincoln: University of Nebraska Press, 1966.

Woodress, James. *Willa Cather: A Literary Life.* Lincoln: University of Nebraska Press, 1987.

My Ántonia, Willa Cather (1918)

Understood by many as an elegy for the frontier-era prairie, *My Ántonia* fictionalizes various elements of Willa Cather's own nineteenth-century childhood on the Nebraska plains. The novel opens with an elaborate introductory frame in which the narrator, Jim Burden, decides to write up his memories of his childhood. Seeking to recapture the sense of wonder he felt growing up on the Midwestern plains, he focuses his thoughts on his childhood friend, Ántonia Shimerda, because more than anyone else she reminds him of "the country" of his youth (5). Pointing to this moment, Susan J. Rosowski characterizes Ántonia as "a coming together of man and nature, a mediator between them" (79), who also functions as a guide in Jim's ecological education.

As children Jim and Ántonia together explore the miles of wine-colored prairie grass that covers the plains, and as Jim grows older, leaves the farm, and eventually relocates to the urban east, his mind often returns to the scenes and images of his youth. The novel ends with his return to the prairie, where he finds Ántonia living happily with her husband and children on a prosperous farm. Formally the novel is divided into five segments, each focused on a different phase of Jim's life: his childhood on the family farm, his teenage years in the town of Black Hawk, his college years in Lincoln, his brief return to the prairie after graduating from college, and his final visit to Ántonia's farm 20 years later.

Many of Jim's childhood recollections reveal a sense of affection for the environment among the frontier settlers. He recalls, for example, his grandmother's admonishment not to fear the badger who lives at the edge of her kitchen garden. She explains to him that even though the badger sometimes kills the family's chickens she refuses to let anyone harm him, for "In a new country a body feels friendly to the animals"; she says, "I like to have him come out and watch me when I'm at work" (19). Several decades later Ántonia voices a similar ethic of friendship for the natural world as she shows Jim around her farm, pointing to the trees in particular. "I love them as if they were people," she confides to him, saying they are constantly "on my mind like children" (253). She regularly wakes during the night and lovingly carries water to them in the dark.

Though agricultural work puts the characters of *My Ántonia* in close and sympathetic contact with the natural world, the novel also carefully registers the difference between cultivated and truly natural environments. Ántonia is anxious about the trees because her fruit orchard is not a native growth, but is instead sustained largely by her husband's careful grafting and her own nighttime watering; and Mrs. Burden's kitchen garden attracts rodents, which in turn attract snakes, who become, as Stephen Trout has pointed out, the targets of her program of "assertive wildlife management," in which she kills all the poisonous snakes she sees and encourages Jim to do the same (106). In fact, the novel mobilizes a particularly troubling interaction between young Jim and a snake to stand in for his relationship to the natural world more generally: while walking across the prairie one day, Jim sees and quickly kills a threatening snake, but then loses control of himself and continues to beat its dead body into an oozing pulp on the ground. Jim and Ántonia both interpret this killing as a coming-of-age moment and Ántonia pronounces him "just like big mans" (41). This logic, which suggests that adulthood and masculinity are connected to the violent domination of the natural world, remains uneasily with Jim for the rest of his life, for as an adult he leverages railroad capital to finance oil-drilling and mining projects throughout the western landscape that he loves so well. Such tensions between human development of the land and the conservation of the natural world inform the novel as a whole, which Patrick Dooley describes as subscribing to an ethic of "homocentric conservation" in which the environment is simultaneously understood as an important entity and an "instrument in the service of human prerogatives."

Cather's sense of the difficult complexities in the relationship between humans and their environment pervades much of her fiction, which eludes any easy categorization of its environmental stance. What is clear, however, is that Cather's Midwest is not the isolating or viciously constricting place depicted by many of her contemporaries like Sherwood Anderson or Sinclair Lewis. Instead, *My Ántonia*, like Cather's other Nebraska novels, is best known for its celebratory images of a prairie landscape valued as a site of wonder and comprehension. One such moment comes when Jim, after graduating from high school, spends a day in the countryside with Ántonia and the other immigrant girls. At sunset they see a plough on the horizon and Jim recalls that, "magnified across the distance by the horizontal light, it stood out against the sun, was exactly contained within the circle of the disk; the handles, the tongue, the share — black against the molten red. There it was, heroic in size, a picture writing on the sun" (185–186). The power of the natural world to transform the ordinary into the heroic informs much of the novel's environmental imagination, and Jim himself is drawn to what he calls "the old pull of the earth, the solemn magic that comes out of those fields" (241).

My Ántonia is the last of Cather's Nebraska novels and marks an important turning point in her career. After completing it she turned her attention to new locales, particularly the desert of the Southwestern United States (which she had visited for the first time in 1915), and never again devoted herself so fully to representing the land in which she spent her youth.

In 1995 *My Ántonia* was adapted into an Emmy Award–winning made-for-television movie. — Rachel Collins

BIBLIOGRAPHY

Cather, Willa. *My Ántonia*. New York: Penguin Books, 1994.
Dooley, Patrick. "Biocentric, Homocentric, and Theocentric Environmentalism in *O Pioneers!*, *My Ántonia*, and *Death Comes for the Archbishop*." *Cather Studies* 5 (2003). Available online. URL: http://cather.unl.edu/cs005_dooley.html. Accessed June 19, 2009.
Rosowski, Susan. *The Voyage Perilous*. Lincoln: University of Nebraska Press, 1986.
Trout, Stephen. "Seeing the Rattlesnake in Willa Cather's *My Ántonia*." *ISLE* 12.1 (2005): 99–114.

Cavell, Stanley (1926–)

Stanley Cavell was born in 1926, in Atlanta, Georgia. Having been taught the piano by his mother, he enrolled as a music major at the University of California at Berkeley. Cavell earned a bachelor's degree from Berkeley before heading to Harvard, where he received his Ph.D. in philosophy. He taught for six years back at Berkeley, but ultimately returned to Cambridge in 1963, later being named the Walter M. Cabot Professor of Aesthetics and the General Theory of Value, acquiring Emeritus status in 1997, receiving a MacArthur Fellowship, and serving as President of the American Philosophical Association. The focus of Cavell's work is rather complex in nature. It is described as centering on "the intersection of the analytical tradition (especially the work of

Austin and Wittgenstein) with moments of the Continental tradition (for example, Heidegger and Nietzsche); with American philosophy (especially EMERSON and THOREAU); with the arts (for example, Shakespeare, film and opera); and with psychoanalysis" (Harvard, par. 2).

Cavell's "ordinary language" philosophy—a broad heuristic approach that he has applied to "literature, language, epistemology, politics, ethics, and culture"—and his interest in "low culture" are often attributed to his "stretching the boundaries between traditional philosophy and more practical modes of cultural criticism" (Brino-Dean 460). Cavell rejects modern skepticism and its Cartesian insistence that we "doubt the very existence of this bare and inert reality" in the absence of "absolute certainty" (Furtak 544–5). He focuses instead on expression and epistemology, and is an important film critic whose psychoanalytic approach to the medium stresses the role of the viewer (Brino-Dean 461), just as his approach to literature, and Thoreau specifically, strongly empowers the reader.

A respected literary critic who has published on Shakespeare, Emerson, Derrida, de Man, Fish, and psychoanalysis, Cavell's inclusion in this volume is due primarily to his 1972 book, THE SENSES OF WALDEN. In it, he joins the target text itself in a process of re-thinking, thereby demonstrating that Cavell is—as Thoreau himself was—an unapologetic iconoclast. Moreover, what is often said of Thoreau, that "his work has proven notoriously hard to categorize" (Hammer x), is equally true of Cavell. Whereas literary critics have historically attempted to simplify WALDEN by means of categorization and classification (be it as nature writing, an epic poem, an ethical manifesto, or otherwise), Cavell instead celebrates its complexity, thus supporting Espen Hammer's contention that he "is a lot less interested in interpretation than in dialogue" (xi). Cavell deems Walden a sacred book for the manner in which it interfaces with readers: as we read Thoreau's text, we become builders of our own, making meaning at each utterance, constructing a world with each word. Cavell's anti-skeptical philosophy is thus quite at home in Walden; after all, just as Cavell encourages his reader to privilege her own unique experience of Walden, so Thoreau seeks no all-encompassing truth, but rather his own personal ethos, all the while exhorting others to follow suit.—David Visser

BIBLIOGRAPHY

Brino-Dean, Terry. "Cavell, Stanley Louis (1926–   )." *The Dictionary of Modern American Philosophers*. 3 vols. Ed. John R. Shook. Bristol: Thoemmes Continuum, 2005.
Cavell, Stanley. *The Senses of Walden*. New York: Viking, 1972.
_____. *The World Viewed: Reflections on the Ontology of Film*. New York: Viking, 1971.
Furtak, Rick Anthony. "Skepticism and Perceptual Faith: Henry David Thoreau and Stanley Cavell on Seeing and Believing." *Transactions of the Charles S. Peirce Society* 43.3 (2007): 542–561.
Hammer, Espen. *Stanley Cavell: Skepticism, Subjectivity, and the Ordinary*. Oxford: Blackwell, 2002.
Harvard University Department of Philosophy: Faculty of the Department: Professor Emeritus Stanley Cavell. Copyright 2007–2008. The President and Fellows of Harvard College. 26 October 2009. http://www.fas.harvard.edu/~phildept/cavell.html.

The Senses of Walden, Stanley Cavell (1972)

Deemed one of the seminal works on HENRY DAVID THOREAU's WALDEN, philosopher Stanely Cavell's *The Senses of Walden* is an atypical work of literary criticism. Seeking not so much to "solve" *Walden* by means of categorical explication, Cavell instead approaches the text with Thoreau's advice in mind: just as Thoreau exhorts us to renew our stale lives and perspectives, so Cavell encourages us to revise our reading of *Walden*.

Utilizing the techniques of New Criticism, and following Thoreau's own injunction to "laboriously seek the meaning of each word and line," Cavell divides his work into three sections, "*Words*," "*Sentences*," and "*Portions*," and contends that *Walden* "is perfectly complete, in that it means every word it says, and that it is fully sensible of its mysteries and fully open about them" (3). Cavell depicts *Walden* as a heroic book, in which America's need for "a modern epic" is satisfied, with "renewed instruction of the nation in its ideals, and a standing proof of its resources of poetry.... The literary ambition of *Walden* is to shoulder the commitment in prose" (6, 30). For Cavell, *Walden* answers EMERSON's plea for a truly *American* literature. In it, Cavell finds an emphatically revolutionary text, one that calls on Americans to liberate themselves, both ethically and literarily, and does so by acknowledging that living, like writing, "will come to a finish in each mark of meaning, in each portion and sentence and word" (27).

Believing it impossible "to discover and settle this land, or the question of this land, once for all," Cavell cites Thoreau's exhortation of Americans to continually reconsider their actions, and do so always with respect to their surroundings (8). Effectively "re-placing" himself by moving to Walden, Thoreau famously aligns himself with Chanticleer by observing, processing, and, ultimately, *sounding*. Bird song inspires Thoreau, according to Cavell: their voices, organic and instinctive, bespeak the prose he seeks, as he aims to "let his words warble and chuckle to themselves" in hopes of a deliberate molting for himself, his country, and *the* country (Cavell 40).

Thoreau's role as one of the first environmentalists is thus tacitly acknowledged, as he stalwartly beseeches us to re-examine our own interaction with the wild: "we have to learn," claims Cavell, "that we have to find ourselves where we are" (97). Hence, identity and place inform each other; finding ourselves means realizing nature. Accordingly, Thoreau aligns nature itself with *Walden*: "for the writer's hoe, the earth is a page" (25). We must live, as Thoreau says, "deliberately," cognizant of the effects of the pen and the hoe. Thus, Cavell's reading of *Walden* is an essentially *ecological* one, keenly aware of process, causality and interdependency.

Walden, for Cavell, is also an ambivalent text; like the rumors surrounding MELVILLE's Moby Dick, it can be ubiquitous and immortal, yet "obsessed with the seasons of a real place ... in Concord, Massachusetts, 'in the Presidency of Polk, five years before the passage of Webster's Fugitive-Slave Bill'" (21, 28). Thoreau thus creates both Walden and *Walden*: the former a distinct locale in New England, the latter an ethereal and eternal workshop housing writer and reader. The problem, as Cavell sees it, is that "So long as we will not take our beliefs all the way to genuine knowledge, to conviction, but keep letting ourselves be driven to more or less hasty conclusions, we will keep misplacing the infinite, and so grasp neither heaven nor earth" (74). We are afforded a rich binary, as it were, yet cannot grasp either, as "The state of our society and the state of our minds are stamped upon one another" (88).

Cavell cites Thoreau's awareness of his own writing as a call to the reader, who must, in turn, be cognizant of her own reading, and the manner in which she perceives — thereby constructing worlds of her own. For Cavell, writing begets reading, which in turn begets further writing, with regard to the act of creation. *Walden* is therefore an invasive text, one that involves itself intimately with the reader, wherever — and whenever — she may be. As Thoreau discusses his experiment in living, she is required to interrogate her own. This forges a certain intimacy, a relationship, which leads Cavell to deem *Walden* "a sacred text" (he details many of Thoreau's biblical borrowings) (14). Those who struggle with *Walden*— and Cavell here names Emerson — are those whose egos block this internal examination. But Cavell is not part of this crowd, as he continuously and transparently reveals his reaction to the text (even when he finds that "*Walden* sometimes seems an enormously long and boring book"), thereby fashioning an intimacy between *The Senses of Walden* and *its* reader (20). Cavell's reader finds a compatriot in another peruser of *Walden*, a liberal sojourner whose thesis is quite tolerant of— indeed, insistent upon — alternate readings.

Ultimately, *Walden* is a hopeful text, Thoreau's good-natured exhortation of his countrymen. Cavell claims success for its hero, citing his ultimate awakening in "The Pond in Winter" chapter, followed by a continued thawing throughout the "Spring" chapter (98). Recognizing that "'Heaven is under our feet as well as over our heads'" entails arriving at a location by which one can witness his own "doubleness," that is, his *place* within the ideal and the material world — in *Walden* and at Walden (99–100). In writing that "The writer of *Walden* is as preoccupied as the writer of *Paradise Lost* with the creation of a world by a word," Cavell demonstrates that places shape texts, which, in turn and simultaneously, form places (110). The "doubleness" is really symbiotic: just as countries are peopled, so people are placed. And "To repeople heaven and earth we have to go back to beginnings" (113). Thankfully, Thoreauvian beginnings — be they springs or morning stars — are everywhere to be found.

It is not difficult to understand why *The Senses of Walden* has been called the most important book ever written about Thoreau's masterpiece. Cavell renders his own poetry, fitting for a critic claiming that interaction with the text is critical to maximizing one's experience of it. Cavell finds in Thoreau not merely a literary relic, but an ethical guide, a fellow seeker over whose shoulder he might steal a valuable glimpse, as his critical textual interface effectively apes Thoreau's own investigative experiment at Walden Pond.— David Visser

BIBLIOGRAPHY

Cavell, Stanley. *The Senses of Walden*. New York: The Viking Press, 1972.
Lewis, R.W.B. *The American Adam*.
Thoreau, Henry David. *Walden*. 1854. Ed. Walter Harding. New York: Houghton Mifflin, 1995.

Columbus, Christopher (c. 1451–1506)

Columbus was a Genoese navigator and explorer considered by the modern Western world to be the first European to discover America. For years, Columbus' primary goal was his "Enterprise to the Indies," the search for a westward route to the Orient for trade in spices, for which he pursued funding for well over a decade. The year 1492 saw him finally persuade Ferdinand V and Isabella of Spain to sponsor an expedition that would hopefully lead to such a discovery. He set out in the *Santa Maria*, with the smaller *Niña* and *Pinta* in tow, fully expecting to arrive in the Orient. Instead, he landed on the islands of the Caribbean, which he subsequently mislabelled the West Indies, and he named the native Arawak people who inhabited these lands "Indians."

Columbus embarked on his second voyage to the "Indies" a year later with no less than 17 ships. The expectation was that he would need them to trade for gold and establish colonies. Columbus spent the next three years surveying the Caribbean archipelago searching in vain for gold finds. Because of his failure, the King recalled Columbus to Spain. Despite returning empty-handed and publicly disgraced, Columbus was yet again allowed to venture off in search of Asia. This venture followed a more southerly route and led to the discovery of Trinidad and the mouth of the Orinoco River. Ferdinand and Isabella forced Columbus out of his recently-awarded governorship of this nascent colony and paid him off by funding his final voyage to the Americas. Thus, the years between 1502 and 1504 saw Columbus exploring the coast of Central America in inadequately equipped ships hoping to find a strait that would lead him to Asia. No route was found and Columbus returned to Spain. On May 20, 1506 he suffered a fatal heart attack caused by reactive arthritis while living in Valladolid. Columbus died still convinced that his journeys had been along the east coast of Asia, in a land that he named the West Indies. Unfortunately this misnomer lingers on, still being used quite frequently to describe the native inhabitants of the Americas even though the people who Columbus first encountered on his voyage were not from the Indies.

The continued misuse of the term "Indies" and all its derivatives speaks forcefully of the important position that Christopher Columbus holds in the annals of American environmental history. His occupation of this position owes much to the publication of his seminal documentary evidence of the existence of the New World. A traditional narrative account of exploration, the diaries of Columbus' voyages are based on some of the most powerful and enduring metaphors of discovery in human history: lands discovered "for the first time" become white spaces on a map to claim and name. Because he was bestowed with the power to first name, and then claim, the lands that he "discovered," and the plants, animals and even peoples that occupied them, Christopher Columbus will no doubt continue to hold the title of discoverer of the Americas for generations to come. In reality, however, he did not really discover anything, as both North and South America had been inhabited for more than ten thousand years when Columbus arrived. The literally hundreds of distinct nations with their own languages, customs, religions, and economic systems that greeted Columbus' arrival in the Americas stand as proof that the lands stumbled upon by a navigator in search of a trade route to the East did not constitute wide, open, virgin space.

Columbus' achievements should not be diminished, however. While the truism that Columbus discovered America is false, the admiral did find the best routes for Europeans to reach the Americas, a fact to which all other ships that followed in his wake for the next 300 years could attest. Additionally, Columbus' explorations initiated sustained contact between European and American peoples. Moreover, they focused the attention and capital of European governments and investors on America, which led them to establish colonies throughout the region over the next century. Finally, and most importantly, his Biblically-inspired accounts of a paradisical environment awaiting European inhabitation and domination, established the mythopeic framework that America, 400 years later, is still struggling to transcend (THE BIBLE).— Christine Cloud

BIBLIOGRAPHY

Cohen, J.M. *The Four Voyages: Being His Own Log-Book, Letters and Dispatches with Connecting Narratives.* New York: Penguin Classics, 1969.

Columbus, Christopher. *The Journal of Christopher Columbus (During His First Voyage).* Paolo Toscanelli, ed. Cambridge: Cambridge University Press, 2010.

Olson, Julius E., and Edward G. Bourne (editors). *The Northmen, Columbus and Cabot, 985–1503: The Voyages of the Northmen; The Voyages of Columbus and of John Cabot.* New York: Scribner's, 1906.

Sale, Kirkpatrick, *The Conquest of Paradise: Christopher Columbus and the Columbian Legacy.* New York: Plume, 1991.

Wilford, John Noble. *The Mysterious History of Columbus: An Exploration of the Man, the Myth, the Legacy.* New York: Alfred A. Knopf, 1991.

Accounts of the Four Voyages of Columbus

Christopher Columbus's textual description of his first voyage to the Americas (1492–1493) took the form of a March 1493 letter to his good friend and sponsor from Lisbon, Portugal, Luis de Santangel. Columbus described in vivid detail his discovery of first "San Salvador" and "Española," lands which the National Geographic Society has deemed to be what is now Samana Cay, in the Bahaman Islands, Fortune Island, Cuba, and the Dominican Republic. Columbus wrote an almost identical letter March 14, 1493, to Raphael Sanchez (d. 1505), one of the three influential New Christians that Luis de Santangel got help from to finance Columbus' first voyage. The goal of writing these letters to his benefactors was no doubt to convince them to provide him with the additional funds that would be needed to embark on subsequent voyages. Little did he know that by the time the Genoese adventurer returned to the Spanish capital in early April, his personal correspondence had been printed and was circulating throughout Europe. Upon reading it, the Spanish monarchs became so delighted that, with the highest of hopes, they instructed Columbus to immediately return to the mysterious yet exciting landscapes described within it. The excitement that the monarchs felt upon reading it speaks to the account's powerful, evocative, yet exaggerated description of the Americas.

The second primary source for Columbus' musings on his adventures in the Atlantic is a logbook that the Admiral had himself kept and then later offered to the Spanish monarchs in 1493. His son Ferdinand wrote a summary of this account in his biography of his father, and the Dominican friar BARTOLOMÉ DE LAS CASAS used it for his *HISTORIA DE LAS INDIAS* which he published in 1558. Since the original and all known copies later disappeared, the journal is known to us today only in the form of Las Casas' heavily mediated copy of it. Later Ferdinand Columbus' Italian translation was published in 1571 by Alfonso Ulloa as *Historie de S. D. Fernando Colombo nelle quali s'ha particolare e vera relazione della vita e de' fatti dell' Ammiraglio D. Christoforo Colombo suo Padre*. Martin Fernandez de Navarrette later published a longer version of it in 1825. It then appeared in English translation in 1893 thanks to Clements R. Markam and the Hakluyt Society.

The journal of the first voyage reads like a discursive map, which would explain why Christopher Columbus is often called the first American landscape writer. Yet the reality is that Columbus wrote his linguistic map of the Americas while still believing that the lands about which he wrote pertained to Asia. Others doubted Columbus' claim to have found a route to the riches of the Orient, however. Columbus wrote his *Relación* in the hopes of convincing these doubters, as well as the King and Queen of Spain, of the veracity of his claims. As a consequence, the journal of the initial voyage in reality *creates*, rather than describes, the lands with which its author first came into contact. It does so through the use of powerful textual images carefully selected for the purpose of reinventing the natural world in which Columbus accidentally found himself. It begins with a description of the gruelling transatlantic crossing of the *Niña*, *Pinta* and *Santa María*, which never hesitates to announce the presence of such natural harbingers of land such as birds, sticks and branches, all of which appear throughout the narrative until land was actually sighted for the first time on October 12, 1492. The journal then goes

on to describe the lands that Columbus and his men first encountered when they disembarked. Columbus's words here evoke the Garden of Eden with their use of paradisiacal vocabulary (THE BIBLE). The trees are all splendid and magical; the flora and fauna are majestic in their beauty. If the landscape constitutes Paradise, the peoples that inhabit it function as the personifications of what humans used to be before their cataclysmic fall from grace. Columbus comments at great length on the beauty of the people who ran around resplendent in their proud nakedness, so much as to appear to be obsessed with their unclothed bodies. This biblical vision of the American natural world ironically led to its destructive exploitation, as it inspired the idea of unending fertility, which later morphed into the romantic anthropocentric notion that these were lands that could be exploited indefinitely, so plentiful was their bounty. Yet the Americas never constituted lands that were free for the taking, given that they were already inhabited when first encountered by the Spanish. This inconvenient truth did not dissuade Columbus from encouraging their exploitation with his unending praise of their seemingly unending ability to provide. Nor did it do anything to prevent the Admiral from bestowing Spanish names upon places that had years ago already been named. After all, in Columbus' eyes at least, if to see is to possess, to name is to reiterate the reality of one's possession.

The descriptions of the rest of Columbus' initial voyage portray Columbus in a similar, if somewhat more ambivalent light. At times he appears to respect the natives he meets, even going so far as to trust them enough to forge alliances with them. Yet at other times the textual Columbus proposes that, once appropriately trained in the Spanish language, religion and customs, the natives he has met would make excellent slaves — despite being cannibals, of course. Columbus' writings on his second voyage cover similar ground in their retelling of the discovery of the Caribbean islands and their vivid yet biased portrayal of the peoples that lived there, principally the Arawaks and the Caribs. Although considerably less famous, the writings that pertain to Columbus' third and fourth voyages are interesting in their own right, describing as they do the trials and tribulations related to tempestuous weather and terrifying attacks by the indigenous peoples with which Columbus and his men were forced to contend when they finally reached the South American continent. Shortly after landing in this unknown region, now thought of as Venezuela, Christopher Columbus' reputation began to suffer the consequences of his poor leadership of the New World colonies with which he had been entrusted, and the crown eventually stripped him of all the titles he had earned, except for those he will probably never lose thanks to the painstakingly detailed description of his travels through new lands: first discoverer and nature writer of the Americas. — Christine Cloud

BIBLIOGRAPHY

Cohen, J.M. *The Four Voyages: Being His Own Log-Book, Letters and Dispatches with Connecting Narratives.* New York: Penguin Classics, 1969.

Columbus, Christopher. *The Journal of Christopher Columbus (During His First Voyage).* Paolo Toscanelli, ed. Cambridge: Cambridge University Press, 2010.

Olson, Julius E., and Edward G. Bourne (editors). *The Northmen, Columbus and Cabot, 985–1503: The Voyages of the Northmen; The Voyages of Columbus and of John Cabot.* New York: Scribner's, 1906.

Sale, Kirkpatrick, *The Conquest of Paradise: Christopher Columbus and the Columbian Legacy.* New York: Plume, 1991.

Wilford, John Noble. *The Mysterious History of Columbus: An Exploration of the Man, the Myth, the Legacy.* New York: Alfred A. Knopf, 1991.

The Conservation Movement

From its nineteenth-century focus on natural resource conservation to its twenty-first-century concerns with global power inequities, American conservationist and environmental movements have profoundly shaped the national environmental imagination. Literature has long been central to America's conservation and environmental movements, and writers from JOHN MUIR to RACHEL CARSON have influenced generations through their writings and participation in social movements.

The conservation movement became visible in the United States during the nineteenth century. Artistic, literary, and intellectual movements admired the perceived wildness of the American landscape, as it appeared to be vanishing with the nation's relentless westward expansion (Nash 96–107). Yet leaders in the conservation movement espoused not only an appreciation for the native land, but an interest in natural history and ecology. Thus, although HENRY DAVID THOREAU is best remembered today for *WALDEN, OR LIFE IN THE WOODS* (1854), he also contributed to natural history with his groundbreaking, "The Succession of Forest Trees." Similarly, George Perkins Marsh sounded one of the earliest alarms in *Man and Nature* (1864). In arguing that environmental destruction was responsible for the collapse of ancient civilizations, Marsh proselytized that human actions may have negative consequences for the natural environment and consequently endanger human populations (Nash 104–105).

By the late nineteenth-century, the scarcity of natural resources and corporations' wasteful use of those resources increasingly concerned Americans. In addition, the scientific forestry practiced in Germany and France influenced early conservationist thought and practice. Gifford Pinchot, the first Chief of the United States Forest Service (1905–1910) and founder of the Yale School of Forestry (1900), espoused a conservationist philosophy. Pinchot defined conservation as "the greatest good for the greatest number for the longest time." He endorsed developing natural resources, but doing so in the most efficient ways possible.

JOHN MUIR, founder of the Sierra Club, was one of Pinchot's contemporaries. An author, naturalist, and advocate, Muir is closely associated with a preservationist philosophy. In contrast to Pinchot's conservationist ethos, Muir found a spiritual value in nature that he prioritized over utilitarian uses. The conflict between Muir and Pinchot escalated over Pinchot's support for sheep grazing in National Forests, and the damming of Hetch Hetchy Valley in Yosemite National Park (Nash 161–181).

Preservationists and conservationists built on advocacy throughout the nineteenth-century for lands to be declared public and held by a state or federal government; and in 1890 Yellowstone became the first National Park. In 1916, President Woodrow Wilson signed the bill authorizing the National Park Service. While the Forest Reserve Act of 1891 created national forest reserves, the federal government placed the Forest Service in charge of those reserves in 1905. The Forest Service operated upon conservationist principles to manage natural resources, while the National Park Service aimed to preserve spiritual, aesthetic, and historical values for future generations (Hays 27–48, Nash 181).

Historians Karl Jacoby and Mark Spence have investigated some of the consequences of these new land designations. National Parks sought to protect nature from humans. They privileged certain forms of human usage (aesthetic, recreational, religious) over others (economic). National Forests prioritized "scientific management" rather than local or traditional use. Many working-class communities that relied on the forests for hunting grounds suddenly found themselves labeled criminal poachers. Similarly, Native Americans, forced onto reservations, were excluded from traditional grounds designated National Parks or National Forests. While earlier in the nineteenth-century, many viewed Native Americans as inseparable from the frontier or wilderness, by the late nineteenth and early twentieth centuries, wilderness was viewed as a place without people. Conservation and preservationist movements existed alongside vibrant progressive-era urban health movements, as described by historian Robert Gottlieb. Alice Hamilton, for example, a contemporary of

Muir and Pinchot, worked at Jane Addam's Hull House in Chicago. Hamilton noted the relationship between urban pollution and disease outbreak, and labored to protect workers from industrial hazards, like lead, arsenic, and mercury. Thus, Hamilton is as important a predecessor to the modern environmental movement as Muir and Pinchot (Gottlieb 83–88).

German biologist Ernst Haeckel is credited with coining the term "ecology" (1869), the study of the relationships among organisms and the environment. The study of ecology, which gained popularity in the United States in the twentieth-century, intertwines with the conservation movement and the management of federal lands, most clearly through the influence of ALDO LEOPOLD. As a wildlife manager for the Forest Service, Leopold participated in predator control programs that sought to protect the local environment and game species through exterminating predator species. He witnessed first hand the results as exploding deer populations devastated ecosystems (Sutter 54–99). In his landmark book, THE SAND COUNTY ALMANAC, Leopold proposed a land ethic, "A thing is right when it tends to preserve the integrity, stability, and beauty of the biotic community. It is wrong when it tends otherwise" (262).

In 1935, Leopold became one of the founding members of The Wilderness Society. According to historian Paul S. Sutter, the increasing availability of automobiles during this period resulted in renewed preservationist efforts to protect wilderness. As cars reached more and more locations, and car camping grew in popularity, conservationists feared that motorized recreation (auto-tourism) significantly threatened the wilderness experience. With the 1964 Wilderness Act, congress officially designated certain lands based on their "primeval character" as wilderness. The Wilderness Act defined wilderness as "an area where the earth and its community of life are untrammeled by man, where man himself is a visitor who does not remain."

The publication of RACHEL CARSON's SILENT SPRING (1962) heralded the birth of the modern environmental movement. Carson, a marine biologist and popular science writer, exposed the devastating effects of DDT on human and animal communities. Along with Carson's book, Paul Erhlich's The Population Bomb (1968), Frances Moore Lappé's Diet for a Small Planet (1971), a catastrophic oil spill in Santa Barbara (1969), Lake Erie's declared death due to eutrophication, and a pollution-caused fire on the Cuyahoga River in Ohio (1969) kept environmental concerns in the public eye (Sale 3–5, 16–17, 19). Simultaneously, David Brower, as president of the Sierra Club, pushed the organization in a more ac-

tivist direction, including publishing full-page ads in the New York Times protesting plans to dam the Grand Canyon (Nash 231). In 1968, an astronaut took the iconic color picture of the blue earth from space. This photograph, suggesting the fragility of the planet and encouraging a holistic approach, contributed to the growing environmental movement (Kirk 41–42). Public attention to the environment culminated in the first Earth Day on April 22, 1970, and 20 million people participated in this national teach-in on the environment, founded by Senator Gaylord Nelson (Sale 24–25).

The concerns of many new environmentalists echoed progressive-era urban health issues rather than traditional conservation. New environmental regulations focused on clear air, clean water, reducing toxic exposures, and disposing properly of wastes (Gottlieb 175–185). Additionally, many participants in 1960s social movements turned away from the perceived plasticity and conformity of the 1950s; going "back to land" suggested a return to authenticity (Gottlieb 140). Indeed, magazines like the WHOLE EARTH CATALOG and Mother Earth News, as well as books like Helen and Scott Nearing's Living the Good Life, inspired some to try homesteading and return to a perceived more natural way of life (Kirk 53–55, 85).

This upsurge in concern led to federal environmental regulations including the Clean Air Act (1955), Clean Water Act (1960), Solid Waste Disposal Act (1965), National Wild and Scenic Rivers Act (1968), National Environmental Policy Act (1969), Water Pollution Control Act (1972), and Endangered Species Act (1973) (Sale xi–xii).

In 1975, EDWARD ABBEY authored THE MONKEY WRENCH GANG, whose eponymous heroes defended the wild through acts of sabotage. Abbey's literature influenced the formation in 1979 of EarthFirst!, the most prominent radical environmental organization in the U.S. The founders, including DAVE FOREMAN and Mike Roselle, objected to the compromises made by more mainstream environmental organizations in determining roadless area designations. With the motto, "No Compromise in Defense of Mother Earth," EarthFirst!'s publicity stunts (like hanging banners) drew media attention to the loss of wilderness. EarthFirst! participants put their bodies on the line to stop logging, road building, and other environmentally destructive activities. Beginning in the early 1980s, EarthFirst! supported "tree sits," wherein participants would live, sometimes for months, hundreds of feet up in old growth trees to prevent their logging (Scarce 58–66). While known for its distinctive tactics, a philosophy of "deep ecology" or biocentrism also fueled the organization. With affinities to Buddhist teaching, deep ecology holds that all life has value in and of itself, and privileges the intrinsic worth of ecosystems over their value and use to humans (Scarce 31–39).

EarthFirst! split in 1990 as participants such as Judi Bari, recognizing connections between environmental issues and other social justice issues including feminism, anti-imperialism, anti-racism, and labor solidarity, challenged Dave Foreman and others who privileged wilderness threats above all other issues (Bari 55–59; Zankin 358–360, 409–415). Organizations such as Rising Tide North America typify the radical environmental movement in the twenty-first century. Such organizations, while linked with EarthFirst!'s radical environmentalism, have also been influenced by the environmental justice movement.

The environmental justice movement confronts the inequitable distribution of environmental risks and the consequences of environmental pollution along lines of race and class. In the late 1970s, Love Canal, a neighborhood in New York situated on 21,000 tons of toxic waste, drew the nation's attention to the plight of communities facing toxic exposure. As communities facing threats similar to those of Love Canal surfaced, accusations of NIMY–ism (Not In My Backyard), were countered by efforts to prevent the production and distribution of such toxics nationally or internationally (Szasz 38–56, 69–83).

Also in the late 1970s, sociologist Robert Bullard applied a civil rights framework to environmental risks, discovering systemic patterns of injustice in the locations of landfills and dumps. The environmental justice movement grew out of communities of color fighting back against their increased exposure to environmental hazards. The environmental justice movement challenged the wilderness focus of the traditional conservation movement, drawing attention to the inequitable distribution of environmental risks in society, and the exclusion of the concerns of communities of color from mainstream environmental agendas. The First National People of Color Environmental Leadership Summit in 1991 developed the central principles of this new movement, recognizing the environment as inclusive of where people live and work (Bullard 19–42). Through the 1990s, changes in the movement of people, goods, and capital, drew attention to global environmental inequities, and natural disasters like Hurricane Katrina suggest the structural manner in which inequitable risks remain.

In 1999, large scale protests at the meeting of the World Trade Organization in Seattle, Washington, heralded the arrival of the global justice movement in the U.S. Protestors represented both environmental organizations and labor unions concerned with the effects of global trade organizations on both labor and environmental regulations. In the face of threats like global warming, the environmental movement increasingly recognizes a need to act internationally, and in coalition with other organizations and social movements.—Sarah Wald

BIBLIOGRAPHY

Bari, Judi. *Timber Wars*. Monroe, ME: Common Courage, 1994. Print.

Bullard, Robert D. "Environmental Justice in the Twenty-First Century." *The Quest for Environmental Justice. Human Rights and the Politics of Pollution*. Ed. Robert D. Bullard. San Francisco: Sierra Club Books, 2005. Print.

Gottlieb, Robert. *Forcing The Spring: The Transformation of the American Environmental Movement*. Washington, D.C.: Island Press, 2005. Print.

Hays, Samuel P. *Conservation and the Gospel of Efficiency: The Progressive Conservation Movement, 1890–1920*. Cambridge: Harvard University Press, 1959. Print.

Jacoby, Karl. *Crimes Against Nature. Squatters, Poachers, Thieves, and the Hidden History of American Conservation*. Berkeley: University of California Press, 2001. Print.

Kirk, Andrew G. *Counterculture Green. The Whole Earth Catalog and American Environmentalism*. Lawrence: University of Kansas, 2007. Print.

Leopold, Aldo. *A Sand County Almanac with Essays on Conservation from Round River*. New York: Ballantine, 1966. Print.

Marsh, George. *Man and Nature*. Seattle: University of Washington Press, 2003. Print.

Nash, Roderick Frazier. *Wilderness and the American Mind*. 4th Edition. New Haven: Yale University Press, 2001. Print.

Pinchot, Gifford. *The Fight for Conservation*. 1910. *Project Guttenberg*. Web. 1 Apr. 2009.

Rising Tide North America. Web. 1 Apr. 2009.

Sale, Kirkpatrick. *The Green Revolution. The American Environmental Movement, 1962–1992*. New York: Hill & Wang, 1993. Print.

Scarce, Rik. *Eco-Warriors: Understanding the Radical Environmental Movement*. Chicago: Noble Press, 1990. Print.

Spence, Mark David. *Dispossessing the Wilderness: Indian Removal and the Making of the National Parks*. New York: Oxford University Press, 1999. Print.

Sutter, Paul S. *Driven Wild: How the Fight Against Automobiles Launched the Modern Wilderness Movement*. Seattle: University of Washington Press, 2002. Print.

Szasz, Andrew. *EcoPopulism. Toxic Waste and the Movement for Environmental Justice*. Minneapolis: University of Minnesota Press, 1994. Print.

Thoreau, Henry David. *The Natural History Essays*. Salt Lake City: Peregrine, 1980. Print.

Thoreau, Henry David. *Walden and Resistance to Civil Government*. 2nd Edition. New York: Norton, 1992. Print.

Zankin, Susan. *Coyotes and Town Dogs. EarthFirst! and The Environmental Movement*. New York: Viking, 1993. Print.

Cooper, James Fenimore (1789–1851)

Through his fiction and nonfiction, James Fenimore Cooper established himself as one of the preeminent mythographers of the early American environment, shaping the essential foundations for the dream of early American man living in harmony with the forest and field. Often, however, this dream conflicted with the desires of others to cultivate the land and exploit its resources for their own profit. Cooper's greatest literary achievement was his series of LEATHERSTOCKING NOVELS: *The Pioneers* (1823), *The Last of the Mohicans* (1826), *The Prairie* (1827), *The Pathfinder* (1840), and *The Deerslayer* (1841). In these tales Cooper presents one of America's most enduring hero archetypes: Natty Bumppo. Bumppo is the voice of the American wilderness for the dominant white European culture, and through his relationship to that wilderness — indeed, through his intrinsically hybrid *being* — the enduring myth of the American frontier itself is born.

Cooper was born in Burlington, New Jersey in 1789, to William Cooper and Elizabeth Fenimore Cooper, but his family soon moved to his father's estate in Cooperstown, New York (founded by his father), and he grew up in the woods and along the shore of Otsego Lake, cultivating an early but decisive affinity and affection for the wild. Cooper entered Yale University at age 13, but was later expelled for a dangerous prank. He then spent a year sailing on a commercial ship before joining the Navy at 17, experiences that, like his earlier wilderness rambles, would figure prominently in his later fiction.

In 1811, Cooper married Susan Augusta Delancey, and spent the next decade raising his family of seven children. He began his publishing career with a European genre — the novel of manners. *Precaution*, published in 1820, was not a great success, but between 1820 and 1850 he published 32 novels and numerous works of nonfiction, including several volumes of travel writing. *Sketches of Switzerland*, the first of five travel narratives Cooper published, provoked hostility by using American landscapes only to show how inferior they were to European ones.

Financial success, and the beginning of Cooper's profound influence on American literature, came with the publication of *The Pioneers* in 1823. Autobiographical elements in the work include characters such as Judge Marmaduke Temple, based on his father, and Templeton, a recreation of the Cooperstown of his childhood. In *The Pioneers*, as in all of the Leatherstocking novels, Cooper attacks the wanton destruction of the waters, forests, and fields for commercial ventures, which he saw in the wilderness clearing of his youth.

From the beginning, the land of the settlers was conceived of as belonging not to the native inhabitants but to the immigrants, for two principal reasons: 1) the intoxicating notion of MANIFEST DESTINY, that Americans were destined to claim not merely their Puritan "promised land" (THE BIBLE), but all of North America, and 2) the proprietorial corollary of the "Protestant work ethic," that the land belonged to those who worked to improve it. Throughout the Leatherstocking novels, and however much his character may otherwise change with age and experience, Bumppo remains an eloquent and charismatic spokesman against the "wicked and wasty ways of civilization" (*The Pioneers*), as settlers rushed to claim and improve the frontier for themselves. In *The Pioneers*, in particular, Bumppo clashes with farmers, like Bill Kirby, who slash and burn the fields irresponsibly. The Bush family of *The Prairie* "scourge the very 'arth with their axes. Such hills and hunting grounds as I have seen stripped of the gifts of the Lord, without remorse or shame!" (75). A generation before HENRY DAVID THOREAU retreated to WALDEN, and two before MARK TWAIN's Huck Finn reckoned he had "to light out for the Territory," Bumppo sought to escape the ever-encroaching civilization, repeatedly trying and failing to find rest on the salutary side of the borderline between the human and nonhuman.

Cooper's time at sea provided him with vivid maritime analogues for the American interior, and his *The Pilot* (1823), *The Red Rover* (1827) and *The Water-Witch* (1830) depicted life on the ocean with the same mythic naturalism — and characters, like John Paul Jones, with the same charismatic otherness — as the Leatherstocking tales' wilderness and their solitary hero.

Influenced by the painters of the Hudson River School and Thomas Cole, with their vast vistas, Cooper's wilderness became a potent symbol of America, *for* America. In contrast to earlier colonial authors, and even "arcadian" idealists like THOMAS JEFFERSON (AMERICAN PASTORAL), Cooper did not portray the frontier as a place that needed to be conquered or domesticated. His depictions of the wilderness and the men who lived there in harmony with the woods and rivers, formed the mythic basis for a new, deeper and more sympathetic understanding and relationship with the American environment. — Patricia Kennedy Bostian

BIBLIOGRAPHY

Franklin, Wayne. *James Fenimore Cooper: The Early Years.* New Haven: Yale University Press, 2007.

Nash, Roderick. "The American Wilderness." *Wilderness and the American Mind.* New Haven: Yale University Press, 1973. 67–83.

Railton, Stephen. *Fenimore Cooper: A Study of His Life and Imagination.* Princeton: Princeton University Press, 1978.

Starobin, Christina. "Who Owns the Land and Who Cares for It?: A Brief Look at Relationships in *The Prairie.*" *2001 Cooper Seminar* (No. 13). Hugh C. MacDougall, ed. The State University of New York College at Oneonta: Oneonta, New York. 96–99.

"The Leatherstocking Tales," James Fenimore Cooper (1823–1841)

James Fenimore Cooper's Leatherstocking Tales center on one of American literature's greatest and most compelling "hybrid" characters, the forester Natty Bumppo, known variously by European characters as "Leatherstocking," "the trapper," and "Pathfinder" and by his Native American companions as "Hawk-eye," "*la longue carabine*" (the long rifle), and "Deerslayer." The series spans Bumppo's formative days on upstate New York's frontiers, his career as a scout in the French and Indian War, and his aged days coming to grips with the encroachment of America's western expansion on his wilderness home. Cooper published five novels focused on different events in Bumppo's life; in order of publication, *The Pioneers* (1823), *The Last of the Mohicans* (1826), *The Prairie* (1827), *The Pathfinder* (1841), and *The Deerslayer* (1841). The novels' publication, however, does not follow Bumppo's life chronology, as *Deerslayer* deals with his youth (1740–55), *Mohicans* (1757) and *Pathfinder* (1750's) with his adulthood, and *Pioneers* (1793) and *Prairie* (1804) with his old age. Among other issues, the novels focus on the clash of settlement and wilderness, how to conserve nature and resources, and the place of Native America in the face of expansion.

As a European character that lives in the wilderness and has adopted the way of life of the Native Americans (Barbara Mann, in fact, claims he has mixed blood), Leatherstocking exists on the unstable "fault line" between the conflicting forces of nature and "civilization" that Cooper believed constituted the essential American dichotomy. This conflict plays itself out in a number of ways in Cooper's novels; for example, through disputes over land ownership on the frontier, clashes between Europeans and Native Americans, and representations of the frontier as a lawless space that has yet to be "civilized." Leatherstocking has an ambiguous place in these conflicts. While he may seem to stand for civilization when he repeatedly claims that he is a Christian "man without a cross" (of pure white blood), his wilderness ways often pit him against civilization. Cooper

confirms Leatherstocking's association with the wilderness by representing him as a Daniel Boone–like figure in *The Pioneers* and *The Prairie*. In these novels of his old age, Leatherstocking retreats further to the west so he may better live his "primitivistic" life, when he finds himself in conflict with the encroaching settlements.

As Arthur Robinson suggests, the conflict in *The Pioneers* between the wilderness and civilization plays out in the novel's dialogue on conservation. Robinson claims that the novel represents three character types that offer three possible responses to the issue of "how the settlers handle their natural resources" (566): those who see an unlimited amount of natural resources present for their own benefit and who therefore shun conservation methods; those who believe conservation should be employed to protect resources, with an eye to the future; and those who only want what they need at the time and have a sentimental attachment to the land. The majority of the settlers fit the first description, and the novel vocalizes fairly clear condemnation of their behavior through Leatherstocking and Judge Temple. Temple fits the second category. While he condemns the wasteful settlers, he does so not out of concern for the environment *per se* but because, as the proprietor of the settlement, he worries that wasteful depletion of resources may inhibit his ability to maximize the gains he can make off his territorial capital. The final category describes Leatherstocking. For Leatherstocking, who has a sentimental, nostalgic attachment to the environment, "The earth is God's product, formed according to his will; any manifold alteration in its natural condition, by 'clearings' in the forest and artificial regulation of his creatures, is sacrilegious" (Robinson 574). Therefore, while one might think that the Judge and Leatherstocking would share a bond over their concern for conservation, they in fact differ in their reasons for this concern: while the Judge acts out of self-interest, Leatherstocking does so because he deeply reverences the environment. The Judge, indeed, breaks Leatherstocking's law, to only take from the environment what one needs to survive, when he introduces settlement and cultivation on the frontier, thus provoking the latter's enmity.

The conflict between these two characters and their value systems exemplifies Cooper's treatment of the civilization vs. wilderness theme. These novels tend to take up the issue in terms of how to settle the West most ethically. Based on his personal predilections as well as his tendency to portray genteel characters like the Judge in a sympathetic fashion, we can conclude that Cooper ultimately sides with the forces of encroaching civilization and economic expansion, as long as such forces follow the Judge's relatively measured, sustainable approach. As a Western believer in progress, Cooper believed that settling the frontier could lead to goods such as greater wealth for the majority, and as a nationalist, he believed that the United States' would dominate the continent (MANIFEST DESTINY). However, at the same time, Cooper sounds a melancholic note in his representation of Leatherstocking. Although unable to reconcile his values with the settlers, Leatherstocking is a noble character who performs valorous deeds and lives by a value system that he earnestly believes in. While Cooper sees Leatherstocking and his ilk as necessarily unfit for life in the settlements, he at the same time sees their ejection as a tragedy. The rise of civilization, while a major achievement for mankind, has its costs for Cooper.

Another of the novel's ethical dilemmas involves the future of Native America. Indeed, Leatherstocking's plight is to some degree one and the same with that of the Native American society that the settlers dispossessed. Similar to Leatherstocking, Cooper's noble Indians, such as Leatherstocking's close friend Chingachgook, Chingachgook's son Uncas, and Hard-Heart, are all admirable figures who show valor in distress and live by strongly felt ethical codes. For Cooper, these characters too must fade in the face of the march of settlement, as their way of life, like Leatherstocking's, is not compatible with civilization. Cooper, in this sense, plays on the Vanishing Indian myth. This myth, which Cooper conjoins with romantic discourses about the "noble savage," indicates that while Native Americans may have admirable characteristics, they are constitutionally incapable of integrating with European civilization due to their lower place on the ladder of human development. In effect, purveyors of the myth denigrate regrettable facts of European colonization's history in the New World, such as the Natives' death due to illnesses they had no immunity against, and the sometimes atrocious military subjugation of technologically inferior Natives to take their lands, to the level of cultural images. These Vanishing Indian figures are typically given a moment to lament their fate, much as Chingachgook does at the close of *The Last of the Mohicans*. However, they are powerless to stop the forces of history. While Cooper's enactment of this myth places him in the camp of writers that used literary and cultural means to support the horrors of Indian Removal, we must also recognize the tragedy which Cooper saw in the Removal, and regarding which, as Barbara Mann claims, Cooper sympathized with Native Americans in contrast to his peers.

While extremely popular in his own day, the intervening years have seen a decline in the critical opinion of Cooper's work, in comparison with that of later American authors such as NATHANIEL HAWTHORNE and HERMAN MELVILLE. However, his complex treatment of the issues described in this discussion render his work of enduring value to students of environmental literature; and in a time of growing environmental awareness and interest in developing sustainable living practices, renewed interest in Cooper is both fitting and rewarding.—John C. Havard

BIBLIOGRAPHY

Cooper, James Fenimore. *The Leatherstocking Tales*. 2 vols. Ed. Blake Nevius. New York: Library of America, 1985.

Mann, Barbara. "Race Traitor: Cooper, His Critics, and Nineteenth-Century Literary Politics." *A Historical Guide to James Fenimore Cooper*. Ed. Leland S. Person. Oxford: Oxford University Press, 2007. 155–86.

Robinson, E. Arthur. "Conservation in Cooper's *The Pioneers*." *PMLA* 82.7 (1967): 564–578.

Cooper, Susan Fenimore (1813–1894)

Born in 1813 in Westchester County, New York, Susan Fenimore Cooper was the eldest surviving daughter of the novelist JAMES FENIMORE COOPER, whose most famous works, the LEATHERSTOCKING TALES, chronicle frontier life and the expansion of European-American settlement in the wilderness. Susan Cooper dedicated much of her literary life to her role as her father's secretary, and later as his literary executor. However, she was an important writer in her own right, notable as the first American woman to author a book of nature writing.

Susan Cooper was born into a well-to-do and successful family headed by her grandfather William Cooper, a judge, member of Congress, and the founder of Cooperstown. As young girls she and her sisters studied writing, geography, arithmetic, and English history at home with their mother. An equally significant part of her education, however, was that offered by the many walks and rides around the countryside with her father and grandfather, which Cooper credits with instilling in her a deep love of nature and the landscape of rural New York. She was briefly enrolled in a girls' school, but more rigorous lessons, especially in French, began as the family prepared to live in Europe. In Paris, in addition to studying such subjects as history, grammar, and several languages, Cooper had lessons in dancing, music and drawing. After seven years of travel and mingling in European society, the family returned home in 1833, with Cooper an accomplished young woman of 20.

Cooper's devotion to her father shaped the course of her life, both personal and literary. She remained unmarried and lived the rest of her life at the family home in Cooperstown. In a family memoir, she recalled, "My dear Father always gave each of us girls a good-night kiss, and blessing, every evening.... This habit he kept up affectionately long after we were grown women; indeed, until the last year of his life" (*Small Family Memories*). In her professional life, she not only served as his copyist and secretary, but followed in his footsteps by writing fiction—first short stories, and later a full length novel, *Elinor Wyllys*, which her father arranged to have published in 1845.

In 1848 Cooper began keeping a written record of her observations of her home county, the farms, fields, villages, and woods around Lake Otsego. Encouraged by her father she revised, researched, and recast her notes into a substantial nature diary, organized around one calendar year. The result, RURAL HOURS (1850), is her most important and successful work, valuable for establishing a detailed portrait of the Cooperstown area as well as raising readers' awareness of the moral importance and physical fragility of the environment. In her later years she continued to write in several genres, including essays on nature, memoirs, fiction, local history, biographical sketches, and works for children. Her philanthropic work was well known in the Cooperstown area, where she founded both a hospital and an orphanage. She died in 1894 at the age of 81.—Anne Kellenberger

BIBLIOGRAPHY

Cooper, Susan Fenimore. *Small Family Memories*. (1883). Available on line. URL: http://external.oneonta.edu/cooper/biographic/memories/1883susan.html. Accessed June 26, 2009.
Johnson, Rochelle, and Daniel Patterson. "Introduction." *Rural Hours*, by Susan Fenimore Cooper (1850). Eds. Rochelle Johnson and Daniel Patterson. Athens: University of Georgia Press, 1998. ix–xxii.

Rural Hours, Susan Fenimore Cooper (1850)

Susan Fenimore Cooper's first nonfiction work, *Rural Hours,* is also the first book of nature writing by an American woman. It takes the form of a nature diary: a collection of near-daily entries organized within one calendar year, beginning in March and ending the following February. The various entries consist of Cooper's detailed observations, musings, recollections, and opinions, each prompted by an excursion into the environs of Cooperstown, New York, her hometown. *Rural Hours* appeared in 1850—four years before THOREAU's *WALDEN*—and went through nine editions in the next 25 years. Its success inspired Cooper to publish other works connected to the environment, including an edition of nature poetry dedicated to WILLIAM CULLEN BRYANT. *Rural Hours,* however, remains her most substantial contribution to the field of nature writing.

One significant issue in discussions of Cooper's contribution to environmental literature has been the question of how best to characterize her approach to the topic: that is, the extent to which Cooper's nature writing conforms to or is limited by the domestic ideology of the day. *Rural Hours,* for example, appeared anonymously—authored simply "by a Lady." In her preface, Cooper also evinces a ladylike modesty, offering readers a "simple record" of her "trifling observations on rustic matters," begun merely for her own "amusement" (3). This conventionally feminine perspective can also be seen in some of her entries on local homes, styles of clothing, gardening, meal preparation, and child-rearing. Indeed, at one point she flatly states that "Home, we may rest assured, will always be, as a rule, the best place for a woman; her labors, pleasures and interests, should all center there, whatever be her sphere of life" (100). Yet the idea that hers are "trifling observations" does not account for the many pages of carefully detailed description, which might better be characterized as the work of a highly informed amateur naturalist. Moreover, Cooper contextualizes much of her painstaking observation of nature with reference to the best science of her day. She was familiar with works by JOHN JAMES AUDUBON, Louis Agassiz, Georges Cuvier, Alexander von Humbolt, and Charles Lyell, among many others. Tina Gianquitto describes her nature writing as being as "accurate as those of the naturalists whose work she both admires and seeks to emulate" (Gianquitto 178). Nina Baym includes Cooper in her study of women and science in the nineteenth century, describing Cooper's project as incorporating a "huge array of print sources, most of them scientific" (Baym 73). Rochelle Johnson and Daniel Patterson confirm that there is "a prodigious depth of research" in *Rural Hours* (xi).

It is, however, Cooper's own deep familiarity with and loving appreciation of nature that gives the book its power and authority. She displays an intimate first-person knowledge of the many varieties of birds, flowers, fruit, grasses, insects, trees and shrubs, and small animals—their comings and goings, the changes in their appearances, the blooming and dying—and offers her constant and scrupulous attention to all she sees. The book builds an impressive sense of place over the course of the year. She knows the girth of the trees and the shifting colors of the leaves, the minute differences between the numerous varieties of birds she observes. Her May 4th entry, for example, records the return of the chimney swallows. She tells readers that there are six species of swallows in the area, four within her own neighborhood, and describes each type. The chimney swallow receives the most detailed attention:

> [It] has no beauty to boast of; it is altogether plain, and almost bat-like in appearance, but in its way, it is remarkably clever and skilful. It is as good at clinging to a bare wall, or the trunk of a tree, as the woodpecker, its tail being shaped like that of those birds.... [T]hey play and chase the insects, and feed and sing after their fashion, with an eager, rapid twitter; they have little to do with the earth, and the plants, and the trees, never alighting, except within a chimney. They feed entirely on the wing supplying their young also, when they are able to fly, in the same manner, and they seem to drink flying as they skim over the water. A cloudy, damp day is their delight, and one often sees them out in the rain [35].

Cooper conscientiously attends to each detail of the birds' shape, activity, sounds and habits. Her mention of "often" seeing them on a rainy day suggests her own frequent presence on wet days, watching intently and taking notes. For all her reliance on learned readings, Cooper ultimately establishes her own authority on the strength of her patient observation and almost exhaustive cataloguing of the results. In entry after entry, Cooper builds a thorough picture of the Cooperstown area — the woods and lake — but also the farms and gardens, fairs and markets. This accretion of detail, the intensity of the scrutiny, the commitment to investigate, and the care in presentation, gradually create a sense of deep love and ethic of responsibility for the environment, which forms the basis of what Michael Bryson identifies as "a rather forward-looking conservation ethic" (Bryson 112).

Perhaps Cooper's most important contribution to establishing an ecological awareness is her repeated documentation of the reduction or disappearance of many different species. Indeed, her awareness of the pressure outside economic forces place on local species contributes to what Timothy Sweet considers her "globalized sense of place-consciousness" (541). She notes the destructive impact of clear-cutting on local trees, the depletion of fish due to dam-building and over-fishing, the disappearance of large predators due to unlimited hunting, the displacement of native flora by European species. She deplores the greed that motivates a landowner to "turn his timber into banknotes with all possible speed," and urges readers to open their eyes to the value of the landscape beyond "dollars and cents" (132). She also inveighs against people's indifference toward, and willful ignorance of, species unique to the American continent, whose preservation is a duty. She warns that many animal species, like the American panther, "have already become so rare in the cultivated part of the country, that most people forget their existence" (314).

The purpose of *Rural Hours* is at least in part to remedy this ignorance. Yet, Cooper does not call for an end to westward expansion; her ideal, like CRÈVECOEUR's before her, is a rural community that maintains a thriving and sustainable use of the land rather than destructive exploitation of it. She celebrates a "middle landscape" between the city and wilderness; a place where human stewardship and cultivation is conducted in a way that respects the irreplaceable beauty, dignity, and wisdom to be found in nature — the Nature that is part of God's revelation to humanity: "A careless indifference to any good gift of our gracious Maker," she insists, "shows a want of thankfulness" (134). The spirit of *Rural Hours* is the antithesis of careless indifference. Unfailingly thoughtful and deeply engaged, Cooper's ambition seems to have been to become the speaking conscience and abiding witness of her home region. As Michael Branch observes, "the fate of the Otsego landscape will depend on how it has been imagined in the past and how it will be imagined in the future" (Branch 79). Cooper dedicated herself to preserving and protecting that image in all its vibrant fullness. — Anne Kellenberger

BIBLIOGRAPHY

Baym, Nina. *American Women of Letters and the Nineteenth Century Sciences*. New Brunswick: Rutgers University Press, 2002.

Branch, Michael P. "Five Generations of Literary Coopers: Intergenerational Valuations of the American Frontier." In *Susan Fenimore Cooper: New Essays on Rural Hours and Other Works*. Eds. Rochelle Johnson and Daniel Patterson. Athens: University of Georgia Press, 2001. 61–80.

Bryson, Michael A. *Visions of the Land: Science, Literature, and the American Environment from the Era of Exploration to the Age of Ecology*. Charlottesville: University Press of Virginia, 2002.

Cooper, Susan Fenimore. *Rural Hours*. (1850). Eds. Rochelle Johnson and Daniel Patterson. Athens: University of Georgia Press, 1998.

Gianquitto, Tina. "The Noble Designs of Nature: God, Science, and the Picturesque in Susan Fenimore Cooper's *Rural Hours*." In *Susan Fenimore Cooper: New Essays on Rural Hours and Other Works*. Eds. Rochelle Johnson and Daniel Patterson. Athens: University of Georgia Press, 2001. 169–190.

Sweet, Timothy. "Global Cooperstown: Taxonomy, Biogeography, and Sense of Place in Susan Fenimore Cooper's *Rural Hours*." *Interdisciplinary Studies in Literature and Environment*. 17.3 (Summer 2010): 541–566. Web. 27 Jan. 2011.

Crane, Hart (1899–1932)

From Hart Crane's early lyric poems to his final epic, *The Bridge* (1930), Crane inscribed the landscape — mediated by architecture — with desire. Geography is experienced through, and merges with, the body; the built environment offers to extend and complete America's promise of liberty and connection. His poems convey a sense of motion, of hallucinatory journeying through fragmented cities and landscapes — gulfs, valleys, gorges, meadows and shorelines — in search of an elusive stable place. The ocean also makes its presence felt: tides and waves splash through most of his poems. But if seas and the vastness of outer space compel and inspire, they also terrify. So it is the structures that link voids to our concealing crevices and shorelines — the liminal spaces — that are the sites Crane's work typically probes and explores. The Brooklyn Bridge is the central trope for telling America's story, emerging from the same locus that WALT WHITMAN evoked in "Crossing Brooklyn Ferry": a nexus of movement of people and bodies of water.

Harold Hart Crane, the only child of Grace and Clarence Arthur Crane, was born in 1899 and died in the sea off the coast of Florida in 1932. He grew up in Warren, Ohio, where his father's maple syrup business grew into a candy empire. When his parents separated, Crane went to live with his maternal grandparents in Cleveland, inhabiting a tower room in their home, a setting which provided him with a sense of power and security. Crane's high school attendance was sporadic, interrupted by trips with his mother, including one to a family plantation off the coast of Cuba, where he made two suicide attempts. An early poem, "C33" (1916) was named after the cell Oscar Wilde inhabited, the perfect symbol of Crane's sense of entrapment as a gay man in the Midwest. In the winter of 1916, Crane succeeded in escaping to the promised land of creative and sexual freedom, New York City. He began to sign himself Hart Crane, leaving behind the name Harold, though his parents continued to use it. His escape, however, was not permanent; financial struggles kept him returning to Ohio, attempting to work for his father but failing to satisfy his demands. The final visit ended disastrously, when his father publicly raged at him for eating with African American employees. Like "C33," Crane's "Black Tambourine" (1921) reveals the nightmare of entrapment, the dilemma of the "black man, forlorn in the cellar," as he identified himself with the oppressed and outcast. Though Crane found work writing advertising copy, the job sapped his spirit and increased his taste for alcohol.

In 1923, Crane returned to New York City, eventually renting an apartment in Brooklyn at 110 Columbia Heights, with a view of the Brooklyn Bridge. It was fortuitous that Crane rented the same apartment from which the son of the bridge's designer, Washington Roebling, crippled by the process of building the bridge, watched his father's work completed. The bridge would eventually become the unifying symbol of Crane's modernist epic. Crane's New York era was marked by periodic excursions to the countryside upstate, where he would recover from his excesses and be rejuvenated. Uprooted by the sale of his childhood home, he purchased land near his friends in Connecticut, but never managed to build on it. Always the need to earn money would drive him back to the city, with all its temptations, ecstasies and debilitations. But even if *For the Marriage of Faustus and Helen* (1923) began by evoking the perennial poetic lament about the city's intrusions on the soul, ultimately this urban island itself, laced with bridges, dark alleys and watery edges, is the landscape that compels Crane most and best expresses humankind's aspiration.

His first book, *White Buildings*, published in 1926, expresses his vision of the ideal city, as Manhattan seemed to be from across the river, and attempts to reconcile the mystical ideal with the modern world. Crane had read ELIOT's *The Waste Land* and found it too grim; he wanted to leave room for joy and laughter (which does not lacerate) in his vision of the human condition in the industrializing world during and after the Great War. Charlie Chaplin had achieved this in his film, *The Kid*, which inspired Crane's "Chaplinesque" (1922) with its "grail of laughter of an empty ash can" and "a kitten in the wilderness" of the city, suggesting the possibility of kindness and rescue amidst the stern gaze of the social order. The book contained the first poem that had earned him money (10 dollars from *The Dial*): "My Grandmother's Love Letters" (1919). The poem describes crumbling letters, found in an attic, where they had merged into the very substance of the structure. It concludes,

Yet I would lead my grandmother by the hand
Through much of what she would not understand;
And so I stumble. And the rain continues on the
    roof
With such a sound of gently pitying laughter [lines
    23–27].

The narrator's love has more to do with the rain than with the shelter, which cannot protect him. Crane must continue to take readers by hand, leading them from "A land of leaning ice" ("North Labrador"), through "Bleecker Street, still trenchant in a void" ("Possessions"), to "New thresholds, new anatomies!" ("Wine Menagerie"). The liminal space of a threshold offers the promise of a freedom prevented by gender codes.

The sea appears briefly in most of the shorter lyrics, finally taking the main stage in the three-part poem "Voyages" (1924), inspired by Crane's love affair with Emil Opffer, a sailor. The sea's erotic promise sings through lines such as these: "Star kissing star through wave on wave unto / Your body rocking!"(III: 13–14). After the completion of this sequence, and "For the Marriage of Faustus and Helen" (the 1923 poem which attempted to recreate the experience of awe that Helen evoked for the ancients, in the modern cityscape), Crane began to conceive of a still longer poem centering on the symbol of the Brooklyn Bridge. In Whitman's day, the river could only be crossed by the ferry he extols in "Crossing Brooklyn Ferry," a poem which delighted in the human parade and sought connection between the poet and future readers. Now the Brooklyn Bridge connected Brooklyn and Manhattan across the East River.

From conception to publication, *The Bridge* was eight years of agony: drunken bouts and despair followed by inspired bursts of writing. The opening inscription from the Book of Job seems innocuous: "From going to and fro in the earth / and from walking up and down in it" could describe the human condition — certainly Crane's condition. But this was actually the original exile, Satan's, account of himself. The poem places Crane in this long line of walkers, beginning with the first rebel, and passing through Whitman, who walked through his *Song of Myself.* Whitman spoke through the voice of another voyager, CHRISTOPHER COLUMBUS, in one of his last poems, and Columbus and his discovery comprise the subject of *The Bridge's* first section, "Ave Maria." Here, earth's "rondure" (line 43) is for Crane, as it was for Whitman, a necessary concept, suggesting the connectedness of past and present; reconciliation, rather than conflict. The poem takes an historical trip through time, grounding the stories in the "macadam" ("Van Winkle," line 1)—the pavement itself. Columbus, Pocahontas (JOHN SMITH), Rip Van Winkle (WASHINGTON IRVING), and others, time travel, trying to make sense of the present landscape by means of the past. In "Cape Hatteras," Crane sees "our native clay" as the "eternal flesh of Pocahontas" (*The Bridge,* "Cape Hatteras," lines 17–18) and directly invokes Whitman, asking "if infinity / Be still the same as when you walked the beach" (lines 47–48). The sense of motion that Crane's rhythm conveys far exceeds the pace of Whitman's walking as the poem gathers force. Columbus's ships become the Wright Brothers' planes (their first flight,

when Crane was just four, had a deep impact on him). Whitman's vision of MANIFEST DESTINY's westward expansion takes to the sky as "taut motors surge, space-gnawing, into flight" (line 102). The sequence concludes with "Atlantis," a poem written much earlier, which required the preceding sequence to justify its hopeful vision. The poem weaves together elements of the American landscape, though its ending suggests that only a mythic island could "hold thy floating singer" (line 88). The Brooklyn Bridge is Atlantis, the lost island whose existence offers hope of redemption for the colonizers' sins upon the continent. It suggests that the violated, feminized body of America, identified with Pocahontas, can, through Whitman's song translated into the modern idiom, be "reclaimed" (*The Bridge,* "Cape Hatteras," line 221).

After the completion of *The Bridge,* Crane received a Guggenheim fellowship, which enabled him to live in Mexico, where he believed he could experience a deeper, more primitive connection to the land's mythic origins than he could find north of the border. His drinking, however, got in the way of any significant output except for his final poem, "The Broken Tower." It was on his voyage home that he leapt to his death. Critical opinions on Crane's achievement have improved since his death. The poems are dense and draw on experiments made by both symbolists and imagists, transformed into what Crane would make his own "logic of metaphor." They reward repeated readings, with a dizzying tour through landscapes wherein the "Promised Land" becomes "Hollywood's new love-nest" and "volcanoes roar" (*The Bridge,* "Quaker Hill," lines 33–38). Crane's greatest works pulsate with the freedom and energy of the urban landscape while the sea laps at the edges of his poems, both as threat and promise. The compelling places are not stable sites, but transitions *between* places — bridges, railway tracks — even rivers lead somewhere else. The Brooklyn Bridge unites, prayerfully, fragments of American life littered throughout the continent, from the vulgar screams of advertisements to the soothing whispers of hidden coves, and offers hope that these can ultimately be redeemed.— Robin Morris

BIBLIOGRAPHY

Crane, Hart. *The Complete Poems and Selected Letters and Prose of Hart Crane,* edited by Brom Weber. New York: Doubleday/Anchor, 1966; New York: Liveright, 2000.

Mariani, Paul. *The Broken Tower: The Life of Hart Crane.* New York: Norton, 1999.

Crane, Stephen (1871–1900)

Few lives in American literary history compare, either in brevity or productivity, to that of Stephen Crane. A college baseball star turned dropout, a failed reporter but later successful correspondent, a denizen of the New York slums who would later call Joseph Conrad and Henry James neighbors in Europe, Crane lived a life varied to the point of contradiction, and, though dead at 28, was prolific enough to fill multiple volumes with his work. The influence of his varied environs notwithstanding, Crane promulgated a naturalist approach to human endeavors; thus, while he is best known for his Civil War classic *The Red Badge of Courage*, his oeuvre may be read as one of mankind's continuous — and pointless — struggle to overcome the uncaring world in which he lives, however briefly.

Stephen Crane was born in 1871, in Newark, New Jersey, the youngest of 14 children, to Methodist minister Jonathan Townley Crane and Mary Helen Peck. Crane's own, later wanderlust may have been borne of his family's continual moving, until finally settling in Asbury Park, New Jersey. Though his father died in 1880, when Crane was only nine, he remained a complex and often antipathetic influence on his skeptical son. Crane attended Military school for a short time, and then university, where he showed a propensity for the written word, but again became rapidly disillusioned, and eventually quit and moved to New York City. There he worked as a reporter, but Crane saw the mere act of relaying facts as mundane, and did not hold the position long.

Without income and low on funds — though still writing — Crane resided in the Bowery, a poor urban neighborhood to which he took famously. His immersion in and observation of this gritty environment inspired his 1893 novella *Maggie, A Girl of the Streets*, the tale of a young woman's road to prostitution. One of the many labels placed on Crane, in the attempt to categorize his elusive sensibility, is that of a realist, and certainly his Bowery experience may be seen in what would be a hallmark of his writing: a focus on working-class, no frills living, and the often anonymous but sometimes quietly heroic day-to-day struggles therein. The environment itself is often invested with true and striking agency, as the ghetto is an irrepressible force that informs and deforms the lives of the characters. This environment exhibits such control, in fact, that free will is regularly subordinated to a grim determinism. Crane's urban cosmos is more dictating force than backdrop. Ghetto life is often grotesque, and refuge is an illusion, as the home is, for Maggie, more dangerous than the street, and her alcoholic mother (ironically

named "Mary") is even more beastly than the brooding father. Such ironic twists are used by Crane to effectively show the subversiveness of the ghetto. Maggie's decision to become a prostitute is, ultimately, an act of self-determination. While the ghetto — and her boyfriend turned pimp — controls all else, she strives to retain control over her own body, and does so by making the one decision that presents itself.

This yearning for self-determination is why suicide is so oddly fitting in Crane's grim world. Maggie, like Edna Pontellier in *The Awakening*, decides upon control at any cost as a means of exerting some sort of control over the environment that has ruled life. Her mother, in the last line of the story, forgives her because she does something that she, as a mother of many children, could never do — retain control of her own body, and at least flail back at the systemic oppression engrained in the Bowery.

Despite *Maggie*'s floundering sales, Crane remained productive, and 1894 saw the serialized publication of his Civil War novel and magnum opus, *The Red Badge of Courage*. This effort was a critical and popular success, and Crane's name became known both in the U.S. and in England. The text is often hailed for its extreme accuracy of detail, especially for someone not yet born when the war occurred — a feat Crane credited to his conversations with veterans of the war. The novel deconstructs the notion of courage, as indicated by a title stressing not the quality itself, but rather a symbolic, surface-level representation thereof. Place itself is often relegated to a certain anonymity with a field or river lying just "beyond" the superficial titles ascribed to them by men. Similarly, the literal "badge" is a wound, but again, only a visible, material, surface-level wound, and the text probes deeper than that; hence the striking lack of significant differentiation between protagonist Henry Fleming's Union side and the opposing confederates — as if the horrific drama of the war was ultimately being all played out for appearances. Henry refers to others as "the tall man," "the loud man," and of course by rank; and taking up his side's banner (a neat, arbitrary symbol of mob mentality) feels vindicated, yet never really seems sure as to what he is doing and why he is doing it. He charges blindly through smoke, essentially running scared through a scarred landscape indistinguishable as either "North" or "South." Henry takes refuge in a "natural cathedral" of sorts, with TRANSCENDENTALIST overtones, but even here, cannot arrive at any truth amidst the chaos. *The Red Badge of Courage* thus suggests a foundational naturalist theme: with the Civil War came the death of hopeful, optimistic idealism. Nature is no longer an

EMERSONIAN fount of epiphanic inspiration, but an unforgiving battlefield unconcerned with human endeavors (AMERICAN NATURALISM).

Crane's new notoriety afforded him the opportunity to combine his desire for adventure with his need of a steady income. Thus, he worked as a war correspondent, and travelled extensively. Nature can even be said to have lent a hand in his ever-evolving view of the universe as uncaring entity. On his way to Cuba prior to the Spanish-American War, he was forced to abandon the sinking *Commodore* and brave hostile seas, the experience of which inspired his classic short story, "The Open Boat" (1897). The tale follows four men in a dinghy who struggle to safely land their small vessel on a shore beset by crashing waves. There is a strong and foreboding existential tone in the narrative, as the correspondent wonders just why he is here in the dinghy — *here* at all; and the tale's refrain is the closest Crane ever approaches to prayer:

> If I am going to be drowned — if I am going to be drowned — if I am going to be drowned, why, in the name of the seven mad gods who rule the sea, was I allowed to come this far and contemplate sand and trees? Was I brought here merely to have my nose dragged away as I was about to nibble the sacred cheese of life? It is preposterous" [286].

These are the thoughts of a man searching for God, searching for equity, fairness and meaning, and utterly denied them all, on a violent sea indicative of nature at large. Ultimately, the sea, the waves, the tides care not at all for the men and their efforts, or for who feels entitled to what. This is neither the evil Puritanical wilderness of the early Americans, nor the Transcendentalists' realm of divine enlightenment. Instead it is the ultimate naturalist space: an indifferent universe, in which one wave crashes methodically one after another.

In between the waves, the cook and correspondent (again, personalizing names are almost entirely foregone; used instead are the players' occupations) argue as to whether the structure on the shore is a life-saving station or a house of refuge. And then they argue about what the difference is. But the tragedy is that none of it matters. No one, ultimately, is saved — "the lucky" merely receive temporary reprieves. As far as planet Earth is concerned, no one gets out alive. And incessant dwelling upon this reality leads to madness. Instead, we argue semantics. "The Open Boat" is a fitting text for a post–Nietzschean era when "God is dead," salvation a pipe dream, and "Shipwrecks are *apropos* of nothing" (283). Nature, ultimately, is not kindhearted and nurturing, nor vengeful and cruel. It is simply indifferent — unconcerned.

The same year that Crane published "The Open Boat," he learned that he was tubercular. He had taken up with Cora Taylor, the madam of a Jacksonville bordello, and she helped him recover from the *Commodore* fiasco. Shortly thereafter, the couple left for Europe where, owing a great deal of money, Crane worked feverishly to square his accounts, paying little attention to his health. Given the brusque naturalism for which he is famous known, perhaps it is fitting that Crane struggled little against his failing health. He and Cora lived well in England until he died in a German sanitarium in 1900. One final home, one last environment, but in the end, changes in venue were mere distractions from the inevitability of death that runs so strongly through Crane's prose. The work he produced has earned Crane labels as a naturalist, realist, symbolist, impressionist, expressionist, and imagist. He drafted novels, short stories, poetry, and journalism. His brief career, day-for-day, may have produced more important American literature than any other author, his productivity rivaled only by the stark vitality that his characters flounder in vain to sustain. — David Visser

BIBLIOGRAPHY

Brown, Bill. *The Material Unconscious: American Amusement, Stephen Crane, & the Economies of Play.* Cambridge: Harvard University Press, 1996.
Crane, Stephen. *Great Short Works of Stephen Crane.* New York: Perennial Classics, 2004.

Crèvecoeur, J. Hector St. John de (1735–1813)

All of J. Hector St. John de Crèvecoeur's works prominently feature the natural environment of colonial America, because to him the largeness and fertility of land in the New World directly contribute to the identity of what he would call "the new man — the American." Though during his youth Crèvecoeur was restless, relocating and taking on new vocations several times, it was his years first as a surveyor and then as a farmer in America that seem to have left him most fulfilled and provided the inspiration for the texts he authored. Crèvecoeur believed that man could have a harmonious relationship with nature, but that too often, especially in Europe, the sad state of human affairs — politics, war, greed, laziness — interfered with that relationship. Though Crèvecoeur appreciates nature's beauty and abundance, it is not the unspoiled wilderness that he praises, as EMERSON, THOREAU, and others would later do. To him the best land is *cultivated* land — land that is productive, ordered, and managed. Farms in America represent a utopia for him because they fall between the untamed wilderness beyond the frontier and the overly developed, overly civilized countries of Europe.

Michel-Guilluame-Jean de Crèvecoeur was born to an affluent family in Normandy, France, in 1735. Trained briefly at a Jesuit College, Crèvecoeur left in 1755 for New France (present day Canada), where he worked as a surveyor and cartographer with a French regiment during the French and Indian War. After the war, Crèvecoeur settled in New York, changed his name to the more British sounding Hector St. John (later expanding his surname to include "de Crèvecoeur"), and became a naturalized citizen in 1765. For the next four years he traveled widely throughout colonial North America, including the Appalachians, the Mississippi Valley, and the Great Lakes.

In 1769 the newly married Crèvecoeur purchased a farm he named Pine Hill in New York, and began writing his most famous work, LETTERS FROM AN AMERICAN FARMER (1783), which describes in idyllic terms his life there. But this tranquil and happy existence came to an abrupt end with the outbreak of the American Revolution. Remaining loyal to the British Crown, which he viewed as a benevolent and protective force in the New World, he attempted to avoid the political turmoil and remain publicly neutral. This move ultimately proved disastrous, however, as the British, wrongly suspecting him of spying for the Americans, imprisoned him for three months. After his release he left his family to the care of neighbors and returned to Europe in 1780.

Crèvecoeur found a publisher for *Letters from an American Farmer* in London in 1782, and the work, describing the lush and fertile lands of the American colonies, gained him entry to the intellectual salons in Paris, where he associated with French and American *philosophes* and political figures (including THOMAS JEFFERSON). The French government appointed him to a diplomatic post in America in 1783, but when he returned to his home in New York he found his treasured Pine Hill farm destroyed by fire, his wife dead, and his children relocated to Boston. He eventually reunited with his children and worked with Thomas Jefferson and others to strengthen political ties between France and the United States. He returned to France in 1793 due to poor health, published *Voyage dans la Haute Pennsylvanie et dans l'état de New York* and a few other works, and died in 1813 in relative obscurity.

Crèvecoeur's *Letters* strongly influenced European conceptions of life in America, and he was one of the first authors to imagine British America as one cohesive geographical unit rather than an amalgam of separate colonies. Europeans were hungry for news of life in the New World, and Crèvecoeur celebrated

the promise of equal opportunity and self-determination in American life, although it is important to note that he claimed such promises only for European Americans. Though he was more sympathetic to slaves and Native Americans than some of his contemporaries, he did not envisage them as candidates for what we today call The American Dream. That said, however, his high praise of the newly forming nation (though criticized by some, including George Washington, for being *too* flattering) introduced the United States as a melting pot of diverse populations that could achieve happiness and fulfillment because of land ownership, as well as freedom from religious and political oppression.—Jacqueline Megow

BIBLIOGRAPHY

de Crèvecoeur, J. Hector St. John. *Letters from an American Farmer*. 1783. Ed. Susan Manning. Oxford: Oxford University Press, 1997.

———. *Voyage dans la Haute Pennsylvanie et dans l'état de New-York*. 1801. Trans. Clarissa S. Bostelmann. Ann Arbor: University of Michigan Press, 1964.

Greeson, Jennifer Rae. "Colonial Planter to American Farmer: South, Nation, and Decolonization in Crèvecoeur." *Messy Beginnings: Postcoloniality and Early American Studies*. Ed. Malini J. Schueller and Edward Watts. New Brunswick: Rutgers University Press, 2003.

Moore, Dennis, ed. *More Letters of the American Farmer: an Edition of the Essays in English left Unpublished by Crèvecoeur*. Athens: University of Georgia Press, 1995.

Philbrick, Thomas. *St. John de Crèvecoeur*. New York: Twayne, 1970.

Wilson, Gay, and Roger Asselineu. *St. John de Crèvecoeur: The Life of an American Farmer*. New York: Viking, 1987.

Letters from an American Farmer, J. Hector St. John de Crèvecoeur (1782)

J. Hector St. John de Crèvecoeur asks in his book *Letters from an American Farmer*, "What then is the American, this new man?" Like other texts written in the period of the Revolutionary War for an audience of Europeans curious to know about life in America, the *Letters* explore the seemingly endless possibilities available to America's inhabitants. Free from the shackles of European monarchy and state-sponsored religion, all of America is a potential Eden (THE BIBLE), an earthly paradise where self-determination allows its citizens to create an ideal society based on agriculture and local industry (AMERICAN PASTORAL). This positive assessment of America's potential takes on a darker tone in the concluding letters as corrupting forces conspire to spoil the promise of America.

The text's protagonist, the fictional Farmer James,

writes 12 letters to describe his life as a Pennsylvania farmer after his decision to emigrate from England. His first two letters provide character sketches of himself, his wife and children, and of Mr. F. B., the fictional reader of the letters that the narrator will write. He gives detailed descriptions of life on his harmonious farm, a life that is filled with a happy family, industrious and friendly neighbors, and, above all, the pleasure of working his own land.

In Letter III, titled "What is an American?," several possible types of the true American are considered and rejected in Crèvecoeur's search to define for his European audience the essential qualities of American identity. Other texts in the late eighteenth century explore the same issue, including Timothy Dwight's *Greenfield Hill*, Thomas Paine's *Common Sense*, BENJAMIN FRANKLIN's *Autobiography* and even parts of THOMAS JEFFERSON's *Declaration of Independence*. What sets Crèvecoeur's account apart from these is that types of Americans in his text are determined not so much by social or cultural forces such as religion, political affiliation, education, or class, as they are by the geography and natural environment of America, which themselves determine the social and cultural forces that will eventually define it. Crèvecoeur claims that men are like plants: they exist in certain climates and assume certain characteristics because of their environments. They are the natural produce of the countryside, determined by their relationship to nature, and not solely the product of historical, social, or cultural circumstance.

In Letters IV through IX, Crèvecoeur continues his presentation of life in three American regions: the Pennsylvania agrarian life, which is the most favorable, followed by whaling life in the Nantucket seaport, followed by slave-owning plantation farming in the South. The hierarchy is predicated primarily upon the use-value of land for its inhabitants. The more intimate the connection between land and worker, the better (and more virtuous) the quality of life. The hierarchy is also based on a balance between savagery and civilization. Natural wilderness areas, neither orderly nor productive, prevent a direct connection between humans and nature, as do overly developed spaces, and both have negative moral implications for their inhabitants.

Geographically and psychologically, the Pennsylvania farm is the ideal place in the eyes of Farmer James because its remoteness allows for enough land to support a family farm, and its proximity to small towns permits social interaction—in churches, schools, and town gatherings. No one is rich here, but people are comfortable in Farmer James's ideal world, the orderly farm. As A. W. Plumstead argues, Crèvecoeur presents the American farm as ideal for

this new breed of man—the American—because a prosperous American needs above all "freedom ... a geographical and political climate that will encourage him to develop his natural genius" (215). Fertile soil, small government, and a lack of interfering laws create an industriousness that the crowded, ancient cities of Europe will not.

Crèvecoeur's glorification of American soil is in direct contrast to contemporary theories put forth by Europeans such as Comte de Buffon, Abbé Raynal and Abbé De Pauw, which held that the natural environments in the New World were of a lesser quality than in Europe. These French *philosophes* argued that America's climate and soil would lead to inferior species of plants, animals, and humans. Crèvecoeur's Farmer James is an insider who can present empirical evidence to contradict the French theories. Not only are America's natural environments not inferior to Europe's; they are actually superior because of the possibility of regeneration and rebirth in the New World. Men in Europe "were as so many useless plants, wanting vegetative mould, and refreshing showers; they withered, and were mowed down by want, hunger, and war; but now by the power of transplantation, like all other plants [men] have taken root and flourished!" (43).

Like the Pennsylvania farmer, the whaling community of Nantucket is happy and moderately prosperous largely because of its relationship to the natural environment. This community's inhabitants farm the sea rather than the land. Using language usually connected to cultivation of the land, Farmer James makes clear that the sea can offer some of the same benefits as farming. The inhabitants of Nantucket "plough the rougher ocean, they gather from its surface, at an immense distance and with Herculian labours, the riches it affords; they go to hunt and catch that huge fish" (87). The industry shown by the people in "cultivating" the ocean creates a Utopia only slightly less ideal than farming does because whaling turns the ocean into "plowable" land. But the sea is not exactly like the land, and therefore inherently less trustworthy. In Pennsylvania, the farmer can take direct "possession of the soil," a task impossible in the ocean, which cannot become private property in the same manner. Still, industry and hard work make Nantucket morally superior to the South (27).

Letter IX covers Farmer James's travels to the South, where he observes first-hand the horrors of slavery. Life in Pennsylvania is defined by the fulfilling vocation of farming, and in Nantucket by whaling and fishing, but South Carolina's inhabitants are lawyers, planters at large plantations, and merchants, none of whom share the farmer's and whaler's direct connection to the natural environment. Farmer John calls the colony's inhabitants "the most wretched people in the world" (162) because the white population live overly civilized lives too distant from the land, and the slave population are subject to the whims of owners who are incapable of feeling the physical and mental pain they inflict. The climate is also problematic; the weather, with its high heat and humidity, "renders excesses" (152), encourages laziness, and incites dissension among neighbors. Lawyers, plantation owners, and merchants may possess greater economic wealth than do Pennsylvania's farmers or Nantucket's whalers, but it is a corrupted sort of wealth, based on "luxuries and refinements" (151), not on "cleared lands, cattle, ... and varieties ... of produce" (55). Farmer James sees a future for Charleston much like that of contemporary Europe — over-civilized towns yielding to decay and ruins, physical manifestations of a life built upon a ruined morality.

Letters X and XI break from the pattern of the first nine, and invoke natural history more explicitly in their exploration of the American landscape. Letter X is a natural history essay with sketches on snakes and hummingbirds, both of which Farmer John has carefully observed on numerous occasions and "with the most minute attention" (170). Letter XI describes a visit to John Bartram's botanical gardens outside Philadelphia, with ebullient praise for the lush countryside. Though the style and purpose of these letters seem almost out of place with the rest of his text, it is clear that Crèvecoeur included them to underscore his praise of British America to his European audience; "Happy the country," he says, "where nature has bestowed such rich treasures!" (177).

The darkest of all the letters, Letter XII, entitled "The Distresses of a Frontier-Man," records how the American Revolution has destroyed Farmer James's chance at happiness. No longer able to find refuge in Pine Hill once war breaks out, he escapes to the frontier where he can forge a new identity, rejecting both European and American identity in favor of an unknown one without laws or political entanglements. Part of the appeal of life as a farmer for James had been that he could maintain his peaceful existence without concern for political conflict; however, he can no longer retain his agrarian neutrality after war breaks out. He will turn to the wilderness to escape the intrusion of war, but he does it to conquer land that had not yet been conquered. He is determined not to become "wild," which he says is possible "as long as we keep ourselves busy in tilling the earth," preserving his sense of control over nature (212).

For an author so enthusiastic about the possibilities for America's inhabitants, it is perhaps a surprise that Crèvecoeur paints the American Revolution as such a destructive force for his fictional Farmer James. Neither Crèvecoeur nor his protagonist supported the idea of separation from England. Life in Europe may have been less free and less natural than in America, but Crèvecoeur longed to maintain the colonial status quo: an America that could rely on the strength of the British Monarchy for stability and security. As James prepares to flee with his family, he asks his audience, "Must I then bid farewell to Britain, to that renowned country? Must I renounce a name so ancient and so venerable?" (197). In the novel's final lines, James asks Mr. F.B. to "mourn ... with me over that load of physical and moral evil with which [I am] oppressed" (217). Though James will attempt to protect his family and way of life by turning to the wilderness, it is clear that he does not expect to find there the idyllic existence of Pine Hill. — Jacqueline Megow

BIBLIOGRAPHY

Branch, Michael P. *Reading the Roots: American Nature Writing Before Walden*. Athens: University of Georgia Press, 2004.

Plumstead, A. W. "Hector St. John de Crèvecoeur," in *American Literature 1764–1789, The Revolutionary Years*. Ed. Everett Emerson. Madison: University of Wisconsin Press, 1977.

Regis, Pamela. *Describing Early America: Bartram, Jefferson, Crèvecoeur, and the Influence of Natural History*. Philadelphia: University of Pennsylvania Press, 1992.

Crichton, (John) Michael (1942–2008)

Michael Crichton received considerable critical and popular acclaim for his novels exploring themes of environmental disaster and systemic breakdown — a breakdown often mirrored in his characters as well as in the world around them. Crichton also authored several nonfiction books and directed movies.

Michael Crichton was born in 1942 in Chicago, Illinois, and grew up in Long Island, New York. His father, an editor and journalist, provided the young Crichton with a strong background in writing by discussing writing and correct use of words over dinner. At the age of 14, Crichton sold a travel essay, about a family vacation, to the *New York Times*. When he commenced study at Harvard College, he intended to pursue a degree in English, but continually received C-grades for his work, and so, in a telling move, switched his major to anthropology. He graduated in 1964 and began studying at the Harvard Medical School the same year. To help pay for medical school, he spent weekends and holidays writing paperback thrillers under the pen name John Lange.

During the same time period, he wrote *A Case of Need* (1968), a thinly-veiled description of people and occurrences at Harvard Medical School, under the pen name Jeffery Hudson. Crichton did not confess to writing the novel until after it was nominated for and then won the Edgar Allan Poe Award for the Best Mystery of the Year. *The Andromeda Strain* (1969), his first best-selling novel, was published shortly before Crichton graduated from medical school. He received his medical degree from Harvard Medical in 1969, and after graduation was a postdoctoral fellow at the Salk Institute in La Jolla, California.

Crichton described his early years of medical school and residency in the first part of his autobiographical book of essays, *Travels* (1988). The second portion of the book recounts his evolution as a writer and the influence of his experiences with success, metaphysics, mysticism, and travel in other countries. His environmentally significant works range in theme from ecological disaster in *State of Fear* (2004), a story about global warming, and bio-catastrophe in *The Andromeda Strain*, to the impact of using technology to tamper with genes in *Next* (2006) and *JURASSIC PARK* (1990). He is often considered a science-fiction writer, but described his own work as "fiction as fact," stressing not merely the possibility but the (often ominous) plausibility, even probability, of his imagined scenarios. As a result of the intensive research he conducted for most of his novels, Crichton, in fact, often lectured on topics related to their central themes, from environmentalism to genetic research, and many other areas of science and policy.

When Crichton spoke on environmentalism in 2003 to the Commonwealth Club in San Francisco, he emphasized perhaps the most central theme in his work, that every action has consequences, often incalculable, and it is imperative that people recognize the potential results of their actions. He also highlighted the importance of assessing the reality of perceived threats and the efficacy of proposed solutions. In the speech, he compared environmentalism to Judeo-Christian religious belief, and related it to mythic structures similar to those he described in *Travels*. Crichton attempted to disabuse listeners of the notion that there ever was an "Eden," or other harmonious paradise, by citing examples of the endless struggles, plagues, and warfare that have characterized both human and nonhuman history. The "romantic view" of nature, he stressed, only exists for those who do not truly *experience* nature. Those who *do* may still maintain spiritual beliefs about aspects of the natural world, but should be released from misleading and even pernicious assumptions about paradisiacal "others" on the other side of the truth.

Ultimately he argued for eschewing the "religion" of environmentalism, for two principal reasons: a non-partisan, peaceful environmental movement based on objective science is needed to successfully achieve positive and sustainable results; and religions typically make claims to absolute knowledge (or faith), but the environment and the problems associated with it are too complex for any one person or group to pretend to such assurance. According to Crichton, the only way to shift environmentalism away from such "religious" error is to enforce more stringent requirements on what constitutes environmental knowledge; and he proposed, moreover, that only through a thorough de-politicization of science may we sure that the so-called facts of any given account are actually *factual*. Novels such as *State of Fear* and *Jurassic Park*, and movies he scripted such as *Twister* (1996), illustrate and imaginatively explore these fundamental convictions of the scientist turned author.

Crichton's awards and honors suggest a measure of his distinctive contribution to contemporary cultural and environmental debate; among them, the Association of American Medical Writers Award for *Five Patients* (1970), the Mystery Writers of America's Edgar Allan Poe Award for *The Great Train Robbery* (1975), a host of awards for the television drama, *ER*, and an ankylosaur renamed the *Crichtonsaurus bohlini* in 2002. — Liz Clift

BIBLIOGRAPHY

Crichton, Michael. "Environmentalism as Religion." *Michael Crichton*. 15 Sept. 2003. Constant C Productions. 5 June 2009, http://www.crichton-official.com/speech-environmentalismaseligion.html.

Nguyen, Hanh. "'Jurassic Park' Author, 'ER' Creator Michael Crichton Dies." *The Chicago Tribune*. November 5, 2008.

Trembley, Elizabeth A. *Michael Crichton: A Critical Companion*. Westport, CT: Greenwood Press, 1996.

Jurassic Park,
Michael Crichton (1990)

Dinosaurs re-created from deoxyribonucleic acid (DNA) found in the blood of amber-entrapped mosquitoes are the centerpiece of Michael Crichton's science-fiction novel, *Jurassic Park* (1990) that examines biological and genetic experiments gone awry. The novel is set in an island theme-park ("Jurassic Park") which is the brain-child of millionaire John Hammond, and filled with supposedly irradiated female dinosaurs. In theory, breeding and stocking only female dinosaurs would forestall reproduction.

By irradiating the dinosaurs, Hammond's team believes they can prevent the dinosaurs from breeding even if a male dinosaur were somehow introduced to the herd. Early in the novel, however, clues exist that the dinosaurs have escaped from their enclosures in the theme park long before they escape within the context of the novel. Before anything is obviously wrong with the park, Ian Malcolm, a mathematician invited to tour the park before it officially opens, expresses skepticism, and illustrates his skepticism by carefully explaining chaos theory, highlighting the idea that simple systems can produce complex systems, and vice versa. He bluntly declares to Hammond that the park cannot be controlled, and this notion, of the uncontrollable complexity of the natural environment, is a central facet of Crichton's environmental perspective.

Hammond begins to resent Malcolm for not sharing his high hopes for the park. Later, Malcolm points out that the distribution of dinosaur height for several different species is a bell-curve, which counters the way in which the animals were released into the park (in three batches)—a typical seed-like trace of the chaos theorized about earlier. Although not revealed until later in the novel, the escape of the dinosaurs supports Malcolm's idea that Jurassic Park—and by extension its optimistic faith in scientific control—is inherently unstable and ultimately doomed.

Due to a series of (plausible) mishaps, including human error and electrical failure caused by corporate espionage, the dinosaurs in Jurassic Park escape from their compounds. The process of natural selection is promptly and brutally illustrated, as Jurassic Park's first guests, along with several employees, find themselves controlled rather than controlling, simply trying to survive, with the dinosaurs establishing predator-prey relationships between the different species. Unlike the prey dinosaurs, however, Hammond and his guests must find ways to outwit and outrun animals that humans were never meant to encounter, thus raising the allegorical stakes of the narrative to a kind of environmental morality tale, which, once having been set in motion, cannot possibly end well.

Throughout the novel, Hammond's unlimited enthusiasm and limited understanding of what he did in creating the park herald his demise. Like much of humanity in similar, uncharted situations, he does not see, or chooses not to see, the dangers in his seemingly controlled environment. Hammond's inability to recognize obvious dangers, combined with his enthusiasm and idealism, suggest that the park he imagines is not the park that exists, a common discrepancy in utopian (and dystopian) societies.

As the creator of the park, Hammond is a god-like figure, and believes that it is thoroughly under his control. He proudly displays the dinosaur compounds covered by motion sensors and high-voltage fences, and the efforts to stock only female animals within the park, recalling similar utopian narratives such as Mary Shelley's *Frankenstein* or Thomas More's *Utopia*. Hammond's utopia is theoretically self-contained and self-supporting, but rapidly disintegrates to reveal the myriad ways in which such a world was effectively doomed to collapse. Like much of Crichton's work, then, *Jurassic Park*, for all its cinematic action, has a ruthless and systematic quality of retrospective diagnosis; looking *back*, as the action rushes forward, on the human arrogance and folly that lies beneath and behind it.

The isolation of the island locale supports the notion of a self-sustained world that has eschewed the evils of the regular world, recalling other tales in which a remote island is the setting for fantastical, utopian schemes, such as Swift's *Gulliver's Travels* or H.G. Wells' *Men Like Gods*. The island location may also provide grounds for suspension of disbelief due to its separation from the "quotidian" mainland. In addition to the literary allusions to islands, the unnatural creation taking place on the island lends to the location shades of the laboratory Shelley creates for Victor Frankenstein. And all of these hermetic factors heighten and intensify the environmental issues at the heart of the novel, rather in the manner of BUCKMINSTER FULLER's "spaceship earth." Although the island is meant to isolate the theme park from the rest of the world, the dinosaurs—symbolic of the unforeseen and unforeseeable forces of nature itself—defeat this false hope as well, and the novel ends by foreshadowing the yet more unsettling sequel to *Jurassic Park*, when the visiting paleontologist notes that the dinosaurs are not looking to escape the island, but to *migrate* from it. Crichton's sequel, *The Lost World* (1995)—clearly recalling the novel of the same name by Arthur Conan Doyle, published a century before—explores the question of what would happen if the dinosaurs not only managed to reproduce, but escape from the island onto the mainland; and both "Jurassic" narratives combine to fuse and update these disparate strands, of fantasy, utopianism and morality tale, in a cautionary fable of environmental hubris and nemesis.—Liz Clift

BIBLIOGRAPHY

Crichton, Michael. *Jurassic Park*. New York: Knopf, 1990.
_____. *The Lost World*. New York: Knopf, 1995.
Gallardo-Torrano, Pedro. "Rediscovering the Island as Utopian Locus: Michael Crichton's Jurassic Park." *Theme Parks, Rainforests and Sprouting Wastelands: European Essays on Theory and Performance in Contemporary British Fiction.* Eds. Todd, Richard and Luisa Flora. Amsterdam: Rodopi, 2000. 17–28.

Crockett, Davy (1786–1836)

David Crockett — Tennessee businessman, soldier, author, and politician — is the foundation for the legendary hero "Davy Crockett," a frontiersman famed for trailblazing, fighting Indians, wrestling bears, riding up Niagara Falls, and other adventures related in tall tales dating back to the 1830's.

The real-life David Crockett was born in 1786 to John Crockett, an Irish immigrant and Revolutionary War veteran, and Rebecca Hawkins Crockett, in Greene County, Tennessee. The elder Crocketts were farmers and operated a tavern. David himself began working at the age of 12, performing a variety of odd jobs including driving cattle and working as a wagoner, professions that allowed him to travel widely and develop skills as a frontier scout.

Deciding at 20 to settle down, David married Mary Finley in 1806, but after seven years of marriage and a succession of failed business enterprises (including keeping a general store and a mill), he decided to resettle his growing family in Franklin County, Tennessee, where he joined the Tennessee militia as a scout. Soon Crockett's militia service found him serving under Andrew Jackson in the Creek War, primarily in what is now Alabama. During the Creek War from 1813–1816, Crockett took part in the burning of several Creek settlements and later tried to rundown unfriendly natives in the Florida swamps. Upon his return home in 1816 he was elected a lieutenant of militia and justice of the peace. With these two elections, Crockett's political career — and his reputation as a masterful storyteller — began. Quick promotion to the positions of town commissioner, a colonel of militia, and state legislator followed, and he was later elected to the U.S. House of Representatives for most of 1827–1835. His (negative) position on the Indian Removal Act, combined with his defection from the Jackson Democrats cost him reelection in 1835, and after this final defeat, Crockett decided to go to Texas. There he joined the ill-fated garrison at the Alamo in San Antonio de Bexar in February 1836, and was among the defenders killed there when Mexican forces attacked on March 6, 1836.

Since the real-life Crockett's Congressional days, Davy Crockett has become an icon in American popular culture. Initially, Crockett's own tall tales and folk humor made him a figure of national prominence. His (ghost-written) autobiography, *A Narrative of the Life of David Crockett of the State of Tennessee* (1834), was widely popular, but so too were other books marketed under his name or plays parodying his image. Similarly, the series of DAVY CROCKETT ALMANACS, marketed under Crockett's name and purportedly describing his adventures during a 22-year period from 1832–1856, sold very well. Crockett's dramatic demise at the Alamo in 1836 only made him more famous, cementing his status as a tough fighting man, capable leader, wilderness guide, and frontier settler, even if most of the stories showing him in these capacities were purely fictional.

Following his death at the Alamo, former Congressman David Crockett — now "Davy Crockett" — truly became a part of America's popular culture, and his exploits emphasized the openness of a wilderness landscape ripe for conquest by enterprising American settlers. Transformed into a national hero virtually overnight, Crockett's new status was later invoked to support the cause of MANIFEST DESTINY, and a motto associated with Crockett, "first, make sure you're right, then go ahead," was widely used to justify American expansion into previously undeveloped territories such as Oregon. The western territories, as portrayed by those in favor expansionism, were a vast wilderness where settlers could quickly establish new towns while living off the land. Consequently, the vast popularity of tall tales associated with the Congressman's fictional persona, and his killing of bears, mountain lions, and buffalo, all helped to popularize the overhunting of these creatures as settlers spread west. The fictional Crockett continually engaged in hunting for sport, rather than for self-sustenance, and like the equally mythologized frontiersman Daniel Boone, he hunted equipped with just his knife, favorite rifle, hunting dogs, and (in Crockett's case) pet bear. Furthermore, this Davy Crockett was not confined to any one specific area, but roamed a vast area, always returning home to either Tennessee or "Kaintuck." It is this fictional and far-roaming Crockett, with his audacious stories of fighting wildcats, riding alligators up Niagara Falls, and killing bears with only his grin, that has become the Crockett that most Americans know best.

Today, the heroic — and fictional — version of Crockett continues to resurface in film and television. While the first extant Crockett film appeared in 1909, perhaps the most recognized films featuring him are *The Alamo* (1960), produced by and starring John Wayne, and the Billy Bob Thornton vehicle *The Alamo* (2004). Additionally, Walt Disney's Davy Crockett television shows, broadcast as part of the *Frontierland* series and starring newcomer Fess Parker, proved to be extremely popular with young Americans during its run in 1954–1956 and afterward. During this time, many youngsters imitated their television hero, dressing as Crockett in raccoon hats, carrying Disney-licensed toy rifles, and singing the show's popular theme song. In the end, the Crockett that Americans have invented for themselves, while based on a real man, is a heroically composite superman, capable of challenging and subduing nature, the wilderness, and anyone who dares challenge the concept of manifest destiny.—Rebekah Greene

BIBLIOGRAPHY

Crockett, David. *A Narrative of the Life of David Crockett of the State of Tennessee.* Intro. Paul Andrew Hutton. Lincoln: Bison Books/University of Nebraska Press, 1987.

King, Margaret J. "The Recycled Hero: Walt Disney's Davy Crockett." *Davy Crockett: The Man, The Legend, The Legacy, 1788–1986.* Ed. Michael A. Lofaro. Knoxville: University of Tennessee Press, 1985. 137–158.

Lofaro, Michael A. "Two Hundred Years: A Crockett Chronology." *Davy Crockett: The Man, The Legend, The Legacy, 1788–1986.* Ed. Michael A. Lofaro. Knoxville: University of Tennessee Press, 1985. xviii–xxiii.

Shackford, James Atkins. *David Crockett: The Man and the Legend.* Ed. John B. Shackford. Lincoln: Bison Books/University of Nebraska Press, 1994.

The Crockett Almanacs,
Anonymous (1835–56)

Published from 1835 until 1856, the immensely popular *Crockett Almanacs* celebrated the life and adventures of DAVY CROCKETT, a legendary figure loosely based on the real-life Tennessee Congressman Colonel David Crockett. As such, they continue a heroic tradition begun with medieval romances that take an authentic historical figure and transform him, here into a larger-than-life character capable of expressing universal concerns about cultural identity and expansionism. The fictitious Davy Crockett is the focal point of the stories and woodcut illustrations included in the *Almanac*, although some stories feature other recurring characters, such as "Mrs. Crockett," "Ben Harding," and "Mike Fink."

The *Crockett Almanacs* were produced by anonymous authors, and the authentic Crockett did not participate in their production. Almanac historians have identified at least 45 different editions, published primarily by Northern printing houses. While the fictional Crockett of the *Almanac* may be viewed today as offensive, the tales do attempt to address conflicts between different racial and class groups, as well as the problems of westward expansion. Thus, the *Almanacs* explore some of the key issues that American society was grappling with in the mid-nineteenth century. Today, the *Almanac* series is highly prized by collectors as an example of mid-nineteenth century American humor.

The *Crockett Almanac* series provided readers with basic information such as calendars and tidal predictions, but this information was minimal in comparison to the number of humorous stories and illustrations to be found on accompanying pages. As an example, the average *Almanac* reader could quickly locate information regarding astronomical observations for "the whole Union, and the Canadas" (*Tall Tales* 1840, 15), but this data was specifically tailored for Boston, New York, Washington, Charleston, and New Orleans. (The 1840 "Nashville" *Almanac*, for example, has 12 pages out of 36 dedicated to these charts.) The emphasis on eastern American cities is important, as the *Almanacs* were actually produced by publishers based in Boston, New York, Philadelphia, and Baltimore rather than in "Nashville" as claimed in the early years of *Almanac* publication.

However, the main emphasis of the *Almanacs* was on the adventures of Colonel "Davy" Crockett. As the 1840 *Almanac* claims on its cover, readers can expect to find "Adventures, Exploits, Sprees, & Scrapes in the West" on every page. Davy is an exciting personality who makes great claims about his capabilities, stating that he "can run faster, dive deeper, stay longer under, and come out drier, than any *chap* this side the big *Swamp*. I can outlook a panther and outstare a flash of lightning: [and] tote a steamboat on my back" ("Tall Tales," xxix). Davy is also an amazingly prodigious traveler. The *Almanacs* are filled with stories of his trips to Mississippi, Alabama, Tennessee, Kentucky, Niagara Falls, and Texas. For these journeys, Crockett uses conventional transportation such as horses or riverboats, but also relies on unconventional means, such as riding a pet alligator up Niagara Falls in an 1846 *Almanac* adventure.

The stories within the *Crockett Almanacs* were (and still are) fascinating partly because of their envisagement of a new world mostly unknown to the (typically) Eastern reader. The series is set in a tripartite world: civilization (the eastern U.S. cities); the frontier settlements of Tennessee awaiting further development to become truly civilized; and the wide-open spaces of the wilderness that Crockett explores while preparing the way for eventual frontier settlements that will evolve into cities. The *Almanac* stories reveal that Davy is only completely comfortable in the arena he knows best: the wilderness. Crockett, the mighty hunter and traveler, has little time for settling down in these stories. Instead, he leaves this task to his wife, children, and various friends. Davy's sole task is to make the West safe for these people to settle.

The vast territory Davy roams is rarely marked, offering only the occasional river or forest. Although he sometimes comes across Indian camps or dangerous animals, these experiences only serve to reinforce the mercantilistic beauties of the land as a place where an adventurous man can roam freely and earn a living for himself and his family. Davy's vignettes never explore the aesthetic beauty that surrounds him because he is constantly on the move, never still long enough —

or much inclined — to appreciate his surroundings. This would require a closer examination of the landscape, something that Crockett's motto, "first, make sure you're right, then go ahead," seemingly forbids. As a product of the American Industrial Revolution and the cause of Manifest Destiny, Davy only reports on the commercial aspects of the land, focusing on how the wilderness can be transformed into goods and services that will support the burgeoning populations of Eastern cities. Davy comes across as plucky and courageous because he knows how to bring the landscape under his control. Likewise, his struggles with the natural world reveal a vast and inviting expanse just waiting for enterprising men to make of it what they will.

The environment that Crockett travels through — and defines for the reader — is one that in which the potential settler could thrive and be comfortable. Davy encounters no mountains, canyons, or valleys. Instead, the land is generally flat, filled with the occasional river and enough trees to support a large population of wildlife. There are no dynamic panoramas capable of startling the reader. Instead, the wilderness is crafted as a place where the reader can improve his current life with relative comfort and ease. Consequently, the animals that Davy hunts — bears, panthers, wolves, and deer — are those familiar to city dwellers whose sole knowledge of the West may come from journals, travel reports, or romance. Other animals native to the Great Plains or the West, such as the buffalo, are rarely mentioned. While the hunting tales that populate the *Almanac* may seem ludicrous, their purpose is twofold: they remind the reader to exercise caution in the wilderness and urge the hunter, no matter how skilled, to always be prepared for emergencies. Davy's limited attention to fauna carries over to the floral world as well: he never makes specific reference to the types of trees he sees or the potential medicinal qualities of plants. He only observes that the land is capable of growing cash crops such as corn, his imagination eschewing all other potential uses for the land.

Besides this simple but profoundly important environmental characterization of the American frontier, the *Almanacs* feature a strong political argument supporting the rapid expansion of America's territory; and the series spurred interest in the cause of Texan independence and annexation, and contributed to increased settlement in the West. As a result, the *Crockett Almanacs* can best be described today as an inspired marketing campaign championing the cause of western expansion. As a symbol of the American cause of "Manifest Destiny," a slogan advocating the expansion of the United States across the entire North American continent, Davy seems capable of accomplishing much of this mission on his own. Yet his purpose in traveling is not to discover the mouths of rivers or even to make contact with (potentially) friendly indigenous peoples, as is the case with other explorers. Instead, he is simply meant to blaze the trail for westward and southward expansion; and the thrust of the *Almanacs* as a whole is to suggest that as settlers follow in Davy's footsteps, American civilization will continue to expand and prosper.— Rebekah Greene

BIBLIOGRAPHY

Lofaro, Michael A., ed. *The Tall Tales of Davy Crockett: The Second Nashville Series of Crockett Almanacs, 1839–1841*. Knoxville: University of Tennessee Press, 1987.

_____. ed. *Davy Crockett's Riproarious Shemales and Sentimental Sisters: Women's Tall Tales from the Crockett Almanacs, 1835–1856*. Mechanicsburg, PA: Stackpole Books, 2001.

Derr, Mark. *The Frontiersman: The Real Life and Many Legends of Davy Crockett*. New York: Morrow, 1993.

Dorson, Richard M., ed. *Davy Crockett: American Comic Legend*. New York: Rockland Editions, 1939.

Meine, Franklin J., ed. *The Crockett Almanacks, Nashville Series, 1835–1838*. Chicago: Caxton Club, 1955.

Rourke, Constance. *Davy Crockett*. New York: Harcourt, Brace, 1934.

DeLillo, Don (1936–)

Born in 1936 — the year, incidentally, in which scientists first synthesized radium E — Don DeLillo grew up in New York City, a Bronx boy in an Italian-American neighborhood, more interested in baseball than writing. It was not until 1964, after earning a degree in Communication Arts and working for awhile in advertising, that he started writing his first novel, *Americana* (1971). Over the next seven years he published five more novels, including his ambitiously researched *Ratner's Star* (1976), a work deeply informed by theoretical mathematics. A half dozen award-winning novels later, he released *Underworld* (1997), a work set in part during the early 1950s of his New York youth. Considered by many his masterpiece, this sprawling historical work earned the author a number of literary awards, including his second Pulitzer Prize nomination. In 1999 he received the Jerusalem Prize for the Freedom of the Individual in Society, an honor that celebrates, among other works, the novel *Mao II* (1991), the author's response in part to the *fatwa* issued two years earlier against novelist Salman Rushdie.

For over four decades DeLillo has interrogated the texture of American culture, in novels about sport, rock and roll, consumerism, paranoia, terrorism, and the threat of nuclear annihilation. His narratives are often driven by modern anxieties, and some are even bleakly comical in conveying, like Kafka or Beckett, a sense of existential dread — unsurprisingly, perhaps, for an author whose cultural touchstones include the Cold War, JFK's assassination, and the comedy of Lenny Bruce. This anxiety and dread is dramatized perhaps most memorably in his popular *WHITE NOISE* (1985): "Some people are scared by the sunsets, some determined to be elated, but most of us don't know how to feel, are ready to go either way." So reflects the novel's narrator on our ambivalence about technology's encroachment upon the natural world — in this case, a sunset whose beauty is tempered not simply with the menacing hues of pollution but also the "Airborne Toxic Event," a rolling fog of mysterious gas looming on the periphery of the town. Compounding the narrator's lurking disquiet is both a mysterious ailment, which may or may not be cancer, and his wife's growing addiction to an experimental drug that promises, with mixed results, to obliterate her own fear of death. DeLillo has a knack for capturing this commingled sense of fear and awe, an often-inchoate uneasiness with technology and culture, struggling for expression against the exhilarating buzz and hum of modernity.

And yet, DeLillo in part rescues us from the edge of terror and dread through his sheer joy in language and invention, churning up anxieties while deftly laying down, like a stonemason at work, line after chiseled line of masterful prose. In a style indebted to literary modernist James Joyce and his fellow experimentalists WILLIAM FAULKNER and ERNEST HEMINGWAY, though often on a narrative scale more akin to filmmakers like Martin Scorsese and Oliver Stone, DeLillo builds a rich aesthetic and semantic texture in his narratives by attending with grace to the nuance and allure of words and their relationships. And in no work, perhaps, does he better capture the sensuousness of language than in his *The Body Artist* (2001), a celebration of language whose ostensible subject is a performance artist coming to terms with her husband's death. Lyrically dense and set at a glacial pace, the novel begs readers to slow down, to linger in those otherwise mundane moments of our lives permeated with what, in a 1988 interview, DeLillo calls the "radiance in dailiness." This radiance he most powerfully evokes in passages describing the natural world: "She moved toward the table and the birds went cracking off the feeder again. They passed out of the shade beneath the eaves and flew into sunglare and silence and it was an action she only partly saw, elusive and mutely beautiful, the birds so sunstruck they were consumed by light, disembodied, turned into something sheer and fleet and scatter-bright."

Here, just at the edge of human perception, the nonhuman world crackles with electricity, and as nature and language take center stage, the displaced observer is always only partly able to discern, just outside her window, a world ringing bright with animation and the luminous morning sunlight. Yes, DeLillo reminds us, it is a world increasingly dominated by technology and industry, and the anxieties that darkly attend (postmodern) life. Yet, though we are often eclipsed by something larger and perhaps menacing — a *fatwa*, for example, or a hyper-real sunset — we still stand enraptured before art and art's nature, finding inspiration and ultimately hope in the language itself, through which we communicate this radiant world to one another. — Zachary Dobbins

BIBLIOGRAPHY

Deitering, Cynthia. "The Postnatural Novel: Toxic Consciousness in Fiction of the 1980s." *The Ecocriticism Reader: Landmarks in Literary Ecology.* Ed. Cheryll Glotfelty and Harold Fromm. Athens: University of Georgia Press, 1996. 196–203.

Kerridge, Richard. "Small Rooms and the Ecosystem: Environmentalism and DeLillo's *White Noise.*" *Writing the Environment: Ecocriticism and Literature.* Ed. Richard Kerridge and Neil Sammells. London: Zed, 1998. 182–95.

Martucci, Elise. *The Environmental Unconscious in the Fiction of Don DeLillo.* London: Routledge, 2007.

Phillips, Dana. "Don DeLillo's Postmodern Pastoral." *Reading the Earth: New Directions in the Study of Literature and Environment.* Ed. Michael P. Branch, Rochelle Johnson, Daniel Patterson, and Scott Slovic. Moscow: University of Idaho Press, 1998. 235–46.

White Noise, Don DeLillo (1984)

Don DeLillo's *White Noise*, his eighth novel, satirizes the absurdities and perils of postmodern America, focusing in particular on the myriad ways in which technological control of the environment has transformed the natural world into an extension of the human. DeLillo's narrator, Jack Gladney, is a death-obsessed professor at a small college, and through him DeLillo charts the destabilizing effects, environmental and psychological, of this transformation. Frank Lentricchia, enumerating some of the reasons why the work was a popular "breakthrough" for DeLillo, notes that its "central event [...] is an ecological disaster," and that the book is "an ecological novel at the dawn of ecological consciousness" (Lentricchia 7).

The novel is divided into three parts, with the middle section devoted to a so-called "airborne toxic event" which forces Gladney and his family to evacuate their town. An industrial accident has released a chemical known as "Nyodene D," producing a gigantic cloud of poisonous gas, at once ominous and alluring: "In its tremendous size, its dark and bulky menace, its escorting aircraft, the cloud resembled a national promotion for death, a multimillion-dollar campaign backed by radio spots, heavy print and billboard, TV saturation. There was a high-tension discharge of vivid light" (151). The interpenetration of the natural and unnatural in this description, the environmental event as a spectacle produced and mediated by technology, epitomizes DeLillo's critique of the confusion, artificiality, and strange lethality of contemporary life. Nature seems no longer to have any claim beyond the human, for "natural" scenes not only seem to be generated by human interventions, but continually remind Gladney and other characters of something they have witnessed previously on television or in the movies. The cultural critic Neil Postman, writing at roughly the same time as DeLillo, makes a similar point about the appropriation of nature's primacy by the media: "There is no more disturbing consequence of the electronic and graphic revolution than this: that the world as given to us through television seems natural, not bizarre" (Postman 79).

As a way of suggesting the ubiquity of technological "white noise" in contemporary culture, DeLillo periodically breaks up Gladney's narrative with snippets of advertising slogans, brand names, or other fragments suggestive of the bewildering eclecticism of late capitalism. One of the sharpest of these links "on-demand" television with the human domination of the environment: "CABLE HEALTH, CABLE WEATHER, CABLE NEWS, CABLE NATURE" (220). As Michael Valdez Moses remarks of this list: "It is precisely by way of technology reducing nature to a postmodern simulacrum (a copy with no original), 'CABLE NATURE,' that man assumes sovereignty over a reality that was once understood to transcend man himself" (Moses 65). Romantic conceptions of nature as a source of inspiration have, as a result of such control, been seriously compromised. "Natural" spectacles are associated with the corrupting human touch, as in the local sunsets which have "become almost unbearably beautiful" (170) since the airborne toxic event. Near the end of the novel, Gladney observes the sunset from a highway overpass and contemplates his own and others' reaction to the phenomenon:

> The sky takes on content, feeling, an exalted narrative life. The bands of color reach so high, seem at times to separate into their constituent parts. There are turreted skies, light storms, softly falling streamers. It is hard to know how we should feel about this. Some people are scared by the sunsets, some determined to be elated, but most of us don't know how to feel, are ready to go either way [(324)].

Not knowing exactly how to feel about the natural world (and many other things) is typical of DeLillo's characters. Natural beauty is hyperbolized and denatured here: a sunset, the trite staple of postcards and tourist photos, becomes overwhelming in its apocalyptic portents, while the poisonous human interference implicated in the breathtaking "natural scene" serves as a reminder of the toxicity of intoxication with beauty. One of DeLillo's literary disciples, Bret Easton Ellis, provocatively echoes this scene in *American Psycho* (1991). Patrick Bateman, the novel's narrator and a possible serial killer (he ultimately suggests he may have only imagined the atrocities he describes), hyperbolizes Gladney's thoughts on the deadliness of sunsets and their implication in consumer culture in his gory contemplation of urban clouds: "I see [in the sky ...] a Gucci money clip, an ax, a woman cut in two, a large puffy white puddle of blood that spreads across the sky, dripping over the city, onto Manhattan" (Ellis 371). For DeLillo and Ellis, nature is not accessible as a presence beyond and greater than the human: it is merely another extension of communal human agency, a spectacle implicated in, and threatening the extinction of, all human interests. A human-engendered death looms in the sky even as the sky delights the senses.

The hyper-consumerism of the postmodern world creates, DeLillo implies, its own illusions about the human triumph over nature. To consume in America is to partake in the illusion of overcoming natural death by encountering a seemingly endless supply and variety of things: endless shopping aisles, endless goods, endless television, all of which suggest an endless consumer, immortally seeking and acquiring. Insulted by a colleague, Gladney goes shopping in order to restore a sense of "endless well-being" (83), finding, in what Jean Baudrillard calls the "primary landscape [le paysage]" of Western affluence, "the final and magical negation of scarcity [..., which] mimic[s] a new-found nature of prodigious fecundity" (Baudrillard 30). Gladney knows, however, that consumer culture can only repress the fear of death in its suggestion of endlessness, offering the aura of immortality while generating its own forms of death and corruption. Told by doctors that his exposure to Nyodene D will likely kill him some day, though it is not clear when, he turns wildly against his own consumption in an attempt to challenge his fear: "I threw away picture frames, shoe trees, umbrella stands, wall brackets, highchairs and cribs, collapsible TV trays, beanbag chairs, broken turntables. [...] There was an immensity of things, an overburdening weight, a connection, a mortality" (262). Even divested of material possessions, however, Gladney remains death-haunted. In a final, deranged effort to make contact with some kind of authentic, "natural" experience, he attempts to murder a rival, but during the act finds himself lost again in simulacra, mimicking cinematic clichés as he attacks and then rescues his victim. Part of DeLillo's point here, which he will elaborate in later novels such as *Libra* (1988) and *Underworld* (1995), is the volatility of the contemporary de-natured world — its solicitation of violence by individuals who model mass media even as they seek to transcend it. — Geoff Hamilton

BIBLIOGRAPHY

Baudrillard, Jean. "Consumer Society." *Selected Writings of Jean Baudrillard*. Ed. Mark Poster. Stanford: Stanford University Press, 1988.
DeLillo, Don. *White Noise*. New York: Penguin Books, 1999.
Ellis, Bret Easton. *American Psycho*. New York: Vintage, 1991.
Lentricchia, Frank. "Introduction." *New Essays on White Noise*. Ed. Frank Lentricchia. Cambridge: Cambridge University Press, 1991.
Moses, Michael Valdez. "Lust Removed from Nature." *New Essays on White Noise*. Ed. Frank Lentricchia. Cambridge: Cambridge University Press, 1991.
Postman, Neil. *Amusing Ourselves to Death*. New York: Penguin, 1985.

Dewey, John (1859–1952)

In many ways John Dewey's long life paralleled the cultural history of America. Unlike his parents, who were both raised on farms, Dewey was born into the first generation of Americans who experienced the radical shift in population, culture, and technology known as the industrial revolution. Dewey's childhood in the small city of Burlington, Vermont was spent hiking and boating near Lake Champlain, but it was also defined by the rapid urbanization occurring across the country. He attended what his parents considered a mediocre and overcrowded school, but excelled as a student and entered the University of Vermont at the age of 15.

After earning a Ph.D. from John Hopkins in 1884, Dewey embarked on a distinguished career teaching and writing about education, social science, and philosophy; and his experiences as a young man in Burlington were a persistent influence on his work on the relationship between the environment, social institutions, and individual freedom. During his career as a university professor at the University of Chicago and Columbia University, Dewey wrote both complex philosophy and popular articles on civic responsibility. One of the first pioneers of American pragmatism, he aligned himself professionally with such "unconventional" thinkers as Charles Sanders Pierce and William James.

In was through pragmatism that Dewey expressed his deep admiration for ecological processes and their value. He believed that the traditional, separate metaphysical categories of "subject" (human) and "object" (nature) hindered our understanding of the complex relationships that define existence. According to Dewey, the reciprocal connection between experiencing subjects and experienced objects creates the foundation for all social and philosophical inquiry. John Stuhr notes that in Dewey, "experience is existentially inclusive, continuous, unified: it is that interaction of subject and object which *constitutes* subject and object — as partial features of this active, yet unanalyzed, totality. Experience, then, is not an 'interaction' but a 'transaction' in which the whole constitutes its interrelated aspects" (4–5). Dewey labeled this belief "radical empiricism," and it would prove to be a foundational concept throughout much of his later work.

Not only did radical empiricism help explain how subjects and objects mutually shape one another; it allowed Dewey to theorize that both humans and nature exist in an ever-changing tide of evolution and contingency. Dewey writes that the natural environment "thus becomes something more than a void in which to roam about, dotted here and there with dangerous things and things that satisfy the appetite. It becomes a comprehensive and enclosed scene within which are ordered the multiplicity of doings and undergoings in which man engages" (*AE* 23). According to Dewey, growth and multiplicity were the only things that could be said to have inherent value because they provoked subsequent changes in dormant or established beliefs. The proliferation and evolution of ideas was intrinsically good, as it produced the materials necessary for further progressive change. As his own cultural history in Vermont had shown, the definition of truth can dramatically shift according to the pressures of its environment, and should therefore be continually reevaluated. Just as fish's gills, for example, are a favorable physical adaptation for breathing under water, they become a liability when the fish is removed from that water; thus we can see that gills are advantageous so long as they are useful, not because they are ideally suited to the nature of a fish.

At the turn of the 20th century, the belief that one's external environment determined truth and identity was an innovative concept, and Dewey's critique of knowledge had a profound impact on the way Americans understood their relationship to the external world. Philosophical tradition had long held that abstract ideas like Truth, Justice, and Beauty were statically defined, and could be attained either through meticulous rationalization or the careful application of facts. Dewey's pragmatism encouraged not only the academic revision of ideas, but a practical application of those ideas to benefit a democratic public. In 1935 Dewey published *Art as Experience*, arguably his most influential work on aesthetics. In it he argued against definitions that identify art with static objects, and instead emphasized the overall artistic experience. He hoped this would erode the notion of a transcendent "fine" art and thus enable the public to see beauty as an experience capable of affecting us outside the narrow confines of the museums.

After the 1940s, both Dewey and pragmatism were marginalized in favor of more analytic philosophers, but his impact on ecological consciousness can best be seen in his insistence that the environment is an essential component of our models of truth and democratic society, even while it is continually in motion.— Chris Findeisen

BIBLIOGRAPHY

Dewey, John. *Art as Experience*. New York: Perigee, 1980.

Martin, Jay. *The Education of John Dewey*. New York: Columbia University Press, 2002.

Popp, Jerome. *Evolution's First Philosopher: John Dewey and the Continuity of Nature*. New York: SUNY, 2007.

Stuhr, John. *Pragmatism and Classical American Philosophy*. 2nd Ed. New York: Oxford University Press, 2000.

Westbrook, Robert. *John Dewey and American Democracy*. Ithaca: Cornell University Press, 1991.

Selected Works of John Dewey

Over the course of his prolific career John Dewey wrote more than 37 volumes of work on a broad range of topics, from democracy, education and social responsibility, to epistemology and art. His willingness and capability to address a wide array of contemporary issues, coupled with his pioneering involvement in social institutions during the years after the Industrial Revolution, made Dewey one of the most influential public intellectuals of the 20th century. His body of work, often associated with the philosophical school of American Pragmatism, exerted a lasting influence on both the content of contemporary environmental ideas, and the ways in which we implement those attitudes in everyday life.

In nearly all his important writings, Dewey touched upon a few keystones that were essential to his philosophical project. One of his central contributions to American thought is the idea that our attitudes toward truth, beauty, and ethical values are socially constructed and must therefore be vigorously scrutinized. In his book *Democracy and Education* (1916) he reminds us how "Men still want the crutch of dogma, of beliefs fixed by authority, to relieve them of the trouble of thinking and the responsibility of directing their activity by thought. They tend to confine their own thinking to a consideration of which one among the rival systems of dogma they will accept. Hence the schools are better adapted, as John Stuart Mill said, to make disciples than inquirers" (211). Unlike previous philosophical traditions, which held "truth" to be a static set of facts or propositions more or less accessible to man, Dewey conceived it as a contingent property of ideas which invited continual reexamination and revision. He believed that many philosophic schools "regard knowledge as something complete in itself irrespective of its availability in dealing with what is yet to be" (215). The vast amount of information continually produced by the physical world, however, coupled with man's limited interpretive capacities, made Dewey skeptical about our ability to formulate totalizing concepts with any degree of certainty; and his skepticism ultimately reflects profound respect for a world that in critical ways exists beyond the scope of human intelligence.

Another important theme in Dewey's work is the celebration of the beauty and variety of ordinary experience. Just as he sees complex philosophical problems both enacted and resolved during the ongoing processes of everyday life, he celebrates the profound aesthetic enjoyment offered by natural and human environments. In his 1934 book *Art as Experience*, Dewey asks why most people feel "repulsion when the high achievements of fine art are brought into connection with common life, the life that we share with all living creatures? Why is life thought of as an affair of low appetite, or at its best a thing of gross sensation, and ready to sink from its best to the level of lust and harsh cruelty?" (20). Here Dewey is countering the impulse to view philosophy, art, and beauty as functions of a human mind somehow divorced from, or even opposed to, worldly or sensual impulses. Instead, Dewey suggests that the "common life" which connects us to all other living beings is the source of aesthetic pleasure, not the cause of intellectual/moral decay. When the art-object becomes the site of our physical, aesthetic experience, we more fully appreciate the system of relationships that went into its physical creation and interpretation. This model thus favors human subjects in continuous relation to their environment, while resisting the impulse to compartmentalize experience into the dichotomous realms of beauty/function, pleasure/work, human/nature.

Dewey also rejects the notion that human beings live in a place somehow removed from the continuities of nature, recognizing that it is impossible to "get outside" nature, just as it is impossible to "get outside" truth. His work attempts to reestablish the connections between humans and their experiences of the natural world, many of which had been devalued in earlier Western philosophical traditions through a complex series of metaphysical abstractions. If Dewey theorized, in the late stages of the Industrial Revolution, that humans and their environment reciprocally determine one another, advances in modern science and industrial capital have provided ample supporting evidence. Bill McKibben writes in his book *The End of Nature* (1989) that in the wake of human-induced climate change no place on Earth is now untouched by mankind. The effects of globalization have shown that the concept of a "Nature" existing apart from humanity is no longer viable, making Dewey's insistence on communities undertaking cooperative action to alter their local and national environments more relevant than ever. However, Dewey's notion of inherent reciprocality not only dictates that humans take seriously their responsibility in shaping the environment, but suggests that environmental pressures determine human interests. "Since no particular organism lasts forever," Dewey writes in *Experience and Nature*, "life in general goes on only as an organism reproduces itself; and the only place where it can reproduce itself is the environment. [...] At every point and stage, accordingly, a living organism and its life processes involve a world or nature temporally and spatially 'external' to itself but 'internal' to its functions" (278). Here Dewey notes that although time and space may exist "outside" living organisms, we nevertheless carry evolutionary and environmental forces internally, through our DNA for example; and in this sense ecological forces are continually present within all living creatures, making our connection to the environment an integral part of our own personal histories.

Although he did not address the issue of ecology in much detail, his work had a profound influence on the history of environmental thought. Pragmatism's insistence that empirical facts clearly reflect social realities cleared a path for ecological science to be considered an essential component of judicial and public policy decisions. Herbert Reid and Betsy Taylor note that "John Dewey did not just espouse a theory of social intelligence; he was a philosopher of 'public intelligence.' Unlike many political scientists, he didn't simply consider public opinion in American society to be both a given force and an elite tool; Dewey pursued a critical theory of the formation of public opinion" (82). As early as 1917 Dewey understood that the rapidly changing world required a new series of interpretive methods if it was to solve the challenges of a new industrial society. In *The Public and Its Problems* he wrote that "If changing conduct and expanding knowledge ever required a willingness to surrender not merely old solutions but old problems it is now" (47). Dewey's work thus encouraged the evaluation of ideas based on their social utility instead of their adherence to established traditions or habits. This enabled later thinkers to talk about nature as something other than a place set apart, either by God or causal necessity; and this in turn helped contemporary thinkers change the dominant environmental paradigm to reflect a model of nature in which humans and the natural environment exist within a complex system of reciprocal and ever-changing relationships. — Chris Findeisen

BIBLIOGRAPHY

Dewey, John. *Art as Experience*. New York: Perigee, 1980.
_____. "Experience, Nature, and Art." *Pragmatism: A Reader*. Ed. Louis Menand. New York: Vintage Books, 1997. 233–364.
_____. "The Public and Its Problems." *The Essential John Dewey*. Ed. Larry A Hickman and Thomas M. Alexander. Bloomington: Indiana University Press, 1998. 46–70.
_____. "Theories of Knowledge." *Pragmatism: A Reader*. Ed. Louis Menand. New York: Vintage Books, 1997. 205–218.
McKibben, Bill. *The End of Nature*. New York: Anchor Books, 1989.
Reid, Herbert G., and Betsy Taylor. "John Dewey's Aesthetic Ecology of Public Intelligence and the Grounding of Civic Environmentalism." *Ethics & the Environment*. 8.1 Spring 2003: 74–92.

Dickey, James (1923–1997)

Poet and novelist James Dickey was born in Buckhead, Georgia, in 1923 to Eugene Dickey, a lawyer, and Maibelle Swift. Dickey enrolled at Clemson College, where he played varsity football. However, after one semester, he enlisted in the Army Air Corps, and eventually in the night-fighter corps during World War II. Having already read Romantic poetry as a boy with his father, in between missions he read modern poetry and tried his hand at writing. On his return, he completed degrees in English and Philosophy at Vanderbilt University, where he also first began writing poetry seriously, and then taught at the Rice Institute, before being called back to duty with the Air Force to train officers for the Korean War.

His military service completed, he spent several years working in advertising in New York and Atlanta, including work on campaigns for Coca-Cola and Lay's Chips. This career paid the bills but left Dickey feeling that he was somehow cheating his creativity. In 1960, he published his first poetry collection, *Into the Stone and Other Poems*; and, convinced he could now earn a living as a writer, he left his advertising job and quickly published *Drowning with*

Others in 1962. It was his volume *Poems 1957–1967*, published in 1967, that brought him significant acclaim, and soon after, he accepted the position of Professor of English and Writer-in-Residence at the University of South Carolina at Columbia, where he taught until his death in 1997. A self-confessed alcoholic, in his latter years he spent time in hospital for jaundice and fibrosis of the lungs. Dickey was married twice, with two sons from his first marriage, to Maxine Syerson, and a daughter with Deborah Dodson.

Dickey's poems are noted for their experimental use of language and form, yet his best known novel, *DELIVERANCE* (1970), is written in sparse and accessible prose. Nonetheless, his oeuvre is unified by its searching depiction of the violence of nature — human, animal and environmental. Humans are certainly viewed as different from animals — in "The Heaven of Animals" the latter are said to have "no souls" (a common Enlightenment view, but not Dickey's, in any simple way) — but away from the "false" civilization of urban environments, humans too can act without conscience. Dickey's primary interest lies in seeing how men behave beyond the rules of civilized society; and he looks to nature as a touchstone and testing ground for masculinity. In Dickey's work, nature is beautiful but brutal, beguiling yet punishing. In the wilderness men become more stereotypically masculine, and women seem to have little or no place. Indeed, significant female characters rarely feature in Dickey's work at all, and are entirely absent, for example, in *Deliverance*.

Dickey's interests in guitar and banjo playing, hunting, woodsmanship, canoeing, and archery, as well as his war-time experience, are all inscribed in his prose and poetry; fighter pilots, football players and Southern backwoodsmen recur throughout his work. His second novel, *Alnilam* (1987), exploited his World War II experiences to explore notions of power abuse in a corps of fighter pilots. Though a move away from the natural setting and threat of *Deliverance*, the novel revisited the idea of natural orders within group dynamics. Less critically well received, his third novel, *To the White Sea* (1993), returned to an untamed wilderness for its setting. Centered on a disturbed soldier forced to parachute into Japan, the tale follows the protagonist's journey from Tokyo to the wilds of the north. While the soldier seems capable in his environment, he becomes almost territorial and kills any humans he encounters, in increasingly depraved ways, an implacable progression anticipating the visceral mythopoeics of CORMAC MCCARTHY.

Dickey cited as his prose influences novelists who he believed strove for poetic intensity and clarity, such as MELVILLE, Woolf, and FAULKNER. His style and thematic concerns have also been likened to HART CRANE and WHITMAN. In addition to his creative writing, Dickey published *The Suspect in Poetry*, a collection of critical essays that was outspoken in its disregard for POUND, Plath and FROST, among others. It was this, along with Henry Hart's biography, *The World as a Lie* (2000), that helped to create an image of Dickey as a rather boorish, macho braggart.

During his writing career, Dickey won a Guggenheim fellowship, was awarded the National Book Award and the Melville Cane Award, and was poetry consultant for the National Library of Congress, a position that is now called poet laureate. Among other notable accolades, he read his poem "The Strength of Fields" at President Jimmy Carter's inauguration in 1977. — Alex Hobbs

BIBLIOGRAPHY

Calhoun, Richard J. and Robert W. Hill. *James Dickey*. New York: Twayne, 1983.

Dickey, James. *Alnilam*. New York: Pinnacle, 1988.

_____. *Deliverance*. New York: Delta, 1994.

_____. *Drowning with Others*. Middletown, CT: Wesleyan University Press, 1962.

_____. "The Heaven of Animals" in *The Whole Motion: Collected Poems, 1945–1992*. Middletown, CT: Wesleyan University Press, 1992.

_____. *Into the Stone*. New York: Scribner's, 1960.

_____. *Poems 1957–1967*. Middletown, CT: Wesleyan University Press, 1967.

_____. "The Strength of Fields" in *The Whole Motion: Collected Poems, 1945–1992*. Middletown, CT: Wesleyan University Press, 1992.

_____. *The Suspect in Poetry*. New York: Sixties Press, 1964.

_____. *To the White Sea*. New York: Delta, 1994.

Hart, Henry. *James Dickey: The World as a Lie*. New York: Picador, 2001.

Deliverance, James Dickey (1970)

Deliverance was the first novel by poet, James Dickey. While his poetry is typically lyrical and full of imagery, his prose in this novel is stark and stripped of his usual melodic description. Yet the theme of remasculinization through nature that runs through his poetic oeuvre is also present here. Like much environmentally significant literature, the novel addresses the confrontation between civilisation and the wild, but also, here, the renegotiation of masculine identity, as four city dwellers seek to reassert their masculinity through mastery of nature. As Theda Wrede summarises: "The narrative hinges on the archetypical hero's quest for self-transcendence through a merger (a blurring of boundaries between self and other) with feminized nature, which, then, reconfirms his masculinity" (178).

Though still critically revered, the novel is also of its time; its violence echoes the escalation in Vietnam, as well as the protests at home, and the shock of the Manson Family murders and the political assassinations of the late sixties. Indeed, in the story of a condemned river, it also struck a tonic chord in the burgeoning environmental movement; 1970 saw the first Earth Day celebration (THE CONSERVATION MOVEMENT). In tone and subject, it owes much to Joseph Conrad's *Heart of Darkness* (1902) and William Golding's *Lord of the Flies* (1954), and shares some similar ground with MARK TWAIN's *THE ADVENTURES OF HUCKLEBERRY FINN* (1884).

Yet praise of the work is not universal; in his portrayal of Southern mountain people, Dickey has been accused of vast oversimplification, forever colouring attitudes towards them. Moreover, when first released, many commented on the novel's sensationalism and its seeming defence of violence and machismo. However, later evaluations have applauded Dickey's subtle use of myth and Jungian archetypes. In the novel, Dickey exploits several of his own interests as plot devices; for example, Dickey enjoyed archery, and bowmanship is inscribed in several key scenes; even his experience working in advertising agencies is utilised in the character of Ed Gentry.

The novel begins when four middle-aged men from Atlanta decide to take a weekend canoeing trip down the southern Appalachian Cahulawassee River before it is flooded to make way for a reservoir which will provide power for their home city. The group — Ed Gentry, a graphic artist and the narrator, Bobby Trippe, a salesman, Drew Ballinger, a soft drink executive — are led by Lewis Medlock, a landlord and self-proclaimed outdoorsman. Seeking to escape civilisation and the emasculating roles they perform in modern life, they look for an environment that is "unvisited and free" (2), in which they can use their "Atomic-survival" instincts (9) and wake from "the sleep of mild people" (31). Lewis in particular arrives at the river with archetypes of lone hunters, frontiersmen, and explorers at the forefront of his mind; these are the stereotypes of men he expects to find on their trip, and he wants the group to emulate their example.

The first major scene of the novel occurs on the journey to the river, when the men stop at a gas station in a mountain community. Urban and rural cultures meet for the first time when Drew, who has brought along his guitar, plays a duet with a young banjo-playing local, who, though mentally deficient and possibly inbred, is a highly gifted musician. It is a subtly ominous scene that suggests camaraderie and commonality, yet at the same time sets the fragile

gentility of the visitors against the "brute" physicality of the locals.

Throughout, Ed's descriptions of nature are filled with awe and trepidation:

> [...] I had not really been aware of the water, but now I was. It felt profound, its motion built into it by the composition of the earth for hundreds of miles upstream and down, and by thousands of years [65].

In the novel's first encounter with wildlife, Ed wakes early to hunt with his bow and arrow; he sights a deer and attempts a shot but misses. This is the first of many failures to master nature with violence. However, although nature itself is an ever present danger, it is the inhabitants of this wilderness who pose the greatest threat to the Atlantans. On this first day of paddling, with Lewis and Drew partnered and further down the river, two mountain men, one carrying a shotgun, surprise the other pair. Forcing Bobby and Ed back into the woods, they tie Ed to a tree and cut him with his own knife then sodomise Bobby. Believing them to be lawless from the outset — "Escaped convicts" or "Bootleggers" (92) — Ed is still astonished by their lack of humanity: "I had never felt such brutality and carelessness of touch, or such disregard for another person's body" (96). Before another act of sexual depravity and extreme emasculation is extorted, the pair are saved by Lewis, who shoots one assailant with an arrow, while the other flees, Ed not quick enough to turn the gun on him. It is clear that rather than the rule of law that the urbanites are used to, here it is survival of the fittest; once they learn this, they take the law into their own hands. From this point in the narrative, the group dynamics begin to feel the strain. Drew wants to go to the police. However, Lewis does not want to alert the authorities because he believes that any trial would lead to them being judged by a jury consisting of the dead man's relatives; he manages to convince Ed and they bury the body.

Yet, having seemingly mastered the inhabitants of the environment, nature itself punishes the group. In a series of difficult rapids that represent "the unbelievable violence and brutality of the river" (124), the river itself assaults the Atlantans, who will benefit from its enforced servitude through the dam. Both Lewis and Drew fall from the canoe; and while Lewis emerges with a broken leg, Drew does not surface at all. Convinced now that the escaped mountain men are stalking them from above the gorge, Lewis presumes that Drew has been shot. Ed assumes responsibility for removing this threat and climbs to the top with the bow. Despite acute fear — "Everything in me was shaking" (162) — Ed is finally able to shoot his prey, although he does injure himself in the process, falling on one of his own arrows. There is some doubt whether this is the same man who attacked them and shot Drew, and, indeed, when they find his body, it is unclear whether he was in fact shot. Nonetheless, back in the gorge, they sink both corpses in the river.

When the remaining three finally arrive at Aintry, they are seen by a doctor and give their story to the sheriff and his deputy. The group devise a shared story about a canoeing accident, and despite the deputy sheriff's suspicions due to his missing brother-in-law, they are allowed to leave, on condition that they do not return. At the novel's close, the characters have returned to their city lives and grown apart, but the wilderness — and "wild" — experience endures, especially in the novel's central protagonist. Despite Lewis's gung-ho approach at the beginning of the novel, it is Ed who truly changes; the experience informs both his masculinity and his broader sensibility thereafter, and his everyday life never quite touches him. As he muses, "And so it ended, except in my mind, which changed the events more deeply into what they were, into what they meant to me alone" (239) and "The river underlies, in one way or another, everything I do" (240).

The novel was adapted into a film of the same name in 1972, starring Burt Reynolds and Jon Voight, and directed by John Boorman; it was nominated for three Academy Awards, including Best film.— Alex Hobbs

BIBLIOGRAPHY

Clabough, Casey Howard. *Elements: The Novels of James Dickey*. Macon, GA: Mercer University Press, 2002.
Conrad, Joseph. *Heart of Darkness*. New York: W.W. Norton, 2005.
Deliverance (1972). Warner Brothers Home Video, DVD, 2007.
Dickey, James. *Deliverance*. London: Bloomsbury, 2005.
Golding, William. *Lord of the Flies*. New York: Perigee, 2003.
Kirschten, Robert, Ed. *Critical Essays on James Dickey*. New York: G.K. Hall, 1994.
Twain, Mark. *The Adventures of Huckleberry Finn*. London: Penguin, 1995.
Wrede, Theda. "Nature and Gender in James Dickey's *Deliverance*: An Ecofeminist Reading" in *The Way We Read James Dickey: Critical Approaches for the Twenty-First Century*. Edited by William B. Thesing and Theda Wrede. Columbia: University of South Carolina Press, 2009.

Dickinson, Emily (1830–1886)

Emily Dickinson lived in Amherst, Massachusetts, from her birth in 1830. Only a handful of her 1775 poems were published in her lifetime. After her death in 1886, her sister Lavinia discovered the forty hand-sewn booklets now referred to as the fascicles, as well as unbound sheets and drafts written on scraps of paper. In 1955, Thomas H. Johnson produced the first edition that preserved Dickinson's wording and some of her unique punctuation. In 1998, R. W. Franklin published *The Poems of Emily Dickinson: Variorum Edition*, in which he reordered the poems based on his research. I will use his poem numbers.

Emily Dickinson was innovative not only in her prosody but also in the range of perspectives from which she wrote on the natural world. Her descriptions of habitat preferences, diurnal and seasonal cycles, sentience in non-human species, and food chain interconnections are ecologically oriented. One unique melding is her evocation of nature as a "haunted house" (F 1403). While this expression incorporates the gothic tone in which NATHANIEL HAWTHORNE depicts the colonial Puritans' discomfort with wild nature as a zone of spiritual danger, Dickinson converts the fear into "mystery" and awe in facing the vast scale of nature. Such depictions unsettle the prevalent anthropocentric attitudes expressed, for example, in EMERSON's famous "transparent eyeball" passage in "NATURE." Her expressions of relativity of viewpoint and indeterminacy of perception link her to modern writers. Finally, one of her poems (F 162) exemplifies the contemporary construct of "swarm logic." From poems that share the exhilaration of spring to poems that probe humanity's place in the ecosystem, Dickinson has contributed richly to the expanding field of ecopoetics.

Dickinson's interest in the natural world began with childhood explorations, such as finding a wild orchid: "the first clutch of the stem is as vivid now, as the Bog that bore it — so truthful is transport" (L 458). "Transport" describes a state of exalted feeling. By adolescence, her outdoor rambles developed into the popular activity of botanizing, gathering plant specimens, which she collected into a Herbarium eventually containing more than 400 local plant species.

She was exposed to both romantic and scientific approaches to nature. In the mid–19th Century, women were just beginning to receive a scientific education. Dickinson studied botany at Amherst Academy (1845–7) and botany and natural history at Mount Holyoke (1847–8). This education supported her keen observations of visible realities, including other species, that balances her more abstract conceptualizations. Although science was shifting into a fully secular profession, its introduction to young women was as colorful as technical. Her botany text, Almira Lincoln Phelps' *Familiar Lectures on Botany*, had an appendix on the "Symbolical Language of

Flowers," a symbol system Dickinson shared with other women writers of her epoch (Petrino 151–2). Yet many of her poems demonstrate her precise knowledge of botanical terminology.

Dickinson's proclamation of a regional perspective in F 256 — "The Robin's my Criterion for Tune ... Because I see — New Englandly" — shows her awareness of relativity of perspective in contrast to the transcendentalists' assumption of universality. Her focus is sometimes on the very locale of her own backyard. To maintain decorum, women were expected to have escorts in wild places, which perhaps explains why Dickinson's explorations dwindled after her dog Carlo's death in 1866. However, she cultivated flowers in the garden and greenhouse of the family Homestead and continued to revel in natural processes. As she told Thomas Wentworth Higginson, whom she invited to be her preceptor in 1862, "the 'infinite Beauty' of which you speak comes too near to seek" (L 2:454). Higginson, a naturalist and writer with a romantic bent, was strongly influenced by Thoreau, to whose essays Dickinson refers approvingly in her correspondence. Critic Barton St. Armand positions the two men as proponents of "poetic natural history" whose interests in nature encompassed both sensory details and spiritual meaningfulness. In contrast to Emerson, who looks through visible nature to a further spiritual reality, they extolled the depths of meaning within the natural world. Dickinson's more naturalistic writing seems convergent with this approach.

Many of Dickinson's poems can be read as dialogues with other writers. The prevalent discourses about nature during her lifetime included the romantic/ sentimental, Calvinist/puritan, transcendental, and scientific. Dickinson sparred with all these positions. She often explored the direct "experience" beyond mental constructions and chose language that conveyed a sense of lived immediacy (c.f. 875, 916). Like her contemporary women writers, Dickinson employed flower symbolism to code human feelings, but her interest in nature was not limited to symbolic figurations. She matched the romantics' intensity of affect and image, but her tone is seldom sentimental and often ironic or gothic. For example, F 1668 describes the "accidental power" of the frost that "beheads" a flower. This view of implacable natural forces challenges the tidy nature of Ralph Waldo Emerson's "Humble Bee" who encounters nothing "unsavory" in his travels. Emerson's writing was an early and strong influence that helped Dickinson define her own divergent project. His poem appeared in a book Dickinson's first tutor gave her in 1853. Comparing Emerson's "Humble Bee" to Dickinson's bee poems helps delineate her ecopoetic project.

In an ecofeminist interpretation of 19th Century thought, males claimed a superior position through their capacity for reason and action, while women were considered creatures of the less-valued body and feelings. A parallel hierarchy is that between humans, deemed active and therefore entitled to exploit passive-coded nature, without regard for sustainability (c.f. Carolyn Merchant). This view is anthropocentric, since it validates human priorities over those of the ecosystem as a whole. Despite his sensitivity to the natural world, Emerson's poem depicts the then-stereotypical active male bee visiting passive female flowers (c.f. Mary Loeffelholz 9–20). Emerson positions himself primarily as an appreciative spectator whose poetic vision allows him to incorporate the "horizon," a transcendent view of the natural/ spiritual world. In "The Humble Bee," his decorous if "burly" bee is a "rover" who will enjoy "dominion" as he moves from flower to flower. The bees in women's writing of the epoch show the other side of this stereotype: most are good providers who stay close to home. In contrast to both approaches, many of Dickinson's 124 bee poems parody gender clichés. She depicts scenes of interaction and immersion, not dominance or domesticity: her bees become inebriated with nectar and sometimes joyfully "lost in balms" (F 205). In contrast to Emerson's viewed horizon are her images of a traveled circumference and the "splendors" of nature envisioned as a varied "menagerie," an aggregate more like a living ecosystem than an abstract ideal (F 319).

A recurrent theme in Dickinson's poems is the reciprocal interaction between bee and flower, as in the assertion that "To make a prairie it takes a clover and one bee" (F 1779)." This bee/ flower dyad depicts a relational rather than hierarchical view of the ecosystem. Ecocritical approaches are relational because they concern the interconnections of individuals and species within the ecosystem. One prime example is the food chain, through which species obtain and provide food for one another. The bee pollinates the flower, while the nectar feeds the bees. This dyad is a small-scale model of an ecological system in which two species are mutually sustaining.

Dickinson's portrayals of interrelatedness among bird and bee populations parallel contemporary ecocritical models that attribute sentience and agency, the capacity to act from their own intentions, to nonhuman species. Dickinson depicts seasonality and process in F 983, where a fly awaits a bee's scheduled arrival. In choosing a non-romantic fly as narrator, Dickinson avoids the sentimental figurations common to her epoch. At the same time, the poem portrays a sentient natural order and seasonal rhythms. Natural processes are purposeful: the caterpillar in F

1523 is "Intent upon its own career" to become a butterfly. Beyond being attractive, the butterfly is an agent with its own "system of aesthetics —/ Far superior to mine." Human valuation is not the only standard. Instead of personifying Nature as one entity, Dickinson presents the natural world as a composite of interacting communities, which she refers to, for example, as the varied melodies of earth (F 895). Dickinson's more naturalistic poems, such as "A narrow fellow in the grass" (F 1096), demonstrate her awareness of habitats: the snake "likes a Boggy Acre." Her persona feels "cordiality" for "Several of Nature's People" whom "I know, and they know me." This syntax implies reciprocity rather than the distanced view of a scientific "objective" observer or the one-way view of Emerson's transparent eyeball. In writing about large-scale splendors of nature, Dickinson can balance a sense of awe with an engagement in science. For example, "The lilac is an antique shrub" (F 1261) uses botanical terminology to present the sunset as a giant flower. The poem contests the Puritan claim that visible nature provides only a dim reflection of heaven's glories by suggesting that this vision of sunset is an immanent revelation complete in itself, for those who fully experience it. Here, the system of sun and earth encompasses humans, but does not grant us center stage.

In "Nature is what we see" (F 721), Dickinson exposes the limitations of human perception to comprehend the vastness of the ecosystem. Each of the three quatrains contrasts human faculties, "see," "hear," and "know," to nature's states: "Heaven," "Harmony," and "Sincerity" ["Simplicity"]. The proposal of the first line is refuted by examples such as "eclipse." Nature encompasses complex processes of production and sustenance, not all of which are visible. Perhaps Nature is "heaven" in the sense of being an all-encompassing whole, as opposed to our partial glimpses. The second quatrain contrasts "what we hear" to "Harmony," implying that the manifold sounds of the environment exceed our capacity to listen. The third quatrain's statement that "Nature is what we know —/ Yet have no art to say" implies an incapacity to fully express what we do experience of the ecological totality. Compared to the creative capacity of nature, our art has a smaller scope. This poem's withdrawal from an attempt to encompass nature through perception could support an ethical stance not limited to anthropocentrism. It contrasts to the famous "transparent eyeball" passage in Emerson's essay, "Nature," in which the poet incorporates a vision of the whole.

Dickinson is often considered a proto-modernist because of her ironic tone and formal experimentation. Her perceptions of the natural world also include innovative insights. Many of Dickinson's poems address transience with a traditional focus on seasonality and the life cycle. Further, though, she depicts transience in moments of perception. As she sums it up in a letter, "All we secure of beauty is it's *evanescences*" (L 781). When we try to "secure" the beautiful life form in art, we find only its trace. For example, in F 370, "Within my garden rides a bird," the reality of a passing hummingbird can only be attested by "just vibrating Blossoms." Without this trace, the persona would be uncertain whether the experience occurred or was projected by "the Garden in the Brain." Such interest in dynamic perception and indeterminacy show her modernistic thinking. Further, F 162 offers a stunning image of ecological interconnectedness and "swarm logic," a construct only defined in the twentieth century. An assemblage of wildlife emerging in spring looks like a giant many-colored organism, "a Peacock's purple Train/ feather by feather — on the plain" where it "Fritters itself away!" Each creature can be separate — they can "Fritter" apart — but they can also function together as a unified group. The comparison to feathers suggests a concrete connectedness. This metaphor well describes bee and ant colonies, now known to function like one giant organism with collective, "swarm logic." The sense of systemic organization continues through the poem, culminating in the final stanza where the myriad forms of wildlife, the "Regiments of Wood and Hill" emerge in the spring and self-organize dynamically, "without" need of a "commander." Such a non-hierarchical emergent order suggests a self-organizing system responsive to seasonal rhythms.

Often, as in F 1365, Dickinson returns to the transport that attunement to natural processes invites.

> A little Madness in the Spring
> Is wholesome even for the King,
> But God be with the Clown —
> Who ponders this tremendous scene —
> This whole Experiment of Green —
> As if it were his own!

Dickinson asks us to question what our role is in "this whole experiment of Green." To assume ownership would be foolish, clownish, but we can be inspired by, and feel kinship with, the natural world within whose boundaries our lives are contained. — Mary Newell

BIBLIOGRAPHY

Baym, Nina. *American Women of Letters and the Nineteenth-Century Sciences.* New Brunswick: Rutgers University Press, 2002.

Dickinson, Emily. *Emily Dickinson's Herbarium: A Fac-

simile Edition. Cambridge: Harvard University Press, 2006.

_____. *The Letters of Emily Dickinson.* Ed. Thomas H. Johnson and Theodora Ward. Cambridge: Belknap Press of Harvard University Press, 1958.

_____. *The Poems of Emily Dickinson: Reading Edition.* Ed. R.W. Franklin. Cambridge: Harvard University Press, 1999.

_____. *The Poems of Emily Dickinson: Variorum Edition.* Ed. R.W. Franklin. Cambridge: Harvard University Press, 1998.

Farr, Judith, and Louise Carter. *The Gardens of Emily Dickinson.* Cambridge: Harvard University Press, 2004.

Grabher, Gudrun, Roland Hagenbüchle, Cristanne Miller, eds. *The Emily Dickinson Handbook.* Amherst: University of Massachusetts Press, 1998.

Keeney, Elizabeth. *The Botanizers: Amateur Scientists in Nineteenth-Century America.* Chapel Hill: University of North Carolina Press, 1992.

Loeffelholz, Mary. *Dickinson and the Boundaries of Feminist Theory.* Urbana: University of Illinois Press, 1991.

Merchant, Carolyn. *Earthcare: Women and the Environment.* New York: Routledge, 1996.

Petrino, Elizabeth A. *Emily Dickinson and Her Contemporaries: Women's Verse in America, 1820–1885.* Hanover, NH: University Press of New England, 1998.

St. Armand, Barton. *Emily Dickinson and Her Culture: The Soul's Society.* Cambridge: Cambridge University Press, 1986.

Sewall, Richard B. *The Life of Emily Dickinson.* New York: Farrar, Streaus and Giroux, 1974.

Smith, Martha Nell, ed. *Dickinson Electronic Archives* http://www.emilydickinson.org/about_us.html.

_____, and Mary Loeffelholz, eds. *A Companion to Emily Dickinson.* Malden, MA: Blackwell, 2008.

Dillard, Annie (1945–)

Depending upon the critic one reads, Annie Dillard, in addition to being a poet, essayist, novelist, and editor, is an inscrutable mystic, an intellectual recluse, an amateur naturalist, a modern Transcendentalist, or "a kind of ecological guru" (Smith 341). By her own account she is "an explorer ... and also a stalker" (Dillard, *Pilgrim* 14), an "unscrupulous observer" (*ibid.* 33), a seeker of mystery, a reader of books, a visitor of monasteries, but most of all a writer, because: "Why are we reading if not in hope that the writer will magnify and dramatize our days, will illuminate and inspire us with wisdom, courage, and the possibility of meaningfulness, and will press upon our minds the deepest mysteries, so we may feel again their majesty and power?" (Dillard, *Writing* 72–73). She is best known for her PILGRIM AT TINKER CREEK (1974), which earned her the Pulitzer Prize and a reputation as an environmental writer of note.

Biographical information on Dillard is sketchy, suggesting that she *is*, in fact, something of a recluse; even her autobiographical texts are admittedly fictionalized to a greater or lesser extent. She was born in 1945 in Pittsburgh, and grew up in a relatively affluent family. Her youth was steeped in religion, books, and the natural world, as recounted in *An American Childhood.* She attended Hollins College in Virginia to earn a bachelor's and a master's degree in English literature, and has lived in places as diverse as Cape Cod and islands off the Washington State coast.

As a child Dillard was a rock- and insect-collector; as a young woman she spent time camping in the Virginia wilderness, which ultimately led to her temporary move to Tinker Creek (in the Roanoke Valley of Virginia) where she researched *Pilgrim at Tinker Creek*, "observing the natural world, taking notes, and reading voluminously in a wide variety of disciplines, including theology, philosophy, natural science, and physics" (*Authors and Artists for Young Adults*). This dual inquiry into the natural world and intellectual history would essentially define the heuristic space of Dillard's later writing.

Highlights of Dillard's oeuvre include *Pilgrim at Tinker Creek* (1974), which earned the Pulitzer Prize; *Holy the Firm* (1977); *Living by Fiction* (1982); TEACHING A STONE TO TALK (1982), named a Best Book of the 1980s by the *Boston Globe*; *An American Childhood*, nominated for a National Book Critics Circle Award; *The Writing Life* (1989); *The Living* (1992); *For the Time Being* (1999); and *The Maytrees* (2007).

Dillard's most significant environmental works include *Pilgrim*; *Holy the Firm*, in which she explores the seeming incompatibility of a divine order and human suffering; and *Teaching a Stone to Talk*, a collection of essays featuring the same acute eye for observation of the natural world that she debuted in *Pilgrim*. *The Living*, Dillard's first novel, is frequently noted for its vivid portrayal of the development of the Pacific Northwest frontier as a backdrop to the characters' lives. *For the Time Being* again takes up the subject of an omniscient, benevolent creator who nonetheless seems to turn a blind eye to suffering. Even in her fiction, Dillard "intersperses narrative vignettes, sometimes casual and other times crucial, with examples of her continuous love affair with nature" (Moore 507).

The narrators in Dillard's environmental works are typically acute, non-intervening observers of the world, somewhat akin to the "transparent eyeball" that EMERSON exalted. And like Emerson, Dillard suggests that to see truly, one must be emptied of self-consciousness and ego. Most critics note Dillard's own "capacity for long scrutiny, careful notetaking, and painstaking remembering" (Smith 350); she herself highlights seeing as the primary human role, and especially the primary writer's role:

Examine all things intensely and relentlessly. Probe and search each object.... Do not leave it, do not course over it, as if it were understood, but instead follow it down until you see in it the mystery of its own specificity and strength Dillard, *Writing* 78].

Such attention, however, is not merely confined to the mundane world, for Dillard views natural phenomena as microcosms through which to explore the divine.

And yet, even in such Emersonian observation, Dillard does not completely absent herself from her writings on the natural world (though some critics express the wish for a yet more personal narrative style). Her books describe raw emotions and a sense of rapture anchored in the body: "What you experience is not purely mental but sensuous as well" (*Authors and Artists for Young Adults*). Even if her style fails to lay bare "her romances..., her griefs, angers, hurts, private joys, deepest longings," Dillard is deeply *present* in her writing; yet she also remains something of a "mystery," akin to the mysteries of the natural world she describes (Smith 353).

A key theme in Dillard's work is the *noninterventionist* role of the human observer (Smith 351). Dillard clearly exhibits more of a poetic than a political agenda. She watches and reports violence, suffering, exuberance, and beauty with a witness's nonjudgmental gaze. She does not comment on the human impact on the environment or call readers to action, and her work is concerned more with the raptures of the natural world than environmental politics — with what might be termed the affective substratum of political life. "In the end," according to the *Environmental Encyclopedia*, "Dillard is a sojourner, a pilgrim, wandering the world, ecstatically attentive to nature's bloodiness and its beauty." "She watches like mad; she records what she observes; she refrains from recommending that anyone do anything about what she sees" (Smith 351).

Another notable feature of Dillard's work is its intertextuality, its tendency to indirectly or directly cite multiple sources, especially American Romantic authors like THOREAU, Emerson and MELVILLE (see Chénetier). Her sources are extraordinarily diverse, ranging from works of Christian mystics and Torah scholars to books on human deformities or scientific reports by entomologists; and they firmly situate her outlook and ideas within the canon of Western intellectual history. However, Dillard does not cite in order to overshadow, question, or correct her source texts (Chénetier), but in order to enrich her own observations and narratives, to juxtapose texts from various backgrounds and reveal their unexplored affinities, illuminating them by that juxtaposition.

Although Dillard became noted as an environmental writer following *Pilgrim*, she has developed a strong following in religious circles for her theological inquiries, highlighted by critical analyses of *Pilgrim*'s mysticism. Her position as a practicing Roman Catholic enhances her popularity among Catholic scholars, and she has been the focus of many book reviews and articles in Catholic publications.

As Peggy Rosenthal notes, "Dillard's stature in American letters is approaching that of her precursor poet-essayist-transcendentalists, Thoreau and Emerson" (*Authors and Artists for Young Adults*). For many, she has revived the romantic tradition of environmental rhapsody, but from a post–Darwinian, post–Big Bang Theory, post-quantum mechanics perspective, one in which postmodern chaos must be reconciled with earlier notions of a self-consistent God (Smith 348, citing John Becker). This locates her among the most significant theological and environmental writers of our time. More broadly, as John Moore claims, Dillard's "work [should be placed] in the company of the best that has been thought and said" (507).— Laura Boynton

BIBLIOGRAPHY

"Annie Dillard." *Authors and Artists for Young Adults* 43 (2002). Reproduced in *Biography Resource Center*. Gale Group. Available online. URL: http://galenet.galegroup.com/servlet/BioRC. Accessed March 9, 2009.

"Annie Dillard." *Environmental Encyclopedia* (2009). Reproduced in *Biography Resource Center*. Gale Group. Available online. URL: http://galenet.galegroup.com/servlet/BioRC. Accessed March 9, 2009.

Chénetier, Marc. "Tinkering, Extravagance: Thoreau, Melville, and Annie Dillard." *Critique* 31.3 (1990): 157–172.

Dillard, Annie. *Pilgrim at Tinker Creek*. 1974. New York: HarperCollins, 1998.

_____. *The Writing Life*. New York: Harper & Row, 1989.

Moore, John Rees. "As the Tide Rises and Falls." Rev. of *The Maytrees*, by Annie Dillard. *Sewanee Review* 116.4 (2008): 507.

Smith, Pamela. "The Ecotheology of Annie Dillard: A Study in Ambivalence." *Cross Currents* 45.3 (1995): 341–358.

Pilgrim at Tinker Creek, Annie Dillard (1974)

Dillard's *Pilgrim at Tinker Creek* received widespread critical acclaim, bestselling status, and a Pulitzer Prize. Although some critics have been frustrated by the difficulty of classifying this "highly unusual treatise on nature" (Reimer 182), few have questioned the book's compelling force or environmental significance.

Dillard describes herself as "no scientist, but a poet and a walker with a background in theology and a penchant for quirky facts" ("Best-Selling Author

Annie Dillard"), and this self-description is exemplified by *Pilgrim at Tinker Creek*, which weaves together meditations on nature, science, theology, and humanity's role in nature, structured around a year's observations near Tinker Creek, in the Roanoke Valley, Virginia. The book aims to "tell [...] some tales and describ[e] some of the sights of this rather tamed valley, and explor[e], in fear and trembling, some of the unmapped dim reaches and unholy fastnesses to which those tales and sights so dizzyingly lead" (Dillard 13).

Pilgrim steadfastly resists categorization: it is not strictly nonfiction, as the personal accounts and theological interludes attest; it is not a novel, as it features little in the way of character-building or plot; it is not a philosophical treatise, as it offers a lyricism and an ecstasy uncharacteristic of the Western philosophical tradition. The book is most often classified as "creative nonfiction," a genre whose name tellingly invokes the same kinds of tensions that are present in *Pilgrim* itself.

Moreover, *Pilgrim* is not a "typical" work of environmental literature. Neither strictly rhapsodic (in the Thoreauvian tradition), nor strictly scientific (like RACHEL CARSON's SILENT SPRING), nor certainly a call to action along the lines of Dave Brower's provocative work, the book revels in the first two traditions without offering the prescriptions and proscriptions of the third. Its juxtaposition of modern scientific observation and mystical/theological ideas makes evaluative fact checking or searches for singular *meaning* both unfruitful and unrewarding. In the end, what the work rewards most is just seeing openly, embracing the text's (and the world's) artfulness: "We must somehow take a wider view, look at the whole landscape, really see it, and describe what's going on here" (Dillard 11). "This is our life, these are our lighted seasons, and then we die.... In the meantime. In between time, we can see. The scales are fallen from our eyes..." (Dillard 129).

Given its unique qualities, it is no surprise, perhaps, that there is a lack of serious critical attention devoted to *Pilgrim*, in spite of the accolades it has earned. Most of the critical attention it *has* earned notes its affinity to the works of the Transcendentalists and the American Romantics. MELVILLE, for example, had a strong impulse to look for metaphysical meaning in natural phenomena, but his focus was darker and less affirmative than Dillard's (see Chénetier, Reimer). Indeed, there are reasons to dissociate *Pilgrim* from the nineteenth-century works to which it is often compared. Critics note, for example, the framework of contemporary science Dillard utilizes that was unavailable to EMERSON and THOREAU. As Pamela Smith explains, citing

John Becker, the ground of scientific certainty was profoundly shaken in the years between Thoreau and Dillard: Darwin's evolution, Einstein's relativity, Heisenberg's uncertainty, and other theories that rocked the solid base on which science was founded, inform *Pilgrim* and give it less of a sense of definitive human purpose and faith in coherence than is present in the nineteenth-century texts to which it has been compared (Reimer 183). Similarly, by Dillard's time notions of unspoiled wilderness and the manifest frontier that earlier authors centralized had largely vanished. And yet, instead of looking lamentingly at the incursions of civilization ("syphilization," as ED ABBEY calls it), Dillard looks *through* a "tamed" wilderness to see more clearly *into* nature (McIlroy 71).

However, while undoubtedly spiritual and theological in character, *Pilgrim* also lacks the unshakable certainty of earlier spirituality. As Gary McIlroy notes, "Less confident than Thoreau that nature would lead her to harmony and coherence, Dillard more willingly explores her negative associations and the philosophical positions which they seem to confirm" (McIlroy 76), and this informs the more personal style that likewise distinguishes *Pilgrim*.

Pilgrim does not offer a meditative reading of natural beauty, but rather a baldly curious one, as Dillard gazes unflinchingly at "grace tangled in a rapture with violence" (Dillard 10), embracing the one and recoiling from the other (but never turning away — always looking). As a result, "underlying even the romanticism of Dillard's book there is always a trace of non–Thoreauvian dread" (McIlroy 81). Dillard's willingness to explore unidealized nature — as in her poring over volumes on parasitic insect behavior and carefully reporting the fate of the frog sucked to death by a giant water bug — sets her apart from her nineteenth-century forebears, and inaugurates a new era of environmental rhapsody that rests on a more realistic, if less certain, foundation.

As Reimer argues, *Pilgrim*'s most dominant characteristic is its graceful movement between the polarized spheres of "the material and the spiritual, the natural and the transcendent," and its unflinching inquiry into both "the beauty and the horror within the natural world" (182). Radaker notes that Dillard's text hangs carefully on a structure constructed of elements as diverse as primitive cosmology (as in the frequent narratives of Eskimo ways of life), contemporary science, and mysticism (125), further frustrating critical exegesis.

Dillard's striking response to the tensions she explores is to embrace both sides of the dialectic with a kind of ecstasy of vision, reveling in the human capacity to grasp and learn from the very struggles and tensions that for Dillard define existence. Unlike the stock Christian answer — to view earthly suffering as a reason to look *beyond* the world to the promise of an afterlife — or philosophical texts that might seek to *overcome* the contradictions they describe, Dillard does not reject, resolve, or reconcile the incompatibilities at the heart of her observations, but rather upholds her own capacity — indeed, her own *responsibility* — to see and bear witness to these tensions (Reimer).

Theologically, *Pilgrim* articulates a critical question that Dillard takes up again in later books, especially *Holy the Firm* and *For the Time Being*, namely, how can we reconcile the notion of a loving, forgiving creator with the horrors inflicted upon the world. The nearest, however, that *Pilgrim* approaches to an answer is the somewhat runic: "That God is unfathomable but definitely there — and there's nothing we can do about it but see, and by our seeing, partake of creation" (Abood).

Still, it is *Pilgrim* that initiated Dillard's fame, that earned her the Pulitzer, and that is still read by generations of students and lovers of nature. "The impact of [Dillard's] vision, shockingly foreign and uncontained, disturbs the accustomed flow of society and challenges current cultural values" (McIlroy 71). It is revolutionary in its inquiry, startling in its multifaceted style, and compelling in its lively call: "The world is wilder than that in all directions, more dangerous and bitter, more extravagant and bright. We are making hay when we should be making whoopee; we are raising tomatoes when we should be raising Cain, or Lazarus.... This is how you spend this afternoon, and tomorrow morning, and tomorrow afternoon. *Spend* the afternoon. You can't take it with you" (Dillard 274).— Laura Boynton Johnson

BIBLIOGRAPHY

Abood, Maureen. "Natural Wonders." *U.S. Catholic* 64.11 (1999): 30–33.

"Best-Selling Author Annie Dillard." Rev. of *Pilgrim at Tinker Creek. Saturday Evening Post.* October 1974: 51.

Dillard, Annie. *Pilgrim at Tinker Creek.* 1974. New York: HarperCollins, 1998.

McIlroy, Gary. "*Pilgrim at Tinker Creek* and the Burden of Science." *American Literature* 59.1 (1987): 71–84.

Radaker, Kevin. "Caribou, Electrons, and the Angel: Stalking the Sacred in Annie Dillard's *Pilgrim at Tinker Creek.*" *Christianity and Literature* 46.2 (1997): 123–143.

Reimer, Margaret Loewen. "The Dialectical Vision of Annie Dillard's *Pilgrim at Tinker Creek.*" *Critique* 24.3 (1983): 182–191.

Smith, Pamela. "The Ecotheology of Annie Dillard: A Study in Ambivalence." *Cross Currents* 45.3 (1995): 341–358.

Teaching a Stone to Talk: Expeditions and Encounters, Annie Dillard (1982)

Annie Dillard's collection of first-person essays, *Teaching a Stone to Talk*, follows the thematic vein of her earlier work by chronicling the development of a particular human consciousness — her own — in the context of a particular place or places. In it she explores, questions, and experiences animals, plants, and natural events through the lens of human knowledge, in all of its forms: cultural, spiritual, scientific. Driving her expeditions and encounters is a very human sense of desire — not for conquest, to discover and possess something, but rather for experience, to find and see something, namely the truth of the world and the presence of God. This is the Dillard that Mike Major describes in 1978, writing about her *Pilgrim at Tinker Creek*, when he says that she has "an artist's eye, a scientist's curiosity, a metaphysician's mind, all woven together in what might be called, essentially, a theologian's quest" (363).

While *Teaching a Stone to Talk* grows from Dillard's prior nonfiction and poetry, it is not simply a straightforward extension of her previous line of thought. The essays are evidence of Dillard's mind reaching up, stretching out, and pushing down into the natural world as she seeks "how to live" (Dillard 15). And when it comes to life, she writes, "there seems to be only one business at hand — that of finding workable compromises between the sublimity of our ideas and the absurdity of the fact of us" (30). Here, as throughout her essays, readers see the tension between what is human and what is not, what is sensible and what is fantastic, what we can know and what will remain a mystery.

In the book's opening essay, "Living Like Weasels," the author's "long glance" with a very "wild" weasel provokes a feeling of awe that deepens into regret and then resolution. She seeks the stark truth of a mystic experience — not necessarily a union with God, but a movement outside of the habitual self, toward a life that contains "something of mindlessness, something of the purity of living in the physical senses and the dignity of living without bias or motive" (15). Yet the weasel's deliberately unconscious way, "open to time and death painlessly, noticing everything, remembering nothing, choosing the given with a fierce and pointed will," can happen for humans only through conscious choice; and thus the essay ends with an exhortation to the reader to make a decision to grab hold of life, "to grasp your one necessity," so that "even death, where you're going no matter how you live, cannot you part" (16).

As Vera Norwood observes, "Dillard is a much

more self-conscious writer" than similarly concerned authors — notably, Isabella Bird, MARY AUSTIN or RACHEL CARSON — in her response to the world around her (341). In fact, Dillard is acutely aware of her own perspective and character, as are her readers, because "[her] primary concern is her individual, personal relationship to God and nature" (Norwood 339). The question "Where (and who) is God?" is a major theme in *Teaching a Stone to Talk*. In "Sojourners," she wonders whether the Earth is our home, infused with the presence of God, or whether we are in exile here from an absent divinity. In "The Field of Silence," she is first stilled by an eternally lonely farm, where "the houses and roadsides and pastures were buckling under the silence," and then surprised to find herself recalling an encounter with angels (136). Like Santa Claus, who she recalls as "God in the Doorway" in another essay, the silent presence in the field is, like nature itself, "misunderstood" by humans (141).

The book's title essay perfectly illustrates Dillard's compassion for those who seek to bridge the gap between human language and the seeming silence of the world. At some point in the past, she suggests, there was a communion of conversation. But "nature's old song and dance" is now "the show we drove from town" (70). Still, people seek to speak with the world: "What have we been doing all these centuries but trying to call God back to the mountain, or, failing that, raise a peep out of anything that isn't us? What is the difference between a cathedral and a physics lab? Are not they both saying: Hello?" (71).

Embracing questions of divinity and cosmology, and ranging from her home island to the Galapagos, Dillard ranges freely through the modern tradition in "Teaching a Stone to Talk," supplementing personal insights with hard evidence, both from firsthand experience and credible second-hand sources. Her style, too, weaves hard facts and evocative images into tightly-knit, highly structured discourse. The questions raised in the essay's first section, which tells the story of Larry — a fellow "crank" who undertakes the serious task of bringing forth a single word from a "beach cobble" — are, through the meditations and musings of the four succeeding sections, brought to a conclusive coda in the last, a single paragraph that begins, "The silence is all there is," and ends, "Pray without ceasing" (76).

Throughout, we hear Dillard's distinctive voice in "the vivid imagery, the perhaps too studied pessimism, the metaphysical speculation, the colloquial style coupled engagingly with quotation from neo–Platonic, Hasidic, or mystical Christian sources" (Lavery 1, 4); but *Teaching a Stone to Talk* is also distinguished by Dillard's fresh perception of death as an individual expedition and encounter. Essays that mark this "new knowledge" include "Total Eclipse," which famously contrasts the probing language of the mind with the animal truth of the flesh, "the dear, stupid body ... as easily satisfied as a spaniel" (99). The contrast brings Dillard to the terrible truth that "all those things for which we have no words are lost," and finally to laughter, for "it is everlastingly funny that the proud, metaphysically ambitious, clamoring mind will hush if you give it an egg" (99). In other essays, such as "On a Hill Far Away" and "Aces & Eights," Dillard returns to the familiar: Tinker Creek and her own childhood. Watching her companion, a young girl, ride a bicycle up a hill, Dillard realizes that in her own life she feels the "momentum" of riding over and down the crest. Connecting her life and her reader's, she writes, "The cards click faster in the spokes; you pitch forward. You roll headlong, out of control. The blur of cards makes one long sound like a bomb's whine, the whine of many bombs, and you know your course is fatal" (167).

Yet, in the next line of the essay, there is no crash. Instead, "the world swings into view again" (167). This is precisely what Dillard desires: the world in view, and her own self shaken enough to be able to see it anew. *Teaching a Stone to Talk* does not promote activism, involvement, or even necessarily participation; it is (characteristically) non-intervening and inconclusive. After the eclipse, for example, "enough is enough. One turns at last even from glory itself with a sigh of relief. From the depths of mystery, and even from the heights of splendor, we bounce back and hurry for the latitudes of home" (103). Yet the significance of her expeditions and encounters, writes Dillard, is always, ultimately, "significance for people. No people, no significance. This is all I have to tell you" (94). — Aubrey Streit Krug

BIBLIOGRAPHY

Dillard, Annie. *Teaching a Stone to Talk: Expeditions and Encounters*. New York: Harper & Row, 1982.

Lavery, David. "Unlicensed Metaphysics: Annie Dillard Revisited." First published in *Religion and Literature* 17.2 (1985): 61–67. Available online. URL: http://davidlavery.net/writings/unlicensed_metaphysics.pdf. Accessed June 1, 2009.

Major, Mike. "Pilgrim of the Absolute." *America* 138 (May 6, 1978): 363.

Norwood, Vera L. "Heroines of Nature: Four Women Respond to the American Landscape." *The Ecocriticism Reader: Landmarks in Literary Ecology*. Ed. Cheryll Glotfelty and Harold Fromm. Athens: University of Georgia Press, 1996. 323–350.

Edwards, Jonathan (1703–1758)

Jonathan Edwards was one of America's greatest philosophers and theologians. He was born in Connecticut to a family of well-known Congregationalist ministers including his father and maternal grandfather. He is often described as a precocious child who had a hunger and curiosity for reading in many different fields, such as mathematics, natural science, theology, ethics, and philosophy, and in his adult life he made contributions to several of these fields. In 1716 he entered Yale College, and upon graduation worked in a several different churches before returning to Yale for a master's degree and becoming a tutor there. In 1725, Edwards was chosen to follow his grandfather as the minister in Northampton Church, where his sermons sparked the revival festivities that would become known as the First Great Awakening (1733–35). In 1758, Edwards was appointed the president of New Jersey College (later known as Princeton), and he accepted, but died a mere six weeks into his term.

While students of literature are most familiar with Edwards' passionate sermons, such as *Sinners in the Hands of an Angry God*, he also wrote extensively in natural philosophy and theology, and was deeply involved in the main philosophical task of his day: developing coherent descriptions of the natural world that drew on philosophical or theological resources, or more pointedly, advancing the debate about the relationship between reason and revelation. Within this conversation, Edwards had a unique voice, in that he sought to ascertain God's relationship to the physical world by engaging Enlightenment and scientific thinking rather than rejecting them. The scientific model of nature that Edwards engaged with and disputed most publicly was the new mechanistic understanding of the physical world, which asserted that the material world was governed by universal laws that could be derived mathematically and were visible to all through observations of the movements of nature. Nature itself was a self-sustaining system, an idea that implied that the world was devoid of God's presence. If there was a role for God it was simply as a creator who was subsequently uninvolved in the world he had created.

This was a radical departure from the teleological conceptions of the world that had persisted since Ancient Greece, as well as the hierarchical notions of the relationship between entities (The Great Chain of Being) that had ordered thinking about nature in the Medieval period (Zakai 16–23).

Edwards resisted these ideas by developing his own theology of nature, which was both teleological and hierarchical, and was based on his theological premises that God was the cause of all being, God was continually active in the world, and God's end was his own glorification. More specifically, Edwards proposes that the material world is but a shadow of the spiritual world, recalling the "shadows" and "forms" of Platonic metaphysics. Thus, the material world may be investigated as a means to access divine reality, which in fact, as for Plato, is the only true reality. Strikingly, however, and in contrast to Platonic idealism, for Edwards the *material* world is merely an idea, and cannot exist without the continued activity of God. Beings (not inanimate nature) are the only spiritual realities and their value is judged on a scale of excellence wherein the most excellent are closer to God. In addition, the order of the world suggests that God created it for intelligent beings and for an end. That end is God's own glory, which in turn means that religious worship is the ultimate end of the human existence. Consequently, those beings that participate in religion are more excellent than those who do not. Edwards thus introduced religion into traditional philosophical teleology, and introduced especially the theological concept of God's own glory as an indisputable theological idea that provides both an end and a framework for his philosophical system. He thus reengaged teleology on theological terms, and incorporated traditional hierarchies, all of which makes his work as appealing to modern creationists as it was to the audience of the First Great Awakening (Miscellanies gg qtd. in Smith, Stout, and Minkema 36).

Furthermore, Edwards interpreted nature typologically, which was a radical idea at the time. Taking his interpretive theory from methods of reading Scripture, Edwards argued that nature and observations of it could point to a greater understanding of God and God's purpose for the world. In doing so, Edwards drew on Aristotelian and Thomistic ideas, along with classical interpretive models such as those of Hugh of St. Victor. As America's earliest and arguably most important theologian, Edwards thus incorporated seminal European ideas into his thinking while positing the inseparability of the material and spiritual worlds.

Although Edwards' philosophical ideas may seem fairly abstract, their concrete expression is vividly apparent in his writings on nature. In "The Spider Letter," for example, Edwards observes the movements of tree spiders and draws theological conclusions about the activity of God in the world, and the intricate design and provisions God has made in creation for even the least of his creatures. He also assails the mechanistic view of the natural world in his work "Of Atoms." Simply put, atoms are dependent on God for their integrity, and since all bodies are composed of atoms, the entire material world is representative of God's immanence. God did not create atoms and then hope that they would stay together, but rather God actively holds atoms together in every moment. And again, in "Images of Divine Things," Edwards describes silkworms and ravens as types or analogies of God's work, and uses Scripture to interpret and integrate these natural creatures in the breathtaking unity of divine creation. Of the silkworm, Edwards writes, "The silkworm is a remarkable type of Christ, which when it dies, yields us that of which we make such glorious clothing" (qtd. in Smith, Stout, and Minkema 17). He goes on to cite Psalm 84 and II Samuel 5, as support for his assertion that Christ became a worm for the sake of humanity, and that with Christ's death humans were clothed in redemption. In describing ravens, Edwards likens them to "devils who with delight prey upon the souls of the dead" (qtd. in Smith, Stout, Minkema 17ff). Scripture is once again invoked to show that the blackness of the raven represents darkness, which in turn is aligned with sin and sorrow. Both nature and scripture, then, point beyond themselves, literally and metaphorically, to divine truths about the spiritual realm. Edwards' theology of nature has thus been described as both pantheistic and a precursor to the TRANSCENDENTALIST ideas of RALPH WALDO EMERSON and HENRY DAVID THOREAU.— Kristel Clayville

BIBLIOGRAPHY

Edwards, Jonathan. *A Jonathan Edwards Reader*. Eds. John E. Smith, Harry S. Stout, and Kenneth P. Minkema. New Haven: Yale University Press, 1995.
Zakai, Avihu. "Jonathan Edwards and the Language of Nature: The Re-Enchantment of the World in the Age of Scientific Reasoning." *The Journal of Religious History* Vol. 26, No. 1 (February 2002): 15–41.

Eiseley, Lorne (1907–1977)

Though recognized as an eminent educator, evolutionary scientist and philosopher, Loren Eiseley is perhaps best known for the poetic essays collected in THE IMMENSE JOURNEY: AN IMAGINATIVE NATURALIST EXPLORES THE MYSTERIES OF MAN AND NATURE (1957). In its effort to determine what it means to be human and possess an identity that functions in accordance with, not in opposition to, the natural world, Eiseley's work typically focuses on the enormous, interlinked complexities of life. His unique environmental perspective, characterized by a masterful integration of science and humanism, centers on his twin preoccupations with "time" and "chance," stressing the important connection between humankind and the environment, and its decisive role in the evolutionary process. A talented story-teller, combining detailed scientific understanding of nature's randomness with mesmerizing prose, Eiseley played a pivotal role in shaping the views of a host of 20th-century environmental thinkers.

Loren Corey Eiseley was born in 1907, in Lincoln, Nebraska, to Clyde Edwin Eiseley and Daisy Corey. The only child of the dejected and disconnected couple, and living on the edge of town, Eiseley spent most of his time alone, cultivating his adoration and appreciation for the natural world. His mother, who had lost her hearing as a child, was a self-taught prairie artist who suffered from paranoia, was prone to destructive behavior, and often left Eiseley feeling isolated. In contrast, Eiseley's father, a salesman who worked long hours for a modest wage, adored his son and was consistently kind and supportive. The marital tensions between his mother and father lead to much instability in the Eiseley home, and created yet another reason for the young Eiseley to seek refuge in the expansive countryside. In addition to these adverse circumstances, Eiseley suffered from tuberculosis, which contributed to his secluded setting. During the Depression, Eiseley, having completed high school, decided to work a series of menial jobs instead of immediately enrolling in university. While this may appear to be a regrettable decision, it was perhaps the most intriguing chapter in Eiseley's life as he delighted in a phase as a wanderer and railway hobo. This period afforded Eiseley the ability to experience humankind and nature in their truest forms — unaffected, uninhibited and unclaimed.

Although his childhood and adolescence were solitary and sorrowful, professionally the multi-faceted Eiseley became something of a sensation, excelling as an archaeologist, anthropologist, educator, poet, scholar and naturalist writer. After obtaining two degrees — a Bachelor of Arts and a Bachelor of Science — from the University of Nebraska, Eiseley went on to earn his MA and PhD from the University of Pennsylvania. A self proclaimed "obscure academician," Eiseley held positions of high distinction at the University of Kansas and Oberlin College in Ohio, ending his career as the head of the Anthropology Department at the University of Pennsylvania. Heir to TRANSCENDENTALISTS like RALPH WALDO EMERSON and HENRY DAVID THOREAU, yet equally an admirer of Charles Darwin and Sir Frances Bacon, Eiseley established himself early as a naturalist writer, publishing many books from the 1950s to the 1970s. Some of the most notable titles are: *The Immense Journey* (1957), *Darwin's Century* (1958), *The Unexpected Universe* (1969), *The Night Country* (1971) and his memoir, *All the Strange Hours: the Excavation of Life* (1975). In addition to these accomplishments, Eiseley was awarded 36 honorary degrees and was a visiting professor at Harvard, Stanford and Yale. Finally, with the assistance of his wife Mabel Langdon Eiseley, the University of Pennsylvania created the Loren Eiseley Library and Seminar Room to commemorate one of the institution's most distinguished scholars.

Eiseley died in 1977, and was buried in West Laurel Hill Cemetery in Bala-Cynwyd, Pennsylvania. His wife, Mabel Langdon Eiseley, with whom Eiseley had no children, was buried next to him on her death in 1986. Their epitaph reads: "We loved the earth, but could not stay." — Katrina Berry

BIBLIOGRAPHY

Buell, Lawrence. *The Environmental Imagination: Thoreau, Nature Writing, and the Formation of the American Culture.* Cambridge, MA: Belknap, 1995.
Christensen, Erleen J. "Loren Eiseley, Student of Time." *Prairie Schooner.* 61:3 (1987): 28–37.
Eiseley, Loren. *The Immense Journey.* New York: Random House, 1957.
Hopson, Janet L. "Strange Hours: Eiseley on Eiseley." *Science News.* 109:7 (1976): 109
"Loren Eiseley." *American Earth: Environmental Writing Since Thoreau.* Ed. Bill McKibben. New York: Literary Classics of the United States, 2008. 337–347.

The Immense Journey: An Imaginative Naturalist Explores the Mysteries of Man and Nature, Loren Eiseley (1957)

Author and anthropologist Loren Eiseley's first and most popular book, *The Immense Journey*, which firmly situates itself within the scope of ecocriticism, consists of a collection of poetic essays that emphasize the important connections between and mutual interdependence of humankind and the environment. The compilation is distinguished by an inspired and characteristic blend of scientific knowledge and artistic vision that provides a unique environmental perspective centered on Eiseley's associated preoccupations of "time" and "chance," which together define the evanescent nature of existence. While many naturalists' essays frequently devolve into desultory ramblings that fail to charm the average reader, Eiseley's unique poetic style — described as the "concealed essay" — utilizes a distinct method that serves to elucidate complex scientific ideas, such as the evolutionary process, for the general public, thus ensuring his provocative narratives a broad and receptive audience.

Eiseley's musings on man and nature begin with the collection's first narrative entitled *The Slit*, which takes place on a timeless prairie. Eiseley, the storyteller on horseback, rides languidly across the vast expanse of grasslands until something catches his eye. Curious, he explores "the Slit" — a prominent fracture in the sandstone walls — where he discovers an animal skull. As he begins to chip away at the rock, exposing the skull, he reflects, "the creature had never lived to see a man, and I, what was it I was never going to see?" (5). In this early passage, Eiseley observes how the story of nature unfolds throughout history, and considers his own story, his own journey: "Forward and backward I have gone, and for me it has been an immense journey" (13). Eiseley's narrative thus becomes a metaphor for the journey of all humankind through the vast dimension of time, space and chance — a journey filled with perplexity, pleasure and impermanence. While Eiseley insists that he does not speak for anyone but himself — since "men see differently, I can at best report only from my own wilderness" (13) — he stresses the importance of each individual's possessing such a wilderness, of the journey *through* it that defines a life well lived.

> Perhaps there is no meaning at all ... save that of the journey itself, so far as man can see. It has altered with the chances of life, and the chances brought to us here; but it was a good journey — long, perhaps — but a good journey under the pleasant sun. Do not look for the purpose [7].

While Eiseley the narrator is a function of time, space and chance, a being permitted and *meant* to exist in a fleeting moment in the evolutionary trajectory of humankind, his stories about this particular place, this specific moment, are in fact timeless artifacts, much like the animal skull, preserving the lineaments and luminous intensity of that moment, in time. This dual role of the environmentally sensitive individual illustrates LAWRENCE BUELL's claim that "each individual must take nothing for granted but [instead] refashion the world for him — or her — self, starting from the premise that personal identity, moral values and social arrangements are all up for grabs" (Buell 8–9).

One of the book's most famous episodes is described in "The Great Deeps," and serves to remind readers of the "primitive roots of the human species, and the connections among all living things." This evolutionary, or co-evolutionary, process is the main thesis of Eiseley's poetic collection of naturalistic essays: "standing thus it finally comes to me that this is the most enormous extension of vision of which life is capable: the projection of itself into other lives" (46).

Despite the fact that everything and everyone are so tightly woven together, Eiseley points out that we are still profoundly unaware of much that exists in space, time and place, and therefore, in order to develop our truest sense of self, our most complete identity, we must situate ourselves more in nature and less in culture. Eiseley is struck by the realization that "a billion years have gone into making" (45) life, as he gazes through the transparent water, meeting the ogling eye of a teeny toad. The eye of this toad, functions for Eiseley as kind of salutary correction of the anthropocentric "transparent eyeball" of EMERSONIAN TRANSCENDENTALISM, a metaphor for the timeless, mystical oneness embracing the human and nonhuman world, resulting in a pragmatic shift in consciousness from an egocentric view of life and the world, to an ecocentric perspective. Eiseley cautions his readers that although

> We teach the past, we see farther backward into time than any race before us ... we stop at the present, or at best, we project far into the future idealized versions of ourselves. All that long way behind us we see, perhaps inevitably, through human eyes alone [57].

One of the more Romantic essays in this collection, entitled *How Flowers Changed the World*, successfully combines the scientific empiricism of Charles Darwin with the poetic prowess of Francis Thompson — two thinkers whom Eiseley greatly admired. Here Eiseley creates an alternate way of looking at "the whole history of the planet Earth" (62) by highlighting the importance of flowers and "their reproductive process" (62), suggesting that ultimately they, in fact, are responsible for "the enormous interlinked complexity of life" (63):

> It was the rise of the flowering plants that provided that energy that changed the nature of the living world. Their appearance parallels in a quite surprising manner the rise of the birds and mammals [66].

Offering a graceful narrative about the history of humankind and nature, while signifying the importance of co-evolution, Eiseley succeeds in illuminating how "the weight of the petal has changed the world and made it ours" (77).

Eiseley's fundamental and far-reaching assertion, that life is story and story life, argued more by the *fact* of *The Immense Journey* than by any explicit claim within it, has elevated American environmental writing (and *reading*) through a salutary self-consciousness regarding both the limits and the unfathomable reach of human understanding. His essential message about humankind and nature, which owes something to the writings of Emerson and THOREAU, is that one can best discover how to live, and best learn what it means to be human, by confronting the essential facts of life through the merging of nature and culture; and through the creation of this 'neo-pastoral' space, the interlinked complexities of life emerge, reminding us that "we can look, but we can never go back" (7). — Katrina Berry

BIBLIOGRAPHY

Buell, Lawrence. *American Transcendentalists: Essential Writings.* New York: Random House, 2006.
_____. *The Environmental Imagination: Thoreau, Nature Writing, and the Formation of the American Culture.* Cambridge, MA: Belknap, 1995.
Christensen, Erleen J. "Loren Eiseley, Student of Time." *Prairie Schooner.* 61:3 (1987): 28–37.
Eiseley, Loren. *The Immense Journey.* New York: Random House, 1957.
Hopson, Janet L. "Strange Hours: Eiseley on Eiseley." *Science News.* 109:7 (1976): 109
"Loren Eiseley." *American Earth: Environmental Writing Since Thoreau.* Ed. Bill McKibben. New York: Literary Classics of the United States, 2008. 337–347.
Scheese, Don. *Nature Writing: The Pastoral Impulse in America.* New York: Macmillan, 1996.

Eliot, T.S. (1888–1965)

Thomas Stearns Eliot was born in 1888, in St Louis, Missouri. He was a late child — the youngest of his brothers and sisters — born to Henry Ware Eliot, president of the Hydraulic-Press Brick Company, and Charlotte Champe Sterns Eliot, a teacher, social worker and passionate advocate for literature. Eliot was a sickly child, forced to wear a corset due to a congenital double hernia. Through his mother, however, he developed an interest in literature. He decided to become a writer at age 14 after reading Edward Fitzgerald's translations of *The Rubáiyát of Omar Khayyám*, a text that prefigures the mystical aspect of his later poetics, for example his interest in Buddhism and Hinduism. Casting a shadow over the family, however, was Eliot's grandfather, William Greenleaf Eliot, who was a Unitarian minister and campaigner. Eliot would rebel against the puritanical religiosity of his family during his years at Harvard University, where he completed postgraduate work in philosophy under tutors such as Barrett Wendall, Irving Babbitt and GEORGE SANTAYANA. Eliot also mingled with the Boston Bohemians, and was able to spend a year in Paris (1910–11). When he moved to London in 1914, Eliot was to find similar succor *via* the Bloomsbury set and the Imagist movement, especially his mentor EZRA POUND.

Eliot's years in Britain were spent first at Oxford University, and later working in London at Lloyds Bank and the publishing house Faber and Faber, but they would be some of the most fruitful of his writing life. Eliot soon met his first wife, the governess Vivienne Haigh-Wood, who would later be committed to a mental asylum. Eliot would not marry again until he was 68, to his secretary Esmé Valerie Fletcher.

Despite the tumult of his personal affairs, Eliot became a British citizen and converted to the Church of England. By his death in 1965, Eliot had attained considerable success as a writer, and was awarded the British Order of Merit and the Nobel Prize for Literature in the same year, 1948.

Because of his connection to England, Eliot is most often thought of in relation to British landscapes such as the city of London and the English countryside ("Burnt Norton," "Little Gidding," or the English historical setting of Eliot's play *Murder in the Cathedral*, for example). Eliot's early experiences in America should not be dismissed, however. In Eliot's poems, there are certainly echoes of the industrial cityscape of St Louis; family vacations in Gloucester, Massachusetts; and the Harvard cloisters of his university years. Anthony Cuda argues that "the pressures of Eliot's creative life" originate "somewhere between the hard claustrophobic inwardness of the city and the open, romantic experiences of the New England shores" (2009: 4). In Eliot's symbolic landscapes, England and New England, London and St Louis are inextricably fused.

Eliot's vision of the environment, however, is not contiguous with earlier traditions of American writing. Early in his career, influenced by the Anglophilia of Harvard professors like Barrett Wendall, Eliot derided American writers, suggesting that NATHANIEL HAWTHORNE, EDGAR ALLEN POE and WALT WHITMAN were inferior artists. Later, however, Eliot's view of American poetry changed considerably. In 1953, Eliot presented an address in St. Louis for the centenary of a university founded by his grandfather. Titled "American Literature and American Language," the speech showed Eliot identifying with writers like Poe and Whitman, and admitting that American literature was emerging as a powerful competitor on the world stage.

For much of his career, however, Eliot's vision of the environment was influenced by European Symbolism and Imagism. As a modernist, his style represented a break from the idealism of Romanticism or the didacticism of Victorian writing. In representing place, Eliot employed startling juxtapositions, experimentation with language, deflation of elevated poetic themes, and objective correlatives wherein physical descriptions came to represent highly complex emotions (cf. Hargrove 1978: 5). Eliot's landscapes are not merely physical and personal places, but environments of the mind that often employ analepsis and prolepsis to juxtapose past, present and imagined settings. The spaces depicted are both American and European, though Eliot's vision of the United States tends to represent either the primitiveness of the frontier or the prim hypocrisy of metropolitan life.

Prefiguring the "Unreal City" of *The Waste Land*, Eliot's early poems portray the American metropolis as a social whirl of insincerity and superficiality. Eliot had experienced the urban sprawl of St. Louis, and, after exploring Boston during his Harvard years, he had begun to rebel against the niceties of New England deportment. Frances Dickey explains that Eliot had become an "inveterate urbanite" (2009: 122), a *flâneur* negotiating urban vice and poverty. The city that emerges in these early poems is not exactly St. Louis or Boston, but a symbolic metropolis which presents an objective correlative for corruption and taintedness. "Preludes" describes the lifting of blinds which expose dingy rooms to unforgiving light, while "Rhapsody on a Windy Night" displays a woman on the threshold inviting in the passer-by. The space between the decent, clean city of the day and the hidden appetites of the city at night are juxtaposed in "*The Boston Evening Transcript*" too, as the narrator delivers a newspaper at twilight. In other poems, Eliot tackles unconventional inhabitants of the city, such as the gender-subverting "Cousin Nancy" and the foreigner "Mr. Apollinax." In later poems, like "Gerontian," the feeling of degeneration is projected on European cities like London, Antwerp and Brussels, and even invades history's cosmopolis of "cunning passageways" (Eliot 1936: 44).

Against the tainted, "civilized" spaces of the metropolis, Eliot often opposes imagery of the sea and rivers, so that in "The Love Song of J. Alfred Prufrock," anaesthetizing yellow fog gives way to a vision of mermaids riding the waves with defiance and freedom. For Eliot, the sea and river symbolize lost freedoms, a meaning which complements their connection to two specific places from Eliot's boyhood. The first is Cape Ann in Massachusetts where Eliot was allowed to go sailing — one of the few physical activities allowed due to his sickliness. Eliot's poem, "Cape Ann," recalls this childhood idyll, urging the reader to hear the New England birdsong; yet this arcadia cannot be maintained: the speaker and reader must let it go. The second significant space is the Mississippi River which Eliot was shown by his nursemaid Annie Dunne when it was overflowing. The river is connected to the passage of time, so that in "Virginia," the inexorable progress of a red river measures out the futility of human existence. The sea, however, is an overwhelming force which, for Phlebus in *The Waste Land* and for Pericles in "Marina," represents oblivion. The symbolism of the river and sea is brought to its full fruition in "The Dry Salvages," which refers to a group of rocks off the coast of Cape Ann. Exploring themes of voyaging, risk and mortality, "The Dry Salvages" describes the "strong brown god" of the river, thwarted by bridge builders, and compares it with the unconquerable ocean that is not only "the land's edge" but the brink of human existence (1943: 35–36). For Eliot, the frontier and wilderness, and the unfathomable power of the sea, offer positive symbolic power even as they terrify.

Much of Eliot's best writing was produced in Britain, but in its recurrent representation of cities and natural spaces, the American landscape haunts the oeuvre. Eliot himself recognized this indelible connection in his poem about "East Coker," a town in Somerset, England that had special significance because Eliot's ancestor, Andrew Eliot, had left East Coker in the seventeenth century to start a new life in Massachusetts. When Eliot died in 1965, his ashes were buried in the town's church, and the inscription on Eliot's commemorative plaque suggests the intricacy of the relationship between Eliot the American and Eliot the Englishman. Quoting the refrain from "East Coker," the plaque reads: "In my beginning is my end. In my end is my beginning."—Zoë Brigley Thompson

BIBLIOGRAPHY

Cuda, Anthony. "The Poet and the Pressure Chamber: Eliot's Life." *A Companion to T.S. Eliot*. Ed. David E. Chinitz. Malden, MA: Wiley Blackwell, 2009: pp. 3–14.

Dickey, Frances. "*Prufrock and Other Observations*: A Walking Tour." *A Companion to T.S. Eliot*. Ed. David E. Chinitz. Malden, MA: Wiley Blackwell, 2009: pp. 120–132.

Eliot, T.S. *Collected Poems 1909–1935*, New York: Harcourt, Brace, 1936.

_____. *Four Quartets*. San Diego: Harvest/Harcourt, Brace, 1943.

Hargreave, Nancy Duvall. *Landscape as Symbol in the Poetry of T.S. Eliot*. Jackson: University Press of Mississippi, 1978.

Miller, James E. *T.S. Eliot: The Making of an American Poet, 1888–1922*. University Park: Pennsylvania State University Press, 2005.

Emerson, Ralph Waldo (1803–1882)

Essayist, poet, lecturer, leader of the American TRANSCENDENTAL movement, and regarded by many as the father of American literature, Ralph Waldo Emerson left an unparalleled legacy to America's understanding of itself and its place in the natural world. With essays such as "NATURE," "EXPERIENCE," "The American Scholar," "The Over-Soul," and "SELF-RELIANCE," Emerson continues to influence and shape American literature, philosophy and environmental thought.

Emerson was born, the fourth of eight children, in 1803, to Ruth Haskins Emerson, daughter of a Boston cooper and distiller, and William Emerson, a Unitarian minister to the First Church, Boston. As ancestors of the original Puritan settlers, the Emerson family had long fostered intellect and education in their children. Emerson would have been exposed to a wide range of intellectual topics at home, particularly in light of his paternal aunt Mary Moody Emerson. Somewhat eccentric and never formally educated, Mary Emerson was nonetheless widely read and conversant on a variety of contemporary issues, and she privately tutored the boys in a broad range of subjects, including Neo-Platonism and Hinduism. In addition to the superior education Emerson received at home, he attended the Boston Latin School from 1812 to 1817. At the age of eight, however, Emerson's father died, leaving his family in financial hardship, and forcing his mother to provide for her family by taking in boarders, appealing for help from relatives, and selling her husband's library.

At fourteen, Emerson entered Harvard, where he began his lifelong practice of keeping a journal, eventually amounting to sixteen volumes. Though Emerson would not be considered an exemplary student, graduating thirtieth in a class of fifty-nine, he received two Bowdoin Prizes for dissertations, the Boylston Prize for declamation, and delivered the class poem at his graduation. After his graduation in 1821, Emerson spent the next three years teaching, but finding the profession unsuitable he entered Harvard Divinity School in 1825 with the intention of following in his father's footsteps. By 1825, he earned his license to minister from the Middlesex Association of Ministers, yet left school because of failing health. Emerson sought warmer climates to improve his health, and so moved south, where he remained until he returned to Boston in 1827 to preach at various Unitarian churches. In 1829, Emerson found a placement as Associate Minister to Henry Ware, Jr., at the Second Church in Boston. During this year, Emerson also met his first wife, Ellen Louisa Tucker. Sixteen months after marrying, however, Ellen died of tuberculosis. With the money Emerson inherited at Ellen's death, in 1832 he resigned the ministry and traveled to Europe. During his travels, Emerson met and conversed with some of the most influential writers of his time, including Thomas Carlyle, John Stuart Mill and Samuel Taylor Coleridge.

Emerson returned to Concord, Massachusetts in 1833 where he began to give lectures, some of his most famous, as a poet and essayist. His lectures covered a wide range of topics, including literature, history, and theology, and contributed to his formation of essays on similar topics. In 1835, Emerson married Lydia "Lidian" Jackson with whom he had four children: Waldo, Ellen, Edith, and Edward Waldo. In

1836, Emerson published "Nature" anonymously, yet soon after delivered his infamous "The American Scholar" to the Phi Beta Kappa at Harvard in 1837 and his "DIVINITY SCHOOL ADDRESS" at Harvard in 1838. The response to Emerson's ideas was immediate and electric, earning him both praise and criticism, yet also gaining him a reputation as one of America's great thinkers. In 1841, Emerson published his *Essays: First Series*, which included such essays as "Self-Reliance" and "Compensation." Between 1836 and 1840, Emerson became involved with a group of young intellectuals, sometimes known as Hedge's Club, or the Symposium, but known today as the Transcendentalist Club, who met to discuss matters of social concern, religion, and philosophy. The club consisted of numerous important American thinkers, including HENRY DAVID THOREAU, MARGARET FULLER, Theodore Parker, George Ripley and Bronson Alcott. He edited the *Dial*, the Transcendentalist Club's publication, from 1842 to 1844, and continued to publish, edit, and lecture for most of his life. While ill and struggling with memory, Emerson still received visitors at his home in Concord, who sought the "Sage of Concord," until his death from pneumonia on April 27, 1882.

Emerson argued that every individual has the innate capacity to access the "Over-Soul," for which the term "God" is inadequate: an almost pantheistic "god-mind" imminent in nature, *human* nature, and humanity's organic relationship to his natural environment. As Perry Miller puts it, "this dread universal essence, which is beauty, love, wisdom, and power all in one, is present in Nature and throughout Nature" (13). From this innate human capacity stems Emerson's resonant principle of "Self-Reliance," fusing the esoteric mysticism of the American Transcendentalist movement with the hardy pragmatism of the American frontier, and crucially shifting transcendental human experience beyond the reach of ratiocinative argument.

Unsurprisingly then, for Emerson, religion and nature are closely allied, the one inscribing in human terms the compelling force and mystery of the other; and both together sanctioning an arm's-length relationship (at best) between the individual and his society. Emerson urged one to follow a personal, if at times ethereal, moral compass, firmly fixed on the Over-Soul. In his address before the Phi Beta Kappa Society at Cambridge, on July 18, 1867, he famously affirmed that "Every law in Nature, as gravity, centripetence, repulsion, polarity, undulation, has a counterpart in the intellect. The laws above are sisters of the laws below"; and this sublime oneness of reality, constantly obscured by our quotidian machinations and concerns, is the sole foundation of truth,

beauty and rightness in the world. — Maureen Anderson

BIBLIOGRAPHY

Emerson, Ralph Waldo. RWE.org — The Complete Works of Ralph Waldo Emerson. The Ralph Waldo Emerson Institute. URL: http://www.rwe.org/. Accessed 17–23 Dec., 2010.

Lothstein, Arthur S., and Michael Brodrick, eds. *New Morning: Emerson in the Twenty-first Century*. New York: State University of New York Press, 2008.

Miller, Perry. "From Edwards to Emerson." *Ralph Waldo Emerson: A Collection of Critical Essays*. Englewood Cliffs, NJ: Prentice-Hall, 1993. 13–31.

Myerson, Joel, ed. *A Historical Guide to Ralph Waldo Emerson*. New York: Oxford University Press, 2000.

Porte, Joel, and Saundra Morris, eds. *The Cambridge Companion to Ralph Waldo Emerson*. New York: Cambridge University Press, 1999.

"The Divinity School Address," Ralph Waldo Emerson (1838)

After he graduated from Harvard Divinity School, Ralph Waldo Emerson served as the assistant pastor of Boston's Second Church, a prestigious Unitarian congregation, but began to have doubts about Christian ritual and belief that came to a crisis following the death of his first wife. He left the ministry and traveled to Europe, where he met William Wordsworth, Samuel Taylor Coleridge, and Thomas Carlyle, three thinkers who inspired his new intellectual direction. In concert with other New England thinkers, Emerson developed the foundations of the uniquely American and environmentally centered philosophy of TRANSCENDENTALISM, which sought to employ reason in comprehending the nature of human life and its place in the universe. In 1836 Emerson published NATURE, a slim volume that became the central text of Transcendentalism. In this context of Emerson's growing fame, the six graduating students of Harvard Divinity School invited their illustrious alumnus to address their graduation ceremony on July 15, 1838.

"The Divinity School Address" begins with a lengthy natural description of the summer of 1838, which seems to have been particularly warm and productive. However, although the introduction's focus on nature is significant, it may strike a modern reader as odd, since the address has become known for its famously divisive theological claims. Indeed, most criticism of the text has focused on this latter aspect of the address, wherein Emerson contends that organized Christianity had made two profound errors, by mistaking the experience of Jesus as normative for all people at all times, and by insisting that God's revelation ended in ancient days. Yet Emerson also uses the address to express his Transcendental worldview, arguing that we must appeal to our native reason to understand that the divine and the human are essentially intertwined in the natural world. To this end, Emerson observes the summertime luxuries of drawing breath, watching the growth of crops and the activity of birds, smelling the odors of pine trees and hay, and enjoying the cool evening spectacle of the starry skies. The vastness of the universe, he says, should make us feel like little children whose world is but a toy. Mention is made of America's fertile soil, its waterways, its mineral resources, its forests, and its wildlife. He refers to the harvests of wine and of corn, and notes specifically that nature has provided us with her bounty in silence without needing to utter a word of explanation. Emerson's introductory goal, therefore, is to reference the cycles of life and of the seasons in order to portray the essential unity and goodness of the natural world apart from and including human beings.

The Transcendentalism that informed "The Divinity School Address" sees nature as a divine entity that is the source of all life and that can be truly known only through our innate intuition or reason, as opposed to our tuition or understanding. It is important to keep these terms distinct when reading Emerson: "reason" is an insight or perception of the laws of nature and the spiritual life that is based in what we know intuitively and that is itself a part of nature; "understanding" comes from precepts taught by secondhand education. Appreciating the beauty and goodness of the natural world can lead to what Emerson calls the "sentiment of virtue," meaning a "reverence and delight in the presence of certain divine laws" (73). These laws include the laws of nature like light, gravity, force, and motion, but also the laws of the "game of human life" like love, fear, and justice; and Emerson argues we can never completely know these laws by being taught them, but only through our inborn intuitive reason. This "sentiment of virtue" may itself lead to the "religious sentiment," which produces the highest human happiness, a joy that Emerson can only characterize (in almost circular fashion) by offering a list of metaphors drawn from nature's beauty: "It is mountain air. It is the embalmer of the world. It is myrrh and storax, and chlorine and rosemary. It makes the sky and the hills sublime, and the silent song of the stars is it" (75). It is this level of intuition that Emerson calls "divine and deifying" (75). God, meanwhile, is neither transcendent and removed, nor locked in the past. Rather, the divine nature is immanent in nature, and humans do not merely possess divinity but in a sense *are* divine and capable of sublime intuition. As one Emerson biographer puts it, the address "is a modern confession of faith, an announcement of the gospel

according to the present moment, a belief not so much in pantheism as hypertheism, a declaration of the divinity of the human" (Richardson 288).

For Emerson, influenced no doubt by his Unitarian roots, Jesus was not a god as understood in the usual sense but a human who realized more fully than any other that all nature is divine and that all people, as integral parts of nature, are themselves divine; hence, there was nothing particular about Jesus apart from his remarkable level of intuition and his teaching that all people are divine. Emerson's accompanying rejection of the miracles of Jesus was highly contentious in his day. Miracles such as the virgin birth or the resurrection are used in the Bible to show the power of God or his human representatives to contravene the workings of nature, which was seen as problematic by Enlightenment science. Emerson, in contrast, simply defines the laws of nature as incontrovertible and argues that all biblical miracles were meant as metaphors. For Jesus, according to Emerson, the true miracle is that the divine is found naturally in human life "at one with the blowing clover and the falling rain" (78).

Emerson's challenge to the graduating ministers, then, was to liberate themselves from blind devotion to ancient rituals, and imitation of past spiritual models like Jesus; to embrace their own inner divinity and rely on their inborn reason; and thereby, to supersede those past models and integrate their lives with nature, returning to a true spiritual wholeness. — Kelly MacPhail

BIBLIOGRAPHY

Cameron, Kenneth Walter. *Emerson at the Divinity School: His Address of 1838 and Its Significance.* Hartford, CT: Transcendental Books, 1994.

Dorrien, Gary J. *The Making of American Liberal Theology: Imagining Progressive Religion, 1805–1900.* Louisville, KY: Westminster John Knox Press, 2001.

Emerson, Ralph Waldo. "The Divinity School Address." *The Portable Emerson.* Rev. ed. Ed. Carl Bode. New York: Viking Press, 1981. 72–91.

Hodge, David Justin. *On Emerson.* Wadsworth Philosophers Series. Australia: Thomson/Wadsworth, 2003.

Richardson, Robert D. *Emerson: The Mind on Fire.* Berkeley: University of California Press, 1995.

"Experience,"
Ralph Waldo Emerson (1844)

Emerson's essay "Experience," from *Essays: Second Series*, introduces a new degree of skepticism in his thinking that was absent from *NATURE* (1836) or *Essays: First Series* (1841). In the essay, Emerson includes a rare glimpse of his personal life by referencing the recent death of his son, Waldo, and lamenting "I grieve that grief can teach me nothing, nor carry me one step into real nature" (288). Stephen E. Whicher believes that in writing the essay Emerson "contrived to rescue his old hope from his new skepticism, the resulting shock of opposites making 'Experience,' as he finally called it, probably his strongest essay. From this time on, however, he habitually assumed the enigmatic nature of his world and the inherent absurdity of that ever-losing winner, man" (Whicher 253). Whereas Emerson's earlier works emphasized the process of integration inherent in human life, "Experience" emphasizes the fragmentation inherent in human existence; but in each case, the singular importance of nature, as touchstone and teacher.

The essay is introduced by a short poem that identifies the seven lords of life, which, according to LAWRENCE BUELL, are mental stages that "start and end in subjectiveness" (Buell 174). The essay itself works through the difficulties of subjectivity by first focusing on human perception: "Our life is not so much threatened as our perception. Ghostlike we glide through nature, and should not know our place again" (286). Emerson is concerned with the difficulties of humankind in striving to properly perceive and understand its existence in the world. David M. Robinson explains that "in *Nature* Emerson had envisioned the attainment (momentary, of course) of a cosmic harmony that revealed the self to be a part of everything around it, in 'Experience' he wrestles with the opposite problem: the inability to bring the self out of a harrowing perceptual isolation" (Robinson 218–219). Emerson reveals, over the course of the essay, that life is a long process and that humankind is entangled in fragmentary moments mistaken as absolutes. "Nature does not like to be observed," Emerson declares, "direct strokes she never gave us power to make; all our blows glance, all our hits are accidents" (288). Nature is itself a process of which humankind can never achieve full knowledge or possession. Instead, humankind simply has its perception of itself and its environment: "Nature and books belong to the eyes that see them. It depends on the mood of the man whether he shall see the sunset or the fine poem. There are always sunsets, and there is always genius; but only a few hours so serene that we can relish nature or criticism" (289). Human perception, influenced by temperament and mood, shapes and attaches meaning to experience, thus "nature and literature are subjective phenomena; every evil and every good thing is a shadow which we cast" (305).

While human perception and subjectivity are the essential *topoi* of "Experience," the physical environment appears in the essay as a means by which Emerson can demonstrate the limitations of humankind to properly perceive and understand. To that end Emerson observes:

We fancy that we are strangers and not so intimately domesticated in the planet as the wild man and the wild beast and bird. But the exclusion reaches them also; reaches the climbing, flying, gliding, feathered and four-footed man. Fox and woodchuck, hawk and snipe and bittern, when nearly seen, have no more root in the deep world than man, and are just such superficial tenants of the globe [297].

Even wildlife cannot lay complete claim upon possession or understanding of the natural world. The creatures of the world are isolated and restricted to the surface of things, due to the fragmentary nature of their subjective experience. In the case of humankind, Emerson chides any attempt to impose values and laws upon the physical environment without the proper perspective: "Nature, as we know her, is no saint. [...] she does not distinguish by any favor. She comes eating and drinking and sinning. Her darlings, the great, the strong, the beautiful, are not children of our law" (297). As Emerson sees it in "Experience," the physical environment exists on its own terms, and it is humankind that must adapt to the challenges of natural history, and be accountable to the larger cosmic process of the natural world.

In the face of such limitations, Emerson advises, "know that thy life is a flitting state, a tent for the night, and do thou, sick or well, finish that stint" (298). To succeed in this endeavor, Emerson suggests humankind must maintain a balance between power and form in order to keep all qualities and impulses from running to excess and ruining the individual. Such balance is important to Emerson because humankind is not the only legitimate interest or force in the world. As he sees it, "life is a series of surprises, and would not be worth taking or keeping if it were not. God delights to isolate us every day, and hide from us the past and the future. We would look about us, but with grand politeness he draws down before us an impenetrable screen of purest sky" (299). Such obstructions are, at times, everywhere in the natural world because "Nature hates calculators" (299). The struggle of human life, as Emerson depicts it in "Experience," mirrors that of natural life, in that it is an organic process that has dynamic and spontaneous aspects requiring an individual to be adaptable and balanced in both power and form.

In "Experience," as in Emerson's oeuvre in general, nature is transformed from an object to be used ("Commodity" in *Nature*) to an entity that has spiritual influences and ramifications on human life ("Idealism" and "Spirit" in *Nature*). In "Experience" the natural world is a reference point for understanding human experience, an independent and compelling entity to which humankind is ultimately accountable. Man is inextricably implicated in the process of the physical environment, and must struggle with the larger process that envelopes human development. That being said, humankind is at all times the focal point of "Experience" and the subject of Emerson's concern. As Emerson notes toward the close of the essay, "I know that the world I converse with in the city and in the farms, is not the world I *think*" (310).— Conor Walsh

BIBLIOGRAPHY

Buell, Lawrence. *Emerson*. Cambridge, MA: Harvard University Press, 2003.

Emerson, Ralph Waldo. "Experience." *Nature and Selected Essays*. Ed. Larzer Ziff. New York: Penguin, 2003. 285–311.

Robinson, David M. "Thoreau's 'Ktaadn' and the Quest for Experience." *Emersonian Circles: Essays in Honor of Joel Myerson*. Ed. Wesley T. Mott and Robert E. Burkholder. Rochester, NY: Rochester University Press, 1997. 207–224.

Whicher, Stephen E. *Selections from Ralph Waldo Emerson: An Organic Anthology*. Riverside Edition. Boston: Houghton Mifflin, 1957.

"Fate,"
Ralph Waldo Emerson (1860)

Emerson first delivered his lecture "Fate" in Boston, in 1851. Nine years later, a final version introduced *The Conduct of Life*, and this volume, with "Fate" and "Power" as its central essays, establishes the main tenets of Emerson's late thought. Confronting the reckless pace of American industrialization, the irreconcilable debate over slavery, and the inexorable approach of the Civil War, Emerson emphasizes individual responsibility in times of political turmoil, and thus departs from the elusive TRANSCENDENTAL-ISM and quasi-mystical tone of his early works.

Throughout the 1850s Emerson drafted and revised "Fate" as his answer to Western philosophy's quintessential question, the Socratic "How shall I live?" (3). In his response, the philosopher curbs earlier optimisms and learns to accept the unavoidable and unpleasant circumstances conditioning human life: "Once we thought, positive power was all," he recalls, "Now we learn, that negative power, or circumstance, is half" (15). Nonetheless, it would be simplistic to read "Fate" as a philosophical counterpoint to Emerson's previous ideas. On the contrary, David M. Robinson sees Emerson as merely facing a new challenge: to reconcile an "increasing recognition of the limits of the possible, and his growing valuation of ethical action" (Robinson 135). Ultimately the essay represents Emerson's attempt to find a balance between man's freedom of action ("Power") and the external and implacable forces constraining it ("Fate"). Providence's limitations still leave room

for man's freedom, and for Emerson, to exercise this freedom constitutes man's ethical obligation. As a result, his notion of "Fate" is no longer the insurmountable wall of the American Calvinists, but a hoop or circular barrier man delineates through trial and error, blindly touching its arc and testing its limits (19, 24). Thanks to "Power" and "ethical action," the barrier never suffocates or oppresses. Instead, man's self-betterment grants enough space within its limits to lead a life of fulfillment and balance — also understood as ecological balance. In fact, Emerson's chief inquiry, "How shall I live?" remains broad enough throughout the essay to invite political, historiographical and environmental interpretations.

Emerson's shifting views on the relationship between the individual and society produced a redefinition of the parallel relationship between the individual and the environment. Earlier in his career, Emerson had found in nature's cycles of renewal and harmonious balance an optimal metaphor for man's inner divinity and innate goodness. In "NATURE" (1836) he affirmed, "In the woods is perpetual youth. Within these plantations of God, a decorum and sanctity reign, a perennial festival is dressed" (18). Nature is timeless, saintly, and harmonious, the same attributes Emerson saw in the benignant individual. From earthquakes to pandemics, "Fate's" catalogue of natural disasters signifies a profound departure from *Nature*'s Arcadian vision: "The diseases, the elements, fortune, gravity, lightning, respect no persons. The way of Providence is a little rude" (12). Ferocious and unpredictable environmental phenomena offer Emerson countless apocalyptic metaphors with which to illustrate man's vulnerability in the face of providence. However, facing the omnipresent possibility of environmental catastrophe, Emerson rejects both triumphalist arrogance and fatalistic despair; and in their place calls for responsibility and agency. Since "every jet of chaos that threatens to exterminate us, is convertible by intellect into wholesome force" (38), man needs to scrutinize nature and identify its mechanisms of causation in order to accommodate and even manage them. Emerson states:

> The annual slaughter from typhus far exceeds that of war; but right drainage destroys typhus. The plague in the sea-service from scurvy is healed by lemon juice and other diets portable or procurable: the depopulation by cholera and small-pox is ended by drainage and vaccination; and every other pest is not less in the chain of cause and effect, and may be fought off. And, whilst art draws out the venom, it commonly extorts some benefit from the vanquished enemy [32–33].

Our first and greatest responsibility is to change the way we look at nature and, then, to extract and put its "venoms" to positive use. "*NATURE*"'s most famous passage, describing the "transparent eyeball," epitomized both the work and its epoch: "I am nothing, I see all" (18). In "Fate" man is no longer a "transparent eyeball" but a visible "I," a historical actor who probes the environment looking for workable, human answers instead of attempting to unify it into an aesthetic and spiritual whole. Andrew McMurry sees Emerson at this point "diagnosing the complexity of the environment and our problematic interaction with it, starting with the question of observation" (McMurry 49). Man's gaze no longer encompasses the environment; instead, the environment, capricious and often cruel, encompasses man.

Thus Nature in "Fate" demands scientific scrutiny rather than, or in addition to, mystical reverie, and apocalyptic prospects animate this demand, as "the planet is liable to shocks from comets, perturbations from planets, rendings from earthquake and volcano, alterations of climate, precessions of equinoxes. Rivers dry up by opening of the forest. The sea changes its bed. Towns and counties fall into it" (7). "Fate" marks the emergence of Emerson's apocalyptic imagination, which will culminate in the famous maxim from "Works and Days" (1870): "No man has learned anything rightly, until he knows that every day is Doomsday" (157) (APOCALYPTIC FICTION). Commenting on the relevance of apocalyptic discourse in environmentalism, LAWRENCE BUELL notes that "to turn utopia into dystopia we need only deny the environment's malleability. If there are land-imposed limits to growth and resistance to human tampering, or if the environment can resist our control, then attempts to control it will produce the death or the revolt of nature" (Buell 308). Similarly, Emerson emphasizes the careful observation of nature in order to prevent thoughtless interaction with the environment, and its apocalyptic consequences. Moreover, were it not for the permanent threat of environmental collapse, man's "Power" would remain quiescent and rusty. In consequence, society would not know how to fight and overcome adversity. We need, then, an apocalyptic threat firmly rooted and operative in our imagination in order to prevent the real eschaton from happening.— Manuel Herrero-Puertas

BIBLIOGRAPHY

Buell, Lawrence. *The Environmental Imagination: Thoreau, Nature Writing, and the Formation of American Culture.* Cambridge, MA: Belknap Press of Harvard University Press, 1995.

Emerson, Ralph Waldo. *The Conduct of Life. The Complete Works of Ralph Waldo Emerson, with a Biographical Introduction and Notes.* Vol. 6. Centenary ed. Boston and New York: Houghton Mifflin, 1903.

_____. "Nature." *Selected Essays, Lectures, and Poems.* New York: Bantam Books, 1990.

_____. "Society and Solitude." *Twelve Chapters.* Boston: Fields Osgood, 1870.

McMurry, Andrew. *Environmental Renaissance: Emerson, Thoreau, and the Systems of Nature.* Athens: University of Georgia Press, 2003.

Robinson, David. *Emerson and the Conduct of Life: Pragmatism and Ethical Purpose in the Later Work.* Cambridge; New York: Cambridge University Press, 1993.

"Nature,"
Ralph Waldo Emerson (1836)

Emerson's "Nature," originally an essay but later published as his first and best-known book, served as a foundational document and profound inspiration for the American TRANSCENDENTALIST movement. With the passion and force of expression characteristic of Emerson's best writing, "Nature" challenged American culture to remake itself and revitalize its relationship with the natural world.

Divided into an introduction and eight chapters, "Nature," "Commodity," "Beauty," "Language," "Discipline," "Idealism," "Spirit," and "Prospects," the work begins with the seemingly dismissive yet provocative claim: "Our age is retrospective" (7). We soon realize that Emerson intends this statement as a scornful indictment of his culture. He challenges his readers to forget their tired habits of looking to the past for insight, and to look instead to present nature: "The foregoing generations beheld God and nature face to face; we, through their eyes. Why should not we also enjoy an original relation to the universe" (7)? The remainder of the essay is an exploration of this profound question and injunction,, and Emerson enthusiastically invites us to join in the inquiry: "Let us interrogate the great apparition, that shines so peacefully around us. Let us inquire, to what end is nature" (7)?

In chapter one, "Nature," Emerson argues that to truly inquire into "the values of nature" (8) or to seek an "original relation with the universe" (7), one must leave books, tradition, and society behind. Yet the reader need not leave the city to admire the stars. "Nature," which for Emerson includes the celestial sphere, may be available to a person in the city: "Seen in the streets of cities, how great [stars] are" (8)! "The stars awaken a certain reverence [...]; but all natural objects make a kindred impression, when the mind is open to their influence," Emerson suggests (9). If alert to nature's impressions, one may recognize the spiritual relationship or unity between natural objects and oneself. In what is certainly the most popular and best-known passage of the book — and indeed, of Transcendentalism itself— Emerson illustrates the perceptive mind's epiphanic interface with the natural world:

> Crossing a bare common, in snow puddles, at twilight, under a clouded sky, without having in my thoughts any occurrence of special good fortune, I have enjoyed a perfect exhilaration. [...] Standing on the bare ground, — my head bathed by the blithe air, and uplifted into infinite space, — all mean egotism vanishes. I become a transparent eye-ball. I am nothing. I see all. The currents of the Universal Being circulate through me; I am part or particle of God [10].

Stripped of his small-minded attention to himself and to the facticity of the material world, the speaker suddenly experiences, in the midst of the town, a moment of divine insight. Here is no yawning chasm or sublime mountain pass, the typical terrain of the Romantic, spiritual encounter. On the contrary, Emerson's pantheistic sublime is omnipresent and diffused throughout the everyday world. In a heightened state of perception lost to or neglected by many adults, the speaker enjoys the "original relation to the universe" of which Emerson writes in the introduction. He shares, in the words of Robert Richardson, his own "primary, firsthand, authentic relation to things" (226). Immediate insight proves more compelling than any history or tradition of insight (Richardson 227).

Whereas in the introduction and "Nature" Emerson discusses the effects of nature on humankind more generally, he examines in the following four chapters the "parts" or facets of our relationship with the natural world; specifically, he considers in "Commodity," "Beauty," "Language," and "Discipline," "nature's "multitude of uses" to humankind (11). In "Commodity" Emerson sets forth the economic benefits of nature and those that appeal to the senses. These are "temporary" benefits, unlike the "ultimate" ones that provide "service to the soul" (11). Humankind puts these "natural benefactors" (11) into service, such as using steam to power boats or by building roads and bridges from the resources of the earth, in various combinations for "mercenary benefit" (12): "The field is at once his floor, his work-yard, his play-ground, his garden, and his bed" (11). But the love of the beauty of nature is a "nobler" pursuit: "Such is the constitution of all things, [...] that the primary forms, as the sky, the mountain, the tree, the animal, give us a delight *in and for themselves;* a pleasure arising from outline, color, motion, and grouping" ("Beauty" 12). These pleasures derive in part from the powers of light, which may make even the most "foul" object beautiful, and from the human eye itself, which is the "best of artists" (12). One may experience the beauty of nature through the "simple perception of natural forms" (12), but an even higher beauty may be seen in the fusion of human will and nature, as in heroic or virtuous acts committed in "a scene of great natural beauty" (13).

We learn in "Language" that nature serves humankind as a vehicle of thought, and Emerson enumerates three ways in which it does so. First, natural facts provide us with language. The words we use, he argues, can be traced to nature: "Every word which is used to express a moral or intellectual fact, if traced to its root, is found to be borrowed from some material appearance" (18). Next Emerson sets forth his doctrine of correspondence. Expounded first and primarily by Emanuel Swedenborg (1688–1772), the doctrine holds that each natural or material object corresponds to some truth in the spiritual or moral world. Emerson writes: "Every natural fact is a symbol of some spiritual fact. Every appearance in nature corresponds to some state of the mind, and that state of the mind can only be described by presenting that natural appearance as its picture" (18). As Barbara Packer notes, "The doctrine of 'correspondence' [...] offered hope that nature itself might be a storehouse of meanings more coherent and more universally accessible than Scripture" (Packer 48). If nature reveals spiritual truths, then the poet can approach nature as if it were a book, and the study of nature becomes an exercise in comprehending its analogies to human life and spirituality (19).

The final four chapters, "Discipline," "Idealism," "Spirit," and "Prospects," elaborate on many of the themes already surveyed. Although Emerson alludes to them in other chapters, he develops his ideas of the faculties of "Reason" and "Understanding" in chapter five, "Discipline." Many Transcendentalists believed that these two faculties comprise our fundamental means of knowing or relating to the world, and the meanings they accorded to the terms often differ from how we commonly use or understand them today. For Emerson, the faculty of Understanding "adds, divides, combines, measures" (23), and is associated with the senses. Our Understanding is what helps us negotiate everyday life, and relies on sensory data and empirical evidence to do so. Since our lives are a constant exercise in the lessons of the material world — "lessons of difference, of likeness, of order, of being and seeming, of progressive arrangement" (24) — nature itself becomes a discipline or a subject of study for the Understanding. Reason, on the other hand, translates these lessons into spiritual truths "by perceiving the analogy that marries Matter and Mind" (23). The faculty of Reason is what allows the speaker to apprehend the "currents of the Universal Being" (10) on a bare common, or share an "original relation to the universe" while admiring the stars. It reconciles the dualism of matter and spirit, body and mind.

In chapter six, "Idealism," Emerson questions whether the natural world actually exists as an absolute fact, or whether it is instead only an expression of spirit. He acknowledges that we naturally resist such a notion, trusting instead to our sensory understanding of the material world. But he concludes in "Idealism" that as our Reason becomes stimulated, by seeing the world in new ways, through the powers of the poet or philosopher, or through the study of religion and ethics, we may begin to see through the veil of materiality to the essence of spirit: "If the Reason be stimulated to more earnest vision, outlines and surfaces become transparent, and are no longer seen; causes and spirits are seen through them" (30).

Emerson explains in "Spirit" that nature is the "organ" (37) through which the universal being speaks to the individual. Nature emanates through and out of us: "Therefore, that spirit, that is, the Supreme Being, does not build up nature around us, but puts it forth through us, as the life of the tree puts forth new branches and leaves through the pores of the old" (38). Humankind, however, has become alienated from nature as from God, and remains in a fallen or degenerated state. In this sense, Emerson's figuration closely resembles the Christian tradition of man's expulsion from Eden (THE BIBLE). In the final chapter, "Prospects," Emerson considers how we might again begin to know nature, redeem our souls, and resume our power as creators of our world. Citing what "a certain poet" sang to him about "some traditions of man and nature" (41), Emerson suggests that we have degenerated ("A man is a god in ruins" (42)) to the point that we no longer recognize ourselves as the spiritual fountainhead of nature.

Today man works on the world with his "Understanding" only, putting it to minor uses, rather than with his "Reason" as well. If we applied our "entire force" upon nature we might accomplish acts like the "traditions of miracles in the earliest antiquity of all nations; the history of Jesus Christ; the achievements of a principle, as in religious and political revolutions, and in the abolition of the Slave-trade" (43). Emerson reiterates here the introduction's claim that we too, like those in ages past, might again behold "God and nature face to face" (7). If we can learn to see nature's "roots in the faculties and affections of the mind" (44) and regain thereby our divine vitality, we might ultimately and benignantly reshape our world.— Todd Goddard

BIBLIOGRAPHY

Cameron, Kenneth Walter. *Emerson's Prose Poem: The Structure and Meaning of* Nature (1836). Hartford: Transcendental Books, 1988.

Emerson, Ralph Waldo. *The Collected Works of Ralph Waldo Emerson*. Edited by R. Spiller, A. Ferguson, et al. Cambridge: Harvard University Press, 1971–.

McKusick, James C. *Green Writing: Romanticism and Ecology*. New York: St. Martin's Press, 2000.

McMurry, Andrew. *Environmental Renaissance: Emerson, Thoreau, and the Systems of Nature*. Athens: University of Georgia Press, 2003.

Packer, Barber L. *The Transcendentalists*. Athens: University of Georgia Press, 2007.

Richardson, Robert D., Jr. *Emerson: The Mind on Fire*. Berkeley: University of California Press, 1995.

Sealts, Merton M., and Alfred R. Ferguson, eds. *Emerson's "Nature": Origin, Growth, Meaning*. 2nd ed. Carbondale: Southern Illinois University Press, 1979.

"Self-Reliance," Ralph Waldo Emerson (1841)

Regarded as a landmark text in American literary and environmental history, "Self-Reliance" has become one of America's most recognized and quoted works of literature. Since its publication in *Essays: First Series*, it has encouraged generations of Americans to break with traditions in order to discover their own authentic mode of being. James C. McKusick writes that his "emphasis on the primacy of individual experience [...] is one of the most vital and recurrent themes in Emerson's writing, and it provided inspiration to numerous American writers in the Transcendentalist tradition, from Henry David Thoreau and Walt Whitman to John Muir and Mary Austin" (114).

Although himself considered one of America's great environmental authors, Emerson's oeuvre evinces a complicated and unstable relationship to the natural world. "Self-Reliance," on its part, attempts to negotiate a space for individuality within the increasingly complex environmental and social systems of 19th-century America, arguing that "Whoso would be a man must be a nonconformist" (122), in an effort to unseat the intellectual traditions that divorce individuals from their intrinsic connection with Nature.

This, however, would prove no easy task. With a conception of Nature that often seems as grand and complicated as nature itself, Emerson had a difficult time maintaining consistent definitions throughout his vast body of work. At times he conceives of Nature as that portion of the environment which exists beyond and, in a sense, in contradistinction to human activity, a sublime entity somehow always beyond the comprehension of our rational mind. While Emerson sees this transcendent force as a positive source of inspiration, the belief that there is a fundamental distinction between humans and the natural world has invited charges of anthropocentrism. Max Oelschlaeger, for example, writes that

"For Emerson consciousness is nothing more than a vehicle to carry him toward a pre-existing conclusion. 'Nature' is not a philosophical inquiry but a literary exercise designed to rest a pre-established belief in God on rational, rather than scriptural, footing. The conceptual focal point is the human soul and God, not nature or the wilderness" (173). Critics have faulted Emerson with over-emphasizing the role of human consciousness in creating natural hierarchies, and much of what Emerson seeks to accomplish in "Self-Reliance" concerns itself with how individuals may reach the divine through their interactions with Nature. Indeed, he asserts that for the self-reliant individual, both works of art and natural scenes are equally "suitors for his notice, petitioners to his faculties that they will come out and take possession. The picture waits for my verdict: it is not to command me, but I am to settle its claims to praise."

Yet, at other times Nature appears as an all-encompassing unity that connects each human soul to both the physical world and the divine realm: "This is the ultimate fact which we so quickly reach on this, as on every topic, the resolution of all into the ever-blessed ONE." In this sense humans cannot help but be encompassed by and subject to the natural processes that guide all other forces on earth. Emerson continues, "We first share the life by which things exist, and afterwards see them as appearances in nature, and forget that we have shared their causes. Here is the fountain of action and of thought. Here are the lungs of that inspiration which giveth man wisdom, and which cannot be denied without impiety and atheism."

Claims of anthropocentrism rely on Emerson's interpretation of Nature as a means to achieve a predetermined and human-centered end, but recent critics rarely give him credit for the extent to which "Self-Reliance" advances the position of an environmentally progressive *mode of life*. To live self-reliantly is to challenge the dominant mode of contemporary American life — a life Emerson saw as overwrought with consumerism and unchecked patriotic fervor. In stressing the common origins of both humanity and the natural world, he suggests that self-reliant, morally responsible behavior both fosters and serves the common interests of all beings within the ecosystem. And in this sense Emerson's vision would prove prophetic. His belief in the interconnectedness of all things dominates current debate about climate change and human consumption, and points to a heightened sense of human accountability toward the environment.

Even without a precise definition of Nature, "Self-Reliance" is clearly an attempt to assert one's individuality in opposition to disingenuous, external influences. Paradoxically, Emerson perceives human society — an amalgamation of individuals — as limiting the intrinsic goodness and welfare of the individual: "when the unintelligent brute force that lies at the bottom of society is made to growl and mow, it needs the habit of magnanimity and religion to treat it doglike as a trifle of no concernment." Emerson's concern with such intrinsic, natural forces — both societal and individual — permeates "Self-Reliance." He asks his readers to be fluid in their judgment, and to embrace their own changing temperaments: "Speak what you think now in hard words, and to-morrow speak what to-morrow thinks in hard words again, though it contradict everything you said to-day" (125). Indeed, Emerson predicts some of the advances Charles Darwin would make a few decades later, claiming that "Power is in nature the essential measure of right. Nature suffers nothing to remain in her kingdoms which cannot help itself. The genesis and maturation of a planet, its poise and orbit, the bended tree recovering itself from the strong wind, the vital resources of every animal and vegetable, are demonstrations of the self-sufficing, and therefore self-relying soul" (130). With human experience so often tainted by (typically religious or political) institutions that claim to understand Nature through adherence to ancient traditions and dogma, Emerson celebrated these "vital resources" and their unique capacity to aid humankind in maintaining contact with its divine origins in nature.

So great are such convictions on Emerson's part, that despite his reverence for the natural world, the author of "Self-Reliance" would most probably have objected to being called an "environmentalist," and avoided associating with current conservation groups like Greenpeace, People for the Ethical Treatment of Animals, and the World Wildlife Foundation. For Emerson was notoriously suspicious of organized movements, even those championing causes with which he empathized. Famously opposed to collective action, he wrote that "an institution is the lengthened shadow of one man" (126). If "Self-Reliance" has an overtly political message, it is surely that we be wary of politics, respecting instead, and bravely embracing in our political lives, those "vital resources" of the individual alone, provided him and sanctioned by Nature. — Chris Findeisen

BIBLIOGRAPHY

Emerson, Ralph Waldo. "Self-Reliance." *Emerson's Prose and Poetry*. New York: Norton, 2001. 120–136.
McKusick, James C. *Green Writing: Romanticism and Ecology*. New York: St. Martin's Press, 2000.
Oelschlaeger, Max. *The Idea of Wilderness: From Prehistory to the Age of Ecology*. New Haven: Yale University Press, 1993.

The Uses of Natural History, Ralph Waldo Emerson (1833–1835)

Ralph Waldo Emerson's "The Uses of Natural History" is the first lecture that reflects Emerson's vocational change from Unitarian minister to public lecturer and naturalist following his eight-month tour of Europe, which included his inspirational visit to the Garden of Plants in Paris (Richardson 97). Emerson read the lecture twice: first in 1833 in Boston, and second in 1835 in Lowell, Massachusetts (Bosco and Myerson 1). The lecture is structured as a defense of the study of natural history, outlining five "advantages" to be gained from the scientific study of nature (Emerson 5, 15). More importantly, the lecture expresses Emerson's vision of the natural world, his perspective of "the relational nature of all things in the universe" and of the environment as "large and thoroughly organic" (Bosco and Myerson 1), themes which are reiterated and expanded on throughout the rest of Emerson's literary oeuvre.

Emerson is profoundly aware of human dependence upon the natural environment. He explains that "it is the earth itself" that makes "the raw material[s]" out of which all of the necessities required for human existence are found and formed: "food, clothing, [and] fuel" (6). The division of labor removes "each process so far out of sight" that human beings are in danger of forgetting their fundamental dependence upon nature's "raw material[s]," so Emerson reminds his audience that "iron came out of a mine, and perfume out of a cat... The water you drink was pumped from a well" (6). He expands upon this theme in "Commodity," the first chapter of "NATURE" (1836), once again considering humanity's relationship with and dependence upon the material world (Richardson 99).

In addition to recognizing that humans rely on their environment, Emerson believes that human health requires regular "habits of conversation with nature" (5). He draws from the ancient Greek fable of the giant Antaeus, who, when he wrestled with Hercules drew strength and found renewal "every time he touched his mother earth" (5). Emerson claims that human beings are like Antaeus, "broken giant[s]" who "in all of [their] weakness" are "invigorated by touching [their] mother earth," or by spending time in and around the natural sphere (5). He criticizes "the bad air, and artificial life of cities," stating "it is good for the body ... to be sent out into the fresh and fragrant fields, and there employed in the laws of the creation" (5). Here Emerson comments on the artificiality of modern life and the negative effects of technological progress, such as pollution.

Emerson also perceives human beings as part of, rather than set apart from, nonhuman nature. This is especially apparent in the description of his visit to the collection of comparative anatomy at the Garden of Plants in Paris. When Emerson views "a perfect series from the skeleton of the *balaena* ... to the upright form and highly developed skull of the Caucasian race of man" (4), he expresses his "singular conviction" regarding the essential unity, the "strange sympathies," between man and nature: "that not a form so grotesque, so savage, or so beautiful, but is an expression of something in man the observer. We feel an occult relation between the very worm, the crawling scorpion, and man" (5). Later in the lecture he similarly posits the existence of a "secret sympathy which connects man to all the animate and to all the inanimate beings around him" (15–16). As LAWRENCE BUELL explains, one of the principal reasons for the traditional hierarchical boundaries between human and nonhuman nature giving way in the nineteenth century is found in the recurring appeals to natural history, the study of which "put nonhuman species and communities on the same footing as the human" (186). Emerson's awareness of the physical similarities between human and nonhuman life forms leads him to situate human beings more holistically within the natural environment.

Indeed, for Emerson, the scientific observation of nature opens up a world of knowledge, knowledge that, in turn, evokes respect for the intrinsic worth of the environment: "Every fact that is disclosed to us in natural history removes one scale more from the eye; makes the face of nature around us so much more significant" (8). Through the scientific study of nature, the individual becomes aware of the way that the earth provides "for human wants" through natural processes that often require "ages for ... completion" (10). The accumulation of "vast beds of fuel" or coal, for instance, is "a great work of Nature in an antiquity that hath no record," but which "contribute[s] to our pleasure and prosperity" in the present (10). Furthermore, knowledge of a natural object or being will "take away the sense of deformity; for, every thing is a monster till we know what it is for" (11). Emerson offers the lobster as an example, explaining that the creature is "monstrous" until it is understood (11). Emerson values scientific knowledge of nature because he believes that it enables human beings to perceive the inherent worth and significance of every living thing.

Indeed, it is, in large part, Emerson's interest and enthusiasm for science that enables his environmental awareness (Richardson 99; Rossi 103). Robert Richardson, who summarizes the conclusion of modern historian Dirk Struik, explains that "Emerson's warm interest in science — his hospitable openness to it — was itself a real contribution, because it helped to create an intellectual atmosphere in which there was no necessary gulf between science and the humanities" (99). The combination of these two discourses — the sciences and the humanities — is apparent as Emerson describes his own visit to the "celebrated Repository of Natural Curiosities, the Garden of Plants in Paris" (Emerson 2). He uses poetic language to describe "the mountain and morass and prairie and jungle," the zoo, where "you walk among animals of every country," and the "botanical cabinet ... where grows a grammar of botany" (2, 3). In contrast to other portions of the lecture, in which Emerson engages the factual, objective discourse of science, here he portrays the "feelings" that his trip "excited in [him]" (2). "The house of stuffed birds fill[s] the mind with calm and genial thought" and "the eye is satisfied with seeing and strange thoughts are stirred as you see more surprising things than were known to exist" (3–4). Emerson's ability to blur the boundaries between objective and subjective experiences of nature resonates with contemporary ecological discourses that, according to Joy Palmer, "do not rely totally on ecological science for their conclusions," but also "value emotional and intuitive knowledge" (86). Emerson recognizes, as Richardson observes, that "what the sciences and the humanities have in common ... is a perennial interest in nature," and this may be his most distinctive bequest to American environmental literature (99).— Laura E. Ralph

BIBLIOGRAPHY

Bosco, Ronald A., and Joel Myerson, eds. *The Selected Lectures of Ralph Waldo Emerson*. Athens: University of Georgia Press, 2005.

Buell, Lawrence. *The Environmental Imagination*. Cambridge: Belknap Press of Harvard, 1995.

Emerson, Ralph Waldo. "The Uses of Natural History." In *The Selected Lectures of Ralph Waldo Emerson*. Athens: University of Georgia Press, 2005.

Palmer, Joy. *Environmental Education in the 21st Century: Theory, Practice, Progress and Promise*. London: Routledge, 1998.

Richardson, Robert D., Jr. "Emerson and Nature." In *The Cambridge Companion to Ralph Waldo Emerson*. Cambridge: Cambridge University Press, 1999.

Rossi, William. "Emerson, Nature, and Natural Science." In *A Historical Guide to Ralph Waldo Emerson*. New York: Oxford University Press, 2000.

Erdrich, Louise (1954–)

(Karen) Louise Erdrich was born in 1954, in Little Falls, Minnesota, and grew up in Wahpeton, North Dakota, where her German-American father and her French-Ojibwe mother worked for the Bureau of Indian Affairs. Erdrich earned a BA from Dartmouth College in 1976 and a Masters degree in the Johns Hopkins writing workshop in 1979. Upon her return to Dartmouth as writer-in-residence, she met again with her former professor and friend Michael Dorris. The couple got married in 1981 and became one of the most famous literary couples in the USA, yet in 1996 they filed for divorce, and on April 10, 1997, Dorris took his own life. Today, Louise Erdrich lives in the Twin Cities, Minnesota, and owns the independent bookstore *Birchbark Books*. She is an enrolled member of the Turtle Mountain Band of Chippewa.

Erdrich's numerous novels represent the interconnectedness of writing, life, family and place. With their focus on community and culture as influenced by and interlocked with individual lives, Erdrich's novels differ from those of the Native American Renaissance, with which she is associated. Her characters are compelling and curiously contradictory, yet they are no "ecological Indians," neither noble nor doomed. As survivors of warfare, harrowing epidemics or deceit, they reveal a profound if subtle environmental awareness in the close connection between individual, community and the land inhabited. Protagonists are interconnected, tied up in relationships that are as passionate as fragile, multifaceted and calamitous. Erdrich does not center her stories on nature, or create a separate place for the environment. In the interwoven stories, all life forms — animals, plants or humans, cultures, genders — are respected and valued. The Ojibwe belief system offers equal reverence for inanimate as much as animate beings and considers transfiguration between animals and humans possible. Resting on these beliefs, Erdrich's stories render the interplay between individual, community and environment, as the most important dynamic, often in stark contrast to human interests.

The value of diversity is expressed not only in the contents of the novel, but also in its narrative mode. Several narrators recount their stories and highlight different perspectives on the world. Individual voices inevitably comment on, contradict, complement and, thereby, interweave with each other's testimony. Hence the juxtaposed stories merge into a larger, organic and ever-unfolding picture of the contested landscapes and multi-ethnic peoples of North Dakota. Individual, communal, cultural and environmental interests cannot be discussed in isolation from each other. They are bonded together in Erdrich's fictional communities, the location where environmental awareness can most effectively be pursued; with the added benefit of strengthening ties, the disruption of which triggered social and environmental disasters in the first place.— Uwe Küchler

BIBLIOGRAPHY

Adamson, Joni. *American Indian Literature, Environmental Justice, and Ecocriticism: The Middle Place*. Tucson: University of Arizona Press, 2001.

Beidler, Peter G. "'The Earth Itself Was Sobbing': Madness and the Environment in Novels by Leslie Marmon Silko and Louise Erdrich." *American Indian Culture and Research Journal* 26. 3 (2002):113–124.

Castor, Laura. 2004. "Ecological Politics and Comic Redemption in Louise Erdrich's *The Antelope Wife*." *NordLit* 15 (2004):121–33.

Jacobs, Connie A. *The Novels of Louise Erdrich: Stories of Her People*. New York: Peter Lang, 2001.

Sarris, Greg, Connie A. Jacobs, and James Richard Giles. *Approaches to Teaching the Works of Louise Erdrich*. New York: Modern Language Association of America, 2004.

Sawhney, Brajesh. *Studies in the Literary Achievement of Louise Erdrich*. Lewiston, NY: Edwin Mellen Press, 2008.

Love Medicine,
Louise Erdrich (1993)

Louise Erdrich's first novel, *Love Medicine* (originally published in 1984, revised and expanded for republication in 1993), chronicles the lives of the Kashpaws and Lamartines, two families living on a Chippewa reservation in North Dakota. The novel spans three generations and the years 1934–84. Considered by some to be more a collection of short stories, the narratives begun in *Love Medicine* are revisited in many of Erdrich's later works such as *The Beet Queen* (1986), *Tracks* (1988), and *The Bingo Palace* (1994). As the tale is told from multiple points of view, and repeatedly circles back to previous events, the ultimate "truth" of the novel is difficult to pin down. This multiplicity of meaning and voice (and even of genre, as both novel and not novel) is in keeping with what Rita Ferrari considers "the fluidity of identity that has come to epitomize so much postmodern self-conception" (Ferrari 146–147). It is also, perhaps, in keeping with Erdrich's own fluid identity as a German-American Chippewa.

Love Medicine strongly suggests that the white world has done little more than defile the more worthwhile, more authentic, Indian way of life; but what is perhaps most striking about this text is the many subtle ways that borders get crossed and traditions intermingle throughout the novel. The multiple narrators, from varied cultural backgrounds and representing three generations, are an obvious example of this. As Ferrari notes, "Erdrich employs a narrative technique that dissolves the boundaries between the seen and the unseen, fact and fiction, memory and event" (Ferrari 146). Boundaries are questioned, and even erased, in myriad other ways in the novel.

In a literal sense, border crossing would seem to suggest physical places and actual land. While stewardship of the environment, or even connection to the land, is not an overt focus of this novel, it undergirds actions and motives throughout, as connection to land is often presented as a more tangible expression of connection to place. Since most of the characters in the novel are Native American, here placement is often painfully linked to *dis*placement and dispossession. Even the reservation that is home to the Kashpaws and Lamartines is not their true ancestral home, but has instead been "allotted" to them by the U.S. government. As one character notes, "[t]he policy of allotment was a joke. As I was driving toward the land, looking around, I saw as usual how much of the reservation was sold to whites and lost forever" (12). Whether or not the land originally "belonged" to them, they have lived on it for generations, and it has become sacred to them; leaving it is akin to leaving family, and self, behind.

The power of home and place, and the danger to one's spirit if it is forsaken, is seen early in the novel in the character of June. Although she dies at the end of the first chapter of the book, memories of her connect the other characters and drive the action of the work forward. In her death scene, as well as in the final lines of the novel when Lipsha is "bring[ing] her home," Erdrich presents some of the most significant border crossings, and explicit connections of humanity and environment, to be found anywhere in her work. In these moments June moves back across the land from the cities of the modern, white world, toward her home on the reservation.

In a further instance of blending and border crossing, Erdrich combines Christian and traditional Chippewa imagery. June walks over snow "like water," and is as fragile as the Easter eggs she has been eating. The use of water recalls not merely the novel's many resonant Biblical references (themselves often focused on crossings — the Red Sea, in the Jews' liberation from Egyptian bondage; the Jordan, into the "promised land"—THE BIBLE), but also evokes a seminal Chippewa tradition; at one point, Lipsha muses on the past existence of the great and "ancient ocean [...] that once had covered the Dakotas and solved all our problems" (367). Moreover, the linking of June's death to water (in Chippewa tradition, the novel tells us, drowning condemns the soul to eternal wandering); and the way that June figuratively haunts the novel and all its characters, suggest that June's death is a kind of metaphorical drowning that condemns her to wander (again echoed in the Jews' 40 years of wandering in the desert after crossing the Red Sea, and before the ultimate crossing of the Jordan). Although she is confident in her course and in her ability to find her way home in the dark and cold, she misjudges the vastness of the distance she must cross. At last her body collapses and is blanketed in snow, but her spirit moves on.

The use of water, here and throughout the novel, is suggestive of both life and death; and Michael D. Wilson further argues that "[t]his image of water foreshadows many instances of tension in the novel between life above the water and those elements below the surface — elements such as the older traditions, the past, or even a willingness to immerse oneself in love for another" (Wilson 123). An example of this kind of immersion and its symbolic connection of water and land, human and environment, can be found in Lulu Nanapush and Moses Pillager's love affair, described in "The Island" chapter. Lulu moves away from her own home and crosses over to be with Moses on an island that "was small and dark and at the center of a wide irritation of silver water" (73). Once on the island, Lulu sinks into an almost elemental kind of existence, thinking only of food, shelter, love for Moses, and nurturing the child that she is carrying. But if the effect of the place on her is powerful and life-changing, the impact on Moses is equally profound: "he was his island [...] he did not exist from the inside out but from the outside in" (83). In these scenes, as frequently throughout the novel, Erdrich literally identifies her characters with the natural elements that surround them. In this way, she suggests that conventional ways of thinking about humanity and the environment as separate entities are limiting, and ultimately threatening to the well-being of both.

Although Erdrich fashions a narrative in which borders are often crossed, and dividing lines — between faiths, families, and truth itself — are often blurred, the psychological and physical results of moving away from the land and thus the traditions that one knows is often hugely damaging. June, Henry Jr., and Nector all seem to suffer psychologically from having involved themselves too much with the white world. Even Marie, who resists being considered Indian for most of her life, realizes in her old age that there is no solace for her in Catholicism or white culture: "Since she had lived among other old people at the Senior Citizens, Marie had started speaking the old language, falling back through time to the words that Lazarres had used among themselves, [...] having seen the new, the Catholic, the Bureau, fail her children, having known how comfortless words of English sounded in her ears" (263).

Throughout the novel, Erdrich simultaneously condemns the inauthentic — Lyman's Tomahawk Factory, Lipsha's store-bought, frozen turkey hearts, Hollywood's portrayal of "Indians," the painting *Plunge of the Brave* — and questions the whole notion of authenticity itself, when human society wanders from the environment that has informed and inspired it. What ultimately unifies and gives meaning to a family is not necessarily its blood-relations; and what makes one "Indian" is not necessarily determined by one's ancestry. As Karla Sanders aptly notes, "[t]he ambivalence created in this attempted reconciliation underscores the difficulty faced by Erdrich's characters in reaching a balance between spheres of past and present, personal and communal, private and public" (Sanders 129). If a general thematic focus can be discerned in this sprawling and heterogeneous work, it may be found in this struggle for an elusive sense of connection and balance between the protagonists' Native American heritage and the white world that so many of the characters seem to be searching for. But just how to find this balance, this "natural" or "real" way of being, is never declared by Erdrich, leaving one to wonder if perhaps it may lie in the *interstices*, both of the narrative and of our lives; not in any one place or way of life, but in the *crossing* between them. — Uwe Küchler

BIBLIOGRAPHY

Erdrich, Louise. *Love Medicine: New and Expanded Edition.* New York: Harper Perennial, 1993.
Ferrari, Rita. "'Where the Maps Stopped': The Aesthetics of Borders in Louise Erdrich's *Love Medicine* and *Tracks*." *Style* 33 (1999): 144–165.
Sanders, Karla. "A Healthy Balance: Religion, Identity, and Community in Louise Erdrich's *Love Medicine*." *MELUS* 23 (1998): 129–155.
Wilson, Michael D. *Writing Home: Indigenous Narratives of Resistance.* East Lansing: Michigan State University Press, 2008.

Farnham, Eliza Wood (1815–1864)

Although absent from the central canon of American literature, Eliza Wood Farnham was a significant TRANSCENDENTALIST in the tradition of EMERSON, BRYANT and FULLER; a leading social reformer and feminist, counting both Margaret Fuller and Elizabeth Cady Stanton as close associates (Hallwas xxvii); and one of America's first and most important environmental writers. Experiencing the early settlement of Illinois and California, Farnham is best known for her travel and nature writing in LIFE IN PRAIRIE LAND (1848), composed of engaging and philosophical encounters with the prairie and American frontier, and *California, Indoors and Out* (1856).

Farnham accompanied her sister to Groveland, Illinois, during the territory's settlement in 1835. Meeting and marrying Thomas Jefferson Farnham in 1836, Eliza was left alone in 1839 when he departed for Oregon on business until his return two years later (Hallwas xvii). *Life in Prairie Land* details her travels in Illinois from 1835 to 1840, and weaves together local realism, popular travel literature, and a romantic response to nature through evocative descriptions of the prairie. Farnham's reflections on her interactions with the frontier environment suggest a transcendental perception of the physical world as a means of comprehending the spiritual.

Farnham traveled by riverboat, stagecoach, wagon, and horseback, critically — and with a woman's eye — observing both the environment, and a variety of settlers from educated Easterners to rough "Hoosiers" and Illinois "Spunkers," and from honest, hospitable farmers to disreputable "stage-house" landlords and horse thieves. Throughout her journey she juxtaposes aspects of nature with humans and their settlements, suggesting that Nature itself inscribes humanity's best and worst characteristics. Individual human tragedy and loss are seen as part of a broader phenomenon, one both natural and sublime. Nature's sequence of death and renewal even shapes the inevitability of the westward movement itself: in her conclusion to *Life in Prairie Land* Farnham asserts that the "free plains and far-reaching streams shall be the theatre of a power and intelligence never yet witnessed!" (269).

After her husband's death in California in 1848, Farnham settled in Santa Cruz where she built her own home, farmed, taught school, married and divorced an abusive husband, and wrote the first book about California authored by a woman. Her personal experiences contributed to a shift in her writing, from youthful idealism associated with Nature to stronger political and social criticism. *California, Indoors and Out* critically assesses Californian society and culture, especially with respect to women's issues. During the Civil War, Farnham served with Dorothea Dix as a volunteer nurse at Gettysburg, where she contracted tuberculosis that led to her death in 1864. Despite her short life and limited output, however, Farnham's direct and sensitive embrace of frontier experience, and her abiding sense of the interdependence of the physical, spiritual and moral realms, both illustrate the progressive environmental currents of her time, and anticipate fundamental elements of the ecofeminism that was yet to come. — Thomas P. Fair

BIBLIOGRAPHY

Farnham, Eliza Wood. *Life in Prairie Land*. 1848. Chicago: University of Illinois Press, 2003.
Georgi-Findlay, Brigitte. *The Frontiers of Women's Writing: Women's Narratives and the Rhetoric of Westward Expansion*. Tucson: University of Arizona Press, 1996.
Hallwas, John. Introduction. *Life in Prairie Land*. By Eliza Farnham. Chicago: University of Illinois Press, 2003. xv–xxxi.

Life in Prairie Land, Eliza Farnham (1848)

Carving out an existence in the largely hostile environment of the nineteenth century American frontier would hardly seem conducive to applying the metaphysics found in EMERSON's NATURE (Hallwas xxvi). Yet, blending the physical with the metaphysical, social activist and feminist Eliza Wood Farnham perceptively analyzes the complex forces shaping the frontier in her best-known work, *Life in Prairie Land*. Unlike popular tales of exploration and conquest, Farnham's narrative provides a distinctively TRANSCENDENTAL account of her encounter with the American prairie, as well as telling insights into the personal lives and social interactions of the settlers. The work details her travels in the Illinois Territory from 1835 to 1840, incorporating realistic vignettes of prairie life, descriptions of the territory's features, and a Romantic response to nature through an often Edenic perception of the prairie. Ultimately Farnham draws on her encounters with the frontier's natural forces to conceive of Nature as a manifestation of both the beautiful and the sublime.

In "Part One" of *Life in Prairie Land*, Farnham describes her journey from St. Louis to her sister's homestead near Groveland in the Illinois Territory. The narrative frequently alternates wry observations of rural conditions and human behavior with far-reaching meditations on the human condition, often metaphorized in natural terms. She humorously satirizes the rustic "Hoosiers" traveling with her, for example, and then contrasts them with the personified Mississippi and Missouri Rivers, those "messengers from the unvexed solitudes" whose "majestic union of powers [...] makes the ocean tremble" (11).

Embracing WILLIAM CULLEN BRYANT's transcendental concept of a guiding force in nature (Hallwas xxvi), Farnham reflects on the profundity of a prairie view: "Nature spoke to us in her own unequivocal language" (27). As THOREAU observed the infinite in the everyday at Walden, Farnham explores the grandeur of the American prairie and the West, but with a similar end: "Living much with nature, makes me wiser, better, purer, and therefore, happier" (134). She revives the timeworn metaphor of the Aeolian harp to describe the interplay between the prairie and her mind: "It yields no sound save the one which first arrested our attention, and this is uttered without ceasing" (45). Farnham associates Nature with the woman homesteader and employs imagery of the household to make connections between the seasonal development of the prairie and the development of a settler's homestead: "The prairie puts on its richest garb about the first of June [...] Nature, like a notable dame, has cleaned house in proper season, got her furniture and ornaments arranged, and now seated complacently in her easy chair, challenges the admiration of beholders." (47). Farnham likewise interprets Nature's duality of beauty and the abominable as a constant challenge to the settlers to cultivate self-discipline and nurture the beautiful, or fail and degenerate, both morally and physically.

The unexpected deaths of both her sister and her small son sorely tested Farnham's convictions of nature's ultimate benignity. Yet these very tragedies, combined with the severity of frontier life and Farnham's deep connection to the environment, led her to a transcendent intuition of nature's sympathy (162): "I no longer brooded in despairing silence over my sorrows. I felt there were infinite love and infinite pity in the divine Mind" (168).

"Part Two" expands the narrative's reach, both in natural and philosophical terms, as Farnham relates her further tours of the territory. Although finding renewal and inspiration in the natural beauty of birdsong, flowering trees, and glorious sunsets, she also embraces the violent extremes of nature as part of an awe-inspiring and complex whole. Visions of the overwhelming scope and devastation of a wild fire ("a sea of roaring flames as far as eye could reach [...] was too sublime a spectacle to turn away from" [155]) or the violence of a prairie storm and its lightning display ("till a mighty flash rends the pall and searches the very soul" [41]) epitomize her concept of the natural sublime. The irrationality of destruction and tragedy, especially in their juxtaposition with the beautiful in nature, become comprehensible when perceived as part of a greater metaphysical matrix, one balancing beauty with terror.

Farnham frequently reflects on the ennobling power of the unspoiled prairie, and describes the decline of the region's Native Americans in elegiac terms: "a race that has dwindled from the strong majesty of freedom, to humility and wasting feebleness" (226). In her very praise of Native American existence and love of the prairie, she asserts the inevitability of "the Indian standing in the attitude of the one who bids farewell" (226). Her descriptions of visible but abandoned pathways or the erosion that exposes ancient graves suggest that as nature's seasons and the land change over time so do the societies of men (227). Nature's cycle of death and renewal even shapes the inevitability of the movement west, as but one manifestation of the prairie's unceasing metamorphoses.

Farnham's concluding observations of Nature intimate an intelligent force at work, an almost Hegelian self-awareness, which encompasses human endeavor as part of a greater process. Thus, while she identifies with the early settlers and their shared appreciation for the prairie's splendor, and recognizes the disadvantages of further human development, she remains optimistic about the arrival of future settlers because of her belief in the positive spiritual influence of the wilderness itself (Georgi-Findlay 39). Ending with intimations of MANIFEST DESTINY, Farnham asserts that the "famishing legions of Europe may find room and abundance" (268) in the great expanse of the American prairie and that the "free plains and far-reaching streams shall be the theatre of a power and intelligence never yet witnessed!" (269).— Thomas P. Fair

BIBLIOGRAPHY

Farnham, Eliza Wood. *Life in Prairie Land*. 1848. Chicago: University of Illinois Press, 2003.
Georgi-Findlay, Brigitte. *The Frontiers of Women's Writing: Women's Narratives and the Rhetoric of Westward Expansion*. Tucson: University of Arizona Press, 1996.
Hallwas, John. Introduction. *Life in Prairie Land*. By Eliza Farnham. Chicago: University of Illinois Press, 2003. xv–xxxi.

Faulkner, William (1897–1962)

The defining moment of twentieth-century American literature — and certainly American literature of the environment — may well have come when William Faulkner realized, after the publication of his novel *Sartoris* (1929), that "my own little postage stamp of native soil was worth writing about and that I would never live long enough to exhaust it" (*Lion in the Garden*, 255). *Sartoris* was the first novel that Faulkner set in his fictional Yoknapatawpha County of rural, northwestern Mississippi, and set the stage for such later, groundbreaking works of fiction as *The Sound and the Fury* (1929), *As I Lay Dying* (1930), *Light in August* (1932), *Absalom, Absalom!* (1936), and *Go Down, Moses* (1942). These works share a commitment to exploring the socio-economic problems of the South after the Civil War, the numerous racial tensions that were a reality of post-war Mississippi, and the unique environment and ecology of this region of the United States. Though Faulkner published fiction until the end of his life, it is this group of Yoknapatawpha novels that many regard as his most important contribution, and the primary reason for his being awarded the Nobel Prize for literature in 1949.

William Cuthbert Falkner (he would later change the spelling to "Faulkner" in an effort to join the Royal Air Force in Canada during World War I) was born in 1897 in New Albany, Mississippi. Faulkner was named after his great-grandfather William Clark Falkner who was, among many other things, a colonel for the South during the Civil War, and who was killed in a duel eight years before Faulkner's birth. As a young child Faulkner's family moved to Oxford, Mississippi, so his father could find work. Faulkner would leave Oxford on numerous occasions, and sometimes for long periods of time — including extended trips to New York, New Orleans, Europe, and Hollywood — but he never failed to return his "postage stamp of native soil."

Though his work is universally esteemed today, Faulker's literary career was punctuated by many ups and downs. Following the end of World War I, Faulkner led a restless life that eventually saw him move to New Orleans to join Sherwood Anderson's literary circle. Later in life Faulkner and Anderson would have a well-documented parting of the ways, but the early support Faulkner received from the Winesburg, Ohio author went a long way in helping him to become a serious writer. During this time Faulkner published his first two novels, *Soldier's Pay* (1926) and *Mosquitoes* (1927). These works were soon followed by much of Faulkner's strongest writing, primarily his Yoknapatawpha novels. However, by the end of World War II Faulkner had faded from the public eye and was all but out of print, having published nothing major since 1942's *Go Down, Moses*. While his career was arguably at its lowest point, Faulkner's standing in the literary world was in part revitalized by the patronage of French philosopher and literary critic Jean-Paul Sartre.

Over the last decade considerable attention has been given to the role that nature, environment, and ecology play in Faulkner's novels, especially those set in Yoknapatawpha County. The prominent literary critic LAWRENCE BUELL has written that "Rarely does Faulkner's mature fiction fail to take shrewd account of southern modernization, especially its casualties and failures, in such a way as to connect people to landscape" (*Writing for an Endangered World*, 172). In general, the novel *Go Down, Moses* has received the most ecocritical attention, as it contains the wilderness cycle of Isaac McCaslin. In "The Old People," "THE BEAR," and "Delta Autumn" Faulkner follows Ike as he is taught the ways of the "big woods" by his Native American mentor Sam Fathers, participates in the hunting and eventual killing of the bear Old Ben, and laments the destruction of the old-growth forests of the Mississippi River Delta. Environmentally focused studies of Faulkner's other works are becoming more common, however, as contemporary topics of farm policy, deforestation, over-hunting, flood management, and ecological degradation appear time and again in works such as *As I Lay Dying, Absalom, Absalom!, If I Forget Thee, Jerusalem* (1939), *The Hamlet* (1940) and *Big Woods*

(1955). Though Faulkner never joined or explicitly spoke out for the environmental movement of his day — led by such figures as ALDO LEOPOLD and RACHEL CARSON — it is evident that the fictional environment he explored and immortalized in Yoknapatawpha County reflected many of the same ecological concerns and, given his immense success and prestige, helped as profoundly to shape the American environmental imagination. — Matt Low

BIBLIOGRAPHY

Buell, Lawrence. *Writing for an Endangered World: Literature, Culture, and the Environment in U.S. and Beyond.* Cambridge, MA: Harvard University Press, 2001.

Faulkner and the Ecology of the South. Eds. Joseph R. Urgo and Ann J. Abadie. Jackson: University Press of Mississippi, 2005.

Faulkner and the Natural World. Eds. Donald M. Kartiganer and Ann J. Abadie. Jackson: University Press of Mississippi, 1996.

Lion in the Garden: Interviews with William Faulkner, 1926–1962. Eds. James B. Meriwether and Michael Milgate. New York: Random House, 1968.

Padget, John B. "William Faulkner." *The Mississippi Writer's Page.* 11 Nov. 2008. The University of Mississippi English Department. Accessed March 9, 2009. http://www.olemiss.edu/mwp/dir/faulkner_william/.

"The Bear," William Faulkner (1942)

One of Faulkner's most anthologized works, the novella "The Bear" was first published in *Go Down, Moses* (1942), a collection of seven related pieces of short fiction that ecocritic Bart Welling describes as "a rich demonstration of Southern modernist nature writing" (473). Like the other stories in *Moses*, "The Bear" centers on Isaac "Ike" McCaslin, detailing his coming-of-age as a woodsman and hunter (from age 10 to 21) and his ultimate refusal to inherit his family's plantation.

"The Bear" takes place in Faulkner's fictional Yoknapatawpha County, from 1877 to about 1890, a self-contained environment mimicking the geography and demographics of late-nineteenth century Mississippi, with its area and inhabitants acting as environmental and social microcosms of the American South after Reconstruction. The novella is divided into five chapters, four of which are set in Big Bottom — "a wilderness of gum, cypress, and oak trees" owned by Major Cassius De Spain (Fargnoli 20). This wilderness is the centerpiece for the story's environmental exposition and argument. It is the home of the bear "Old Ben," and the last remaining primal wilderness in Yoknapatawpha, "whose edges were being constantly gnawed at by men with plows and axes who feared it because it was wilderness" (185).

As the story opens, Ike is 16 and again joining the

annual hunt for Old Ben. For the hunters — in a vivid reminder of MELVILLE's white whale in MOBY DICK— Old Ben is a totemic animal of the woods, perhaps even of nature itself. Critic John Lyndenberg comments, "at the same time sacred, and dangerous or forbidden, [... Ben] is truly animistic, possessing a soul of his own, initiating action, not inert like other creatures of nature" (162). The aged and elusive bear is seemingly impervious to bullets, and has one paw mauled from a bear trap, recalling the scars on Moby Dick. Anticipating Santiago's reverence for the marlin in HEMINGWAY's THE OLD MAN AND THE SEA, Ike and his half–Indian mentor Sam Fathers revere Old Ben both for what he has survived and for what he represents: the timeless being and ways of the natural world.

Ike has a number of encounters with Old Ben. The first time he sees him face to face he is alone in the woods, having abandoned his gun, watch, and compass. He has undertaken "a condition in which ... all the ancient rules and balances of hunter and hunted had been abrogated"— he has returned to a natural state (198). Ben appears "not as big as he had dreamed it but as big as he had expected, bigger, dimensionless against the dappled obscurity" (200). Here the narrator, like the hunters, conflates the bear with the woods, and they are joined for a time in unity with Ike, who has (foreshadowing later events) set aside the trappings of civilization in favor of a simpler existence.

On a later hunt Ike has a chance to take a clear shot at Old Ben, but at the last moment leaps in to save the life of the fyce-dog he has used to corner the bear. Sam later trains the only hunting dog truly capable of hunting Old Ben. Lion is a vicious Airedale mix caught by Sam in Big Bottom. Boon Hogganbeck, an inept hunter who at one point misses five point-blank shots at Old Ben, takes to Lion and becomes his keeper until the day of the hunt that brings down the dog, the bear, and Sam Fathers. When Lion meets Old Ben, the bear fatally wounds him with one vicious swipe, moving Boon to leap upon his back, stabbing Old Ben and killing him. In the chase Sam Fathers collapses, dying a few days later. He and Lion are buried in Big Bottom. These events serve to strengthen the emotional and metaphysical bond between the wilderness (including the domesticated Lion), the bear, Sam Fathers, and Ike. More broadly, throughout the novella, Sam sees himself as approaching obsolescence in a way that mirrors Big Bottom. Having nurtured Ike to become an exceptional woodsman, and with Old Ben now gone, his usefulness has passed, and his death marks the end of an era in Yoknapatawpha — a fact made clear in the story's closing section.

This last section offers the novella's most explicit criticism of the modern world's desecration of the natural landscape of rural Mississippi. Two years after the death of Old Ben, Ike "went back to the camp one more time before the lumber company moved in and began to cut the timber" (301). Major de Spain has sold the cutting rights of Big Bottom as the railroads steadily encroach upon the places Old Ben once roamed. Ike visits the graves of Lion and Sam Fathers, who he imagines as "not held fast in earth but free in earth and not in earth but of earth ... dark and dawn and dark and dawn again in their immutable progression and, being myriad, one: and Old Ben, too" (313). In the closing scene, he meets Boon Hogganbeck, who has trapped a group of squirrels but is trying to repair his rifle: "He didn't even look up to see who it was. Still hammering, he merely shouted back at the boy in a hoarse, strangled voice: 'Get out of here! Don't touch them! Don't touch a one! They're mine!'" (315).

Such ownership is, for Ike, one of the most abhorrent aspects of modern man's relationship to nature. None can own the land — not "any white man fatuous enough to believe he had bought any fragment of it ... [nor] Indian ruthless enough to pretend that any fragment of it had been his to convey" (183). In the novella's temporally disruptive fourth section Ike explains to his cousin Cass why he is repudiating his claim to the family plantation. Invoking evidence ranging from THE BIBLE to the McCaslin family ledger and the American Civil War, Ike states that not only does man have no right to claim land, but the Southern landowners are cursed by God as a punishment for enslaving the black race. He sees himself as fundamentally outside this struggle because "Sam Fathers set me free," by teaching him that he comes not from the tainted McCaslin blood, nor from the exploitive culture that has tainted it, but from the land itself (287).— Daniel E. Burke

BIBLIOGRAPHY

Faulkner, William. *Go Down, Moses.* New York: Vintage International, 1970.
Lyndenberg, John. "Nature Myth in Faulkner's the Bear." *Bear, Man, and God: Eight Approaches to William Faulkner's the Bear.* Ed. Francis Lee Utley, Lynn Z. Bloom, and Arthur F. Kinney. New York: Random House, 1964.
Welling, Bart. "A Meeting with Old Ben: Seeing and Writing Nature in Faulkner's *Go Down, Moses.*" *Mississippi Quarterly,* 55 (2002): 461–96.

Fitzgerald, F. Scott (1896–1940)

F. Scott Fitzgerald offers a challenge to environmental approaches to literature as his fiction focuses on navigating the perils of relationships and social class in predominantly urban and suburban environments. However, his memorable portraits of "flappers and philosophers" during the Jazz Age ultimately shed light on a new sense of cultural geography at the turn of the century, revealing how environments and individuals are shaped by cultural practices.

Francis Scott Key Fitzgerald was born in 1896 in St. Paul, Minnesota, to parents Edward and Mollie (McQuillan). The family connections to his namesake were distant (Francis Scott Key was Fitzgerald's second cousin, three times removed), and his parents name choice reflects a desire to create an ambitious legacy for their son. Edward was the president of the American Rattan and Willow Works, a St. Paul furniture company, which failed in 1898. The Fitzgerald family moved to Buffalo, New York, after Edward gained employment with Procter & Gamble as a wholesale grocery salesman. After a decade in sales, however, Edwards lost his job, and the Fitzgerald family returned to St. Paul in 1908, to live with Mollie's parents. The young Scott Fitzgerald saw his father's unemployment — and the family's subsequent financial struggles — as a crisis, one which permanently defeated his father's spirit and which would shape his own definitions of success and financial security. Due to his family's financial situation, Fitzgerald felt like an outsider while attending the St. Paul Academy. He was quickly labeled a "show off" due to his boasting and other antics, as he attempted to mitigate his outsider status. Fitzgerald was not without friends, however, and the social activities of his childhood — secret clubs, football, bob parties, and attempts to understand the mysteries of the opposite sex — would eventually provide material for his first novel, *This Side of Paradise* (1920).

Several of Fitzgerald's short stories explore the changes that occurred in the physical and cultural geography of American regions during the first few decades of the twentieth century. Edmund Wilson argues that "Fitzgerald is as much of the Middle West of large cities and country clubs as Sinclair Lewis is of the Middle West of the prairies and little towns" (32). In addition to *This Side of Paradise*, Fitzgerald's short stories "Bernice Bobs Her Hair" and "Winter Dreams" examine the romantic triumphs and defeats of young people as they navigate through a more prosperous Middle West. Fitzgerald taps into his experiences with Zelda in the South, and his own youthful fascination with his father's stories of the Civil War in Maryland, in his short story "The Ice Palace," which explores Southern graveyards and the St. Paul Winter Carnival through the eyes of Georgian Sally Carrol Happer and her Minnesotan fiancé Harry Bellamy. In "The Diamond as Big as the Ritz," Fitzgerald finds the isolated geography of the Far West a suitable location for a fantastic fable of a man corrupted by his attempts to protect the source of his outrageous wealth — a mountain-sized diamond. Although Fitzgerald's critique of the excesses of the 1920s is expressed most clearly in this last story, the regional places in many of his stories frame and inform optimism, bitter remorse, love, jealousy, and self-reflection.

Concepts of regionalism also inform *The Great Gatsby*, which is, according to narrator Nick Carraway, "a story of the West, after all" (184). Carraway's sense of regional determinism explicitly contrasts with titular character Jay Gatsby's attempts to remake himself in a fictionalized Long Island, in order to win back the love and affection of Daisy Buchanan. Matthew J. Bruccoli labels Fitzgerald's approach to place in *Gatsby* as impressionistic, as Fitzgerald uses language to express "the emotions associated with actual and fictional settings" (" The Text" 192). Many of the novel's places — the city ash heaps, Gatsby's lavish mansion, and Daisy Buchanan's dock — showcase Fitzgerald's emotional rendering of modern landscapes. These places represent LEO MARX's conception of "complex pastoralism," as Fitzgerald questions the idealization of place through juxtapositions of the ideal and the corrupt. The novel's concluding scene, Nick Carraway's imagining of the "fresh, green breast of the new world" that appeared before the eyes of Dutch sailors as they first arrived in the Americas, celebrates an idealized pastoral landscape while simultaneously dramatizing the disparity between such a landscape and the modern condition. — Kelsey Squire

BIBLIOGRAPHY

Bruccoli, Matthew J. *Some Sort of Epic Grandeur: The Life of F. Scott Fitzgerald.* 2nd revised edition. Columbia: University of South Carolina Press, 2002. Print.
_____. "The Text of *The Great Gatsby.*" *The Great Gatsby.* Ed. Matthew J. Bruccoli. New York: Simon & Schuster, 1995. 191–194. Print.
Fitzgerald, F. Scott. *The Great Gatsby.* Ed. Matthew J. Bruccoli. New York: Simon & Schuster, 1995. Print.
Marx, Leo. *The Machine in the Garden: Technology and the Pastoral Ideal in America.* London: Oxford University Press, 1964. Print.
Wilson, Edmund. "F. Scott Fitzgerald." *Literary Essays and Reviews of the 1920s and 30s.* New York: Library of America, 2007. 30–36. Print.

Foreman, David (1946–   )

Dave Foreman's youth illustrates a political reversal: born in 1946 in New Mexico, he grew up as a conservative Republican. After graduating from the University of New Mexico in 1968, he worked as the Southwest representative for the Wilderness Society throughout the 1970s, identifying as a moderate environmentalist. But over the course of the decade, he became persuaded that wealthy, powerful interests such as petrochemical, logging, and mining companies were blindly pursuing profits to the detriment of the environment (and therefore the future), and that government agencies were essentially complicit in this process. Environmentalist organizations like the Sierra Club seemed ill suited to the job of fighting this powerful and dangerous alliance.

So Foreman and a group of friends in 1980 founded EarthFirst! Philosophically drawing upon EDWARD ABBEY's THE MONKEY WRENCH GANG, EarthFirst! advocated sabotaging equipment like bulldozers, removing survey stakes, spiking trees, and other aggressive means to prevent the development (which they would call "loss") of America's remaining wilderness. Yet Foreman left EarthFirst! in 1990 to pursue other avenues of environmental activism, a transition he details in CONFESSIONS OF AN ECO-WAR-RIOR (1991).

Foreman has published several books and owns an environmentalist publishing house. He has served as editor of *Wild Earth* magazine and chair of the Wildlands Project. He has been arrested several times, and is generally regarded as a radical, inflammatory activist who inspires strong responses, whether in support or condemnation of his actions.

His major works include *Ecodefense: A Field Guide to Monkeywrenching* (1987), an ecotage how-to manual that he co-edited, which contends that ecotage aims to damage property, not harm people; but critics maintain that workers can easily be injured or killed by monkeywrenching, especially by shattered chainsaw blades from spiked trees. His 1991 *Confessions of an Eco-Warrior* is an autobiographical and philosophical treatise on monkeywrenching, and a meditation on the evolution of Foreman's own environmentalism. *Confessions* also presents a plan for managing remaining wilderness areas, advocating the preservation of wilderness *as* wilderness, empty of roads or amenities, unserved by rescue patrols, even uncharted on maps. Such areas would exist for rugged recreational purposes but also as preserves of wilderness for its own sake, testament to a non-anthropocentric worldview. Foreman's less famous works include *The Big Outside*, which he published with Howie Wolke in 1989; *Defending the Earth*, co-written with Murray Bookchin in 1991; and *The Lobo Outback Funeral Home* (2000). He has also contributed articles to anthologies about environmentalism and to environmental periodicals.

The theme for which Foreman's works are most noted is monkeywrenching, cited as evidence of his radicalism. Foreman is here indebted to Abbey's *The Monkey Wrench Gang*, although *Confessions* points out the long history of American civil disobedience

to which ecotage is heir. Whether reckless or sage, Foreman's controversial wilderness advocacy succeeds in drawing notice. Indeed, he is to environmental activism what Edward Abbey is to environmental literature — the rugged, renegade poet figure who inspires admiration, condemnation, praise and blame. For many, Foreman is *the* face of radical environmentalism and deep ecology in the United States. — Laura Boynton Johnson

BIBLIOGRAPHY

Archer, Jules. *To Save the Earth: The American Environmental Movement.* New York: Viking, 1998. Print.

Bookchin, Murray. *Defending the Earth: A Dialog Between Murray Bookchin and Dave Foreman.* Boston: South End Press, 1991. Print.

Davis, John, ed. *The EarthFirst! Reader: Ten Years of Radical Environmentalism.* Salt Lake City: Peregrine Smith Books, 1991. Print.

McDaniel, Carl. "Restoring Wildlands: Dave Foreman and Preserving Biodiversity." *Wisdom for a Livable Planet: The Visionary Work of Terri Swearingen, Dave Foreman, Wes Jackson, Helena Norbert-Hodge, Werner Fornos, Herman Daly, Stephen Schneider, and David Orr.* San Antonio: Trinity University Press, 2005. Print.

Confessions of an Eco-Warrior, Dave Foreman (1991)

Dave Foreman is perceived — and in such a case perception is half the truth — as a "a relentless and provocative advocate for preserving the American wilderness" (Paul 134), who "instructs by subverting the unquestioning, radicalizing the conventional and otherwise shaking things up" (Klockenbrink 16). It is certainly his reputation as subversive that has won Foreman international attention, beginning in 1980 when he co-founded EarthFirst! (THE CONSERVATION MOVEMENT). The activist organization was the political expression of Foreman's broader attempt to counter the joint interests of government and industry, whom he saw as colluding to forestall environmentalist progress. However, in 1990, having earned himself and his organization a reputation for radicalism, Foreman left EarthFirst! to pursue other paths of activism.

Confessions of an Eco-Warrior (1991) is Foreman's major published work, although he also co-edited *Ecodefense: A Field Guide to Monkeywrenching* (1987). *Confessions* outlines Foreman's environmentalist philosophy, his ideas to preserve and expand wilderness areas, and his experience with EarthFirst! Although the book is often summarized as narrating Foreman's departure from EarthFirst!, this is certainly not its major thrust; similarly, its defense of monkeywrenching, while rhetorically powerful, often distracts critics from other, equally salient features of the book.

As Klyza notes, "There are three main themes in

this collection of essays: (a) the difference of deep ecology from mainstream environmentalism and other conceptions of the public interest, (b) the importance of wilderness, and (c) the rationale and use of monkeywrenching or ecotage" (584). These three function as major environmental themes of the work, but *Confessions* goes beyond philosophical treatise to present practical *plans* for wilderness preservation, historical analysis of the successes and failures of conservation, and concrete pros and cons of monkeywrenching.

Confessions' most prominent environmental feature is its exploration of "deep ecology," which dates to the 1970s, and as Klyza explains, can be described as a "truly radical" offshoot of preservationism, one that "advocates policies typically far in excess of those advocated by the preservationist groups and [...] based on a fundamental restructuring of human society" (578). Unlike preservationism, deep ecology emphasizes the health of ecosystems as a basis for decisions, even over and above human welfare. Foreman puts the metaphysics of deep ecology more poetically: "Why does a man with a lifespan of seventy years think it proper to destroy a two-thousand-year-old redwood to make picnic tables? To kill one of thirty breeding female Grizzlies in the Yellowstone region because she ate one of his sheep?" (192).

Still, *Confessions* receives more attention for its advocacy of monkeywrenching, although Foreman lists and discusses common objections to the practice before defending its morality and effectiveness. As Foreman defines it:

> Monkeywrenching, ecological sabotage, ecotage, ecodefense, or "night work"—these are all terms for the destruction of machines or property that are used to destroy the natural world. Monkeywrenching includes such acts as pulling up survey stakes, putting sand in the crankcases of bulldozers, rendering dirt roads in wild areas impassable to vehicles, cutting down billboards, and removing and destroying trap lines... [M]onkeywrenching is nonviolent and is aimed only at inanimate objects, *never* toward physically hurting people... It is not major industrial sabotage; it is not revolutionary. Ecotage is not necessarily the most important tool for conservationists; it is merely one of the many approaches that may be valid and effective, depending on the circumstances... [118].

Such careful presentation and discussion of the practice's dangers makes Foreman's ultimate support more convincing.

Confessions devotes significant attention to developing national wilderness-preservation plans, and to evaluating the effectiveness of the conservation movement. Foreman advocates a national wilderness management plan by which stretches of land would be closed to human use altogether, allowed to revert to natural circumstances. By his plan, such areas would not even be mapped, much less supplied with tourist infrastructure or services.

Foreman also discusses EarthFirst! and his reasons for leaving the group (a departure that came not long after Foreman's arrest and investigation by the FBI in conjunction with EarthFirst!'s activities). In agreement with many critics, Foreman notes that one of EarthFirst!'s major accomplishments is simply its radicalism *per se*. By redefining radical environmentalism, the organization has tempered the reputations of more moderate groups such as the Sierra Club and the Nature Conservancy, in essence *creating* the category of "moderate" environmentalist by taking over the radical position on the spectrum.

In spite of its radical outlook, *Confessions* received little of the attention or demands for fact-checking that have spurred debates over other environmentalist works, such as the more recent An Inconvenient Truth by Al Gore, perhaps due to Foreman's marginalization as a radical; indeed, the public's tendency to dismiss the claims of its "radical" elements may have partly motivated Foreman's departure from EarthFirst!; but if he hoped to court a moderate audience with *Confessions*, its militant rhetoric (noticeable in the very title) could hardly help.

Cheryll Glotfelty notes that early environmentalist rhetoric — exemplified by Rachel Carson's Silent Spring— harnessed the force of military rhetoric, and capitalized on lingering Cold War anxieties, to motivate powerful responses in audiences and help them perceive the ecological threat as a real menace. But, as Glotfelty concludes, military rhetoric might no longer be the most apt choice for a movement that seeks to preserve and promote life:

> In the heat of environmental backlash, perhaps it is time to question whether the trope of war — with its battles, its victories and defeats, its ecowarriors and enemies, its moral crusades and mortal fear — is an appropriate tool for solving environmental problems and making intelligent decisions. Perhaps in Carson's day, war was a necessary and appropriate context in which to conceptualize environmental issues. But, thankfully, the Cold War is over. Should people who are committed to enlightened stewardship of the earth continue to invoke it? [Glotfelty 168].

Ultimately, then, it may be more its rhetorical than political failings that have left the provocative and informative *Confessions* unjustly undervalued, in comparison to EarthFirst!, to the broader work of Foreman himself, and to similar works of American environmental literature. — Laura Boynton Johnson

BIBLIOGRAPHY

Foreman, Dave. *Confessions of an Eco-Warrior.* New York: Crown, 1991. Print.

Glotfelty, Cheryll. "Cold War, Silent Spring: The Trope of War in Modern Environmentalism." *And No Birds Sing: Rhetorical Analyses of Rachel Carson's* Silent Spring. Ed. Craig Waddell. Carbondale: Southern Illinois University Press, 2000. 157–173. Print.

Klockenbrink, Myra. "In Short: Nonfiction." *New York Times Book Review* 16 June 1991: 16. *Academic Search Premier.* Web. 16 July 2009.

Klyza, Christopher McGrory. "Framing the Debate in Public Lands Politics." *Policy Studies Journal* 19.3/4 (1991): *Academic Search Premier.* Web. 16 July 2009.

Paul, Nancy. "Audio Reviews." *Library Journal* 117.18 (1992): 134. *Academic Search Premier.* Web. 16 July 2009.

Franklin, Benjamin (1706–1790)

Benjamin Franklin was born in 1706 in Boston, Massachusetts. Although his parents hoped that he would enter the clergy, they had little money and were only able to pay for his formal schooling until the age of 10. After briefly apprenticing for his brother James, who founded *The New-England Courant*, Franklin ran away to Philadelphia at age 17 and was subsequently estranged from his family for much of his life.

After a brief foray in London, Franklin returned to Philadelphia in 1726 and was a widely recognized public figure by 1733, when he first began publishing *Poor Richard's Almanack.* He continued publishing the *Almanack* until 1758, using it as a "vehicle for conveying instruction among the common folk" (qtd. in Isaacson 96). Franklin's endeavors to instruct his readers reflected his broader personal philosophy of self-improvement, which was most fully articulated in his posthumously published autobiography. In addition to chronicling the major events of his life, *The Autobiography of Benjamin Franklin* proposes 13 virtues, which together outline a philosophy that glorifies the struggle for individual perfection, and grounds his claims for preserving and improving the natural world inhabited by such individuals.

Although Franklin is not widely recognized for his contributions to environmental studies, he was in fact one of America's first environmentalists. One of his most notable contributions was his championing of what he called "public rights" against the interests of corporations and individuals whose actions were detrimental to the public welfare. His first battle for public rights occurred in 1739 when he led a group in petitioning the Pennsylvania Assembly to stop tanneries in Philadelphia's central commercial districts from dumping waste into a tributary of the Delaware River. While companies fought him on the grounds that regulations would impinge on their private rights as businesspeople, Franklin claimed that the dumping, which was causing property devaluation and spreading sickness and disease, was impeding the "public rights" of those living and working nearby. Although Franklin's success marked a small victory, the case set an important precedent in establishing the rights of the public to live in a sanitary and safe environment.

Franklin was also instrumental in leading a Philadelphia commission during the 1760s to help regulate trash collection and water pollution. While garbage disposal and water purification are public services that we largely take for granted today, Franklin's ideas on public health were novel and strikingly innovative in the eighteenth century for their insistence that the government play a major role in regulating public health and safety, and in protecting the environment upon which they clearly depend.

Franklin's contributions to the study of the environment were not, however, limited to the political realm. For example, on October 21, 1743, he fortuitously — although aided, of course, by his intelligence and curiosity — discovered that storms do not always travel in the direction of the prevailing winds, as was thought at the time. As with many of Franklin's discoveries, his conclusions are not often recognized in their own right, although they had a lasting impact on the field of meteorology.

Many of Franklin's contributions to the study of the environment still have not been given due recognition. In a 2009 article, for example, Steven Johnson describes Franklin's collaboration with Joseph Priestly in discovering that "the air we breathe is not some unalienable physical phenomenon, like gravity or magnetism, but is rather something that has been specifically manufactured by plants" (28). Johnson explains that "with Franklin's help, [Priestly] was able to grasp and describe the far-reaching consequences that [the process of plants producing breathable air] would have on our understanding of the earth's environment" (32). And yet, he goes on to say, Franklin's contribution — and even, to an extent, the discovery itself — continues to go unrecognized because the implications of Priestly's experiments "took almost 200 years to evolve into a coherent discipline" (32). Thus, while we may not often recognize Franklin directly in contemporary environmental studies, his scientific and socio-political contributions in fact provided the foundation for many later advances in the field.

Franklin died in 1790 at the age of 84, but — as we have seen — his impact on environmental studies was not confined to his own lifetime. Indeed, his will called for the construction of a fresh water pipeline for Philadelphia, which led to the establishment of the Philadelphia Water Commission. Franklin's concern for the health of the environment was not a casual interest or a political tool, but something that he cared passionately about and fought to preserve even after his death.— Adam Meehan

BIBLIOGRAPHY

Isaacson, Walter. *Benjamin Franklin: An American Life.* New York: Simon & Schuster, 2004. Print.
Johnson, Steven. "Green Ben." *American History* 44.3 (2009): 26–33. Print.

Frost, Robert (1874–1963)

Robert Frost was born in 1874 in San Francisco, California, to a journalist father, William Prescott Frost, Jr., and a Scottish, Swedenborgian mother, Isabelle Moodie. Frost's father, however, died of tuberculosis in 1885, leaving the family penniless. This event precipitated a move back to New England, the landscape with which Frost is most often associated. Supported by his grandfather in Massachusetts, Frost received good schooling and studied at Dartmouth and Harvard. Family responsibilities, however, meant that Frost did not complete his degree. After a tumultuous courtship, he married his school classmate Elinor White, and after a stint as teachers, they took up poultry farming in New Hampshire. Though Frost had a large family, he was to suffer considerable personal loss, including the deaths of four children, the suicide of one child, mental illness in the family, and the death of his wife in 1938. Yet from such humble beginnings and cruel personal tragedies, Frost went on to be one of America's foremost poets, honored by the U.S. senate in 1953 and given a gold medal by Congress in 1960 in recognition of his work.

Frost is most often thought of as a pastoral poet, but the image of him as an unschooled, rural savant belies the classical learning which informed his writing. Frost's vision of rural subjects was especially inspired by his reading of Virgil's *Eclogues* and *Georgics* (AMERICAN PASTORAL). Virgil captured the speech and life of rural characters to introduce political themes which disturbed the tranquility of the pastoral arcadia. Frost's rustic speakers are similarly employed to reveal and explore the problems both of life in the countryside and of American society in general. In his poetics, Frost stresses the need for human characters to appear in poems about nature. Using the metaphor of the stage, Frost emphasizes that it is not enough to have nature as a backdrop: there must always be "a human foreground" (1966: 34). In Frost's modern eclogues and georgics, the human foreground enables a political subtext to be drawn out of the natural backdrop. "The Self-Seeker," for example, features a visitor's conversation with a terribly mutilated man, based on Frost's own friend Carl Burrell whose legs were injured in a box factory accident. In "The Ax-Helve," the French Canadian lumberjack, Baptiste, confiscates the speaker's ax because of its shoddy workmanship, and drawing on old traditions of craft, creates a new ax-helve which will endure better than the machine-made one. Both of these poems explore the effects of industrialization on the rural idyll, and both critique the human cost of American industrialization.

If the male speakers of Frost's poems offer intriguing critiques of rural life, his female characters and narrators are often represented as extensions of the land and nature itself, threats to domestic order, and only ever temporarily managed or controlled. Sometimes the portrayal is realist in character; in "Home Burial," the wife laments the loss of her child, refusing her husband's every offer of help or support; while in "Hill Wife," a lonely marriage breaks down when the wife finally slips away into the landscape and freedom. More often though, Frost's women are mythical representatives of the irrational powers of nature, as in "Paul's Wife," where the beloved is carved from a tree trunk, or in "The Witch of Coos" and "The Pauper Witch of Grafton," where the women, defined by the places from which they originate, have powerful magic at their disposal. These pioneering female characters are as much a part of the American landscape as the natural world itself, and they represent the country's untamed quality, which is praised especially in Frost's later poems like "The Gift Outright."

Although he is most thought of as a poet of rural life, Frost experienced life in cities like San Francisco, London and Boston, as well as the New England countryside. He does, however, engage with the pastoral in a manner rejected by his cosmopolitan, modernist contemporaries, and he complicates the traditional pastoral mode that sets the *locus amoenus* or "pleasant place" of nature against the corruption of the city. In poems like "Ghost House," "In the Home Stretch," and "The Need of Being Versed in Country Things," rural life is depicted with sensitivity and vividness, but is far from idyllic. Alongside the sublime beauty of nature, Frost represents the suffering of country people and the deterioration of the idealized New England landscape. Having lived the life of a New England farmer, and witnessed the industrialization of traditional agriculture, Frost could not be a reversionist in the mode of HENRY DAVID THOREAU. He did, however, associate himself with the tradition of New England writers which included RALPH WALDO EMERSON and Henry Wadsworth Longfellow. Out of this tradition, Frost would write on themes such as the relationship between man and nature, and the possession of land, producing memorable poems on the colonial mindset of New England such as "The Vanishing Red" or "Our Hold on the Planet."

If Frost's poetry was written in an increasingly industrialized America, it also emerged in the context of a post–Darwinian world. During his studies at Harvard, Frost encountered ideas about faith and science through American thinkers like William James, Josiah Royce and GEORGE SANTAYANA. Frost's own interpretation of Darwin suggested that scientific discoveries need not strip the mystery from the world for the poet. Commenting on John Keats' disquiet at the discovery of the causation of the rainbow, Frost affirmed that "knowledge of its causation could not spoil the rainbow for me" (1966: 64). For him, there is mystery, magic even, in the microcosmic routines of the rural world. Frost described himself as a "Synecdochist," suggesting that the small objects or seemingly insignificant people described in his poems represent a larger interconnectedness between the poem and the world. In "Hyla Brook," for example, the drying up of a stream becomes a synecdoche for the forfeiture of the natural world, and the loss inherent in modernity. Similarly, the spider web in "Design" ultimately provokes larger post–Darwinian questions about the creation of the universe and the possibility of faith.

In this post–Darwinian world, Frost's poetry could not simply reproduce the poetics of Romantics like Thoreau, Wordsworth or Keats, but he did find new allegiances and influences during his years living in England from 1912 to 1914. In London, Frost met EZRA POUND and W.B. Yeats, but his time in Dymock, Gloucestershire brought his most intense friendship, with the Anglo-Welsh poet Edward Thomas. British nature writers, including the English Romantics, are a source of dialogue for Frost in poems like "The Mountain," where a herdsman persuades the speaker that climbing the peak is a waste of time rather than a sublime Romantic quest for knowledge. Frost's first collection of poetry *A Boy's Will* was published in England in 1913, to sympathetic reviews from Ezra Pound and others, and his first American editions were published in 1915.

Frost went on to publish over 30 collections of poetry, and by the end of his life had become a kind of American sage, deeply involved in the country's cultural and political life. His poetry also became more political, articulating, for example, his reactionary politics in response to Franklin D. Roosevelt's "New Deal" in the 1930s. In "An Equalizer" and "A Semi-Revolution," Frost mocks government schemes for public health and Marxist notions of revolution against class hierarchies. One of his most controversial later poems, "Two Tramps in Mud Time," describes the narrator's reaction to two tramps that emerge from the woods hoping to be paid to split wood. In poems like these, Frost explores the limits of social conscience and the worthiness of selflessness.

In the 1960s, Frost would explore the problems and perplexities of American society when he read "The Gift Outright" at the inauguration of President John F. Kennedy; and in 1962, a year before his death, Frost would play yet another role in the American scene as a somewhat controversial special cultural envoy to Soviet Premier Nikita Khrushchev. Through all his poetical and political activity, Frost became at last a kind of national institution, but remained — and yet remains — a poet most associated with the rural environment. The American landscape was Frost's enduring inspiration and passion, a place as mysterious and worthy of contemplation as poetry itself. — Zoë Brigley Thompson

BIBLIOGRAPHY

Faggen, Robert. *The Cambridge Introduction to Robert Frost*. Cambridge: Cambridge University Press, 2008.
_____. *The Collected Prose of Robert Frost*. Ed. Mark Richardson. Cambridge: Belknap Press/Harvard University Press, 2007.
_____. *Interviews with Robert Frost*. Ed. Edward Connery Lathem. New York: Holt, Rinehart and Wilson, 1966.
_____. *Robert Frost and the Challenge of Darwin*. Ann Arbor: University of Michigan Press, 2001.
Frost, Robert. *Complete Poems*. New York: Holt, Rinehart and Winston, 1964.
Parini, Jay. *Robert Frost: A Life*. Basingstoke: Macmillan, 2000.

Fuller, Margaret (1810–1850)

Long noted as a journalist, critic, and feminist associated with the American TRANSCENDENTALISM movement, Margaret Fuller remains relevant today in part because her work continues to exert a powerful influence on America's sense of, and attitude toward, the environment. Born Sarah Margaret Fuller in Cambridge, Massachusetts in 1810, Margaret was the first child of Timothy Fuller (1778–1835), a U.S. Representative from Massachusetts, and Margaret Crane Fuller. Timothy Fuller believed that his daughter should have an education equal to that of a boy's of the time. Consequently, he taught her to read and write at a very young age and later included Latin, Greek, and French instruction in their lessons. Fuller's formal education began when she matriculated at Cambrigeport's Port School in 1819. From 1821 to 1822, Fuller attended the Boston Lyceum for Young Ladies, and then in 1824, the School for Young Ladies in Groton, Massachusetts.

After the death of her father in 1835, Fuller began teaching to help support her family. She taught first at Temple School in Boston and later at the private Green Street School in Providence, Rhode Island. In 1939, Fuller returned to Boston, where she began to hold conversations with the city's female elite; topics included economic, political, and social issues that affected women. During this time, Fuller became the first female member of the Transcendentalist Symposium Club, a group of intellectuals that felt that "the knowledge of reality is arrived at intuitively rather than through objective experience." Her affiliation with this group led to RALPH WALDO EMERSON offering her a position at the Transcendentalist journal, *The Dial.* Fuller served from 1840 to 1842 as the editor of *The Dial,* a publication to which she contributed much of her own writing. Because of her role at *The Dial,* Fuller gained recognition as a notable figure in the American transcendentalism movement. She spent time at George Ripley's Brook Farm, a communal experiment which encouraged its participants to work together as they balanced labor and leisure (UTOPIAN COMMUNITIES).

In 1843, Fuller traveled by train, steamboat, carriage, and on foot, to make a roughly circular tour of the Great Lakes region of America. After her tour, Fuller's journal of the trip was published in 1844 under the title *SUMMER ON THE LAKES, IN 1843.* Fuller's first original book-length work, *Summer on the Lakes* is perhaps best described as a portfolio of sketches, poems, stories, anecdotes, dialogues, reflections, and accounts of a leisurely journey to the northwestern frontier. After reading the book, Horace Greely offered Margaret the position of literary critic and social commentator for the *New York Daily Tribune.*

When Fuller took the helm as the literary editor of the *New York Tribune* in the fall of 1844, she also began the process of publicly sharing her personal opinions on a range of political, social, environmental, and cultural issues. With each newspaper column she wrote, Fuller expressed her developing political identity as she began speaking out for women's rights and other types of reform — including abolitionism and social reform that would improve the human rights of mentally ill and prison populations. Along with these *Tribune* essays and her *Summer on the Lakes, in 1843,* Fuller is known for writing a key early feminist text called *Woman in the Nineteenth Century* (1845), which argues for the spirituality of women. Considered by many to be her most famous work, the book we know as *Woman in the Nineteenth Century* first appeared in essay form in *The Dial* in July, 1843, under the title "The Great Lawsuit. Man versus Men. Woman versus Women"; Horace Greely en-

couraged Fuller to expand it, and it was republished in book form in 1845.

Just one year later, Margaret Fuller went on assignment to Europe as the *Tribune*'s first female correspondent. While in Italy, she met the Italian revolutionary Giovanni Angelo Ossoli, a man with whom she had a relationship and a son, Angelo Eugene Philip Ossoli, who was born in 1848. It is unclear whether Ossoli and Fuller ever married, and Fuller did not inform her mother about Ossoli or Angelino until 1849. On July 19, 1950, all three members of the family perished at sea just off the coast of Fire Island, New York, as they were traveling to the United States. Fuller's body was never recovered.

Within a week after her death, Horace Greeley suggested to Emerson that a biography of Fuller, to be called *Margaret and Her Friends,* be published. At the time of her death, Fuller had many admirers, including the early Women's rights' advocates Elizabeth Cady Stanton and Susan B. Anthony (who saw Fuller as an important influence on American women), and authors such as HENRY DAVID THOREAU, WALT WHITMAN, Elizabeth Barrett Browning, and EDGAR ALLEN POE (who respected her writing despite personal differences). Indeed, Fuller, through her writings and the profound influence that they had on 19th-century America, managed in a "single decade to fashion herself into her generation's most famous cosmopolitan intellectual" (Capper 3). Fuller's place in American letters has been secured not only by her connections to American transcendentalism and the Women's Rights movements, but also because of the environmental concerns reflected in her important treatise, *Summer on the Lakes, in 1843.* — Heather Duerre Humann

BIBLIOGRAPHY

Capper, Charles, and Cristina Giorcelli, eds. *Margaret Fuller: Transatlantic Crossings in a Revolutionary Age.* Madison: University of Wisconsin Press, 2007.
Dickenson, Donna. *Margaret Fuller: Writing a Woman's Life.* New York: St. Martin's Press, 1993:
Murray, Meg McGavran. *Margaret Fuller, Wandering Pilgrim.* Athens and London: University of Georgia Press, 2008.
Slater, Abby. *In Search of Margaret Fuller.* New York: Delacorte Press, 1978.
Steele, Jeffrey. *Transfiguring America: Myth, Ideology, and Mourning in Margaret Fuller's Writing.* Columbia and London: University of Missouri Press, 2001.

Summer on the Lakes, in 1843, Margaret Fuller (1844)

Margaret Fuller's first original book-length work, *Summer on the Lakes,* is a portfolio of sketches, poems, stories, anecdotes, dialogs, and reflections, with multiple narrative voices. In the book, Fuller mixes commentary on contemporary politics with references to THE BIBLE, allusions to Greco-Roman mythology, and excerpts from Shakespeare. The text, however, functions primarily as Fuller's intense meditation on the land, a record of her internal journey of self-exploration, and an account of the three months she spent at the Great Lakes and in the prairie-region states.

In 1843, Fuller, already an established figure in the TRANSCENDENTAL circle of EMERSON and THOREAU, traveled with a small group of friends that included Sarah Freeman Clarke, a fellow transcendentalist who later illustrated Fuller's book, making a roughly circular tour of the Great Lakes region. Fuller and the group began their trip on May 23, 1843. The group traveled by train, steamboat, carriage, and on foot, from Niagara Falls and Buffalo in New York State, through the Great Lakes on a five-day lake voyage, to Illinois and into the Wisconsin territory, ending their journey with a nine-day stay at Mackinac Island. *Summer on the Lakes* records these travels through what was considered, in mid–19th century America, to be the far western frontier of the country.

While on the trip, Fuller "had no guidebook, kept no diary"; nor, in fact, did she know exactly how many miles the group traveled — either per day or in total — as she later confides in her book (Fuller 67). She simply wrote, in a kind of timeless present, about the people and places she encountered, finding frequent occasion to praise the landscape she traversed, which she saw as reflecting the heterogeneity of the American environment. For these reasons, *Summer on the Lakes* is an important example of 19th-century American nature writing.

Fuller, however, was not interested in simply recording the topographical details of the places she visited; instead, she was concerned about the "spirit" of the places she had traveled and wanted to give a "poetic impression of the country at large" (Fuller 67). Drawing on historical sources, contemporary travel books, and her own firsthand experience of life in these locales, Fuller used the opportunity of visiting the frontier to meditate on the state of her own life and of life in America — both as they existed and as she hoped they might one day become. Thus, her account of a leisurely journey to the Great Lakes region is both an external and an internal travelogue, with national implications.

Throughout the book, Fuller ruminates about her fellow travelers and the landscape, revealing her own ambivalence about 19th-century America's identity. As Fuller critic Anne Baker points out, a particular strength of the book is that Fuller also meditates on the "act of seeing" in *Summer on the Lakes* (91). The

result is a particularly rich form of autobiography; not merely a portfolio of sketches and reflections on her Great Lakes journey, but a record of her internal journey of self-exploration, and by extension that of educated, white America itself. Although aspects of the book are highly personal, *Summer on the Lakes* offers its readers more than simply one woman's personal journey. It also offers a pointed critique of American history and 19th-century "progress" by examining how westward expansion had affected the environment and individuals, including displaced Native Americans.

The work is composed of seven chapters, but critics tend to divide the book up into its four stated parts, all of which highlight the national theme of America as the world's pastoral arcadia (AMERICAN PASTORAL). The four "pastorals" that comprise the book include: the pastoral of simplicity, represented by an American's escape from New England and the fashion and jargon associated with that region; the pastoral of organic nature, shown through the trope of the American West as a wild, yet cultivable, garden; the pastoral of diverse organic culture, represented by the West as a place where old-world values flourish and whose inhabitants both practice and celebrate folk arts; and the ultimate pastoral of America as a boundless and fecund land.

The episodic nature of the work has presented challenges to critics and readers alike since the time of its initial publication. Fuller scholar Dorothy Z. Baker contends that the root of this "difficulty is primarily generic" (97), but though its cause may be singular, its nature is multi-faceted, being alternately described as a sketchbook, a TRANSCENDENTALIST travelogue, a social and political tract, and an autobiography — to name only the most popular labels applied to the text.

What further complicates these questions of genre is the two editions of Summer on the Lakes, the original 1844 edition and the 1854 edition edited by her younger brother, Arthur B. Fuller, which he published after her death in 1850. The version published by her brother omits several meditative and narrative passages as well as the tale of Mariana, one of the book's best known episodes, which offers a semiautobiographical account of Fuller's challenges as a woman in 19th-century American society. Many critics now suspect that Arthur Fuller objected to this tale because of the homosociality reflected in it, and its suggestions of the superiority of women.

For all the challenges presented by the book, however, *Summer on the Lakes* remains an important and far-reaching exemplar of early American nature writing because of the myriad environmental concerns reflected and explored within it. The book also marks a pivotal position in Fuller's development as a writer, Transcendentalist, and feminist, particularly because of her impressions of the "women of the west," which both hearken back to the feminist views she espoused in "The Great Lawsuit" and anticipate her influential feminist study, *Women in the Nineteenth Century*.— Heather Duerre Humann

BIBLIOGRAPHY

Baker, Anne. *Heartless Immensity: Literature, Culture, and Geography in Antebellum America*. Ann Arbor: University of Michigan Press, 2006.

Baker, Dorothy Z. "Excising the Text, Exorcising the Author: Margaret Fuller's *Summer on the Lakes, in 1843*." *In Her Own Voice: Nineteenth-Century American Women Essayists*. Ed. Sherry Lee Linkon. New York: Garland, 1997. 97–112.

Fuller, Margaret. *Summer on the Lakes, in 1843*. Urbana and Chicago: University of Illinois Press, 1991.

Murray, Meg McGavran. *Margaret Fuller, Wandering Pilgrim*. Athens and London: University of Georgia Press, 2008.

Slater, Abby. *In Search of Margaret Fuller*. New York: Delacorte Press, 1978.

Smith, Susan Belasco. Introduction. *Summer on the Lakes, in 1843*. Urbana and Chicago: University of Illinois Press, 1991. Vii–xxii.

Steele, Jeffrey. *Transfiguring America: Myth, Ideology, and Mourning in Margaret Fuller's Writing*. Columbia and London: University of Missouri Press, 2001.

Fuller, Richard Buckminster, Jr. (1895–1983)

Richard Buckminster Fuller, Jr., known to friends and family as "Bucky," was a notable futurist, architect, engineer, author and lecturer, best known for inventing and popularizing the geodesic dome.

Born into a venerable New England family, Fuller was sent to Harvard, from which all Fuller men since 1760 had graduated. Expelled from the school in his first year, however, for using his tuition money to entertain chorus girls in Manhattan, Fuller would never complete a college degree, though he would spend decades as a professor and was awarded a host of honorary degrees and distinctions. In the years after Harvard he worked in a textile mill and various meatpacking plants before entering the Navy as an officer during World War I. During the war, Fuller met and married Anne Hewlett, with whom he would have two children and would remain until their deaths, one day apart, in 1983.

After the war, Fuller went to work for his father-in-law, but had little success as a businessman. In 1927, unemployed and near bankruptcy, Fuller contemplated suicide until he had what he described as a life-changing mystical experience: finding himself in dialogue with what he called "Universe," he was told that his life was not his to take and that he belonged to Universe. Fuller then embarked on a lifelong experiment to determine what, if anything, an individual could do on behalf of all humanity, often referring to himself as "Guinea Pig B"— the "B" for Bucky.

Philosophically Fuller eschewed specialization, preferring to function as a "comprehensive, anticipatory design scientist" or "comprehensivist." He considered himself a world citizen and viewed the planet as a massive spaceship ("Spaceship Earth") that has supported human life for millions of years through its ingenious design. Thus the ideal way to achieve human reform was to use Design Science to competently reform the environment, rather than attempting to directly reform humans themselves. In this pursuit Fuller designed a variety of imaginative, often fantastical projects, utilizing ecological principles like recycling and "ephemeralization"— doing ever more with ever less. These designs included a three wheeled car (Dymaxion Vehicle), a waterborne city (Tetrahedronal City) and an aluminum house that cost the same as a car and could be assembled in a day (Dymaxion House). While these experiments garnered much media attention, few were ever realized and none were mass produced. Fuller's only significant commercial success as a designer was the geodesic dome, a spherical structure that encloses more space with less material and more structural integrity than virtually any other building. First patented in 1954, thousands of the distinctive domes would be built within his lifetime.

While Fuller's impact as a designer was never fully realized, he authored, co-authored or contributed to more than 50 books, and circumnavigated the world many times as a lecturer and teacher. His enduring message was that Design Science had the capability to avert environmental catastrophe, and that if humanity were to survive aboard Spaceship Earth, it would require technological innovation and social teamwork.— Paul Falzone

BIBLIOGRAPHY

Kenner, Hugh. *Bucky: A Guided Tour of Buckminster Fuller*. New York: William Morrow, 1973.

Lorance, Loretta. *Becoming Bucky Fuller*. Cambridge: MIT Press, 2009.

Miller, Dana, et al. *Buckminster Fuller*. New York: Whitney Museum of American Art, in association with Yale University Press, 2008.

Sieden, Lloyd. *Buckminster Fuller's Universe: An Appreciation*. Cambridge: Perseus Books, 2000.

Utopia or Oblivion: The Prospects for Humanity, Buckminster Fuller (1969)

Utopia or Oblivion: The Prospects for Humanity is a collection of essays by Buckminster Fuller, Jr., first published in 1969 by Bantam Books and reissued in

2008 by Lars Müller Publishers. The title is based on two quotes from physicists referring to the then burgeoning arms race. The first, from John R. Platt is that "The world is now too dangerous for anything but Utopia" (in Fuller 155). The second, from Jerome Wiesner, is that "The armaments race is an accelerating downward-spiral to Oblivion" (*ibid*.). Fuller's basic thesis is that for the first time in human history we have the technological capacity to provide for the physical needs of all people on Earth. Because we also have the technology for total destruction through nuclear holocaust, Fuller argued that it was essential that we prioritize creating "maximum abundance" for all humanity.

Fuller bases his ideas of "maximum abundance" on a criticism of two flawed assumptions of the "old economics." The first is Thomas Malthus' claim that there has always been and will always be an insufficient amount of resources to support humanity. Historically this belief led to social Darwinism's "survival of the fittest," which encouraged the domination of "great pirates" (Fuller's name for masters of commercial and political power) who accrued wealth for themselves at the expense of others. In fact, claims Fuller, higher standards of living lead to slower population growth, and technology has created mechanisms that allow for the universal and equitable distribution of resources.

The second incorrect assumption of the "old economics" is the Newtonian principle that the universe is normally at rest and that the tendency of matter is toward entropy. In fact, says Fuller, Einstein has shown that the universe is in a state of continual transformation, and the Law of Conservation of Energy, which states that matter cannot be created or destroyed, means that this energy is a finite resource that can be harnessed and redistributed. The human mind, meanwhile, is the ultimate anti-entropic mechanism, and humanity's ultimate purpose in the universe is to be an anti-entropic force, reducing chaos and becoming active crew members aboard "Spaceship Earth" through the practice of design-science. Fuller writes, "Energy cannot decrease. Knowhow can only increase. It is therefore scientifically clear that wealth which combines energy and intellect can only increase." (229)

Fundamental to Fuller's vision of a utopian future is his profound disregard for politics and political parties of all types. As he repeatedly states in the book, in slightly different formulations: if all the world's industrial machinery were to disappear overnight, billions of people would starve to death within a matter of months, but if every politician and political party were to disappear, humanity as a whole would be fine and perhaps even better than they are now.

Fuller notes that the average human lifespan in the U.S. was extended from 42 years to 70 years between 1895 and 1965, and the percentage of people with a high standard of living — better than that enjoyed by the monarchs of a century before — went from 1 percent in 1900 to 44 percent by the mid 1960's. He writes that this industrialization and improvement of the human condition in the 20th century was largely the unintended result of war. He claims that virtually all advanced technology began as government subsidized weapons technologies, which, through technological obsolescence or an end to hostilities, were adapted for consumer use in home markets. Fuller differentiates between weaponry, which he called "killingry" and technology meant to improve people's standard of living, which he called "livingry." He estimates the average lag time between killingry innovation and livingry application at roughly 25 years. The goal for design science is to make innovations for the improvement of all humanity the primary intention rather than a side effect of design.

Fuller believed that the ideal way to achieve reform was to use design science to competently reform the environment, rather than attempting to reform humanity itself. Ecological principles were key to the success of this design science. For Fuller, fossil fuels represented an energy "savings account" which short-sighted designers had decided to use as a primary source of energy. Instead, he claimed that the energy required for universal wealth and a high standard of living should come from "the harnessable ocean tides, wind, sunpower, and alcohol producing vegetation..." (241). He conceived of an age of "Accelerating Ephemeralization" in which virtually all of the planet's mined ores would be recycled into newer and better technologies. This drive toward ephemeralization — finding new ways to do ever more with ever less — was key to the success of the "great pirates" who required lighter, faster, and more spacious vessels to use in plundering. In recent years these same practices of ephemeralization were applied to technological innovations in airplane weaponry. Fuller complained that designers of land-based structures never asked how much a building weighed, but designers of water and airborne vessels could not design without knowing this. Fuller's goal was to apply nautical principles to terrestrial design for purposes of designing more advanced livingry. In this way, man could "participate consciously and somewhat more knowingly and responsibly in his own evolutionary transformation." (145)

Because it is a collection, *Utopia or Oblivion* is not meant to function as either a discreet work or as a scientific treatise. As one early reviewer put it, the book was "likely to appeal to the imaginative reader rather than the scientific disciplinarian" (Bettison 79). Buckminster Fuller was legendary not only for his tendency to coin new phrases and to offer hyperbolic predictions for the future, but for the colorful manner in which he did so. Environmentalist BILL MCKIBBEN writes that, "I once interviewed R. Buckminster Fuller. That is to say, I once held a microphone in front of his mouth while he embarked on a stunning, elliptical, and semi-connected 20-minute ramble that touched on everything from rocket travel to architecture to why he wore three watches..." (464). Fuller was legendary for his ability and propensity to lecture for four or five hours at a stretch, often without notes or prepared materials of any type. Because the 12 chapters that comprise *Utopia or Oblivion* are based primarily on talks delivered by Fuller to professional and academic audiences throughout the 1960s, the book tends to be more circuitous and unfocused than Fuller's purely textual works, and many anecdotes, statistics and citations are often repeated, showing up almost verbatim from one chapter to the next. At the same time, this redundancy allows the reader to discover the themes and information that were most salient for Fuller. What emerges is the portrait of a thinker with a profound belief in the ability of technology and science to overcome human challenges, and a spirited appeal to the passengers aboard Spaceship Earth to become active in ensuring the survival of their planet and their species.—Paul Falzone

BIBLIOGRAPHY

Bettison, David. Book Review: Utopia or Oblivion: The Prospects for Humanity. *Journal of Sociology*, Jan 1975, vol. 11: pp. 78–79.

Fuller, R. Buckminster, Jr. *Utopia or Oblivion: The Prospects for Humanity*. New York: Bantam Books, 1969.

McKibben, Bill, ed. *American Earth: Environmental Writing Since Thoreau*. New York: Literary Classics of the United States, 2008.

Gaines, Ernest J. (1933–   )

Short story writer, novelist and essayist, Ernest J. Gaines was born, the eldest of 12 children, on the River Lake Plantation in Point Coupee Parish in Oscar, Louisiana, in 1933. His was the fifth generation of a sharecropper family, and Gaines grew up in the original slave quarters of the plantation. He left the region at 15 in 1948, to attend high school in Vallejo, California, reunited with his mother and stepfather, who had left during World War II. For two decades, from 1984–2004, he divided his time between California and a writer-in-residence position at the University of Louisiana at Lafayette, and in 2004 returned to settle on part of the original

plantation of his birth, physically relocating the original plantation church to his property.

Unsurprisingly, Gaines' work articulates the social, political, and economic position of society's most vulnerable citizens: the poor, voiceless, invisible, and downtrodden. Raised in the "quarters" by his aunt, Augusteen Jefferson, whose disability forced her to crawl about the house, Gaines would later model a number of his highly sympathetic female characters after her. Influenced by intensely "local" American authors such as ERNEST HEMINGWAY and WILLIAM FAULKNER, as well as the Russian novelist Ivan Turgenev, Gaines greatest influences were the storytellers in the quarters; the women and men who sat on the "garries" (porches) of residents' homes and spun tales. It was as a result of these neighborly associations that Gaines—at the behest of his aunt—began writing letters on behalf of the members of the community.

When he left the South, his visits to the library in Vallejo were literary quests in search of books containing stories reflective of his former home; stories about the people on the plantation, their speech, habits, and affection for the land; tales that reminded him of the oak trees in Louisiana, the bayous, swamps, fields, sugarcane rows, rivers, fields, and churches. During his residence in California, he missed hearing the "voices of his people" in song and prayer, and his frequent returns to the region testify to his deep and creative affection for his indigenous surroundings. For the last 10 ten years, in fact, on the last Saturday in October, Gaines and his wife Dianne, have held a Beautification Day ceremony on the burial grounds of the former quarters, in honor of the ancestors buried on the land. The tombs are washed, the grass is cut, and flowers are planted.

In *A Lesson Before Dying*, and other fictional works, Gaines pays homage to the rural Louisiana environment of his childhood by evoking the memory of the community's economic dependency upon sugar cane, pecan trees, and the harvesting of crops, including peas, corn, beans, and potatoes. During his formative years he learned the importance of an undesecrated environment, and still, to this day, champions the joys of Southern life untouched by modern industrialization and development. As a child, he swam and fished in the pristine waters of the False River, across from the Point Coupee Plantation. His first novel, *Catherine Carmier*, initially titled "The Little Stream," was a reflection of his respect for the purity of the False River and his attachment to the land surrounding it. His subsequent fictional works, specifically *Of Love and Dust*, speak to his advocacy of the environment and the guardianship of his native land.

While Gaines is not generally regarded as a folklorist, his work embraces a culturally diverse regional community that includes blacks, whites, Cajuns, and Creoles. Bayonne, the fictional community in his canon, is often compared to Faulkner's Yoknapatawpha County.

Catherine Carmier (1964) depicts the racial antagonism between Creoles and blacks, and serves as the thematic precursor for *Of Love and Dust* (1967). *Bloodline* (1968), his only collection of short stories, shows his attachment to the land and his strong sense of allegiance to the region. The bestselling *The Autobiography of Miss Jane Pittman* (1971) established Gaines on the international literary stage, and *A Gathering of Old Men* (1983) was critically acclaimed for giving voice to male characters as agents for social change. Both works were turned into major motion pictures. His signature tale of father and son separation, *In My Father's House* (1978), received less enthusiastic reviews but serves as an eloquent argument for the achievability of redemption. *Mozart and Leadbelly* (2005) is an influential collection of stories and essays in which Gaines describes the critical influences on his life, and why he became a writer. The work, which came out 12 years after *A Lesson Before Dying*, takes its title from the diverse musical influences in his life on the Point Coupee Plantation, through his writing career in California and Louisiana. The essays reveal the heroic efforts of the plantation people, and he speaks fondly of the sights, sounds, and smells of the bayou. Most notably, the author writes of the source of *A Lesson Before Dying* and how "Jefferson's Diary," the most prominent chapter in the novel, originated. The collection also includes two previously published stories, "My Grandpa and the Haint" and "The Turtles," Gaines' first published short story which appeared in *Transfer* magazine in 1956, when he was a student at San Francisco State College [University]. A fierce believer in the unadorned countryside of his upbringing, he writes, in *Mozart and Leadbelly*, regarding his early search for works reflective of his rural background, that he wanted to "smell that Louisiana earth, feel that Louisiana sun, sit under the shade of one of those Louisiana oaks, [and] search for pecans in that Louisiana grass in one of those Louisiana yards next to one of those Louisiana bayous, not far from a Louisiana river."

Following a successful career in writing and teaching (at the University of Louisiana at Lafayette), Gaines' return to the plantation speaks to his unwavering desire to be close to the forces that helped shaped him. As much as he pays respect to the elders of the community during his early years on the plantation, he also champions the importance of the environment by infusing his works with a sacred reverence for the land. Thus, his work not only speaks to his sense of time, place, and community, it also articulates his deep and abiding appreciation for the environment which helps sustain him. — Lillie Anne Brown

BIBLIOGRAPHY

Doyle, Mary Ellen. *Voices From the Quarters: The Fiction of Ernest J. Gaines.* Baton Rouge: Louisiana State University Press, 2002.
Estes, David C. *Critical Reflections on the Fiction of Ernest J. Gaines.* Athens: University of Georgia Press, 1994.
Simpson, Anne K. *A Gathering of Gaines: The Man and the Writer.* Lafayette: Center for Louisiana Studies, 1992.

Garland, Hamlin (1860–1940)

Hannibal Hamlin Garland's life spanned a wide and tumultuous period in American history, one in which the country underwent dramatic and perpetual change. Accordingly, Garland was used to change from a young age. His father Richard Hayes Garland was a hardworking farmer with a recurring urge to move further West for new opportunities in Iowa and Wisconsin. Garland was much closer to his mother Isabelle (née McClintock), who encouraged his education and interest in reading. It was with her support that he eventually traveled East to Boston — a move that would prove immensely influential.

While in Boston, Garland dedicated himself to his education, though with little means to support himself. During this time, he encountered important works of contemporary science, including those of Charles Darwin and Herbert Spencer, but he was especially influenced by the work of the political economist Henry George, who argued that people should own what they create, but that the land and all of nature belongs to humanity in general. This early eco-sensitive philosophy, reminiscent of Native American wisdom, would inspire Garland to write fiction fiercely advocating a host of reforms, in particular regarding the situation of the American farmer. It was also in Boston that Garland would meet William Dean Howells, with whom he formed a lifelong and influential friendship.

Garland returned from the East with a new perspective on the agricultural life and communities he had come from. The burdens of this life, and the bleak opportunities for personal improvement, which he observed — especially for women like his mother — inspired the stories comprising his most celebrated work, *Main-Travelled Roads* (first published 1891). In his introduction to the collection, Howells praised its portrayal of the farming life as "ungarnished and unvarnished," placing Garland alongside other noted Regionalist writers such as Sarah Orne Jewett, Bret Harte, and Mary Wilkins Freeman.

The uncompromising realism of Garland's depictions of farming life in the Midwest is also notable for its challenge to THOMAS JEFFERSON's agrarian ideal, which until then had remained the dominant trope of agricultural America (AMERICAN PASTORAL). When, in "Up the Coolly," Garland describes the farm to which the main character returns, "with all its sordidness, dullness, triviality, and its endless drudgeries," Jefferson's image of the God-elected arcadian farmer seems dangerously unrealistic. The poignant vulnerability of some of Garland's characters to their environment, and to the unreformed political systems beyond their control, lead him to be sometimes grouped with AMERICAN NATURALISTS such as STEPHEN CRANE, whom Garland himself helped introduce to a wider audience; while Garland's harsh depictions of the Midwest would also influence writers such as Sherwood Anderson and Sinclair Lewis.

But Garland's fiction is not all bleak. On the whole, it maintains a rugged and hard-won, perhaps peculiarly American, sense of optimism. The overarching theme of his work involves the labor and struggle intrinsic to the relationship between the land and those who work it. Garland later expanded this theme, with less success, to various CONSERVATIONIST interests (including mining and forestry) and other causes (including the condition of Native Americans). Garland also stayed attuned to the limitations upon, and opportunities for, women in harsh environments. The high points of his later work were the autobiographical books of the Middle Border series, which revisited the settings and themes of *Main-Travelled Roads*; the second installment in this series won Garland a Pulitzer Prize. Garland's old age saw his work wane in critical esteem, but its vivid and realistic evocation of rural American life still instructs, and his sensitive exploration of human struggles with, and responsibility for, the environment still resonate today.— Eric Morel

BIBLIOGRAPHY

Garland, Hamlin. *Main-Travelled Roads*. Lincoln: Bison Books, 1995.
McCullough, Joseph. Introduction. *Main-Travelled Roads*. Lincoln: Bison Books, 1995.
Newlin, Keith. *Hamlin Garland: A Life*. Lincoln: University of Nebraska Press, 2008.

Ginsberg, Allen (1926–1997)

Allen Ginsberg was born in Newark, New Jersey in 1926. His father Louis was a poet, and in the 1970s he and Allen would do joint poetry readings promoted as the "Battle of the Bards." Ginsberg attended Columbia in the 1940s and during that time became acquainted with other key figures of the Beat movement, including William S. Burroughs, JACK KEROUAC, and Neal Cassady. Ginsberg gained notoriety when he read part of *Howl* at the Six Gallery in San Francisco in 1955. Soon after, *Howl* was published, seized, and its publisher Lawrence Ferlinghetti put on trial for printing and distributing obscene material. In October 1957, Judge Clayton W. Horn deemed that *Howl* had "redeeming social values" and was therefore not obscene. Throughout his life, Ginsberg fought against the censorship of his own and others' works, and actively participated in other social causes such as the anti–Vietnam war protests, the peace movement, and gay liberation.

Beginning in the early 1960s, Ginsberg traveled widely in Europe and Asia, where he sought out religious teachers. Like many of the Beats, he explored heightened consciousness through drugs and, especially, eastern spirituality: "The Orient, particularly India and Japan, became meccas and sites of inspiration and wisdom for the American Beats that birthed the counterculture of the 1960s. The interest in the East was, in principle, a quest for a deeper way of knowing the self and living a more contemplative, integrated, ecological and holistic life" (Dart 51). A Buddhist, Ginsberg founded the Jack Kerouac School of Disembodied Poetics at the Naropa Institute in Boulder, Colorado, with Anne Waldman in 1974. In addition, his travels further opened his eyes to what he would refer to as America's "plastic consciousness," and the resulting imperative that Americans "*have* to be responsible for our own salvation's sake" (*Family Business* 87). Humanity is part of nature — "Everything is holy!" ("Footnote to *Howl*"). We cannot ignore this relationship and promote some ideological construct that destroys our environment:

> Living like beasts,
> befouling our own nests,
> Smoke & Steam, broken glass & beer cans,
> Auto exhaust–
> Civilization shit littering the streets,
> Fine black mist over apartments
> watercourses running with oil
> fish fellows dead —["Wings Lifted Over the Black Pit"]

In letters to his father, Ginsberg often criticized America's reliance on oil, and its disinterest in finding alternative sources of energy: "It would be wise for the U.S. to develop solar, wind, & other decentralized electric sources. The whole fight over preserving oil resources is something characteristic of oil-interest capitalist monopoly & industrial-military alliance on a mentally & economically static plan of fixation"; indeed, America's reliance on oil is an addiction and as "neurotic as a junky looking for a fix. That's part of the whole context" (*Family Business* 355). The analogy is a telling one. Like Burroughs, Ginsberg placed governmental policies in their larger contexts, linking, for example, the war on drugs to energy policies. Ginsberg would argue for an ecological and economic benefit to the decriminalization of drugs, particularly marijuana: "Thus the junk problem should be decriminalized and medicalized, and hemp, now a problem, should be transformed into an asset for the failing family farm to help reinhabit the countryside and provide some sustainable product (cloth, rope, et al.) as alternative to plastic consciousness" (Foreword xvi).

The threat to the ecosystem posed by nuclear weapons is also a factor in Ginsberg's environmental awareness. The extremes of the "rational ethos" that created the atom bombs that destroyed Hiroshima and Nagasaki, and continued to threaten the planet throughout the Cold War, cast a shadow over much Beat writing:

> Redemption and earthly salvation for Ginsberg and others took the form of a belief in a transcending spirit that represented the ultimate and inviolate unity of things of nature, which no system of humanity could ever fully dissolve. Awareness itself, the reckless plunge and immersion into the whole of experience, was an act of personal salvation because it renewed the feeling of complete participation of self with the world and because it pushed back the limits set around life by the new rational ethos [Christensen 216].

In part, Ginsberg's concern for personal and earthly salvation are an extension of the work of his two great poetic precursors WALT WHITMAN and William Blake, who "both insisted on politics as an extension of the self—rather than as matters of compromise and concession or as something imposed from without" (Foster 86). Thus, Ginsberg's ethical view of humanity cannot be separated from our responsibilities to the planet. In other words, our environmental responsibilities are, ultimately, responsibilities to ourselves. This is key to Ginsberg's visionary stance:

> We're not our skin of grime, we're not our dread bleak dusty imageless locomotive, we're all golden sunflowers inside, blessed by our own seed & hairy naked accomplishment-bodies growing into mad black formal sunflowers in the sunset, spied on by our eyes under the shadow of the mad locomotive riverbank sunset Frisco hilly tincan evening sitdown vision ["Sunflower Sutra"].

If we do not recognize this responsibility "for our own salvation's sake," Ginsberg states in a letter to his father, "It's a piece of arrogance & stupidity you could find in science fiction, about a bunch of slobs who tore down their own planet and died" (*Family Business* 373–4).—Jim Daems

BIBLIOGRAPHY

Dart, Ron. *Thomas Merton and the Beats of the North Cascades*. Expanded edition. North Vancouver: Prospect Press, 2008.
Foster, Edward Halsey. *Understanding the Beats*. Columbia: University of South Carolina Press, 1992.
Ginsberg, Allen. Foreword. *The Beat Book: Writings from the Beat Generation*. Ed. Anne Waldman. Boston: Shambhala, 1996.
_____. *Collected Poems, 1947–1997*. New York: HarperCollins, 2006.
_____, and Louis Ginsberg. *Family Business: Selected Letters Between a Father and Son*. Ed. Michael Schumacher. New York: Bloomsbury, 2001.

Glasgow, Ellen (1873–1945)

Ellen Glasgow was a Pulitzer Prize–winning novelist whose 19 novels and other works of short fiction, poetry, and criticism appeared over a nearly 50-year career. Glasgow was born in 1873 in Richmond, Virginia, the eighth of 10 children. Her father, Francis Thomas Glasgow, was a wealthy landowner and managing director of Tredegar Iron Works, the main supplier of munitions to the Confederacy. Her mother, Anne Jane Gholson, was related to several prominent Virginia families. They embodied the hard-edged Calvinism and the fading aristocratic traditions that Glasgow was to examine in her fiction. She is considered a regionalist and a realist, whose novels, most notably *VEIN OF IRON* (1835), explore the social mores, generational tensions, evolving gender norms, and increasingly industrial landscape of the American South.

As a child, Glasgow spent the summers at Jerdone Castle, a large estate north of Richmond, purchased by her father when she was about six. Julius Raper reports that she "ranged about the fields of corn and tobacco, through the broomsedge and scrub pine, and on into the virgin woods. Summers there she gave to natural things — earth, sky, hills, fields, trees, grass, flowers — for which she developed a lasting affection" (150). Glasgow was a small and sickly child, considered too delicate for school. Much of her early education consisted of her own reading — favorite authors were Fielding, Dickens, and Meredith — and later she was attracted to the work of Thomas Hardy. Still later, under the influence of her much-admired brother-in-law, Walter McCormick, she began to read works of philosophy, including Spencer, Mill and Huxley. Most influential was her reading of Darwin; her experiences drew her to a Darwinian world view, where forces of nature and competition favor the strong.

In her posthumously published autobiography,

Glasgow referred to "the many tragedies of my life," beginning with her mother's chronic nervous illness and early death in 1893. Glasgow's biographer, Susan Goodman, describes her "antipathy" to her father and the resulting family tensions (20–21). In the years after her mother's death, Glasgow was again devastated by the death of her mentor, Walter McCormick, the loss of a beloved sister to cancer, and later her favorite brother's suicide. Perhaps equally devastating was the onset of hearing impairment. Although she lived an active and social life, Glasgow's partial deafness caused her to be, to some extent, socially isolated and dependent on others. Self-conscious about her increasing deafness, she did her best to conceal her condition and continued to seek cures, reluctantly using an amplifying device later in life. Her first desire when she obtained a hearing aid was to listen to the sounds of nature (Goodman 113).

One source of solace was her deep and life-long love for animals. Glasgow was famously attached to her own pet dogs, and was involved in promoting animal rights, once giving a speech on "The Moral Responsibility of Man to Animals" (Goodman 114). She was deeply sympathetic to the suffering of animals, and at her death left part of her estate to the Society for the Prevention of Cruelty to Animals.—Anne Kellenberger

BIBLIOGRAPHY

Glasgow, Ellen. *The Woman Within*. New York: Harcourt Brace, 1954.
Goodman, Susan. *Ellen Glasgow: A Biography*. Baltimore: John Hopkins Press, 1998.
Raper, Julius Rowan. "Barren Ground and the Transition to Southern Modernism." *Ellen Glasgow*. Ed. Dorothy M. Scura. *Tennessee Studies in Literature*, Vol. 36. Knoxville: University of Tennessee Press, 1995. 146–161.

Vein of Iron, Ellen Glasgow (1935)

Ellen Glasgow's 18th published novel follows the fortunes of a family with deep roots in Virginia history, from the turn of the 20th century to the Great Depression. The "iron" in the title is less a reference to the village of Ironside, where much of the novel is set, than to the determined character of its protagonists. In her non-fictional *A Certain Measure*, Glasgow notes that her aim in this novel was not to trace the fortunes of individuals, but to explore this inherent sense of fortitude over time and under stress; she writes: "From the beginning, I had known that I was engaged upon a family chronicle, that I was studying not a single character or group of characters alone, but the vital principle of survival, which has enabled races and individuals to withstand the destructive forces of nature and of civilization" (169).

Human life is cast a Darwinian struggle for food and shelter. Non-human nature is seen as having "destructive" powers in the novel, but also as offering a source of strength and stability, especially to the female characters.

The novel follows the lives of the Fincastles, grandmother, father and daughter, over 35 years. It opens with Ada as a child, but recounts the back-story of the family on the land, stretching back five generations. The grandmother's unswerving strength of character, devout Calvinism, and devotion to her family enable her to endure the reverses of the Civil War and the loss of several children. The family struggles against financial ruin when her son John relinquishes his ministry, rejecting "the God of Abraham" for a principled and philosophic acceptance of "the God of Spinoza" (45). Many years later, Ada's out-of-wedlock pregnancy forces the family to leave the Manse and live among poor city-dwellers, as the nation's economy collapses in the 1930s. After years of reversals and stoic self-sacrifice, Ada returns to her childhood home, trusting her inner "vein of iron," inborn yet refined by experience, which allows her to continue on undefeated by forces that destroy others.

The novel opens with the village children tormenting the "idiot" boy—a scene that seems to illustrate the violent and destructive qualities of both nature and civilization. The boy is described in repulsive, animalistic terms: "his small dull eyes squinted between inflamed eyelids" as he "squawked with rage" (3). Toby is a victim by birth—like the rabbit whose cries little Ada recalls hearing as it was being "torn to pieces" by dogs. She questions the natural evil she perceives, asking "Why did God make idiots?" (65). In a later encounter with Toby, an adult Ada reflects, "he was a creature like herself ... more repulsive than any animal, but born as she and an animal were born, to crave joy, to suffer loss, and to know nothing beyond" (166).

In the novel, non-human nature has no fixed meaning. Amy Berke notes that although Glasgow "refused to present a purely mechanistic, material universe, ... [she also] refused to return to either romanticism or Transcendentalism as a philosophical stance for understanding nature" (7). Nature is a force that can elevate or destroy. The natural world is sometimes seen as possessing a mysterious power—often a benevolent power, especially when accessed by women—but at other times as being brutal and indifferent. Ada grows up with the naïve assumption that the human and nonhuman world are in harmony with each other and with her. When she experiences the bitter disappointment of losing her fiancé to another woman, this connection is shattered:

"Until this moment of anguish, she had felt that she was a part of the Valley, of its religion, its traditions, its unspoken laws, as well as of its fields and streams and friendly mountains" (161). She suddenly realizes with revulsion, "Life contained no security. Horror waited everywhere to pounce upon happiness, as the hawk pounced on the small bird" (167–8). As Marcelle Thibeaux notes, nature "in some instances becomes a metaphor for the violence and cruelty of the world and the conditions of life for which one must have the vein of iron to survive" (160).

Nature, however, is also the setting for whatever genuine happiness the world of the novel has to offer. When Ada experiences love, it is in a hunter's cabin in the wilderness by the Indian trail. The natural world is not unjust or deliberately cruel, in contrast to much of human society; and the personal betrayals, the horrors of a world war, the economic forces that impose poverty and misery on millions, and the ethic of selfish consumerism are as destructive as anything in nature. John Fincastle ponders the moral atmosphere in the modern city: "whatever could not feed the machine was discarded as rubbish. Everything, from the aimless speeding of automobiles down to the electric dust in the sunlight appeared to whirl on deliriously, without a pattern, without a code, without even a center" (293). Sick and exhausted, John painfully travels to the Manse to save the expense of a city funeral. His self-sacrifice brings the family back to the land and allows Ada to rebuild from a "center."

Ada's return is seen by Lucinda MacKethan as part of "a design that could be called matriarchal" (90). Ada comes to work the land and restore the Manse; here she feels "the dead generations behind her ... lending her their fortitude; they were reaching out to her in adversity" (461). The continuing tradition of her female forbearers offers her hope, as do the seeds in the ground. The novel ultimately highlights a few undisputed and fundamental values that tend to thrive most when rooted in the earth: strength, generosity, devotion to family, and inner courage. What Raper called the "irreversible determinism" (6) of Glasgow's earlier novels had softened by the time she wrote *Vein of Iron*, replaced by a belief in an individual's ability to offer resistance to destructive forces, through a matriarchal ethic of "love and respect for all living beings" (MacKethan 104).— Anne Kellenberger

BIBLIOGRAPHY

Berke, Amy. "Darwinism and the Spiritual Impulse in the Works of Ellen Glasgow and James Lane Allen." *Ellen Glasgow Newsletter* 54 (2005): 7–10.

Glasgow, Ellen. *A Certain Measure: An Interpretation of Prose Fiction.* New York: Harcourt, Brace, 1943.

_____. *Vein of Iron.* New York: Harcourt, Brace and World, 1963.

MacKethan, Lucinda H. "Restoring Order: Matriarchal Design in *The Battle Ground* and *Vein of Iron.*" *Ellen Glasgow: New Perspectives.* Ed. Dorothy M. Scura. *Tennessee Studies in Literature,* Vol. 36. Knoxville: University of Tennessee Press, 1995. 89–105.

Raper, Julius Rowan. *From the Sunken Garden: The Fiction of Ellen Glasgow, 1916–1945.* Baton Rouge: Louisiana State University Press, 1980.

Thiebaux, Marcelle. *Ellen Glasgow.* New York: Fredrick Ungar, 1982.

Gore, Al, Jr. (1948–)

Al Gore, Jr., is a prominent politician and environmentalist in the era of climate change. A politician, lecturer, writer, and sustainable technology advocate, Gore's environmental proclivities guided his work as Representative, Senator, and Vice President between 1976 and 2001. His climate change work is best known through his bestselling books, *Earth in the Balance* (1992) and AN INCONVENIENT TRUTH (2006).

Al Gore, Jr., was born in Washington D.C. in 1948 to mother Pauline LaFon Gore and father Al Gore, Sr., Representative in the U.S. House and later Senator from Tennessee. In June 1969 Gore graduated from Harvard University with a degree and high honors in government. His national political career began in 1976 when he was elected to the U.S. House of Representatives. In the wake of the Love Canal chemical scandal during his first term, Gore co-sponsored the first bill to clean up Superfund sites (Turque 137). In 1984 he won a seat in the U.S. Senate, where he served until 1992. In his first four years as Senator, Gore showed dedication to toxic waste issues, and was among the early cautionary voices on climate change, but his voting record shows lesser commitment to environmental positions than other Senators of his class, such as Daniel Moynihan and Tom Harkin (Turque 217). His environmental self-education took a leap in the last years of his first term (1988–1990), however, when he traveled to the South Pole, the Brazilian Amazon, and the Aral Sea to witness impacts of increased global temperatures and deforestation. These experiences would lay the foundation of his global environmental vision in the coming years. He ran for president in 1988, but failed to secure the Democratic nomination on his platform of nuclear arms and environmental regulation. In retrospect, he confessed that he "began to doubt my own political judgment ... I simply lacked the strength to keep on talking about the environmental crisis constantly whether it was being reported in the press or not" (quoted in Turque, 216). Instead, Gore redirected his environmental convictions into the pages of a bestselling book.

Earth in the Balance: Ecology and the Human Spirit (1992) is a polymath's inventory of the causes of and concerns about climate change, written early in the era of public awareness. The book was published a half year before Gore became Vice President. Gore's writing blends an enthusiasm for metaphor with detailed histories of climate events and civilizations, scientific analysis of climatology, and appeals for spiritual and material investment in the reduction of emissions. It concludes with a "Global Marshall Plan" that lays out a strategy for human civilization to begin cooperative steps towards mitigation. In the plan, Gore advocates stabilizing human populations, developing and sharing new technologies, reorienting global economies toward sustainable use and factoring in the economic effects of environmental degradation, forging international climate treaties, and generating global consensus through active and inclusive education programs. Biographer Bill Turque calls the book "an environmental call to arms, a midlife confessional, and a meditation on spiritual poverty in a bloated secular world, written with a hortatory urgency that places it firmly in the tradition of Rachel Carson and Jeremy Rifkin" (230). Gore's eloquence, tending toward the grandiose, enlivens his extended political analysis and scientific detail. *Earth in the Balance* is a classic in climate change philosophy, and served as a model for generalist books on climate change written by scientists in the 1990s and 2000s.

During his Vice Presidency, Gore stepped back from the strong positions on climate regulation he had voiced in *Earth in the Balance*. His influence emerged in muted form in the Clinton-Gore campaign proposals to increase automobile efficiency, protect the Arctic National Wildlife Refuge from drilling, and lower carbon dioxide emissions to 1990 levels by 2000—a pledge from the 1992 Earth Summit in Rio (Turque 257). The last of these proposals proved elusive, with the failure of an emissions-reducing BTU tax in 1993, a Republican congressional takeover in 1994, and Gore's self-distancing from the 1997 White House debate about new air quality standards that would limit smog and soot in urban areas (Turque 334). Eventually, with Gore's support, EPA administrator Carol Browner gained Clinton's approval for stricter regulation of air quality. Gore attended the Kyoto Accords in December 1997, and through intensive negotiations with European nations and Japan, Gore dedicated the United States to a 7 percent reduction in emissions from 1990 levels by 2008–2012 (Turque 336). To date, the United States is the only one among 192 nations not to sign and ratify its Kyoto pledge. Throughout his eight-year term as Vice-President, Gore reminded Clinton of their espoused environmental commitments.

Al Gore's indelible loss to George Bush in the November-December 2000 presidential elections hinged for weeks on ballots from Florida, a state with 25 electoral votes, where major environmental concerns vied with economic growth to spark voter interest. In January 2000 Clinton administration Interior Secretary Bruce Babbitt and EPA Administrator Carol Browner expressed opposition to an airport development project in Homestead, Florida, where the Air Force kept a base between Everglades and Biscayne National Parks. Historian Monika Mayr has argued that candidate Gore's ambivalent stance on the Homestead Airport development project cost him critical support from environmentalists in South Florida. Despite his extended record of environmental stewardship, Gore maintained that a compromise between environmental and economic priorities could be met in the Homestead case, but he would not give specific measures of acceptable compromise during his campaign. In the last days before the election Gore's campaign manager Katie McGinty appealed to prominent South Florida environmentalists, including local Sierra Club and Audubon leaders, not to forget Gore's strong record of environmental advocacy. Ralph Nader, the Green Party candidate stridently opposed the airport, publicly criticized Gore for not openly stating his support or opposition for an airport between two national parks. Gore lost the state of Florida by 537 votes (Mayr, 125–134).

Following the election, President Clinton signed into law the Comprehensive Everglades Restoration Plan, and the Homestead Airport project was scrapped by the Air Force in preference for mixed-use development.

Again a private citizen, Gore resumed his climate change advocacy with the blockbuster book, lecture tour, and film documentary, *An Inconvenient Truth: The Planetary Emergency of Global Warming and What We Can Do About It* (2006). Appealing to a popular audience, and casting aside much of the science and policy detail of his earlier work, the triad of book, lecture tour, and documentary is an accessible and inclusive call to action. Gore suggests that widespread denial and apathy in developed countries can be explained because "the truth about the climate crisis is an inconvenient one that means that we are going to have to change the way we live our lives" (284). The film won an Academy Award for best documentary (2007), and Al Gore was awarded the Nobel Peace Prize in 2007, shared with the Intergovernmental Panel on Climate Change. Gore's current work includes an ongoing campaign for clean energy called *Repower America*, a partnership with the environmental entertainment syndicate *Live Earth*, and his chairmanship of Generation Investment Management LLP, an investment firm that integrates sustainability research into equity analysis.—Laura Boynton Johnson

BIBLIOGRAPHY

Gore, Albert, Jr. *Earth in the Balance: Ecology and the Human Spirit.* New York: Houghton Mifflin, 1992.
_____. *An Inconvenient Truth: The Planetary Emergency of Global Warming and What We Can Do About It.* New York: Rodale Books, 2006.
Kaufmann, Joseph. *The World According to Al Gore: An A-to-Z Compilation of His Opinions, Positions, and Public Statements.* Los Angeles: Renaissance Books, 1999.
Mayr, Monika. *Everglades Betrayal: The Issue That Defeated Al Gore.* Minneapolis: Two Harbors Press, 2008.
Turque, Bill. *Inventing Al Gore.* New York: Houghton Mifflin, 2000.

An Inconvenient Truth, Al Gore (2006)

An Inconvenient Truth began as a documentary film about global warming starring former vice-president Al Gore and directed by Davis Guggenheim. The same year the film was released Gore published a book entitled *An Inconvenient Truth: The Planetary Emergency of Global Warming and What We Can Do About It* (Rodale Press). The book is billed as a "Companion to the Academy Award®–Winning Best Documentary Feature" and is essentially a reiteration of the film, even illustrated with the same photos and graphs displayed in the film, and with stills of Gore's lecture scenes from the film. (As the film and book are inseparable parts of the same cultural event, and virtually identical in content and style, they will here be treated as effectively one.)

An Inconvenient Truth won two Academy Awards in 2007, one for Best Documentary Feature and the other for Best Original Song (contributed by Melissa Etheridge). Also in 2007, Al Gore shared a Nobel Peace Prize with the International Panel on Climate Change for their collective work on global warming, with Gore's work exemplified by *An Inconvenient Truth.*

An Inconvenient Truth is structurally intricate, alternating images of natural habitats and photographs from Gore's personal history with narratives of his life, and "live" fragments of Gore delivering his now-famous lecture on global warming. Gore uses the images of nature and the stories from his own life (for example, his son's life-threatening accident at age six, his sister's death from cancer) to create a personalized image of himself and his political career; and through this intimacy he indirectly defends global warming and environmentalism *as personal issues,* relevant not only publicly and collectively but privately. What is

more, he calls attention to Congress's repeated failure to address the issue and implies that this failure is a result of *his own* inability to draw enough attention to its urgency. These pathos-inspiring aspects of the work humanize Gore and lend him an "everyman charm" that is "as crucial to the documentary's success as his seemingly strong grasp on the science" (Bartlett 36; see also Rosteck and Frentz 3). Gore's construction of his political, scientific, and personal credibility is widely viewed as integral to the work's appeal.

Gore's scientific credibility depends on his lecture's presentation of evidence of global warming, which he accomplishes through graphs, maps, and charts. He begins by summarizing the work of Roger Revelle, one of his university professors and the first person to record CO_2 levels in the atmosphere. Gore goes on to cite numerous experts to support his claims, many of whom he introduces as friends or close colleagues. He attributes losses we have already experienced—glacier melts, the break-up of the Larsen B ice shelf, the Katrina disaster, deadly droughts and flooding in China, heat waves, and even the violence in Darfur—at least in part to global warming. To a lesser extent Gore projects these consequences into the future and asks us to intervene to counteract accelerating climate change. Throughout, he presents an image of himself as authoritative, learned, and personally acquainted with the relevant research, having traveled to various test sites and interviewed researchers. Alongside the studies and statistics he introduces, Gore builds a case for his audiences' *moral responsibility* to act against climate change.

The work's personal interludes, although sometimes criticized as detracting from its philosophical point, also cushion Gore's message and help audiences identify with him, which is likely to help in his goal of getting people to "feel ... that global warming is not just about science and that it is not just a political issue. It is really a moral issue" (Gore 10). It is also possible to read these interludes as serving to counteract the stoic image Gore earned during his 2000 presidential campaign; at one point Gore even makes a joke about his political career, introducing himself with "I used to be the next president of the United States." In Bartlett's words, "Such populist touches contribute to an informal, personal take on the issue that ... demands an emotional rather than a critical response from its audience" (36). After the film's release many commentators publicly wondered whether it was intended to launch Gore into the 2008 presidential race; and the fact that he did *not* run has tempered some of the more scathing speculations about Gore's motives in releasing the film and book.

Much of the criticism surrounding *An Inconvenient Truth* concerns the extent to which it exaggerates global warming, or strategically manipulates data to support Gore's point. Critics question, for example, the degree to which the graphs Gore presents oversimplify data (especially in the now infamous "hockey-stick graph" found on p. 65 in the book) and contend that his attribution of cause dangerously glosses real-world complexities, as when he connects violence in Africa to global warming. They also question the accuracy of his claims about polar-bear deaths and global warming-inspired intensification of storms, and likewise the truth of his assertion that Lake Chad's draining has been due to global warming. Many of the work's assertions about global warming — especially those that posit cause-effect relationships — will likely never be proved or disproved to the satisfaction of every critic, and the recentness of the research means that predictions about climate change are constantly changing with new data and new interpretations of data. However, the very prevalence and virulence of critiques of *An Inconvenient Truth* do more to shore up its cultural significance than to dismiss it as unworthy of serious attention. Indeed, the attention garnered by *An Inconvenient Truth* led Gore to re-release his 1992 work, EARTH IN THE BALANCE: ECOLOGY AND THE HUMAN SPIRIT, which more broadly examines a range of environmental problems, and explores how everyday human actions can contribute to (or reverse) environmental degradation. Ultimately, and perhaps most critically, *An Inconvenient Truth* helped to produce an American audience more amenable to environmentalism in general.

Perhaps the most curious and widespread characterization of *An Inconvenient Truth* is as an apocalyptic or fear-mongering work. Although it is certainly rhetorically powerful and calls attention to the possibility of future disaster, the work is hardly apocalyptic compared to the canon of environmental jeremiads in American environmental literature. Compared to seminal works such as SILENT SPRING and *The Population Bomb*, Gore's work presents a more reasoned, scientific approach to ecological problems, making every effort to present "apocalyptic" scenarios as avoidable through coordinated political action. Moreover, he spends less time than he might on the victims of present and future calamities caused by global warming, leaning instead to less personal projections conveyed through graphs. Thus characterizations of the work as "a factual fear piece" (Bartlett 34) or a "politicized environmental jeremiad" (Rosteck and Frentz 3) fail to consider its moderated presentation, especially compared to earlier, more fiery environmentalist works.

In the end, *An Inconvenient Truth* is perhaps best remembered not for its technical merits or its portrayal of a more humanized Al Gore, much less for its factual (in)accuracies, but rather for its memorable argument for global-warming's exigency. Indeed, the work may go down in history simply for making global warming an issue once again, at least to a public that had widely forgotten about climate change since the late–'80s and early–'90s campaign against CFCs. The work has inspired a huge body of literature on the topic, from skeptical responses to heartfelt defenses. It has made climate change relevant not just as a campaign issue but as a personal crusade, no doubt contributing to a recent renaissance of environmental concern (particularly in the U.S., where environmental issues had been neglected in the years leading up to the work).

The film earned nearly $50 million globally in box-office sales (Bartlett 34), and the book reached the #1 spot on the *New York Times* bestseller list, reflecting their persuasive appeal to broad audiences. It is fair to say that Gore has succeeded in his goal of making countless people "*feel* that global warming is [...] really a moral issue," and one that we confront everyday. — Laura Boynton Johnson

BIBLIOGRAPHY

Bartlett, Myke. "Representations of the Apocalypse: Debating the Merits of *An Inconvenient Truth* and *The Great Global Warming Swindle*." *Screen Education* Issue 53 (Autumn 2009): 34–41.

Gore, Al. *An Inconvenient Truth: The Planetary Emergency of Global Warming and What We Can Do About It*. Emmaus, PA: Rodale Press, 2006.

An Inconvenient Truth: A Global Warning. Dir. Davis Guggenheim. Paramount, 2006.

Rosteck, Thomas and Thomas S. Frentz. "Myth and Multiple Readings in Environmental Rhetoric: The Case of *An Inconvenient Truth*." *Quarterly Journal of Speech* 95.1 (2009) 1–19.

Harriot, Thomas (1560–1621)

Although Thomas Harriot is renowned as a sixteenth-century mathematician, scientist, cartographer, and navigator, his literary reputation is founded on A BRIEFE AND TRUE REPORT OF THE NEW FOUND LAND OF VIRGINIA (1588), arguably the first book about English colonial experience in North America. This slim volume — republished in 1590 alongside famous engravings by Theodor de Bry — offers a snapshot of how the English saw sixteenth-century flora and fauna, as well as Indian life, in coastal North America.

Thomas Harriot (variously spelled "Hariot," "Harriots" and "Heriots") was born in Oxfordshire, England, in 1560, but very little is known about his first decades. We do know, however, that he graduated from Oxford with considerable scientific understanding and then became an applied mathematics instructor in London, focusing on instrumental navigation. After ingratiating himself into the company Sir Walter Raleigh, Harriot began offering navigational training to the members of the first Roanoke expedition in 1584. In April of the following year, Harriot sailed for Virginia (modern day North Carolina) under the leadership of Sir Richard Grenville, lending this second Roanoke voyage both his scientific prowess and record-keeping abilities. Equally significant, he acted as interpreter among the Native inhabitants. Prior to embarking, Harriot had studied Algonquian languages with two Roanoke Indians who had been brought to Europe, and most scholars agree that this knowledge gave him a much better understanding of the Native culture in Virginia than most of his contemporaries. Even so, by June 1586 the Roanoke colony was near collapse. Relationships with the Indians had reached a boiling point, and fleeing imminent disaster Harriot and company returned to England.

Harriot's day-to-day records of his New World experiences no longer exist, but after returning home, at Raleigh's encouragement he composed *A Briefe and True Report*— unquestionably his greatest literary work and a critical contribution to environmental literary history. Making no claim to objectivity about Roanoke colony history, the book is instead a persuasive promotional tract designed to entice future colonists and encourage financial backers. At the same time, *A Briefe and True Report* presents an assessment of Virginian natural history; and like many similar accounts, Harriot's descriptions of natural phenomena brim with the rhetoric of use. For instance, he first lists "commodities" which "for distinction sake I call Merchantable" and then describes those that provide "sustenance of mans life," each entry focusing as much on the commodities to be found as on the profits that might be gained from them (Harriot 6). Harriot also carefully describes the "manners of the people of the countrey" (22), and his writing in every section demonstrates what Wayne Franklin calls "a seriousness of purpose, and a depth of energy, rare among his contemporary Englishmen" (Franklin 106).

In the decades following his North American adventure Harriot continued his career as scientist and mathematician, but charges of atheism and heresy forced him to retreat into privacy. After his death from nasal cancer in 1621, most of Harriot's voluminous notes and papers remained unpublished, as they do to this day.— Tom J. Hillard

BIBLIOGRAPHY

Fox, Robert. *Thomas Harriot: An Elizabethan Man of Science*. Burlington, VT: Ashgate, 2000.

Franklin, Wayne. *Discovers, Explorers, Settlers: The Diligent Writers of Early America*. Chicago: University of Chicago Press, 1979.

Greenblatt, Stephen. *Shakespearean Negotiations: The Circulation of Social Energy in Renaissance England*. Berkeley: University of California Press, 1988.

Harriot, Thomas. *A Briefe and True Report of the New Found Land of Virginia*. 1588. New York: Dover, 1972.

Lorant, Stephen, ed. *The New World: The First Pictures of America*. New York: Duell, Sloan & Pearce, 1946.

Rukeyser, Muriel. *The Traces of Thomas Harriot*. New York: Random, 1971.

A Briefe and True Report of the New Found Land of Virginia, Thomas Harriot (1588)

Harriot's is an early promotional text, describing the American "landscape in terms of both the challenges of its strangeness and the potential for its commodification" (Phillippon 128). While, as Timothy Sweet notes, such a text is most certainly not a green text, it is worthy of "the attention of anyone interested in a general consideration of ecocritical and ecological issues" (401). Harriot's purpose is explicitly clear in the structure of the text. The first part comprises "merchantable" commodities; the second, commodities that afford sustenance and victual; and the third, the nature and manner of the inhabitants. The first section, then, is essentially a catalogue of saleable commodities. A whole series of resources are individually listed and a paragraph provides some naturalistic description and comments on their uses, at times reliant on information from Native peoples. These range from medicinal commodities to things like iron, wood, and pearls.

Part Two is a similar catalogue of foodstuffs such as corn, beans, peas, and melons. These commodities are cultivated by the Native peoples of the region, and Harriot includes comments on how the ground is properly prepared for these crops. It is interesting to note that tobacco is treated as a medicinal plant in this section. Harriot sees Native methods of cultivation as "careless" (15), but this conclusion sits oddly with his comment that growing corn is less labor intensive than planting wheat. He then turns to what can be harvested from nature without cultivation, moving through roots, fruits, nuts, and on to beasts, fish, and fowl. The landscape is essentially there to be exploited for its resources.

Harriot's account of the manners and nature of the inhabitants in the third section of *A Briefe and True Report* continues to pay attention to their use of natural resources. This is often done to assess the usefulness of particular commodities to the English; and here also, much of Harriot's description, particularly in terms of geography, is primarily motivated by a colonial eye—the means of fortification of Native villages and their weapons are clearly an issue in relation to English intentions for the land, playing a part in "the imperial hopes and dreams" of its author (Phillippon 127). Harriot notes, in terms of the establishment of trade, that the Natives have a desire for English "trinkets," which will make them friendly and "have greater respect for pleasing and obeying us" (25). Indeed, technology such as a ship's compass is thought by the Natives to be a gift from god to the English, signifying the greatness of the English god in relation to their own. Religion, Harriot subversively recognizes, will also aid in colonial purposes. Particularly in relation to the diseases brought to America by the English, the Natives ask for the English to pray to their god to prevent sickness and for good crops. Harriot makes the observation that disease follows the English as they explore the area. While the Native peoples feel that disease may be the result of the English god, Harriot rationalizes this as being a just punishment by his god for supposed Native conspiracies against the English. Harriot's observations on religion can lead to an ecocritical reading following from Lynn White, Jr.'s "The Historical Roots of Our Ecological Crisis." When Theodore de Bry republished the work in 1590, he included illustrations by John White, but the first illustration was of Adam and Eve, further suggesting links between Christianity, the environment, and colonialism in the sixteenth century (THE BIBLE).

Thus, *A Briefe and True Report* can be seen as a foundational text of what Alfred W. Crosby calls *ecological imperialism*:

> imperialism not only altered the cultural, political, and social structures of colonized societies, but also devastated colonial ecologies and traditional subsistence patterns [...]. European diseases were unwittingly (and more rarely deliberately) introduced to other parts of the globe, where they decimated indigenous populations and thus facilitated European military and technological conquest. More importantly, introduced crops and livestock not only supported conquering armies and colonizing populations but, in what Crosby calls "the Neo-Europes" (settler colonies), radically altered the entire ecology of the invaded lands in ways that necessarily disadvantaged indigenous peoples and annihilated or endangered native flora and fauna on which their cultures (and sometimes their very lives) depended [Ashcroft, Griffiths, and Tiffin 76].

Harriot's *A Briefe and True Report* marks a beginning of this process in the Americas.

An ecofeminist reading of Harriot's text is also possible. The name Virginia is in honor of the "Virgin" queen, Elizabeth I. As New Historicist critics such as Stephen Greenblatt have argued, the period is marked by "the transformation of power relations into erotic relations" (169) that mediate the desires of male courtiers in relation to a female monarch. Though Harriot does not explicitly gender the land, reading his text through the name given to this region opens such a possibility. As Greg Garrard states,

> The gendered landscape that seemed to be the fulfilment of Old World fantasies of endless plenitude generated a fundamental ambivalence, however, with a kernel of irremediable guilt. As a nurturing maternal presence, the land could be the object of puerile but essentially harmless regressive fantasies. However, as a desirable Other of a self-consciously virile frontier society, the land might well become a lover to be subdued by aggression [51].

Harriot's process of cataloguing commodities can be seen as analogous with the literary technique of the blazon—"an encomium for a beloved, beautiful woman" (Holman and Harmon 60)—evident in sonnets of the period. For example, in Sonnet XV of *Amoretti*, Edmund Spenser writes,

> Ye tradefull Merchants that with weary toyle
> do seeke most pretious things to make your gaine:
> and both the Indias of their treasures spoile,
> what needeth you to seeke so farre in vaine?
> For loe my love doth in her selfe containe
> all this worlds riches that may farre be found [1–6].

The itemization of the beloved's body that follows in Spenser's sonnet (based on comparisons with merchantable commodities) establishes control over the feminine other, and is commensurate with the intention of Harriot's cataloguing of commodities.

Hence, while not a "green text" by our contemporary standards, Harriot's work provides a fascinating and immensely influential early European description and *conception* of the environment; one which lies at the roots of our current environmental crises, rationalizing our exploitation of nature.—Jim Daems

BIBLIOGRAPHY

Ashcroft, Bill, Gareth Griffiths, and Helen Tiffin. *Post-Colonial Studies: The Key Concepts*. Rpt. New York: Routledge, 2004.

Garrard, Greg. *Ecocriticism*. Hoboken: Taylor & Francis, 2004.

Greenblatt, Stephen. *Renaissance Self-Fashioning: From More to Shakespeare*. Chicago: University of Chicago Press, 1980.

Harriot, Thomas. *A Briefe and True Report of the New Found Land of Virginia*. Frankfurt, 1590.

Holman, C. Hugh, and William Harmon. *A Handbook to Literature*. 5th ed. New York: Macmillan, 1986.

Phillippon, Daniel. "United States Environmental Litera-ture Before the Twentieth Century." *Teaching North American Environmental Literature.* Eds. Laird Chris-tensen, Mark C. Long, and Fred Waage. New York: The Modern Language Association of America, 2008. 126–38.

Sweet, Timothy. "Economy, Ecology, and Utopia in Early Colonial Promotional Literature." *American Literature* 71: 3 (Sept. 1999): 399–427.

Harrison, Harry (1925–   )

While Harry Harrison's science fiction ranges from traditional cowboy-in-space narratives to alternate American Civil War histories, he is best known out-side the science fiction community for works that explore the fear of overpopulation and its attendant environmental and social damage. In these texts he suggests that the solution to their eerie, almost pre-scient problems is an ecocentric, rather than anthro-pocentric worldview.

Harrison was born in 1925 as Henry Maxwell Dempsey to Henry Dempsey, a printer, and Ria Kir-jassoff Dempsey, a grade school teacher until her marriage. Due to the Great Depression, Dempsey worked irregularly, leading to frequent family moves. Harrison claims this is why he spent much of his childhood reading science fiction pulp magazines like *Amazing Stories* and *Astounding Science Fiction.* After graduating from high school in 1943 Harrison was drafted, an experience that led both to a strong dislike for the military and to his later literary interest in war. He entered Hunter College in New York City in 1946 to study art, and after graduating illustrated comics.

A bout of tonsillitis left Harrison well enough to work but his hands too shaky to draw, and his first short story, "Rock Diver," was the result. Interest-ingly, his first agent, hired to sell the story, was FRED-ERIK POHL, author of THE SPACE MERCHANTS. In 1954 Harrison met and married Joan Merkler. Shortly after their marriage Harrison and his family moved to Mexico where Harrison wrote *Deathworld* (1959), his first novel, which features vivid descrip-tions of an Earth-like planet with a psychically aware natural environment that is attempting to destroy invading human colonizers. The colonizers, failing to recognize the sensitivity of their environment, have split into factions that now fight both each other *and* the planet; and this theme, of environmental vi-olence (due to lack of awareness) leading to social violence, weaves throughout the *Deathworld* sequels and much of Harrison's later work.

As Harrison's family continued to move every few years between Europe and America, his concern with overpopulation continued in short stories such as "A Criminal Act," describing a world where having chil-dren over the legal limit is punishable by death, and "Roommates," which would eventually evolve into the novel MAKE ROOM! MAKE ROOM! Published in 1966, the work is more notable for its compelling set-ting and description than its mystery plot: in a heavily overpopulated New York, scarce water and land resources dictate a miserable life of bare subsis-tence for all but the super-wealthy elite. The novel argues strongly for conservation and population con-trol, especially in the form of the then controversial birth control. *Make Room!* was adapted for film in 1973 as *Soylent Green,* Harrison's best-known work, winner of a Nebula award and nominated for a Hugo. *Soylent Green* reworks *Make Room!*'s murder mystery into a moral saga whose grisly solution to overpopulation suggests the most dire consequences for failure to think ecocentrically.

While environmental awareness in Harrison's other work tends to be muted, these noted texts' in-sistence that humanity must curb its desires in def-erence to what a sensitive earth can sustainably sup-port explains both their haunting immediacy and continued popularity. — Amber Pearson

BIBLIOGRAPHY

Harrison, Harry. *Make Room! Make Room!* Boston, MA: Gregg Press, 1979.

_____, Paul Tomlinson, and Michael Carroll. *The Official Harry Harrison Website.* Available online. URL: http://www.harryharrison.com/. Accessed June 17–19, 2009.

"Soylent Green." *The Internet Movie Database.* Available online. URL: http://www.imdb.com. Accessed June 17–19, 2009.

Soylent Green. Dir. Richard Fleisher. MGM: 1973.

Stover, Leon. *Harry Harrison.* Boston, MA: Twayne, 1990.

Make Room! Make Room!, Harry Harrison (1966)

According to LAWRENCE BUELL, a common envi-ronmentalist problem is that, once we begin to extend rights to all humans and nonhumans, we find ourselves caught between "the relative claims of an anthropocentric or humankind-first ethics versus a nonanthropocentric or ecosystem-first ethics of whatever kind. What values to assign to the welfare of endangered people as against the welfare of en-dangered nonhumans and/or bioregions?" (*Writing* 227). This problem frames and drives the narrative in Harry Harrison's *Make Room! Make Room!* As di-verse characters collide in a resource-depleted, vastly overpopulated New York City, we see the multiple, overlapping lives, "places" and concerns that occupy the city space. This allows Harrison to explore en-vironmental fears while avoiding a narrative that falsely dichotomizes environmental concerns; instead employing multiple characters and viewpoints to speculate about the effects that human actions can have on the environment, and envisioning how those actions may create situations of unequal access to sustainable living conditions.

In *Make Room!* the city is so vividly described as to appear at times almost itself a protagonist, and its ecocentric concerns become the reader's. Ecocentrism, Lawrence Buell explains, is a way of thinking that "define[s] human identity not as free-standing but in terms of its relationship with the physical environment and/or nonhuman life forms" (Buell, *Future* 101). Harrison's narrative directly demands an ecocentric response from its readers; after projecting that in 2000, the U.S. alone would require the entire planet's resources, the prologue demands, "In which case, what will the world be like?" (Harrison 9). Harrison's story is the ominous answer, one he wants readers to envision as their own future. With his richly described setting, Harrison creates New York as a virtual place for his readers, encouraging an accompanying virtual bioregional awareness. Deepening this place-sense is the prologue to Part 1, which recites the history of the space of New York City, which is well read as an example of Dan Flores' bioregional history: "The narrative line of bioregional history is essentially imagining the stories of different but sequential cultures occupying the same space, and creating their own succession of 'places' on the same piece of ground" (Flores 52). Just as bioregionalism allows us to understand place in the landscape's own terms, and make ecocentric ethical decisions, historical bioregionalism allows us to project that understanding into the past — and, in Harrison's case, into the future.

The result is an insistence that human beings curb their own desires in favor of what the planet can support. Examples of a conservationist ethic brought about by necessity abound, from reusable writing surfaces to a detailed water management system. However, as characters within the book argue over overpopulation, a "deep ecology" voice emerges in Sol:

> So mankind gobbled in a century all the world's resources that had taken millions of years to store up, and no one on the top gave a damn or listened to all the voices that were trying to warn them, they just let us overproduce and overconsume, until now the oil is gone, the topsoil depleted and washed away, the trees chopped down, the animals extinct, the earth poisoned, and all we have to show for this is seven billion people fighting over the scraps that are left, living a miserable existence — and still breeding without control [Harrison 169].

Sol's description of people as breeding animals blurs species boundaries, amplifying the sense of unfairness in human destruction. Deep ecology is marked by this type of biotic egalitarianism: no one species has rights that allow it to destroy other species. Arne Naess, deep ecology's founder, called for a reduced human population. Subsequent thinkers have suggested that overpopulation is more pressing than problems such as racism or sexism (Buell, *Future* 137). As a result, deep ecology is often challenged as being antihuman or ecofascist — as Shirl challenges Sol in the novel, countering with an anthropocentric "Yet it does seem an intrusion of privacy, Sol. Telling people they can't have any children" (Harrison 169).

The environmental justice movement seeks to redress inequities in who benefits or suffers from various environmental practices, demanding that environmentalists pay attention to the ways in which institutionalized bodies of power contrive to provide a less-sustainable environment for minority and disadvantaged groups. Sylvia Hood Washington notes that "There is an inextricable relationship between poverty and environmental racism and the Environmental Justice Movement. It is evidenced by the fact that it is usually poor and minority communities who are on the front line, protesting and demanding relief from environmental inequities" (34). In *Make Room!* Billy Chang's murder of Mike O'Brien is driven by his life as a minority inhabitant of the boat town, where he experiences more of the hardships of antienvironmental practices than do other inhabitants of the city; the murder occurs when Chang and O'Brien finally confront the disparity between their lives. City riots are started by groups like the Eldsters, whose poverty and age renders them powerless to prevent environmental inequity. Ecofeminist criticism explores the disturbing parallels in *Make Room!* between the masculinized violence performed against nature, resulting in an unsustainable environment, and the violence that results in women's limited role in this society: female characters are caught in a double bind as mothers — producers of more people, emblems of overpopulation — or dependent on sexually pleasing others, thus risking pregnancy. The social injustices in the New York of *Make Room!* are thus inextricable from, and windows upon, the accompanying environmental injustices.

Although individual characters may lean more towards an ecocentric or anthropocentric view, through the novel format Harrison is able to establish a dynamic dialectical context in which his future New York confronts us with simultaneous and compelling questions of environmental ethics and environmental justice. Even more than *Soylent Green*, the popular 1973 film adaptation of the novel, *Make Room!* offers a telling example of Buell's ideal critical environmental imagination at work, wherein "the soundest positions ... will be those that come closest to speaking *both* to humanity's most essential needs and to the state and fate of the earth and its nonhuman creatures independent of those needs, as well as to the balancing if not the reconciliation of those two" (Buell, *Future* 127).—Amber Pearson

BIBLIOGRAPHY

Buell, Lawrence. *The Future of Environmental Criticism: Environmental Crisis and Literary Imagination.* Malden, MA: Blackwell, 2005.
_____. *Writing for an Endangered World.* Cambridge, MA: Belknap Press, 2001.
Flores, Dan. "Place: Thinking about bioregional history." *Bioregionalism.* Ed. Michael Vincent McGinnis. London: Routledge, 1999.
Harrison, Harry. *Make Room! Make Room!* Boston, MA: Gregg Press, 1979.
Washington, Sylvia Hood. *Packing Them In: An Archaeology of Environmental Racism in Chicago, 1865–1954.* Lanham, MD: Lexington Books, 2005.

Hawthorne, Nathaniel (1804–1864)

The novels and short-stories of Nathaniel Hawthorne, an American-born Romantic, explore themes of alienation, guilt, sin, and evil, as part of human experience and as reflected in the natural world. Hawthorne uses rich imagery to describe the setting of his stories and novels, with emphasis on the surrounding nonhuman environment, even when writing about life in a village or town. Nature, as Hawthorne conceived it, represented a simpler and ultimately more authentic form of existence than that fabricated by the actions and creations of humanity.

Born in Salem, Massachusetts in 1804, Hawthorne grew up in Massachusetts and Maine, and attended Bowdoin College from 1821–1824. After graduating he worked as a writer, and contributed to journals and magazines from 1825–1836. In 1828 he self-published his first novel, *Fanshawe*. Hawthorne's second published work, *Twice-Told Tales* (1837), established his reputation as a master storyteller, and an excerpt from one story in this collection, "The Great Stone Face," exemplifies Hawthorne's attitude to nature.

> Some ... show the soundness of their judgment by affirming that all the beauty and dignity of the natural world existed only in the poet's fancy. Let such men speak for themselves, who undoubtedly appear to have been spawned forth by Nature with a contemptuous bitterness; she having plastered them up out of her refuse stuff, after all the swine were made. As respects all things else, the poet's ideal was the truest truth.

In 1841, Hawthorne invested $15,000 in the Brook Farm UTOPIAN COMMUNITY, which he believed would provide an ideal place to raise a family and work on his writing. Although Hawthorne joined Brook Farm, he was skeptical of movements intended to reform society, a central aim of America's utopian communities. Less than a year later, he left the community, disillusioned with its inability to address the essential needs of civilized, and indeed communal, life. His skepticism of the idealistic vogue of his time extended also to TRANSCENDENTALISM. Though he knew transcendentalists RALPH WALDO EMERSON and HENRY DAVID THOREAU personally, he acknowledged that he had little confidence in writers, artists, and other intellectuals because these professions did not put food on the table, and was particularly critical of Thoreau's venture to the woods by Walden Pond, writing that Thoreau had opted out of creating a livelihood.

The Scarlet Letter (1850) proved Hawthorne's first critical and popular success, and was based in part on his experiences as a surveyor in Salem, Massachusetts. Unlike the townspeople, steeped in Puritan intolerance and with their backs firmly turned away from nature and the natural, the wilderness does not judge or sentence, and the often socially-tormented protagonists of the novel find an ease and space in nature that is deprived is them in the claustrophobic atmosphere of the town (a sensation shared by Hawthorne himself). The forest in *The Scarlet Letter*, like those in other works by Hawthorne, is personified and often reaches out (or "in") to human "outsiders" who are exceptionally good or bad. The *House of Seven Gables* appeared the next year, and is notable both for the resonance it suggests between natural phenomena such as the weather and human moods and actions, and for its skilful anatomization of the Puritanical tendency to stand off and opposite to nature, interpreting, judging, explaining, but never participating in it—at best being *in* but not *of* it. In 1852, Hawthorne published THE BLITHEDALE ROMANCE, which was based on his experiences in the Brook Farm Utopian Community, and traces, as does so much of his work, the roots of human problems to humanity, reflecting both his intransigent skepticism of social reform and his privileging of the nonhuman.

Although Hawthorne is best known for *The Scarlet Letter*, he was also a celebrated short story and "fable" writer, essayist, and poet. In 1862, he published *Our Home*, a series of travel sketches documenting his time in England, and exploring the deleterious effects of denuding the natural environment. Several of his short stories are widely anthologized and of enduring environmental significance. On the surface, "YOUNG

GOODMAN BROWN" is a traditional tale of temptation in the woods, inhabited here by "the Wicked one," who holds a staff shaped like a snake and baptizes members of Goodman Brown's community in evil. Beneath this fabular exterior, however, lies a searching exploration of the pernicious effects of humanity's demonization of the unknown and nonhuman; and when the eponymous protagonist adjures his wife — the aptly named Faith — to look toward heaven, that she might resist the temptation of this evil, we are reminded of the Puritans' denatured and displaced conception of that heaven. Here, as in his "Rappaccini's Daughter," wherein the wild is brought even closer to home in the form of a poisonous garden, Hawthorne, like EDGAR ALLAN POE and HERMAN MELVILLE after him, invests the natural environment with supernatural correlatives, even extensions, of the human spirit, arguing not merely for the physical interdependence of the human and nonhuman, a common theme in environmentally sensitive literature, but for something far deeper and more typical of Native American narratives: the delicate but inescapable connection between the soul of man and the felt *animus* of the world around him. — Liz Clift

BIBLIOGRAPHY

Bloom, Harold, ed. *Nathaniel Hawthorne*. New York: Chelsea House, 1986.

Hawthorne, Nathaniel. *The Snow Image: And Other Twice-Told Tales*. New York: Thomas Y. Crowell, 1899.

Mellow, James R. *Nathaniel Hawthorne in His Times*. Boston: Houghton Mifflin, 1980. Reprint, Baltimore: Johns Hopkins University Press, 1998.

The Blithedale Romance, Nathaniel Hawthorne (1852)

Hawthorne's third novel-length work, *Blithedale Romance* reminisces about and expands upon his experience in the 1840s utopian community of Brook Farm in West Roxbury, Massachusetts (UTOPIAN COMMUNITIES). *Blithedale* depicts the environment and human existence as coexistent and contingent realities in a direct exploration of the interaction between human society and the natural world. While the natural setting of this dramatic romance seems, at first glance, to be merely decorative and coincidental, Hawthorne continually depicts the natural world interacting, often profoundly, with the human. Indeed, the personages at the Blithedale Farm, like the Brook Farm participants of Hawthorne's own experience, find themselves necessarily and deeply exploring the relation between the thinking person and the natural world. Beginning with an idealized natural environment, Blithedale develops into a place

of hard work that eventually forces the main character to see his relation with the environment in much more realistic terms.

Certainly, the picturesque setting of Blithedale provides a strange sort of utopian world, a world evoked by frequent mentions of the Garden of Eden (THE BIBLE) or a pastoral Arcadia (AMERICAN PASTORAL). Brian Black describes the renewed environmental relations of nineteenth-century Americans who saw interactions with primitive nature as a desirable end: "As society became more industrialized, developed, and urban, a contrary impulse attracted some Americans to seek innocence in raw nature" (83). Like THOREAU and other contemporaries, Hawthorne views the natural world as a way of correcting an overly capitalistic worldview. Rather than simply romanticizing the natural environment, however, Hawthorne shows life at Blithedale Farm as a place where hard work is essential. Acting as a "tutor in the art of husbandry," the hard-working farmer Silas inspires Miles Coverdale, the main character, to participate in the natural world around him, to hoe the clods of the earth, and ultimately to become a "husbandman" of the ground (13). Such interaction with the land involves more than half-hearted commitment. After hoeing the earth repeatedly, Coverdale disappointedly states, "The clods of earth, which we so constantly belabored and turned over and over, were never etherealized into thought. Our thoughts, on the contrary, were fast becoming cloddish" (Hawthorne 66). As a result, he decides he must give up being a farmer if he wants to be a thinker and poet. In her eco-criticism on *The Blithedale Romance*, Kelly Flynn outlines the basic distinction between mental and manual labor, claiming that Hawthorne's concern in *Blithedale* is to elide those differences — an elision that fails because of the spectator status increasingly taken on by the narrator-character Coverdale (145). As Coverdale withdraws from any involvement with the natural world, it becomes more and more brutal, climaxing in an awful death by drowning. Flynn concludes that Coverdale's withdrawal from his natural environment, like Hawthorne's own withdrawal from the Brook Farm community, indicates that "[t]he land can never be appropriated by manual labor; it can only be rendered comprehensible by the intellectual labor of the author" (153). Such a conclusion suggests an imaginative human interaction with the environment that is congenial to both the human world and the natural world.

To overlook the irony that resounds in the lines spoken by Coverdale, however, is to see only the surface of Hawthorne's environmental concerns in *Blithedale*. Michael Newbury points out that the misassumption of some critics that Hawthorne had no agreement with the utopian goals of Blithedale completely misses the mark by failing to take into consideration his desire for shared labor (696–97). Furthermore, Hawthorne comments on his Brook Farm experience in the "Custom-House" preface to *The Scarlet Letter,* noting that "it lay at my own option to recall whatever was valuable in the past," which included "the nature that is developed in earth and sky" (27). Without the stinging authorial irony, *Blithedale* would represent little more than a helpless wallowing in Coverdale's self-pity. Such irony, with regard to the narrative voice, indicts the narrator's estrangement from the natural world — an estrangement that underscores the theme of missed opportunities marking the narrator's life. Coverdale's failure occurs because he withdraws from, rather than fully participates in, the world around him — not limited to, but certainly including, the natural world.

Hawthorne shows Coverdale gradually becoming aware of the effects of human actions on the environment. Coverdale gives the first hint of such environmental awareness in his description of the actions of one of their company "who showed no conscience in such matters [... but] rifled a cherry-tree of one of its blossomed boughs" (58). Although this statement could be mistaken as a tongue-in-cheek remark, Coverdale's later comments also indicate a cautious approach to human interaction with the natural environment. He imagines that "Nature, whose laws I had broken in various artificial ways, comported herself towards me as a strict, but loving mother, who uses the rod upon her little boy for his naughtiness, and then gives him a smile, a kiss, and some pretty playthings, to console the urchin for her severity" (62). A more beneficial human interaction with the natural world occurs when Coverdale discovers a hideout in the boughs of a great pine tree where he can spy out the scenery. His cozy relation with this tree places Coverdale in a strange, albeit temporary, union with his environment: "The branches yielded me a passage, and closed again, beneath, as if only a squirrel or a bird had passed" (98). For Coverdale, this natural nest becomes a "hermitage" from which he can watch the human and natural worlds in action.

Even though Coverdale, like the human society of the urban areas of his time, misunderstands the interaction of humans and nature, and often exploits and misuses nature, the natural environment still finds a way to act upon and inform his consciousness. At one point, Coverdale imagines himself in a relation with nature similar to that of an American Indian: he supposes that a certain piece of primitive forestland would provide a good place for a wigwam

that does not interfere with the natural world (118). When Priscilla, the wan city girl, encounters "the pleasant air" of Blithedale, Coverdale describes her reaction to her environment, comparing her to "plants that one sometimes observes doing their best to vegetate among the bricks of an enclosed court, where there is scanty soil, and never any sunshine" (50–51). Upon his return to the busy, unsettling city, the invigorating effect of the fresh air at Blithedale contrasts sharply with the lethargic "dusky element of city-smoke" and the "thick, foggy, stifled element of cities" (145–46). The city thus provides a much less salutary atmosphere for human mental and physical health than does the rural countryside.

In the end, Coverdale views nature as an unavoidable reality that interacts with even the most urban human society. He describes the growth of plants and gardens behind the houses as more natural than any of the more artificially arranged plants at the front of houses. In the rear especially, Coverdale sees Nature's pervasive presence: "Bewitching to my fancy are all those nooks and crannies, where Nature, like a stray partridge, hides her head among the long-established haunts of men!" (149). When he visits Blithedale one last time, he notes the moss that has softened and covered the traces of a woodpile of a "former possessor of the soil" (211). Thus, he recognizes the ultimate transience of human possession of the soil, and the continuing impulse of nature to return to its primitive freshness. — Steven Petersheim

BIBLIOGRAPHY

Black, Brian. "Speaking for Nature." *Nature and the Environment in Nineteenth-Century American Life.* Westport, CT: Greenwood Press, 2006. 75–94.

Flynn, Kelly M. "Nathaniel Hawthorne Had a Farm: Artists, Laborers, and Landscapes in *The Blithedale Romance." Reading the Earth: New Directions in the Study of Literature and the Environment.* Ed. Michael P. Branch et al. Moscow: University of Idaho Press, 1998. 145–54.

Hawthorne, Nathaniel. *The Blithedale Romance.* New York: Penguin, 1983.

_____. *The Scarlet Letter.* New York: Penguin, 2003.

Newbury, Michael. "Healthful Employment: Hawthorne, Thoreau, and Middle-Class Fitness." *American Quarterly* 47.4 (1995): 681–714.

"My Visit to Niagara," Nathaniel Hawthorne (1835)

Hawthorne's "My Visit to Niagara" is one of many nature essays about Niagara Falls written in the nineteenth century. The essay self-consciously engages with the difficulties involved in trying to write seriously about the natural environment while contending with nineteenth-century American readers' expectations of the genre of travel writing and tourism brochures. Christopher Mulvey suggests that the challenge of an author like Hawthorne was to discover "what kind of voice could be found with which to talk about Niagara that would not expose the writer as gushing fool or insensitive boor" (55). As a result, "My Visit to Niagara" offers a much more direct engagement with the natural world than most of his other writing, and represents, at the same time, an attempt to critique cultural desires and anxieties about human interaction with the natural world.

For nineteenth-century travelers in America, Niagara Falls exerted a powerful and symbolic influence on the imagination, and Hawthorne's approach to the falls was well aware of what was expected of the traveler: "Never," he begins his account, "did a pilgrim approach Niagara with deeper enthusiasm, than mine" (244). Like other pilgrims approaching a shrine, he knows the expected response, but he expresses consternation at his actual response: "I am quite ashamed of myself here. Not that I ran, like a madman, to the falls, and plunged into the thickest of the spray—never stopping to breathe, till breathing was impossible; not that I committed this, or any other suitable extravagance. On the contrary, I alighted with perfect decency and composure..." (244). Hawthorne's reaction to the falls indicates an awareness of a natural world that is alive with its own pulse. "The noise of the rapids," writes Hawthorne, "draws the attention from the true voice of Niagara" (247). This "true voice" allows him to experience an intimacy with the falls that is not pre-formed by the expectations and descriptions of tourists who have written about the falls. "Oh, that I had never heard of Niagara till I beheld it!" mourns the narrator. "Blessed were the wanderers of old, who heard its deep roar, sounding through the woods, as the summons to an unknown wonder, and approached its awful brink, in all the freshness of native feeling. Had its own mysterious voice been the first to warn me of its existence, then, indeed, I might have knelt down and worshipped" (246). In her study of Niagara Falls, Elizabeth McKinsey describes them as an "icon of the American sublime" for Hawthorne and other nineteenth-century writers. In SUMMER ON THE LAKES, for example, MARGARET FULLER writes of Niagara's sublimity, declaring, "the cataract seems to seize its own rhythm and sing it over again, so that the ear and soul are roused by a double vibration" (4). For Hawthorne and Fuller both, the natural world is a force with a vitality of its own that includes the human and nonhuman.

At the very end, the narrator seems to forget all he has learned, showing how difficult it is to shed romantic ideals about Nature and to embrace Nature as a vibrant force. Supposing himself to have overcome the disappointments and pitfalls of most observers, the narrator states, "[t]he solitude of the old wilderness now reigned over the whole vicinity of the falls. My enjoyment became the more rapturous, because no poet shared it—nor wretch, devoid of poetry, profaned it: but the spot, so famous through the world, was all my own!" (250). Thus, he takes up the idea of possessing Nature once again. But within the narrative itself, such possession is shown as mere illusion, and the Falls themselves possess a presence and force that cannot be possessed by any human. Mulvey claims that Hawthorne manages to find "a relatively successful voice that is midway between those of WASHINGTON IRVING and Henry James" (55). Neither adopting a wholly picturesque view of the landscape that ignores the immanence of the natural world, nor advocating a realist approach that sees nothing transcendent in nature, Hawthorne's narrator sees nature as both immanent and transcendent. The rhetoric of the sublime invites both reverence and awe before nature as a dynamic force, and an awareness of the human place within a cosmos that includes humans within the larger order of the natural environment.—Steven Petersheim

BIBLIOGRAPHY

Hawthorne, Nathaniel. "My Visit to Niagara." *Tales and Sketches*. Ed. Roy Harvey Pearce. New York: Library of America, 1982.

Fuller, Margaret. *Summer on the Lakes, in 1843*. 1844. Urbana: University of Illinois Press, 1991.

McKinsey, Elizabeth. *Niagara Falls: Icon of the American Sublime*. New York: Cambridge University Press, 1985.

Mulvey, Christopher. "New York to Niagara by Way of the Hudson and the Erie." *The Cambridge Companion to American Travel Writing*. Ed. Alfred Bendixen and Judith Hamera. New York: Cambridge University Press, 2009. 46–61.

The Scarlet Letter,
Nathaniel Hawthorne (1850)

Nathaniel Hawthorne's magnum opus, *The Scarlet Letter*, explores an array of differing attitudes toward nature. Although some may seem little more than romanticizations of the natural world, Hawthorne ultimately presents nature as a reality in which humans participate rather than merely a reflection of human values. Hawthorne contrasts Puritan suspicions of the natural world with TRANSCENDENTALIST reverence, and searchingly ranges between these two poles. Where he notably differs from the Puritans is in their demand that nature be controlled, and where he differs from the Transcendentalists is in their idealization of nature as a simple purveyor of truth. *The Scarlet Letter* positions humanity as an integral part of nature, but posits also that nature has a rich, primary existence outside of human control. Thus, under the sheen of an often heavily romanticized nature is the suggestion of an ecological relation to the earth.

The most influential and emblematic Puritans in Hawthorne's work typically view the natural world with suspicion and distrust; and in *The Scarlet Letter* this world is firmly rooted in the forest, that dark "other" always just beyond the outskirts of white European civilization. Many of Hawthorne's Puritans view the forest as the domain of the devil, and the abode of devil-worshiping witches and their fellow heathen Indians. Mistress Hibbins, herself a suspected witch, speaks the suspicions of the community when she tells Hester that she has seen Dimmesdale "take an airing in the forest": "Aha! We know what that means, Hester Prynne!... Many a church member saw I, walking behind the music, that has danced in the same measure with me, when Somebody was fiddler, and, it might be an Indian powwow or Lapland wizard changing hands with us!" (*SL* 209). For most of Hawthorne's Puritans, enmity toward and fear of the forest are the natural and justifiable results of its haunting by the devil and his minions.

John Endicott (1588–1665), the administrator of a Massachusetts plantation and Puritan leader, who functions in many of Hawthorne's historical tales as "the Puritan of Puritans" (*Selected* 180), calls the natural landscape of the new world a "howling wilderness" where wild animals and "savages" compete with "a rugged soil and wintry sky" to menace the Puritan community (*Selected* 222). Though such a conception of nature fits the harshest Puritans in *The Scarlet Letter,* the main characters of Hawthorne's romance do not share this view. As the heroine of the work, Hester Prynne's relation to the natural world — like her relation to the Puritan community — is far more nuanced and complex, and far more open to environmental benefaction. Hester frequently escapes from societal constraints by going off to the woods. But unlike YOUNG GOODMAN BROWN, the eponymous character of Hawthorne's earlier short story of a witches' meeting in the forest, who sees the forest as a site "of wickedness, in this dark world" (*Selected* 146), Hester finds there a place sympathetic to her own nature, even though the sunbeams often elude her. They find, however, her daughter Pearl; and Pearl's affinity to the natural world seems partly owing to the simple fact that she has not been poisoned *against* it by stern Puritan parents, but has instead been allowed to develop and explore her own natural vivacity. When she goes into "the great black forest" (as the Puritans conceive it), it becomes her "playmate," with the plants and animals inviting her into their wildness: "The truth seems to be," adds the narrator, "that the mother-forest, and these wild things which it nourished, all recognized a kindred wildness in the human child" (*SL* 178). The forest is amenable not only to Pearl and her mother but to the rivals Chillingworth and Dimmesdale as well. Both men find in nature a kind of panacea — Chillingworth, a natural panacea where he can gather herbs; Dimmesdale, a spiritual panacea where he can refresh his spirits and return to society reinvigorated. Although these four characters do not all participate in the natural world in the same way, they all treat it with far more respect, and as a result benefit from it far more, than the hostile and anthropocentric character (and world) of the Puritan Endicott.

While Hawthorne's Puritans generally viewed nature as a place of "bad" spirituality (the abode of the devil), the Transcendentalists viewed it as a site where the connection between human and divine was most evident. Hawthorne's view of the natural world is decidedly closer to that of the Transcendentalists, but by no means identical to it. Although Hawthorne overtly distances himself from the Transcendentalists in his writings, he nonetheless sees nature as a kind of teacher — but of a curiously mimetic sort. As Darrell Abel points out, for Hawthorne "nature was not thoroughly mediate but compellingly immediate.... Persons were more likely to project their moods and thoughts, often distempered, *on* nature than to find mysteries 'figured in flowers'" (42). This "qualified Transcendentalism" is evidenced by the *Scarlet Letter*'s treatment of its central romance. Describing Hester and Dimmesdale's passionate tryst in the woods, the narrator comments on the relation between "wild" nature and human nature, invoking in this scene "the sympathy of Nature — that wild, heathen nature of the forest, never subjugated by human law, nor illumined by higher truth — with the bliss of these two spirits!" (177). Most of Hawthorne's Puritans would roundly applaud one part of the narrator's description of nature, and as roundly reject the rest of it. Conceiving of the forest as a "wild, heathen nature" seems at first to justify the Puritan's general antipathy toward it; but such justification is quickly undermined by Hawthorne's description of the natural world as "sympathetic" to human nature. As Melissa Pennell notes, Hawthorne's use of the word "subjugated" is also highly significant here: "The word subjugated reflects the attitude of Puritans (and the later American culture that endorsed westward expansion) toward nature (MANIFEST DESTINY). Nature must be brought under human control, ordered, cultivated, and tamed. The Puritans feared unregulated human nature; they held the same views toward physical nature" (82).

Ultimately, however, Hawthorne's text raises more questions about nature than it answers. As Nina Baym notes, the typical Puritan significations concerning nature and civilization, which both frame and contextualize any hermeneutic understanding here, do not hold in Hawthorne's text: "Wildness and evil are not necessarily identical; the forest, where Indians and the Devil dwell, is also the abode of nature, which the community must destroy in order to erect its civilization. Is nature evil, or only untamed? Is everything that is untamed evil? Why does every heart have secrets, and if every heart does, might not the forest, where they can be shown, be more the abode of honesty than the town, where law and order require inhibition, suppression, and concealment?" (44). Questioning the dominant views is an important concern for Hawthorne, and his challenges to seventeenth-century Puritan *and* nineteenth-century Transcendentalist conceptions of nature suggest that such profound questions deserve intense scrutiny rather than premature, didactic closure.

Hawthorne's personifications of nature — the sunshine dancing through the trees, the brook murmuring its secrets, the heart of nature offering sympathy to the humans in its bosom — typically serve to illustrate and inspire a romantic impulse toward the natural world. However, Hawthorne's treatment of nature is neither merely reactive in a Puritan sense nor wholly romantic. The space separating and connecting the human, the natural, and the supernatural is above all a space of *possibility* in *The Scarlet Letter*. And while Puritans may too quickly cleave the natural to the supernatural, the Transcendentalists may too readily reduce the natural to the human. The narrator's voice alternately applauds, questions and rejects individual characters' attitudes; but finally and most generally intimates that our relation to the natural world is both an important indicator of our individual character and a critical locus of opportunity for our betterment, and the betterment of humankind.— Steven Petersheim

BIBLIOGRAPHY

Abel, Darrell. *The Moral Picturesque: Studies in Hawthorne's Fiction*. West Lafayette, IN: Purdue University Press, 1988.

Baym, Nina. *The Scarlet Letter: A Reading*. Boston: Twayne, 1986.

Hawthorne, Nathaniel. *The Scarlet Letter*. 1850. Ed. Thomas E. Connolly. New York: Penguin, 2003.

_____. *Selected Tales and Sketches*. Ed. Michael J. Colacurcio. New York: Penguin, 1987.

Pennell, Melissa McFarland. *Student Companion to Nathaniel Hawthorne*. Westport, CT: Greenwood Press, 1999.

"Young Goodman Brown," Nathaniel Hawthorne (1835)

"Young Goodman Brown," one of Hawthorne's most anthologized tales, is at once a moral meditation of universal scope, and a revisionist critique of Massachusetts' early settlers, their dogmatic excesses and their skewed understanding of the environment. The story contemplates a dramatic divide between man and nature, as its eponymous protagonist travels from the village of Salem, a microcosm of American Puritanism, into the uncharted space of the enclosing forest. Accompanied by a devilish doppelganger, Brown's trajectory is both geographical and spiritual. He enters a wilderness that symbolizes human nature's darkest recesses, taking "a dreary road, darkened by all the gloomiest trees of the forest, which barely stood aside to let the narrow path creep through, and closed immediately behind" (66). The dense, untamed stratum of the American frontier turns the latter into a site of psychic repression. One sees this in the invisible — yet assumed — presence of those Indians that had been removed from their original settlements by Brown's direct ancestors. As the Devil reminds Brown, "it was I that brought your father a pitch-pine knot, kindled at my own hearth, to set fire to an Indian village" (67). Thus, the wilderness lies mostly unexplored, yet it resonates with repressed historical guilt, echoing the Puritan obsession with the original sin and subsequent fall of mankind. For John S. Hardt, "this forest is a version of the Garden of Eden, albeit a darkened one already controlled by the serpent" (252) (THE BIBLE).

Hawthorne turns the Salem surroundings into the antithesis of Eden: a setting of eternal retribution, not reward. This anti-pastoral tone gains traction in the story's climax, when a solitary clearing in the woods hosts an antithetical community gathering in which Salem's public sainthood is replaced by a pagan descent into vice, the local church by a Satanic counterpart "bearing some rude, natural resemblance either to an alter or a pulpit, and surrounded by four blazing pines" (72). This Dantesque powwow revolves around this anti-church, whose natural elements (fire, trees) compromise the values of purity, thrift and restraint allegedly upheld by Salem's civilization. Far from expanding his horizons, Brown's discovery of his fellow citizens' tainted souls leads him to a perpetual state of paranoia and isolation. Hawthorne asks readers, "Had Goodman Brown fallen asleep in the forest and only dreamed a wild dream of a witch-meeting?" (75); and his question urges us to share in Brown's agonizing suspicion and excruciating paradox: greater knowledge only makes hesitancy more painful.

Many scholars read "Young Goodman Brown" in terms of Brown's theological quest for evidence of God, but the same doubt that motivates his search ultimately dooms it, since Brown's "doubt of goodness is equally a faith in evil" (Colacurcio 304). The Faustian warning that knowing too much is dangerous relates "Young Goodman Brown" with other tales compiled in Hawthorne's *Mosses from an Old Manse* (1846). "The Birthmark" and "Rappaccini's Daughter," for example, caution readers against the implicit risks in man's engineering of nature, a nature that is divinely arranged and only for God to command. Man's tampering with it, a result of the Enlightenment urge for positivistic science and rational observation, leads to abject creations which — like Rappaccini's lethal garden and Georgiana's surgically-removed cheek — are no longer "God's making, but the monstrous offspring of man's depraved fancy" (Hawthorne 198). Although "Young Goodman Brown" diverges from the scientist-playing-God trope, Hawthorne still debates whether or not human knowledge should have boundaries.

From an eco-critical perspective, the nonhuman environment in "Young Goodman Brown" exists partly as an unfathomable 'other' and partly as an allegorical device that materializes Puritan anxieties. The landscape in "Young Goodman Brown" tightly correlates with the protagonist's moral, spiritual and psychological state, and this allows critics like Reginald Cook to relate "Young Goodman Brown" to other famous mindscapes of American letters such as EDGAR ALLAN POE's oneiric opening of "The Fall of the House of Usher" (39–40). And like Poe, Hawthorne explores the deeper and more unsettling question whether there can *be* a true landscape that is not at once a mindscape. In the original preface to *Mosses*, Hawthorne's contemplation of Concord's bucolic surroundings leads him to ponder if natural forms can actually exist without our psychological filtering: "Which, after all, was the most real — the picture, or the original? — the objects palpable to our grosser senses, or their apotheosis in the stream beneath?" (280–81). Rooting our analysis in this question, we can read "Young Goodman Brown" as a story about man's profound inability to "read" nature, to access it outside the frame of his own perception and its ideological tunnel visions. LAWRENCE BUELL expresses a similar frustration when he affirms, "one can 'speak a word for Nature, for absolute freedom and wildness,' as Thoreau did, but self-evidently no humans can speak *as* the environment, *as* nature, *as* a nonhuman animal" (7). At its most insightful, "Young Goodman Brown" interrogates the Puritan construction of the wilderness as a moral setting, even if it, like its protagonist, cannot ulti-mately confirm if there is a natural world outside the self.

This essentially epistemic failure transforms nature into a mirror that mocks man's epistemological pretensions. In "Youth Goodman Brown," several scenes introduce a personified wilderness that mocks Brown's bewilderment. When an enraged Brown calls his wife Faith in despair, "the echoes of the forest mocked him, crying, "Faith! Faith!" Or in the following scene:

> The whole forest was peopled with frightful sounds — the creaking of the trees, the howling of wild beasts, and the yell of Indians; while sometimes the wind tolled like a distant church bell, and sometimes gave a broad roar around the traveller, as if all Nature were laughing him to scorn. But he was himself the chief horror of the scene, and shrank not from its other horrors [71].

Even if he partly shares the early New Englanders' fear of and aversion for the forest, Hawthorne also cautions against their excessive allegorizing of nature. The apex of Brown's despair overlaps with an authorial detachment in which Brown and Brown alone becomes "himself the chief horror of the scene." Still far from the eco-centrism described by Lawrence Buell as the fundamental requisite of environmental literature and "nature writing," Hawthorne's anthropocentric expression of the American wilderness is, nonetheless, not merely self-aware, but aware of the self's intimate relationship to that wilderness. — Manuel Herrero-Puertas

BIBLIOGRAPHY

Buell, Lawrence. *The Future of Environmental Criticism: Environmental Crisis and Literary Imagination*. Malden: Blackwell, 2005.
Collacurcio, Michael J. *The Province of Piety: Moral History in Hawthorne's Early Tales*. Durham: Duke University Press, 1995.
Cook, Reginald. "The Forest of Goodman's Brown Night: A Reading of Hawthorne's 'Young Goodman Brown'" *New England Quarterly*. 43.3 (Sept. 1970): 473–81.
Hardt, John S. "Doubts in the American Garden: Three Cases of Paradisal Skepticism." *Modern Critical Interpretations: Nathaniel Hawthorne's "Young Goodman Brown."* Ed. Harold Bloom. New York: Chelsea House, 2005.
Hawthorne, Nathaniel. *Nathaniel Hawthorne's Tales*. Ed. James McIntosh. New York, London: Norton, 1987.

Hay, John (1915–2011)

Widely considered the dean of twentieth-century American nature writing, John Hay authored some 16 books and hundreds of shorter pieces, describing the need for a revival of awareness of the natural world that humanity, in its rush toward modernization, has long forgotten.

John Hay was born in Ipswich, Massachusetts, in 1915, to Clarence Leonard Hay and Alice Appleton Hay, but soon moved into the social and political circles of Manhattan. Grandson to John Milton Hay — personal secretary to Abraham Lincoln and secretary of state to William McKinley and THEODORE ROOSEVELT, as well as a poet and biographer — Hay was brought up in a world readymade for an inquisitive child, as Clarence would allow his son to accompany him on business to Central America in his work as archaeological curator for the New York Museum of Natural History. After completing his studies at Harvard, where he earned the nickname Foggy Hay for his dreamy attitude, Hay contacted the poet Conrad Aiken, who invited the young freelance writer and his wife, Kristi, to live with him at his Cape Cod home. Acting as mentor, Aiken also convinced Hay, before his being drafted into service during World War II, to purchase a parcel of land at nearby Dry Hill, a plot that would become, for nearly 60 years, Hay's home and principal subject, until the Hays retired permanently to Maine.

From the publication of his first collection of poems, *A Private History* (1947), the connection to the Cape Cod environment (and the natural world generally) and its effect on the psyche, as evidenced in verse, became a central theme in a lifetime of writing. *The Run* (1959), his first book-length work to engage the nonhuman world, is a natural history of alewives that visit Cape Cod. Garnering popular and critical attention, the book provided Hay with the encouragement and financial security to pursue this genre. Hay's style continues the THOREAUVIAN tradition, through fellow Cape-Codder Henry Beston, as it relentlessly pursues a reconnection to our local spaces through tireless observation. Works like *The Great Beach* (1963, winner of the prestigious John Burroughs Medal for natural history), and *A Beginner's Faith in Things Unseen* (1995), kept Hay's gaze trained homeward. His works range widely in terms of his local subjects; however, the writer returned again and again to avian life, as in *Spirit of Survival* (1974), and to environmental concerns, particularly as he saw humanity's estrangement from nature as ultimately an ethical problem, as in *The Defense of Nature* (1969), THE UNDISCOVERED COUNTRY (1981), and *The Immortal Wilderness* (1987). As Hay writes, "If I can write well enough so that people can prick up their ears and their senses ... if I can do it in some sort of ethical, moral fashion so that people will listen — I realize they won't listen very much — it's about all you can do." Apart from his writing, Hay was involved with numerous nature projects, including the founding, in 1954, of the Cape Cod Museum of Natural History. Seeing education as an antidote

to the human-nature schism, he was also, from 1972–1987, visiting professor of environmental studies at Dartmouth College. Hay passed away in his Maine retreat in early 2011, leaving behind a mass of unpublished work and personal journals, a rich testament to his commitment to writing everyday.

Because of the highly regional aspects of his work, Hay remains a somewhat underground figure in environmental writing. Nonetheless, owing to his lengthy career, one can see Hay's influence as a compassionate, concerned observer of the nonhuman world, on generations of writers, including Scott Russell Sanders, BARRY LOPEZ, ANNIE DILLARD, JAMES DICKEY, and David Gessner, who has called Hay a "prophet" for his Jeremiadic qualities in addressing environmental concerns years before a contemporary movement even existed. Gessner writes that where we might see simply old-fashioned nature writing, in actuality "John's ideas ... *are* subtly radical," in that they shift our environmental presence and active attention out of mere journalism and into the political arena. — Tom Hertweck

BIBLIOGRAPHY

Gessner, David. *The Prophet of Dry Hill: Lessons from a Life in Nature*. Boston: Beacon, 2005.

Hay, John. *Mind the Gap: The Education of a Nature Writer*. Reno and Las Vegas: University of Nevada Press, 2004.

Huntington, Cynthia. "John Hay." *American Nature Writers Vol. 1*. Ed. John Elder. New York: Scribner, 1996. 349–62.

Trimble, Stephen, ed. *Words from the Land: Encounters with Natural History Writing*. 1988. Expanded ed. Reno and Las Vegas: University of Nevada Press, 1996.

The Undiscovered Country, John Hay (1981)

Shortly before he shipped off to service overseas in World War II, John Hay took the advice of his mentor and friend, the poet Conrad Aiken, to purchase a parcel of land near Aiken's own home on Cape Cod. Aiken's suggestion to buy, meant to give the young serviceman something concrete to come home to, turned out to be prophetic. That used and abused acreage, called Dry Hill, would become not just a sanctuary for Hay, but in some ways his entire world. More than a retreat from the horrors of globalized warfare, the Dry Hill–Cape Cod space emerged in Hay's life as home and subject matter for a writer who wrote prodigiously about little else but the area immediately surrounding the spartan accommodations he and his wife quietly enjoyed for nearly 60 years.

Like THOREAU, who famously "traveled extensively in Concord," Hay became the chief tourist, caretaker, popularizer, and natural historian of the

Cape, doing much for its literary and tourist reputation, and developing a preservationist's ecological mindset in an age before environmental thinking attained its current vogue. While Hay's popularity as a nature writer was secured by the publication in 1959 of *The Run*, an insightful, lyric natural history of the Cape's alewife (a native herring), *The Undiscovered Country* (1981) chronicles the Cape as Hay knew it best. Harnessing the inertia emerging out of the nascent environmental movement in the years following passage of the Wilderness Act (1964), the Clean Air and Water Acts (1963 and 1972), and the celebration of the first Earth Day (1970), he writes in the introduction, "We were born into the great democracy of nature, no matter how far we seem to have strayed, and more and more people are looking for ways to be its citizens again." *The Undiscovered Country*, in its concern with reacquainting ourselves with the biotic community of the earth by illustrating one person's experience of getting to know a relatively small portion of it, spurs the reader's interest in regaining our place in a world otherwise gone astray.

In Part One, "Dimensions of the Past," Hay tells the story of his return from military service and his settling in at Dry Hill. Hay recounts his return in a register familiar to readers of veterans' narratives, where trauma dominates the writer's response to his return from combat; while Hay spends no time on what he as seen and experienced as a soldier, it is clear enough that the war was a traumatic experience. The natural world, however, proves a tonic to this fatigue by providing a welcome distraction to his war-weary mind. "Dimensions" therefore illustrates the process of Hay's natural history self-education — from simple naming to more complex ecological interconnectedness — as he comes to learn the constituent elements and movements of his new home. In fact, it is this education itself that makes the place a home. Spending time contemplating the sea, which he sees as "wonderfully indifferent to my complaints," Hay comes to understand his return as the discovery of something new, despite his having been here before. "So it had been for thousands of years: the original exercise, the inescapable condition. And although our age seemed to have cast itself out beyond all moorings, this was where the New World came into view again." This re-visioning of place encourages the reader to see how even the ostensibly familiar can become remarkable again, and anticipates Barry Lopez's vision of ethical ecological thinking in his *Rediscovery of North America* (1992). Hay's awe and humility reappear frequently throughout the first part of the book, as the narrator confronts elements and patterns, much larger than himself, at work. Hay

is capable of seeing himself in and amongst things, and not claiming dominion over them.

In Part Two, "Live with Me," he chronicles various particular experiences he encounters as a resident of a place that to an outsider might appear a windswept coastal desert, but on closer inspection is teeming with life and drama. Throughout the section Hay invokes a number of tropes that have become standard motifs for contemporary nature writers, some of which he had developed in his earlier work. These include the notion of the ecological Indian, biotic wholeness in a form similar to Gaia, and probing the banal or maligned aspects of the natural world in order to engage a larger ecological point. In the chapter "Chroniclers of the Year," Hay discusses so-called "nuisances" (like earwigs) in order to critique the notion of utility. As he writes, "When we dismiss any 'wildlife,' plants as well as animals, as useless to us, or insignificant, we risk doing the same to the whole passage of the earth around the sun." In other words, one small part entails the whole. This refiguration of knowledge, gleaned from daily lived experience, exemplifies Hay's method of discovery. What was once simply setting or background noise now comes to the fore as an integral part of a finely tuned web of relations waiting to be noticed by the conscious — and conscientious — mind.

Near the end, in a chapter uneventfully called "Hunger and the Crickets" (because the most impressive knowledge comes from the seemingly uneventful), Hay expresses his project most clearly as an embodied and lively philosophical practice, that will be more than enough for one lifetime. "I think I can say this much, though I am still groping, still probing the darkness of unknowing," he writes:

> The things we do, or fail to do, become more significant as they are involved in the concentricity of the world. You listen best when other lives are listening. Any minor act we take is heightened by the full vigor and engagement of its surroundings. Nothing we say can be completely empty or idle except insofar as it is isolated from an environment that busies itself with us, as we in turn occupy ourselves to its advantage. We become more than we are when there are other than ourselves, whether of foreign speech, or no speech at all, to measure our lives by. We are superior only to the degree that we share that superiority. The truth is a composite thing. This new country, this older wilderness that spawned us, exists by reason of the inclusion of infinite force, danger, and opportunity. The only reality is in participation.

Rather than sit back and passively record details, Hay's interaction with earthly matters and literary reflection on the world are themselves both morally benign and intellectually rigorous. In this way, Hay's

Undiscovered Country presents a project more THOREAUVIAN than EMERSONIAN: action and thinking must take place simultaneously in order to produce a meaningful existence. Thus the "country" of Hay's title ultimately reveals itself to be the metaphysical truth of his own existence, just as much as the Cape Cod geography in which he lives and which prompted the book. To be in a place, to come to terms with it, requires interaction with that place in thought and action. This merging of mind and matter fulfills the ethical and intellectual obligations of the active, meaningful life he advocates in all of his works, but which receives its fullest explication here in an holistic ecological vision of living mindfully on — and with — the earth. That it took Hay some 35 years to write the story of his arriving and learning to live in the place he called home should therefore come as no surprise, as that learning process would take a lifetime or more, and even then present only suggestions as answers to the question of how to live. The active search is all that should matter, and be enough for a life well lived.— Tom Hertweck

BIBLIOGRAPHY

Federman, Donald. "Toward an Ecology of Place: Three Views of Cape Cod." *Colby Literary Quarterly* 13 (1977): 209–22. Print.

Hill, Jen. "John Hay." *Twentieth-Century American Nature Writers*. Ed. Roger Thompson and Scott J. Bryson. Detroit: Gale, 2003. Print.

Lopez, Barry. *The Rediscovery of North America*. 1990. New York: Vintage, 1992. Print.

Hemingway, Ernest (1899–1961)

From his birthplace in Oak Park, Illinois, Ernest Hemingway went on to explore, with unrivalled veracity, the nature and human significance of a host of disparate environments around the world. His unadorned and mesmerizing prose is an icon of Modernism, bringing an acute sense of language to bear on the overwhelming human and environmental realities of the first half of the 20th-century, and typically paying close attention to environmental details, focusing on animals, weather, food, and landforms as focal points for his stories.

Hemingway spent portions of his childhood in Northern Michigan, and this ecosystem figures prominently in many of his works. For example, in several short stories Hemingway situates his semiautobiographical character Nick Adams, at different ages, near the shorelines of Lake Michigan, where Nick experiences both epiphanies and existential dread in this glacially formed landscape. The literary scholar Thomas Strychacz has noted how Hemingway's Northern Michigan scenes rely on concepts of nature inherited from Native Americans, as well as from American TRANSCENDENTALISM (82). Hemingway's Northern woods, moreover, serve as spiritual registers even when the characters themselves seem spiritually void.

A distinctly Modernist concept of the environment emerges from Hemingway's oeuvre, as well. *A Moveable Feast* begins:

> Then there was the bad weather. It would come in one day when the fall was over. We would have to shut the windows in the night against the rain and the cold wind would strip the leaves from the trees in the Place Contrescarpe. The leaves lay sodden in the rain and the wind drove the rain against the big green autobus at the terminal and the Café des Amateurs was crowded and the windows misted over from the heat and the smoke inside [3].

The passage begins with vivid seasonal imagery involving rainstorms, temperature shifts, and plant life — and then ends in a gritty city with public transit and obscured visibility. In characteristically Modernist fashion, Hemingway evokes a nature that is fragmented and eludes objectification: the natural environment surrounds, flows through, and encompasses human culture, as in this description of Paris.

Hemingway is often cited for his aura of outdoorsy masculinity, but it is critical to understand that he was first and foremost a *writer*. Hemingway was just as taken (if not more so) with the wildness of words as he was with trout, tigers, and rugged terrain. The Hemingway scholar Peter Hays puts it succinctly: "his greatest accomplishment was with language" (137). Where one might assume, then, that the memorable scenes of hiking, fishing, boating, or hunting are what make Hemingway's works environmentally significant, the primary wilderness is one of words. As the critic Fredric Jameson has shown, the form of Hemingway's writing complicates what can otherwise seem to be simplistic descriptions of the natural world (408–413). Indeed, Hemingway's writing is almost always as interested in language itself as it is in whatever subject the writing appears to be about. It is useful therefore to think about Hemingway as a writer who encountered language *itself* "environmentally."

Consider the first sentences of *For Whom the Bell Tolls*, a novel about the Spanish Civil War:

> He lay flat on the brown, pine-needled floor of the forest, his chin on his folded arms, and high overhead the wind blew in the tops of the pine trees. The mountainside sloped gently where he lay; but below it was steep and he could see the dark of the oiled road winding through the pass. There was a stream and the falling water of the dam, white in the summer sunlight.

"Is that the mill?" he asked.

"Yes" [1].

This is a classic example of Hemingway's environmental sensibility: the scene begins with the close textures and sounds of pine trees, and then zooms out to include a framing landscape view. The interjection of dialogue suggests that it is not enough to perceive topography; the characters need words to describe and confirm their sense of place. Hemingway's writing hovers on irreducible thresholds between the external world and the human mind, and in this regard the works are key environmental literary texts.

Another compelling environmental aspect of Hemingway's work is how his style itself is often described through recourse to a natural metaphor: the "iceberg theory" of writing. Hemingway argued that, as only the tip of an iceberg is exposed above the surface of the water, likewise writing should not reveal everything, but only express the bare-minimum of action, dialogue, and plot. Meanwhile, the remaining bulk of thought, feeling, and emotion remains hidden under the surface of the text (consider his discussion in *Death in the Afternoon*, 192). This schema conceives of language itself as a kind of environment: a cold, deep sea in which massive icebergs drift, poking out from the page but hiding a great deal, as well. Such a framework posits an extra, deeper layer of environmental imagery, beneath the actual content of the writing. According to the iceberg theory, acts of writing are essentially reflections of an arctic phenomenon, no matter what a story is about.

For example, *The Sun Also Rises* catalogues a seemingly endless series of drunken parties and inane conversations among American expatriates in Europe. But this is merely the tip of the iceberg; beneath the surface of the words accumulates the swelling violence of World War I, a sense of despair at the futility of so-called "progress," and general cynicism concerning the viability of romantic love in the modern world. At one point in the novel, when the main character Jake and his friend Bill are headed on a fishing excursion in the hills near the Basque town of Burguete, Hemingway provides the following account of their walk, a vivid example of classic environmental imagery:

It was a beech wood and the trees were very old. Their roots bulked above the ground and the branches were twisted. We walked on the road between the thick trunks of the old beeches and the sunlight came through the leaves in light patches on the grass. The trees were big, and the foliage was thick but it was not gloomy. There was no undergrowth, only the smooth grass, very green and fresh, and the big gray trees well spaced as though it were a park.

"This is country," Bill said [122].

Just before this passage the two had been bantering, but then Bill mentioned Jake's war wound, which shuts down the conversation. The novel transitions into a picturesque landscape scene as a way to avoid Jake's inner-subjective quagmire; this avoidance is reflected in Hemingway's use of apophasis, or the mentioning of things not present (*no* gloominess, *no* undergrowth), drawing the reader's attention to these things while also claiming that they are *absent*. Bill's understated pronouncement that what surrounds them "is country" marks the tip of the dialogic iceberg. There is a great deal left unsaid; a critical mass concealed and congealed beneath the surface of words, which deflects our attention to a spectacular (but incidental) forest. The iceberg theory reveals the operative "environment" to be consisting not merely of the greenery in this passage, but also *how* this greenery functions in the broader environment of the story: the verdant description suggests a vast and looming world of things, only some of which can be glimpsed through words.

Hemingway's works are highly sophisticated in terms of their environmental aesthetics. He was obviously enthralled by landscapes and animals, and constantly saw the human world *through* them, but it is essential to realize that language itself was just as captivating to the writer, and just as wild.— Christopher Schaberg

BIBLIOGRAPHY

Hays, Peter. *Ernest Hemingway*. New York: Continuum, 1990.
Hemingway, Ernest. *Death in the Afternoon*. New York: Scribner, 1932.
_____. *For Whom the Bell Tolls*. New York: Scribner, 1940.
_____. *A Moveable Feast*. New York: Scribner, 1964.
_____. *The Sun Also Rises*. New York: Scribner, 1926.
Jameson, Fredric. *Marxism and Form*. Princeton, NJ: Princeton University Press, 1971.
Strychacz, Thomas. "In Our Time, Out of Season." *The Cambridge Companion to Ernest Hemingway*. Ed. Scott Donaldson. Cambridge: Cambridge University Press, 1996.

The Old Man and the Sea, Ernest Hemingway (1952)

One of the best known works of Ernest Hemingway (1899–1961), *The Old Man and the Sea* tells the story of Santiago, an old fisherman on the north coast of Cuba who hooks a huge 18 foot marlin far out to sea. After valiantly fighting the fish for three days he finally catches it, only to have it soon devoured by sharks. Written in Hemingway's characteristically unadorned yet vivid and suggestive style, the novella rapidly became a classic; it won the Pulitzer Prize and was mentioned specifically when Hemingway was awarded the Nobel Prize for Literature. Through the experience of Santiago, Hemingway argues that traditional fishing methods — and the modes of life analogous to them — maintain our links with nature, with the animals we harvest, and ultimately with our own humanity.

In many ways, *The Old Man and the Sea* represents a pivotal moment in the development of the fishing industry in particular, and animal harvesting in general. It depicts tensions between traditional methods and the use of new technologies in communities facing increasing international economic competition. The first factory fishing trawlers appeared in the mid-fifties, and longlining in the early sixties; and along with increased demand since the 1950s, these pressures on fish stocks have reduced the numbers of top marine predators, like the blue marlin Santiago catches, by 90 percent. Conversely, the older generation of Santiago's fishing community rely on traditional means that could never have decimated our planet's renewable marine resources as new technologies have done. The difference between these worldviews — and worlds — is elegantly suggested by Hemingway in the simple choice of gender with which the fishermen describe the sea: Santiago "always thought of the sea as *la mar* which is what people call her in Spanish when they love her ... the younger fishermen, those who used buoys as floats for their lines and had motorboats, bought when the shark livers had brought much money, spoke of her as *el mar* which is masculine. They spoke of her as a contestant or a place or even an enemy" (33). Such "improvements," including a fish house and shark processing factory that now flank the village, will eventually decimate the fishermen's own livelihood and end their way of life (11–12).

Santiago, in contrast, is an integrated part of his natural surroundings. When he departs for his extraordinary day of fishing, he interprets natural signs that an untrained eye would miss: he looks for the tiny plankton the fish feed on, he evaluates the light of the sun on the water and the shape of the clouds on the land to ascertain the weather (38–39), and he watches a bird circling and fish jumping far away to guess what larger fish may be nearby (36–42). Hence, although most men would feel lost and alone out of sight of land, Santiago claims "A man is never lost at sea" (99) and, upon seeing a flight of ducks, remarks that no one is ever alone on the sea (67).

Traditional fishermen rely on nature and develop an intimate relationship with it, just as Santiago relates to different sea creatures, like the Portuguese man-of-war, turtles, dolphins, and flying fish, as old friends or enemies. In an extended passage, he remembers a female marlin he caught whose mate jumped clear of the water to see her one last time as she was hoisted on board and clubbed to death; the old man recalls, "He was beautiful ... and he had stayed" (54–55), by which he anthropomorphizes the marlin and thinks, "That was the saddest thing I ever saw with them" (55). As the three-day fight with the marlin drags on, Santiago feels the same devotion toward it and swears he loves this fish (58, 60). Facing a moral dilemma, he pities the fish but must kill it to make his living, even as he admits that such great fish "are more noble and more able" than the people that eat them (70). When the final fight begins, he calls out, "You are killing me, fish.... But you have a right to. Never have I seen a greater, or more beautiful, or a calmer or more noble thing than you, brother. Come on and kill me. I do not care who kills who" (102); and when Santiago harpoons the marlin, he says regretfully, "I have killed the fish which is my brother" (105).

Although much has been made of Santiago as a suffering Christ figure, the marlin suffers just as much, and of course dies after three days. Moreover, the text focuses on her blood, which trails out of her heart and down to the depths of the ocean, swelling forth when the first sharks attack, when Santiago feels as if he himself has been mutilated with her (104, 113, 122). In some of Hemingway's best-known lines, Santiago prepares himself for more sharks, arguing "man is not made for defeat.... A man can be destroyed but not defeated" (114). His stoic resilience in fighting the marlin, defending his catch, and respecting it as his brother show Santiago's humanity as a traditional fisherman. Compare, for instance, his four hand-forged and carefully baited hooks with the thousands of hooks used in longlining, and one has an immediate sense of the difference of scale between traditional fishing and modern industrial methods that lack respect for individual fish, ecosystems, or communities. Moreover, Santiago's relationship with the boy, Manolin, represents a possible continuation of the long tradition of training younger men to live off nature with sustainability and respect.

As an inseparable part of his environment, Santiago is himself a predator, but one with the bare tools of a boat, a hook, and fishing line. Indeed, he approaches a primitive or even bestial condition as the battle with the marlin wears on. Fearing the rebellion of his wounded body, for example, he eats a raw tuna and two flying fish from its stomach in an almost ritualistic attempt to gain their strength (65, 86). He shakes shrimp out of a patch of seaweed, pinches off their heads, and chews them whole (108).

His hand starts to cramp, but he sees it as more of a claw, perhaps like that of a bird or a crustacean (64). Yet, Santiago's humanity remains after the sharks have consumed the marlin's carcass, and he continues to Cuba with the skeleton. He again feels regrets killing the great fish, and tries to justify it by recalling that the marlin would have fed many people, but then reflects that they are unworthy to eat him because the fish had so much dignity and was a true brother (83). Santiago tells himself "You were born to be a fisherman as the fish was born to be a fish.... You did not kill the fish only to keep alive and to sell for food.... You killed him for pride and because you are a fisherman. You loved him when he was alive and you loved him after" (116). It is this sacred respect for his vocation, for the fish he harvests, and for traditional modes of life, that raise Santiago's tale, and its broader metaphorical ecology, to the level of modern myth.— Kelly MacPhail

BIBLIOGRAPHY

Bloom, Harold, ed. *Ernest Hemingway's The Old Man and the Sea*. New York: Bloom's Literary Criticism, 2008.
Brenner, Gerry. *The Old Man and the Sea: Story of a Common Man*. New York: Twayne, 1991.
Fleming, Robert E., ed. *Hemingway and the Natural World*. Moscow: University of Idaho Press, 1999.
Hemingway, Ernest. *The Old Man and the Sea*. New York: Scribner's, 1952.
Love, Glen A. *Practical Ecocriticism: Literature, Biology, and the Environment*. Charlottesville and London: University of Virginia Press, 2003.

Hogan, Linda (1947–   )

Linda Hogan is a Chickasaw novelist, poet, essayist, teacher, and environmental activist. Both her written and activist work seek to demonstrate her spiritual and political belief in the interconnectedness of all beings. "Spirituality necessitates certain kinds of political action," Hogan notes in an interview, "If you believe that the earth, and all living things, and all the stones are sacred, your responsibility really is to protect those things. I do believe that's our duty, to be custodians of the planet" (Coltelli 79).

Linda Hogan was born in Denver, Colorado, in 1947 to Charles Henderson, a Chickasaw, and Cleona Bower Henderson, a non-native. Because her father joined the military to support their family, Hogan moved often throughout her childhood. Shy and lonely as a child, she began writing poetry in her 20's as a way to "[anchor herself] to the earth, to matter, to the wholeness of nature" (*Woman* 57). Hogan earned a Master's degree in English and creative writing in 1978 from the University of Colorado at Boulder, and has since taught at universities throughout the country. In 1979 she adopted two daughters of Oglala Lakota heritage, both of whom had been severely abused and neglected. Her daughters later became the inspiration for the tormented female characters in her novel *Solar Storms*. In addition to her environment-focused writing and academic work, Hogan volunteered for many years at wildlife rehabilitation centers in Minnesota and Colorado, and has also been an active participant in antinuclear and pacifist movements. She currently lives in Oklahoma, where she is the inaugural Writer in Residence for the Chickasaw Nation.

Her recent memoir, *The Woman Who Watches Over the World* (2001), describes her struggle with a painful neuromuscular disease and the amnesia she suffered after falling off a horse. In this book and *Dwellings* (1995), a collection of essays, Hogan intersperses autobiography with natural history in order to reveal how the "geography of the human spirit" connects with the geography of the living earth (*Woman* 16); while her SWEET BREATHING OF PLANTS (edited with Brenda Peterson) blends fiction, poetry and natural observation to extend and nuance this connection.

Hogan's poetry and prose elegantly demonstrate her political conviction that the oppression of indigenous people and the destruction of the environment result from an economic greed that threatens the survival of all earth's inhabitants. In her many books of poetry Hogan has addressed issues of environmental protection, the urban relocation of Natives, racism, and poverty. Each of Hogan's four novels centers on a different environmental crisis that has drastic effects for indigenous people. *Mean Spirit* (1990) depicts the rampant corruption and environmental devastation of Oklahoma's oil-frenzied boomtowns in the 1920s. At the end of the novel Michael Horse echoes Hogan's own philosophy when he adds a chapter to the Bible which replaces the idea that "man has dominion over the creatures of the earth" with the concept that "all living things are equal" (273). In *Solar Storms* (1995) Hogan fictionalizes the movement that arose in the 1970s to oppose Quebec's massive James Bay hydro-electric project, which destroyed natural habitats as well as the hunting grounds and sacred places of Cree/Inuit people. The novel charts Angel Wing's quest to understand how the physical abuse she suffered as a child actually originates in the colonial decimation of her tribe's homeland. Hogan contrasts the dam builder's conception of the land as an exploitable resource with a philosophy that emphasizes the need for reciprocity between humans and the environment, which are inextricably joined on a "cell-deep" level (137). Hogan's latest novel, *People of the Whale* (2008), addresses the controversial resumption of whale hunting by a fictional tribe on the northwest U.S. coast. Implying the need for global alliances between indigenous people fighting poverty and environmental devastation, the novel links the destruction of oceanic ecosystems in the U.S. with the demolition of the forest homelands of indigenous people in Vietnam during the war.

An influential figure in the growing movement for environmental justice, Hogan continues to write and lecture on environmental issues throughout the world, insisting that ecological renewal ultimately depends on recognizing the interconnectedness and intrinsic value of all beings.— Summer Harrison

BIBLIOGRAPHY

Champion, Laurie, and Rhonda Austin, eds. *Contemporary American Women Fiction Writers: An A-to-Z Guide.* Westport, CT: Greenwood Press, 2002.
Coltelli, Laura. *Winged Words: American Indian Writers Speak.* Lincoln: University of Nebraska Press, 1990.
Hogan, Linda. *Mean Spirit.* New York: Ivy Books, 1990.
_____. *The Woman Who Watches Over the World: A Native Memoir.* New York: W.W. Norton, 2001.
_____. *Solar Storms.* New York: Scribner, 1995.

The Sweet Breathing of Plants: Women Writing on the Green World, Eds. Linda Hogan and Brenda Peterson (2001)

Linda Hogan's and Brenda Peterson's edited collection of essays, poems and personal ruminations in *The Sweet Breathing of Plants,* meditates on the intimate relationship women have had with their natural environment. The anthology, supported by scientific data and meticulous observation, uses the unique voice of each woman to reveal physical, emotional, and spiritual relationships between women and plant ecology. Poetic and lyrical, each piece describes a personal journey into the green world and the subsequent awakening to the intelligence of plant life. These sojourns inspire us to awaken our own senses and attune ourselves to the intricate, intelligent world of plants we depend on, yet foolishly ignore. This relationship with the green world is essential to our identity, argue the writers, and unless we seriously attend to it we are doomed to destroy our planet and ourselves.

The first of the six sections of the anthology, appropriately named "A Passion for Plants," begins with a description of the individual authors' passions for various plant forms, from the humble mold to the evolved orchid. The slow-growing, ancient orchid has adapted to every kind of environment, and therein lies the necessity to pay attention to one of many such marvels of the plant world. A plethora of interesting information about plant parts, forms of pollination, and variety of adaptive engineering is explored, as is the sensual bounty of the green world. Yet, we deplete with rampant consumerism and poor policy this plenitude that Annick Smith explores in "Huckleberries," exhorting us to enact and adopt policies for gathering wild, medicinal plants and berries that currently support our game industry. Additionally, novelists Isabel Allende and ZORA NEALE HURSTON explore the beauty and fragrance of flowers that make them fixtures of human ceremonies, and the subsequent association of flowers with the feminine. But flowers also give off a variety of foul odors too, mimicking various rotting smells to attract and ward off pollinators and predators. However, what fascinates Sharman Russell is that so many things smell like one another, revealing nature's efficiency, and reminding us that we all come from the same primordial soup.

The second section, "Keepers of the Plants: Native Women," consists of three poems, one entitled "Bamboo" by Hogan herself, five prose pieces, and a combination prose/poetry piece by indigenous women, revealing their intuitive understanding of the plant world in their role as nourishers and healers. The sacred *Peyote* and *La Limpia* ceremonies are described, and the *La Limpia*, which is a ritual cleansing of fear, is especially highlighted because as Paula Gunn Allen posits, fear is the root cause of our destructive impulses. These ceremonies, in addition to carefully gathering plants, stones, and special eggs, honor the spirit of all past life forms, thereby revealing the eternal continuum of life, death, and regeneration. They seek cures by restoring the fine balance between humans and their natural environment.

Linda Yamane describes her pleasure of the outdoors through the act of basket weaving, where the careful gathering of sedge runners is both a physical experience and a spiritual reminder of our intricate interconnectedness to the web of life. Anita Endrezze in her poem "Corn Mother," and Nobel Prize winning activist Rigoberta Menchu in her piece "Maize," pay tribute to the humble corn for her plentiful gifts. Paula Allen articulates a holistic way of looking at pain and suffering that could curb our egotistical and destructive impulses, claiming that "being good, holy, and/or politically responsible means being able to accept whatever life brings ... includ[ing] everything ... [we] usually think of as unacceptable, like disease, death and violence" (80). She views the human body as a microcosm of our planet, "replete with creatures that live in and on it" (80). Pain, suffering, and dying are inescapable conditions of life, but by desperately seeking to escape them, we "bring great harm to the delicate and subtle balance of the vital processes of planetary being" (Allen 80).

A highlight of the relatively short third section, "Collecting Myself," is Alice Walker's dense, bud-like poem "The Nature of this Flower is to Bloom." Marjory Stoneman Doughlass in "The Grass," ruminates on the color, texture, and dance of light on the ancient sawgrass in Lake Okeechobee where the new grass literally grows from the decaying rot of the dead grass. Trish Maharam narrates plant cuttings traveling from garden to garden, carrying with them stories and memories of people and gardens, creating an invisible web of plants and people. Finally Molly Peacock in "State of Grace," says that to look truly at a flower is a state of grace approximating Buddhist mindfulness.

The fourth section, "The Science of Green," celebrates remarkable scientific contributions by women in our understanding and preservation of the green world. RACHEL CARSON's seminal work on DDT brought about the banning of the noxious pesticide and Barbara McClintock's pioneering work on maize genetics revolutionized scientific thinking. Sandra Steingraber as a cancer survivor traces the long lasting effects of carcinogens in pesticides and ends with a call to duty: "From the right to know flows the duty to inquire- and the obligation to act" (190). The section ends with Linda Shepherd urging us to think of weeds not as pests but as plants whose value has yet to be discovered, offering the science of combination planting as an alternative to pesticides.

The fifth section "The Forest for the Trees," begins with Kathleen Norris recounting early North American settlers' Herculean efforts to plant and nurture trees in the prairie of the western United States. But the vast, open, treeless prairie has its own beauty and utility, allowing us to experience the other forces of nature such as wind and light in their purest form. Diane Ackerman takes us on a visual walk in the electrifying rainforest where every nook and cranny of forest space is utilized. Rainforests have innumerable varieties of species but each species is limited in number and therein lies the fragility of rainforests where the loss of a few plants means the loss of a species. Both Laura Foreman and Stephanie Kaza lament forest logging, Foreman for forestry experts' single-minded devotion to just certain varieties of trees at the expense of others, and Kaza for our insatiable need for wood products. Kaza grieves over the unacknowledged wood that held the crucified body of Christ and wonders "if Jesus was embraced by the spirit of the tree in his painful death" (236). She connects Jesus' sacrifice to the sacrifice of the plant world and wonders how much will be destroyed "before we

find the tree behind Jesus" (237). Similarly, Brenda Peterson likens the felling of trees to the killing of our grandparents who are a storehouse of wisdom brought on by maturity that "teaches us limits and respect for those limits within and around us" (242). She champions the pagan way of life wherein the spirit of all living things was revered, and trees worshipped, and she urges us to embrace such ways of life.

The last section, "Flora for Fauna," lists numerous observations of different animals seeking out specific plants to cure their illnesses, and reminds us that many of the ingredients in modern day pharmaceuticals were at one time plant-derived. From the chimpanzee that feeds on specific varieties of *Aspilia* leaves at dawn, to the vegetarian piranha that feeds on the fruits of trees lining the Amazon river, this section catalogues animal adaptation and understanding of their habitat, urging humans to do the same. Mary Troychak claims that simply protecting endangered species from extinction without protecting their habitats and interactions with other life forms is myopic and doomed to fail. Her ruminations on the yellow pigment, the carotenoids, allows her to come to the profound conclusion that plants give us the gift of vision, for no animal produces carotenoids by itself, only plants do. This meditation on carotenoids leads to Sylvia Earle marveling at life forms under great depths of water that survive in minimal light. The section ends with a poem by Pattiann Rogers in which the incongruous juxtaposition of the huge whale and tiny iris baffles our narrow ratiocination, and opens up space for wonder.

The Sweet Breathing of Plants is as eclectic as nature itself, and as full of fascinating information and instruction, ultimately compelling readers to heed the sanctity of their green planet through mindful attention to nature's detail and variety.— Sukanya B. Senapati

BIBLIOGRAPHY

Cook, Barbara J. Ed. *From the Center of Tradition: Critical Perspectives on Linda Hogan.* Boulder: University Press of Colorado, 2003.

Fiandt, Julie. "Autobiographical Activism in the Americas: Narratives of Personal and Cultural Healing by Aurora Levins Morales and Linda Hogan." *Women's Studies* 35.6. (2006): 567–84.

Hogan, Linda. *Seeing Through the Sun.* Amherst: University of Massachusetts Press, 1985.

_____, and Brenda Peterson. Eds. *The Sweet Breathing of Plants.* New York: North Point Press, 2001.

Scholer, Bo. "A Heart Made of Crickets: An Interview with Linda Hogan." *Journal of Ethnic Studies.* 16.1. (1988): 107–17.

"Home on the Range," by Brewster Higley (1873)

Brewster Higley was born in 1823, in Rutland, Ohio. He studied medicine in Indiana, where between 1849 and 1864 he was married to three different women, all of whom died. In 1866, Higley wed his fourth wife, Mercy Ann McPherson. This was an unhappy marriage, and in 1871 he left her and his three children from his previous marriages and went west. While he was living in a one-room dugout on the banks of the Beaver River in Smith County, Kansas, he wrote a poem that has since become one of the best-loved and most widely-recognized American folk songs: "Home on the Range."

In his essay, "The Land Sings its History," Carl L. Biemiller argues that folk music can tell us as much about American history as any textbook (25). "Home on the Range" is no exception to this tradition. As is typical of American folk songs, it arose from obscure origins, was passed on orally, and has been revised and rearranged as it traveled through time and the American landscape. As a result, the poem/song can be seen as a record of changing material realities and ideological currents in American society. Moreover, because it is a nature poem, its adaptation over time reflects profound changes in the American environment and the relationship of the American people *to* that environment.

The poem, which Higley initially called "Oh Give Me a Home Where the Buffalo Roam," was first published in the Smith County Pioneer in 1873. The words were as follows:

Oh, give me a home where the buffalo roam
Where the deer and the antelope play,
Where never is heard a discouraging word
And the sky is not clouded all day.

A home, a home where the deer and the antelope
    play,
Where never is heard a discouraging word
And the sky is not clouded all day.

Oh, give me the gale of the Solomon vale,
Where light streams with buoyancy flow,
On the banks of the Beaver, where seldom if ever
Any poisonous herbage doth grow.

Oh, give me the land where the bright diamond sand
Throws light from the glittering stream
Where glideth along the graceful white swan,
Like a maid in her heavenly dream.

I love these wild flowers in this bright land of ours;
I love, too, the curlew's wild scream.
The bluffs of white rocks and antelope flocks
That graze on our hillsides so green.

How often at night, when the heavens are bright,
By the light of the glittering stars,

Have I stood there amazed and asked as I gazed
If their beauty exceeds this of ours.

The air is so pure the breezes so light,
The zephyrs so balmy at night.
I would not exchange my home here to range
Forever in azure so bright.

A year after Higley wrote the poem, which he later renamed "Western Home," fiddler Dan Kelley put the words to music. The resulting song became an instant favorite among settlers on the frontier. Its optimism offered hope in hardship, and its depiction of a utopia amidst pristine nature gained appeal as the area of unsettled land receded (AMERICAN PASTORAL). The constant refrain of "a home, a home" also resonated with itinerant cowboys, and the song quickly spread from campfire to campfire across the plains.

Over time, the song was changed by the people who adopted it, to reflect their particular places and preoccupations (Tinsley 215). One example of this is "Colorado Home," the 1885 version of the song by Leadville prospector Bob Swartz that extols the land's rich natural resources.

Oh, give me the hill and the ring of the drill,
In the rich silver ore in the ground;
And give me the gulch, where the miners can sluice,
And the bright yellow gold can be found.

In 1908, folklorist John Lomax made the first recording of the song, sung by Bill Jack McCurry, an African-American who had worked as a cook in cow camps and knew many songs by heart (Lomax 424). This recording was significantly different from Higley's original, the changes presumably made during the song's thirty years wandering the frontier territories of American society, or by Lomax himself, who admitted to "[rephrasing] some unmetrical lines" (62). All local references were omitted, and Lomax added a new title, "Home on the Range," based on a line that does not appear in Higley's poem (Mechem 24).

In Lomax's version, first published in 1910, the penultimate line of the poem was altered to make "range" a noun rather than a verb, replacing "I would not exchange my home here to range" with "I would not exchange my home *on* the range," and the final line was changed from "forever in azure so bright" to "for all of the cities so bright." This new wording invests the "range" with a heavy symbolic value, distinguishing the rural from the urban and extolling the virtues of nature after the closing of the frontier and the increasing growth of urban centers. The singer would now be committed to the range as a specific physical place, and rather than being unwilling to exchange his home there for the night sky, the singer is now unwilling to exchange it for "all of the cities so bright."

A further change in the Lomax version added a poignant note to this celebration of the American landscape:

The red man was pressed from this part of the West
He's likely no more to return,
To the banks of Red River where seldom if ever
Their flickering camp-fires burn.

This acknowledgment of the genocide of Native Americans highlights the irony at the heart of a poem that unknowingly memorializes a vanishing world (Mussleman 1). Higley describes the very natural resources that were the stakes in the battle for the West, of which he as a homesteader was part (West 18). Less than a decade after the poem was written, there were no buffalo left to roam the plains. The gold rush, which is featured in the Swartz version, offered a new frontier in the exploitation of the natural resources of the "New World." The westward push of settlement caused the recession of habitat for wildlife like the deer and antelope and of Native Americans' way of life, a fact that this new verse, added anonymously some time between Higley's writing and Lomax's recording, so movingly addresses.

By the 1930s, there were at least 10 different versions of sheet music for "Home on the Range." The song was now known all over the world, and in 1934 it was the most popular song on the radio, a popularity largely attributed to Franklin D. Roosevelt's endorsement of it as his "favorite song"; but Russell K. Hickman points out that "the refrain which had helped to dispel the gloom of the Grasshopper Days in Kansas, and had brought renewed hope to the hard pressed pioneer throughout the West, was a most appropriate song for the Great Depression and the era of the New Deal" (20). Thus, part of the unparalleled appeal of the song may be attributable — much like the appeal of the pastoral through the ages — to its function as a mythopoeic medium for the nostalgic re-imagining of the rural for those living in the gritty urban American cityscapes that epitomized Depression era America.

In 1947, "Home on the Range" became the official state song of Kansas, the "official" version reverting back to an almost identical form to the original that appeared in the *Pioneer*. Of course, by that time there were no buffalo roaming in the state, but one member of the legislature joked that "knocking out buffalo and putting in Jersey milk cow would naturally hob with the meter of the thing" (Miner 318). The irony of such a statement might have been lost in a period when Kansan legislators sought to encourage the expansion of agricultural productivity, which had reached unprecedented levels during the Second World War (Richmond 282).

Today, the chorus of "Home on the Range" is still well-known, but the song's bucolic sentimentality often lends itself less to nostalgia than to parody; and its omission of the hard facts of Western settlement have produced ironic renditions such as Tori Amos' "Home on the Range: Cherokee Edition." In an age of increased awareness of environmental degradation and the consequences of unthinking promotion of progress and development, this idealized description of abundance and harmony with nature must take on new significance as the history of the song continues to unfold.— Catherine Cooper

BIBLIOGRAPHY

Biemiller, Carl L. "The Land Sings Its History." *The Country Gentleman*. July 1948. 25, 78–79.
Hickman, Russell K. "The Historical Background of 'Home on the Range.'" Barlag Collection, La Porte Co. Historical Society, 1–20.
"Home on the Range." *Wikipedia, The Free Encyclopedia.* 21 Jan 2009, 20:58 UTC. 4 Feb 2009, http://en.wikipedia.org/w/index.php?title=Home_on_the_Range&oldid=265557372.
Lomax, John Avery. *Adventures of a Ballad Hunter.* New York: Macmillan, 1947.
Mechem, Kirke. *The Story of Home on the Range.* Kansas State Historical Society, Kansas Historical Quarterly, November 1949.
Miner, H. Craig. *Kansas: The History of the Sunflower State, 1854–2000.* Lawrence: Published in association with the Kansas State Historical Society by the University Press of Kansas, 2002.
Mussulman, Joseph. "An Anthem." *Discovering Lewis and Clark,* http://www.lewis-clark.org/content/content-article.asp?ArticleID=459.
Richmond, Robert W. *Kansas: A Land of Contrasts.* 3rd Ed. Saint Charles, MO: Forum Press, 1974.
Tinsley, Jim Bob. *He Was Singin' This Song.* Orlando: University Presses of Florida, 1981.
West, Elliott. *The Way to the West: Essays on the Central Plains.* Albuquerque: University of New Mexico Press, 1995.

Hurston, Zora Neale (1891–1960)

Zora Neale Hurston published four novels (*Jonah's Gourd Vine*, 1934, THEIR EYES WERE WATCHING GOD, 1937, *Moses, Man of the Mountain*, 1939, and *Seraph on the Suwanee*, 1948), two works of folklore (*Mules and Men*, 1935, *Tell My Horse*, 1938) one autobiography (*Dust Tracks on a Road*, 1942) and many short stories and articles in her lifetime. Some of her works have been published posthumously, most notably her play *Mule Bone: A Comedy of Negro Life*, written with Langston Hughes.

Zora Neale Lee Hurston was born to John and Lucy Potts Hurston in 1891, in Notasulga, Alabama, but the Hurston family moved to Eatonville, Florida, an entirely Black town, shortly after her birth. Eatonville occupied a special place in Hurston's memory (she later claimed it was her birthplace), and is frequently represented in her work. Her early love for literature focused on the Bible, mythology, and the folk tales she heard on the front porch of Eatonville's mayor. Hurston attended local schools until the death of her mother in 1904, when she was sent to Florida Baptist Academy in Jacksonville. Moving from all–Black Eatonville to racially mixed Jacksonville provided Hurston with a kind of racial awakening, but she was forced to withdraw from the school after a year for failure to pay tuition, and did not return to school until the age of 26, when she was living in Baltimore. She shaved 10 years off her age to qualify for free schooling, and maintained the younger age most of the rest of her life. After a stint in New York, where she attended Barnard University and was sometimes affiliated with the Harlem Renaissance, she began occasional research tours of the South. These were funded by her patron, Charlotte Mason, and two Guggenheim grants. Despite this prestige, she died in anonymity. Her work was not widely appreciated during her lifetime, and was brought to national prominence after her death largely by the work of Alice Walker.

There are two coherent strands in Hurston's work that distinguish her from the Harlem Renaissance writers: her portrayal of the relationship between Blacks and nature, and her emphasis on locality. The two strands, however, are profoundly connected: for Hurston the swamps of Florida were somewhere she could be without the specter of race hanging over her — a return to the idyllic Eatonville. Thus, while most of the Harlem Renaissance writers were focused on overtly political issues, as in Richard Wright's *Native Son*, Hurston was concerned with a people's relationship with the land they lived on. For her the folklore of the people was inextricably tied to the landscape, and she consciously invoked an earlier folk tradition of hoodoo and religious services held in the woods. Nature was a force that made people what they were. And whereas the Harlem Renaissance writers were principally concerned with Blackness and Whiteness, Hurston was concerned with Blackness and nature, whose color-blind landscape, especially that of her native Florida, forms not merely a backdrop to her writings, but an integral part of them.— Jeremy Elliott

BIBLIOGRAPHY

Boyd, Valerie. *Wrapped in Rainbows: The Life of Zora Neale Hurston.* Surrey, Great Britain: Virago Press, 2003.
Hurston, Zora Neale. *Dust Tracks on a Road.* 1942. New York: Harper Perennial, 2006.
_____. "What White Publishers Won't Print." 1947. *African American Literary Theory: A Reader.* Ed. Winston Napier. New York: New York University Press, 2000. 54–57.

Their Eyes Were Watching God, Zora Neale Hurston (1934)

For decades *Their Eyes Were Watching God* has been a staple of American and multicultural literature courses. When read from an environmental perspective the text highlights the effects on personal development of divisive gendered and racialized environments, and reveals the ways nature leads the protagonist, Janie, toward self-fulfillment. *Their Eyes* follows Janie's lifelong journey toward self-realization, and emphasizes the challenges to her development presented by the racist and sexist environment of the American south between the abolition of slavery and the Civil Rights Act. Each stage of Janie's journey is closely aligned to and influenced by the distinct environment and culture in which it occurs. However, her early connection with the natural world remains prominent, as Janie, a biracial woman often located socially and economically in the gap between black and white cultures, looks to the natural world to teach and guide her when no other, cultural models are available.

Their Eyes Were Watching God opens with Janie returning to the all-black town of Eatonville, Florida, after burying her third husband, Tea Cake Woods. Having left town with Tea Cake a year and a half earlier, Janie, formerly the wife of the mayor of Eatonville (during her second marriage), walks back into town at sundown, wearing a pair of overalls, barefoot, and alone. From the storefront porch, the townspeople watch her return, gossiping that Tea Cake, who was 20 years her junior, has taken her money and left her for a younger woman. When Janie gets home her friend Phoeby comes to her place to hear the story, and as Janie sits soaking her feet and eating the "mulatto rice" Phoeby has brought, she describes where she has been, beginning not when she left Eatonville, however, but when she was born.

As she relates her tale to Phoeby, Janie explicitly identifies her life with the natural world, stating it was "like a great tree in leaf with the things suffered, things enjoyed, things done and undone. Dawn and doom was in the branches" (8). Raised by her grandmother, her conscious life began in adolescence after sitting for days under a pear tree in blossom (10). She identifies her womanhood with, and creates an idealized image of love through, her connection with this tree. Watching bees pollinate the tree's blossoms in a nearly ecstatic reverie, she exclaims, "So this was a marriage!" (11). Nature thus teaches Janie what her grandmother cannot, and Janie reveres this image of marriage the rest of her life, as it guides her through two unsatisfying marriages. The dialogue Janie enters into with nature in her adolescence allows her to make choices that defy social norms and ultimately lead to self-realization at the end of the novel. Inspired and fortified by the image of the pear tree in blossom, she is able to leave her financially secure but loveless first marriage; and thoughts of the pear tree help her endure her second marriage to power hungry Jody Starks, enabling her finally to abandon wealth, comfort, and social convention in hopes of attaining the pear tree's promise of true union, with her third husband, Tea Cake. Even after Tea Cake's sudden death, Janie's continued dialogue with the natural world provides essential wisdom and ultimately peace.

Written in the bold narrative style characteristic of the folktales Hurston collected as an ethnographer in the Caribbean and the American south, *Their Eyes* is told by a benignant, all-knowing third-person narrator whose voice opens and closes each chapter of the book. The narrator has a deeply metaphorical voice full of folk wisdom, and weaves metaphors from the natural world, like that of Janie's pear tree, throughout the novel. In the opening of the book, for example, the narrator introduces the leitmotif of Janie's horizon, and then returns to this at the end to illustrate her personal growth: "She pulled in her horizon like a great fish-net. Pulled it from around the waist of the world and draped it over her shoulder.... She called in her soul to come see" (184).

The novel is shaped by the four main stages of Janie's personal development, with each new stage strongly influenced by her changing environment. The first occurs in the West Florida town of her birth, as well as on the farm she moves to with her first husband, Logan Killicks. At this time Janie's life is determined almost entirely by the racist and sexist environment of the American south in the early 1900s. Janie's grandmother insists, for example, that Janie marry an older man she does not love because she "can't die easy thinkin' maybe de menfolks white or black is makin' a spit cup outa you" (19). As a biracial woman in the American south without any family besides her grandmother, Janie has no option but to marry Killicks. After her grandmother passes away, however, Janie's enduring dialogue with the natural world concludes her first stage of development: "She knew things that nobody had ever told her. For instance the words of the trees and the wind [...]. She knew now that marriage did not make love. Janie's first dream was dead, so she became a woman" (23–24). Through this dialogue Janie finds the courage to leave her loveless marriage and try again, in another place, with Jody Starks.

The second stage takes place in Eatonville, Florida, where she lives with Jody and reluctantly presides over the town as wife of the mayor. Because Eatonville is an all-black town Janie escapes some of the more direct effects of racism, but finds patriarchal norms redoubled in her husband. Jody jealously guards her, making her cover her hair in public and never allowing her to participate in events of the town, claiming they are beneath her. Like a tree in dormancy, however, Janie nurtures throughout the marriage an internal life she does not share with the world: "She had an inside and an outside now and suddenly she knew not to mix them" (68). At last, in a moment of both self-reclamation and self-assertion, Janie stands up to Jody when he insults her intelligence and womanhood, as her internal and external selves unite in a challenge to such patriarchal abuse; and when Jody dies she is ready to claim the full experience of love she learned from the pear tree in blossom years ago.

For the self-actualized adult Janie "the entrance of Tea Cake Woods into Janie's life signifies the moment when her concept of horizons solidifies into real possibilities" (Dressler 2006, 8). Bucking social norms, she leaves the security of Eatonville to go with a man 20 years her junior to a sugar plantation in South Florida called "the muck." And there, for the first time in her life, Janie is happy, as the freedom of the transient life on the muck allows her and Tea Cake to live outside the artificial strictures of society. But life on the muck proves environmentally unsustainable, when a hurricane destroys their home and ultimately takes Tea Cake's life. However, when he dies Janie is able to return to Eatonville satisfied that, although brief, she achieved the promise of true marriage that she had been taught by the pear tree in adolescence. — Kimberly L. Rogers

BIBLIOGRAPHY

Dressler, Allison. "Connecting Nature with the Empowered Self." *Portals: A Journal in Comparative Literature* vol. (4), 2006. Available online. URL: http://userwww.sfsu.edu~clsa/portals/2006/dressler.html. Accessed June 29, 2009.

Merchant, Carolyn. "Shades of Darkness: Race and Environmental History." Available online. URL: http://www.historycooperative.org/journals/eh/8.3/merchant.html. Accessed June 29, 2009.

Washington, Mary Helen. "Foreword" in *Their Eyes Were Watching God* by Zora Neale Hurston. New York: Harper & Row, 1990.

Ideologies: Manifest Destiny, the American Dream, and the Land of Opportunity

The term "Manifest Destiny" first appeared in an editorial by John O'Sullivan in the *Democratic Review* in 1845. O'Sullivan argued for the annexation of Texas, which he said would begin to fulfill "our manifest destiny to overspread the continent allowed by Providence for the free development of our yearly multiplying millions " (qtd. in Kluger 398). O'Sullivan's rhetoric quickly became a national mission: after the annexation of Texas, Americans annexed Oregon County, California, Mexican lands in the Southwest, Alaska, and Hawaii. It was the impetus behind the Mexican and Spanish-American Wars.

The full scope of Manifest Destiny in the mid-nineteenth century reflects a notion that had been embedded in the national psyche long before it was articulated as such. The Puritans arrived in America already convinced that they were fulfilling their "manifest destiny" upon a continent bequeathed to them by God (THE BIBLE); JOHN WINTHROP's famous sermon, "A Model of Christian Charity," given aboard the vessel *Arbella* before landing in 1630, asserted that the Puritans were God's chosen people who would make of their new home "a city upon a hill."

The Puritans found proof of God's will and their role in enacting it within nature itself: just as God's existence was evident in the ordered design of nature, His blessing upon their mission was made clear by the New World's spectacular abundance. These Puritanical notions died hard: writing over two hundred years later, HERMAN MELVILLE asserts in the novel *White Jacket* (1850):

> And we Americans are the peculiar, chosen people — the Israel of our time; we bear the ark of the liberties of the world. Seventy years ago we escaped from thrall; and, besides our first birthright — embracing one continent of earth — God has given to us, for a future inheritance, the broad domains of the political pagans, that shall yet come and lie down under the shade of our ark.... We are the pioneers of the world; ... sent on through the wilderness of untried things, to break a new path in the New World that is ours... [506].

Melville's assertion that the "wilderness of untried things" has been given to his "race" by God demonstrates the unbroken line of reasoning that links early Puritan rhetoric with that of nineteenth century thinkers, writers, and policy-makers, who found it useful in rewriting the landscape, particularly the American West, as peculiarly American (5). ROBERT FROST's poem, The Gift Outright" (1960), delivered at John F. Kennedy's inauguration more than a hundred years after Melville's *White Jacket*, reveals how firm a grasp this logic has had on the American imagination: "The land was ours before we were the land's. /She was our land more than a hundred years /Before we were her people" (348).

Kris Fresonke notes that "[r]egardless of what landscapes [nineteenth-century nature] writers described, they were expert at having seen it already: it was brave, new, Arcadian, ... usually non–Mexican, free of slave, lousy with resources, virgin, unoccupied, and most of all, *ours, by design*" (15). Melville inadvertently articulates the underlying belief that made the land "ours, by design": the perceived superiority of the Anglo Saxon race. The Puritans justified their taking of inhabited lands by determining that anything or anyone who obstructed the way of God's chosen people were doing devil's work; a devil and the forest he inhabited could be destroyed if it impeded the white man's push for progress (Kluger 35). By the nineteenth century, the relentless hunger for land resulted in the Indian Removal Act of 1830, and the shameful "Trail of Tears" as Cherokees were forced off land and sent on a journey that would kill a quarter of the tribe (Heidler and Heidler 90); westward expansion in the 1850s displaced tens of thousands more Native Americans, decimated entire tribes, and rendered all but extinct the American Buffalo (New York Public Library 22–25).

While writers such as WALT WHITMAN, RALPH WALDO EMERSON, and particularly HENRY DAVID THOREAU may have been discomfited by the opportunistic impulses of Manifest Destiny, they found it difficult to refute: they could not resist the narrative of American progress that nature seemed to be telling, even in the face of an expansionist politics they increasingly abhorred. For instance, though Thoreau spent a night in jail for civil disobedience in order to protest the Mexican War, he plaintively ruminated in "Walking," "I think that the farmer displaces the Indian even because he redeems the meadow and so makes himself stronger and in some respects more natural" (qtd. in Fresonke 5–6). JAMES FENIMORE COOPER, whose literary creation, Natty Bumpo (in five novels published between 1823 and 1841) champions his adopted Native American family and his beloved forest, equivocates: the noble savage may be preferable to the crass masses savagely seeking their fortunes, but not necessarily to the noblemen Cooper also admired (Newlin 29).

There is no question that American settlers from the Puritans onward justified their exploitive treatment of the indigenous population and the environment itself as the prerogative of their race. If the land was theirs for the taking, it was also conceived as an inexhaustible resource and an eternal virgin (though in his exploration of the defining characteristics of American literature, D. H. LAWRENCE would ask pointedly, "Can you make a land virgin by killing off its aborigines?" [qtd. In Newlin 28]). In his *THE SIGNIFICANCE OF THE FRONTIER IN AMERICAN HISTORY*

(1893), historian FREDERICK JACKSON TURNER asserted that "the demand for land and the love of wilderness freedom drew the frontier ever onward" (8).

Turner himself acknowledged what more recent historians of the American West have emphasized, that pioneers, the U.S. government, and powerful economic interests conquered the West by overpowering native peoples and Hispanic forerunners (Heidler and Heidler 23). And Turner brings his romanticized vision literally down to earth when he acknowledges that farmers moved westward in search of fresh, free soil after they had exhausted their own land by failing to rotate crops (10). Nearly 50 years later, JOHN STEINBECK would chronicle the devastating results of these practices in the novel THE GRAPES OF WRATH (1939), an ironic retracing of the journey westward during the Great Depression, which follows the Joad family on their exodus out of the Dustbowl.

Yet Turner's thesis of the "rugged individual" having his way with an "unmastered continent"(8) has had a tenacious grip on the national imagination, providing the fuel that stokes the amorphous American Dream, a phrase not coined until 1931 by James Truslow Adams in *The Epic of America*, but summarized in the Declaration of Independence as the right to "life, liberty, and the pursuit of happiness" and expressed fully in the boundless opportunity perceived to be offered by the vast continent itself. Turner credits our frontier heritage with instilling in Americans a sense of "perennial rebirth": "the West offered an exit into a free life and greater well-being among the bounties of nature." (29). This rendering of the American Dream, in which the very landscape is regenerative, is lovingly realized in the concluding stories of ERNEST HEMINGWAY's *In Our Time* (1925), especially "A Big Two-Hearted River," in which the protagonist Nick Adams, shell-shocked after serving in the First World War, is restored while fishing alone in Michigan's Upper Peninsula. Turner's thesis of "perennial rebirth" also speaks to the perception engendered by the seemingly limitless frontier, that one can always pick up, move on, and reinvent himself, an impulse and hope expressed throughout American fiction, epitomized in MARK TWAIN's THE ADVENTURES OF HUCKLEBERRY FINN (whatever Twain's misgivings about Manifest Destiny may have been) as well as "road" novels such as JACK KEROUAC's *On the Road* (1957).

While the concept of the frontier has been responsible for the American Dream's promise of renewal, the American landscape has also been revered as the "Land of Opportunity" because of its capacity to deliver personal fortune to those who conquer it. Perhaps no novel has been more emphatically associated with the illusory American Dream than F. SCOTT FITZGERALD's *The Great Gatsby* (1925); yet while the Jazz Age novel may not immediately strike the reader as one concerned with the frontier, at the end of the novel, Nick Carraway mournfully realizes, "I see now that this has been a story of the West after all" (176). If so, it is a West that now exists only in the imagination: "the transitory enchanted moment man must have held his breath in the presence of this continent" is past, and the "fresh, green breast of the new world" has been defiled to make way for Gatsby's garish house (180). Robert Beuka argues that *The Great Gatsby* anticipates the massive suburban development after World War II that would make the American Dream of home ownership a reality for so many Americans. Land ownership has been a part of the American Dream since the first settlers arrived; JEFFERSON felt that democracy could only flourish among a citizenry of independent landholders (Kluger 43). Yet more recent novels remind the reader that the bounty of the wilderness has been sacrificed in the realization of that dream. Richard Ford's novel *Independence Day* (1996) is a "road novel" that chronicles a father and son's weekend journey out of the suburbs west to Bumpo's beloved forest, Cooperstown, New York. Yet if the journey is arduous, it is because of traffic, bad fast food, and sleazy highway motels. Cooperstown itself has been reduced to the Baseball Hall of Fame. CORMAC MCCARTHY takes Ford's observations to their horrific logical extreme in his post-apocalyptic novel, THE ROAD (2006) (APOCALYPTIC FICTION). In a destroyed landscape, even the imagination has been robbed of a bountiful wilderness.— Kathryn Knapp

BIBLIOGRAPHY

Beuka, Robert. *SuburbiaNation: Reading Suburban Landscape in Twentieth-Century American Fiction and Film.* New York: Palgrave Macmillan, 2003.

Fitzgerald, F. Scott. *The Great Gatsby.* 1925. New York: Scribner, 2004.

Fresonke, Kris. *West of Emerson: The Design of Manifest Destiny.* Berkeley: University of California Press, 2003.

Frost, Robert. "The Gift Outright." *The Poetry of Robert Frost.* New York: Henry Holt, 1979.

Heidler, David S., and Jeanne T. Heidler. *Manifest Destiny.* Westport, CT: Greenwood Press, 2003.

Kluger, Richard. *Seizing Destiny: The Relentless Expansion of American Territory.* New York: Vintage Books, 2008.

Melville, Herman. *Redburn: His First Voyage; White Jacket, or The World in a Man-of-War; Moby-Dick or, The Whale.* New York: Library of America, 1983.

Newlin, Paul. "The Prairie and 'The Prairies': Cooper's and Bryant's Views on Manifest Destiny." In *William Cullen Bryant and His America: Centennial Conference Proceedings, 1878–1978.* Ed. and introd. Stanley Brodwin. Ed. and introd. Michael D'Innocenzo; Ed. Joseph G. Astman. New York: AMS,1983, 27–38.

New York Public Library American History Desk Reference. Second Edition. New York: Hyperion, 2003.

Turner, Frederick Jackson. "The Significance of the Frontier in American History." 1893. *The Turner Thesis Concerning the Role of the Frontier in American History.* Ed. George Wallace Taylor. Boston: D. C. Heath, 1956. 1–33.

"Iroquois Creation Story" from *Sketches of the Ancient History of the Six Nations*

The Iroquois creation story reveals a complex attitude toward the natural world. All that is found in the universe is the result of the creations of either a "good mind" or a "bad mind" within a primordial world. Inextricable links between humans and nonhuman nature are established in this creation myth, infusing the natural world with sacred signatures and showing humans' dependence upon and participation in a dynamic natural world. The myth variously and memorably suggests that human life is part of a larger circle of life, and that ecological sensitivity is essential for proper human understanding of the surrounding nonhuman environment.

Despite their multivalent essences, animals are linked to humanity from its very beginning in the Iroquois creation myth. Some animals are "monsters" of the deep who precede the later creation, some are created by a good force, and others are malformed by a bad force. The natural world itself appears as a given, with a lower world of water and sea creatures, and an upper world of sky people (not to be confused with humans). As a sky woman falls to the lower world, the sea "monsters" gather to prepare for her arrival, and a turtle offers his back as a surface for her to rest upon. She lands on the back of the turtle on which "a small quantity of earth was varnished" (5), and the turtle's back expands to become the earth. Here a sea creature becomes the very substance of the earth, which in turn provides a place for humans and land animals to breed and thrive, illustrating the intricate nature of interrelations between humans, animals, and the earth itself. The woman dies while giving birth to twins, two boys known as the good mind and the bad mind. The good mind retains the sacred touch of the sky people by bringing light, life and souls to the earth, but the bad mind turns away from his upper world lineage. The good mind created "numerous species of animals of the smallest and greatest, to inhabit the forest, and fishes of all kinds to inhabit the waters," but the bad mind formed only reptilian creatures "injurious to people" (7). As in many other creation stories, the good mind shapes human figures out of the clay of the earth and "by his breathing into their nostrils he gave them living souls" (7) — a striking echo of God's creation of mankind in the Hebrew Genesis (THE BIBLE). The

bad mind's attempt to do the same, however, results in the creation of apes rather than humans. The distinctions between human and nonhuman life are not simple, however. As Susan Kalter points out, the Iroquois account "draws a relatively solid line between human beings and animals" and yet "animals play a central role, far more central than their role in similar Western tales of the foundation of the earth or the creation" (14). Animals, then, lack a homogenous line of descent, and do not fall unequivocally into a category of good or bad, though they are part of the essential fabric of earthly life with some sharing the "good" creation of humans.

Vegetation appears as an unequivocal natural good, but natural landscapes receive the same kind of double treatment as animals do in the Iroquois creation myth. In Iroquois cosmology, William Fenton locates twenty "concepts" underlying their understanding of the world, identifying the first as "[t]he native earth. The earth, our mother, is living and expanding continually, imparting its life-giving force to all growing things on which our lives depend" (49). The back of the turtle which forms the surface of the earth sprouts with vegetation as it expands, supplying life to all growing things on earth. The good mind "continued the work of creation, and he formed numerous creeks and rivers on the Great Island" (7). The bad mind, however, disfigured the work of his good twin by making dangerous landscapes, including "numerous high mountains and falls of water, and great steeps" (7). Not surprisingly, given their vastly differing motivations, the good mind and bad mind eventually battle for the right to rule the universe, tearing up the natural landscape in their battle. When the bad mind lost, he was forced to descend below the earth. The bad mind's misuse of the natural landscape, whether in creating dangerous terrain or in inciting battle that used the natural landscape as weapons of war, implies an underlying ethical concern with how best to use the land. The good mind's triumph, along with the fact that he had earlier "restored the Island to its former condition" after his brother's disfigurations (7), suggests that the natural landscape retains its goodness through the work of the good mind, whose sacred acts hold sway on the earth as he retires to the sky. The landscape then, like the vegetation rooted in it, is itself a great good that can be misappropriated, as it was by the bad mind, for destructive or malicious purposes.

In the Iroquois creation story, the natural world functions as the basis for the circle of life in which humans participate, even as that world changes to make way for the creation of new life. Rather than the result of the body/spirit duality that characterizes much of Western thought, disharmony with the natural world is caused by the bad mind that opposes the good mind. The latter ultimately succeeds in infusing the natural world with light as he creates and re-creates the natural world into a good world, and the bad mind descends from the earth as he transmogrifies into the Evil Spirit. Christopher Vecsey and Robert W. Venables thus emphasize the concept of an "encompassing creation" in American Indian thought, noting that "the sacred circle [of life] expresses a physical and spiritual unity" (x). Good and evil are not divided into the Puritan binary of "physical" and "spiritual," but into the sacred, life-breathing creations of a "good mind" on the one hand, and the half-creations and disfigurations of a "bad mind" on the other. The ecological sensibility of the Iroquois creation myth thus sees human life as contingent upon a dynamic circle of life, at once sacred and natural.— Steven Petersheim

BIBLIOGRAPHY

Cusick, David. "A Tale of the Foundation of that Great Island, Now North America — The Two Infants Born, and the Creation of the Universe." *David Cusick's Sketches of the Ancient History of the Six Nations.* 1828. Ed. Paul Royster. Faculty Publications, UNL Libraries. Available online. URL: http://digitalcommons.unl.edu/library science/24. Updated on January 24, 2006.

Fenton, William N. "This Island, the World on the Turtle's Back." *The Great Law and the Longhouse: A Political History of the Iroquois Confederacy.* Norman: University of Oklahoma Press, 1998. 34–50.

Kalter, Susan. "Finding a Place for David Cusick in Native American Literary History." *MELUS* 27.3 (2002) : 9–42.

Vecsey, Christopher, and Robert W. Venables. Introduction. *American Indian Environments: Ecological Issues in Native American History.* Ed. Christopher Vecsey and Robert W. Venables. Syracuse: Syracuse University Press, 1980. ix–xxv.

Irving, Washington (1783–1859)

Washington Irving's works of early 19th-century romantic fiction fail to fall neatly into any one class or category specific to environmental literature or nature writing. His widely read and still popular fiction, much of which, like FAULKNER later on, he set in familiar, yet fictive places in those always-evolving spaces between urban areas and pastoral locales, resists ecocritics' efforts to "index" the tales (Branch 282). Though written before THOREAU—"the progenitor of the American nature writing tradition" (Branch 282)— Irving's short stories are not examples of the kind of natural history that colonial-era writers produced, nor can they be categorized as rambles, farm-life essays, or early versions of the genre that speaks in the grand style of what Thomas J. Lyons describes as "man's role in nature" (278), such as the

essays of EMERSON. Ultimately, Irving's works suggest that the philosophic underpinnings of various branches of ecocriticism may in fact be insufficient and somewhat simplistic.

Primarily owing to its uniquely American pastoral settings (AMERICAN PASTORAL), Irving's fiction tempts some critics to focus on the role of the "natural" world, while at the same time enticing others to assert that nature and culture in these works, like others of this era, are interchangeable (Buell 21–22). However, a closer look at his oeuvre suggests that these various approaches — and more generally, these eco-critical lenses — tend to obscure rather than illuminate the significance of his work as it pertains to environmental literature.

To understand Irving's fiction in terms of the role it plays in the development of environmental literature, one must be mindful that he wrote before the concept of the genre existed, and that he did so for an audience mostly uninterested in environmental concerns. Moreover, one must be cognizant that Irving created complicated, fictional, framed worlds that metaphorically re-presented the world beyond the book for personal and political reasons. This re-presentation of reality complicates critical efforts to examine Irving's fiction and, in the process, to assert with certainty what makes it, in the final analysis, an example of environmental literature.

Born in New York in 1783, Washington Irving, named for General George Washington, was among the first American artists to enjoy international acclaim while earning his living by his pen. He produced volumes of essays, sketches, histories, biographies, and fiction over the course of his long and prolific career, and many of these underlined the importance of place on Americans and their nascent culture.

Irving came to his craft as a writer indirectly, having been raised by a merchant father among brothers likewise interested in the business of buying and selling. Irving studied law, but was an uninspired student, distracted by his interests in the theatre and the art scene associated with it. Fortunately, his brothers nurtured his ambitions, vague though they were initially; and eventually his inclinations found an outlet in the form of letters he wrote to *The Morning Chronicle* in 1802, and then satirical essays for the literary magazine *Salmagundi* in 1807. It was while producing various pieces for the magazine that he happened upon the conceit of writing under pseudonyms, a technique that paradoxically soon made him famous.

Writing under the name "Diedrich Knickerbocker," Irving completed his first major and timely, yet timeless, book, *A History of New York* (1809). An instant success, the book provided Irving notoriety and, in the process, an audience both at home and abroad. It did not, however, ensure his financial solvency, as he would struggle to protect the copyright, of this work and others, from European bootleggers for the remainder of his career.

His next work, a collection of short stories and essays, was written under the name Geoffrey Crayon and published in 1819, while Irving was residing in Europe. Titled *The Sketchbook of Geoffrey Crayon, Gent.*, it included such classics as "Rip Van Winkle" and "The Legend of Sleepy Hollow." These stories, like many others he would write subsequently, were often set in pastoral landscapes and picturesque locales occupying those areas on or near the rugged, open land specific to eighteenth- and nineteenth-century America. In this regard, they represent the ways that Irving's fiction blended extant European tales with American places and characters to create an essentially new and unique type of literature, one that looked at local landscapes with a certain artistic, culturally convoluted sensibility.

Born at a time when New York City had a population of only about 23,000, Irving, like many of his contemporaries, turned to the community rather than the countryside when pursuing his artistic aims. As one of his earliest biographers wrote of New Yorkers such as Irving living near the turn of the 17th and 18th centuries, "In their gay, hospitable, and mercurial character, the inhabitants were true progenitors of the present metropolis." A child of his historical cultural zeitgeist — one where "A newspaper had been established in 1732, and a theater had existed since 1750" — Irving identified in his youth as much with the town's budding "metropolitan air" as he did with its "rural aspect" (Warner 9).

Still, he had considerable and long-lasting exposure to the natural world beyond the city's borders during his childhood. Edward Wagenknech, in his 1962 biography *Washington Irving: Moderation Displayed*, asserts that Irving learned early in life to "relish the beauties of nature," and he points to statements Irving made near the end of his life about the impact this beauty had on him and his art: "I have been greatly delighted with the magnificent woodland scenery of Ohio, and with the exuberant fertility of the soil, which will eventually render this State a perfect garden spot"; a revealing statement followed by the equally illuminating assertion, "Many parts of these prairies are extremely beautiful, resembling cultivated countries, embellished with parks and groves, rather than the savage rudeness of the wilderness" (40). The tone of his reflections, and the distinctions he made between the cultivated European landscapes and the more savage, rude but

uniquely American environment, underscore the nature of his characteristic temperament and how it informed his writing.

Thus, while Irving was, in the words of his most recent biographer, "strongly affected by [his] sojourns into the countryside" (Jones 20), the effect was always colored by his interest in art, and his pastoral sensibility. Of a trip he took to the frontier at the age of 20 — at the time when his literary skills had begun to sharpen and his voice to emerge — Irving states in his journal, for example, "I was at an age when imagination lends its coloring to everything [...] and the stories of the Sinbads of the wilderness made the life of a trapper and fur trader perfect romance to me" (Jones 24). Throughout his life, Irving persisted in this way of viewing the natural world, often looking at it through what he describes as 'a romantic medium that gives an illusive tinge to every object'" (Hedges 40). This predilection to be moved not by the natural but by the once-removed and picturesque, combined as it is with Irving's artistic sensibility, is perhaps represented best by the fact that the story of "Rip Van Winkle" was inspired not by a trip to the Catskill mountains but instead by a picture Irving had seen of those mountains while living in Europe.

When considering the role of the cultural and natural landscapes in Irving's life and literary work, it is critical to note that most of his writing was done in Europe, where gothic ruins and bucolic scenery differed from the more culturally adolescent and relatively pristine landscape in much of the United States during the first half of the 19th century. Still, despite his romantic proclivities, and his having spent his most productive years writing about American settings while living in Europe, Irving represents a critical stage in the development of American literature of the environment. He viewed the landscape through a romantic lens not unlike that of such naturalists as William Bartram and Alexander Wilson, and in turn inspired the work of such seminal figures as JOHN JAMES AUDUBON and JAMES FENIMORE COOPER (Branch 294). Moreover, in the process of producing profitable fiction located against semi-historical backdrops in the United States, and featuring characters speaking in dialect, he helped engender a literary environment that would foster the works of essayists such as Henry David Thoreau and Ralph Waldo Emerson, and novelists such as MARK TWAIN and Bret Harte. — Colin Irvine

BIBLIOGRAPHY

Branch, Michael P. "Indexing American Possibilities: The Natural History Writing of Bartram, Wilson, and Audobon. *The Ecocriticism Reader: Landmarks in Ecology.*

Ed. Cheryll Glotfelty and Harold Fromm. Athens: University of Georgia Press, 1996. 282–302.

Buell, Lawrence. *The Future of Environmental Criticism: Environmental Crisis and Literary Imagination*. Malden, MA: Blackwell, 2005.

Hedges, William L. *Washington Irving: An American Study, 1802–1832* (The Goucher College Series). Westport, CT: Greenwood Press, 1965.

Jones, Brian Jay. *Washington Irving: An American Original*. New York: Arcade, 2008.

Lyon, Thomas. "A Taxonomy of Nature Writing." *The Ecocriticism Reader: Landmarks in Ecology*. Ed. Cheryll Glotfelty and Harold Fromm. Athens: University of Georgia Press, 1996. 276–281.

Wagenknech, Edward. *Washington Irving: Moderation Displayed* New York: Oxford University Press, 1962.

Warner, Charles Dudley. *Washington Irving*. Boston: Houghton, Mifflin, 1884.

A Tour on the Prairies, Washington Irving (1835)

Given that the vast untouched prairies that once covered most of the mid-section of the North American continent have become an all-but-forgotten landscape, vanquished for the most part by two centuries' of intensive agriculture and industrialization, the mere existence of Washington Irving's *A Tour on the Prairies* ought to be considered a blessing. Most accounts of the trans-Mississippi West in the first half of the nineteenth century were written by men who were explorers, trappers, hunters, or soldiers first, and authors second, at best. This is not to discount the invaluable and compelling travelogues of LEWIS AND CLARK, Zebulon Pike, and Edwin James (among others), but Irving's narrative of his trek through the North American interior contributes a refreshing, and much needed, literary component to the larger story of American expansion and settlement that is missing in these more description-oriented texts. This is not to say that Irving's text is without problematic ambivalence, however. One reason why *A Tour on the Prairies* continues to be an important text is the seeming transparency with which Irving describes his participation in a number of the same colonizing acts that would eventually lead to the prairie's decline and degradation: depicting the grasslands as a "desert" or "wasteland," participating in a number of hunting expeditions for bison and other animals now vanished from the prairie, and especially revealing an uneven (at best) or antipathetic (at worst) relationship with the prairie's indigenous human inhabitants. In many ways, Irving's expedition and the work it produced might be seen as precursors to the sort of "ecotourism" and subsequent travel writing that has, for better or worse, become a mainstay of American popular culture.

At the time of its writing, Irving was among a handful of highly successful American authors, and the fact that he turned his attention to the frontier regions of the country, as opposed to its more populated and cosmopolitan East, is something of a surprise. Moreover, unlike JAMES FENIMORE COOPER in his *The Prairie* (1826), a fictionalized account of the same region, Irving actually visited the prairie himself in order to write about it. Though Irving's prose is meticulously sculpted, and at times reads much like a fictionalized account, he nonetheless conveys the experiences of a participant in the journey, an early witness and documentarian of life on America's prairie frontier. The opening sentences of the work, for example, offer Irving's early assessment of the prairie environment: "It consists of great grassy plains, interspersed with forests and groves and clumps of trees, and watered by the Arkansas, the grand Canadian, the Red River, and all their tributary streams. Over these fertile and verdant wastes still roam the Elk, the Buffalo, and the wild horse in all their native freedom" (13). While the idea of a "fertile and verdant waste" might sound contradictory to a modern audience, the image of the prairie as a wasteland was quite common in Irving's time.

This is especially true of the more southern prairies that Irving traversed. Beginning in the East, Irving's travels eventually led him on a southwesterly route, passing through Ohio, Kentucky, and Missouri before entering the tall- and mixed-grass prairies of Kansas and Oklahoma, then the heart of the "Indian Territory." Because one of the defining characteristics of a prairie ecosystem is its relative aridity, coupled with the "oceans of grass" that earlier travelers to these regions encountered, Irving and other writers commonly associated this landscape with a desert: both feature a lack of rain, a lack of trees, and a generally unstable climate. Coming from the forests of Europe or the Northeast, the openness of the land that Irving and his fellow travelers encountered was often disorienting. Irving expounds on this later in the book, writing that "We have consciousness of being far, far beyond the bounds of human habitation; we feel as if moving in the midst of a desert world.... The silence of the waste was now and then broken by the cry of a distant flock of pelicans stalking like spectres about a shallow pool. Sometimes by the sinister croaking of a raven in the air, while occasionally a scoundrel wolf would scour off from before me and having attained a safe distance, would sit down and howl and whine with tones that gave a dreariness to the surrounding solitude" (135). Though *A Tour on the Prairies* is not dominated by such melancholy reflections, these scenes are prevalent enough to allow the reader to realize just how foreign and mysterious this grassland environment was to most Euro-Americans encountering it for the first time. Such ambivalence is also reflected in Irving's treatment of the native fauna of the prairie, especially the bison and the wild horse — the pursuit of which dominates much of the text. After giving chase and killing a bison, for example, Irving writes of the "mixture of the awful and the comic in the look" of the bison, and expresses true remorse for mortally wounding the animal, deciding to "put him out of his misery" to save him from prairie scavengers (136–137). This lamentation comes late, however, and does not counterbalance the enthusiasm with which Irving writes of these hunts throughout the text.

In addition to such observations of prairie ecology, *A Tour on the Prairies* provides a detailed look at the relationship between Native Americans and the increasing numbers of Euro-Americans moving onto their home grounds, but one from a decidedly (and given Irving's fame, damagingly) Euro-centric perspective. Guy Reynolds elaborates on the importance of Irving passing through "the Indian Territory of eastern Oklahoma at a time when such trips were intimately framed by Indian policies. Irving set out from Fort Gibson on 10 October 1832; the leader of the party was one of the three Indian commissioners; the tour took place in the immediate aftermath of the Indian Removal Act of 1830. Irving travelled at the moment when Jackson's policy of removing Indians from south-eastern states such as Georgia, in order to place them in homelands further west, was beginning to operate" ("The Winning of the West," 90). The prairies of Kansas and Oklahoma at the time of Irving's tour, therefore, were a place of ongoing change, resettlement, and even violence. That Irving has a sense of this himself is evident in his own assessment of the local native populations, built largely upon the rumors and gossip of the guides and soldiers traveling with him, wherein the Osage, Creek, and Delaware are mostly regarded as "friendly" Indians, while the Pawnee are largely cast as villains. At several points, Irving and his companions are alarmed by fears of being raided by the Pawnee. The majority of these alarms are unfounded, but the rhetoric of Irving and his fellow Euro-Americans concerning this group never softens or relents, and ultimately provides a telling glimpse of the profoundly ambiguous and highly-colored early attempts to "understand" the American frontier: "There is always some wild untamed tribe of Indians who form for a time the terror of a frontier, and about whom all kinds of fearful stories are told. Such at present was the case with the Pawnees who rove the regions between the Arkansas and the Red River, and the

prairies of Texas ... for like their counterparts, the sons of Ishmael, their hand is against every one, and every one's hand against them" (58). — Matt Low

BIBLIOGRAPHY

Branch, Michael. *Reading the Roots: American Nature Writing Before Walden.* Athens: University of Georgia Press, 2004.

Burstein, Andrew. *The Original Knickerbocker: The Life of Washington Irving.* New York: Basic Books, 2008.

Irving, Washington. *A Tour on the Prairies.* New York: The Library of America, 2004.

Jones, Brian Jay. *Washington Irving: An American Original.* New York: Arcade, 2008.

Reynolds, Guy. "The Winning of the West: Washington Irving's *A Tour on the Prairies.*" *The Year Book of English Studies* 34 (2004): 88–99.

Jeffers, Robinson (1887–1962)

Perhaps the most important environmental aspect of the poetry of Robinson Jeffers is its loosely defined but fiercely expressed belief in "Inhumanism." This idea, a call to "uncenter" human self-importance, was deeply ecological several decades before any widespread public acceptance of environmentalism as a viable topic or practice. In Jeffers' account we must shift our "emphasis from man to notman," rejecting our self-importance as a species in exchange for a "reasonable detachment" that allows us to see ourselves situated in a larger web.

Jeffers was born in 1887 in Allegheny, Pennsylvania, the elder son of respected Bible scholar the Reverend Dr. William H. Jeffers (who sternly "slapped" Greek and Latin into his son, by Jeffers' own account) and Annie Robinson Tuttle (herself a descendant of notable Puritans). Jeffers attended boarding school in Leipzig, Zurich, and Geneva, and David Perkins regards Jeffers' eventual homesteading in Carmel, California as a response to his uprooted early years. Jeffers studied postgraduate literature (and briefly medicine) at USC, and forestry at the University of Washington — an academic mix that foreshadows the unique blend of his lifetime interests.

Jeffers' main poetic *topos* is the violent, primeval turbulence of the Pacific Coast. James Daly, in an early review (*Poetry,* August 1925) refers to a "tidal recurrence" in Jeffers' poetry, a free verse based on alternating measures mimicking the nearby sea. Jed Rasula sees Jeffers at Carmel as a monomaniac poet peering out like a watchman on the Western shore, gleaning lessons and parables from the seemingly senseless clash of its elements. Jeffers' half-century stay at Carmel was no vacation retreat but an obsessive vigil, a facing-down of nature's fierceness. During the roaring Jazz-Age 1920's, Jeffers set a notably self-denying counter-example by living a stern life at Big Sur, purged of most practical comforts.

Despite having "enisled" himself and his small family, Jeffers attracted visitors ranging from the actor James Cagney to the mystic Krishnamurti. He used a fisherman's block-and-tackle apparatus to lift his Tor House's stones into place, and his stonemasonry set a model for his poetry, similar to GARY SNYDER's metaphor of "riprap" (a cobbling used in hillside walkways) for his own carefully placed, hard-chiseled verse. While many of his peers were engaging in poetic collages (blending elements from classical and contemporary sources), Jeffers was working on his own collage of a home environment. His (still surviving) house is part Tudor barn, part Spanish mission, its Hawk Tower featuring a porthole from the ship Napoleon used to flee Elba, and its walls studded with lava shipped from Mt. Vesuvius, arrowheads from Michigan, tile from a temple devoted to Ishtar, and a huge stone from Yeats' tower smuggled home in Jeffers' suitcase following a 1929 trip to Ireland. This rugged attention to detail is mirrored in the poet's emphasis on spare, carved images and carefully balanced lines.

Jeffers saw the coastal Monterey mountain range as a landscape in which people lived lives reminiscent of the legends of classical Greece and Rome. Big Sur's Mediterranean climate likewise deepened his sense of neo-classicism. His poetic scenes and subject matter — swirling tide pools, continental erosion, tectonic slide — were at once modern (in their emphasis on disruption) and timeless (in their focus on unending geologic dramas). In stark contrast to the sentimentality often associated with nature verse, Jeffers' work is marked by scenes of competition and cruelty, of killer whales hunting sea lions and hawks scanning the Western horizon for prey.

Despite its reputation as a kind of secular utopia, California has also long been a metaphor for American exhaustion. The state serves as a kind of end zone for MANIFEST DESTINY's westward expansion; for Jeffers it is the final brink of Western accomplishment. One poem likens its coastline to "Euphrates mud" and to "Niles shore," again treating the Pacific coast as a climaxing of classical tendencies. In Jeffers' view, California is a forfeiting end but also a "wild future, wild as a hawk's dream," an intense and epical zone in which to assess our Western heritage and all of its treasures and traumas, where sand grains are finely shaped measures of change, and sea foam is an expression of a rabid rage and fury.

Such an environment offered Jeffers' "transhuman" gospel much of its material. In "Mangrave," our planet is a "particle of dust by a sand-grain sun" in which human claims to significance are pathetic. A line like "It is all truly one life, red blood and tree-sap," does not express a New Age optimism, but instead demotes the human creature to merely one specimen in a vast crowd of carbon-carriers. We were initially born of "unstable proteins," and register only as a "pin-point fleck" on any telescope pointed our way. Our species is a "sick microbe" in Jeffers' perspective, and nature's "broken balance" may be primarily attributed to human intervention. Jeffers viewed his verse as a tool with which to scour off excess sentiment: "one christens each poem, in dutiful/ hope of burning off at least the top layer of the time's uncleanness." David Perkins regards Jeffers as a lyric inheritor of such "exposers of fantasies" as Freud and Schopenhauer, Jung and Havelock Ellis — all figures intent on debunking too-comfortable beliefs supporting human specialness.

Indeed, 1948's *The Double Axe* centers largely on a character called the Inhumanist. "Human" derives from *humus* or ground (as does "humble"), and in Jeffers' unforgiving view, humanity can never be sufficiently humiliated. Man is "no measure" in such a vision, opposing the long-held belief (adapted, unfairly, from Socrates) that the human form is the central gauge of all value. While Jeffers is certainly engaged in an unabashed attack on all forms of human self-elevation, he is deliberately lacking in D.H. LAWRENCE's belief in sex as a renewing force. Jeffers' breaking of taboos aims to assess human frailty and folly through a clear-eyed lens, but he does not see a reversion to animal grace as a possible source of purity. Jeffers' ecological emphasis is radical because it does not mean to reassure his fellow humans but instead to trouble their sense of their position on the planet's pecking-order.

Human empire is therefore a mere fleeting bubble when viewed through a transhuman lens. Jeffers infamously claimed he would prefer killing a man to killing a hawk, a claim employed by some critics to pigeonhole him as a poet whose bitterness prohibited him from dealing with the more gentle and tender portions of our emotional range. Similarly, LOREN EISELEY referred to Jeffers' "Greek mask" of a face, a face that caused him to be rejected from jury duty in a homicide case for the "assumed cruelty of his countenance."

Still, Jeffers was no sponsor of violence for violence's sake, and he held a dim view of the "social Darwinism" used to extend nationalist causes. His protest of the United States' entering World War II earned him outrage from many fellow writers — *The Double Axe* may be the only volume of verse to ever require a Publisher's Note disavowing a poet's pacifism. Still, Jeffers fell out of favor in the post-World War II climate for reasons formal as well as moral: in an academic climate in which small, carefully modeled poems of refined emotion and irony were the favored mode, Jeffers' excursions were seen as unwieldy and overheated.

Oddly, Jeffers the renouncing man opposed the renunciation of much Modernist poetry, and what he viewed as its "narrowing" of verse, removing music and vividness in the name of formal innovation. On the contrary, he tried to reclaim a novelistic scope for modern verse; *The Alpine Christ* (1916, unfinished) is a cosmically vast, Shelleyan poetic drama. Moreover, he aimed at a science-savvy poetry addressing permanent objects, not concerned with trends or fashions but by with verifiable truths — "rock-solid" topics, in his own phrase.

Jeffers died in 1962 at a low ebb in his public profile, but soon an upsurge in environmental activism restored his place as a formative figure in American eco-poetics. William Everson titled his study of Jeffers *Fragments of an Older Fury*, treating his subject as an artist mainly attentive to the eternal, primal energies that lie below our claims to civilization. Bill Hotchkiss' 1975 critique calls attention to Jeffers' "Sivaistic vision," likening his poetry to the Hindu deity's violent refreshing of reality — killing in order to cleanse. Tim Hunt refers to Jeffers as a poet of "shocking claims" in his preface to *Robinson Jeffers and a Galaxy of Writers*— claims soon vindicated by ensuing schools of human-demoting "green" literature. Gradually, more official bodies are coming to recognize Jeffers' status. The U.S. Post Office even issued a commemorative Jeffers stamp in 1973, and an annual Fall Festival in Carmel tours Jeffers' home as an example of a life lived at a geographic and principled extreme.— John Reder

BIBLIOGRAPHY

Eiseley, Loren. "Preface" to *Not Man Apart: Photographs of the Big Sur Coast.* (David Ross Brower, ed.) San Francisco: Sierra Club, 1969.
Everson, William. *Robinson Jeffers: Fragments of an Older Fury.* Berkeley, CA: Oyez Press, 1968.
Hotchkiss, Bill. *Jeffers: The Sivaistic Vision.* Auburn, CA: Blue Oak Press, 1975.
Tim Hunt (ed.). *Robinson Jeffers and a Galaxy of Writers: Essays in Honor of William H. Nolte.* Columbia: University of South Carolina Press, 1995.
Karman, James. *Robinson Jeffers: Poet of California.* San Francisco: Chronicle Books, 1987
Rasula, Jed. *This Compost: Ecological Imperatives in American Poetry.* Athens: University of Georgia Press, 2002.

Jefferson, Thomas (1743–1826)

Principal author of The Declaration of Independence, minister to France, third President of the United States, and founder of the University of Virginia, Thomas Jefferson engaged with the American landscape in numerous and influential ways. The third of eight children and the eldest son of an early Virginian family, the nine-year-old Jefferson inherited some 5,000 acres and over a hundred slaves when his father died; later he would personally design and build his beloved Monticello upon this working Virginian slave plantation. In 1762 he graduated from William and Mary, and at 29 married the 23-year-old widow, Martha Wayles Skelton; the two would have six children together, only two of whom lived into adulthood. After Martha died, it is alleged that Jefferson took Sally Hemings, a young quadroon slave, as his mistress; he never remarried. Jefferson died at Monticello on July 4, 1826 at the age of 83.

Despite an impressive career of diplomacy, politics, and writing, which took him around the Colonies and across Europe, Jefferson never lost his love for, or centeredness on, his paternal lands. Such affection is most visible perhaps in Jefferson's NOTES ON THE STATE OF VIRGINIA, a collection of essays written in response to the queries of a French diplomat seeking specific information about the United States. (Though written in 1781, *Notes* was not published until 1787.) While Jefferson carefully details information about the boundaries, resources, flora, fauna, settlements, and history of his State, he also advances now famous arguments that have implications far beyond the immediate description of Virginia. Most notably, by compiling a list of known species along with their average or measured weights in Query VI, Jefferson directly refutes the Old World belief that New World animals were lesser in size, number, and quality because of the supposed primitiveness of the landscape. In fact, Jefferson's extensive chart shows that the New World has a greater diversity of species, many of which (e.g., bison) are much larger than Old World animals. Such an argument extended to the peoples of the United States who, Jefferson argues, are not degenerate or devolved in comparison to Europeans: "The United States contain three millions of inhabitants; France twenty millions; and the British islands ten. We produce a Washington, a Franklin, a Rittenhouse. France then should have half a dozen in each of these lines, and Great-Britain half that number, equally eminent" (191).

In 1803, interested in preventing any European power from gaining too much power in nearby lands, as well as in increasing American knowledge about the West, President Jefferson sent MERIWETHER LEWIS AND WILLIAM CLARK westward with the stated purpose of seeking out a direct water route to the Pacific. Though Lewis and Clark and their "Corps of Discovery" would not find the desired direct water route, they did, as per their instructions, conduct extensive research on the climate, ecology, resources, and native peoples, as well as create maps of the area over which they traveled — all information later of much interest to white Americans and their mid- and late-nineteenth-century ideas of MANIFEST DESTINY.

While Lewis and Clark were journeying, Jefferson began trying to buy the port of New Orleans through which much American commerce passed. When Napoleon, in need of funds for his war efforts, and reeling from the loss of Haiti, offered the entirety of the Louisiana Territory, Jefferson jumped at the opportunity; and with the 1804 treaty, Jefferson thus doubled the size of the young republic, despite some home opposition which pointed to the fact that the Constitution supplied no mechanism for acquiring territory.

In that foundational document of the United States, The Declaration of Independence, Jefferson wrote of King George III (monarch of Great Britain): "He has plundered our seas, ravaged our coasts, burnt our towns, & destroyed the lives of our people" (21). Though this complaint was just one of a litany of grievances against the King, it demonstrates Jefferson's early and keen awareness of the political importance of the land. Despite his eminence as President, Ambassador, author, and architect, he was first and last a gentleman-farmer, one who believed strongly in the importance of environmental integrity for the creation of the independent and almost self-sufficient nodes of family and community, critical to the pastoral ideal of Jeffersonian democracy (AMERICAN PASTORAL). — Lydia G. Fash

BIBLIOGRAPHY

Ambrose, Stephen E. *Undaunted Courage: Meriwether Lewis, Thomas Jefferson, and the Opening of the American West.* New York: Simon & Schuster, 1996.

Bernstein, Richard B. *Thomas Jefferson.* New York: Oxford University Press, 2003.

"Biography of Thomas Jefferson." The White House. Available online. URL: http://www.whitehouse.gov/about/presidents/thomasjefferson/. Accessed June 14, 2009.

Burns, Ken, Sam Waterston, Ossie Davis, and Geoffrey C. Ward. *Thomas Jefferson.* [Alexandria, VA]: PBS Home Video, 2004.

Ellis, Joseph J. *American Sphinx: The Character of Thomas Jefferson.* New York: Alfred A. Knopf, 1997.

Jefferson, Thomas. *Notes on the State of Virginia.* In *Thomas Jefferson: Writings,* edited by Merrill D. Peterson, 123–325. New York: Library of America, 1984.

Miller, Robert J. *Native America, Discovered and Conquered: Thomas Jefferson, Lewis & Clark, and Manifest Destiny.* Westport, CT: Praeger, 2006.

Peterson, Merrill D. *Thomas Jefferson and the New Nation; A Biography.* New York: Oxford University Press, 1970.

Notes on the State of Virginia, Thomas Jefferson (1787)

Jefferson's *Notes on the State of Virginia* were, as he informs us, "written in Virginia in the year 1781, and somewhat corrected and enlarged in the winter of 1782, in answer to Queries proposed to the Author, by a Foreigner of Distinction, then residing among us" (124). The answers Jefferson sent to this François Marbois, secretary to the French legation, were published in France, "but with such alterations as the laws of the press in that country rendered necessary" (Jefferson 124). Jefferson then continued to revise the text, and finally published it in 1787. The 23 "Queries" range in subject from the natural environment of Virginia to culture (such as the laws, government, religion, manufacturing, towns, colleges, roads, and Native peoples of the region), and Jefferson's "answers" regarding the physical environment blend, in interesting and significant ways, into observations regarding the social institutions of the state. Thus, in his *Notes*, Douglas Anderson claims, Jefferson "sought to move from surfaces to depths and back again, across the natural and cultural landscapes of his region" (235). Such movement, always graceful and well-integrated in the broader compass of the work, is made possible not merely by Jefferson's exceptional intellect and writerly skill, but also by his bold synthesis of Christian and classical, Arcadian worldviews (THE BIBLE and AMERICAN PASTORAL).

Beyond this unified perspective, Jefferson shows wonderful attunement to the intrinsic beauty and character of the Virginia landscape throughout the first 12 questions, relating to the natural environment. The junction of the Shenandoah and the Patomac Rivers, for example, with its rushing waters and mountains, is a sight "worth a voyage across the Atlantic" (143); and "the passage of the Patomac through the Blue Ridge is perhaps one of the most stupendous scenes in nature" (142). But he is concerned here with more than the merely picturesque mixture of the "placid and delightful," "the wild and tremendous" (Jefferson 142–3). The landscape is perceived through the critical eighteenth-century concept of the sublime. Here, at the rivers' junction, for example, "the mountain being cloven asunder, she [Nature] presents to your eye, through the cleft, a small catch of smooth blue horizon, at an infinite distance in the plain country, inviting you, as it were, from the riot and tumult roaring around, to pass through the breach and participate in the calm below. Here the eye ultimately composes itself" (Jefferson 142–3). Beyond its susceptibility to an eco-feminist reading of this "cleft," the passage illustrates the essential aesthetic architecture of the sublime, detailed further in his account of the "Natural Bridge over Cedar Creek," "the most sublime of Nature's work":

> Though the sides of this bridge are provided in some parts with a parapet of fixed rocks, yet few men have resolution to walk to them and look

over into the abyss. You involuntarily fall on your hands and feet, creep to the parapet and peep over it. Looking down from this height about a minute, gave me a violent head ach [sic.]. If the view from the top be painful and intolerable, that from below is delightful in an equal extreme. It is impossible for the emotions arising from the sublime, to be felt beyond what they are here: so beautiful an arch, so elevated, so light, and springing as it were up to heaven, the rapture of the spectator is really indescribable! [148].

Such descriptions — fusing the European aesthetic concept with the American landscape — are significant for another reason that is equally central to the thematic core of the *Notes*. The natural grandeur contributing to Jefferson's sublime musings arises from the convulsive natural processes that create these scenes, and there is a critical link here to the wider revolutionary context surrounding the composition of Jefferson's text, particularly as the word "convulsion" recurs throughout the natural *and* cultural sections of the *Notes*. Specifically, the sublime contributes to Jefferson's implied counter-argument to the views of European natural philosophers: "Celebrating the state's glorious prospects, Jefferson offered a powerful rebuttal to the claims of the Comte du Buffon and other European natural philosophers that the New World's inferior natural endowment inevitably led to the degeneracy of animal species, including humans" (Onuf 103). The elevation of spirit prompted by the experience of the sublime in the American landscape awakens something higher, to counter the notion of New World degeneration in the interplay of the American landscape and American man. This relates to Jefferson's classically informed view of the superiority of husbandry over manufacture: "Those who labour in the earth are the chosen people of God, if ever he had a chosen people, whose breasts he has made his peculiar deposit for substantial and genuine virtue" (290). A deep, emotional connection to the land is thus central to the American identity for Jefferson; and it is critically threatened by a manufacturing-based economy:

The loss by the transportation of commodities across the Atlantic will be made up in happiness and permanence of government. The mobs of great cities add just so much to the support of pure government, as sores do to the strength of the human body. It is the manner and spirit of a people which preserve a republic in vigour. A degeneracy in these is a canker which soon eats to the heart of its laws and constitution [291].

Here we see a dramatic inversion of the European natural philosophers' notion of "degeneracy," and one perfectly commensurate with Jefferson's description of the American sublime: establishing and maintaining an intimate relationship to the land may well make America superior to the more urban and industrial Europe.

There is one significant concern challenging this relationship between Americans and the environment in Jefferson's text, primarily for the gentry, and that is a dependence on tobacco. For Jefferson, tobacco cultivation "is a culture productive of infinite wretchedness" (Jefferson 293). Not only does this cultivation deplete the soil, but it sunders the idealized bond between the American husbandman and the land, through its dependence on slave labor. The sensitive man capable of experiencing the sublime may momentarily identify with the natural environment, much like Jefferson's description of the "sensible" tobacco plant responding to "the change in the temperature of our climate" (293), but his emotional response to his fellow, enslaved human beings toiling in these fields remains extremely ambivalent.

More than any other single factor in the complex moral equation at work both in Jefferson's *Notes* and other writings, the institution, and even more importantly, the fundamental assumptions supporting slavery, call into question the relationship between white, Euro-American man and nature itself. Interestingly, and tellingly, Jefferson shows more respect for Native peoples than he does for African-Americans in the *Notes*, perhaps recalling his association of husbandry and virtue, as Natives "lived principally on the spontaneous productions of nature," which was already being adversely affected by the "abridgement of territory" brought about by white settlement (Jefferson 221). Like Jefferson's "sensible" tobacco plant, Native culture was withering away as its resources were depleted and "Spirituous liquors, the small-pox, [and] war" (221) took their toll. African-Americans, on the other hand, possessed "real distinctions which nature has made," and the animosities that slavery had created "will probably never end but in the extermination of the one or the other race" (Jefferson 264). While Jefferson's point is relevant to the slow destruction of Native cultures in America, he seems incapable of recognizing the obvious parallel evident in the case of African-Americans and their culture. And his telling use of the word "nature" here, indicating what Anderson refers to as Jefferson's "moral blindness" (238), leaves the *Notes* in particular, and Jefferson's worldview in general, vulnerable to deconstructive critique, with his sublime idealizations of nonhuman nature revealing a darker and more exploitive subtextual relationship between human beings and the environment. — Jim Daems

BIBLIOGRAPHY

Anderson, Douglas. "Subterraneous Virginia: The Ethical Poetics of Thomas Jefferson." *Eighteenth Century Studies* 33.2 (Winter 2000): 233–49.

Jefferson, Thomas. *Notes on the State of Virginia. Thomas Jefferson: Writings.* Ed. Merrill D. Peterson. New York: Library of America, 1984. 123–335.

Onuf, Peter S. "'We shall all be Americans': Thomas Jefferson and the Indians." *Indiana Magazine of History* 95.2 (June 1999): 103–41.

Kerouac, Jack (1922–1969)

Jack Kerouac was born (he claimed) Jean Louis Lebris de Kerouac, to French-Canadian parents, in 1922, in Lowell, Massachusetts. Coming of age during the Depression, Kerouac's childhood was largely "a dark and gloomy time" (Charters 28). However, he early revealed a vivid imagination that allowed him to escape into fantasies inspired by pulp magazines and film. Along with this uncommon imagination, the young Kerouac also had a budding interest in the natural world. Having grown up in the watershed of the Merrimack and Concord, he especially loved rivers. John Suiter explains that "he had from an early age been attracted to them as sources of mystery and experience" (198). As one who travelled continually across America in later life, Kerouac made many crossings of the Mississippi, Delaware, Susquehanna, Ohio, Hudson, and other rivers. Suiter points out, in fact, that Kerouac considered calling his magnum opus, *On the Road*, "Rain and Rivers."

Although Kerouac was sensitive and imaginative from an early age, he also possessed an interest in sports. He was a talented running back in high school and earned football scholarships to Notre Dame and Columbia University, ultimately opting to attend Columbia. This was the first time that he left the shelter of his home in Lowell. He soon dropped out of the university, however, after fracturing his tibia during his first season. It was during this time that he met ALLEN GINSBERG, William S. Burroughs, and others, who Kerouac began calling the Beat Generation. For Kerouac, "beat" not only possessed the common connotations of "dead beat," "down and out," etc., but also entailed a celebration of the group's refusal to conform to social conventions and expectations. He described the Beats as "characters of a special spirituality who didn't gang up but were solitary Bartlebies staring out the dead wall window of our civilization" (*Portable* 599). The Beats saw themselves — and were largely seen by mainstream society — as "others," misfits who sought something more "authentic" than the cookie-cutter American life, and who rejected the bourgeois ideology of the American Dream.

Ginsberg, Burroughs, and other Beats are featured prominently (under aliases) in Kerouac's most famous novel, the semi-autobiographical *On the Road* (1957). *On the Road* is a novel of both the city and the country. Kerouac's proxy in the book — Sal Paradise — revels in the excitement of city life, but also envisions the possibility of spiritual enlightenment outside of urban America. "Somewhere along the line," Paradise says, "I knew there'd be girls, visions, everything; somewhere along the line the pearl would be handed to me" (8). His quest takes him into the West for the first time in his life, where he discovers that the "authentic" American character lives not only in its cities but on its roads, in its towns, and across its diverse landscape. His journey also takes him into Mexico, where he confronts a primitive nature like none he has come in contact with before: "We took off our T-shirts and roared through the jungle, bare-chested. No towns, nothing, lost jungle, miles and miles, and down-going, getting hotter, the insects screaming louder, the vegetation growing higher, the smell ranker and hotter until we began to get used to it and like it" (293). This scene can be read as a microcosm of the experience of Kerouac and the other Beats, who confronted life — whether in the city or the country — with reckless abandon. It is also representative of Kerouac's goals as a writer primarily concerned not with writing "realistic" depictions of events, but with capturing the essence of the thoughts and feelings that he experienced and framing them in the broader context of American and ultimately human experience. Kerouac's travels across America, as reflected in *On the Road*, spurred a lifelong interest in the relationships between the people and ideas of America's urban and rural geographic spaces.

After finishing *The Subterraneans* in the fall of 1953, Kerouac reread WALDEN and "thought the only life for him would be to leave civilization and live like Thoreau" (Charters 201). Spurred by THOREAU's mention of Hindu philosophy, Kerouac explored Ashvagosa's *The Life of the Buddha*, which led to a deep and prolonged immersion in Eastern Studies, particularly between the years of 1953 and 1956. In the spring of 1956, Kerouac moved into a cottage with his good friend and poet GARY SNYDER in Mill Valley, north of San Francisco. Snyder, whose own relationship to Buddhism was profoundly influential for Kerouac, convinced him to take an eight-week job as a fire lookout on Desolation Peak in northwestern Washington. While solitude was a lifelong interest for Kerouac, biographer Ann Charters explains that "it's possible that the summer of 1956 was the only period in Kerouac's life in which he could have tried to live the life of solitude he'd written and talked about so much" (Charters 262). During his eight weeks on Desolation Peak, he "lived in a primitive wooden cabin, the windows of which opened to a view of the surrounding peaks stretching for miles in every direction. There were no other human beings in sight" (263). Kerouac's time on the peak was one of the most profound and challenging experiences of his life, and one which became both an inspiration and subject for his subsequent writing.

The Dharma Bums (1958), which was based on Kerouac's life in the years between *On the Road's* composition in 1951 and its release in 1957, culminates with narrator Ray Smith's final days as a lookout on Desolation Peak. While *On the Road* is Kerouac's most recognized novel, many critics view *The Dharma Bums* as the culmination of Kerouac's life-long fascination with the relationship between urban and wilderness life and experience. While Smith enjoys wild nights at parties, poetry readings, and jazz clubs in the city, he also develops a love for the hitchhiking, mountaineering, and bicycling introduced to him by his friend Japhy Ryder, who is based on poet Gary Snyder. As he descends Desolation Peak in the final chapter of the book, Smith looks at the surrounding landscape with reverence and awe, having gained a newfound appreciation for the wilderness.

While Kerouac was fascinated by the excitement of the urban lifestyle, he never lost sight of the importance of nature, not only as an alternative to the city, but as a critical element in the elusive search for spiritual balance in life. His fondness for the natural world pervades his writing, which in turn, along with that of the other Beat Generation writers, played a significant role in galvanizing the bourgeoning environmental movement in the 1960s, and continues to inspire readers to explore the American wilderness, without and within. — Adam Meehan

BIBLIOGRAPHY

Charters, Ann. *Kerouac: A Biography.* San Francisco: Straight Arrow Books, 1973. Print.

Kerouac, Jack. *On the Road.* New York: Penguin, 2003. Print.

_____. *The Portable Jack Kerouac.* Ed. Ann Charters. New York: Viking, 1995. Print.

Suiter, John. *Poets on the Peaks: Gary Snyder, Philip Whalen & Jack Kerouac in the North Cascades.* Washington, D.C.: Counterpoint, 2002. Print.

The Dharma Bums, Jack Kerouac (1958)

Published a year after Kerouac's most famous novel, *On the Road,* and at the apex of his fame, *The Dharma Bums* is in many ways a starkly different book from the previous work. *On the Road* secured

Kerouac's reputation as the "king of the Beat Generation," while *The Dharma Bums* provided a model emulated by the hippies a few years later, a model exemplified and prophesied by the novel's central character Japhy Ryder (Kerouac's fictional name for the poet GARY SNYDER). Both works are based on actual events, both are concerned with portraying alternatives to the post–World War II consumerist culture, and both feature a frenetic lifestyle; but while *On the Road* focuses on "the fast-paced, urban way of life which Dean Moriarty represents," *The Dharma Bums* "embraces the much more balanced, nature-centered world of Ryder" (Phillips 53).

The action takes place in 1955 and 1956, while Kerouac was negotiating the publication of *On the Road* with Viking Press. During this time, Ann Charters explains, Kerouac "spent what was probably the happiest three months of his life" (Charters 520). In late 1955, and the months that followed, Kerouac, under the influence of Snyder, intensified his immersion in Buddhist thought and practice, and experienced a profound intimacy with the natural world.

The Dharma Bums is dedicated to Han Shan, an 8th-century Chinese Buddhist whose writings Snyder was translating when Kerouac met him. In the novel, Ryder describes Han Shan as a "scholar who got sick of the big city and the world and took off to hide in the mountains" (Kerouac 20). Some of Synder's early translations, which were later published on their own, appear in *The Dharma Bums*, and the philosophy behind Han Shan's poetry helps establish the tone and central theme of the novel: "Cold Mountain path goes on and on, long gorge choked with scree and boulders, wide creek and mist-blurred grass, moss is slippery though there's been no rain, pine sings but there's no wind, who can leap the world's ties and sit with me among white clouds?" (20). Although there are obstacles and entanglements on the long path to enlightenment, Han Shan asserts they can ultimately be overcome with such a simple leap, and serves as an embodiment of the Dharma (truth) for Ray Smith (Kerouac's fictional persona) and Ryder. For Smith and Ryder, the Dharma is encountered when they confront the essential realities of existence with the assistance of the wild, natural world.

Nature may be used as a metaphor in Han Shan's poem, but it is more than just symbolic, particularly in the novel. After a sharp critique of educational institutions as "grooming schools for the middle-class non-identity which finds its perfect expression [...] in rows of well-to-do houses with lawns and television sets," Kerouac explains that as an alternative "the Japhies of the world go prowling in the wilderness to hear the voice crying in the wilderness, [...] to find the dark mysterious secret of the origin of [...] civilization" (39). Smith, Ryder, and a third companion Henry Morley, do just this when they travel to the Sierra Nevada to climb Matterhorn peak. Although Smith is overcome by fear near the summit, and does not make it to the top, he is inspired when he sees Japhy "running down the mountain in huge twenty foot leaps" (85) after summitting the peak. Smith realizes that he "can't fall off a mountain" and bounds down after Ryder, catching up to him only after he follows a deer trail: "I trusted the instinct of my sweet little millennial deer and true enough just as it was getting dark their ancient trail took me right to the edges of the familiar shallow creek (where they stopped to drink for the last five thousand years) and there was the glow of Japhy's bonfire" (88).

Just as in the famous Zen ox-herding pictures, however, Smith must come down out of the wilderness and return to the realities of daily living. And while he, like Ryder, remains critical of the dominant society's "system of work, produce, consume, work, produce, consume," he revels in the society of his peers and enjoys the fruits of the system, albeit on a simplified level: he shops at the Salvation Army and drinks cheap gallon-jugs of wine. Ryder envisions as an alternative to the dominant system "a great rucksack revolution [with] thousands even millions of young Americans wandering around with rucksacks going up to the mountains to pray" (97).

Smith later spends Christmas with his mother in North Carolina, and continues to find solace in natural surroundings: "Behind the house was a great pine forest where I would spend all that winter and spring meditating under the trees and finding out by myself the truth of all things" (132). His brother-in-law, however, criticizes his unconventional lifestyle, and Smith argues about Buddhism with his family, who encourage him to "stick with the religion" he was born with (144). This aspect of the novel in part represents Kerouac's own attempts to reconcile his Catholic upbringing and belief with his Buddhist studies and convictions (Giamo).

In the spring Smith journeys west again, along the way succumbing to the temptations of city-life and quickly being disillusioned by them. After spending an "insane day" getting drunk and smoking marijuana with "a bunch of evil Mexican Apaches," Smith remembers his "perfect white sand gulch" and the place where he would sleep that night. He leaves the "evil city" (Kerouac 155–156) for the peace and solitude of the wild, natural world; but when he returns to the West coast he again takes up a dissolute lifestyle, supplemented by hikes and religious discussions with Ryder (who himself falls prey to similar temptations).

After Ryder leaves for Japan, however, to study at a Zen monastery, Smith, with Ryder's encouragement, secures a position as a firewatcher on the isolated Desolation Peak in the high Cascade Mountains, where his Dharmic journey finally culminates in lasting enlightenment; and the novel concludes with Smith leaving the mountains and going "back to this world" after spending a summer attaining a "vision of the freedom of eternity [that] was mine forever. The chipmunk ran into the rocks and a butterfly came out. It was as simple as that" (243). The reader has the impression at the end of *The Dharma Bums* that the narrator has come to a fundamental realization of truth and beauty, and in some critical way overcome attachment to the material world and the suffering that comes with it. We are lead to believe that he has escaped the world's ties and sat among the clouds of enlightenment through his eight weeks of solitude, and that he is now prepared to return to the "evil city" and expound the Dharma.

Kerouac himself alternately called *The Dharma Bums* a potboiler, written quickly and without revision for money, and an example of his theory of spontaneous prose. The novel undeniably lacks unity and at times suffers artistically; the critic Warren French argues that the novel "is better remembered for its striking passages than digested as a whole" (French 55). But when these "striking passages" are taken as a whole, we find a work of lyrical, stimulating, and mystical reverence both for the natural world and for our relationship to it. — Michael Beilfuss

Bibliography

Charters, Ann. *Kerouac: A Biography*. San Francisco: Straight Arrow Books, 1973.
French, Warren G. *Jack Kerouac, Twayne's United States authors series*. Boston: Twayne, 1986.
Giamo, Benedict. "Enlightened Attachment: Kerouac's Impermanent Buddhist Trek." *Religion and Literature* 35 (2–3): 173–206, 2003.
Kerouac, Jack. *The Dharma Bums*. New York: Penguin, 1976. Original edition, 1958.
_____, and Ann Charters. *Selected Letters, 1940–1956*. New York: Penguin Books, 1996.
Phillips, Rod. "'Forest beatniks' and 'urban Thoreaus': Gary Snyder, Jack Kerouac, Lew Welch, and Michael McClure, Modern American Literature*. New York: P. Lang, 2000.

Kingsolver, Barbara (1955–)

"First, picture the forest. I want you to be its conscience, the eyes in the trees.... This forest eats itself and lives forever." In these opening lines of *The Poisonwood Bible* (1998), Barbara Kingsolver reveals her characteristic grace and introspection as an accomplished novelist, essayist, short story writer, and poet. Her work often portrays an ineluctable sense of wonder and respect for the natural world, paired with a passionate dedication to social change. Having grown up in the American South, in Appalachia, lived much of her adult life in the American Southwest, in Arizona, and traveled and lived in Africa and Europe, Kingsolver brings a rich worldliness to the intimate portraits of her storytelling. She reflects deeply on the interrelation between the human organism and its animal, vegetable and mineral counterparts, infusing her fiction and nonfiction alike with an ecological consciousness at once passionate and shrewd, stirring and candid.

Born in Annapolis, Maryland in 1955, and raised in rural Kentucky, Kingsolver was profoundly affected by the wild hills and woods in which she grew up, as well as by the more domestic issues of class and racial segregation that plagued the area. A "wrinkle on the map that lies between farms and wildness" (*Prodigal Summer*, x), Kingsolver's hometown of Carlisle in Nicholas County, Kentucky, depended on tobacco farming for its agricultural wealth. But like many other neighboring towns, there remained in Carlisle a clear division between the poor tobacco farmers and its middle- and upper-class merchants. While the latter lived comfortably in town, the former struggled to maintain their farms in the same wilds in which Kingsolver wandered throughout her childhood — growing intimately familiar with both the land and its people. Her ability to move comfortably between town and country, coupled with her keen observations of endemic injustices, helped nurture the liberal, humanistic conscience so vividly and cogently expressed in her writing (Snodgrass, 8).

Kingsolver's apparently "amphibious" nature was firmly grounded in the dynamic compassion and social activism of her parents, Dr. Wendell R. Kingsolver, a rural family physician, and Virginia Lee Henry Kingsolver, an avid birdwatcher and nature rambler. When Kingsolver was seven years old, her family moved to the former Republic of Congo on a two-year medical exchange, living in a small village without electricity and running water while both parents worked for the public health. It was this experience in particular that inspired *The Poisonwood Bible*, written over 35 years later. In the preface to this novel, Kingsolver thanks her parents directly for bringing her "to a place of wonders," teaching her "to pay attention," and setting her "early on a path of exploring the great, shifting terrain between righteousness and what's right" (x).

In addition to nurturing Kingsolver's resolute moral compass and her love of nature, the Kingsolver parents instilled in all their children a fond and disciplined appreciation for books and reading. Kingsolver herself read fiction alongside anatomy and physiology, prose alongside poetry, and discovered "that literature could enable her to live many lives besides her own and that language — words — has power and beauty" (DeMarr 3). She consequently went on to earn both her bachelor's and master's degrees in biology from DePauw University and the University of Arizona, respectively, while also taking a few creative writing courses along the way. Since 1985, Kingsolver has been working as a freelance journalist and author, producing numerous award-winning works across a wide range of genres. Her first novel, *The Bean Trees* (1988), is now widely adopted in college courses across the nation, and has helped pave the way for some of her most well-known works. From *The Poisonwood Bible* and *PRODIGAL SUMMER* (2000) to *Animal Dreams* (1990), *Pigs in Heaven* (1993), and *The Lacuna* (2009), Kingsolver's novels consistently return to the enlightening intersections of the natural world as biological system and human diversity as a comparable cultural system of imperfection and promise (Leder 1). Likewise, her essay and short story collections, such as *Homeland and Other Stories* (1989), *High Tide in Tucson* (1995), and *Small Wonder* (2002), as well as her 1992 book of poems, *Another America,* explore an ecology of individualism and community informed by her experiences both abroad and in her native environs. In 2007, Kingsolver released her first nonfiction narrative, *Animal, Vegetable, Miracle: A Year of Food Life*, in which she documents her family's move back to a farm in rural Virginia and their efforts at eating locally. As both memoir and journalistic investigation, *Animal, Vegetable, Miracle* celebrates the life cycles of animal and vegetable harvests alongside those of the human mind; it offers a story of how a return to our agricultural roots can help us not only to grow good food, but to reform bad habits — to understand the challenges and benefits of "realigning our lives with our food chain" (*Animal, Vegetable, Miracle*, 6).

Although sometimes accused of an idealism that is more escapist than activist (Leder 20), Kingsolver effectively weaves together political and spiritual themes, social and environmental concerns. She highlights ecological responsibility as a wellspring for human rights advocacy, and vice versa. Her varied works emphasize the importance of place to identity and the necessity for shared education to better ourselves and our world.— Janelle A. Schwartz

BIBLIOGRAPHY

DeMarr, Mary Jean. *Barbara Kingsolver: A Critical Companion.* Westport, CT: Greenwood Press, 1999.

Kingsolver, Barbara. *Animal, Vegetable, Miracle: A Year of Food Life.* New York: Harper Perennial, 2007.

_____. *Barbara Kingsolver: The Authorized Site.* http://www.kingsolver.com.

_____. *The Poisonwood Bible*. New York: Harper Flamingo, 1998.

Leder, Priscilla, ed. *Seeds of Change: Critical Essays on Barbara Kingsolver*. Knoxville: University of Tennessee Press, 2010.

Snodgrass, Mary Ellen, ed. *Barbara Kingsolver: A Literary Companion*. Jefferson, NC: McFarland, 2004.

Prodigal Summer, Barbara Kingsolver (2000)

Prodigal Summer is Barbara Kingsolver's fifth novel, first published in hardcover edition in 2000 (and followed by the first paperback edition in 2001). Kingsolver is best known for writing elegant, lush novels, as well as equally graceful short stories, poems and essays, often centered on the interrelationships of people and the landscapes they inhabit, and typically located in the rural American South or American Southwest. *Prodigal Summer*, a national bestseller, relates the interwoven tales of three idiosyncratic human characters living and working in rural Kentucky, against the subtly but insistently informing backdrop of the life cycles of local flora and fauna. Ecology and economy correspond and diverge, clash and harmonize in what *The New York Times* called "an improbably appealing book with the feeling of a nice stay inside a terrarium." Catching a glimpse of what Kingsolver herself writes in the novel's dedication as "wildness, where it lives," *Prodigal Summer* offers readers a memorable sense of the majestic paradox of the natural world: everlasting fecundity alongside inevitable poverty and extinction, the devastation of loss and the hope of renewal. This "wildness" acts as a defining trope through which to gain an intimate understanding of both nature's vital cyclicality and the analogous resiliency (and dependency) of the human condition.

Kingsolver opens her novel firmly ensconced in one of its three interwoven tales, "Predators," quickly introducing her reader to the first of several distinctive characters tied passionately to the land of Appalachia. Deanna Wolfe, a National Forest Service employee, wildlife biologist and recluse, is both "frustrated" and "happy" to be "following tracks in the mud she couldn't identify" (1). For two years she has been living in a secluded cabin deep in the Appalachian Mountains, a verdant place demonstrative of life's flourishing in myriad and complex forms — a stark contrast to the impoverished marriage from which she had earlier escaped. As an expert on coyotes, her life in these mountains has been focused on tracking and studying the movements of a new family of these scarce yet necessary predators. Hunted almost to extinction by resident humans, the coyote, argues Deanna, is as vital a piece of the regional ecosystem as the farming of tobacco is to Kentucky's economic stability. And so she sees this top predator's return to Zebulon Mountain as a propitious sign. While acting as steward, guardian and groundskeeper of this particular Appalachian mountain area and its denizens, Deanna explores (and portrays) the region as an intricate system dependent on the delicate balance between predator and prey.

Such balance, however, is complicated and upset (beyond the disappearing coyote or other potential losses, both floral and faunal) when Eddie Bondo, a young hunter from Wyoming, interrupts Deanna's imposed isolation, and challenges both her conception of husbandry and her most intimate knowledge of herself. He appears as a predator himself, an animal at once fearful and wonderful:

> And there he stood, looking straight at her. He was dressed in boots and camouflage and carried a pack larger than hers. His rifle was no joke — a thirty-thirty, it looked like. Surprise must have stormed all over her face before she thought to arrange it for human inspection. It happened, that she ran into hunters up here. But she always saw them first. This one had stolen her advantage — he'd seen inside her [3].

"She wanted to watch him walk, to watch his body without his knowing it" (8). He is an intruder in a foreign territory, a threat, like the fescue hay and kudzu plants that have since overgrown — suffocated — the native grasses of the area, and fatally disoriented and displaced indigenous birds like the bobwhite quail (138). His presence thus reminds us of the tension between the richness and beauty of life's varied abundance and its unchecked, invasive reproductions. Eddie Bondo appears on Zebulon Mountain, Deanna's mountain, just as "spring heaved in its randy moment. Everywhere you looked, something was fighting for time, for light, the kiss of pollen, a connection of sperm and egg and another chance" (9). In a season fundamentally communal and fruitful, the natural world, including Deanna and this new male, fall prey to what Kingsolver describes as the "aggressive copulations that seemed to be collisions of strangers" (6).

Prodigal Summer might be read as an ecofeminist text, a novel that dwells on (and in) what Barbara Bennett defines as the "interconnectedness of all things" to reveal "a society based on cooperation and balance rather than dominance and hierarchy" (63–63). Not only, then, may we read the evolving story of Deanna Wolfe through its internal holisms, drawing analogies between the dense landscape of Appalachia and the deep intricacies of the human heart and mind; we are made to understand how the land itself sutures together the lives and livelihoods of a variety of seemingly incommensurable, though elaborately involved characters. Interlaced with Deanna's tale of "Predators" are the narratives of "Moth Love" and "Old Chestnuts," both of which move the reader off the mountain and into the small town of Egg Fork, in rural Zebulon County. Continuing the theme of conflict and rebirth, these additional stories add the complex fabric of human society to nature's already delicate and vulnerable tapestry.

In "Moth Love" we meet Lusa Maluf Landowski, a lepidopterist from Lexington, of Polish-Jewish and Palestinian descent, who had moved from the city, "from the other side of the mountains" (33), to Egg Fork, where her husband Cole Widener farmed tobacco on his family's homestead. But the untimely death of Cole leaves Lusa alone in an unfamiliar environment, and even more of an outsider now that she has inherited the largest share of the Widener farm. As she "struggles ... to fit into the tightly knit Widener family," Lusa replaces tobacco with goats in an attempt to keep "the family farm productive and intact" (Hanson 254). She is at once protective of and co-creative with the land she occupies, respectful of its past and hopeful for its future. As Lusa continues to align herself with her new home, she comes to recognize what Kingsolver herself experienced as the dynamic "interface between farms and wilderness" (Brace 17). Like many of Kingsolver's works, *Prodigal Summer* contains emerging and enlaced narratives wrought with the autobiographical details of its author. The strong land ethic with which Deanna and Lusa approach life in Appalachia echoes that with which Kingsolver was raised and raises her own children. This eco-consciousness is in turn reciprocated by the natural world and its ability to "empower and liberate the individual" (Hanson 258), be it Kingsolver or her (often female) characters.

Further representative of what many have described as Kingsolver's RACHEL CARSON–like perspective, evoking a sense of wonder and delight in the natural world, but also "challeng[ing] readers to treat the Earth with respect" (Hanson 258), is the third of *Prodigal Summer*'s interwoven tales, "Old Chestnuts." Centered on long-time resident of Egg Fork, retired agriculture teacher and chestnut tree enthusiast, Garnett S. Walker III, the narrative explores the conflict between thoughtful land management and ignorant husbandry. Just as Garnett Walker, now in his late seventies, continues to work at producing a blight-resistant strain of the all-but-extinct American chestnut tree, he is himself plagued by the organic farming practices (and other similar "indecencies") of his 75-year-old neighbor, Nannie Rawley. The irony of laboring to restore a lost species

of tree in the midst of a feud over pesticide use throws the urgency — and embattled state — of ecological conscience into stark relief.

"We must change our perspective of community," states Bennett, "and see it as a system of cooperation for the betterment of all rather than the competition for the success of a few" (64). The way in which the seemingly innate antagonism between Garnett Walker and Nannie Rawley evolves ultimately into an abiding attraction, manifested in the closing image of Nannie embraced by Garnett "like a calm little bird inside the circle of his arms" (427), displays the potential for just such a change in perspective. Like the metamorphosis of a caterpillar into a moth, or the development of a tree from seed, transformation is as instinctive to nature as it is to humankind, proving finally that we "are only one part of life on earth" (Barbara Kingsolver's Authorized Site). "Solitude is a human presumption," challenged by *Prodigal Summer*'s compelling fusion of the human and nonhuman in the "the web pulling mate to mate and predator to prey, a beginning or an end" (444). — Janelle A. Schwartz

BIBLIOGRAPHY

Bennett, Barbara. "Through Ecofeminist Eyes: LeGuin's 'The Ones Who Walk Away from Omelas.'" *English Journal.* 94:6 (July 2005): 63–68.

Brace, Marianne. "To Have and Have Nothing." *Independent* [London]. 8 July 2001: 17. Print.

Hanson, Susan. "Celebrating a Lively Earth: Children, Nature, and the Role of Mentors in *Prodigal Summer*" in *Seeds of Change: Critical Essays on Barbara Kingsolver*, Priscilla Leder, ed. Knoxville: University of Tennessee Press, 2010.

Kingsolver, Barbara. *Barbara Kingsolver: The Authorized Site.* http://www.kingsolver.com.

_____. *Prodigal Summer.* New York: HarperCollins, 2001.

Maslin, Janet. Book Review of Barbara Kingsolver's *Prodigal Summer*, "BOOKS OF THE TIMES; 3 Story Lines United by the Fecundity of Summer." *The New York Times.* 2 Nov 2000. Accessed 28 May 2011. http://www.nytimes.com/2000/11/02/arts/02MASL.html.

Kirkland, Caroline Matilda Stansbury (1801–1864)

With a literary career ranging from editor of the *Union Magazine of Literature and Art*, to numerous articles such as "The Significance of Dress" and "Literary Women," to a biography of George Washington, Caroline Kirkland attained her literary recognition primarily through three works detailing her experiences on the Michigan frontier from 1837 to 1843. Despite moments when she reflects on the natural beauty and splendor of a wilderness scene, Kirkland's writing evinces a realistic, often sarcastic attitude that challenges the inflated romantic descriptions common to popular reports of the western territories. More particularly, Kirkland presents a feminine perspective that critically details the difficulty of balancing domestic responsibilities with frontier freedoms in advancing frontier culture.

Born in 1801 into an intellectual family, Kirkland received an academically challenging Quaker education at her Aunt Lydia Mott's school. After Kirkland completed her professional teacher training, she met and later married William Kirkland in 1828 and moved to Detroit in 1835 to teach at the Detroit Female Seminary. *A New Home, Who'll Follow?* (1839) presents a largely biographical yet fictional account of Kirkland's initial experiences of her family's settlement in Pinckney, Michigan in 1835. Her first-person narrator, Mary Clavers, is a well-educated, cultivated Eastern woman who experiences, as Kirkland herself did, cultural and social isolation among those with generally less education and of lower social standing. She satirically comments on habits, conventions, cleanliness, fashion, and literary tastes of the Montacute (Pinckney) community, often finding humor in their pretentious and unrefined behavior.

Because *A New Home* had deeply offended her neighbors, Kirkland tempered FOREST LIFE (1842), her second treatment of life in Pinckney. Nonetheless, through the revived persona of Mary Clavers, Kirkland continues her critical and, at times, facetious examination of life on the Michigan frontier, mocking the idealized portraits of pioneer settlements, encouraging personal and domestic refinements, targeting recognized disreputable figures such as dishonest land speculators, and highlighting the difficulties, successes, and eccentricities of other pioneers.

After their land investment near Detroit failed, the family returned to New York in 1843, and both Caroline and William resumed writing and teaching. In 1845, Caroline Kirkland published WESTERN CLEARINGS, compiled from the periodical sketches of her western adventures previously published in *Knickerbocker*, *The Gift*, *Graham's*, and *Godey's*. Although other contemporary frontier accounts, such as those of MARGARET FULLER and ELIZA FARNHAM, address the Native American condition, Kirkland's texts noticeably lack substantive discussion of the regional Indian tribes.

After William's death in 1846, Caroline continued to edit *Sartain's Union Magazine of Literature and Art* and to write professionally on cultural and social topics. Committed to her work for the U.S. Sanitary Commission (later the Red Cross), Kirkland opened a Metropolitan Fair to raise funds for the Commission on April 4, 1864 and died in her sleep from a stroke on April 6. Among nineteenth-century frontier writers, Caroline Kirkland stands out as a realist and a cultural critic whom EDGAR ALLAN POE, in "The Literati of New York," aptly commends: "Her mere style is admirable, lucid, terse, full of variety, faultlessly pure, and yet bold." — Thomas P. Fair

BIBLIOGRAPHY

Georgi-Findlay, Brigitte. *The Frontiers of Women's Writing: Women's Narratives and the Rhetoric of Westward Expansion*. Tucson: University of Arizona Press, 1996.

Kolodny, Annette. *The Land Before Her: Fantasy and Experience of the American Frontier 1630–1860*. Chapel Hill: University of North Carolina Press, 1984.

Poe, Edgar Allen. "The Literati of New York." *Essays and Reviews*. New York: Viking, Library of America, 1984.

Zagarell, Sandra A. "Introduction." *A New Home, Who'll Follow?* (1843) Caroline Kirkland. New Brunswick: Rutgers University Press, 1990.

Forest Life, Caroline Stansbury Kirkland (1842)

Caroline Kirkland achieved both fame and some notoriety with the publication of her first major work, *A New Home, Who'll Follow?* (1839), which realistically (and satirically) recounted her experiences with her new family homestead and the community of Pinckney, Michigan in 1837. Although *A New Home* was well received by the general public, her neighbors saw through the thinly disguised representations and protested their portrayal. Consequently, Kirkland depicted more affirmative elements of the pioneer experience in *Forest Life*, while addressing the problems and shortcomings that she believed continued to inhibit the progress of the western settlements.

After apologizing for any offenses in her previous work, Kirkland dismisses the distorted, idealized vision that politicians, land agents, and travel writers often provide of frontier settlement, with a parody of their hyperbolic style: "I borrowed from a political friend the optics he had used in travelling through the state ... certain that I should now be able to give the most fascinating and satisfactory accounts of all I saw and heard" (I, 17). Through her "magic glasses" (I, 17) she observes: "luxurious sugar-maples and lofty elms, with fantastic arbors," "youths and maidens habited with the simplicity of Arcadia," "pillared palaces of painted pine," or cottages "roofed with golden thatch," odors "of ineffable purity and power," and "gushing streams of crystal water" (I, 19–22) (AMERICAN PASTORAL). A "girl of seraphic beauty" accidentally breaks the glasses, restoring Kirkland's objectivity and the realism she favors, and the child now appears as "a dirty little urchin" (I,

22–23). However, Kirkland importantly acknowledges the possibility that despite the distortion she censures, the images contain "like some other dreams, much of 'the inner life of things'" (I, 24).

Having suggested the potential of the frontier and its inhabitants, Kirkland severely criticizes the exploitive and reckless clearing of the land, as an illustration of the settlement's skewed values. For Kirkland, the westward expansion of civilized society holds greater importance than the mere acquisition of property. Although she recognizes the vigorous pioneering spirit involved in continually pushing the frontier west, as appropriate to an earlier time, she condemns in her time the despoliation of ancient trees for soon vacated farmlands, as much as the civilized settlements' neglect of the domestic needs of the women and children (I, 28). She notes: "The very notion of advancement, of civilization, of prosperity, seems inseparably connected with the total extirpation of the forest" (I, 43). Kirkland's emphasis on civilization refers more to the elevation of the spirit and intellect than to mercantile expansion or promotion of luxuries and class. The potential for individual growth and independence associated with frontier life fails, in her estimation, if cultural development and intellectual growth do not follow.

Similar to the regional journeys described by MARGARET FULLER (*SUMMER ON THE LAKES*) and ELIZA FARNHAM (*LIFE IN PRAIRIE LAND*), Kirkland moves beyond the Montacute (Pinckney) focus of *A New Home* and describes a tour of the local region, to reveal the complex and often contradictory values exhibited by the settlers. Supporting her concern for frontier refinement, she details the several household enhancements and improved manners of Mrs. Ainsworth after her extended eastern visit. Kirkland modifies her broad support of Eastern influences in her indictment of the wealthy Margold family's discourteous and pretentious behavior towards the generous poverty of the Gastons, financially ruined by the failed financial development schemes of Eastern banks. She takes politicians to task for their self-interest and shortsighted failure to see the need for building roads and schools. Incorporating a scientific style integrating specific terms and explanations, Kirkland also defends Michigan's natural beauty, noting the variety of lakes, grasslands, and clear air (I, 129–131). Unlike Farnham's often elevated descriptions of natural beauty, Kirkland's treatment notably lacks references to the sublime (I, 88–89).

To broaden and nuance her complex account of the western experience, Kirkland discusses several elements of pioneer life: the education of children, the changing social roles and expectations, and the handling of unexpected hardships. She incorporates a frontier parable relating the successful struggles of young Seymour Bullitt in his quest to attain Caroline Hay as an exemplary victory of compassion, hard work and purpose, over vanity, social position and artificial style (I, 237–250; II, 3–45). Employed as a hand to study the methods of the prosperous Mr. Hay, an initially unsophisticated Seymour leaves to study in a Western city and returns as a mature man with a sophisticated business understanding. The indulged Caroline, currently more estranged from frontier life, similarly returns from a socially focused stay with her aunt in an Eastern city. Through a series of hardships and losses, Seymour reveals an industrious, virtuous and steadfast character that now wins an enlightened Caroline's love. Although his efforts earn Seymour a lucrative offer to manage an Eastern business, he stays to improve his local interests. Kirkland's morality tale celebrates both the positive character of settlers like Seymour, and the need to apply both skills *and* moral character, to improve the frontier settlements.

Kirkland also recounts her meeting with the Englishman Sibthorpe and uses his liminal interactions, as a foreigner, with the Western experience, as another means of interpretation. She regards his romantic views of nature as a reminder of frontier ideals, including his impassioned discussion with an innkeeper about the hypocrisy of racist sentiment in "the land of liberty," and the importance of quality and action over a preference for wealth (I, 205). She also expands upon his struggles in creating a pioneer homestead through a packet of family letters (II, 62–146). Kirkland balances the Sibthorpes' enthusiasm for the pleasures of the Michigan wilderness and a new home, against the pragmatic difficulties of creating a homestead and their adjustment to the paucity of materials and help available to them. Kirkland admires the Sibthorpes' idealism and presents it as a critical and sympathetic component of the national motivation for westward expansion; however, her counterpoint of the attendant difficulties in establishing and maintaining a homestead underscores the demanding reality of the experience.

Kirkland concludes *Forest Life* with two stories further illustrating the character diversity of the region and emphasizing the positive attributes of the land and people. She speaks of Mrs. Parshalls' story of endurance and compassion, and of the Ardens and Beamers' tale of love, vanity, and forgiveness. In her final, personal commentary, Kirkland reiterates the difficulties of frontier life but asserts the personal benefits of nature and community available to those who settle the west. — Thomas P. Fair

BIBLIOGRAPHY

Georgi-Findlay, Brigitte. *The Frontiers of Women's Writing: Women's Narratives and the Rhetoric of Westward Expansion.* Tucson: University of Arizona Press, 1996.

Kirkland, Caroline. *Forest Life.* 1844. Upper Saddle River, NJ: Literature House/Gregg Press, 1970.

Kolodny, Annette. *The Land Before Her: Fantasy and Experience of the American Frontier 1630–1860.* Chapel Hill: University of North Carolina Press, 1984.

Western Clearings, Caroline Kirkland (1845)

"The wild new country, with all its coarseness and all its disadvantages of various kinds, has yet a fascination for the settler in consequence of a certain free, hearty tone, which has long since disappeared if indeed it ever existed, in parts of the country where civilization has made greater progress" (Kirkland 1). Thus Caroline Kirkland begins her *Western Clearings* (1845), with "Land-Fever," an explanation of the rampant land speculation which drew so many to the Michigan wilderness, and the negative effect it had on settlers and the land itself. Hospitality and domesticity gave way to fierce battles for land. Men, who had little experience of the frontier, would set out alone, unwilling to share their location with other speculators, and unprepared to face the unfamiliar environment and its dangers.

Rachel Borup thus argues that Kirkland stands in opposition to male frontier voices such as JAMES FENIMORE COOPER's. Where the male authors typically describe the West in terms of the outdoors and individual mastery, Borup argues that Kirkland "moves the story of the West indoors," and focuses on domesticity. Even as Kirkland spends a significant part of her narrative in *Western Clearings* (1845) on the rhythms of rural agricultural life in the Michigan woods and prairies, she also writes about the importance of home and good husbandry on the frontier.

Domesticity is valued in the country and includes work outside. All will quickly grow wild again without constant cultivation — not only the crops, but the house gardens as well. In "Idle People" and other essays, Kirkland states that in the "western wilds" nature demands labor. Idleness will not be rewarded, and in fact can be detrimental to both the family's and the community's welfare. Nature, lush in its natural state, must be hedged in and cultivated in order for its human inhabitants to survive. Kirkland views the coarsening of people's manners with far less facetiousness in *Western Clearings* than she did in *A New Land* (1839), and exhibits a more nuanced and sympathetic understanding, stressing that one's survival is dependent on a new standard of civilized behavior; indeed, that what *constitutes* civilized behavior in this environment is fundamentally and importantly different — an attitude far ahead of its time.

In the penultimate essay of the collection, "Half-Lengths from Life," for example, white hands imply a lack of connection to the land. Anna is working to earn money for the family in their time of need. Her brother objects, urging her to think of her beautiful "lady's" hands. Anna scoffs at the idea of being ladylike on the frontier. "Of what use are white satin hands in the country?" she argues (192). She is brown from gardening — much more important in the country than the urban status of being a "lady."

Success in this Michigan wilderness is measured by how domesticated the land has become. Kirkland adapts the traditional frontier text to a female perspective; all nature is improved by a woman's hand. Fruits are made into jams, a clearing into a garden, a sturdy log cabin into a cottage. Although Tom, a character in "Ambuscades," is able to hunt raccoons and squirrels from his cabin window, he has also domesticated his home for his mother's sake by cultivating fruit trees and filling the cabin with furniture. This domestication is not done for his own comfort — his land is a farm in name only, and populated with deer and other wilderness inhabitants — but for his mother who needs the civilization that domestication implies.

Kirkland devotes most of her book to the description of the domestic value of good husbandry as seen by women, but in "Harvest Musings," the ripened wheat under a full harvest moon provides her with the opportunity to feminize the male work of cultivating winter crops. Her description of the cradle scythe used to harvest the grain marks one of the most eloquent passages in the book (58).

The idea of improvement — what it means to improve one's material possessions as well as oneself — is another constant theme Kirkland's works. Scott Peoples notes that "The Bee Tree" focuses on "the flawed economic theory of Silas Ashburn," a man whose family is barely held together even though "Silas [...] works, as he says, 'like a tiger'" (67). Silas's land is run-down and poorly maintained, situated in a swampy area that is ruining the health of his family. Unable to focus on land cultivation, he is obsessed with the honey that can be found in the bee-tree of the story's title. But Silas's real problem is that he is unable, and ultimately unwilling, to work hard enough to shape his environment to his needs.

Good husbandry is the fundamental sign of success on the frontier, a notion expressed in the very title of *Western Clearings.* Taking care of the environment ensures not only one's survival, but one's new-found civility. Thus Kirkland works an important variation on the traditional American theme of survival, exploring it from the domestic and female viewpoint, largely absent from the standard frontier texts of the period.— Patricia Kennedy Bostian

BIBLIOGRAPHY

Borup, Rachel. "Bankers in Buckskins: Caroline Kirkland's Critique of Frontier Masculinity." *ATQ* 18.4 (2004): 229–247.

Kirkland, Caroline. *Western Clearings.* New York: Wiley & Putnam, 1845.

Kolodny, Annette. "The Literary Legacy of Caroline Kirkland: Emigrants' Guide to a Failed Eden." *The Land Before Her: Fantasy and Experience of the American Frontiers, 1630–1860.* Chapel Hill: University of North Carolina Press, 1984. 131–158.

Peeples, Scott. "'The Servant Is as His Master': Western Exceptionalism in Caroline Kirkland's Short Fiction." *ATQ* 13.4 (1999): 305.

Krakauer, Jon (1954–   )

Born in Massachusetts and raised in Oregon, Jon Krakauer is a mountaineer and writer recognized for significant works of environmental narrative journalism, particularly INTO THE WILD (1996) and *Into Thin Air* (1997). After receiving a degree in Environmental Studies from Hampshire College in 1976, Krakauer worked as a fisherman and carpenter, eventually becoming a freelance writer. Beyond his full-length works, he has published in major American magazines such as *Outside, Rolling Stone,* and *National Geographic,* in addition to editing several works on mountaineering, adventure, and exploration.

When he was eight, Krakauer was invited to climb a 10,000-foot peak with family friend Willi Unsoeld, who would later summit Everest, and the experience convinced Krakauer that his passion was mountains. In 1974 he ascended peaks in the Brooks Range and published his first article, about the experience, in *The American Alpine Journal.* In 1977 he made a difficult traverse of the Devil's Thumb in Alaska. Recounting that experience in the British magazine *Mountain,* Krakauer revealed two key themes of his later work: the test of individual will against an often hostile natural world, and a fascination with extreme personalities who undertake tremendous physical trials in remote and perilous regions. The article was republished in the collection *Eiger Dreams* (1990) and as part of *Into the Wild.*

One of Krakauer's most notable works, *Into the Wild* tells the true story of Christopher McCandless, a young man who relinquished all his money and possessions to travel the United States and Mexico before dying alone in an abandoned Alaskan camp. Krakauer's second, equally successful full-length work was *Into Thin Air,* which recounts the tale of the "Everest disaster" of May 11, 1996, when a storm developed on the mountain in late afternoon, stranding climbers near the summit. Krakauer details the small decisions and mistakes that resulted in the death of eight people. The work criticizes the commercialization of Mount Everest, and reflects Krakauer's insistence on human accountability to the environment, a theme equally prominent in *Into the Wild. Into Thin Air* was adapted for television in 1997.

In an interview with the *New York Times* after the Everest tragedy, Krakauer attempted to address why people subject themselves to the physical demands of high altitude climbing, noting that "There's something about being afraid, about being small, about enforced humility that draws me to climbing." In a recent film made for the Sundance Channel, he extols the virtues of the "primordial place, the world not made by man," where you can get a "glimpse of eternity." His writing explores the ways that wild places become sites for cathartic experiences, and his protagonists typically seek profound connection with the wilderness; however, he is careful to remind readers of the moral consequences of the human presence in the non-human environment.

After a six-year hiatus from book publishing, Krakauer returned with *Under the Banner of Heaven* (2003), an expose of fundamentalist Mormonism. In 2009 he was scheduled to release a book chronicling the death of Pat Tillman, killed in action in Afghanistan, but was unhappy with the manuscript and withdrew the book from publication.— Marguerite Helmers

BIBLIOGRAPHY

Egan, Timothy. "At Home With: Jon Krakauer; Back from Everest, Haunted." *The New York Times,* 23 May 1996. Available online. URL: http://www.nytimes.com/1996/05/23/garden/at-home-with-jon-krakauer-back-from-everest-haunted.html. Accessed June 16, 2009.

Jacobson, Kristin J. "Desiring Natures: The American Adrenaline Narrative." *Genre* 35, no. 2 (2002): 355–82.

Krakauer, Jon. *Eiger Dreams: Ventures Among Men and Mountains.* New York: Lyons & Burford, 1990.

———. *Into the Wild.* New York: Villard, 1996.

———. *Into Thin Air: A Personal Account of the Mount Everest Disaster.* New York: Villard, 1997.

———. *Under the Banner of Heaven: A Story of Violent Faith.* New York: Doubleday, 2003.

Manning, Peter K. "High Risk Narratives: Textual Adventures." *Qualitative Sociology* 22, no. 4 (1999): 285–299.

Penn, Sean, and Jon Krakauer, Sean Penn + Jon Krakauer. Film. Directed by Joe Berlinger, 2007. Sundance Channel.

Weissman, Larry. "Interview with Jon Krakauer." Random House *Bold Type.* Available online. URL: http://www.randomhouse.com/boldtype/0697/krakauer/interview.html. Accessed June 16, 2009.

Into the Wild,
Jon Krakauer (1996)

Into the Wild is a work of biographical investigative journalism that raises profound questions about man's proper relationship to the environment. Revised and expanded from a 9,000 word magazine article titled "Death of an Innocent" in *Outside* magazine in 1993, Krakauer's story of Christopher J. McCandless has become a classic and controversial work of outdoor fiction, which is regularly placed on lists of great travel and adventure books of the 20th century, and has fostered a documentary and a Hollywood feature film. Krakauer specializes in outdoor and adventure writing; his bestselling work, *Into Thin Air*, for example, critiqued the high-altitude climbing industry with its account of the ill-fated ascent of Mount Everest in 1996.

The protagonist of *Into the Wild* is Christopher McCandless, who in the spring of 1990, after graduating from Emory University, donated his money to charity, packed his 1982 Datsun B210, and began traveling. His dream was to be self-sufficient, maintaining only those possessions needed to survive. In the process he abandoned all communication with his family in suburban Washington D.C. and took on a new name, Alexander Supertramp. Echoing TRANSCENDENTALIST ideas he wrote to a friend, "The joy of life comes from our encounters with new experiences, and hence there is no greater joy than to have an endlessly changing horizon, for each day to have a new and different sun" (57). Inspired by the work of JACK LONDON, McCandless dreamed of a "great Alaskan odyssey" (45) in which he would test his survival skills in a remote and unforgiving environment. Thus, on April 28, 1992, McCandless walked "into the wild" on the Stampede Trail, eventually camping in an abandoned school bus 25 miles west of Healy, Alaska, and north of Denali National Park. He packed a fishing rod, a .22 caliber rifle, binoculars, a sleeping bag, one 10-pound bag of rice, and a field guide to edible plants. Four months later he was dead at age 24. How he died remains a point of controversy and is one of the enduring fascinations of the book.

Although the narrative of McCandless' "Alaskan odyssey" follows the formula of the hero's quest, the book is not structured chronologically. Readers know the outcome on the first page: this hero will not survive his test. Krakauer organizes the book thematically and episodically. Thus, like a highway or river, the tale meanders and often doubles back on itself. Chapter headnotes are integral to understanding McCandless's story, as they contain excerpts from works by London, Leo Tolstoy, and MARK TWAIN, which

help to position him within a lineage of other wilderness pioneers, particularly HENRY DAVID THOREAU and JOHN MUIR. Consequently, *Into the Wild* can be read both as a spiritual manifesto and as a philosophical narrative about the human relationship to nature. McCandless sought to renounce the commodification of late twentieth-century capitalism for an existence dependent on the land, believing material wealth to be "shameful, corrupting, inherently evil" (115). He internalized the mythos of self-sufficiency, the primacy of nature, and a dream of rugged American individualism on the frontier. As Susan Kollin writes, for McCandless Alaska was a blank spot on the map, "terra incognita awaiting his arrival" (41).

Among its thematic aims, *Into the Wild* draws attention to the persistent need to define the terms "wild" and "wilderness," and to describe who truly has access to them. Krakauer notes in his preface to the published book version of McCandless's story, that one of the "larger subjects" of the tale is "the grip wilderness has on the American imagination." While the environment (variously cast as nature or the wilderness) is always present at the core of McCandless' consciousness, and at the core of the book, the extent to which it may, in the end, be a cultural or imaginary construct is frequently tested by Krakauer. Quoting from Roderick Nash's *Wilderness and the American Mind*, Krakauer points out that wilderness and the frontier played an important part in the developing mental life of Americans because they "offered an escape from society" and allowed "the Romantic individual to exercise the cult that he frequently made of his own soul" (Nash, qtd. 57). Exclaiming in his journal, "Jack London is King," McCandless did not seem to recognize the irony of basing his concept of Alaska on the fiction of a writer who had spent very little time in the north. London was responsible for constructing the "imaginary geography" of Alaska (to borrow a term from Edward Said), and it was into this simulacrum of the wilderness as constructed by London that the pseudonymous Alexander Supertramp ventured.

Ironically, Krakauer's *Into the Wild* has mythologized McCandless own life, leading to "bus tourism," pilgrimages to the bus where photographs are snapped and posted to blogs. Since the publication of *Into the Wild*, two films have taken up the subject. Sean Penn directed an artful interpretation of the story in a 2007 release by Paramount starring Emile Hirsch as McCandless; and in the same year, director Ron Lamothe released a documentary titled *The Call of the Wild* that followed McCandless's path through the American landscape. Both films draw attention to the persistent hold that the idea of the wilderness has on the American imagination and the collective psyche of the nation. A confused and unstable, but highly-charged amalgam of beauty, sublimity, and mythic significance, the wilderness "trail" leads ultimately to the unknown, both in the external landscape and in what Krakauer calls "the inner country of [one's] own soul" (183). It is a country apart, a place beyond the corruptions of the city, to which people "escape" to find solitude, peace, and a renewed sense of identity. Thus Krakauer concludes that "an extended stay in the wilderness inevitably directs one's attention outward as much as inward, and it is impossible to live off the land without developing both a subtle understanding of, and a strong emotional bond with, that land and all it holds" (183).— Marguerite Helmers

BIBLIOGRAPHY

Bryson, George. "Theories Differ on the Cause of McCandless' Death." *Anchorage Daily News* 8 October 2007. Available online. URL: www.adn.com/intothewild/v-printer/story/219344.html. Accessed June 7, 2009.

Call of the Wild. Dir. Ron Lamothe. Terra Incognita Films, 2007.

"Film Captures Young Man's Journey 'Into the Wild.'" Interview with Jon Krakauer. *NPR All Things Considered.* 20 September 2007. Available online. URL: http://www.npr.org/templates/story/story.php?storyId=145648 27 Accessed June 9, 2009.

Into the Wild. Dir. Sean Penn. Paramount, 2007.

Kollin, Susan. "The Wild, Wild, North: Nature Writing, Nationalist Ecologies, and Alaska." *American Literary History* 12.1/2 (Spring-Summer 2000): 41–78.

Krakauer, Jon. *Into the Wild.* New York: Random House, 1996.

Raskin, Jonah. "Calls of the Wild: On the Page and on the Screen." *American Book Review* (May-June 2008): 3.

Said, Edward. *Orientalism.* New York: Vintage, 1978.

Krutch, Joseph Wood (1893–1970)

Joseph Wood Krutch came to nature writing in his fifties, in the midst of a long, varied, and prolific career, one marked by notable achievements and awards, including the 1954 National Book Award for *The Measure of Man* and, toward the end of his life, in 1967, the American Academy of Arts and Sciences' Emerson-Thoreau Medal for "distinguished achievement in the broad field of literature." Long before he published his first collection of nature essays, *The Twelve Seasons,* in 1949, he had established a national reputation as a social critic, a book reviewer, the longtime drama critic for *The Nation,* a literary biographer, and a professor of English at Columbia University. Once his identity as a New York intellectual was secure, this quintessentially urban intellectual was free to pursue his latent interest in the natural world, first at his weekend retreat in Con-

necticut, and then, after retirement from Columbia, in a home just outside Tucson, Arizona.

By the mid 1950s and until his death in 1970, Krutch was widely known as a writer of thoughtful, often amusing essays containing his observations of wild animals, native plants, climate, and seasonal change; but even during this period he continued to publish social criticism and essays on a broad array of topics. In particular, he was recognized as a nature writer of the desert landscape of the American Southwest. In the 1960s his fame extended to television viewers when a former student recruited him as the naturalist host of multi-part documentaries broadcast on NBC about the Southwest, the Grand Canyon, and Baja California (Margolis 224–25). Passages from his books on these topics formed the majority of the programs' scripts. These programs received both critical and popular acclaim, and did much to raise public awareness of the American environment and environmental issues; the Grand Canyon series won the Edison Award for Excellence in Television. In addition, Krutch's numerous contributions to magazines, Sierra Club books, and natural history book series, as well as his frequent appearances on television and radio talk shows, gave him "national standing and [a] popular reputation" until the end of this life (Margolis 229).

Born in 1893 to a comfortable, conservative family in Knoxville, Tennessee, Krutch earned an undergraduate degree from the University of Tennessee and then eagerly left the South to study for his Ph.D. in English at Columbia University in New York City, where he became a close and lifelong friend of poet Mark Van Doren (Margolis 27–30). On the eve of the Great Depression, in 1929, he published *The Modern Temper,* a critically acclaimed book that summed up the anxieties of high Modernism, emphasizing humanity's isolation in the world, questioning life's meaning once traditional religion seemed irrelevant, and expressing a resulting spiritual angst and emotional despair. Eventually, he found an antidote to this despair in the natural world, gaining solace through fellowship with small creatures such as frogs, salamanders, and beetles that carried on with their lives despite the constraints of climate and the limitations of size and lifecycle.

Krutch's shift in focus from an urban landscape to a rural one occasioned a rereading of the works of HENRY DAVID THOREAU in the 1940s and led him to write a biography of the New England TRANSCENDENTALIST, which was published in 1948. Like Thoreau, and like the other major influences on his nature writing, ALDO LEOPOLD and entomologist William Morton Wheeler, Krutch was struck by the interdependence, yet fragility, of all natural life

(McClintock 49–58). In his view, Thoreau "always sought in his intercourse with living things and even with the very hills and fields themselves ... that warm and sympathetic sense of oneness, that escape from the self into the All..." (*Henry David Thoreau* 172). This theme emerges in practically every Krutch essay, including his first, "April: The Day of the Peepers," which he concludes with a quiet cheer for the small springtime tree toad: "'Don't forget,' I whisper to the peepers; 'we are all in this together'" (*Twelve Seasons* 13).

In his nature books, Krutch writes for a popular audience; nonetheless, literary allusions — and humorous twists on their implications — are characteristic of his style. For example, in a much anthologized essay, "Love in the Desert," Krutch describes jack rabbits with the help of Wordsworth, cowbirds with references to Jean Jacques Rousseau and WALT WHITMAN, tarantulas using a phrase from Algernon Charles Swinburne's poetry, and the asexual reproduction strategies of many plants and animals with a nod to "Is Sex Necessary?" by James Thurber and E.B. White (*Voice of the Desert* 167–80). He employs these allusions both as touchstones of social norms and human expectations, and as comparisons between the learned world of letters and the more exotic and wonderful (though perhaps more humble in status) lives and places he observes. While explicating how spring courtship rituals begin early in the desert, Krutch does not resist a gratuitous literary aside: "Though I have never noticed that either of the two kinds of doves which spend the whole year with us acquire that 'livelier iris' which Tennyson celebrated, the lizard's belly turns turquoise blue, as though to remind his mate that even on their ancient level sex has its aesthetic as well as its biological aspect" (168). The typical approach and purpose of Krutch's essays emerge among their allusions; they are shaped by first-hand observation, an informal, often off-hand questioning of assumptions and apparent causes, and a primary desire to understand the nonhuman world. Krutch's voice is kindly, droll, and informed but not expert; he is led by his senses and his curiosity. He wants to know more than he does, but he likes entertainment too. Collectively, these techniques create the appealing persona and ethos of an educated individual who aspires to be a naturalist; through them Krutch good-naturedly tutors readers in ecology, and more surreptiously, in a quiet but telling reverence for nature.

Consequently, Krutch's essays are easy on readers, guiding them gently to perceive a unity with the natural world but rarely challenging public policy, capitalism, or materialism. Only occasionally, as in "Conservation is Not Enough," does Krutch directly expound on the broad risks of a "homocentric point of view" (*Voice of the Desert* 202):

We have three tigers — the economic, the physical and the biological — by the tail and three tigers are more than three times as dangerous as one. We cannot let any of them go. But it is also not certain that we can hold all of them indefinitely. Many a despot has discovered that it was just when his power seemed to have been made absolute at last that the revolution broke out. And it may be that just about three hundred years was necessary to expose the fallacy of the ideal [of theologically sanctioned human dominance and exceptionalism] born in the seventeenth century" [*Voice of the Desert* 203].

Though he can be frank, for the most part Krutch teaches with a light, patient touch, hoping readers agree with his critique of society and turn away from short-sighted values, views, and habits.

After he turned to publishing nature essays, Krutch became active in establishing nature writing as a distinct genre. In 1950 he published a landmark anthology, *Great American Nature Writing*, with a scholarly 70-page prologue that traces the western influences of philosophy, theology, and science on humanity's relationship to nature from the middle ages to the twentieth century and, then, defines nature writing from Thoreau onward. The most important criterion for nature writing, according to Krutch, is the conviction of the oneness of all. In addition, he views nature writing as the work of "artists," not merely scientists or explorers, who "seek literary means to communicate the personal experience of living in contact with the natural world," once they have "absorbed" the lessons of the natural science of their day (21). Krutch identifies two trends in the genre since Romanticism, one led by "lovers of the sublime in nature [and the other by] watchers of living things" (32). Additional pervasive themes include "the search for peace, the dream of the golden age, and that whole nostalgia for a more primitive way of life" (60) (AMERICAN PASTORAL). This volume was commercially successful enough to be reprinted in book club editions.

Krutch's standards for nature writing are characteristic of his time, as seen in the work of contemporaries such as Edwin Way Teale and LOREN EISELEY, before the more apocalyptic and disturbing voices of the 1960s emerge. Krutch writes to help readers make connections between their daily lives and the natural world; he is no radical. Despite his conviction that limited human influence over the natural world is surely the wisest strategy for the survival of humanity and of all life, his essays usually stop short of warnings and proscriptions. — Elizabeth Giddens

BIBLIOGRAPHY

Krutch, Joseph Wood. *Great American Nature Writing.* New York: William Sloane, 1950. Print.

_____. *Henry David Thoreau.* New York: William Sloane, 1948. Print.

_____. *The Measure of Man: On Freedom, Human Values, Survival, and the Modern Temper.* New York: Bobbs-Merrill, 1954. Print.

_____. *The Modern Temper: A Study and a Confession.* 1929. New York: Harcourt, Brace, 1956. Print.

_____. *The Twelve Seasons: A Perpetual Calendar for the Country.* New York, William Sloane, 1949. Print.

_____. *The Voice of the Desert: A Naturalist's Interpretation.* New York: William Sloane, 1954. Print.

Margolis, John D. *Joseph Wood Krutch: A Writer's Life.* Knoxville: University of Tennessee Press, 1980. Print.

McClintock, Jimes I. *Nature's Kindred Sprits: Aldo Leopold, Joseph Wood Krutch, Edward Abbey, Annie Dillard, and Gary Snyder.* Madison: University of Wisconsin Press, 1994. Print.

Las Casas, Bartolomé de (1474–1566)

Bartolomé de Las Casas, a Spanish priest and New World chronicler, wrote some of the most important and controversial works of the sixteenth century.

Las Casas journeyed to Hispaniola (now the island comprised of Haiti and the Dominican Republic) from Spain in 1502, where he was allotted an *encomienda*—a land grant authorizing the owner to enslave its inhabitants. In 1513 Las Casas participated in the conquest of Cuba, where he was given another *encomienda*. As he Christianized the indigenous populations, however, he became increasingly enraged by Spanish mistreatment of them, and his sympathies were heightened by similar objections from Dominican friars. Finally, in 1514 Las Casas renounced his *encomiendas*, freed his slaves, and began a lifelong critique of Spanish injustices against inhabitants of the New World.

Las Casas won a symbolic victory in 1542 when Charles I abolished the *encomienda* system, but colonial protests led the king to revoke the abolishment in 1545. Las Casas returned to Spain in 1547, where he continued to publicize the issue. Most famously he debated Juan de Sepulveda, who argued on Aristotelian terms that some populations — specifically New World peoples — were naturally suited for slavery. "The consensus of the time and since has been that Las Casas got the better of the debate," especially as his response to Sepulveda's 3-hour speech lasted 5 days (*World Eras*). Although his work had little effect on contemporary *events* in the New World, his lifelong quest to make the world *aware* of those events influenced international opinion of Spain for centuries to come.

Las Casas' writings are less about the environment

of the New World than about its inhabitants. However, his *History of the Indies* performs a vital historical role: as Henry Raup Wagner notes, it "remains the most valuable single account of the discovery of the New World.... [Las Casas] used and preserved for us masses of documentary material, the most priceless being the diary of Columbus' first voyage" (qtd. in *Hispanic Biography*). Its major environmental contribution lies in its preservation of early descriptions of New World landscapes.

Las Casas is most famous for his BRIEF ACCOUNT OF THE DESTRUCTION OF THE INDIES (1522), which describes in excruciatingly vivid detail episodes of Spanish violence against indigenous peoples, and by extension the land. The work drew international attention to the injustices of the Conquest. He also wrote a philosophical tract, *Apologetic History of the Indies*, an Aristotelian argument against Native American enslavement.

Las Casas' works stand out from other writings of the period because of his inflammatory indictment of the Spanish. By many accounts, he initiated international debate about the treatment of conquered populations. Thus he has had less influence on American environmental awareness than on human rights history. However, insofar as environmental issues overlap with the rights of Native Americans, Las Casas' work lays a foundation for environmental ethics based on fair treatment of and self-determination for original inhabitants.— Laura Boynton Johnson

BIBLIOGRAPHY

"Bartolomé de Las Casas." *American Eras, Vol. 1: Early American Civilizations and Exploration to 1600* (1998). Reproduced in *Biography Resource Center.* Gale Group. Available online. URL: http://galenet.galegroup.com/servlet/BioRC. Accessed June 24, 2009.

"Bartolomé de Las Casas." *Dictionary of Hispanic Biography* (1996). Reproduced in *Biography Resource Center.* Gale Group. Available online. URL: http://galenet.galegroup.com/servlet/BioRC. Accessed June 24, 2009.

"Bartolomé de Las Casas." *World Eras, Vol. 1: European Renaissance and Reformation (1350–1600)* (2001). Reproduced in *Biography Resource Center* Gale Group. Available online. URL: http://galenet.galegroup.com/servlet/BioRC. Accessed June 24, 2009.

A Brief Account of the Destruction of the Indies, Bartolomé de Las Casas (1552)

A Brief Account of the Destruction of the Indies presents a vivid catalog of the 16th-century Spanish Conquest of the West Indies. Written by Bartolomé de Las Casas, a Spanish priest and New World chronicler famous for his opposition to Spanish mistreatment of indigenous populations, the narrative is vivid, brutal, violent, and — unfortunately — broadly accurate.

Las Casas details unprovoked massacres of native populations; violent torture of leaders in service of locating gold; brutal rapes; forced enslavement; the pillaging and burning of homes and temples; the separation of families; the forced relocation of populations; and the painful, prolonged, public slaughter of captives to intimidate others into submission. It is an altogether horrifying read, and stands out dramatically in the corpus of writings by Spanish explorers primarily for its radical stance against the doctrine of Native American inferiority.

A Brief Account departs from many colonial writings because of its rhetorical (rather than strictly documentary) purpose; that is to say, Las Casas was more invested in persuading readers into belief than in preserving geographic or narrative details of the Spanish exploration. Some of Las Casas' other works, like the *History of the Indies*, present more straightforward *reports* of the Conquest. *A Brief Account*, on the other hand, seeks to convince audiences of the injustice of subjugating Native American populations. As such, it has faced accusations of inaccuracy and exaggeration because its aim is more suasive than archival. Still, the dominant consensus seems to be that while Las Casas may have exaggerated the numbers of natives slaughtered by the Spanish, he did not invent the brutality or widespread scope of that slaughter.

Although *A Brief Account* is much less overtly concerned with the environment than with human rights, it arguably constitutes the first dissent against imperialist views of the New World as a font of resources to be pillaged. By drawing attention to the rights of indigenous peoples, Las Casas laid the foundation for an environmental ethics based on native land rights, implicitly suggesting that there were prior claims to ownership of the New World. Moreover, insofar as the common colonial view conflated indigenous populations with their environment — seeing the one as a source of forced labor and the other as a source of riches — Las Casas' opposition to the instrumental view of New World inhabitants might be seen as inviting questions about the instrumental view of the land. Thus by demanding humane treatment of Native Americans, Las Casas indirectly highlights the Spaniards' gross misuse of the *land* underwritten by the same imperialist ideology.

A Brief Account also stands out as an environmental text for its notable *lack* of information about New World landscapes. Most explorers' diaries — like most works of environmental literature — devote a great deal of attention to geographic descriptions and measurements, chronicling the spoils of exploration and compiling reports for future expeditions.

A Brief Account, by contrast, positions such description as of secondary importance. When it *does* provide such description, it is almost always as a backdrop for human events, making it a more poignant and humanistic read than many writings of the explorers. Still, the *tone* of Las Casas' descriptions, marveling at the fertility and expansiveness of the land, is often similar to that of explorers' accounts.

Las Casas describes "[t]he Spanish Island, which has a most fertile soil, and, at present, has a great reputation for its spaciousness and length, containing in perimeter 600 miles" (11). He details Marien, "more fertile and large than the kingdom of Portugal [...]. [I]t abounds with Mountains, and is rich in Mines of gold and Orichalcum, a kind of Copper Metal mixed with gold..." (19). His descriptions of Native Americans position them as innocent and friendly, their greatest fault being their ignorance of Christianity: "The inhabitants of this place excel all other Indians, either in polite or prudence or in leading a regular life and morality, truly deserving to be instructed in the knowledge of the true God" (52). As these descriptions attest, Las Casas describes the landscape in superlative terms, emphasizing fertility and boundlessness.

Still, these environmental descriptions are few and far between. On the one hand, this constitutes a deemphasis of environment, and on the other hand, it *refuses* to indulge the typical colonialist mindset, looking at the environment not as an inventory of resources newly owned by Spain but as the home of other peoples whose rights Las Casas defends. By *not* detailing the spoils of conquest, Las Casas potentially opens the question of Spanish right to ownership.

But *A Brief Account* also adopts another, more noteworthy position with respect to the natural environment. Las Casas repeatedly connects New World depopulation (at the hands of the Spaniards) with desertification, suggesting that the Spaniards' brutality constitutes an attack not just on the indigenous people *but on the physical continent as well.* Carrying this argument to its conclusion suggests that, in murdering New World inhabitants, the conquistadors essentially destroyed their prized new territory. For example, Las Casas describes Cuba post–Conquest as "now uncultivated, like a desert, and entombed in its own ruins"; St. John and Jamaica are likewise left "uninhabited and desolate"; and "[t]he Lucayan Islands on the North Side, adjacent to Hispaniola and Cuba," formerly more lush than "the Royal Garden of Sevil [...], with a healthful and pleasant climate" are now "wild and uninhabited" (12–13). By Las Casas' account, the depopulation of the New World equally devastates its environment:

We are sure that the Spaniards, by their bar-barous and wretched actions, have absolutely depopulated as much as ten countries on the main land, all of greater extent than Spain, Arragon and Portugal put together, above 1000 Miles in all. The main land now lays desolate and ruined, when as formerly no other Country what-soever was more populated [13].

These incarnate devils laid waste and desolate four hundred miles of most fertile land, contain-ing vast and wonderful provinces, most spacious and large valleys surrounded with hills, forty miles in length, and many towns richly abound-ing in gold and silver. They destroyed so many and such considerable regions, that there is not one spare witness left to relate the story... [69].

The "cruelties and brutishness" (46) of the Span-iards that Las Casas describes literally *lay to waste* the land, not just depopulating it but destroying it by presumably rendering it infertile, dry, and desert-like. This portrayal constitutes Las Casas' most prevalent and interesting environmental theme. By his account, the Conquest was not just an assault on innocent populations (although this is obviously the major element) but also an assault on the land, an environmentalist perspective centuries ahead of its time.

And Las Casas' vivid critique of the Conquest con-tinues to be relevant; the historical pattern of dual abuses of "conquered" populations and their ancestral lands is still active, and still inspiring debate. But the long, continuous history of violating native rights in the New World in pursuit of natural resources illus-trates the extent to which Las Casas' message has gone unheard. Thus, when we consider issues like oil drilling in the Amazon — where multinational corporations have been accused of decimating an-cestral lands at nominal compensation to inhabitants and then refusing to safely clean up the resulting waste — we may hear echoes of Las Casas' own ob-jections. — Laura Boynton Johnson

BIBLIOGRAPHY

De Las Casas, Bartolomé. *A Brief Account of the Destruction of the Indies.* 1552. Miami: BN, 2008.

Lawrence, D(avid) H(erbert) (1885–1930)

D. H. Lawrence was born in 1885, in Eastwood, a small coal mining town in the county of Notting-hamshire, England. The circumstances of his up-bringing — including the industrial character of his hometown, his father's occupation as a collier, his family's poverty, and the friction between his par-ents — had a profound effect on his life and work,

which often investigates the impact of industrializa-tion on humanity and the natural world.

Lawrence's novels are rife with a sexuality that is deeply rooted in humanity's primal connection to the environment. Each of his most famous novels, including *Sons and Lovers* (1913), *The Rainbow* (1915), *Women in Love* (1920), and *Lady Chatterley's Lover* (1928), feature protagonists who struggle to reconcile their primal urges and emotions with the conventions and expectations of the modern world. His charac-ters, who live predominantly in mining communities like Lawrence's own hometown of Eastwood, are often alienated by the rapid industrialization of the English countryside, and are only able to achieve physical and psychological well-being when they re-connect with their natural surroundings.

Much of his poetry, including his most acclaimed collection *Birds, Beasts and Flowers* (1923), is also concerned with nature, and its profound and in-eluctable influence on man. *Birds, Beasts and Flowers* features poems on animals, trees, and even fruits. One of his most anthologized poems, "Snake," is wrought with symbolic connections between the human and animal world, ultimately suggesting that our anxiety toward nature is a result of our inability or unwillingness to confront it honestly and with an open mind.

While Lawrence is not an American writer *per se*, his landmark work of literary criticism, STUDIES IN CLASSIC AMERICAN LITERATURE (1923), offers unpar-alleled insight into the American environmental imaginary. With chapters on BENJAMIN FRANKLIN, J. H. CRÈVECOEUR, JAMES FENIMORE COOPER, NATHANIEL HAWTHORNE, EDGAR ALLAN POE, HER-MAN MELVILLE, WALT WHITMAN and others, Law-rence considers the lives and work of a host of Amer-ica's most important and influential writers. Several of these authors, most notably Herman Melville, were not acclaimed at the time and owe their dis-covery largely to Lawrence. The final chapter of the book, which celebrates Walt Whitman's "message of American democracy," claims that a soul is known "not by anything, but just itself. The soul passing unenhanced, passing on foot and being no more than itself" (177). In appropriating this claim from Whit-man, Lawrence draws a connection between the uniquely American consciousness, a desire for soli-tude, and communion with nature.

Although his time in America was brief, it is said that Lawrence's happiest years were spent on his ranch just outside of Taos, New Mexico. He once wrote, "I think New Mexico was the greatest expe-rience from the outside world that I ever had. It certainly changed me forever [...] The moment I saw the brilliant, proud morning shine high up over the deserts of Santa Fé, something stood still in my soul, and I started to attend" (*Phoenix* 142). Though he died in France, in 1930, from tuberculosis, his ashes now reside in a small chapel east of Taos.—Adam Meehan

BIBLIOGRAPHY

Ellis, David. *D.H. Lawrence: Dying Game, 1922–1930*. Cambridge: Cambridge University Press, 1998. Print.

Kinkead-Weekes, Mark. *D.H. Lawrence: Triumph to Exile, 1885–1930*. Cambridge: Cambridge University Press, 1996. Print.

Lawrence, D.H. *Phoenix*. London: Whitefriars Press, 1936. Print.

_____. *Studies in Classic American Literature*. New York: Viking Press, 1968. Print.

Worthen, John. *D.H. Lawrence: The Early Years, 1885–1912*. Cambridge: Cambridge University Press, 1991. Print.

Studies in Classic American Literature, D. H. Lawrence (1923)

Although an English citizen, D. H. Lawrence (1885–1930) was driven to leave Britain after World War I because of his German wife and outspoken pacifist views. He spent the rest of his life in a voluntary exile that sometimes brought him to America, where he published *Studies in Classic American Literature,* a collection of twelve essays initially written as journal articles, in which Lawrence discusses BENJAMIN FRANKLIN, HECTOR ST. JOHN DE CRÈVECOEUR, JAMES FENIMORE COOPER, EDGAR ALLAN POE, NATHANIEL HAWTHORNE, Richard Henry Dana, HERMAN MELVILLE, and WALT WHITMAN. Lawrence's diverse commentary is intuitive and impressionistic, mixing praise with exasperation. He sees American literature as inherently shaped by its natural environment, a vast and often wild continent; yet he criticizes the American psyche for inevitably trying to conquer or idealize nature, for rejecting the land's Native peoples and their claims of belonging, and for thwarting nature by relying on technology. He urges Americans to embrace the spiritual aspects of nature and to acknowledge the interdependence of all things.

Lawrence posits that the quintessential American desire, whether to idealize or to destroy nature, is an attempt to control the wild. The first tendency, to idealize, is illustrated for him by the writing of Crèvecoeur, who is pilloried as a false "man of the land" whose LETTERS FROM AN AMERICAN FARMER (1782) gained him a celebrity in Europe that he exploited after abandoning his farm and family. Lawrence calls Crèvecoeur an emotional liar who spins tales about nature as if he were its true child, whereas in reality he romanticizes an imaginary wilderness in order to "put NATURE in his pocket" to sell to a Europe fascinated by his image of the New World (25–26). For the same reasons Lawrence mocks the Brook Farm project of the American TRANSCENDENTALISTS when examining Hawthorne's BLITHEDALE ROMANCE (1852), which was based on the short-lived collective-farming experiment (UTOPIAN COMMUNITIES). Lawrence has no patience with these "famous idealists and transcendentalists [who] met to till the soil and hew timber in the sweat of their own brows, thinking high thoughts all the while, and breathing an atmosphere of communal love, and tingling in tune with the Oversoul, like so many strings of a super-celestial harp" (104). He claims their experiment failed due to their frequent quarrels, dislike of hard labor, and because they "left off brookfarming, and took to bookfarming" (105).

In American literature, Native peoples often represent the wilderness, and thus suffer from the same American desire to conquer or idealize nature. Lawrence castigates Franklin, who thought the drunkenness of Natives was "the design of Providence to extirpate these savages in order to make room for the cultivators of the earth, [for] it seems not improbable that rum may be the appointed means. It has already annihilated all the tribes who formerly inhabited all the seacoast" (15). Lawrence likewise criticizes Crèvecoeur for his false representation of Native Americans as "noble Children of Nature ... like so many cooing doves" (30). In evaluating Cooper's portrayal of Natives, summarized as wish-fulfillment, Lawrence sets out the grievances of Native Americans against whites and concludes that the "Red Man died hating the white man. [...] He doesn't believe in us and our civilization, and so is our mystic enemy, for we push him off the face of the earth" (35). Lawrence argues that there exists a white American "desire to extirpate the Indian. And the contradictory desire to glorify him. Both are rampant still, to-day" (36).

Lawrence treats American sea tales as separate from its land stories and claims Americans "have never loved the soil of America as Europeans have loved the soil of Europe. America has never been a blood-home-land. Only an ideal home-land" (111). Hence, much classic American writing turns to the sea, the mother of all. Lawrence calls Dana the communicator of "a profound mystic vision" of the eternal expanses of sea and air where the puny human can become "elemental like a seal, a creature" (114). Yet Dana records a conflict against "the vast, almost omnipotent" sea where "Man fights the element in all its roused, mystic hostility to conscious life" (124). Oddly, Lawrence makes almost no allusion to the environmental aspects of Melville's MOBY DICK

(1851). He applauds Melville's authentic descriptions of sailing, the South Seas, the whaling industry, giant squid, aquatic mating rituals, and so on; but his real interest lies in explaining the symbol of the great white whale, which he takes to represent "the deepest blood-being of the white race" (160–161).

Early in the work, Lawrence bluntly summarizes what he perceives as the American ethos: "Some insist [...] on the plumbing, and some on saving the world: these being the two great American specialties" (vii–viii). He characterizes Whitman as too invested in the machinery of urban industrial America and pictures him speeding along in a motorcar "going whizz over an unwary Red Indian, [...] oblivious of the corpses under the wheels" (167). Moreover, he challenges Whitman's reputation as the poet of the body, insisting that "Everything was female to him: even himself. Nature just one great function" (168). Yet, although he replaced sensuality with utility, Whitman "was the first to smash the old moral conception that the soul of man is something 'superior' and 'above' the flesh" (171); hence he embraces "the soul living her life" (173). In this sense, Lawrence reveals some ambivalence toward Whitman, applauding his celebration of life, but assailing his vision of the human as a functionary within the mosaic of the urban industrial space, set apart from the individual's natural spiritual existence.

Lawrence is likewise enamored with the basic technology of the sailing ship in Dana's narrative, as opposed to later industrial technology like steam engines. He claims that "The more we intervene machinery between us and the naked forces the more we numb and atrophy our own senses [and] take the miracle of life from us.... We do not know what we lose by all our labour-saving appliances" (125). As Armin Arnold observes, Lawrence laments that America, "instead of being free, [is] chained by her machines and her industry" (49). Thus, Lawrence's interest in Poe, for example, centers on the latter's concern with immediacy and intimacy. Poe sees humans as organic beings who depend on contact with the natural world's air, food, and water, and who seek the sort of radical, sensual love favored by Lawrence, with "each losing itself in transgressing its own bounds" (66, 80). Writing of Poe's *The Fall of the House of Usher* (1839), Lawrence highlights the protagonist's awareness of sentience in vegetation and inanimate objects like stones, recognizing the environmental interdependence of humans, animals, plants, and inanimate figures as "a physical oneness" (78).

Lawrence believes humans must revere their inner nature and their natural environment in order to sustain their own humanness. He urges, "Believe in your own Holy Ghost" (102), and warns that there "comes a new generation to sweep out even the ghosts, with these new vacuum cleaners. No ghost could stand up against a vacuum cleaner" (104). Lawrence concludes that the use of technology, so prevalent in America, to control nature, to free us from labor, to maintain our urban fortresses, and to allow us to idealize the natural world even as we destroy it, will not only undermine our essential, life-supporting connections to the environment but corrupt the *human* nature at the core of our being.— Kelly MacPhail

BIBLIOGRAPHY

Arnold, Armin. *D.H. Lawrence and America*. London: Linden, 1958.
Blanchard, Lydia. "Lawrence as Reader of Classic American Literature." *The Challenge of D. H. Lawrence*. Eds. Michael Squires and Keith Cushman. Madison: University of Wisconsin Press, 1990. 159–175.
Lawrence, D. H. *Studies in Classic American Literature*. 1923. New York: Viking Press, 1964.
Swigg, Richard. *Lawrence, Hardy, and American Literature*. London and New York, Oxford University Press, 1972.
Worthen, John. "'Wild Turkeys': Some Versions of America by D.H. Lawrence." *European Journal of American Culture* 24:2 (2005): 91–103.

Leopold, Aldo (1887–1948)

Few authors in the American environmental canon offer such a clearly focused articulation of their ideas, beliefs, and values as Aldo Leopold in *A SAND COUNTY ALMANAC* (1949), a text regarded by many as a touchstone of twentieth-century American environmental writing. As it was published posthumously, Leopold never had the opportunity to expand on its many moving and often revelatory passages, including the long look at the life of a tree in "Good Oak" and the famous "fierce green fire" lamentation of a dead wolf in "Thinking Like a Mountain"; nor was he able to expand on his famous "land ethic" that closes the work. Yet those looking for insights from one of America's most important advocates of the primacy and importance of the natural world will find much in the lifetime's worth of personal correspondence, essays, and articles that Leopold produced in an active, though too brief life of fieldwork, scholarship, and teaching. Indeed, those who stop with *A Sand County Almanac* miss out on Leopold's deeper elaboration of the many topics and themes that inform that work, bolstered both by academic expertise and life experience, in individual articles and essays on, among other things, land management, forestry, hunting, farming, wilderness, public and private property, outdoor recreation, environmental education, and ethical and aesthetical concern for the natural world.

With the exception of the six years he attended school in the East, at Lawrenceville School and Yale University, Aldo Leopold's life was spent in comparatively remote outposts of early twentieth-century America: he was born in the Mississippi River town of Burlington, Iowa in 1887, cut his teeth in the field of land management as a forester in the Southwest, and died in 1948 battling a grass fire near his "shack" in rural Wisconsin; and all of these places may be seen influencing both his life and writing. Burlington at the turn of the twentieth century may not have been at the forefront of progressive American politics or the burgeoning conservation movement, but it did provide an ideal setting for the young Leopold to develop a sincere, even spiritual, appreciation of the natural world around him. Leopold's family was entrenched in the history and culture of the region, and both his father Carl and his grandfather Charles Starker had a reputation for being amateur naturalists and avid outdoorsmen. The forests, bottoms, and bluffs of the upper Mississippi offered fertile ground for Leopold to develop quickly into a proficient naturalist himself, with a fondness for bird watching. At age 15 Leopold began his first bird journal, which he used to document observations he had made of various bird species on his daily "tramps" into the woods. He took these journals with him on expeditions around the Burlington area, and on family vacations, and continued the practice of identifying new bird species and observing migration patterns after he moved to Lawrenceville, New Jersey to finish high school. This self-initiated environmental education was as important to Leopold's development as the more formal training he would receive later in life.

Leopold began his formal study of the natural world when he enrolled at Yale University in 1905, with the goal of graduating from the Yale Forest School. Marybeth Lorbiecki's concise biography of Leopold draws particular attention to a summer stint at the Yale Forest School Camp in the Pocono Mountains of Pennsylvania, wherein "Nature was gradually becoming for [Leopold] something that could be measured, managed, and put to human use" (*A Fierce Green Fire*, 34). Leopold's attendance at the Yale Forestry School from 1907–1909 is significant for a number of reasons, not least of which is the influence of its founder, Gifford Pinchot. Pinchot is best known as the early head of the Forest Service, where he helped create the National Forests, and as a conservationist advocate for "wise use," an attitude often contrasted to the preservationist outlook of JOHN MUIR and his followers. As Leopold began his career with the Forest Service in the American Southwest, including his first major assignment at the Apache National Forest in Arizona, he continued to wholeheartedly subscribe to Pinchot's ideas that land management was first and foremost about fairly distributing natural resources among the loggers, ranchers, farmers and other human agents with a commercial interest in the land.

A significant element in this wise-use approach to the land was Leopold's lifelong interest in game management, another practice that he attempted to regulate in the forests of the Southwest. Still operating under the belief that human interests came first, Leopold's early game management practices entailed killing off natural predators like wolves and mountain lions to ensure that large numbers of deer, antelope, and turkeys remained for human hunters. However, it was during this time that Leopold would undergo an experience that transformed his views on game management and on human relationships to the environment in general. This is the event documented in the "Thinking Like a Mountain" section of *A Sand County Almanac*, where Leopold recounts killing a mother wolf and her pups while on a surveying expedition in the Arizona mountains. Having shot "with more excitement than accuracy" at the wolves, Leopold goes on to detail one of the most famous conversion experiences in all of American environmental literature: "We reached the old wolf in time to watch a fierce green fire dying in her eyes. I realized then, and have known ever since, that there was something new to me in those eyes — something known only to her and to the mountain" (*A Sand County Almanac*, 130). Partly as a result of this epiphanic moment, Leopold soon began to turn away from the Pinchot-inspired policies of land management, and to express a greater concern for all elements of the natural world, culminating at last in the creation of his distinctive "land ethic."

After finishing his career with the Forest Service in the Southwest, Leopold resettled his family in Madison, Wisconsin, to pursue work in the private sector — a fateful decision as it turned out. First, the change of jobs allowed Leopold to finish and publish his first book-length publication, *Game Management* (1933), which eventually led to his being hired by the University of Wisconsin as a faculty member of the nation's first graduate program in game management; and then in 1935, Leopold was able to purchase a stretch of land outside of Baraboo, Wisconsin, which would become known as "the Shack" and which provided his family the opportunity to enact the sort of land restoration that Leopold was increasingly calling for on a regional and national scale. Through his ongoing work with his family at "the Shack" and his students at the University of Wisconsin, Leopold was able to explore and impart his own developing sense of a deeper and more intimate relationship between humanity and the environment, an attitude neatly summarized in an essay he wrote near the end of his life: "I am trying to teach you that this alphabet of 'natural objects' (soils and rivers, birds and beasts) spells out a story, which he who runs may read — if he knows how. Once you learn to read the land, I have no fear of what you will do to it, or with it. And I know many pleasant things it will do to you" (*River of the Mother of God*, 337).— Matt Low

BIBLIOGRAPHY

Leopold, Aldo. *The River of the Mother of God and Other Essays*. Eds. Susan J. Flader and J. Baird Callicott. Madison: University of Wisconsin Press, 1991.
_____. *Round River: From the Journals of Aldo Leopold*. Ed. Luna B. Leopold. London: Oxford University Press, 1972.
_____. *A Sand County Almanac*. London: Oxford University Press, 1949.
Lorbiecki, Marybeth. *Aldo Leopold: A Fierce Green Fire*. Guilford, CT: Falcon, 2005.
Meine, Curt. *Aldo Leopold: His Life and Work*. Madison: University of Wisconsin Press, 1991.
Newton, Julianne Lutz. *Aldo Leopold's Odyssey*. Washington, DC: Island Press, 2006.

A Sand County Almanac, Aldo Leopold (1949)

Published posthumously, Aldo Leopold's *A Sand County Almanac* belongs among the short list of seminal books associated with environmental literature. Written over a span of 11 years from 1937 until 1948, the book represents the culmination of Leopold's prolific career as a forester, wildlife manager, conservationist, ecologist, and professor. Similar in form to THOREAU's *WALDEN* (1854) and echoing themes JOHN MUIR touches on in *THE MOUNTAINS OF CALIFORNIA* (1894) and *My First Summer in the Sierra* (1911), *A Sand County Almanac* brings together these and other 19th-century influences with an increased emphasis on scientific rigor and environmental ethics. In this way, the book draws upon previous published environmental literature along the lines of Gilbert White's *The Natural History of Selborne* (1789) and Darwin's *Voyage of the Beagle* (1839) while influencing American writers from diverse backgrounds (Tallmadge 110), including RACHEL CARSON, EDWARD ABBEY, WALLACE STEGNER, and Arne Næss, among others.

A Sand County Almanac is made up of four separate but thematically connected sections, each of which speaks to the central importance of developing and enacting what Leopold describes near the end of the book as a "Land Ethic" (237). "Part I: A Sand County Almanac" takes for its structure the calendar year — an anthropocentric conception of time — and imposes upon this human construct descriptions of seasonal events and discussions of larger, ecological patterns underlying these seemingly isolated occurrences. "The sketches of Part I, written for the most part in the present tense, describe the life [Leopold] and his family live now" on their recently purchased plot of land in. In "January," as well as other chapters in this first part, Leopold models how one should participate in and learn from nature. He introduces, through unadorned depictions, mundane but significant events on and around his plot of land and the iconic "shack," a "chicken-house-turned-cowshed" that he and his family converted into a modest cabin (Flader 53). In each anecdote, he presents himself as both an interested and an uncertain participant, suggesting in this way that nature has much to teach those willing to learn.

In Part I, Leopold often takes the reader back metonymically, through particular events, to topics that consider "the wider reaches of evolutionary time" (103). In this way, the opening section of the book enjoins readers to think ecologically by practicing the intuitive "art of drawing deductions" (67). The purpose of this type of sustained, patient study, suggests Leopold with each new episode, is to develop the capacity to make inferences based on informed speculation, or what he refers to later in the text as "perception" (292). The main such inference one must make is that — as is the case with all species of plants and animals that invariably battle for survival in nature over time — individuals in particular and civilization as a whole must be vigilant and guard against creating a society that promises its members "freedom from want and fear" (4).

The scope of what readers soon recognize as subjective yet trenchant investigations into the relationship between mankind and nature broadens in Part II, which includes many of Leopold's most progressive ideas regarding conservation and ecology. In this second section, which was written in the decades prior to the writing of Part I (Ribbens 103), Leopold draws on research and, in some cases, previously drafted essays that focus on issues tied to work he had done in Illinois and Iowa, Arizona and New Mexico, Chihuahua and Sonora, and elsewhere. Written primarily in the past tense, these essays are organized episodically and "depict the transformation of the narrator from an ignorant, insensitive, restless, and ordinary person (someone much like the reader) into the vibrant, perceptive, wise, and serene observer of Part I" (Tallmadge 114).

Of the essays included in Part II, the most prominent is "Thinking Like a Mountain," one that grew out of Leopold's work in New Mexico as a Forest

Service Assistant, and later as Director, during the first phase of his career (Philippon 301). In this essay, he reflects on the mistakes he made while carrying out Forest Service policies and failing to appreciate the interdependent quality of the land. In the process of recalling a time when he shot a wolf from a distance and arrived at its side in time to watch the light leave its eyes, he introduces the works' central themes, of humility and responsibility, which form the basis of the environmental ethic outlined later in the book. Noting that his actions were both legal and short-sighted, he conveys through his account of what he calls the "fierce green fire" in the dying animal's eyes the paradoxical idea that we cannot have peace without danger, and that we should thus not equate progress with such things as "safety, prosperity, comfort, long life, and dullness" (141). Returning in this context to Thoreau's famous dictum "In wildness is the preservation of the world," Leopold complicates and renews the time-worn homily by drawing upon his extensive fieldwork, as well as his expertise as a professor of conversation biology, stating, "Perhaps this is the hidden meaning in the howl of the wolf, long known among mountains, but seldom perceived among men" (141).

The third section, "Part III: A Taste for Country," explores topics tied to land aesthetics, sustainable farming, ecological education, and environmental ethics. These essays redefine a number of concepts specific to education and economics by insisting that they be understood not in anthropocentric but in ecological terms. After declaring in the opening essay that "Poor land may be rich country, and vice versa" (177), Leopold re-presents this apparent contradiction, stating in "The Round River," that "The last word in ignorance is the man who says of an animal or plant: 'What good is it?,'" and adding that "If the land mechanism as a whole is good, then every part is good, whether we understand it or not" (190). He then applies this line of reasoning to topics such as private and public lands, "clean farming" (199), and the "profit motive" (201). Effectively deconstructing conventional (by human standards) thinking associated with concepts such as profit and progress, he lays the groundwork for the final section of the book, wherein he calls readers to reconsider much of what they know and how they think about "the land," and their concomitant responsibility for its health.

In Part IV, "The Upshot," *A Sand County Almanac* fleshes out Leopold's seminal "Land Ethic," a set of sweeping principles that the author has, in the book's preceding sections, been tangentially addressing. Here at last Leopold explicitly challenges readers to alter their thinking about familiar ideas specific to conservation, ecology, and ethics. He calls for paradigmatic changes in conception and, as importantly, behavior among individuals and societies, especially those who understand nature as something separate from and ultimately "useful" to mankind.

Greater than the sum of its parts, *A Sand County Almanac* is considered by many academics, politicians, ethicists, and activists as the cornerstone of contemporary environmental thinking, and continues to shape discussions and policies pertaining to conservation and ecology.— Colin Irvine

BIBLIOGRAPHY

Flader, Susan. "Aldo Leopold's Sand Country." *Companion to A Sand County Almanac*. Ed. J. Baird Callicott. Madison: University of Wisconsin Press, 1987. 40–62.

Leopold, Aldo. *A Sand County Almanac: With Essays on Conservation From Round River*. 1949. New York: Oxford University Press, 1966.

Philippon, Daniel. *Conserving Words: How American Nature Writers Shaped the Environmental Movement*. Athens: University of Georgia Press, 2004.

Ribbens, Dennis. "The Making of *A Sand County Almanac*." *Companion to A Sand County Almanac*. Ed. J. Baird Callicott. Madison: University of Wisconsin Press, 1987. 91–109.

Tallmadge, John. "Anatomy of a Classic." *Companion to A Sand County Almanac*. Ed. J. Baird Callicott. Madison: University of Wisconsin Press, 1987. 110–127.

Lewis, Meriwether (1774–1809) and William Clark (1770–1838)

Meriwether Lewis and William Clark are the most famous authors of any early American exploration narrative. They conducted their famed travels across North America in 1804–06 as leaders of the first U.S. government-sponsored scientific expedition to explore the lands between the Missouri River and the Pacific Ocean. The two explorers kept detailed journals of their observations and experiences, which were later published in a long string of editions beginning in 1814, most notably as *The Lewis and Clark Journals: An American Epic of Discovery*. In addition to its value as a landmark text of natural history, Lewis and Clark's *Journals* are an important illustration of the growing dichotomy between science and romanticism in the American view of the natural environment in the early nineteenth century.

Meriwether Lewis was born in Virginia in 1774 to a prominent family that counted THOMAS JEFFERSON among its neighbors. His parents were Lucy and William Lewis, the latter an army officer who died of pneumonia in 1779. Meriwether Lewis spent all but three years of his youth in Virginia, and took early to outdoor pursuits. When he was 13 Lewis began managing his father's farm, and simultaneously began taking tutoring lessons in Latin, mathematics, and science. After joining the military in

1794 he served in a variety of posts of increasing prestige that eventually led to an appointment in 1801 to serve as President Thomas Jefferson's secretary. Jefferson and Lewis soon began planning the president's top project, an expedition across the continent that would be known as the Corps of Discovery.

William Clark was born in 1770 to John and Ann Clark. Like Lewis he was born in Virginia, but in 1784 his family relocated to the Kentucky frontier, where he had little chance of a formal education. With five brothers who all served as officers in the Revolutionary War, Clark was destined for a military career. He began participating in militia activities as a teenager, and got his chance to join the army in 1789. During this period Clark met Lewis in the army and the two became friends. After four years Clark resigned from the army for personal reasons, and in 1803 Lewis contacted him with an invitation to join his upcoming western expedition.

That year, upon completion of the Louisiana Purchase, the United States suddenly owned nearly a million square miles of western territory about which it knew very little. The primary goal of the Lewis and Clark expedition, as described by Jefferson in his extensive instructions to the two explorers, was to identify a water route across the continent for the purposes of commerce. However, Jefferson's interests lay more in the scientific realm, and he directed them to take detailed observations of the land, weather, animals, plants, and people they encountered along the way. The expedition began in 1804 with a plan to travel by water up the Missouri River, and from there to portage across land until reaching an imagined river that would connect them to the Columbia River and, thereby, to the Pacific Ocean.

In May of 1804 the Lewis and Clark expedition began traveling north by boat. Armed with the expedition's own precise measurements and careful observations, modern historians have identified Lewis and Clark's route as having passed along the Missouri River as far as Montana, at which point they were forced to travel on foot across Idaho, eastern Washington, and eastern Oregon until locating an outlet to the Columbia River and making the rest of their way to the Pacific Ocean by boat.

In terms of their goal of identifying a water route across North America, Lewis and Clark's expedition was a failure; they had been forced to travel more than three hundred miles by land, much of it across difficult, mountainous territory. Yet the overall expedition was considered a great success. The explorers had collected an enormous amount of valuable information about the western territory, and they were greeted like heroes upon their return in 1806. Lewis turned over the expedition journals and

a substantial collection of specimens from the trip to President Jefferson, who shared them with scientists and natural historians of the time.

As a reward for their successful efforts, both explorers were appointed to positions in the Louisiana Territory, Lewis as governor and Clark as superintendent of Indian affairs. Although Lewis was charged with preparing the expedition journals for publication, he never completed the task, dying in 1809 of apparent suicide. Meanwhile, Clark married and went on to become governor of the Missouri Territory. He picked up where Lewis left off and commissioned a lawyer, Nicholas Biddle, to compile and publish the expedition journals, which were finally released for the first time in 1814 under the title, *History of the Expedition under the Command of Captains Lewis and Clarke.*

Lewis and Clark's writings convey a view of the natural environment that blends romantic, scientific, and survivalist themes, reflecting the multifaceted experience of early Western explorers. As naturalists they profoundly advanced science by describing and collecting a tremendous number of species that were new to Euro-American culture. As literary authors they offered what Frank Bergon has dubbed "the equivalent of a national poem, a magnificent epic for an unfinished nation." To a country still in its uncertain adolescence, the *Journals* fed into a powerful source of nationalism: the vast Western landscape. They were also the first to provide maps and other critical details of the United States' new western territories that would guide future pioneers. From Lewis's romantic flourishes, evocative of later paintings by Hudson River School artists, to Clark's concise, objective measurements, the *Journals* document not only the state of North American ecosystems at the time, but also some of America's most fundamental parameters for our complex human relationship to the natural world. — Kim Leeder

BIBLIOGRAPHY

Ambrose, Stephen E. *Undaunted Courage: Meriwether Lewis, Thomas Jefferson, and the Opening of the American West.* New York: Simon & Schuster, 1996.

Danisi, Thomas, and John C. Jackson. *Meriwether Lewis.* Amherst: Prometheus Books, 2009.

Foley, William E. *Wilderness Journey: The Life of William Clark.* Columbia: University of Missouri Press, 2004.

Cutright, Paul Russell. *Lewis and Clark: Pioneering Naturalists.* Lincoln: University of Nebraska Press, 2003.

Furtwangler, Albert. *Acts of Discovery: Visions of America in the Lewis and Clark Journals.* Urbana: University of Illinois Press, 1993.

Lewis, Meriwether, and William Clark. *The Lewis and Clark Journals: An American Epic of Discovery.* Edited by Gary E. Moulton. Lincoln: University of Nebraska Press, 2003.

The Lewis and Clark Fort Mandan Foundation. "The Corps." Discovering Lewis & Clark. Available online. URL: http://www.lewis-clark.org/content/content-channel.asp?ChannelID=56. Accessed June 29, 2009.

Woodger, Elin, and Brandon Toropov. eds. *Encyclopedia of the Lewis and Clark Expedition*. New York: Facts on File, 2004.

London, Jack (1876–1916)

Though Jack London is remembered today mainly as a writer of adventure stories for young adults, in his own time he was one of the most famous and prolific American authors. An amateur student of natural science, London spent much of his life out of doors, with stints as a fisherman, investigative reporter, prospector, sailor, hobo, and rancher — lifestyles that would be reflected in his writing. Beneath the surface of London's entertaining stories, we find an engaging portrait of the life-world of nonhuman animals and an exploration of the relationship between humans and the natural environment.

Jack London was born in 1876 in a working-class district of San Francisco, to a single mother. As a young man he was an avid reader, and was largely self-educated through time spent at the Oakland Public Library. By the age of 13 London was working in a cannery, a job he soon quit to become an oyster pirate in San Francisco Bay. In 1893 he spent seven months aboard a sealing schooner, writing an award-winning journalistic account of the experience. When London returned to the U.S. later that year the country had entered a period of economic depression, and he found himself unemployed and roaming the countryside as a tramp, an experience he would later recount in the influential travel narrative, *The Road* (1907). It was during this period of hardship that London converted to socialism, a political position he held for the rest of his life and illustrated in works such as the sociological study *The People of the Abyss* (1903) and the dystopian novel *The Iron Heel* (1908). In 1897 he traveled to the Yukon Territory to take part in the Klondike Gold Rush, and although he was unsuccessful as a prospector, the experience furnished him with material for his best-known works: the novels THE CALL OF THE WILD (1903) and *White Fang* (1906), and the short-story "To Build a Fire" (1908).

London is typically classified, along with Stephen Crane, Frank Norris, and Theodore Dreiser, as a member of the Naturalist school of American writers. Influenced by the novelistic theories of Emile Zola, as well as by Charles Darwin and the social philosopher Herbert Spencer (coiner of the term "survival of the fittest"), naturalists explored the ways in which characters are affected by heredity and by the surrounding natural and social environment. The movement has sometimes been labeled "pessimistic" because characters seem to lack free will and instead are determined by antagonistic outside forces. However, it could also be argued that these writers cogently (and admirably) criticized the belief that humans are above or separate from nature. In many of London's works, for example, we encounter animals that are more suited to their environments than their inept and self-absorbed human counterparts.

The poet Carl Sandburg has said of *The Call of the Wild* that it is "the greatest dog story ever written." In the novella, a pampered house pet named Buck is stolen from his California home and sold north to work as a sled dog in the Yukon, where he is forced to adapt to the harsh physical conditions of the northern climate and the brutal competition of the sled-dog team. The wilderness atmosphere awakens a primitive urge in the animal, and he becomes ever wilder, eventually leaving human civilization behind to become the leader of a wolf pack. *White Fang*, published a few years later, shows the opposite progression: a wild wolf dog becomes increasingly tame, ending as a family pet. London found himself embroiled in an ongoing debate over the accuracy of animal representations when President TEDDY ROOSEVELT and naturalist JOHN BURROUGHS accused him and other writers of being "nature fakers." Undaunted, however, London would continue to explore such themes throughout his work, for example in the post-apocalyptic "re-wilding" that occurs in *The Scarlet Plague* (1912).

London devoted most of his energies later in life to building and improving upon a ranch he had purchased in the Sonoma Valley of California, where he took great interest in soil conservation, organic fertilizers, animal breeding, and the latest scientific farming techniques. The beauty of the ranch and its landscape are captured in the pastoral back-to-the-land novel *The Valley of the Moon* (1913). Unfortunately, London's rural sentiments, like those of many of his contemporaries, were tainted by racism and anti-immigrant xenophobia. Nonetheless, his transformation of the area into an experimental farm provided an early example of agricultural reform. Jack London died at home on his ranch at the relatively young age of 40. In the 1960's the ranch and the surrounding area were designated a state park. — Tristan Sipley

BIBLIOGRAPHY

"Introduction to Jack London Ranch Album," in *The World of Jack London Website*. David A. Hartzell, Manager. Available online. URL: http://www.jacklondons.net/intro.html. Accessed March, 9 2009.

Jack London Online Collection. Site maintained by Roy

Tennant and Dr. Clarice Stasz. Sponsored by Sonoma State University Library. Last update 25 July 2006. Available online. URL: http://london.sonoma.edu/ Accessed March 10, 2009.

"Jack London." *Norton Anthology of American Literature, Short 5th Edition.*

Labor, Earle. *Jack London.* New York: Twayne, 1974.

Locke, Michelle. "The Call of the Wild Organic Farmer." *Los Angeles Times,* Sunday, July 2, 2006. Available online. URL: http://articles.latimes.com/2006/jul/02/news/adme-jack2. Accessed March 10, 2009.

London, Jack. *The Call of the Wild* (1903). Annotated and Illustrated. Ed. Daniel Dyer. Norman: University Oklahoma Press, 1997.

Lutts, Ralph H., ed. *The Wild Animal Story.* Philadelphia: Temple University Press, 1998.

Tavernier-Courbin, Jacqualine. "*The Call of the Wild* and *The Jungle*: Jack London's and Upton Sinclair's Animal and Human Jungles." *Cambridge Companion to Realism and Naturalism.* Ed. Donald Pizer. Cambridge: Cambridge University Press, 1995.

The Call of the Wild, Jack London (1903)

Set during the 19th-century Klondike gold rush, Jack London's novella *The Call of the Wild* traces a domesticated dog's devolution into a primordial beast. Its protagonist is Buck, a 140-pound mixed-breed dog whose unique combination of St. Bernard and Scotch shepherd traits make him resemble a large wolf. First introduced as a "sated aristocrat" ruling over the Santa Clara Valley home of Judge Miller, Buck is stolen and shipped to the Klondike for use as a sled dog (London 6). This series of events marks the beginning of Buck's devolution, a process that culminates in his departure from human civilization when his master, John Thornton, dies and he answers the titular "call" by joining a pack of wolves. London reverses this plot in *White Fang*, a novella written three years later in which a wolf-dog hybrid from the Klondike becomes domesticated and returns with his master to the latter's Santa Clara Valley home. Although both novellas take up similar themes, *The Call of the Wild* is arguably a more successful exploration of the intertwined roles of heredity and environment in shaping the individual.

London's story of devolution is heavily influenced by his interest in 19th-century naturalist Charles Darwin's theory of evolution; and the stark, brutal environment of the Klondike serves as an ideal setting in which to dramatize a Darwinian struggle for existence. Although Buck leads "a lazy, sun-kissed life" at Judge Miller's place, London quickly establishes his inherent fitness by pointing out that Buck "had saved himself by not becoming a mere pampered house-dog. Hunting and kindred outdoor delights had kept down the fat and hardened his muscles" (15, 6). Still, Buck's transition to the North-land is sudden and harsh. Sold to a dog-breaker who beats him into obedience and then sells him, Buck then witnesses the brutal death of Curly, a friendly Newfoundland who is eaten alive by a pack of huskies after unwittingly antagonizing one of them. These experiences introduce Buck to "the law of club and fang," a concept akin to Darwin's (in fact Spencer's) "survival of the fittest," which Buck must learn "unconsciously" in order to survive (15, 21). By observing more experienced dogs, he discovers how to defend himself, make a warm bed in the snow, and steal food; and this capacity for learning marks Buck as "fit to survive in the hostile Northland environment. It marked his adaptability, his capacity to adjust himself to changing conditions, the lack of which would have meant swift and terrible death" (21).

As London's use of Darwinian language suggests, the environment exerts a twofold influence on Buck's development. First, it shapes him in an immediate, physical sense: his feet, previously "softened" by domestication, become calloused, his muscles "hard as iron" (28, 22). Second, and more profoundly, it has already instilled in him inherited traits which facilitate his adaptation. Buck experiences these traits as memories, a trope which also appears in *Before Adam*, London's 1907 serialized novel in which the human narrator "remembers," in the form of vivid dreams, the experiences of a primordial ancestor. This reemergence of "instincts long dead" enables Buck to learn, almost automatically, "to fight with cut and slash and the quick wolf snap"— skills which enable him to kill and replace Spitz as the team's lead dog (22). Ultimately, it is Buck's unique combination of inherited traits which, sharpened by his education "in the fiercest of schools," makes him "as formidable a creature as any that roamed the wild": "His cunning was wolf cunning, and wild cunning; his intelligence, shepherd intelligence and St. Bernard intelligence" (79). London emphasizes the innateness of Buck's superior fitness by contrasting him with two other varieties of "Outside dogs": purebred dogs like pointers who are "bewildered and spirit-broken by the strange savage environment," and "mongrels of indeterminate breed" who are "without spirit at all" (51). Unlike the hybrid Buck, who inherits the best characteristics of two robust breeds, these dogs prove unable to adapt to the harsh Northland and quickly perish.

Accompanying Buck's transformation is a moral decline characteristic of naturalistic devolution plots. Frank Norris, London's contemporary and fellow naturalist, seemed especially preoccupied with this theme, most notably in *Vandover and the Brute* (published posthumously in 1914) and *McTeague* (1909).

Yet while Norris's Vandover feels "the brute in him ... forever seeking a lower level, wallowing itself lower and lower into the filth and into the mire," London portrays Buck's moral regression as both necessary and positive (Norris 233). In abandoning his "moral nature," Buck frees himself of "a vain thing and a handicap in the ruthless struggle for existence" (London 21). Moreover, some of the novella's most ecstatic moments feature Buck indulging remorselessly in graphic violence. For example, the rabbit hunt which precedes his defeat of Spitz fills Buck with a bloodlust that enables him to experience "the sheer surging of life, the tidal wave of being, the perfect joy of each separate muscle, joint, and sinew" (34). Subsequently killing Spitz cements his status as "the dominant primordial beast who had made his kill and found it good" (36). This moral decline has frequently been read allegorically, a move encouraged by London's characterization of Buck's bloodlust as only a more intense manifestation of "that stirring of old instincts which at stated periods drives men out from cities to forest and plain to kill things by chemically propelled leaden pellets" (33–34). Frederic Taber Cooper thus criticized London's representation of human nature in 1909, arguing, "There is a vast difference between thinking of man as a healthy human animal and thinking of him as an unhealthy human beast — and the Call-of-the-Wild school of fiction is tending toward precisely this exaggerated and mistaken point of view" (qtd. in Auerbach 26).

The Call of the Wild does indeed glorify some acts of violence — perhaps most disturbingly, Buck's brutal attack on the Yeehat Indians in a "relentlessly graphic paragraph" which, critic James R. Giles notes, problematically exploits the Yeehats' status as racial others in order to justify Buck's revenge for the death of John Thornton (188). Yet, as Giles also suggests, these troubling scenes nevertheless form part of the novella's more significant contribution: its implicit critique of the anthropocentric logic that uncritically valorizes civilization and reason, and consequently devalues nature, instinct, the primitive, and the animal. London not only elevates these traditionally devalued categories but also suggests — particularly by reversing Buck's devolutionary trajectory in *White Fang*— that the boundaries between nature and culture, instinct and reason, are not rigidly fixed but fascinatingly malleable. Thus, in an essay responding to President Theodore Roosevelt and others who objected to the apparent attribution of something like reason to Buck, London overtly criticizes the "homocentric" perspective that fails to recognize the "kinship" between humans and animals suggested by Darwinian continuity (qtd. in Auerbach 25). In this way he anticipates the more complex understanding of the implications of Darwin's theory which would develop over the course of the 20th century. Moreover, London offers his own idiosyncratic brand of hope to those who share his skeptical views of civilization. In 1906 poet Carl Sandburg praised *The Call of the Wild* not only as "the greatest dog-story ever written" but also as "a study of one of the most curious and profound motives that plays hide-and-seek in the human soul. The more civilized we become the deeper is the fear that back in barbarism is something of the beauty and joy of life we have not brought along with us" (230). Yet the continuity which London posits between humans and the natural world suggests that we have not lost the ability to experience the beauty of barbarism.— Karalyn L. Kendall-Morwick

BIBLIOGRAPHY

Auerbach, Jonathan. "'Congested Mails': Buck and Jack's 'Call.'" *Rereading Jack London.* Ed. Leonard Cassuto and Jeanne Campbell Reesman. Stanford: Stanford University Press, 1996. 25–45.

Giles, James R. "Assaulting the Yeehats: Violence and Space in *The Call of the Wild.*" *Twisted from the Ordinary: Essays on American Literary Naturalism.* Ed. Mary E. Papke. Knoxville: University of Tennessee Press, 2003. 188–201.

London, Jack. *The Call of the Wild.* 1903. *The Call of the Wild, White Fang, and Other Stories.* Ed. Earle Labor and Robert C. Leitz, III. Oxford: Oxford University Press, 1990. 1–88.

Norris, Frank. *Vandover and the Brute.* 1914. *Frank Norris: Novels and Essays.* Ed. Donald Pizer. New York: The Library of America, 1986. 1–260.

Sandburg, Charles A. [Carl Sandburg]. "Jack London: A Common Man." *Tomorrow Magazine* 2 (1906): 35–39. Rpt. in *Jack London: A Study of the Short Fiction.* By Jeanne Campbell Reesman. New York: Twayne, 1999.

Lopez, Barry (1945–   )

Barry Lopez, a self-described natural history writer of both fiction and nonfiction, examines the nonhuman world in an attempt, ultimately, to better understand human interactions; and the exploration of his own relationship to the environment is a critical element in this attempt.

Born in Port Chester, New York in 1945, Barry Lopez spent several years of his childhood in the Mojave Desert. While living in the desert, he raised pigeons, and Lopez points to the raising and releasing of those pigeons as his introduction to the complexity of life. His family returned to New York when he was 11, and Lopez later attended the University of Notre Dame for his undergraduate studies, continued through to a Masters degree in 1966, and then moved to Oregon. In Oregon, Lopez studied under Barre Toelken, a folklorist, who inspired him to investigate anthropology with a focus on how other cultures interacted with the land. He earned a second Master's degree in anthropology in 1968 from the University of Oregon. His immersion in the American West and Pacific Northwest is evident in many of his works.

His essay collection, OF WOLVES AND MEN (1978) won the JOHN BURROUGHS Medal, given to distinguished works of natural history. The book links natural history with cultural criticism by first examining wolves as a species and then exploring various cultural perspectives on them. In 1986, ARCTIC DREAMS: IMAGINATION AND DESIRE IN A NORTHERN LANDSCAPE won the National Book Award for nonfiction. Here, Lopez combines research from a host of academic disciplines with his own experiences in the Arctic, arguing against human detachment from the nonhuman environment, even going so far as to include a note to his readers about the goal of the book, advocating a "more particularized understanding of the land ... as if it were another part of civilization itself" (11). In the essay "Narrative and Landscape," Lopez suggests that the way in which a person perceives both named and unnamed relationships with nature is largely shaped by where on the planet a person travels, what that individual touches and perceives, and the patterns he or she observes in nature.

Lopez's early writing focused on Native American folktales, which he collected and edited, and at the same time wrote short stories. Even his earliest writing is informed by recurring themes that would dominate his life and work, such as a profound and profoundly respectful sense of place, human responsibility to the earth, and questioning how people reach an understanding of their surroundings and themselves. As Lopez explores and writes about the natural world, he goes through an awakening process comparable to that of HENRY DAVID THOREAU. Like Thoreau, Lopez never suggests that one may ever have a complete or even satisfactory awareness of the natural world, but his essays intertwine natural facts with his personal experiences of a place, in order to deepen our understanding of the land and create connections between the reader and the place. To this end, Lopez strives for a delicate and shifting —living— balance between the factual and the subjective. He must make his own experiences understood and meaningful, using language accessible to his readers, and this limits the amount of technical or scientific jargon he can employ.

Despite this, Lopez relies heavily on scientific inquiry in order to convey and support his meaning. At the same time, he finds reliance on scientific fact to be troubling, because in order to obtain it humans must invade animals' space, and both organize and relate to the world in anthropocentric terms. He ex-presses concern that scientists view the evolution of humans as a consequence of natural selection and evolution, rather than formation by a god, finally asking "Why can't it be both?" (Lueders 17).

Lopez wants to help people discover connections with the rest of the human and nonhuman world, and believes that writers have an obligation to provide stories people can "feel comfortable in," without inherently reinforcing certain beliefs about the world. Instead, Lopez argues, people should finish a story simply feeling they have a better and more sympathetic understanding of the subject than when they began. Likewise, he hopes to inspire deeper compassion, and a greater sense of obligation, through his stories and essays, rather than the typical focus on rights (and conflict) in American culture, in part because of his belief that this will best aid Americans in reconnecting with one another and with place.

Lopez classifies himself as a natural history writer, concerned with relationships embracing more than just humans and the land, the "complex biological, social, economic, and ethical relationships" based on hierarchal thinking about the world. His sense of natural history writing eschews genre classification, and instead forms part of a "literature of hope." To foster this hope, Lopez relies on metaphor, as he sees, in this uniquely human capacity, a strong yet supple bridge to the natural world, expressing as it does the human ability to incorporate alternate perspectives into one's own thoughts or views. In a 1988 conversation with E.O. WILSON, Lopez refers to such metaphors as a means of overcoming things that bewilder our senses, through the use of parallel stories providing different levels of meaning (Lueders 16).

Flowing naturally from these views is Lopez' conviction that "Nonfiction writers have taken over territory abandoned by American fiction writers," because it is the former who explore more deeply and sensitively the relationships between man and 'the other'" (qtd. in Slovic 145). And indeed, much of the hope that informs his writing centers on its message of harmony or agreement with, rather than separation from, the environment — what he calls "the dream of the people" in Arctic Dreams (12). That work explicitly strives for such harmony by making every effort to appreciate an unknown people and/or landscape and then convey this appreciation in a vibrant and memorable form.

Like the TRANSCENDENTALISTS, Lopez hopes to create a unique body of literature that heightens awareness of our connections and obligations both to our fellow human beings and to the nonhuman world. However, unlike the transcendentalists, Lopez embraces intellectualism, approaching human inter-action with the natural world, and the process of sci-entific inquiry, with equal and healthy skepticism, questioning why a partnership cannot exist between science and religion, and exploring the devastating impact that this intellectual division has had on the way humans view and treat the world around them.—Liz Clift

BIBLIOGRAPHY

Bass, Rick, John Daniel, Gavan Daws, Pamela Frierson, John Haines, Linda M. Hasselstrom, John Hildebrand, Edward Hoagland, William Kittredge, Barry Lopez, Nancy Lord, Christopher Merrill, Dan O'Brien, David Rains Wallace, Peter Wild and John A. Murray. "The Rise of Nature Writing: America's Next Great Genre?" Manoa, Vol. 4, No. 2, 1992, 73–96.

Drew, Bernard A. *100 Most Popular Nonfiction Authors.* Westport, CT: Libraries Unlimited, 2008, 230–33.

Lopez, Barry. *Arctic Dreams.* New York: Vintage Books. 1986.

_____. *Crossing Open Ground.* New York: Vintage Books, 1989.

_____. *Of Wolves and Men.* New York: Touchstone, 1978.

Lueders, Edward G. (ed). *Writing Natural History: Dialogues with Authors.* Salt Lake City: University of Utah Press, 1989.

Seaman, Donna. *Writers on the Air: Conversations about Books.* Philadelphia: Paul Dry Books, 2005.

Slovic, Scott. *Seeking Awareness in American Nature Writing.* Salt Lake City: University of Utah Press, 1992.

Arctic Dreams: Imagination and Desire in a Northern Landscape, Barry Lopez (1986)

Arctic Dreams, Barry Lopez's sixth book and winner of the National Book Award, is considered a modern classic of environmental literature. The non-fictional novel illustrates his penchant for meticulous research and forbidding landscapes, which is also seen in his other works of fiction and non-fiction, such as OF WOLVES AND MEN (1978), *Desert Notes* (1976), and *About This Life* (1998) (Campbell 82). Lopez spent five years researching *Arctic Dreams,* traveling with Eskimos, marine ecologists, landscape painters, oil company employees, and the crew of a shipping freighter; and the resulting work is part human history, part natural history, and part medi-tation. Lopez evokes the Arctic environment, both in body and soul, by focusing each chapter on one phenomenon of the region. These fall into three cat-egories: animal (polar bears, muskoxen, narwhals, among others), the physical environment (ice, snow, light), and humanity (Eskimos, modern scientific and industrial workers, and the history of European exploration); with each considered from multiple perspectives. Using a technique typical of classic na-ture writers like THOREAU, Lopez offers detailed sci-entific descriptions as well as poetic musings about his subject (Grewe-Volpp 133). However, it is his deft evocation of the perspective of the phenomenon *itself* that makes *Arctic Dreams* a landmark of envi-ronmental literature.

Chapter 5, devoted exclusively to narwhals, epit-omizes Lopez's technique, which weaves together sci-ence, myth, and first-hand reportage to create a col-lage-like picture of the natural world, and sense its intrinsic perspective. He begins with his own aston-ishing first encounter with the narwhal. Flying over the Bering Sea in a research plane, Lopez and the sci-entists spotted two male narwhals lying on the surface of the ocean below (127). No one had ever seen narwhals in this location before, and the sighting shocked everyone in the plane. Lopez repeatedly presents his reader with such memorable moments, and in each case offers possible explanations; in this case, based on the thickness of the ice around them, the narwhals could have been full-time residents of the area, or they could have come from known nar-whal habitats the previous fall (127). However, as renowned eco-critic LAWRENCE BUELL notes, Lopez resists these easy scientific explanations (8), instead musing on the implications of attempting to reduce what one sees to *any* scientific explanation. The kernel of indisputable information, for Lopez, is a dot in space; interpretations grow out of the desire to make this point a line, to give it a direction. But the directions in which it can be sent, the uses to which it can be put, in a culturally, professionally, and geographically diverse society, are almost without limit. (127)

This instinctive caution regarding interpretation and explanation is what Buell identifies as Lopez's respect for "out there," which is "the ultimate au-thority, to which both laboratory result and field-camp explanation must appeal..." (Buell 93). The appearance of the narwhals is one example of the un-predictable behavior of "out there" (the nonhuman world), which can always "contradict what has been documented as fact" (Grewe-Volpp 133). According to Buell, this is what makes *Arctic Dreams* unique; it "is an environmental text distinguished for its ex-ceptional sensitivity to the limits of objective repre-sentation when the writer is placed in a totally un-familiar setting" (Buell 92). And this respect for the "limits of objective representation" is a major theme of the novel, coloring Lopez's approach to every as-pect of the Arctic.

After the initial report of the sighting, Lopez skill-fully inscribes other perspectives, canvassing what is known about the narwhal, from clear and dispas-sionate scientific observation to poetic descriptions of fascinating and distinctive features of the animal. He also describes the animal's mythic past during the Middle Ages when narwhal tusks were mistaken for evidence of the existence of unicorns (142). Finally, and most memorably, Lopez considers the perspective of the narwhal itself, comparing the narwhal's experience of the world to our own:

> ...it has a highly discriminating feeling for depth and a hunter's sensitivity to the slight turbulence created by a school of cod cruising ahead of it in its dimly lit world.... How different must be "the world" for such a creature, for whom sight is but a peripheral sense, who occupies, instead, a three-dimensional acoustical space. Perhaps only musicians have some inkling of the formal shape of emotions and motivation that might define such sensibility [138].

In order to evoke such native perspectives Lopez draws upon all of his sources of information, employing "scientific and personal observation as well as philosophical speculation aimed at letting a distant ecosphere 'speak'" (Grewe-Volpp 130).

Lopez's approach to nature writing illustrates his broader conviction about how we should approach nature in general; the consideration of multiple perspectives is not merely a literary tool, but the core of his environmental message:

> The land retains an identity of its own, still deeper and more subtle than we can know. Our obligation toward it then becomes simple: to approach with an uncalculating mind, with an attitude of regard.... To intend from the beginning to preserve some of the mystery within it as a kind of wisdom to be experienced, not questioned. And to be alert for its opening, for the moment when something sacred reveals itself within the mundane, and you know the land knows you are there [Lopez 228].

In this way, *Arctic Dreams* deepens our understanding of both how we affect the natural world and how we are affected by it, and answers the call of eco-critics and environmentalists alike, for images of the relationship between humans and the environment that illustrate the true complexity and reality of that relationship.—Lauren Mitchell Nahas

BIBLIOGRAPHY

Buell, Lawrence. *The Environmental Imagination: Thoreau, Nature Writing, and the Formation of American Culture*. Cambridge, MA: Belknap Press of Harvard University Press, 1995.

Campbell, SueEllen. "Review: Arctic Dreams: Imagination and Desire in a Northern Landscape by Barry Lopez." *Environmental Review*: ER 11, no. 1 (Spring 1987): 82–84.

Evans, Alice. "Leaning into the Light: An Interview with Barry Lopez." *Poets and Writers Magazine*, April 1994.

Grewe-Volpp, Christa. "How to Speak the Unspeakable: The Aesthetics of the Voice of Nature." *Anglia—Zeitschrift für englische Philologie* 124, no. 1 (August 2006): 122–143.

Lopez, Barry Holstun. *Arctic Dreams: Imagination and Desire in a Northern Landscape*. New York: Vintage Books, 2001.

Of Wolves and Men, Barry Lopez (1978)

Barry Lopez's *Of Wolves and Men* was a National Book Award finalist when first published in 1978, and has come to exemplify the author's interdisciplinary style, a deft fusion of literary acumen, ecological awareness and ethnography. *Of Wolves and Men* is not just about wolves, but about how little is actually known about wolves — in other words, Lopez is interested in the mythologies that circulate around these iconic but often misunderstood animals. And, of course, as humans are the creators of such mythologies, the book is as much about humans (and their creation). The book is also about how humans *visualize* wolves: Lopez's writing is typically woven around visual culture, from historical photographs, to an Eskimo print of wolves eating a caribou (84), to illustrations of the wolf and the crane attached to the eponymous Aesopian fable (260).

Lopez introduces his book by placing the act of writing in the foreground, and thereby seeking to embed the reader in a detailed (if also entirely mediated) environment:

> I am in a small cabin outside Fairbanks, Alaska, as I write these words. The cold sits down like iron here, and the long hours of winter darkness cause us to leave a light on most of the day. Outside, at thirty below, wood for the stove literally pops apart at the touch of the ax. I can see out across the short timber of the taiga when I am out there in the gray daylight [1].

This is a prime example of what the literary scholar Timothy Morton calls "ecomimesis," when environmental writing attempts to "break the spell of language" and "go beyond the aesthetic dimension" (30–31). Lopez is calling on his readers to get *into* a scene — or as his next sentence puts it, "Go out there" (1); and the "there" in this sentence is both the Alaskan terrain and the *inside* of the book, a landscape of the mind. Lopez acknowledges a distance from his subject (he is *writing* here, not looking at wolves) precisely in order to achieve "a sense of the surrounding environment, not by being less artful, but more so" (Morton, 31). This is a common tactic throughout *Of Wolves and Men*, by which Lopez reminds his readers that, finally, the real environment of this text is not the behaviors and habitats of wolves, but rather the (un)knowing human mind in relation to all lupine things, and by extension the world in which they (and not we) are at home. As Lopez writes: "...in the wolf we have not so much an animal that we have always known as one that we have consistently *imagined*" (204) — a notion equally applicable, by analogy, to the natural environment as a whole.

Thus Lopez begins the first chapter with a visual directive to the reader: "Imagine a wolf moving though the northern woods..." (9). The following paragraph goes on to flesh out this imaginary scene, and the sentences are rife with figurative language: "The wolf's body, from neck to hips, appears to float over the long, almost spindly legs and the flicker of wrists, a bicycling drift through the trees, reminiscent of the movement of water or of shadows" (9). The third paragraph, however, strikes a quite different, but equally characteristic tone, scientific and declarative: "The wolf is three years old. A male. He is of the subspecies *occidentalis*, and the trees he is moving among are spruce and subalpine fir on the eastern slope of the Rockies in northern Canada (10). This type of stylistic shift typifies what environmental critic LAWRENCE BUELL describes as Lopez's distinctive role, as a "roaming" ethnographer, "gleaning insights more from interdisciplinary study and place-based informants ... than from staying put" (69). *Of Wolves and Men* follows an indeterminate yet cumulative pattern of "roaming" between personal narratives, rumors, pictures, field accounts, and observations. This methodology allows Lopez to draw something of an open and inclusive perimeter around his subject, which he defines as "a variable creature" (83).

The literary scholar Susan Kollin has shown how "Lopez dismantles notions of Alaska as a pastoral or wilderness retreat, a place somehow cut off from the rest of the United States or the world" (46). So while certain passages from *Of Wolves and Men* linger on classic environmental imagery and specific ecosystems, the book continually shifts ground, requiring the reader to recalibrate and come to terms with outlying horizons of knowledge and experience. Indeed, *Of Wolves and Men* focuses on the lore and legends of wolves in order to expand a general sense of consciousness about how humans, in Lopez's words, "...struggle to come to grips with the nature of the universe" (204). The scope of this book is thus at once narrowly focused on wolves, and almost endlessly expansive.

In one section Lopez explains a social phenomenon between wolves and ravens: ravens will often follow wolf tracks in order to discover (and clean up) fresh kills. In the next few paragraphs, Lopez follows this ecological dynamic into the realm of play, and relates stories of how ravens and wolves have been observed to tease one another and engage in games of tag, for fun (67–68). Such a move from scientific documentation to fanciful speculation is a signature feature of Lopez's writing.

As Peter Wild writes in his book on Lopez, "*Of Wolves and Men*, founded on the premise that men have created varying concepts of wolves, tells perhaps more about the human psyche than it does about the physical wolf loping along in isolation through the centuries" (26). *Of Wolves and Men* appears to have a fairly traditional "environmental" subject, yet there are ways in which this book can be understood to have anticipated contemporary intersections between critical theory and environmental studies, such as recent discussions of the human–animal conjunction (e.g., Agamben, Derrida, Haraway, and Wolfe). Near the end of the book, Lopez writes:

> I think, as the twentieth century comes to a close, that we are coming to an understanding of animals different from the one that has guided us for the past three hundred years. We have begun to see again, as our primitive ancestors did, that animals are neither imperfect imitations of men nor machines that can be described entirely in terms of endocrine secretions and neural impulses. Like us, they are genetically variable, and both species and the individual are capable of unprecedented behavior. They are like us in the sense that we can figuratively talk of them as beings some of whose forms, movements, activities, and social organizations are analogous, but they are no more literally like us than are trees [283–284].

This passage shows what the philosophical stakes are for Lopez in taking animality seriously as a subject of investigation; these sentences also demonstrate how, for Lopez, the wolf is both utterly unique and a metonymy for life at large.

Of Wolves and Men is a hybrid manifesto on behalf of "human inquiry" and against "dogmatic certainty" (285), and its resistance to be strictly defined in terms of any one genre is in part what makes it such a significant environmental literary text. Barry Lopez's work ranges across diverse subjects and fields of speculation, as one can tell from his more recent short story collections *Field Notes* and *Light Action in the Caribbean*, but *Of Wolves and Men* offers an early indicator of how Lopez's environmental sensibility functions as an elastic point of consciousness between humans and the world. — Christopher Schaberg

BIBLIOGRAPHY

Agamben, Giorgio. *The Open: Man & Animal*. Stanford: Stanford University Press, 2003.
Buell, Lawrence. *The Future of Environmental Criticism:*

Environmental Crisis and Literary Imagination. Malden, MA: Blackwell, 2005.

Derrida, Jacques. *The Animal That Therefore I Am.* New York: Fordham University Press, 2008.

Haraway, Donna. *When Species Meet.* Minneapolis: University of Minnesota Press, 2007.

Kollin, Susan. *Nature's State: Imagining Alaska as the Last Frontier.* Chapel Hill: University of North Carolina Press, 2001.

Lopez, Barry. *Of Wolves and Men.* New York: Scribner's, 1978.

Morton, Timothy. *Ecology Without Nature: Rethinking Environmental Aesthetics.* Cambridge: Harvard University Press, 2007.

Wild, Peter. *Barry Lopez.* Boise: Boise State University, 1984.

Wolfe, Cary. "Flesh and Finitude: Thinking Animals in (Post)Humanist Philosophy." *SubStance* Issue 117 (Volume 37, Number 3), 2008.

Lowell, Robert (1917–1977)

The life and poems of Robert Lowell contract and expand unpredictably. An invocation of the planet, for example, can signify both the recognition of vast ethical responsibilities and a rampant ego. Lowell was famously attracted, in "empathy and protest," to the grand men of history, such as Caligula and Calvinist theologian JONATHAN EDWARDS (Hart xxi). In an early poem, "Mr. Edwards and the Spider," killing a spider is portrayed as so far-reaching an act that the thought of being burned by God is welcomed. Leaving the Episcopalianism of his parents and converting to Catholicism in 1941, then converting out of it in the 1950's, Lowell never abandons the creation of ethical allegories. What his poetry ultimately seeks to reveal are the connections between social justice, democracy, and the natural world. His conscientious objection to World War II in 1943, and participation in the March on the Pentagon in 1967 to protest the Vietnam War, demonstrate his belief in the force of singular actions, which can remove the singular great man from consideration.

In his global orientation, Lowell "addresses the very contemporary phenomenon of survival," according to Nicholas Fraser (92). Many of his poems fretfully, yet stalwartly contemplate the major anxiety of the twentieth century: "the chafe and jar" of worldwide war and nuclear devastation ("Fall 1961" line 6). Significantly, Lowell remarked, America was "founded on a Declaration, on the Constitution, on Principles, and we've always had the ideal of 'saving the world.' And that comes close to perhaps destroying the world" (Alvarez "A Talk" 105). Lowell wants his readers to experience and recognize the numbing power of American ambition, before acting against its numbing effects. To do so, he often contrasts a racked speaker with a nonhuman or natural force, such as an animal, a public park, or the element of water. His much-admired poem "Waking Early Sunday Morning," from *Near the Ocean* (1967), begins with the resilience of salmon:

> O to break loose, like the chinook
> salmon jumping and falling back,
> nearing up to the impossible
> stone and bone-crushing waterfall —[lines 1–4]

The poem seems to close mournfully, "Pity the planet, all joy gone / from this sweet volcanic cone" (105–106), and its recurring *o*-sounds heightens the reader's sense of the earth as "a ghost / orbiting forever lost / in our monotonous sublime" (110–112).

Much as in the work of HART CRANE, water, for Lowell, is the medium wherein human ambition is most exposed to indifference. "The Quaker Graveyard in Nantucket," an early poem, is an elegy for Lowell's cousin who died at sea, but the poem cannot always disentangle this specific death from the deep pull of "Ahab's void and forehead" (line 15) — where Ahab from MELVILLE's MOBY DICK represents an obsessive desire to amputate from the self everything outside the self. Lowell's interest in the movements of the sea is also an interest in the mind's shifting beliefs, and he wonders how best to keep alive the fluidity of thought and nature. The popular poem "For the Union Dead" is about the death of an aquarium in contemporary Boston, which is contrasted with the still-standing statue of Civil War hero Robert Gould Shaw and his regiment of black soldiers. Why is commemorating "the dark downward and vegetating kingdom / of the fish and reptile" (lines 10–11) less important, or more difficult to achieve, asks the poem, than the commemoration of man's noble failures. At the end of the poem, the lost aquatic life is reincarnated: "giant finned cars nose forward like fish; / a savage servility / slides by on grease" (66–68). Such imperfect forms of survival, memorably rendered by Lowell, are the work of poetry and metaphor.

The first three books of poems and the first quarter of his fourth, *Life Studies* (1959), contain formally thick poems — tough and odd diction, self-conscious literariness, a commitment to rhyme — and many are sustained by the vigor of APOCALYPTIC FICTION. In "Where the Rainbow Ends," Lowell's Boston is being weighed in "the pans / Of judgment" (lines 14–15). Granted "wisdom, exile" (29), Lowell's speaker is told to "Stand and live" (29), and in this way he says goodbye to his New England heritage and religion. The overreliance on apocalypse in his early poems testifies to what Selim Sarwar calls Lowell's "awareness of a grand divine purpose mislaid and frustrated" (118).

In the rest of *Life Studies* and his next collection

For the Union Dead (1964), however, "the angry voice of the visionary is tuned down to the tired confessional musings of a convalescent" (Sarwar 123). Lowell's new subject, instead of prophecy, becomes the unceasing revelation of himself to the world. It is for this reason that he is known as the originator of "confessional" poetry: his mental health, hospitalization, hectic marriages, and the family he renounced are his new muses. As Lowell himself puts it, "I thought that civilization was going to break down, and instead *I* did" (Alvarez "Robert" 77). Exploring the extent to which global crises overlap with his internal crises, Lowell both risks and shrinks from hubris. For this reason, the term "confessional" means more than simply self-obsession; it means that an environment's metabolism is imprinting itself directly onto the poet's consciousness. In "Skunk Hour," a disturbed Lowell wanders up an empty hill, and as he declares, "I myself am hell" (line 35), the poem replaces Lowell's personal hell with the "moonstruck eyes' red fire" of a mother skunk (40). The appearance of this absurd beast of the night directs our attention to a form of survival that is free of anxiety: scavenging for food. This fantasy is alarming and comical, though only slightly deflating, because the anguish of American greatness would like to pawn itself off on the skunk, but is prohibited from the act of personification. Lowell's work repeatedly arrives at this difficult point: one cannot effortlessly imagine being safe from earthly provocations which "will not scare" (48).

Similar to this interruption of "hell," Lowell's images of paradise and the pastoral (AMERICAN PASTORAL) are often invaded and undermined, as in his attack on wealthy paranoiacs in "Central Park" ("Behind each bush, perhaps a knife" [53]), or as in the later poem "We Took Our Paradise" ("Can one bear it; in nature / from seed to chaff no tragedy?" [15–16]). Lowell is suspicious of tragedy's absence, but drawn to tragedy as much as to nature's rejection of tragedy; ultimately he is doomed, as he puts it in "This Golden Summer," to "imagine / the shadow around the corner... / downstairs ... behind the door" (14–16). These dark thoughts occur after the speaker steps on his cat: "Our cat, a new mother, put a paw / under my foot, as I held a tray" (9–10). The non-human literally and existentially gets under the human's foot. Without reference to the unknowable ways of God in the allegory of "Mr. Edwards and the Spider," Lowell reveals instead a no less important and lengthy chain of sublunary connections, extending from his own paranoia to the accident, her pain, and finally, his own inescapable accountability.— Jonathan Gaboury

BIBLIOGRAPHY

Alvarez, A. "Robert Lowell in Conversation." *Robert Lowell: Interviews and Memoirs.* Ed. Jeffrey Meyers. Ann Arbor: University of Michigan Press, 1988. 74–78.
_____. "A Talk with Robert Lowell." *Robert Lowell: Interviews and Memoirs.* Ed. Jeffrey Meyers. Ann Arbor: University of Michigan Press, 1988. 99–108.
Fraser, Nicholas. "Grace of Accuracy." *Harper's* 311 (2005): 92–98.
Hart, Henry. *Robert Lowell and the Sublime.* Syracuse, NY: Syracuse University Press, 1995.
Lowell, Robert. *Day by Day.* New York: FSG, 1978.
_____. *Selected Poems: Revised Edition.* New York: FSG, 1978.
Sarwar, Selim. "Robert Lowell: Scripting the Mid-Century Eschatology." *Journal of Modern Literature* 25 (2001/2002): 114–130.

Manifest Destiny *see* Ideologies

Marx, Leo (1919–   )

Marx is best known as the author of THE MACHINE IN THE GARDEN: TECHNOLOGY AND THE PASTORAL IDEAL IN AMERICA (1964), a seminal study of the evolving relationship between industrial and pastoral ideologies in American literature and culture. The work appeared during the dawn of the modern environmental movement, and has played a vital role in shaping the burgeoning field of ecocriticism over the past half century. Marx is a Senior Lecturer, William R. Kenan, Jr. Professor of American Cultural History (emeritus), and member of the Program in Science, Technology and Society, at the Massachusetts Institute of Technology.

Marx grew up in the Rockaway Peninsula, a popular summer resort area on the south shore of Long Island. As a youth, he spent much of his free time swimming and boating in the ocean, and he counts his experiences with the Boy Scouts, on the Island and in Manhattan, as a strong influence on his environmental awareness: "The Manhattan troop was very privileged — owned a cabin in the Ramapo mountains north of NYC on land we shared with the Jackson Whites — the strange people who were made up of escaped slaves, deserting Hessian soldiers of the Am[erican] Rev[olution], and native Americans. We did a lot of serious camping — white water canoeing in the Adirondacks and serious climbing (we climbed Khatadin — up to the famous knife edge)" (Marx). Marx spent four years on small ships in the U.S. Navy during the Second World War, and saw up close the results of military-industrial interventions into diverse natural environments. After returning home, he often explored the backwoods of Maine, where his wife's family has a house.

From an early age, Marx was a fan of the writings of HENRY DAVID THOREAU (on whom he wrote his senior honors thesis) and HERMAN MELVILLE. He completed his doctorate, which became the basis for *The Machine in the Garden*, in Harvard's History of American Civilization program in 1949. Marx then taught at the University of Minnesota and Amherst College, making foundational contributions to their American Studies programs, before moving to M.I.T. in 1976. Besides his most famous work, he has published widely on topics related to the intersection of urban and natural environments, and the rise, and often forbidding implications, of our technocratic culture. His works include *The Pilot and the Passenger* (1988), (with M.R. Smith) *Does Technology Drive History?: The Dilemma of Technological Determinism* (1994), and (with Bruce Mazlish) *Progress: Fact or Illusion?* (1996). Marx is often classed — along with such scholars as Henry Nash Smith, John William Ward, Annette Kolodny, Richard Slotkin, and Alan Trachtenberg — as one of the founding members of the so-called "Myth and Symbol School" of American Studies, which looks to recurring thematic patterns in literary and cultural work in order to identify essential truths about the national imagination. He has also edited a number of canonical works of "environmental literature" by authors such as Thoreau, NATHANIEL HAWTHORNE, and MARK TWAIN. — Geoff Hamilton

BIBLIOGRAPHY

Buell, Lawrence. *The Environmental Imagination: Thoreau, Nature Writing, and the Formation of American Culture.* Cambridge, MA: Belknap Press of Harvard University Press, 1995.

Garrard, Greg. *Ecocriticism.* The New Critical Idiom. London ; New York: Routledge, 2004.

Marx, Leo. Personal communication. Aug. 29, 2011.

Meikle, Jeffrey L. "Leo Marx's the Machine in the Garden." *Technology & Culture* 44.1 (2003): 147–159.

M.I.T. Program in Science, Technology and Society. "Leo Marx." 2011. Available online. URL: http://web.mit.edu/sts/people/marx.html. Accessed Aug. 20, 2011.

Trachtenberg, Alan. "Myth and Symbol." *The Massachusetts Review.* 25.4 (Winter 1984): 667: 673.

The Machine in the Garden, Leo Marx (1964)

Published at the nascence of the modern environmental movement, *The Machine in the Garden* has proven a widely influential work for both American literary criticism in general and ecocriticism in particular. What began as Marx's doctoral dissertation at Harvard, became, in the words of LAWRENCE BUELL, "The best book ever written about the place of nature in American literary thought" (Buell 11). Greg Garrard explains that "This key text does not mention ecology or environmentalism directly, but clearly situates its discussion in relation to the increasingly problematic place of technology in the American landscape" (Garrard 36).

The central argument of the book focuses on the recurring image in American literature and landscape painting of some form of technology interrupting an idyllic scene situated in a natural environment. Marx begins by investigating a "little event" recorded in NATHANIEL HAWTHORNE's journal, where the author is peacefully enjoying a bucolic scene near Concord, Massachusetts. Images of nature are blended harmoniously with images of society, but then a train intrudes with its piercing whistle and disrupts Hawthorne's reverie. Marx observes that "the noise arouses a sense of dislocation, conflict, and anxiety. [...] Most important is the sense of the machine as a sudden, shocking intruder upon a fantasy of idyllic satisfaction" (13, 29). Marx traces the recurrence of such scenes throughout nineteenth- and early twentieth-century American literature in authors such as HENRY DAVID THOREAU, HERMAN MELVILLE, MARK TWAIN, Henry James, WILLIAM FAULKNER, ERNEST HEMINGWAY and F. SCOTT FITZGERALD. However, he explains that the conflicting emotions aroused by the contrasts between nature and civilization have long been a topic of literature. This "complex pastoral," as he calls it, is juxtaposed to the "sentimental pastoral," which merely praises nature and assumes life is always easier when lived close to nature (AMERICAN PASTORAL). The former has its roots in Virgil's *Eclogues*, and Marx connects the complex pastorals of the ancient world to those of the new world through the English Renaissance, devoting an entire chapter to a discussion of Shakespeare's "American Fable," *The Tempest*, to demonstrate the "conflicting European preconceptions of the American landscape: innocent natural paradise and savage natural wilderness" (Meilke 151).

Marx is primarily concerned with this "middle landscape," the traditional location of the shepherd in complex pastoral works. On one side exist the burdens and pressures of the sophisticated city with its crowds and modernity, on the other side are the fears and dangers of the wilderness with its "violent uncertainties." In between the two is the ideal pasture, the place where the humble shepherd negotiates a truce, living in harmony with nature and translating its resources, both material and spiritual, into a language comprehensible and useful to the urban culture. For Marx, this "middle landscape" finds a particular relevance in American history, culture, and literature, different and perhaps more genuine than the idealistic pastorals of ancient Rome or the English Renaissance. In America, and especially in the colonies, the realities of the wilderness facing the frontier settler called for an uneasy but fecund synthesis of the natural world and the juggernaut of technological progress.

Marx traces the growth and development of the pastoral ideal in American writing from its foundations in simple and sentimental praise of nature to the more complex conception of an agrarian culture. He cites Robert Beverley's History and Present State of Virginia (1705) as an example of a text that extols the New World as the new Garden of Eden. Beverley's writings rely on what Garrard calls a "cornucopia" view of the natural world. He celebrates the plenty and the innocence that he finds in the uncultivated regions of colonial Virginia. But Marx points out inconsistencies in Beverly's garden idyll, as in its description of atrocities committed by the Native Americans after its celebration of their innocent and "primitivistic" communion with nature. Beverley's simple and largely sentimental view is contrasted with later writings by J. HECTOR ST. JOHN DE CRÈVECŒUR, who celebrates a cultivated landscape rather than the wilderness, searching for a balance somewhere between the wild frontier in America and the ornate and highly cultivated gardens of Versailles.

The discussion of de Crèvecœur's work leads to an examination of THOMAS JEFFERSON's defense of agrarianism, which in turn leads to a discussion of the tensions implicit in the confrontation between nature and "the machine." Jefferson wrote that "Those who labor in the earth are the chosen people of God," and imagined an American pasture stretching west across the continent that would take a thousand years to cultivate. Marx explains that Jefferson's ultimate goal is a society based on "sufficiency, not economic growth" (127). While even Jefferson recognized that the competing interests of industrialization would easily overtake his agrarian ideal, Marx argues that it was not just the convenience and comfort that comes from industrialization that encouraged its rapid growth; rather its nearly universal acceptance was partially the result of the rhetoric of a few influential individuals who developed a philosophy of progress and celebrated mechanization and industrialization as an embodiment of the "ultimate laws of nature" (161). Thinkers who followed Jefferson, such as the Scottish writer Thomas Carlyle, continued to decry the sense of alienation and dehumanization which accompanied mechanization and industrialization, but were in many ways handicapped by a lack of compelling terminology to counter the claims of industrialists. They could not compete with what Marx calls the "mechanized sublime" of Daniel Webster.

Although industrialization easily won the debate and consumed the culture's attention and intention, many artists and writers still resisted the lure of unswerving industrial and mechanical progress; hence the trope of the machine invading the garden. Technological and industrial progress may be inevitable and even celebrated, but Marx warns us of its dangerous consequences when not critically examined. As F. Scott Fitzgerald suggests in The Great Gatsby, the same force of history which gave us the modern city and all its wonders also transformed the "fresh green breast of the new world" into the "valley of ashes."

Marx's approach was criticized most famously by Bruce Kuklick, who took issue generally with what he called the "myth and symbol school." Nevertheless Marx continued throughout his career to pursue the themes and topics first addressed in The Machine in the Garden, revisiting and refining his arguments, and adapting them to the modern world and contemporary issues. The birth and vigorous growth of ecocriticism and the environmental movement in general, the continued and unsustainable depredation of nature, and our culture's dedication to the possibility of infinite technological progress, all suggest that Marx's themes and arguments are as relevant today as they were when he wrote the book; just as they were for Hawthorne when the train whistle first intruded on his pastoral reverie. — Michael Beilfuss

BIBLIOGRAPHY

Buell, Lawrence. The Environmental Imagination: Thoreau, Nature Writing, and the Formation of American Culture. Cambridge, MA: Belknap Press of Harvard University Press, 1995.

Garrard, Greg. Ecocriticism. The New Critical Idiom. London and New York: Routledge, 2004.

Marx, Leo. "Pastoralism in America." Ideology and Classic American Literature. Eds. Sacvan Bercovitch and Myra Jehlen. Cambridge: Cambridge University Press, 1986. 36–69.

Meikle, Jeffrey L. "Leo Marx's the Machine in the Garden." Technology & Culture 44.1 (2003): 147–159.

Reed, T. V. "Myth and Symbol School." 2007. Theory and Method in American Cultural Studies. Available online. URL: http://www.wsu.edu/~amerstu/tm/myth.html. Accessed August 1, 2009.

Mather, Cotton (1663–1728)

Two of Mather's works are important environmental writings: a series of letters known as Curiosa Americana (1712) and his book of natural philosophy, The Christian Philosopher (1721). In these works, although he emphasized Christian orthodoxy, Mather influenced a changing worldview in colonial America from Puritanism — the adherence to absolute faith — to Deism, which finds God through reasoning and observations of the natural world.

Cotton Mather was born in Boston, Massachusetts, and belonged to one of the most powerful New

England families. His maternal grandfather was the Reverend John Cotton, an early Puritan leader in England and in the New World. His grandfather Richard and father Increase were, like Cotton, Puritan ministers who influenced both the religious and political life of the Massachusetts colony (Increase's diplomatic efforts proved instrumental in obtaining a new charter for New England in 1691 from King James II). Mather himself was an erudite and educated man, having entered Harvard in 1674 at the age of 11, well ahead of other students. Graduating at 15 in 1678, he immediately began a successful preaching and writing career, receiving his M.A. from Harvard at the age of 18.

Mather was ordained, after several invitations, as a pastor in Boston's Old North church in 1685. He maintained this public role until his death, preaching among the Puritan settlers and working in the service of what he saw as the founding generation's original mission: adherence to the revealed word of Scripture, achieving the state of purity in the church, and cultivating piety, or deep religiousness, in the individual self. Mather married three times. His first marriage was to Abigail Phillips in 1686 with whom he had nine children. After her death in 1702, Mather married Elizabeth Hubbard, with whom he had six children; she died in 1713. He married Lydia Lee George in 1715 and had no children. Of his fifteen children, nine died in infancy, and only two — Samuel and Hannah Mather — survived him.

Devotion to Puritan religious values determined Cotton Mather's life and work: many of his 440 published works are sermons, Biblical commentaries, and instructions for the clergy. Magnalia Christi Americana (1702), intended as a history of the church of New England from its founding in 1620 to 1698, is considered his greatest work. An ecclesiastical history, Magnalia also abounds with details of daily life, such as Mather's descriptions of attacks on the English and Dutch settlements by "Indians" and the French, the history of Harvard College, and biographies of the New England governors. Mather's commentary on the Salem witch trials, Wonders of the Invisible World (1693), is considered his most controversial book. In it, Mather expressed support for the Salem court, even though he did not participate in the trials or executions of the alleged witches. Mather believed in the existence of witches as the sign of the Devil's presence in New England and as an announcement of Judgment Day, which he thought was imminent in his century. It is important to note that, like his writings on the natural world, Curiosa Americana and The Christian Philosopher, Wonders of the Invisible World reflected the beliefs of both the educated and uneducated in the American colonies, including a sense that the new continent was a land possessed by the Devil before the settlers arrived, and that supernatural forces and beings were therefore native to the place itself.

The belief in the invisible supernatural world, combined with Mather's inquisitive observations, is especially evident in Curiosa Americana. In this series of letters to the Royal Society in London, the highest intellectual authority of the English-speaking world, Mather contributed keen observations of natural phenomena in America, corresponding with the English naturalist John Woodward. His letters described the flora and fauna native to the New World, medicinal plants and their uses in American medicine, as well as hurricanes, earthquakes, and rainbows. At the same time, some of the letters referred to the existence of mermen and two-headed snakes, conjectured that certain fossilized teeth and bones belonged to a giant, and gave unusual interpretations of medical conditions. The Royal Society rejected some, but published the majority of these letters, electing Mather to its membership in 1713.

Mather's The Christian Philosopher: A Collection of the Best Discoveries in Nature, with Religious Improvements (1721) amalgamates Puritan religious views with a scientific emphasis on natural phenomena, indicating a critical movement in colonial thought toward rationalism. The book compiles scientific data about physical categories such as light, stars, planets, minerals, insects, reptiles, and human beings, juxtaposed with exaltations of God, numerous Biblical references, observations of nature, and aesthetic judgments. With Christian Philosopher, Mather joined a larger movement of thinkers who were responding to Newton's principles of motion and gravity, and to his groundbreaking discoveries on the order of the natural world. Following English authors such as Robert Boyle, the author of The Christian Virtuoso (1690) and George Cheyne, the author of Philosophical Principles of Natural Religion (1705), Mather strove to address the relationship between the natural world and God, reiterating the argument from design: a claim that the wonderful order of nature points toward God as its supreme designer. The Christian Philosopher and Mather's scientific work has been sometimes understood as an aberration of Mather's orthodox Puritan thought; however, many scholars agree on Mather's utmost importance in ushering in the scientific era and naturalist thought to colonial America. — Lejla Kucukalic

BIBLIOGRAPHY

Lovelace, Richard F. The American Pietism of Cotton Mather: Origins of American Evangelicalism. Grand Rapids: Christian University Press, 1979.

Middlekauff, Robert. "Cotton Mather." American National

Biography Online. February 2000. Available online. URL: http://www.anb.org/articles/01/01-00580.html. Accessed May 11, 2009.

Silverman, Kenneth. *The Life and Times of Cotton Mather.* New York: Harper & Row, 1984.

Smolinski, Reiner. "How to Go to Heaven, or How Heaven Goes? Natural Science and Interpretation in Cotton Mather's 'Biblia Americana' (1693–1728)." *New England Quarterly*: 81: 2 (Jun 2008): 278–329.

McCarthy, Cormac (1933–   )

Born Charles McCarthy in 1933, the oldest son of a successful lawyer, McCarthy changed his name to Cormac, the Gaelic equivalent, in keeping with his Irish ancestry. His early years were comfortable, in a house staffed by maids and with ample land to play in. Yet throughout his adult life, McCarthy has lived frugally in the country, in a dilapidated farm that he has renovated himself. He currently lives in El Paso with his third wife, Jennifer Winkley, and his young son, John Francis.

McCarthy does not enjoy the celebrity his writing has brought him; in an interview with *New York Times'* Richard B. Woodward, he said he would rather keep the company of scientists than other writers. He rarely gives interviews, and when he does, he does not encourage questions about writing or himself. In his only television interview, with Oprah Winfrey in 2008, he gave a little more detail, speaking about his dislike of semicolons and quotation marks for dialogue, preferring to write in "simple declarative sentences."

McCarthy is now well known for his fiction. However, until *All the Pretty Horses* (1992), none of his previous works had sold more than 2,500 copies, despite critical praise. Alongside his ten novels, McCarthy has published two plays and has also written several screenplays, although only *The Gardener's Son* (1996) has been published.

Characteristically, his work is violent, austere, gloomy, and overwhelmingly masculine. The threat and wonder of the natural world is a recurrent theme throughout his work, but perhaps it is most obvious when situated at the heart of the novel, becoming something of a malevolent or benevolent character in itself. Many of his novels revolve around criminal or outcast protagonists and their encounters with wild and unforgiving landscapes; for example, *The Orchard Keeper* (1965), in which old Arthur Ownby attempts, in the face of a complex and rather grotesque mystery, to teach a local mountain boy his knowledge of mountain craft. Here, McCarthy's depiction of nature and its impact on the fortunes of the characters won the author great praise.

Reminiscent of the work of JACK LONDON, the plots of McCarthy's acclaimed Border Trilogy revolve around animals: in *All the Pretty Horses*, two boys find trouble on account of a stolen horse; in *The Crossing*, the narrative follows Billy Parham's attempt to return a trapped wolf to the northern mountains of Mexico; and in the last, *Cities of the Plain*, John Grady tries to heal every sick and injured animal he finds. Throughout, McCarthy draws an evocative portrait of nature as a living, even wilful entity that can be both beautiful and incredibly dangerous; a thematic revisited in his most recent novel, THE ROAD (2006).

McCarthy has often based his fiction on actual events; *Child of God* (1973), *The Gardener's Son*, and BLOOD MERIDIAN (1985) being notable examples. And his novels often require extensive research; in particular, he always visits the settings of his works to collate information on the landscape and the people, paying special attention to local dialects.

Along with its striking natural imagery, McCarthy's work is also renowned for its violence; and this can sometimes divide critics, as in the case of *Child of God*, which was centred on a necrophilic murderer who lived in an underground cave with rotting corpses. *Blood Meridian*, however, was seen by most critics as an unflinching and veracious portrayal of a shameful period in American history, one mired in suffering and violence. Widely praised as the beginning of a new stage in his writing, with scenes largely set in the West rather than the Appalachia of his earlier novels, the work was nonetheless criticized by some for wandering too far from his imaginative roots.

Throughout McCarthy's career, critics have cited similarities in tone, theme and environmental sensibility with authors as diverse as MARK TWAIN, WILLIAM FAULKNER, HERMAN MELVILLE, AND EDGAR ALLAN POE. He has received the Pulitzer, the National Book Award, and the James Tait Black Memorial Prize, amongst others. Alongside Philip Roth, Thomas Pynchon and DON DELILLO, he is, according to Harold Bloom, one of the four major American novelists of our time.

Several of his novels have been adapted into films; most successfully, *No Country for Old Men* (2007), which won an Academy Award, and *The Road* (2009).

His papers are held by Texas State University at San Marcos.— Alex Hobbs

BIBLIOGRAPHY

Bloom, Harold. "Dumbing Down American Readers." *Boston Globe*, September 24, 2003. Available online. URL: http://www.boston.com/news/globe/editorial_opinion/oped/articles/2003/09/24/dumbing_down_american_readers/. Downloaded on January 19, 2011.

Frye, Steven. *Understanding Cormac McCarthy.* Columbia: University of South Carolina Press, 2009.

No Country for Old Men (2007). Walt Disney Video, DVD, 2008.

The Oprah Winfrey Show. July 8, 2008. Available online. URL: http://www.oprah.com/oprahsbookclub/Oprahs-Exclusive-Interview-with-Cormac-McCarthy-Video. Downloaded on November 20, 2010.

The Road (2009). Sony Pictures Home Entertainment, DVD, 2010.

Woodward, Richard B. "Cormac McCarthy's Venomous Fiction." *New York Times* April 19, 1992. Available online. URL: http://www.nytimes.com/books/98/05/17/specials/mccarthy-venom.html. Downloaded on November 11, 2010.

Blood Meridian, Cormac McCarthy (1985)

With *Blood Meridian*, his fifth novel, Cormac McCarthy departed from the lush mountains of the Appalachian South which had provided the setting for his earlier work, and instead turned to the merciless deserts of the American Southwest in the wake of the Mexican-American War (1846–8). Based on actual events, *Blood Meridian* chronicles the reign of terror of the Glanton Gang, a posse of bounty hunters who repeatedly clashed with Apache and Comanche marauders as they razed fledgling settlements along the new U.S.–Mexico border. The novel offers a scathing indictment of American expansionism and its ideological rationalization, "a counter-narrative to the overly sanitized rhetoric of Manifest Destiny" (Eaton 160). McCarthy's revisionism is particularly concerned with the environmental devastation — epitomized in the extermination of the buffalo — that accompanied the expansion of American borders in the nineteenth century. One of the most startling features of the novel, moreover, is the way its indictment depends upon the development of an environmental consciousness — and not only a human consciousness of the environment, but also the environment's own (seeming) consciousness of its exploitation by human hands.

As *Blood Meridian* insists, territorial expansion is fundamentally driven by the politico-economic imperative to possess and control access to valuable natural resources. The American expansion into what was once the Mexican Northeast was expressly driven by the imperative to mine and cultivate the rich Californian soil. But the expansionist mindset is not content simply to own the land: it must ensure that the land is occupied and its occupants subdued in order to demonstrate dominance over them. *Blood Meridian* incarnates and literalizes this mindset in the form of the monstrous Judge Holden, the *de facto* leader of the Glanton Gang. The Judge is a seven-foot-tall albino with an overpowering intellect, an unquenchable thirst for violence, and a chillingly totalitarian worldview that posits environmental exploitation as a means of assuring one's social superiority:

> Whatever exists, he said. Whatever in creation exists without my knowledge exists without my consent. [... A]nonymous creatures, he said, may seem little or nothing in the world. Yet the smallest crumb can devour us. Any smallest thing beneath yon rock out of men's knowing. Only nature can enslave man and only when the existence of each last [natural] entity is routed out and made to stand naked before him will he be properly suzerain of the earth. [...]
> The Judge placed his hands on the ground. [...] This is my claim, he said. And yet everywhere upon it are pockets of autonomous life. Autonomous. In order for it to be mine nothing must be permitted to occur upon it save by my dispensation. [...] The freedom of birds is an insult to me. I'd have them all in zoos [198–99].

The Judge's swelling sense of his *own* autonomy leaves, at last, no room for the autonomous existence of any other living thing.

The investment of the environment with a sort of consciousness — expressing a resistance to human domination and an interest in human annihilation — is one of the novel's most intriguing features. The narrator of *Blood Meridian* — whoever or whatever that may be — seems at times to construe the environment as a vast, sentient entity that observes, largely antipathetically, the various creatures and objects it contains:

> In the neuter austerity of that terrain all phenomena were bequeathed a strange equality and no one thing nor spider nor stone nor blade of grass could put forth claim to precedence. [... H]ere was nothing more luminous than another and nothing more enshadowed and in the optical democracy of such landscapes all preference is made whimsical and a man and a rock become endowed with unguessed kinship [247].

Moreover, the "optical democracy" mentioned in this passage is not merely a subject for the narrator to remark upon but seems like the very basis of the narrator's own observational practices. In other words, *Blood Meridian* rejects the notion that human beings hold a position in the environment over and above that of anything else they exist alongside; and thus, as David Holloway writes, the novel "diminish[es] language as an agency of human cognition, binding [its] aesthetic ever more tightly to a phenomenal world upon which language might otherwise go to work" (Holloway, "'Optical Democracy'" 192). As such, the narrator of *Blood Meridian* emerges as a consciousness that is at least empathetic to the conscious environment it observes and perhaps even is the environment itself. Mimicking what is described above as the environment's equalization of everything it observes, the narrator registers "[m]inute details and impalpable qualities [... so precisely] that the prejudices of anthropocentric perceptions are disqualified," and instead offers "a kind of perception before or beyond the human. This is not a perspective *upon* the world [...] but an immanent perspective that already *is* the world" (Shaviro 153–54).

Effectively, then, *Blood Meridian* depicts the environment's view of its own exploitation by human beings whose purpose in exploiting it is ultimately to brutalize one another; and to the extent that the novel advances an indictment of American expansionism, environmental exploitation is fundamental to its indictment. Finally, however, McCarthy concedes that the nineteenth century was essentially defined by the institutionalization of such exploitation when he concludes *Blood Meridian* with an epilogue set several decades after the end of the Glanton Gang's narrative, in which a man with a post-hole digger proceeds across an open field to mark the footprint of what will eventually become a fence (337). Fencing, of course, suggests the formal segmentation and occupation of the land and the socio-political legitimization of its exploitation; and by raising these suggestions on its final page *Blood Meridian* anticipates the opening pages of its successor, *All the Pretty Horses*, the first volume in Cormac McCarthy's acclaimed *Border Trilogy*. That novel finds its protagonist, John Grady Cole, disgusted by the ubiquitous fencing of the Southwest and thus compelled to retreat to Mexico on "a quest for reconnection with some undefined but older, notionally purer or more authentic landscape" (Holloway, *Late Modernism* 61)—ironically, and futilely, since *Blood Meridian* demonstrates that absolute environmental purity is unattainable for human beings insofar as the source of that impurity is humankind.—Daniel Davis Wood

BIBLIOGRAPHY

Eaton, Mark A. "Dis(re)membered Bodies: Cormac McCarthy's Border Fiction." *Modern Fiction Studies* 49.1 (Spring 2003): 155–80.
Holloway, David. *The Late Modernism of Cormac McCarthy*. London: Praeger, 2002.
_____. "Modernism, Nature, and Utopia: Another Look at 'Optical Democracy' in Cormac McCarthy's Western Quartet." *Southern Quarterly* 38.3 (Spring 2000). 186–205.
Kollin, Susan. "Genre and the Geographies of Violence: Cormac McCarthy and the Contemporary Western." *Contemporary Literature* 42.3 (Autumn 2001): 557–88.
McCarthy, Cormac. *Blood Meridian*. 1985. New York: Vintage, 1992.
Shaviro, Steven. "'The Very Life of the Darkness': A Reading of *Blood Meridian*." *Perspectives on Cormac McCarthy*

(Revised Edition). Ed. Edwin T. Arnold and Dianne C. Luce. Jackson: University Press of Mississippi, 1999. 145–58.

The Road,
Cormac McCarthy (2006)

In Cormac McCarthy's post-apocalyptic novel *The Road*, the world is in tatters and ruins. The remains of an advanced civil society are visible in rare Coke cans, wobbly-wheeled grocery carts, occasional jars of food, and a skein of empty roads, bridges, and streets that wend through the blasted terrain. However, the novel is not a science-fiction allegory of a world like ours, but rather a gloomy prediction of a near future that is very much grounded in our present.

The nameless man and boy who we follow throughout the novel are tasked with "carrying the fire." This means avoiding the roving cannibals and thieves who inhabit the wasted terrain. Fire might serve as a metaphor for morality or civility in the novel; for the most part, however, fire simply functions on a literal level, as the two main characters try to avoid freezing on their quest south, where they hope it will be warmer—and perhaps more civilized. Along the way, the man and boy encounter sparsely distributed but familiar objects, suggesting that late 20th-century American culture has resulted in an apocalyptic landscape of remains.

Early in the novel the man and boy encounter an abandoned supermarket with "a few old cars in the trashstrewn parking lot" (22). This is a standard landscape setting for the novel, and the pervasive emptiness of the geography causes the remains to appear in stark relief. For example, in the supermarket the man makes a precious discovery:

> By the door were two softdrink machines that had been tilted over into the floor and opened with a prybar. Coins everywhere in the ash. He sat and ran his hand around in the works of the gutted machines and in the second one it closed over a cold metal cylinder. He withdrew his hand slowly and sat looking at a Coca Cola.
> What is it, Papa?
> It's a treat. For you.
> What is it?
> Here. Sit down.
> He slipped the boy's knapsack straps loose and set the pack on the floor behind him and he put his thumbnail under the aluminum clip on the top of the can and opened it. He leaned his nose to the slight fizz coming from the can and then handed it to the boy. Go ahead, he said.
> The boy took the can. It's bubbly, he said.
> Go ahead.
> He looked at his father and then tilted the can

and drank. He sat there thinking about it. It's really good, he said [23].

The narrative buildup to this scene causes the Coke can to be a glistening feature in the overwhelmingly drab topography of the novel. However, the can is hardly a good omen. With its stark singularity and its "slight fizz," the soda drink functions as a bittersweet reminder of mass production and consumer culture — indeed, in this scene the man and boy take pleasure in the very sort of object that has tilted humans toward a catastrophic contemporaneity.

Later in the novel, the man ponders the de-linking taking place between his memory of the world and the world that remains:

The names of birds. Things to eat. Finally the names of things one believed to be true. More fragile than he would have thought. How much was gone already? The sacred idiom shorn of its referents and so of its reality. Drawing down like something trying to preserve heat. In time to wink out forever [89].

Here, the existence of things is directly tied to their names; and when the signifiers go, the signified goes with them. The prediction is not hopeful for a world of things whose idiom has lost its value. Shortly thereafter, we can see the process taking place:

He looked at the boy. I've got to go for more wood, he said. I'll be in the neighborhood. Okay?
Where's the neighborhood.
It just means I wont be far.
Okay [95].

The word "neighborhood" has lost its meaning for the boy, for whom "neighborhood" means nothing in a landscape of dead wood and charred roads. The idea of the neighborhood remains intact for the man, but the boy contradicts this idea, and shows it to be a mere remnant of thought, no longer remaining as material reality. This disappearance of neighborhoods is paradoxically good news for the environment (as suburban neighborhoods tended to result in dark ecology), but also bad news for the human survivors, who are not used to existing outside the conveniences of advanced consumer society. The boy represents a transitional stage of the species, adapting to a world where certain words have lost their meaning.

In *The Road* we continually witness shifts between prior and current meanings, and these changes are often calcified in the built environment. For instance:

They passed through towns with messages scrawled on the billboards. The billboards had been whited out with thin coats of paint in order to write on them and through the paint could be

seen a pale palimpsest of advertisements for goods which no longer existed [127–128].

The billboards and their layered meanings indicate what the narrative calls "the richness of a vanished world" (139) — this is a fraught richness, a textual surface that is both dense with meaning yet also evacuated, and losing significance by the day. The narrative meanders through this world in a documentary fashion, noting "odd things scattered by the side of the road. Electrical appliances, furniture. Tools" (199). Toward the end of the novel, the scenes continue to degrade, time turning into "days sloughed past uncounted and uncalendared. Along the interstate in the distance long lines of charred and rusting cars. The raw rims of the wheels sitting in a stiff gray sludge of melted rubber, in blackened rings of wire" (273). McCarthy employs the close attention of environmental aesthetics, but reorients this tactic and brings it to bear on the remains of Americana.

At one point along the way, the man and the boy discuss the fate of "the states" and the geophysical tenacity of "the road." While the state-level governmental systems of the U.S. have collapsed, the road remains with nothing to "uproot" it, at least not "for quite a while," as the man remarks. This conversation is sparked by a physical arrangement of the roadmap that the man and the boy use to travel south:

The tattered oil company roadmap had once been taped together but now it was just sorted into leaves and numbered with crayon in the corners for their assembly. He sorted through the limp pages and spread out those that answered to their location.
We cross a bridge here. It looks to be about eight miles or so. This is the river. Going east. We follow the road here along the eastern slope of the mountains. These are our roads, the black lines on the map. The state roads.
Why are they the state roads?
Because they belong to the states. What used to be called the states.
But there's not any more states?
No.
What happened to them?
I dont know exactly. That's a good question.
But the roads are still there.
Yes. For a while.
How long a while?
I dont know. Maybe quite a while. There's nothing to uproot them so they should be okay for a while.
But there wont be any cars or trucks on them.
No.
Okay [42–43].

The Road demonstrates how the degradation of civil society cannot be disentangled from the ecological baseline of the world: for the man and the boy, the icy rains and gray skies are as hostile and looming as the scattered hoards of other people who threaten to rob, kill, and/or eat them. There is a productive ambiguity about the novel in the sense that the cause of the ecological catastrophe is kept obscure, thus allowing for the human presence to be a flashpoint for apocalyptic imagery, and also a sort of mere medium through which we understand apocalyptic effects (climate change, food scarcity, unchecked violence, contaminated water, etc.). In other words, in *The Road* the ecological catastrophe has both *already occurred*, and is *ongoing*.— Christopher Schaberg

BIBLIOGRAPHY

Gwinner, Donovan. "'Everything uncoupled from its shoring': Quandaries of Epistemology and Ethics in *The Road*." *Cormac McCarthy: Continuum Studies in Contemporary North American Fiction*, Ed. Sara Spurgeon. New York: Continuum, 2011.

Kollin, Susan. "'Barren, silent, godless': Ecodisaster and the Post-Abundant Landscape in *The Road*." *Cormac McCarthy: Continuum Studies in Contemporary North American Fiction*, Ed. Sara Spurgeon. New York: Continuum, 2011.

McCarthy, Cormac. *The Road*. New York: Vintage, 2006.

Phillips, Dana. "He Ought Not Have Done It: McCarthy and Apocalypse." *Cormac McCarthy: Continuum Studies in Contemporary North American Fiction*, Ed. Sara Spurgeon. New York: Continuum, 2011.

McKibben, William Ernest "Bill" (1960–)

Bill McKibben was born in 1960 in Lexington, Massachusetts. His father was a well-known journalist for newspapers such as the Wall Street Journal and the Boston Globe, and McKibben followed his own love of words into his father's profession by covering the basketball team for his local paper while in high school. He received his B.A. from Harvard University, and while there, was president of *The Harvard Crimson* newspaper. After graduation he joined the staff of *The New Yorker* for a five-year stint (1982– 87) writing the "Talk of the Town" column. After leaving *The New Yorker*, Bill relocated to the Adirondack Mountains of upstate New York, where he continued to write as a freelance journalist and to take on book-length projects. To date he has written 12 books and countless essays appearing in publications such as *Mother Jones*, *The Washington Post*, and the *New York Review of Books*, among others. He has received such prestigious awards as the Guggenheim and Lyndhurst Fellowships, and the Lannan Prize for non-fiction writing. He currently resides in Vermont with his wife Sue Halpern, and is a scholar in residence at Middlebury College.

McKibben is one of the most famous American environmental writers, and yet his foray into specifically environmental topics was almost an accident. While writing at *The New Yorker*, McKibben learned that "great journalism could produce critical thinking," and he was content to use his passion for research, investigation, and writing to further explore and unveil the tension between the individual and the community through other pressing practical problems such as homelessness and the manifold ills of consumerism (McKibben 2008). Through his early journalistic work, McKibben elaborated the virtues of community membership and accountability by focusing on local solutions for local problems. Ironically, McKibben's own interest in the local nearly kept him happily entrenched in writing about particularly urban problems. Only upon leaving *The New Yorker* and its urban oasis for a rural setting did he begin chronicling and analyzing his own experiences of nature, and thus the Adirondack Mountains moulded McKibben into their advocate by exploiting his greatest strengths: his focus on experience and the local — even as one's location changes over a lifetime — and his ability to relate his passions to others through mesmerizing and personable prose.

The twin hallmarks of McKibben's environmental writing are his focus on experience, and his nearly archaeological investigation of the cultural and philosophical underpinnings of Western thought that have led to current American attitudes toward the environment. In his first and best-known book, THE END OF NATURE (1989), McKibben introduced global warming to a skeptical American readership, digesting an immense amount of scientific data and rendering it intelligible for lay readers, while also interspersing this hard data with his own subjective experiences of nature, and those of American nature writers such as HENRY DAVID THOREAU, WENDELL BERRY, and RACHEL CARSON. And so, from the early period of his environmental writing, the history of thinking about nature and experiencing it were yoked together.

After his first book, McKibben continued writing about the environment but within the context of broader social problems. In *The Age of Missing Information* (1992) McKibben compared a day of watching television to a day spent in the wilderness, noting the different kinds of attention required and the various genres of information that are available to the television watcher and the person experiencing nature. In *Hope, Human and Wild* he writes about the ways that people in other countries live lightly on the earth, while in *The Comforting Whirlwind: God, Job, and the Scale of Creation* he approaches our attitudes toward the environment from an explicitly religious perspective (THE BIBLE). In his later works,

McKibben tackles the challenges of human overpopulation, local versus global economies, and the potential dangers of genetic engineering, while also offering readers highly literary accounts of his own athletic experiences of cross-country skiing and hiking through New England, in which he muses on embodied human existence and mortality (McKibben 2000).

Throughout his writing on the environment, McKibben has constantly returned to the patient, painstaking, almost archaeological effort of unearthing lost aspects of the American experience of nature, and connecting thought about environmental problems with action in the world. For him, technology and the pace of modern life have served to narrow the American experience of the natural world. In order to expand the possibilities for experience (and action), McKibben has not only written about his own experiences of nature, but encouraged and organized environmental activism in his community in Vermont, through his position at Middlebury College, and through forging new location-diverse communities of activism via the internet.—Kristel Clayville

BIBLIOGRAPHY

McKibben, Bill. *The Bill McKibben Reader: Pieces from an Active Life*. New York: Holt, 2008.
_____. *Long Distance: A Year of Living Strenuously*. New York: Simon & Schuster, 2000.
Rustin, Susanna. "A Life in Writing: Bill McKibben." *The Guardian* on the Web. Available online, URL: http://www.guardian.co.uk/books/2010/dec/06/bill-mckibben-interview.

The End of Nature,
William McKibben (1989)

The End of Nature, William "Bill" McKibben's first book, was published in 1989 and reprinted with an introduction by the author in 1999 and 2006. It is part of the distinctly American genre of Environmental Apocalyptic literature (APOCALYPTIC FICTION), while also resonating with the literature of the Wilderness Debate, which is an ongoing conversation among academics and environmentalists about the value of human life against the backdrop of endangered ecologies. While certainly at home in this genre and conversation, the book also blends scientific and philosophical writing with autobiography, provides an overview of the environmental movement to date, and is the first book to explain the science behind global warming to a general audience (xiii).

The main argument of *The End of Nature* is that nature and the very idea of nature have ended, due to the imprint of human activity on all areas of the wild. Not only does the end of nature have an effect on the physical world, but it also drastically changes the way humans think with and about nature. Thus, McKibben's main claim is organized around human effects on nature, which create a feedback loop that forever alters the way that humans are able to think about themselves and the world around them. Unlike HENRY DAVID THOREAU or JOHN MUIR before him, McKibben cannot take for granted that the sky will always be safe from the human destruction of nature; instead, he takes their observations on the inviolability of the sky as the starting point for his own argument that the end of nature has arrived, by focusing specifically on the human impact on the atmosphere.

The End of Nature is divided into two parts: the present and the near future. In the first part, McKibben explains the science behind the atmospheric changes, the interactions between chloroflurocarbons (CFCs) and ozone, the problems with carbon dioxide and methane and the vicious feedback loops that make tackling these problems nearly impossible. McKibben also describes the changes in polluting technology that have developed since RACHEL CARSON wrote *SILENT SPRING*. Traditional pollutants, like DDT, had local effects, but new atmospheric pollutants have global effects. The immediate consequences of pollution are a global problem, but may no longer belong to any particular locale. In addition, human power has transcended human presence. Tampering with the atmosphere means that humans can control the weather in places that are currently uninhabited. Thus, even the idea of nature is now extinct because all wild places have been "humanized."

In the second part of the book, McKibben predicts that we will follow one of two paths to solve our environmental problems: the path of defiance or the path of humility. The path of defiance is marked by our continued reflex to master nature and to adapt nature to our needs, rather than adapting ourselves to nature. This path is undergirded by a deep and unreflective anthropocentrism leading ultimately to genetic engineering. While we once only tried to dominate nature from the outside, this will mark a move toward dominating nature from the inside. McKibben argues that this is the second end of nature, but that this end is more devastating because it is deliberate, while the first end of nature was accidental and naïve on our part. In contrast, the path of humility requires us to think of ourselves as merely one species among many, which leads McKibben to discuss environmental philosophies, such as biocentrism, the Gaia Hypothesis, and Deep Ecology, all of which involve a commitment to austerity. McKibben notes that he and his wife have started to "prune and snip [their] desires" in the wake of the greenhouse effect (159). McKibben admits to wanting more and more in his own life; being austere is not easy, yet we must not allow our desires to be the engine of our actions if we are to halt global warming.

Ultimately, McKibben fears that we will choose the path of defiance due to the paralysis and inertia of affluence, the near exponential increase in population, and social problems like poverty, which pit environmental concerns against humanistic ones. Nonetheless, he urges us, even more passionately as a result, to rely on our special gift of reason to tackle this problem, but to couple it with restraint. Unlike other creatures, "we could limit ourselves voluntarily and *choose* to remain God's creatures instead of making ourselves gods (182)." The only hope McKibben offers us is that through reason, restraint and austerity we can circumvent, if not avoid, the second end of nature.

Running parallel to his main argument about the human impact on the environment is an argument about the changing environment's impact on humans. McKibben's choice of temporal divisions for his book is not superficial. He argues that we have completely broken with the past; that our present is not different merely in degree, but in *kind* from the historical periods that preceded it. He points to the limits of human reason and the end of certain modes of human thinking, describing the innate human perception of space and time as inadequate to recognize and respond to the current environmental problems. We think our natural world will always change gradually, but that is because it has in the past. All of pre-history and history as we know it has shown that nature changes very slowly, but we are speeding up the process of change. Our previous thoughts of nature as eternal and separate from us are being overridden by concrete changes in the world, and this clash of ideas tests our perceptions. Unfortunately, our ability to perceive changes in nature cannot keep pace with our ability to augment nature or develop new technologies to master it. We think of nature as permanent and stable, and these enduring conditions of nature allow us to abstract the concrete ideas of "permanence" and "stability" for conceptual use in other areas of our lives. But without the concrete conditions, the abstract ideas are also endangered. In addition, nature has played a large role in ancient and contemporary religions, so we stand to lose the naturalistic language that we use to describe the indescribable. Eventually, McKibben worries that our language itself will suffer due to a lack of external physical referents, and consequently we may not be able even to *think* of ourselves as part of something greater than ourselves. Underlying both of McKibben's arguments are firm convictions about the definition and value of wildness and the embeddedness of humans in a natural world to which they owe everything — even the ability to communicate meaningfully with one another.

The End of Nature was well-received by popular audiences, and is widely thought to be the *Silent Spring* of its generation. That said, McKibben has received some criticism for merely acknowledging arguments against his position — that humans are part of nature so everything they do is natural, and that humans have been interfering with nature since tools and agriculture were invented — rather than fully explaining or dismantling these arguments. Furthermore, McKibben claims not to be making a moral argument, yet his apocalyptic rhetoric, and the language of sin that he uses to describe human action in nature and humanity's future orientation, as well as his musings on God, all bear unmistakable traces of a prophet warning humanity to pay more — and more humble — attention to the starry heavens above. — Kristel Clayville

BIBLIOGRAPHY

McKibben, Bill. *The Bill McKibben Reader: Pieces from an Active Life*. New York: Holt, 2008.
_____. *The End of Nature*. New York: Random House, 2006.

McPhee, John (1931–)

John McPhee's career as a highly respected and rigorous writer of literary nonfiction culminated with the publication of *Annals of the Former World*, for which he received the Pulitzer Prize in 1999. *Annals* comprises five pieces that McPhee published over two decades, and it enunciates themes explored throughout his work: the intricacy of human entanglement in natural ecosystems, and the abiding primacy of Nature over the brevity of human history.

John McPhee was born in Princeton, New Jersey, to Harry Roemer McPhee, a sports physician at Princeton University, and Mary Ziegler McPhee, a schoolteacher. Except for a few years spent in New York and abroad, his life has been centered in Princeton, and he still teaches one course in "The Literature of Fact" at the University. He attended the Princeton public schools, where he explored the foundations of his craft through his high school English teacher's demanding composition assignments. To this day he tightly structures his prose, reads aloud while composing, and edits scrupulously — even reading his final drafts aloud to his wife, Yolanda Whitman. McPhee believes, however, that his most influential education was at Camp Keewaydin, a summer camp for boys near Middlebury, Vermont, where he was a camper and then counselor for 16 years. So many of his subjects derive from the love of the outdoors developed at the camp, that he characterizes of some of his books as "Keewaydin stories" (Pearson 3–5).

After graduating from high school in 1948 McPhee attended Deerfield Academy, where his teachers helped him recognize his vocation as a writer. In 1949 he enrolled at Princeton, where he wrote for the University's literary magazines, honing his style and descriptive skill in hopes of one day writing for *The New Yorker*. After receiving his B.A. in English in 1953, he studied literature at Cambridge and traveled in England for a year, a trip that provided the subject of a freelance piece for *The New Yorker*, "Basketball and Beefeaters" (1963). Its publication prompted a change in McPhee's career as a freelancer and reporter for *Time*, and in 1965 he became a staff writer for the magazine he long admired, a position he has held ever since. His first assignment covered all–American basketball star Bill Bradley, who became the subject of his first book, *A Sense of Place* (1965) (Howarth 24–27).

Since then McPhee's career has unfolded at the prodigious rate of one book every 16 months (johnmcphee.com). McPhee emerged among the impassioned voices of the 1960's literary nonfictionists, such as John Hersey and RACHEL CARSON, many of whom were reexamining human relationships to the environment. McPhee explores his subjects, from oranges to bark canoes, with a penchant for factual detail that some find daunting. This scientific disposition is manifest in his meticulous descriptions of technologies and geographies, especially as he traverses the fortieth parallel with geologists in *Annals* or navigates the Alaskan wilderness in *Coming into the Country* (1975). Such descriptions give his work a masterful sense of place; however, McPhee sees his writing as primarily character-driven. He spends months traveling with intriguing people, often in remote settings, such as the disappearing New Jersey pine forests in THE PINE BARRENS (1968), Georgia's threatened rural hills in *Pieces of the Frame* (1975), and the vanishing Louisiana bayous in *The Control of Nature* (1989).

Critical reception of McPhee's work has been overwhelmingly positive, with three general criticisms: that he praises his heroes too much, that he writes too often about rocks, and that he does not take stands on controversial issues (Howarth 36). Critic Brian Turner argues, however, that McPhee is a highly rhetorical writer, whose work intends to persuade through its skillful arrangement. Rather than adopt a polemical or editorial tone, McPhee instead uses his characters to voice the intricacy of environ-

mental controversies, and he orchestrates the fragments of the story to appeal to a reader's intellect. While other literary nonfictionists foreground their own presence in a text, McPhee believes that "the reader is the most creative thing in a piece" (Pearson 18). In his groundbreaking *Encounters with the Archdruid* (1971), for example, McPhee travels with Sierra Club Director David Brower, chronicling the militant conservationist's encounters with miners, developers, and dam builders, whose views McPhee represents with equal insight. With this reverence for complexity, McPhee invites creative readers to assess the relationship of Brower, his rivals and themselves, to the environment, through a critical yet empathetic lens.—R. Lindsay Dunne

BIBLIOGRAPHY

Howarth, William. "Introducing John McPhee." *Coming into McPhee Country*. Eds. O. Alan Weltzein and Susan N. Maher. Salt Lake City: University of Utah Press, 2003. 19–53.
"John McPhee: 1999 Pulitzer Prize Winner." Available online. URL: www.johnmcphee.com. Accessed 15 March, 2009.
McPhee, John. *Annals of the Former World*. New York: Farrar, Straus, & Giroux, 1998.
_____. *Coming into the Country*. New York: Farrar, Straus, & Giroux, 1977.
_____. *The Control of Nature*. New York: Farrar, Straus, & Giroux, 1989.
_____. *Encounters with the Archdruid*. New York: Farrar, Straus, & Giroux, 1971.
_____. *Pieces of the Frame*. New York: Farrar, Straus, & Giroux, 1975.
_____. *The Pine Barrens*. New York: Farrar, Straus, & Giroux, 1968.
Pearson, Michael. *John McPhee*. New York: Twain, 1997.
Sims, Norman (Ed). "The Literary Journalists" and "John McPhee." *The Literary Journalists*. New York: Ballantine Books, 1984. 1–28.
Turner, Brian. "Giving Good Reasons: Environmental Appeals in the Nonfiction of John McPhee." *Coming into McPhee Country*. Eds. O. Alan Weltzein and Susan N. Maher. Salt Lake City: University of Utah Press, 2003. 162–184.

The Pine Barrens, John McPhee (1968)

John McPhee's fourth work of literary nonfiction, *The Pine Barrens*, is a portrait of life in the remote and often misunderstood Pinelands of southern New Jersey, "the halfway point between Boston and Richmond — the geographical center of the developing megalopolis" that will one day connect the entire northeastern corridor (5). Yet, the area sustains a unique culture, language, and lifestyle, despite the fast-paced American society that encroaches on its borders. In the text's masterful descriptions of the woods, and its sensitive and humorous portrayal of the people known as "pineys," it marks a significant change in McPhee's critical preoccupations. By the mid–1960s the young writer had published books about basketball player Bill Bradley, the orange-growing trade, and elite private school headmaster Frank Boyden. In *The Pine Barrens*, however, Mc-Phee's interest in place moves from the sidelines to the center of his work, where it has remained ever since.

As in all literary nonfiction, the structure of *The Pine Barrens* is key to understanding its purpose. In an interview with Norman Sims, McPhee explains that "Structure is the juxtaposition of parts, the way in which two parts of a piece of writing, merely by lying side-by-side, can comment on each other without a word spoken" (Sims 13). *The Pine Barrens* has a simple form compared to many of McPhee's later spiraling or tri-part works. Eight of the book's nine chapters address some aspect of the Pines' environment or culture, from its natural topography and botany to its economy, history and folklore, with each chapter focusing on the intersections of the unique material, personal, and social meanings of the place. That this 1,000 square miles of wilderness could even exist, let along thrive, in the middle of the most densely populated state in the Union is itself an improbability; and the writer portrays its vitality and obscurity as almost magical, a place where towns arise and just as quickly vanish, where "God's water" runs pure and untapped just below one's feet, where the sandy roads seem to shift continuously, and where only the fabled residents can navigate the woods without fear of being lost. The rarity of untainted wilderness is here juxtaposed with the proximity of rampant civilization to convey the central argument of *The Pine Barrens*: the land itself has given rise to the Pines culture, and this environment — in which people and nature count equally — is now threatened by deforestation.

We see clearly in *The Pine Barrens* the trademarks of McPhee's now well-known approach to exploring environmental conflict. While some critics have argued that he refuses to take sides on political issues, Brian Turner suggests that McPhee backgrounds himself and instead uses his characters to communicate the nuances of a place and the complexity of environmental controversy surrounding it. In order to capture a sense of life in the Pine Barrens McPhee takes readers into the home and life of Frederick Chambers Brown, a 79-year-old resident of the town of Hog Wallow (population: 25), located at the center of the Pines. The scene in which McPhee meets Fred demonstrates the former's keen observation and intuitive selection of telling details, what Lawrence Buell would call those "quotidian, idiosyncratic intimacies that go with 'place'" (Buell 63).

For example, McPhee finds Fred's house near a cranberry bog in the woods, and writes that what attracted him to it was the pump in the yard: "It was something of a wonder that I noticed the pump," he comments, "because there were among other things, eight automobiles in the yard ... and maybe a thousand other things" (6–7). Readers are likely to remember the first sight of Fred Chambers, "seated, eating a pork chop" for breakfast, "dressed in a white sleeveless shirt, ankle-top shoes, and undershorts" (7), in a house with seven current calendars, a meat cleaver, and a billy club on the peeling floral walls (10). Through conversations and travels with Fred, Fred's taciturn neighbor Bill Wasovwich, and the Buzbys, who own the general store in Chatsworth (population: 306), McPhee depicts a people who are friendly and welcoming to those who respect their woods, but suspicious of outsiders who may criticize or threaten their way of life.

It is important to note that while *The Pine Barrens* carefully chronicles this way of life, it does not adopt the detached style of traditional ethnography. Mc-Phee brings an empathetic and respectful eye to his interactions with the residents of the Pines, and challenges the stereotypes held by many in New Jersey of the "degeneracy" and "mental deficiency" of the residents (47). McPhee relates how, in 1913, Elizabeth Kite, "a psychological researcher, published a report called 'The Pineys,' which had resulted from two years of visits" in the Pine Barrens. Though Miss Kite, who became known and loved by many in the Pines, was studying a small segment of the population of interest to her psychological research on what was then called "feeble-mindedness," her report was promulgated by the press and some politicians as a general statement about life in that area of the state. The stigma has never worn off. McPhee deliberately counters the stereotype by showing that the Pines' people sustain a fully functional culture of their own. Far from the "hostile and semi-literate people" of the stereotype, they are revealed to possess a rich history and folklore, and a unique intelligence born of their intimacy with the land. For example, while many outsiders believe that shiftless "pineys" cannot keep a steady job, they are actually continuously working in harmony with the economic cycles provided by their environment: "sphagnum in the spring, berries in the summer, coaling when the weather is cold. With the plentitude of the woodland around them ... pineys are bored with the idea of doing the same thing all year long, in every weather" (55). At the end of Chapter 3 McPhee lets his characters themselves speak for the worthiness of their lifestyle, and as one resident tells him, "It's a privilege to live in these woods" (58).

While the first eight chapters focus primarily on the Pines people themselves, the ninth, rather ironically entitled "Vision," steps outside to describe some of the development plans proposed over the last century for new cities in the Pines, including one in the mid-sixties for a jetport and a city of a quarter million people. However, no grand-scale, controlled development has ever come to fruition, McPhee observes, while "over a million people have bought or otherwise acquired lots in the Pine Barrens on which no houses have ever been built" (147). It seems from this history of failed plans that the Pines would be safe from destruction, that the conservationists and the pineys would preserve their land and their culture with it. But what McPhee sees as the real threat to the area is not the lunacy of grand-scale, controlled development, but the small, unregulated building that is chiseling away at the edges of the woods. While many have accused McPhee of hedging his environmental advocacy later in his career, he does not veil his stance in this early work, musing in closing that "people may one day look back upon the final stages of the development of the great unbroken Eastern City and be able to say at what moment all remaining undeveloped land should have been considered no longer a potential asset to individuals but an asset of the society at large — perhaps a social necessity" (56). *The Pine Barrens* thus emerges as McPhee's first piece of social ecology, insisting on the importance of wilderness places and the cultures they support, and laying the foundation for decades of work to follow. — R. Lindsay Dunne

BIBLIOGRAPHY

Buell, Lawrence. *The Future of Environmental Criticism: Environmental Crisis and Literary Imagination*. Malden, MA: Blackwell, 2005.

McPhee, John. *The Pine Barrens*. New York: Farrar, Straus, & Giroux, 1967.

Sims, Norman. *The Literary Journalists*. New York: Ballantine Books, 1984.

Turner, Brian. "Giving Good Reason: Environmental Appeals in the Nonfiction of John McPhee." *Coming into McPhee Country: John McPhee and the Art of Literary Nonfiction*. Eds. O. Alan Weltzien and Susan N. Maher. Salt Lake City: University of Utah Press, 2003. 162–84.

Melville, Herman (1819–1891)

Considered one of the world's great writers of the sea, Herman Melville engaged with the environment in complex and sometimes contradictory ways. Born in 1819, in New York City, Melville hailed from cultivated stock, a descendent of English and Dutch families both celebrated for their roles in the Revolutionary War. The third of eight children born to Allan Melvill and Maria Gansevoort Melvill, Herman enjoyed a brief period of relative prosperity during his early childhood. His gentleman-merchant father, however, squandered the family fortune, suffered business collapse and bankruptcy, and died by the time Herman was 12 years old. Forced by financial difficulties and debt to quit his schooling, Melville tried his hand at a number of odd jobs, such as bank clerk, bookkeeper in his older brother's soon-to-fail fur business, field hand on his uncle's Berkshire farm, and teacher. In 1839 Melville shipped from New York to Liverpool and back as a sailor aboard the merchant vessel *St. Lawrence*, and began a life-long infatuation with the sea. Soon after returning from a trip where he knocked about the Great Lakes, the Mississippi River, and the frontier towns of Illinois, Melville embarked on an eventful second cruise, one which would find him away from home for nearly four years, and greatly broaden his connection with the world at large.

On January 3, 1841, Melville sailed from New Bedford to the South Seas on the maiden voyage of the whaleship *Acushnet*, but after six months at sea he deserted ship with Richard Tobias Green at Nukuheva harbor in the Marquesas Islands of the South Pacific. Here Melville spent roughly one month of rather liberal captivity with the natives of the Typee (Taipi) valley, before escaping to sail aboard the Australian whaling ship *Lucy Ann*. Imprisoned in Tahiti for his alleged mutinous behavior in a shipboard revolt, Melville subsequently absconded from another lax confinement to wander the island and the neighboring Eimeo, afterwards boarding yet another whaleship, Nantucket's *Charles and Henry*. Closing the book on experiences that would furnish his first two novels, *Typee* (1846) and *Omoo* (1847), Melville shipped aboard the U.S. Navy frigate *United States* in Honolulu, and reached port in Boston on October 3, 1844.

Returning home, Melville married Elizabeth Shaw (daughter of Chief Justice Lemuel Shaw), with whom he would have four children, and began a prolific writing career that would see him pen nine novels and numerous short stories between the years 1845 and 1857. Although his early novels were bestsellers, Melville's later works — fraught with metaphysics, philosophical digressions, and sharp social criticisms — failed to win public acclaim. Earning little more than $10,000 for his collected works during his lifetime, Melville never managed to support himself through his writing, a fact that eventually forced him to take a job at the New York customs office in 1866. Suffering bouts of heavy depression, compounded by the deaths of his sons Malcolm and Stanwix, Melville spent the latter portion of his life writing poetry that few would read, and sank into virtual anonymity by the time of his death in 1891. Melville's literary fortunes experienced a reversal during the "Revival" of the 1920s, however, which witnessed the posthumous publishing of *Billy Budd* in 1924, and found both the author and his prose-masterpiece *MOBY-DICK* (1851) moving toward the center of the American canon.

Designated a central writer of American Romanticism, as well as a proto-modernist whose work foreshadows the literary innovations of writers such as James Joyce, Melville has since found recognition for an environmental vision considered to have anticipated the twentieth-century work of ALDO LEOPOLD, among others. In his early fiction Melville often positions the nature of the South Seas in terms of a perpetual garden paradise. Describing constant climates, enchanted wilds, and Adam-and-Eve–like natives in *Typee* and *Omoo*, he envisions a static environment akin to a new Eden. Elsewhere, however, nature is cast as a sinister lapsarian presence, as in *The Piazza Tales'* (1856) "The Encantadas." Chronicling the nightmare-inducing Galapagos tortoises, the "special curse" (765) of eternal desolation, and the volcanic wasteland of Narborough, he writes that "In no world but a fallen one could such lands exist" (766). Moreover, despite Melville's long-standing fascination with the polar opposites of nature-as-garden and nature-as-fallen-world, there is evidence of a larger and more complicated environmental understanding in his early fiction, as is indicated by his description of the active and ongoing creation of the Coral Islands in *Omoo*, as well as his observations regarding the rapid and fatal spread of the scrub guava bush following its foreign introduction.

In addition to supplying such ethico-religious conceits, nature also figures for Melville as a reflection of the human mind. This TRANSCENDENTALIST approach appears at times in *Moby-Dick*, and again in *Pierre* (1852), in which nature operates as the "supplier of that cunning alphabet" whereby "man reads his own peculiar lesson according to his own peculiar mind and mood" (397). In a separate register, nature — particularly the sea — also functions as an agonistic arena of Darwinian violence, as evoked by *Moby-Dick*'s "universal cannibalism of the sea; all whose creatures prey upon each other, carrying on eternal war since the world began" (1087). If not utterly hostile, nature is at best indifferent to human existence in the latter scenario. Humans are not elevated above nature, but rather are part of— indeed, locked into — the fray. Melville's tendency to destabilize human dominion, in fact, is the environmental stance for which he is most lauded. In *Mardi* (1849) Melville's philosophical mouthpiece Babbalanja claims that "'Mardi [The World] is not wholly ours.

We are the least populous part of creation. To say nothing of other tribes, a census of the herring would find us far in the minority. And what life is to us, — sour or sweet, — so is it to them'" (1234). Introducing a doctrine of interspecies equality, Melville extends the notion of a shared planet even beyond the animal kingdom: "'Mardi is alive to its axis. [...] Think you there is no sensation in being a rock? — To exist, is to be; to be, is to be something'" (1114). Mardi, an archipelago microcosm of the globe, is a thoroughly interdependent web of human, animal, and elemental life.

In his most famous case of environmentally aware writing, *Moby-Dick*, Melville is credited for creating in the eponymous White Whale, the only nonhuman character in the nineteenth-century American literary canon to rival the centrality of the pond in THOREAU's WALDEN. A naturalist text of sorts, the novel works through its cetological chapters to educate the reader about whales, while at the same time challenging the species line between human and nonhuman. By applying human characteristics to whales in general (in chapters such as "The Grand Armada" and "Schools & Schoolmasters") and Moby Dick in particular, Melville fosters "a unity between humanity and nature, a unity derived from an emotional and social kinship" (Schultz 100). This unity is undercut, of course, by the bloodshed of the numerous whale hunts; and if *Moby-Dick* is about an interspecies fraternity, it is no less a statement about nature's ability to strike back at the hand that oppresses. Although the White Whale becomes a destroyer in the end, the novel suggests that the humans aboard the *Pequod* might represent the more bestial and destructive species of the two. This is not a position that Melville ever reached unequivocally in his work, however, and his environmental legacy remains, like the environment he himself depicted, a vastly complex, interdependent, ever-unfolding and impressing enigma. — Scott Moore

BIBLIOGRAPHY

Buell, Lawrence. "*Moby-Dick* and the Hierarchies of Nation, Culture, and Species." *Writing for an Endangered World: Literature, Culture, and Environment in the U.S. and Beyond.* Cambridge, MA: Belknap Press of Harvard University Press, 2001. 205–214.

Delbanco, Andrew. *Melville: His World and Work.* 2005. New York: Vintage, 2006.

Melville, Herman. *Mardi and a Voyage Thither.* 1849. From *Melville: Typee, Omoo, Mardi.* Eds. Harrison Hayford, Hershel Parker, and G. Thomas Tanselle. New York: Library of America, 1982. 647–1316.

_____. *Moby-Dick, or The Whale.* 1851. From *Melville: Redburn, White-Jacket, Moby-Dick.* Eds. Harrison Hayford, Hershel Parker, and G. Thomas Tanselle. New York: Library of America, 1983. 771–1408.

_____. *The Piazza Tales.* 1856. From *Melville: Pierre, Israel*

Potter, *The Piazza Tales, The Confidence-Man, Uncollected Prose, Billy Budd*. Eds. Harrison Hayford, Hershel Parker, and G. Thomas Tanselle. New York: Library of America, 1984. 616–833.

_____. *Pierre, or the Ambiguities*. 1852. From *Melville: Pierre, Israel Potter, The Piazza Tales, The Confidence-Man, Uncollected Prose, Billy Budd*. Eds. Harrison Hayford, Hershel Parker, and G. Thomas Tanselle. New York: Library of America, 1984. 1–421.

Moore, Bryan L. "Herman Melville and Anti-Anthropocentric Personification." *Ecology and Literature: Ecocentric Personification from Antiquity to the Twenty-First Century*. New York: Palgrave Macmillan, 2008. 117–120.

Parker, Hershel. *Herman Melville: A Biography Volume 1, 1819–1851*. Baltimore: Johns Hopkins University Press, 1996.

_____. *Herman Melville: A Biography Volume 2, 1851–1891*. Baltimore: Johns Hopkins University Press, 2002.

Schultz, Elizabeth. "Melville's Environmental Vision in *Moby-Dick*." *Interdisciplinary Studies in Literature and Environment* 7, no. 1 (2000): 97–113.

Moby-Dick: or, The Whale, Herman Melville (1851)

Although Ishmael, *Moby-Dick*'s narrator, is describing a painting in a sailor's inn, the following slyly self-reflective observation equally characterizes Melville's classic story of the sea: "A boggy, soggy, squitchy picture truly, enough to drive a nervous man distracted. Yet there was a sort of indefinite, half-attained, unimaginable sublimity about it that fairly froze you to it..." (Melville 13). In sea-narrative tradition, the novel is wide-ranging and even self-contradictory, yet it is this "indefinite" quality that allows *Moby-Dick* to evoke the vast reach and significance of whaling as a global industry, and its effects on both humans and nonhumans. We must not forget, however, that supporting the novel's "unimaginable sublimity" is a firm narrative substratum. Richard White reminds us that, "work itself is a means of knowing nature" (White 171), and Melville, a sailor himself, wrote a sailor's book, about a specific group of workers and their relationship to their environment.

Unexpectedly, for a sea adventure, *Moby-Dick* opens with two chapters about language: "Etymology," which outlines the large, far-flung and fascinating word-family of "whale," and "Extracts," an eclectic compilation of sayings about whales. As structuralists like de Saussure point out, language is a representational act. However, because the word is not intrinsic to the thing itself, because there is an actual, real whale that will always escape my attempts to capture it by naming or describing it, any representational effort will always fall short; and these chapters seeming attempts to literarily "capture" whales remind us that no language can accurately recreate the natural world. *Moby-Dick* thus begins

by suggesting that the natural world is always both a construct and something inescapably beyond, eluding the reader just as Moby Dick eludes Ahab.

Explaining his decision to join a whaling crew, Ishmael says, "It is a way I have of driving off the spleen, and regulating the circulation" (Melville 3), and his depression ultimately leads him to seek the natural sublime. For Immanuel Kant the sublime occurs after our sense of self as complete is challenged by the confrontation with something far greater than ourselves, an experience which, like the "whale" above, eludes representation — for example, the apparent infinity of the sea, which is a very real, physical challenge, as well as an aesthetic one. In confronting this challenge, we discover a unique faculty or capacity within ourselves, something uniquely human, a kind of super-charged moral or aesthetic appreciation of nature; and the pleasurable discovery that we contain something large enough to respond successfully to such immensity marks the sublime moment. Ishmael finds sublimity in "The Mast-Head," suspended above the immensity of the sea, and after surviving this challenge to his comprehension — indeed, his very existence — experiences a deep sense of peace and communion with nature. By contrast, in "The Whiteness of the Whale," Ahab's failure to come to terms with this challenge results in a constantly unstable, threatened self, the result of which, Melville suggests, is necessarily violence. As Ishmael comments, in the face of such a constant threat "Wonder ye then at the fiery hunt?" (Melville 212).

The middle bulk of *Moby-Dick* is given over to vivid and meticulous descriptions of whaling, interspersed with often esoteric meditations on man and his place in nature. Like most of Melville's work, *Moby-Dick* draws much from Melville's own sailing experience. Hester Blum posits what she calls a "sea eye" to describe writing such as Melville's. Encompassing — indeed, fusing in a profoundly significant manner — both labor and contemplation, a "sea eye" unites the practical experience of being a sailor, the sailor's own analysis of and reflection on that experience, and the literary work of sea narratives that combines them, forming "knowledge that has a material, and thus institutional, existence" (Blum 131) for the reader.

LAWRENCE BUELL calls *Moby-Dick*'s world the first moment of global capitalism: "It is the first canonical work of Anglophone literature to anatomize an extractive industry of global scope" (Buell, *Writing* 205). Ishmael's ocean is a globalized place where economic forces draw together multiple nationalities, ethnicities, and even species in ways that critically blur our dry-land divisions. The "savage" Queequeg is ultimately as civilized as Ishmael, whereas Ahab's quest renders him barbaric. The human and non-human are themselves blurred, as Ishmael describes whales in human terms and vice versa, and as Ahab and Moby Dick take on each other's characteristics. Ultimately *Moby-Dick* encourages readers to stop thinking about oceans or whales as owned resources, in favor of a more complex sense of a globalized industrial environment, with competing descriptions and ownership claims, which is exploitive of people and the environment, but which, as a hybrid space, offers possibilities for understanding identity and environment that are not available elsewhere.

As *Moby-Dick* nears its end, ecofeminism helps explain Ahab's increasingly obsessive, violent hunt. Lawrence Buell describes ecofeminism as a field where "inquiry starts from the premise of a correlation between the history of institutionalized patriarchy and human domination of the nonhuman" (Buell, *Future* 19). This correlation is well illustrated by the power structures in place on the Pequod, which are entirely shaped to serve Ahab's violent relation towards his environment. Violence creates a ready-made relationship to the natural world, one that favors human agency, human power, and human needs. Ultimately, whaling aboard the Pequod eroticizes predation, performing and reflecting masculine sexual violence. Ahab's desire to harpoon nature and bring it under control attempts to conquer the world's challenge to the self by eliminating the world. This explains the violent ejaculatory image of Ahab's revenge: "He piled upon the whale's white hump the sum of all the general rage and hate felt by his whole race from Adam down; and then, as if his chest had been a mortar, he burst his hot heart's shell upon it" (Melville 200). By contrast, in "A Bosom Friend" and "Nightgown," Ishmael's loving relationship with Queequeg destabilizes such aggressive masculinity. The celebration of sperm in "A Squeeze of the Hand" suggests both community and an ecosystemic view of whaling and its commercial ramifications. Moreover, Ishmael's elaborate, engaged descriptions of whales and procedures are an alternative to Ahab's rage, as is Starbuck's pragmatic view that revenge does not produce oil.

It is important to remember that, as Buell points out, there is no "save the whales" message in *Moby-Dick* (Buell, *Writing* 209); though the book questions the whaling industry, Ishmael is a sailor, not an activist. Yet *Moby-Dick*'s complex understanding of whaling as an expression of man's broader relation to the environment remains current and incisive, and this explains in part its frequent adaptation to television and film, as well as its centrality in the environmental canon. — Amber Pearson

BIBLIOGRAPHY

Blum, Hester. *The View from the Masthead: Maritime Imagination and Antebellum American Sea Narratives.* Chapel Hill: University of North Carolina Press, 2008.
Buell, Lawrence. *The Future of Environmental Criticism: Environmental Crisis and Literary Imagination.* Malden, MA: Blackwell, 2005.
———. *Writing for an Endangered World: Literature, Culture, and Environment in the U.S. and Beyond.* Cambridge, MA: Belknap Press, 2001.
Melville, Herman. *Moby-Dick or, The Whale.* 1851. New York: Penguin Books, 2003.
Wenzel, Christian Helmut. *An Introduction to Kant's Aesthetics: Core Concepts and Problems.* Malden, MA: Blackwell, 2005.
White, Richard. "'Are You an Environmentalist or Do You Work for a Living?': Work and Nature." *Uncommon Ground: Rethinking the Human Place in Nature.* Ed. William Cronon. New York: W. W. Norton.

Momaday, N. Scott (1934–   )

Tsoai, "Rock-tree," located in northeastern Wyoming and known to most as Devils Tower, is central to the narrative of the Kiowa's migration from the mountain west to the southern plains, and its creation is a foundational story of the Kiowa cosmogony. Yet few associate Devils Tower with the Kiowa; instead, it is best known for its appearance in movies like *Close Encounters of the Third Kind* (1977) and its popularity as a rock climbing destination. The latter in particular has received some recent publicity, as the Lakota (for whom Devils Tower is Mato Tipila, "bear lodge") have asserted their right to worship at Devils Tower without constant intrusion from rock climbers. That any association remains between Devils Tower and the Kiowa is owed in large part to Kiowa writer N. Scott Momaday, who includes the story of Tsoai in no less than five of his major works, including his novels *HOUSE MADE OF DAWN* (1968) and *The Ancient Child* (1989), his memoirs *The Way to Rainy Mountain* (1969) and *The Names* (1976), and his collection of essays *The Man Made of Words* (1997). As Momaday tells it in each of these works, virtually unchanged as it appears among them, the creation of Tsoai looked something like this:

> Eight children were at play, seven sisters and their brother. Suddenly the boy was struck dumb; he trembled and began to run upon his hands and feet. His fingers became claws, and his body was covered with fur. Directly there was a bear where the boy had been. The sisters were terrified; they ran, and the bear after them. They came to the stump of a great tree, and the tree spoke to them. It bade them climb upon it, and as they did so it began to rise into the air. The bear came to kill them, but they were just beyond its reach. It reared against the tree and scored the bark all around with its claws. The seven sisters were

borne into the sky, and they became the stars of the Big Dipper [*The Names*, 55].

Placed beside Momaday's retelling of this story, other claims to Devils Tower, as a "climber's paradise" or "sci-fi mecca," pale in comparison. Indeed, few natural features of the American landscape can claim to have so rich an origin story as Tsoai, thanks in large part to the work of Momaday.

The story of Tsoai lends a rich element to each of the individual works in which Momaday includes it, but its placement in *The Names* is arguably the most compelling. *The Names* is both memoir and profound family history, with Momaday tracing his genealogy back four generations, his lineage comprised of Kiowa, Cherokee, and Euro-American ancestors. The use of the Tsoai story is contextualized in a larger account of how Momaday was given his Kiowa name, Tsoai-talee ("Rock-tree boy") by the elder Pohd-lohk, in part because Momaday's parents had taken him to Devils Tower when he was just six months old. As a result Momaday has long identified with the boy in the Devils Tower story, and thus the bear as well. In interviews Momaday often speaks openly about his attachment to "rock-tree boy": "I identify with the bear because I'm intimately connected with that story. And so I have this bear power. I turn into a bear every so often. I feel myself becoming a bear, and that's a struggle that I have to face now and then" (*MELUS*, 82). In *The Ancient Child* Momaday draws out his connection to the bear most fully, with the semi-autobiographical character Locke Setman being told at one point, "You are *Set*; you are the bear; you will be the bear, no matter what" (271).

Though the example of Tsoai reveals Momaday's strong identification with the Kiowa forbears he traces back from his father, his early days were actually comprised of a self-described "Pan-Indian experience" ("About N. Scott Momaday," 188). Momaday, whose given name is Navarre Scott Momaday, was born in Oklahoma and lived for a time on the Kiowa reservation with his father's family. His parents, both teachers, then took a series of positions on reservations of the Navajo, Apache, and other indigenous cultures of the American Southwest, before settling on the Pueblo reservation in Jemez, NM. After graduating from the University of New Mexico and teaching for a time himself, Momaday completed a Ph.D. at Stanford University in 1963, studying under the tutelage of Yvor Winters. Momaday later taught at Stanford, as well as the University of California (Santa Barbara and Berkley), the University of Arizona, and even the University of Moscow. In addition to a distinguished career as a writer and academic, Momaday has received a number of prestigious awards, including a Guggenheim fellowship, a Western Heritage Award, a Pulitzer Prize (for *House Made of Dawn*), and a National Medal of Arts. He is commonly referred to as the "dean of Native American writers," and continues to be recognized, alongside LESLIE MARMON SILKO, LOUISE ERDRICH, SIMON J. ORTIZ, and Sherman Alexie, as transforming the status of Native American literature and helping it receive the popular and critical attention it has long deserved.

Arguably more so than any other native writer, however, Momaday is deeply attuned to the physical environments of the American landscape that play such a prominent role in all of his writing. The story of Tsoai is just one example where a feature of the land is bestowed with a unique narrative life of its own. Other landscapes in Momaday's writing are imbued with similar distinction, even sacredness: the sun-burnt plains of Oklahoma in *The Way to Rainy Mountain*, the mesas and valleys of the Jemez Reservation in *House Made of Dawn*, and the Medicine Wheel of the Bighorn Mountains in *The Man Made of Words*, are but a few examples from Momaday's oeuvre. In addition to landscapes, Momaday also deals extensively with animal life, particularly in his poetry and fiction. The adoption of the bear persona is one clear manifestation of his attachment to animals, but others stand out as well. Take, for example, his poem "Angle of Geese," an image and expression he repeats in his writing and that he describes as "So much symmetry!—/ Like the pale angle of time / And eternity" (*In the Presence of the Sun*, 21). Of the presence of animals in Momaday's writing, Anishinaabe scholar Gerald Vizenor proclaims that "[Momaday] turns metaphors of authored animals into an unrevealed presence, the tensive myths of creation and native solace.... The mere mention of the bear is traced in sound, motion, and the memories of the characters" (137).

Momaday writes in his essay "An American Land Ethic" that he "is interested in the way that a man looks at a given landscape and takes possession of it in his blood and brain. For this happens, I am certain in the ordinary motion of life. None of us lives apart from the land entirely; such an isolation is unimaginable" (47). It is uncertain whether Momaday's title is an invocation of ALDO LEOPOLD's "land ethic" from *A SAND COUNTY ALMANAC* (1949), but what is certain is that Momaday shares a similar sense of responsibility toward the ethical treatment of the American environment. His work shows strong cultural and aesthetic associations with the land, but it is his unflinching belief in the sacredness of the natural world that truly defines Momaday's unique connection — and contribution — to it. — Matt Low

BIBLIOGRAPHY

Givens, Bettye, and N. Scott Momaday. "A MELUS Interview: N. Scott Momaday. A Slant of Light." *MELUS* 12.1, Native American Literature (1985): 79–87.

Hager, Hal. "About N. Scott Momaday," in *House Made of Dawn*. New York: HarperPerennial, 1999, 187–193.

Momaday, N. Scott. *The Ancient Child*. New York: HarperCollins, 1989.

_____. *House Made of Dawn*. New York: HarperCollins, 1968.

_____. *In the Presence of the Sun: Stories and Poems, 1961–1991*. New York: St. Martin's Press, 1992.

_____. *The Man Made of Words*. New York: St. Martin's Griffin, 1997.

_____. *The Names*. Tucson, AZ: Sun Tracks, 1976.

Vizenor, Gerald. *Fugitive Poses*. Lincoln: University of Nebraska Press, 1998.

House Made of Dawn, N. Scott Momaday (1968)

N. Scott Momaday's Pulitzer Prize winning first novel, *House Made of Dawn*, is one of the most respected and influential pieces of Native American Literature ever written. It is also one of the most frequently studied and written-about novels in that canon. Like LESLIE MARMON SILKO's *CEREMONY* (1977), the work explores the struggle of Indian people to maintain a sense of tradition and responsibility to land and community in a contemporary world; and both novels feature protagonists who struggle with addiction and psychological fragmentation after their experiences with war. *House Made of Dawn* tells the story of Abel, a young Kiowa man, who has recently returned to the fictional Pueblo "Walatowa" in New Mexico after fighting in World War II. Abel seems to be suffering from post-traumatic stress disorder and arrives home drunk and unable to recognize his grandfather, Francisco. The novel is somewhat unconventional in style, frequently presenting information in the form of achronological memories, and shifting between multiple narrators, but its focus rests largely if loosely on Abel and his impact on the lives of the other characters.

The story centers on Abel's continuous struggle to establish a stable and sustainable identity in the world. His general sense that he has no "place," or is not truly connected to the place that he lives, stems from an early sense that he is different from the others in Walatowa. From a young age Abel feels singled out because he does not know who his father is. All he knows is that his father was a "Navajo, [...] or a Sia, [...] an outsider anyway," and that this "made him and his mother and [his brother] Vidal somehow foreign and strange" (11) Later, Abel's mother and Vidal die of illness and Francisco raises Abel alone. Abel's sense of disconnection only increases when he returns from the war and discovers that although he is back in the place where he grew up, he cannot seem to conform to the pattern of life there. Abel "had tried to pray, to sing, to enter into the rhythm of the tongue but he was no longer attuned to it" (58). Abel's struggle to squeeze his disparate and fragmented understanding of the world into the monolithic life on the reservation leaves him only further fragmented and alone.

After being humiliated by an Albino man at a local ceremony, Abel responds by killing the man. Although his true reasons for the murder are not clear in the novel, it is evident that Abel's violence is not in keeping with traditional methods for excising evil from the reservation. Abel's violence is thus further evidence of his profound disconnect from his people and his culture.

After six years in prison, Abel is released into the care of the Indian Relocation Program. He is living in Los Angeles and soon gets a job at a factory where he meets Ben Benally, a Navaho man who also grew up on a reservation. Even though Ben and Abel form a strong friendship and frequently talk about their childhood, the two men respond to life in the city in completely different ways. Where Abel struggles, Ben accommodates himself to the world he finds himself in. He succeeds because he has largely relinquished his Indian traditions and values. He believes that "you have to change. [...] You have to forget about the way it was, how you grew up and all. Sometimes it's hard but you have to do it" (148). Ben's and Abel's responses to life off the reservation can be viewed here as a microcosm of the struggle of a vanishing culture. Ben and Abel seem to suggest two approaches to living in a world that is no longer receptive to Indian cultures and traditions.

The importance of land and the environment is evident everywhere in the novel. The text begins and ends with mirroring phrases: "*Dypaloh*. There was a house made of dawn. It was made of pollen and of rain, and the land was very old and everlasting," and "*House made of pollen, house made of dawn. Qtsedaba*." These flanking words signal a focus on man's place within nature that resounds throughout the novel. The significance of the land and the environment in Kiowa tradition, and Native American culture more generally, cannot be overstated. The novel explores the collision of man, nature, and time. It considers the struggle to find a way to exist in a human way amongst the forces of nature and time, and in a natural way amongst the forces of man and progress.

The exact meaning and significance of environment is complicated in this novel, however, because of Abel's general sense that he is out of place. A particularly compelling example of this complication is seen in the contrast between Abel's experience in the Eagle Watcher's Society, and Francisco's boyhood bear hunt. Francisco came of age in a time when the "race for good hunting and harvests" was still run. His understanding of what it is to be Kiowa is based on traditions that Abel only partially understands. He is attuned to the land that he farms, and was raised and initiated into a culture that recognized the reciprocal relationship of man and nature. Francisco's bear hunt is presented in the novel as a test of patience, skill, and cunning that Francisco passes with grace and steadfastness. He kills the bear he has been tracking for days and returns to his people as a man. Abel has a similar experience when he first ventures out with the Eagle Watcher's Society and skillfully captures an impressive female Golden Eagle. But rather than feeling proud of his accomplishment, he is "filled with longing" at the thought of the eagles in flight. Perhaps seeing the eagle, "bound and helpless" in a sack, as a kind of reflection of his own mental state, Abel is filled with "shame and disgust" and strangles the bird.

At the end of the novel, Abel prepares his grandfather's body for burial in the traditional way and participates in the enigmatic "race of the dead" at dawn. Fraught with luminous but ambiguous intensity, the final images of the novel suggest that Abel has at last found a place with his people, and has made peace with his past, his world and himself.— Kimberly O'Dell Cox

BIBLIOGRAPHY

Momaday, N. Scott. *House Made of Dawn*. New York: Perennial Library, 1989.

Scarberry-Garcia, Susan. *Landmarks of Healing: A Study of House Made of Dawn*. Albuquerque: University of New Mexico Press, 1990.

Schweninger, Lee. *Listening to the Land: Native American Literary Responses to the Landscape*. Athens: University of Georgia Press, 2008.

Teuton, Sean Kicummah. *Red Land, Red Power: Grounding Knowledge in the American Indian Novel*. Durham: Duke University Press, 2008.

The Way to Rainy Mountain, N. Scott Momaday (1969)

Momaday's *The Way to Rainy Mountain* illuminates the crucial connection between the natural landscape and human language. In essence, the book is an account of Momaday's effort to connect with his Kiowa heritage through the process of storytelling and mythmaking. Momaday's "cultural memoir" presents an interesting case study for the eco-critic, as it introduces some valuable ideas about how the human and nonhuman communities can interact through the power of language.

In Rainy Mountain, Momaday presents the reader with the history of the Kiowa migration east from the Yellowstone area to southwestern Oklahoma, which he personally retraces en route to his grandmother's grave at Rainy Mountain. The book is an extension of Momaday's first publication, The Journey of Tai-Me (1967), and the general account of the migration is also repeated in his Pulitzer prize-winning novel, HOUSE MADE OF DAWN (1968). Rainy Mountain is divided into three sections. The first, "The Setting Out," recounts the beginning of Kiowa history, and describes vital aspects of Kiowa religion and culture, including the Sunboy, the Ten Grandmother Bundles, the Tai-me, the Sun Dance, and the peyote altar. The second section, "The Going On," focuses primarily on life on the Great Plains, including arrow making and buffalo hunts. The final section, "The Closing In," emphasizes images of Euroamerican encroachment and the termination of the "golden age" of Kiowa culture (85). Structurally, each chapter within the three main sections juxtaposes three voices: the first describes Kiowa mythology; the second provides an historical/anthropological perspective; and the third articulates Momaday's personal reflections. Even as Rainy Mountain traces the decline of traditional Kiowa culture, the combination of these three voices emphasizes the significance of storytelling as a tool of endurance, as Rainy Mountain itself manifests the power of what Momaday calls the "living memory and the verbal tradition which transcends it" (86).

Momaday's tale of the journey to Rainy Mountain, as much as the journey itself, binds human culture together with the physical landscape. For Momaday, the land as it exists in personal and collective memory is as potent and real as the land itself. Indeed, the inspiration behind Momaday's journey is not the land per se, but his grandmother's *memory* of the land: "[Aho] could tell of the Crows, whom she had never seen, and of the Black Hills, where she had never been. I wanted to see in reality what she had seen more perfectly in the mind's eye, and traveled fifteen hundred miles to begin my pilgrimage" (7). That Aho can tell stories about cultures and places she has never seen illustrates the efficacy of language: again, the land as it exists in the "mind's eye" is as crucial and vital as the land "in reality." It is through language, through Aho's stories, that human perception of the landscape and the physical landscape merge and become inseparable. In the final chapter of "The Closing In" section, Momaday reiterates the importance of connecting with the land through memory and story, imploring his reader to "concentrate his mind upon the remembered earth" and to "give himself up to a particular landscape in his experience, to look at it from as many angles as he can" (83).

The capacity for language to bridge the gap between human perception and the natural environment is an integral part of its power. Indeed, as Lawrence Evers points out in his examination of Momaday's "sense of place," it is through words that cultural landscapes are created and a symbolic order is established that helps to explain the meaning of the world around us (213). Momaday articulates this fact most directly through the three voices that comprise Chapter VIII of the book. Here, the "mythological" voice relates the story of the sun's twin children who find themselves trapped in the cave of a giant. In order to escape suffocation after the giant builds a smoky fire, the twins recall the advice of grandmother spider: "If you ever get caught in the cave, say to yourselves the word *thain-mom*, 'above my eyes'" (32). After multiple recitations of this word, the smoke does in fact rise above their eyes and the giant ultimately lets them go. This narrative demonstrates the ability of language to impose a kind of order on reality. The message of this myth is emphasized by the historical voice that follows it: "A word has power in and of itself. It comes from nothing into sound and meaning; it gives origin to all things. By means of words a man can deal with the world on equal terms" (33). That is, words assign meaning to the world and offer humans the opportunity to *create* the world on their own terms so that they may stand in better relation to it. The word *thain-mom* imposes an order on nature, as it is an expression of grandmother spider's own understanding of how the natural world operates: smoke rises. Momaday's personal recollection about his own grandmother in this section illustrates this same principle: in an effort to confront evil, Aho would say *zei-dl-bei*, which means "frightful." As Momaday explains, "It was not an explanation so much, I think, as it was a wading off, an exertion of language and disorder" (33). To name a thing is to come to know it better and to enter into a closer relationship with it. This chapter skillfully depicts the way in which language can empower humans by providing them with the means to better understand and articulate themselves and their relationship to the world around them. When this "exertion of language" is directed toward the landscape, the reciprocal relationship between the human and nonhuman is made manifest.

Inasmuch as language is vital to humans in their effort to connect with the land, however, the Kiowa emergence narrative serves as an important reminder of the fact that the land always comes first. Indeed, as Elaine Jahner notes, Momaday is careful to assert the primacy of the land as a source for the human imagination. She writes, "Momaday's writing implies that creation in a very real sense does begin with the land. The perspective that the land imposes inspires the imagination to find meaning in life" (219). That the Kiowa people come forth from the land through a log certainly emphasizes this point: "You know, everything had to begin, and this is how it was: the Kiowas came one by one into the world through a hollow log" (16). This mythic narrative aligns the Kiowas closely with the land, as their culture was literally birthed from the bowels of the earth. The Kiowa emergence narrative creates a *symbolic* order where Kiowa identity must be measured in terms of the land, because the earth, in essence, is their mother. Implicit in this creation myth is an understanding of the intricate relationship between the land, humans, and language. The story itself reemphasizes the role that language plays in framing the association between human culture and the natural world.

The theory of language articulated in *Rainy Mountain*, and the celebration of the landscape encountered along "the way," are recurrent themes in Momaday's oeuvre. As Mathias Schubnell asserts, "Nature and the American landscape are central features of Momaday's writings" (63). Indeed, many of the materials and ideas expressed in *Rainy Mountain* can be found throughout the pieces collected in *The Man Made of Words: Essays, Stories, Passages* (1997), especially in essays like "A First American Views His Land" and "An American Land Ethic." *Rainy Mountain* is therefore part of a larger body of work that establishes Momaday as a key American environmental writer and thinker.—Matthew Cella

BIBLIOGRAPHY

Evers, Lawrence J. "Words and Place: A Reading of *House Made of Dawn*." *Critical Essays on Native American Literature*. Ed. Andrew Wight. Boston: G. K. Hall, 211–230.

Jahner, Elaine. "A Critical Approach to American Indian Literature." *Studies in American Indian Literature: Critical Essays and Course Designs*. Ed. Paula Gunn Allen. New York: MLA, 1983. 211–224.

Momaday, N. Scott. *The Way to Rainy Mountain*. Albuquerque: University of New Mexico Press, 1969.

Roemer, Kenneth M., ed. *Approaches to Teaching Momaday's* The Way to Rainy Mountain. New York: MLA, 1988.

Schubnell, Matthias. *N. Scott Momaday: The Cultural and Literary Background*. Norman: University of Oklahoma Press, 1985.

Schweninger, Lee. *Listening to the Land: Native American Literary Responses to the Landscape*. Athens: University of Georgia Press, 2008.

Morrison, Toni (1931–   )

Toni Morrison's novels are widely considered to represent a distinctly African-American environmental ethic. Complicating traditional perspectives on nature with close attention to the social forces that construct our relationship to the environment, Morrison's work insists upon the inextricability of the social from the natural.

Toni Morrison was born Chloe Anthony Wofford in 1931, in Lorain, Ohio, to George and Ella Ramah Wofford. The family had a penchant for storytelling and reading that led the Wofford children to seek out books at an early age. Morrison earned her B.A. from Howard University in 1953 and her M.A. in English from Cornell University in 1955. She worked as an editor at Random House for 18 years and taught at several institutions including Howard and Princeton. While she has published in a variety of genres, including essays, plays, and operas, Morrison is best known for her novels, most notably *The Bluest Eye* (1970), SONG OF SOLOMON (1975), *Beloved* (1987), *Paradise* (1998), and *A Mercy* (2008). In 1993 she became the first African-American woman to win the Nobel Prize for Literature.

Elizabeth Dodd writes of ecocriticism that "African Americans seem largely absent from this burgeoning literary, cultural, and critical movement" (1095). She argues that there is a general neglect of writers such as Morrison, whose work "treats far more visibly questions of social place, as constructed through race" than the natural as such (*ibid.*). However, Morrison's contribution to the study of environmental literature has been, among other things, to emphasize the relationship between race and the environment. In *Beloved*, for instance, the beauty of the wild plantation and the reduction of human beings to the condition of livestock under slavery results in a situation where "the construction of nature as refuge so prominent in mainstream environmental thought simply does not hold true" (Wallace and Armbruster 215).

However, Morrison's work does not merely critique this "mystical" tradition in environmental literature, but engages with environmental themes to challenge equally entrenched assumptions about African-American literature. In *Song of Solomon*, for example, protagonist Milkman Dead experiences a constructive destabilization of self in the face of nature. This challenges tendencies in the African-American novel to see as its political goal the invention of stable forms of agency in the pursuit of self-determination. Morrison's work thus strikes a difficult balance by emphasizing "the spiritual possibilities of human interaction with more-than-human life-forms ... within a complex web of cultural and historical contexts" (Berry 164).

Morrison's latest novel, *A Mercy*, criticizes colonization as a hubristic effort to impose human dominance upon nature and white dominance upon oth-

ers. Here, however, environmental conquest is not merely analogous to the conquest of human communities, but is seen as the very justification for slavery, as African and indigenous slaves are taken in order to combat the harsh conditions of nature. Morrison, then, continues to bring questions of race and environment together in crucial ways that illuminate the study of Black literature and environmental thought.—Rachel Greenwald Smith

BIBLIOGRAPHY

Berry, Wes. "Toni Morrison's Revisionary 'Nature Writing': *Song of Solomon* and the Blasted Pastoral." *South to a New Place: Region, Literature, Culture.* Ed. Suzanne Whitmore Jones & Sharon Monteith. Baton Rouge: Louisiana State University Press, 2002. 147–164.
"Chronology." *Toni Morrison: Conversations.* Ed. Carolyn C. Denard. Jackson: University Press of Mississippi, 2008. xix–xxiii.
Dodd, Elizabeth. "Forum on Literatures of the Environment." *PMLA* 114.5 (1999): 1094–1095.
Langer, Adam. "Star Power." *Toni Morrison: Conversations.* Ed. Carolyn C. Denard. Jackson: University Press of Mississippi, 2008. 206–213.
Wallace, Kathleen R., and Karla Armbruster. "The Novels of Toni Morrison: 'Wild Wilderness Where There Was None.'" *Beyond Nature Writing: Expanding the Boundaries of Ecocriticism.* Ed. Karla Arm & Kathleen R. Wallace. Charlottesville: University Press of Virginia, 2001. 211–230.

Song of Solomon, Toni Morrison (1977)

Toni Morrison's *Song of Solomon* is among her most highly regarded works of fiction, and certainly one of the most interesting from an ecocritical point of view. The novel not only won the National Books Critics Award and was cited by the Swedish Academy in awarding Morrison the 1993 Nobel Prize in Literature; in 1996 it was chosen by Oprah Winfrey for her influential book club, because it expressed "the mysterious primal essence of family bond and conflict" (Oprah), and was thus recommended as valuable reading material also for a popular audience interested in issues of race, kinship and gender. However, in recent years a number of scholars have urged us to see how in the novel these issues are intimately related to ecocritical and eco-feminist concerns. Already in 1985, the black feminist literary critic Barbara Christian pointed to the centrality of nature to African-American community building in *Song of Solomon*, and Kathleen Wallace and Karla Armbruster suggest in a 2001 essay that Morrison's work is notable for "exploring how the natural world has been used as an instrument of oppression but has simultaneously provided a source of sustenance and comfort" to black women and black communities more generally (213). *Song of Solomon* is a particularly interesting example in this regard because it interrogates nature-human interactions from an African American point of view, and offers insights into the complex relationship between racial, gender, and environmental violence.

Most critics read *Song of Solomon* as a coming-of-age story focusing on the young African American Milkman Dead, whose life is shaped by both his father Macon II, a materialistic and emotionally barren slumlord, and his aunt Pilate, a charismatic and slightly mysterious woman who smells "like a forest" (27), sways "like a willow" (30), and looks like "a tall black tree" (38). The novel opens on the day before Milkman's birth in an unnamed town in Michigan when a local insurance agent promises people that he will fly and then jumps to his death from the roof of the very same hospital in which Milkman is about to be born. Milkman's birth is thus overshadowed by a man's unsuccessful attempt to soar into the clouds, and when old enough to understand that humans cannot actually fly he is deeply disturbed by that recognition. Although his life is marked by the affection, care, and nurture of the women in his extended family, he does not seem to appreciate his multiple privileges and, like his father, is unable to feel empathy and compassion for others. He has little understanding and respect for Pilate's dedication to African-American cultural traditions, and he only uses and eventually abandons her troubled granddaughter Hagar, who, unable to bear his rejection, tries to kill him several times and finally dies of a broken heart. In spite of these tragic occurrences, however, the tree-like Pilate becomes Milkman's spiritual guide when he travels to the ancestral home of his father's family in Shalimar, Virginia, in search of a lost bag of gold that was allegedly taken by a man involved in the murder of his grandfather.

Milkman's initial motivation for his journey to the rural South is purely materialistic. Together with his friend Guitar, a black radical, he tries to recover the lost bag, but as his quest progresses his objectives begin to change. As Ann Imbrie has pointed out, his journey to "a simpler, more primitive and 'natural' world" allows him to be "educated in a new way, in lessons the city cannot teach him" (477). The northern, urban world Milkman leaves behind is a world in which making money takes precedence over generosity and compassion, in which racial prejudice separates people from each other, and in which violence ruins human relationships. Pilate is the exception to this rule. Not only has she a close connection to both her ancestors and the land, she also helps the oppressed women of her family and is able to see the high price her older brother Macon pays emotionally and spiritually for his adoption of capitalism and

tyrannical patriarchy. While Macon symbolizes the corrupting and disrupting effects of capitalism, Pilate stands for a connection with nature and the legacy of the family's black ancestry. This is why she can guide Milkman to a different understanding of his history and his place in nature. The characters' shared belief system and understanding of the natural world are of central importance in *Song of Solomon*, and, as Barbara Christian has pointed out, central also to the way in which Morrison weaves her story (75). Milkman's journey from the urban North to the rural South is a journey back in time, both into the history of his family and into the history of African-American people more generally, and he slowly begins to understand the complex relationship they have with the natural world.

In this new environment he not only learns about the unsustainable farming practices of his grandfather Macon Dead I, who died defending his land, and about his great-grandfather Solomon, who according to local legend escaped slavery by flying back to Africa on the wind. Going through a traditional hunting ritual, he also begins to develop a new understanding of the natural world around him, "where all a man had was what he was born with, or had learned to use" (277), and he starts thinking about the meaning of language "back in the time when men and animals did talk to one another, or a man could sit down with an ape and the two converse; when a tiger and a man could share the same tree, and each understood the other; when men ran *with* wolves, not from or after them" (278). If his ancestors could talk to animals, he wonders, "and the animals could talk to them, what didn't they know about human beings? Or the earth itself for that matter" (278). Moved by a new understanding of the world around him, Milkman is finally able to connect with human and nonhuman others, including his former friend Guitar, who is now trying to take his life, but for whom he nevertheless feels affection.

According to the black feminist bell hooks, "collective black self-recovery takes place when we begin to renew our relationship to the earth, when we remember the way of our ancestors" (39). In *Song of Solomon*, such renewal takes place on the last pages of the novel, and it is Milkman's aunt Pilate who makes it possible. Stacy Alaimo argues in *Undomesticated Ground* (2000) that nature "serves not only as an oppositional space" in *Song of Solomon*, but also "as a symbolic means of celebrating Pilate and the matrix of gender, race, and class positions she represents" (138). Although the protagonist of the novel is male, he can only arrive at his moral and spiritual enlightenment through a woman's guidance and an acceptance of her values and beliefs: "You want my life," shouts Milkman at the end, knowing that Guitar is lying in dark with his rifle, "you need it?" (337). And then he leaps forward, knowing from Pilate and the history of his family that "if you surrendered to the air you could ride it" (337). Morrison leaves open whether Milkman, like his fabled great-grandfather, has learned to fly or whether he jumps to his death, but she leaves little doubt that he has found a way of life that is much more fulfilling than being Dead.—Alexa Weik von Mossner

BIBLIOGRAPHY

Alaimo, Stacy. *Undomesticated Ground: Recasting Nature as Feminist Space*. Ithaca: Cornell University Press, 2000.
Christian, Barbara. "Community and Nature: The Novels of Toni Morrison." 1980. Reprinted in *Toni Morrison*. Ed. Harold Bloom. Broomall, PA: Chelsea House, 2003. 75–93.
hooks, bell. *Belonging: A Culture of Place*. London and New York: Routledge, 2009.
Imbrie, Ann E. "'What Shalimar Knew': Toni Morrison's *Song of Solomon* as a Pastoral Novel." *College English* 55.5 (Sep., 1993): 473–490.
Morrison, Toni. *Song of Solomon*. 1977. New York: Vintage, 2004.
Wallace, Kathleen R., and Karla Armbruster. "The Novels of Toni Morrison: 'Wild Wilderness Where There Was None.'" *Beyond Nature Writing: Expanding the Boundaries of Ecocriticism*. Eds. Karla Armbruster and Kathleen R. Wallace. Charlottesville and London: University Press of Virginia, 2001. 211–230.
Winfrey, Oprah. "*Song of Solomon*." *Oprah's Book Club Collection*. October 18, 1996. August 27, 2011. http://www.oprah.com/oprahsbookclub/About-Toni-Morrisons-Book-Song-of-Solomon.

Morton, Thomas (1576?–1647?)

Thomas Morton's life and work challenge the authority of the Puritan narratives detailing America's early development. Although some early historians acknowledge Morton's colonial contribution, subsequent conservatively aligned scholars marginalized Morton's position in both American history and American literature. Recent scholarship, however, increasingly reveals Morton's significant historic role in New England's early settlement and his potential as America's first poet. His major work, NEW ENGLISH CANAAN (1637), celebrates the glories and possibilities of the new land and satirizes both the Puritans' adverse response to the wilderness and their racist view of Native Americans.

Incomplete records place Morton's birth around 1576 into Devon gentry. Details in Morton's writing suggest he was "the Son of a [sic] souldier" (145), had "been bred in so genious a way" (66), and had benefited from a gentrified lifestyle that included hunting and falconry. With its high Anglican and Royalist loyalties and its maintenance of folkways,

the west country of Devon also profoundly affected Morton's character and perceptions. Existing records from 1593 place him in London at the Inns of Court, specifically as a student at Clifford's Inn. Morton's exposure to the satiric and literary culture of the Inns of Court, including his associations with writers like Ben Jonson (Shea 57), shaped his stylistic development. He entered the service of Sir Ferdinando Gorges in 1624 as a minor partner of a new colony in Massachusetts that ultimately became "Ma-Re Mount" or Merrymount in 1626. However, his success created a moral, political, and economic conflict with the Puritan Plymouth Colony (Dempsey 128), and eventually the Puritan leadership manipulated charges of immorality and illicit gun trade in order to arrest, try, and banish him to the Isles of Shoals off New Hampshire.

Upon his return to England, Morton wrote *New English Canaan*, which extols both New England's settlement and Merrymount's success, and satirizes the Puritans and their policies and practices. Morton embraces the new world and its people and exults in the rich diversity of the animals, plants and minerals, even the water, claiming their superiority to European equivalents. In "The Second Book" he exclaims: "The more I looked, the more I liked it. And when I had more seriously considered of the beauty of the place; with all her fair endowments, I did not think that in all the known world it could be paralleled" (53). He describes the Native Americans' nobility and celebrates life's pleasures and folk traditions such as the Maypole, while simultaneously exposing Puritan brutality, corruption, and bigotry.

Morton and his political allies managed the revocation of the Massachusetts Bay Colony charter, and he returned triumphantly to New England in 1642. However, increased Puritan political power in England quickly led to his arrest, trial, and imprisonment for Royalist sympathies and sedition. His petition for clemency because of his age and health obtained his release to Gorges' supporters in Agamenticus (York), Maine, where he died around 1647.—Thomas P. Fair

BIBLIOGRAPHY

Dempsey, Jack. *Thomas Morton of "Merrymount": The Life and Renaissance of an Early American Poet*. Scituate, MA: Digital Scanning, 2000.
Morton, Thomas. *New English Canaan*. 1637. Ed. Jack Dempsey. Scituate, MA: Digital Scanning, 1999.
Shea, Daniel B. "'Our Professed Old Adversary': Thomas Morton and the Naming of New England." *Early American Literature*. 23.1 (1988): 52–69.

New English Canaan,
Thomas Morton (1637)

Denigrating Thomas Morton as a libertine, an adventurer, and a seditionist, colonial accounts of the Massachusetts Bay Colony and subsequent conservative historians have assigned him a marginal space in American history and literature (Major 2). However, both in his life and work, Morton challenged the conventional understanding of the Puritan period and offered an alternative portrayal of the early settlement. His *New English Canaan*, in particular, tells of the founding and success of his colony of Merrymount and his subsequent conflict with the Puritan authorities in Plymouth; and his enthusiastic view of the new world, the land and its indigenous people, challenges the racism and cynicism of the traditionally accepted Puritan perception.

A three-part prose and poetry description of his New England experiences, Morton's text praises the environment and Native Americans while satirizing the bigotry and corruption of Puritan society. Moreover, it celebrates regional and traditional English festivals at Merrymount, including the May Day Revels that offered a mixture of cultural celebration, interaction with the Native Americans, and occasion for trading, including the sale of guns. The Puritan authorities considered the events to be immoral and illegal; consequently, they arrested, tried and banished Morton to the Isles of Shoals off the New Hampshire coast. But Morton obtained passage to England in September of 1628 and gained freedom upon his arrival. While busily applying his political connections and the power of the English courts in order to revoke the Massachusetts Bay Colony's charter and effect his return to New England, Morton wrote *New English Canaan* (Dempsey 262).

In "The First Book," he celebrates Native Americans' qualities, and challenges the Puritans' superstitious and racist perceptions of them as fearful terrors and savage, ignorant creatures to be used but not tolerated as equals. Morton associates the indigenous people with the land and nature, viewing them as inherently complementary. He even establishes a classic pedigree for North American tribes by connecting them to "the scattered Trojans" (18). Moreover, he refutes the concept of heathen savagery through parallels he establishes with Christianity, citing the Native American creation stories and the people's belief in the existence of God, Hell and the immortality of the soul (42). He also praises their respect for their elders (28), their "subtlety" or sharpness of mind (37), and their superior physical senses (40), in order to establish their equality with the English. Balancing his realistic portrayal, Morton also discusses the damaging vices of pride (32) and drunkenness (46). Overall, however, he perceives and depicts much more to praise in the natives than to criticize: "According to human reason, guided only by the light of nature, these people lead the more happy and freer life, being void of care which torments the minds of so many Christians. They are not delighted in baubles, but in useful things" (50).

"The Second Book" directly addresses the rich and varied characteristics of the North American environment, especially as they shaped Morton's own experience in New England. In it, Morton offers the earliest and most complete catalogue of biological forms and geological elements indigenous to the northeast, "exult[ing] in its wildlife," while "The orthodox, on the other hand, either ignored [...] or disparaged it" (Zuckerman 261). His attention to detail is that of a scientist as well as nature lover, and the number and diversity of entries in each category exemplify a rich, varied, and complex ecosystem, vastly exceeding its Biblical counterpart: "Canaan came not near this country. As for the milk and honey which that Canaan flowed with, it is supplied by the plenty of birds, beasts, and fish, whereof that Canaan could not boast herself" (91). Morton equates the country's riches with the richness of possibility for those seeking prospects in New England, condemning those who fail to recognize or to explore fully the numerous advantages offered. His view of New England's splendors challenges the corrupt and brutal landscape so characteristic of the Puritan narratives, and posits, instead, a land of infinite opportunity.

Morton's biting satire of his Puritan opponents generates "The Third Book" and contrasts the harmonious descriptions of the people and land established in the first two books with the repressive Puritan beliefs and culture. The most allusive and complex of the three sections, "The Third Book" incorporates numerous classical and mythical references as well as "the tradition of the masque and its vulgar play within a play, the antimasque" (Shea 56). This complex literary format recounts both the Plymouth Colony's early history and Morton's own experience, often adopting a spurious Puritan perspective, of "the Brethren of Plimoth" (105). The narrator concludes many sections with questions that challenge the veracity of the Puritan accounts and support Morton's assertions in "The First Book." Episodes supposedly critical of the Native Americans detail their being tricked, abused, or murdered, while other accounts ultimately vindicate or ennoble them. Morton mocks Puritan repression with a discussion of the Revels' sexual activities, most notably in "The Song" (137–139). He burlesques the Puritan authorities as the "Nine Worthies," and in "The Poem"

(149–154) ridicules Puritan justice, focusing on his own banishment to the Isles of Shoals. To repay the betrayal of his former associate John Endicott, Morton portrays him as comic Captain Littleworth: "A great swelling fellow, of Littleworth" (164), whom Mine Host (Morton) outwits. The subsequent discussion of Mine Host's conflict with the "great Joshua surnamed Temperwell [John Winthrop]" (169) condemns the destruction of Morton's property and the cruelty, rigidity, and self-righteous hypocrisy of the Separatists' society. He compares his exile metaphorically to Jonas (Jonah) being swallowed by a whale, and Morton as Jonas prophesies his victorious return with a warning to "Repent, you cruel Separatists, repent" (198).

Thomas Morton's actual return coincided with the Puritans' defeat of Charles I in England, which prevented Morton's triumph and led to his exile and death in Maine. However, *New English Canaan* strongly advances Morton's vindication from the falsehoods spread by the Plymouth Colony's leadership, and promotes his claim for consideration as America's first poet.— Thomas P. Fair

BIBLIOGRAPHY

Dempsey, Jack. *Thomas Morton of "Merrymount": The Life and Renaissance of an Early American Poet*. Scituate, MA: Digital Scanning, 2000.

Major, Minor Wallace. "William Bradford Versus Thomas Morton." *Early American Literature*. 5.2 (1970): 1–13.

Morton, Thomas. *New English Canaan*. 1637. Ed. Jack Dempsey. Scituate, MA: Digital Scanning, 1999.

Shea, Daniel B. "'Our Professed Old Adversary': Thomas Morton and the Naming of New England." *Early American Literature*. 23.1 (1988): 52–69.

Zuckerman, Michael. "Pilgrims in the Wilderness: Community, Modernity and the Maypole at Merrymount." *The New England Quarterly*. 50.2 (1977): 255–277.

Mueller, Marnie (1942–)

Marnie Mueller was born as Margaret Grace Elberson in 1942, the daughter of Don Elberson and Ruth Siegel Elberson, and the first Caucasian American to be born in the Tule Lake Japanese American Segregation Camp in Newell, California, where both of her parents worked during World War II. Mueller spent her early childhood years in the confined space of the camp, an experience that despite her young age left a lasting impression on her.

In 1963 Mueller joined the Peace Corps, which had been established only two years earlier at the initiative of John F. Kennedy, and she happened to commence her tour of duty on the very day Kennedy was shot. Mueller notes in an interview that her "involvement in the Peace Corps was probably the defining episode of my adult life" ("Author Interview"). Stationed as a community organizer in an impoverished *barrio* of Guayaquil, Ecuador, she was faced with the precarious living conditions and environmental health status of the community, and with the agonizing fact that as a Peace Corps volunteer she really had no means to improve them. Moreover, she became increasingly aware of the massive destruction that oil exploration was wreaking on the Ecuadorian rainforests, and recognizing the role that organizations like the Peace Corps played in maintaining the oil companies' interests, she at last became utterly disillusioned with her volunteer work.

After her return from Ecuador, Mueller served as a community organizer in East Harlem in New York and became the Program Director of the public Pacifica Radio station (WBAI). Soon after, she married the German Fritz Mueller, with whom she still lives in New York City. In 1994 Mueller published her first novel, GREEN FIRES, with the non-profit Curbstone Press. Drawing on her Peace Corps experience in Ecuador, Mueller centers her story on an environmental justice conflict between the indigenous population, the Ecuadorian government, and American oil exploration companies. The novel received an American Book Award, a Maria Thomas Award for Outstanding Fiction, and a Best Books for the Teenage Award from the New York City Public Library, all in 1995. Five years later Mueller published her second novel, *The Climate of the Country* (1999), which, as Ralf Seliger has pointed out, is "a kind of prequel to *Green Fires*" (Seliger) and which also heavily draws on Mueller's own experience. Set in the Tule Lake Japanese American Camp, the novel depicts the camp's oppressive and culturally repressive practices against Japanese American detainees, and the struggle of its main protagonist (whom Mueller modeled after her father) to alleviate the plight of the victims. In her third and latest novel, *My Mother's Island* (2002), Mueller depicts an American woman's deathwatch for her estranged mother in the unfamiliar environment of Puerto Rico, in the process of which she comes to terms both with her mother and with her own past.

Mueller was a fellow at the renowned MacDowell Artist Colony in 2001 and has been a lecturer at high schools and universities, as well as at special-interest venues, speaking on subjects related to her novels. In 1999 Peter Jennings included her as a "voice of the twentieth century" in both his ABC documentary *The Century: America's Time* and his book of the same title. In 2004 Tom Jagninski produced a documentary about Mueller, entitled "Marnie Mueller, Novelist," which traces the intricate ways in which history, ecology, biography, and imagination merge in her fiction.— Alexa Weik

BIBLIOGRAPHY

Gale Reference Team. "Mueller, Marnie Grace Elberson (1942–)." *Contemporary Authors*. Andover, UK: Thomson Gale, 2002.

Mueller, Marnie. "Author Interview." *Curbstone Press Website*. Available online. ULR: http://www.curbstone.org/ainterview.cfm?AuthID=21. Accessed June 25, 2009.

_____. *The Climate of the Country*. Willimantic, CT: Curbstone Press, 1999.

_____. *Green Fires: A Novel of the Ecuadorian Rainforest*. Willimantic, CT: Curbstone Press, 1994.

_____. *My Mother's Island*. Willimantic, CT: Curbstone Press, 2002.

_____. *Personal Website*. May 5, 2005. Available online. URL: http://www.marniemueller.com. Accessed June 25, 2009.

Seliger, Ralf. "Tule Lake Travail: Marnie Mueller's Novel Exposes Internment Camps." *Metroactive*. February 25, 1999. Available online. ULR: http://www.metroactive.com/papers/metro/02.25.99/cover/lit-mueller-9908.html. Accessed June 25, 2009.

Green Fires: A Novel of the Ecuadorian Rainforest, Marnie Mueller (1994)

Set in the Ecuadorian rainforest during the late 1960s, Marnie Mueller's debut novel *Green Fires* skillfully interweaves an impressive array of related themes, foregrounding the fundamental conflict between environmental preservation efforts on the one hand, and economic and political interests on the other. With its compelling descriptions of the endangered environment of the tropical rainforest, *Green Fires* reminds us of the fragility of this vital ecosystem and of the dangers involved in the mindless exploitation of its natural resources. Mueller's first-person narrator, the half–Jewish American Annie Saunders Schmidt, knows Ecuador from her tour of duty as a Peace Corps volunteer in Guayaquil; but it is only when she returns for her honeymoon with her German husband Kai that she fully understands the country's precarious environmental situation. When the newlyweds join the Indian Mingo on a trip into the Ecuadorian *Oriente* region to go bird watching, they soon find themselves in the middle of a violent conflict between oil exploration companies, the Ecuadorian government, and the indigenous population. Drawing heavily on her own experience as a Peace Corps volunteer in Ecuador during 1963–65, Mueller uses her main character to voice a powerful critique of the involvement of seemingly benevolent American institutions in the violent actions which, in their reckless pursuit of economic interests, destroy both the precious rainforest and the traditional ways of life of its human inhabitants.

The action of the novel takes place on three different temporal levels. While the main plot is set during a few days in 1969, in the remote *Oriente* in the Northeast of Ecuador, the events of two other, earlier periods play an important role in the development of the story. Annie's difficult childhood as the daughter of a Jewish mother and gentile father emerges as the starting point of an identity struggle that is aggravated when she experiences failure as a Peace Corps volunteer in the Ecuadorian seaport of Guayaquil, and reaches its painful climax when she is involved in the environmental justice battle that is at the heart of the novel. Whereas Annie's past (and unsuccessful) efforts as a community organizer were focused on securing access to clean air and water for the inhabitants of the impoverished *barrio* Cerro Santa Ana, she is now involved in the desperate struggle of indigenous people to defend their natural habitat.

In *Green Fires* Mueller foregrounds the conflicting interests and agendas that characterize environmental justice conflicts in general, and the exploration and exploitation of the equatorial rainforests in particular. Writing her novel in the early 1990s, she sets it back in the 1960s when American oil companies first began exploring the Ecuadorian jungle for oil. As Carlos Herrera notes, "the environmental disaster in indigenous lands in the tropical rain forest" caused by American companies such as Texaco, "is worse than the spill of the Exxon Valdez ... in Alaska" (Herrera), and its detrimental consequences for the indigenous population in the area has inevitably led to conflict. In *Green Fires* the American oil company Somaxo considers the natural resources of the *Oriente* a valuable source of profit, and the Indians who live in the region as obstacles to those profits. The interest of the Ecuadorian government is to improve its country's economic status, and it too has little concern for the ecological space of the rainforest or the people who live in it. The Indians, on the other hand, want to continue their life as they have for centuries, in close connection with the local environment and undisturbed by outside intruders. All the other characters in the novel, be they missionaries, Peace Corps volunteers, travelers or fugitive Nazis, see themselves as well-meaning helpers or friends of the Indians and seem to have a predominantly aesthetic and/or political relationship to the rainforest. What is at stake, for them, is on the one hand the preservation of this precious ecosystem, and on the other the protection of what each of them considers an "innocent people" (240). They all have vowed, for different reasons, to "help the Roani speak for themselves" (288)—and they all fail miserably.

Indeed, the only group that really has no voice at all in the novel is the Roani themselves. Their spokesman, in a sense, is Mingo, a transcultural wanderer between indigenous and western worlds who was educated by missionaries and who now sells arms to the indigenous people so that they can defend themselves against the government's intruders. But not even Mingo, we learn in the novel, is a reliable interpreter of the wants and needs of the Indians. His attempt to unite and arm them against an overly powerful opponent is what leads, ultimately, to the escalation of the conflict and to the bombing of their settlements with napalm and white phosphor, killing many of them and thoroughly destroying the natural environment around them.

Mueller offers no solutions to the complex environmental problems she depicts, and while the novel's representation of unabashed violence against both humans and nature can sometimes be difficult to bear, her work never resorts to a simplistic binary of good versus evil. If the plot of *Green Fires* sometimes reminds one of *Heart of Darkness* (1899), the novel presents us with characters very different from Conrad's, but no less mysterious. Annie's journey into the heart of the Ecuadorian rainforest helps her understand the enormity of the environmental injustice that is happening there, but the motivations of the people involved in the struggle remain convoluted and obscure. "Would the story have been less ambiguous in a running narrative?" Annie wonders towards the end of the novel, after having found out she has no means to preserve the Roani's story on tape. "Would a hero have emerged?" (290). The answer is that there are, in fact, a number of "heroes" in the novel, but that none of them, and certainly not Annie, is a typical American hero, in possession of full and unrestricted agency and thus able to "win" the battle. As it is, Mueller's novel embraces the often painful ambiguity and relativity that environmentalists confront on a daily basis, suggesting in the end the simple but compelling truth, that even in the face of uncertainty and improbable odds we can only continue to fight for environmental preservation and justice as well as we can.— Alexa Weik

BIBLIOGRAPHY

Adamson, Joni. *American Indian Literature, Environmental Justice, and Ecocriticism: The Middle Place*. Tucson: University of Arizona Press, 2001.
Herrera, Carlos. "Ecuador: Oil Exploitation and Environment Rape." *Axis of Logic*. March 5, 2006. Available online. URL: http://www.axisoflogic.com/artman/ publish /article_16093. shtml. Accessed June 25, 2009.
Mueller, Marnie. *Green Fires: A Novel of the Ecuadorian Rainforest*. Willimantic, CT: Curbstone Press, 1994.
Shrader-Frechette, Kristin. *Environmental Justice: Creating Equality, Reclaiming Democracy*. Oxford and New York: Oxford University Press, 2002.

Muir, John (1838–1914)

John Muir, scientist, explorer and writer, is a pivotal figure in the development of both the conservation movement and nature writing (THE CONSERVATION MOVEMENT). Muir was born in 1838, in Dunbar, Scotland, but his father, a fundamentalist Christian and strict disciplinarian, moved the family to the United States when Muir was 11 in an effort to gain more religious autonomy.

In 1860 Muir left home, and in subsequent years explored a host of different life paths, from college student to schoolteacher, inventor, factory foreman, engineer, and sawmill operator. During his time at the University of Wisconsin he developed a love for botany, and this new hobby set him on a lifelong quest to discover new plants, which introduced him to his second great love: wilderness exploration. The combination of these two passions would eventually lead Muir to the Yosemite Valley in California, and around the world. His devotion to these interests only intensified when, in 1867, a sawmill accident temporarily blinded him. According to his biographer Donald Worster, the experience had a profound impact on the young naturalist; he resolved to "throw down his tools, abandon forever any career in industry or invention, and seek his own independent way on earth" (Worster 114). From that time until his marriage, Muir worked only to support his travels in the wilderness.

After completing his famous "1,000-mile walk" through the southern United States and Cuba, he arrived in San Francisco in 1868 and immediately headed to the Yosemite Valley. Initially Muir worked as a sheepherder in the mountains, and this work provided him with a small income and plenty of time for botany and journal-writing. Muir later collected and revised the journals produced during the summer of 1869 to create one of his most important works, *My First Summer in the Sierra* (1910). That summer of exploring the mountains was a pivotal experience for Muir; it "awakened the deepest and most intense passion of his life, a long moment of ecstasy that he would try to remember and relive to the end of his days" (160). In the following passage from that text Muir describes sleeping on a boulder that lay at the foot of a waterfall, and the passage illustrates his enthusiastic and spiritual understanding of nature, as well as his penchant for immersing himself in his surroundings:

After dark, when the camp was at rest, I groped my way back to the altar boulder and passed the night on it,—above the water beneath the leaves and stars,—everything still more impressive than by day, the fall seen dimly white, singing Nature's old love song with solemn enthusiasm, while the stars peering through the leaf-roof seemed to join in the white water's song. Precious night, precious day to abide in me forever. Thanks be to God for this immortal gift [*My First* 49].

Muir lived and worked in the Yosemite Valley for the next six years, and gradually began writing during the winter to support himself, spending the summers exploring the great wildernesses of the west coast. Over time he developed a reputation as an expert back-country guide. Muir's out-going personality and eccentric "mountain-man" persona, coupled with his role as guide, allowed him to easily befriend the politicians, scientists, and dignitaries that visited Yosemite in the summer. It also allowed him access to many influential people. His most famous trip was with then–President THEODORE ROOSEVELT, whom he guided through Yosemite in 1903 and convinced of the importance of protecting the valley. The people Muir met also had a profound effect on him. While guiding geology professor Joseph LeConte in 1870, Muir discovered his own love of geology. Discussions about the geological origins of Yosemite that occurred during this trip, and others like it, caused Muir to become interested in the study of glaciers. He taught himself geology, and in 1871, produced his first geological publication, "Yosemite Glaciers," which argues that glaciers were responsible for the formation of the valley; then a novel theory, Muir's explanation has now been accepted as fact.

Also during this period, Muir began writing for the conservation movement, and became a reluctant political reformer. He was a central figure in efforts to designate Yosemite and other parts of the west as National Parks, and in 1890 he published "Treasures of Yosemite" and "Features of the Proposed Yosemite National Park" in *Century* magazine to support the cause. Muir's influence on these issues is illustrated by the fact that his description of the proposed park's borders in the latter essay closely mirrored the boundaries eventually established by politicians when Congress passed the Yosemite bill later that year. Even that considerable influence, however, had its limits: 23 years after this initial success with Yosemite, Muir was unable to convince the government to save the Hetch Hetchy Valley, Yosemite's twin, lying just north of it. In 1913 the government agreed to allow the damming of Hetch Hetchy in order to provide water to San Francisco.

In addition to these political achievements, Muir's increasingly skilful attempts to depict the science, spirituality, and sublimity that he saw in nature helped to establish and define nature writing as a genre (Worster 562), effecting a critical Copernican shift from human- to nature-centred perspective:

"Building on parson-naturalist Gilbert White, Concord's HENRY DAVID THOREAU, and JOHN BURROUGHS," Muir's writing "focused more on nature and its workings or meanings than on the trials and triumphs ... of humankind" (Worster 462). According to environmental literature scholar LAWRENCE BUELL, Muir's writing "satisfied ... a 'taste for realism' that characterized the late nineteenth century," an era when the natural sciences were beginning to gain considerable influence and prestige (qtd in Worster 341). However, Muir's writing always maintained a "tension," Worster notes, between science and religion (342). Muir saw science as a way to unlock the mysteries of nature, and thus, of God's work. This did not undermine that work, in Muir's view, but merely allowed us to better understand and appreciate it (Worster 208). In his own words, "Beauty is God, and what shall we say of God that we may not say of Beauty" (qtd in Worster 208).

In his thoughts on conservation, Muir was no radical. He viewed nature as essential for "human health — mental, physical, and economic" (Worster 308). However, he disagreed with those who ignored the first two elements in favor of the last. Muir saw nature as a tonic for the materialist excesses of urban life, and felt that certain special places should be set aside for this purpose alone (Worster 222), a view echoed later by more radical environmentalists like the influential EDWARD ABBEY. Perhaps Muir's greatest contribution to the conservation movement lay simply in the pure passion and love of nature inspired by his writings. His factual, yet inspiring descriptions of natural phenomena aimed to show the public that everything — even the fiercest storms and most forbidding glaciers — was a part of a glorious and harmonious plan (Worster 340), substantiating the often rarified speculations of the earlier TRANSCENDENTALISTS like EMERSON and Thoreau. His ultimate goal, modest but enduring, was simply to promote the appreciation of nature and celebrate nature's beauty in all its myriad detail. The end of one of his most popular essays, "A Wind-storm in the Forests," illustrates well his celebratory and infectious enthusiasm:

> When the storm began to abate, I dismounted and sauntered down through the calming woods. The storm-tones died away, and, turning toward the east, I beheld the countless hosts of the forests hushed and tranquil, towering above one another on the slopes of the hills like a devout audience. The setting sun filled them with amber light, and seemed to say, while they listened, "My peace I give unto you."
>
> As I gazed on the impressive scene, all the so called ruin of the storm was forgotten, and never before did these noble woods appear so fresh, so

joyous, so immortal [*Mountains* 256].— Lauren
Mitchell Nahas

BIBLIOGRAPHY

Muir, John. *The Mountains of California*. New York: Century, 1922.
_____. *My First Summer in the Sierra*. Boston: Houghton Mifflin, 1911.
The Sierra Club. "Chronology (Timeline) of Life and Legacy of John Muir." The Sierra Club online. URL: http://www.sierraclub.org/john_muir_exhibit/framein dex.html?http://www.sierraclub.org/john_muir_exhibit/ john_muir_day_study_guide/biographical_timeline.html. Accessed on Aug 2 2008.
Worster, Donald. *A Passion for Nature: The Life of John Muir*. Oxford: Oxford University Press, 2008.

"The American Forests," John Muir (1897)

In 1896, John Muir joined the National Forest Commission, a group of scientists appointed by the Department of the Interior, as they traveled through American forests gathering information to make recommendations about how best to manage these national resources. The next summer *The Atlantic Monthly* published "The American Forests," an essay Muir wrote that introduced the Commission's work to a broad public, and provided a religious and pragmatic argument for the kind of forest management he supported.

The nuanced stance on federal forest preservation that Muir articulates in this essay — combining religious, aesthetic, economic, and nationalist arguments to urge the necessity of federal, and preferably military, protection of western forests — reflects the divisions within the Commission and the American public between "rational, development-oriented conservationists ... and the aesthetically oriented preservationists" (Williams 179). Both sides believed forests should be managed and used by humans, but only the latter group valued aesthetic forms of "use." When Muir revised "The American Forests" and published it as the final essay in *Our National Parks* (1901), he dedicated the book to Charles Sprague Sargent, the Harvard botanist who led the National Forest Commission. By doing so, Muir reiterated his support of Sargent's preservationist views over the more economically oriented position of Gifford Pinchot, who also participated in the Commission and later became the first Chief of the United States Forest Service. In "The American Forests" Muir provides a succinct articulation of his religious reasons for preserving tracts of wild forest while also arguing that such preservation made practical, economic sense.

The essay begins with a mythic frame that gives American forests an exceptional status: "The forests of America, however slighted by man, must have been a great delight to God; for they were the best he ever planted" (331). This divine care justifies Muir's portrayal of America as an Eden that contained "the largest, most varied, most fruitful, and most beautiful trees in the world" (331) (THE BIBLE). He moves from region to region describing the American forests as an eternal paradise where humans, animals, and plants dwelled harmoniously, with "enough and to spare for every feeding, sheltering beast and bird, insect and son of Adam" (335). This Edenic existence fell, however, when "the steel axe of the white man rang out" (335). It is not the entrance of humans or the introduction of agriculture to which Muir attributes this fall — the development of human civilization may require buffalo to be replaced by cattle and sections of forest to be converted into fruit orchards and cornfields. Instead, Muir condemns the sinful actions of shortsighted settlers, who "in the blindness of hunger, ... claiming Heaven as their guide, regarded God's trees as only a larger kind of pernicious weeds" (336). It is this arrogant attitude that Muir claims causes the destruction of God's best forest gardens.

The religious tone of this introduction establishes Muir's ultimate reasons for valuing wild forests — he fears that soon "not a grove will be left to rest in or pray in" (337)—but he follows this with an appeal to the more pragmatic members of his audience. Citing Pinchot's research on the forest management practices of other countries, Muir argues that the United States needs to learn from nations that manage their forests centrally. In contrast to these governments, Muir characterizes the federal government as a "rich and foolish spendthrift" who plunders and wastes its "magnificent" inheritance (340).

A combination of poor laws and weak enforcement has left the Western forests vulnerable to an array of forest "destroyers" (353): mill companies, railroads, miners, shepherds, and shake makers. As he catalogues these destroyers, Muir becomes most incensed when describing their waste: lumber companies are "grossly wasteful" (351), blasting the "sublimely beautiful" (350) Sequoias with gunpowder and using only portions of the trees they cut; miners and railroad companies carelessly allow their fires to burn whole hillsides; shepherds burn off the trees to promote the growth of meadows and allow their sheep to turn fertile slopes into bare dirt. Even though the shake makers use only a small portion of each tree they cut, Muir treats these "[h]appy robbers" with more sympathy because at least they enjoy a comfortable and independent existence in the forests (356). Muir concludes his litany of destruction by claiming that "from five to ten times as much is destroyed as is used, chiefly by running forest fires that only the federal government can stop" (356). As a final warning, he cites THOREAU's description, in THE MAINE WOODS, of desperate Eastern loggers who, after decades of waste and mismanagement, are forced to harvest increasingly scrubby trees, and Muir insists the same fate awaits the once abundant Western forests.

Muir concludes his essay by urging "the government to begin a rational administration of its forests" that will ensure they remain "a never failing fountain of wealth and beauty," emphasizing his consideration of both pragmatic and aesthetic concerns (359, 360). Until now, corruption has kept Congress from addressing this issue, but Muir quotes EMERSON's "Compensation" to support his belief that progress will prevail and the woods will be saved from their destroyers (362). Returning to the religious narrative with which he began, Muir invites his readers and the federal government to stop this destruction and instead to participate in God's careful gardening: "Through all the wonderful, eventful centuries since Christ's time — and long before that — God has cared for these trees, saved them from drought, disease, avalanches, and a thousand straining, leveling tempests and floods; but he cannot save them from fools, — only Uncle Sam can do that" (364–65). Muir's religious frame is not only "consistent with his world view," but it also connects wilderness preservation with the "Evangelical reforming spirit" that lay behind much of the Progressive efforts to reform society via the government (Williams 181). So although Muir expresses a view of forest management that values religious and aesthetic uses, he agreed with conservationists like Pinchot that "the federal government had a key role to play in enacting restrictions on forest use. Unlike Thoreau, he did not conceive of wilderness in the ideological terms of 'absolute freedom,' one meaning of which was a complete negative freedom beyond the reach of governments" (Dorman 153). The destruction that Muir witnessed in the Western forests made this earlier conception of wilderness untenable for him. And while the battles between conservationists and preservationists only escalated in the early twentieth century, Muir's biographer Donald Worster argues that because of "The American Forests" and Muir's other essays, the federal government increasingly recognized the need to manage its forests wisely (356). — Jeffrey Bilbro

BIBLIOGRAPHY

Dorman, Robert L. *A Word for Nature: Four Pioneering Environmental Advocates, 1845–1913.* Chapel Hill: University of North Carolina Press, 1998.
Muir, John. "The American Forests." *Our National Parks.* Boston: Houghton, Mifflin, 1901. 331–65.
Nash, Roderick Frazier. *Wilderness and the American Mind.* 4th ed. New Haven: Yale University Press, 2001.
Williams, Dennis. *God's Wilds: John Muir's Vision of Nature.* College Station: Texas A&M University Press, 2002.
Worster, Donald. *A Passion for Nature: The Life of John Muir.* New York: Oxford University Press, 2008.

The Mountains of California, John Muir (1894)

Adapted from essays published 1875–1882, Muir's first book recounts his extensive — and often ecstatic — experiences traveling in the wilderness in and around California's Sierra Nevada mountains. Unlike his later book about these same mountains, *My First Summer in the Sierra* (1911), *The Mountains of California* is not a single, cohesive narrative. Its 16 chapters reveal a diverse mix of genres, some resembling short stories or narrative sketches ("A Near View of the High Sierra," "The River Floods"), others reading like natural history ("The Water-Ouzel" "The Bee-Pastures"), while one is constructed as a reference work ("The Forests").

The chapters are united, however, by their setting among the Sierra, and by Muir's euphoric praise of the mountains' singular character and beauty. Describing a rainstorm over the Sierra, for example, he declares that "scarcely a drop can fail to find a beautiful mark [...]. Good work and happy work for the merry mountain raindrops" (485). However, it is important to note that when Muir praises the "beauty" of nature (as he does in almost every paragraph) he means something far more complex than its superficial, sensory appeal. "A Near View of the High Sierra," describing Muir's chance meeting with two artists in the wilderness, perhaps best articulates what sort of beauty he seeks to encounter in his mountaineering and express in his writing. Early in the piece, he muses that he wishes to "carry colors and brushes" with him on his travels, "and learn to paint" the "glorious picture" presented by the mountains (345); and here he seems to be aligning nature writing with painting, suggesting that his written pieces are essentially prose portraits of natural scenery. However, though they initially seem similar, Muir's work and the work of the artists are shown to sharply diverge: "the artists went heartily to their work and I to mine" (347).

In narrating the events that follow, Muir expresses the higher purpose of his writing: to capture in prose nature's deep harmony and structure. This is nature's true "beauty." Leaving the artists behind to paint a handsome and "typical alpine landscape" (347), Muir ventures deeper into the wilderness. While the artists only appreciate the superficially beautiful, Muir can appreciate even those scenes that are "less separable [...] into artistic bits capable of being made into warm, sympathetic, lovable pictures" (344). This deeper appreciation is earned only through the extensive experiential knowledge of the writer/mountaineer: "it is only after [the mountains] have been studied one by one, long and lovingly, that their far-reaching harmonies become manifest" (357). In other words, the "beauty" and "harmony" Muir senses in nature are not superficial or visual but structural and intuited.

When he suggests that nature's structure is harmonious, however, he does not mean that it is necessarily gentle or hospitable. Indeed, if there is a nature writer who sees the "grandeur" in the Darwinian view of nature — that is, in the generative force of struggle and violence — it is Muir. In "A Wind-Storm in the Forests," for example, he praises the destructive powers of hail, lightning, snow, winds, and avalanches. These are the tools of "Nature's forestry," a benevolent natural demolition that through its destructive agency actually fortifies life. "The manifest result of all this wild storm-culture is the glorious perfection we behold" (465). Muir, in other words, sees beyond the immediate violence of nature to sense the deeper, harmonious structure of which that violence is a part. To bear witness to this (chaotic) harmony, Muir suggests, is the ultimate human experience.

Like the TRANSCENDENTALISTs he admired Muir insists that we can learn from nature, that nature "has always something rare to show us" (467). But Muir, one might say, climbs several perilous footholds higher in the cliff of intense experience than ruminative path-strollers like EMERSON or THOREAU. Because violence and struggle are part of nature's harmony, Muir's pursuit of experience in nature often verges on the extreme and dangerous. Indeed, ecocritic LAWRENCE BUELL indicts him for being at times "quite foolhardy and imperious" in seeking to validate his vision of nature's harmony "by showing that he could experience even the most hostile environments as friendly" (194). In "The River Floods," for example, Muir turns storm-chaser, abruptly leaving a friend's home to "enjoy" a ferocious storm in the wilderness (467).

If transcendentalism valued nature's power to quietly enlighten its observer, Muir values nature's power to quiet the observer entirely, body and soul. The aesthetic spectacle that is nature can negate the self, can make you "secure from yourself." You can be "dissolved in it" until "you are all eye" (395). This seeming allusion to the "transparent eyeball," of Emerson's NATURE (1836), however, can be misleading. Insisting that nature's beauty exists to enlighten the human spirit, Emerson locates man at the center of nature (albeit as appendage of the divine). In Muir's vision humans are just a small and largely ex-

pendable part of nature; and what humans behold in nature is not, as Emerson claimed, a revelatory metaphor for the human spirit, but a reality greater than (and largely indifferent to) humankind.

From a contemporary perspective informed by environmentalism, we might see Emerson's perspective as "anthropocentric," and Muir's (at least in this book) as "ecocentric," attributing to nature a value independent of, and even opposed to, human interests. As environmental historian Donald Worster observes, The Mountains of California "was meant to be an interpretation of a world that humans had not made [...]. Such a world where people were not dominant." Thus, Muir "tried to erase himself and indeed all humans from his pages" (341). In fact, the sheer intensity of his ecocentrism leads Muir to make statements that, divorced from context, may at times seem cheerily misanthropic. In the introductory chapter, "The Sierra Nevada," he expresses something like amusement in observing that people have built their homes on the "flanks of volcanoes," and declares that he can "hardly fail to look forward to its [that is, Mt. Shasta's] next eruption" (322). Indeed, human safety — including his own safety — is not a priority in The Mountains of California, and at times Muir seems to valorize death. Wilderness, he admits, can quite literally kill you: "True, there are innumerable places where the careless step will be the last step" (363). But in another sense, a spiritual sense, the wild is "safer" than the "doleful chambers of civilization" (363, 364). Wilderness, Muir insists, will "save you from deadly apathy, set you free, and call forth every faculty into vigorous, enthusiastic action" (364). Though it endangers his body, wilderness energizes Muir because it allows him to see beyond himself, beyond conventional human perspective altogether, and to sense the (violent) harmonies of nature of which he and we all are part.

The Mountains of California was published two years after Muir helped found The Sierra Club, but as Worster notes, it is not an explicit "conservation tract" (341). There are certain paragraphs that speculate on the possibility of a species' extinction, or that warn of environmental hazards like "the sheep evil," that is, overgrazing (Muir 547). These, however, are few and far between. The book is less interested in intervening in specific conservation issues than in testifying to the power of nature as an aesthetic spectacle and in articulating a radically ecocentric worldview. That being said, this worldview "certainly had political and ethical implications," as Worster suggests (341); implications that would inform both Muir's later writings and his incipient career as chief public advocate of natural preservation. It is for this reason, we may assume, that despite its almost complete neglect of politics, *The Mountains of California* became, according to historian Michael P. Cohen, "the Sierra Club's chief text, a political book" (284).— Erich Werner

BIBLIOGRAPHY

Buell, Lawrence. *The Environmental Imagination: Thoreau, Nature Writing, and the Formation of American Culture.* Cambridge, MA: Harvard University Press, 1995.

Cohen, Michael P. *The Pathless Way: John Muir and American Wilderness.* Madison: University of Wisconsin Press, 1984.

Cronon, William. "Note on the Text." In *John Muir: Nature Writings.* New York: Modern Library, 1997. 850–853.

Muir, John. "The Mountains of California." In *John Muir: Nature Writings.* New York: Modern Library, 1997. 315–547.

Worster, Donald. *A Passion for Nature: The Life of John Muir.* Oxford: Oxford University Press, 2008.

Steep Trails, John Muir (1918)

Steep Trails is a collection of articles and letters John Muir wrote over the course of 29 years, assembled four years after his death. Many of the texts had not been previously published or were published locally prior to this book. Each essay is sharply focused on a specific place, often on its nonhuman features such as geography, flora, or fauna. When human life comes into view, Muir concentrates on particular regional features, especially those that are idiosyncratic, such as Mormon marriage traditions or Nevada's farming culture. Though the style of the essays varies considerably, their characteristic approach is travelogue, and Muir's keen naturalist's eye, great physical energy, and high enthusiasm are constants in the collection. Introducing a 1994 edition of the book, Edward Hoagland finds it "among [Muir's] best" because in it we see Muir's "feeling of gaiety and spontaneity after a series of strenuous, exuberant hikes" (Hoagland ix).

Steep Trails focuses on the American West, detailing Muir's roamings as far east as Utah and the Grand Canyon, as far south as Los Angeles, as far north as Victoria, Canada, and as high in altitude as 14,411 feet (the current measurement of Mt. Rainier, in Washington state, very close to the altitude Muir reports for it, despite his editor's incorrect attempt to claim its measure as 13,394 feet [Muir 186]). While the book devotes significant space to Muir's accounts of time spent in Nevada, Utah, and Arizona, its greatest portion focuses from Mt. Shasta, in California, northward, including considerable attention to Oregon, Washington, and the southern portions of Canada's British Columbia.

These Pacific Northwestern regions garner much acclaim from Muir for their great rivers, their striking, snow-bound volcanic mountains, and particularly their stately and enormous trees. The trees, massed in impressive forests, seem to Muir to dwarf everything human: "Notwithstanding the tremendous energy displayed in lumbering [...], the woods of Washington are still almost entirely virgin and wild, without trace of human touch, savage or civilized" (172). Muir's account of the people of this region, however, is rather more muted in its praise, noting for instance that although the loggers of Puget Sound near Seattle are "altogether free from quick, jerky fussiness" due to their daily physical labor, they also grow into a "tired, somewhat haggard appearance" as they age (177).

As Roderick Nash reports, Muir became a "champion" for wild country partly as an antidote to Western civilization (Nash 122). However, a nineteenth-century faith in a certain kind of progress animates much of the book in ways that can seem surprising. Muir appears, for instance, to accept as natural and inevitable the supplanting of Native Americans by Euro-American settlers (Worster 227), and he appears unresolved at times about how to engage nature. He is ready for a place like Oregon to surrender its "Natural wealth" (193), which he finds "open and ripe for use" (195).

Muir does not fail to register numerous suggestions about preservation, however. Immediately after noting that "the sugar pine makes excellent lumber," for example, and calling it "too good to live" as it "is already passing rapidly away before the woodman's axe" (219), he suggests establishing a "park of moderate extent" in Oregon to protect sugar pines, a proposal that he also raises for the Mt. Shasta region in northern California (74). And as Donald Worster points out, Muir's tireless efforts to preserve particularly beautiful tracts of land as parks or forest preserves were remembered as central to his life achievements in the newspaper obituaries that followed his death (Worster 461–462). This pragmatic element of Muir's work — offering policy proposals — is akin to his persistent quantitative approach to much of what he studies in *Steep Trails*, whether it is counting the hairs on wild sheep in the book's first chapter (4), comparing mountains' elevations (20), or carefully reporting plant life in Mormon towns by counting leaves (e.g., 93). But Muir, like THOREAU before him, almost invariably embeds these facts in a broader perspective by way of some final story, comment, or metaphor, as when he concludes his scientific account of Mormon lilies by taking note of the one, rare Mormon woman whom he thought lived up to a metaphoric comparison to these flowers he so admires.

Admiration is the characteristic emotion of Muir's many descriptions of animals in the book, whether it is the rattlesnake he finds and tolerates at his feet (108), the Douglas squirrel who locates "without any apparent guidance" leftover horse feed (46), or the wild sheep, an "admirable alpine rover" not unlike Muir himself (228). Indeed, his enthusiasm for animals and landscapes often seems greater than that for people, and his strong preference for mountains also emerges in these sketches. Yosemite Valley is a case in point. The object of constant reference (as in 50, 106, 187, 250–251), the valley is even employed as a kind of adjective: "yosemitic" (89); and this usage aptly characterizes a book that approaches the world in a vigorously particular way, as if there were no general category of mountain valley or tree, but rather only particular examples, such as Yosemite or Oregon ash. Such usages also illustrate the book's profoundly place-centered approach.

In *Steep Trails*, as in other Muir works like *My First Summer in the Sierra* and THE MOUNTAINS OF CALIFORNIA, some of the most gripping narratives develop from the author's mountaineering adventures. His climbing accounts are marvelous simply as tales of personal gumption, but more importantly bear Muir's signature in their insistence on praising the outer world more than on proving the traveler's inner strength. His constantly outward orientation, his focus on what is beyond or in addition to the human self, marks much of his work as profoundly environmental, and fosters a surprising humility that tempers and complements his ebullient joy. Muir loved to wander widely, to talk, as Worster explains, to anyone he could (Worster 4–5), and to sing praises of the world he found. So it is not surprising that this characteristic collection of essays ends by noting that in careful study of the wonders of nature's life, we "enrich and lengthen our own" (272).— Ryan Hediger

BIBLIOGRAPHY

Hoagland, Edward. "Foreword." *Steep Trails*. John Muir. San Francisco: Sierra Club Books, 1994.
Muir, John. *Steep Trails*. 1918. San Francisco: Sierra Club Books, 1994.
Nash, Roderick. *Wilderness and the American Mind*. Third Edition. New Haven: Yale University Press, 1982.
Worster, Donald. *A Passion for Nature: The Life of John Muir*. Oxford: Oxford University Press, 2008.

Gloria Naylor (1950–   )

Bestselling novelist, essayist, educator and screenwriter with her own production company (One Way Productions), Gloria Naylor is a leading figure in the African-American feminist movement. She was born in 1950, in New York City, to Roosevelt Naylor and Alberta McAlpin Naylor, who had recently moved to the city after spending their lives as sharecroppers in Mississippi. Though Naylor never experienced that punishing but deeply earth-centered life, it would form a consistent and fecund counterpoise to her urban upbringing, and figure prominently in her literary work. As a young child, Naylor was extremely shy; her mother presented her with a writing journal, and Naylor's love of writing flourished. Through her school years she wrote steadily, penning numerous short stories, until the assassination of Martin Luther King in 1968. This tragedy caused a crisis of reflection in the young author, and she decided to become a missionary for the Jehovah's witnesses, remaining in this role until 1975. At the age of 25, Naylor left her missionary work to pursue a degree in English at Brooklyn College; after graduating in 1981, she went to Yale, and received an M.A. in African American studies in 1983; thereby laying the two principal intellectual foundations of her future writing.

Naylor's writing consistently explores the liminal space between the urban environment of her youth, and the rural life of her parents' experience, with the former rarely benefiting from the comparison. Her first novel, the bestselling *The Women of Brewster Place* (1982), depicts the claustrophobic and often debilitating inner-city lives of seven African American women, isolated even from the rest of the city by a huge wall, and from nature by the city on the other side. The visceral symbol of the wall, echoed in countless more subtle and insidious forms throughout the novel, is literally overcome by the novel's end, when it is physically torn down by the women.

In contrast to this violent but cathartic "negative" virtue — seemingly the only one possible for those so deeply mired in the unnatural environment — Naylor's *MAMA DAY* (1988), divided now between New York City and Willow Springs, a small island between Georgia and South Carolina, reaches across the human "wall" to what has been walled *out*. Here nature, portrayed unflinchingly in all its destructive force, is nonetheless a healer — perhaps the only healer possible for the city's man-made "cures." After this second novel, Naylor returned to the city she knew so well, and what might be termed the apophatic anatomy of urban salvation, with *Baily's Café* (1992), *The Men of Brewster Place* (1998) and *1996* (2005).— Candace A. Henry

Mama Day, Gloria Naylor (1988)

Gloria Naylor's third novel, *Mama Day*, takes place in two disparate settings: New York City and Willow Springs, a fictional barrier island off the coasts of South Carolina and Georgia but belonging to neither. The novel's New York sections tell the story of Cocoa Day and her relationship with George Andrews. Abandoned at birth, George grew up in a state home for boys and has always lived by the motto of the home's director: "only the present has potential." Cocoa was raised by her grandmother Abigail and her great-aunt Miranda "Mama" Day, the island's matriarch, midwife, and nurse; and she visits Willow Springs every August. It is during one of these visits home that Cocoa and George's love for each other, and the possibility of blending two belief systems and ways of life, are tested against malevolent forces on the island.

Willow Springs is a community with a particularly strong sense of place and history. The town owes its existence to the mythic Sapphira Wade, a "true conjure woman" who could "walk through a lightning storm without being touched" and who, in just a thousand days convinced her master/lover/husband to "deed all his slaves every inch of land in Willow Springs" (3). Sapphira Wade is the "grand mother" of the island, and though herself mythical and unknown — "the *name* Sapphira Wade is never breathed out of a single mouth in Willow Springs" — her legacy is actual and has ensured the inhabitants of the island ownership of their land for all generations to come.

The front matter of the novel, consisting of a family tree and map of the island, signals the centrality of both history and place. Significant locales infused with the power of memory and ritual abound in the novel. Dr. Buzzard's camp in the woods, Abigail's house, "the other place," and the island of Willow Springs itself — all function under specific rules defined largely by their physical makeup and their relation to the natural laws that encompass them. And whether exploring bakeries in the outer boroughs of New York or looking for choke-cherry trees in the woods of Willow Springs, the characters in the novel must become open to and aware of their environments if they have any hope of finding help or pleasure in them. Unlike the developers who periodically invade the island hoping to entice land owners into selling their beach-front property, the residents of Willow Springs understand the folly of fighting against a nature that would knock them into "the bottom of the marsh first hurricane [blew] through here" (4). The rapacious misuse of nature, as seen in the developers and in Ruby's vindictive root magic, is unwelcome and punishable.

Critic Daphne Lamothe considers a further and more profound function of nature in the novel, suggesting that "[t]he characters' navigation of this landscape, the weaving together of places, becomes a metaphor for the constitution of memories, for the weaving together of narratives about those memories" (158). This metaphorical intertwining of generations, places, and traditions is equally instantiated in Miranda's tending of the garden at the other place, in the way she teaches George a lesson by dragging him through the difficult East Woods, and in the way she uses housekeeping and gardening to teach Bernice patience and Reema proper childcare. For all the novel's mystical qualities, there would be no magic, no power, without the physical realities of the land and people who respect and know them well.

Redolent with shades of her Shakespearean namesake, Miranda, Sapphira Wade's great-granddaughter, is the novel's most powerful advocate for the harmonious balance of man and nature, combining the power of the natural world and the power of history in her abilities as a healer and a seer. Without an understanding of the personal history preceding her she would find no power in nature. However, she knows that the natural world, and the place of humanity within it, is not static or assured. Lamothe notes Naylor's "interest in the ideas of traditional rootedness and collective identity" (159), and this is particularly evident in Miranda's view of the natural world and its place in human rituals.

When a hurricane threatens to destroy Miranda's garden at "the other place" she mourns this potential loss because of the many years she took to restore it after the last big storm. It is significant that the garden was returned to its original state rather than being improved upon. As critic Paula Gallant Eckard suggests, "the past [in Naylor's fiction] becomes a multi-dimensional, prismatic entity that shapes familial, community, and cultural history" (121). Even though Miranda can only guess why the garden was laid out as it was, she has resurrected it faithfully. However, this desire to maintain the past as it was is not an all-encompassing one. When the town's ritual of Candle Walk (a secular holiday involving the exchange of gifts that "came from the earth and the work of your own hands") begins to change, many of the older residents fear the loss of their tradition (110); but Miranda reasons that by the time people stop practicing or talking about the practice of Candle Walk, "it won't be the world as we know it no way — and so no need for the memory" (111).

Miranda is the keeper of memory and the seat of the collective identity of the island. Childless herself, she has delivered so many babies, and nursed so many sick men and women, that the island has come to think of her as "[e]verybody's mama" (89). Her connections stretch far back along generational and historical lines and extend, tendril-like, throughout the community, but her voice is not the only one of importance. Consciously drawing on ZORA NEALE

HURSTON'S THEIR EYES WERE WATCHING GOD and its depiction of a community waiting to be taken or spared by violent nature, Naylor enters the mind of the community as a whole as a hurricane bears down on Willow Springs. Serving as a kind of refrain to Hurston's "eyes [...] watching God," Naylor's storm scene shows the residents of Willow Springs turning away from the storm-watches of the mainland "so folks can sit in the quiet, a respectful silence, for the coming of the force" (249). As Miranda reminds Abigail, "[i]t ain't got nothing to do with us, we just bystanders on this earth" (228). It is the *quality* of their bystanding, however, that so distinguishes these islanders, and the novel ultimately derives both its power and peace from this interconnectivity — of people and the natural world, of individuals and their neighbors, of families, of history.— Kimberly O'Dell Cox

BIBLIOGRAPHY

Eckard, Paula Gallant. "The Prismatic Past in *Oral History* and *Mama Day*." *MELUS*. 20.3 (1995): 121–135.
Hurston, Zora Neale. *Their Eyes Were Watching God*. 1937. New York: Harper Perennial, 1990.
Lamothe, Daphne. "Gloria Naylor's *Mama Day*: Bridging Roots and Routes." *African American Review*. 39.1–2 (2005): 155–169.
Naylor, Gloria. *Mama Day*. 1988. New York: Vintage, 1993.

Oliver, Mary (1935–   )

Mary Oliver's poetry and essays explore the relationship between the human and non-human world, and challenge the notion that humans can exist apart from or opposed to nature.

Born in 1935 in Cleveland, Ohio, and now living in Provincetown, Massachusetts, Oliver dropped out of college to pursue her writing, but has taught or been a writer-in-residence at several colleges, including Duke University and Sweet Briar College. She draws much of her inspiration from the natural world and wrote about her personal connection to the environment in the essay "Winter Hours," bluntly affirming that without nature she would not be a poet (98). She claims to speak on behalf of nature, rather than about it, and argues that humans are connected to the world by "a thousand unbreakable links" (102).

Among her influences, Oliver lists RALPH WALDO EMERSON, RACHEL CARSON, ALDO LEOPOLD, and Mary Shelley, all of whom, she claims, encourage being both part of the world and a dreamer (*Winter Hours* 20). Reflecting the TRANSCENDENTALISM of Emerson, Oliver imagines that living and nonliving objects possess "other identities that are inhuman but neither unconscious or mute" (McNew 66). Her poetry examines the boundaries between the human and nonhuman world, seeking "natural communion" and the deepest springs of humanity. In poems like "August" and "Wings," in her *House of Light* (1990), Oliver writes from the perspective of an object or nonhuman entity, enacting the consciousness she believes exists in every natural thing of the world. Oliver's work remains grounded in that world even when musing on death, and this latter is a constant presence in her poems, which are dominated by themes of loss, limitations, and the chance for renewal. Death is a critical part of the life cycle, as Oliver writes in "Ghosts": "In the book of the Earth it is written: / *nothing can die*" (*Primitive* 28–30); here describing the thick grasses growing where bison droppings once fertilized the ground, and illustrating the interdependence of living things. In addition, her poems contain a strong sense of place, focusing primarily on the Ohio of her upbringing and the area of New England where she now lives.

The title poem of her first book, *No Voyage and Other Poems*, won first prize from the American Society of Poetry in 1962. Oliver won the Pulitzer Prize for her book of poetry, *American Primitive* in 1984 and the National Book Award for Poetry in 1992 with *New and Selected Poems*.— Liz Clift

BIBLIOGRAPHY

Harde, Roxanne. "Mary Oliver." *Contemporary American Women Poets*. Ed. Catherine Cucinella. Westport, CT: Greenwood, 2002.
Look, Marie. "Mary Oliver." *World Literature Today*. 81.4 (July-August 2007): 52(1).
McNew, Janet. "Mary Oliver and the Tradition of Romantic Nature Poetry." *Contemporary Literature*. 30.1 (Spring 1989): 59–77.
Oliver, Mary. *American Primitive*. New York: Little, Brown, 1984.
_____. *House of Light*. Boston: Beacon Press, 1990.
_____. *No Voyage and Other Poems*. Expanded Edition. New York: Houghton Mifflin, 1965.
_____. *Winter Hours*. Boston: Mariner Books, 2000.

Red Bird,
Mary Oliver (2008)

In *Red Bird*, renowned poet and nature-writer Mary Oliver's 23 book of poems, she continues her literary exploration and intimate dialogue with the animal, plant, and human world. Famously sparse in a world of material and verbal excess, *Red Bird* is Oliver's largest collection, containing 61 poems exploring such themes as the author's inevitable death, aging, spirituality, and the value of human accomplishments when viewed from a larger, ecological perspective. In *Red Bird* Oliver's "keen observation of the natural world and her gratitude for its gifts" (frontispiece *Red Bird*) leap to the forefront, spoken to the reader in Oliver's direct and lean poetic voice.

Oliver uses concrete images sparingly — a single red bird in a frozen landscape, for example — but the sheer precision of such images allows them to resonate with visual and metaphoric power.

The title poem, "Red Bird," begins the book with the simple stanza, "Red bird came all winter/ firing up the landscape/ as nothing else could" (1); but implied here are the continued daily observations of the speaker, her habitual awareness of her surroundings, and her gratitude and reliance on the red bird that fires up the landscape she inhabits. Such gratitude subverts the typical human-animal hierarchy: "perhaps because the winter is so long/ and the sky so black-blue,/ or perhaps because the heart narrows/ as often as it opens —/ I am grateful that red bird comes all winter" (1). Oliver thus places human life within a broader ecological framework in which bird and human interact on equal terms, where human life is not dominant, but a part of nature, and where the speaker, burdened by the length and darkness of winter, is reanimated by the flash of a single bird.

Throughout *Red Bird* Oliver returns to the notion of human life as one small part of a larger ecosystem. In the poem "Straight Talk from Fox" a fox recounts the joy experienced in licking dew from leaves, smelling the fat of ducks, finding a rabbit with a fast-beating heart, and traveling dark, deserted roads outside of town (11). Written from the point of view of the fox, the narrator tells readers he has witnessed human life by peeking in our windows. Comparing his life to that of humans, he exclaims, "What I am, and I know it, is/ responsible, joyful, thankful. I would not/ give my life for a thousand of yours" (11).

Oliver often records wisdom received from observing the natural world. In "Luke" she celebrates the dog's transcendent joy as it sniffs flowers in a field: the dog "adored/ every blossom,/ not in the serious,/ careful way/ that we choose/ this blossom or that blossom —... but the way/ we long to be —/ that happy/ in the heaven of earth —/ that wild, that loving" (3). In "I will try" Oliver learns from the red bird ways to deal with the grief caused by the recent passing of her lover: "I did not come into this world/ to be comforted./ I came, like red bird, to sing" (75). In "So every day" and "There you were, and it was like spring," the poet feels peace and renewed energy to rejoin the world by thinking of her lover, not as gone, but as everywhere — in the flowers, trees, birds, and wind — part of the earth and heavens, everywhere (70,72).

The poems in the middle section of *Red Bird* deal most directly with environmental issues. In "Red," for example, Oliver writes of finding a gray fox dead in the road, and then another, two days later, most likely the mate, struck but not yet dead (41–2). Even in the face of such offenses, however, she avoids environmental didacticism, shaping "From This River, When I Was a Child, I Used to Drink," as call and response, exploring the pollution of a once-clean river in a dialogic manner (44). Musing on the threat of global warming, she states both her faith and doubt in the poem, "Watching a Documentary about Polar Bears Trying to Survive on the Melting Ice Floes," when she affirms that all is part of God's plan, but worries that God's plan *might* have been that humans would be better than they are (45).

Red Bird demonstrates Oliver's continued commitment to seeing and writing herself as one person within a vast and dynamic ecosystem, while as the second book written after the death of her lover, it highlights the wisdom and healing offered by eco-conscious practice. — Kimberly L. Rogers

BIBLIOGRAPHY

Oliver, Mary. *Red Bird*. Beacon Press: Boston, 2008.
Seaman, Donna. "Review: *Red Bird* by Mary Oliver." *Booklist*. 1 March 2008, pp. 44.

Ortiz, Simon J. (1941–)

A storyteller and teacher, Simon J. Ortiz has emerged as a significant voice in 20th- and 21st-century American literature through his poetry, fiction, and essays. Using the Acoma people as representative of humanity in general, and incorporating different voices and perspectives from both the past and the present, Ortiz explores his and his people's connection to the land — and their disjuncture from it.

Born in 1941, Simon Ortiz grew up on the Acoma Pueblo, in New Mexico, attended Indian schools in McCartys, Santa Fe, and Albuquerque, and graduated from Grants High School in 1960. Before beginning college, Ortiz worked for about a year at the Kerr-McGee uranium processing plant at Ambrosia Lake, an experience he explores in *FIGHT BACK*. After a three-year army enlistment, Ortiz attended the University of New Mexico from 1966 to 1968. Ortiz next accepted a fellowship at the University of Iowa International Writing Program, and later returned to UNM as a counselor/part-time instructor. A grant from the National Endowment for the Arts propelled Ortiz into national recognition and led to his first publication, *The Naked in the Wind* (1971), exploring, like all of Ortiz's work, the varied and inextricably interwoven elements of land, culture and community.

Ortiz has received recognition from the National Endowment for the Arts, Lila Wallace — Reader's Digest Fund Award, the Lannan Foundation's Artists in Residence, "Returning the Gift" Lifetime Achievement Award, WESTAF Lifetime Achievement Award, and the New Mexico Governor's Award for Excellence in Art, among others. In addition to having served as a member of the Acoma tribal government, he has taught at San Diego State, the Institute of American Indian Arts, Navajo Community College, the College of Marin, the University of New Mexico, Sinte Gleska College (SD), the University of Toronto, and Arizona State University.

Central to Ortiz's perception of the individual and the world is his belief in the inextricable bond between the people and the land. Themes of emergence and integration, and of a movement from ignorance or confusion to understanding and eventual connection to the land and people, are central to the work not merely of Ortiz, but other Southwestern authors like SCOTT MOMADAY, Welch, and LESLIE MARMON SILKO. Ortiz creates competing views and interpretations of the factors that tie the individual to the land, the past to the present, the physical to the spiritual, and Acoma (and places like Acoma) to America itself. His later works demonstrate a progression from his earlier focused anger over the exploitation of indigenous people to a more subtle inclusivity that addresses, regardless of race, all victims of corporate/ government malfeasance. Additionally, Ortiz's use of Keres, the traditional Acoma language, along with English, adds nuance and complexity to his expression, and evokes both his personal identification with Acoma and a sense, in the reader, of the historic and timeless in his poetry and prose. Ortiz also reconfigures the traditional Coyote symbol, both to represent himself on occasion and as a general representation of the human in a natural world.

Two of Ortiz's early works, *Going for the Rain* (1977) and *A Good Journey* (1977), incorporate a cyclic physical journey to represent a journey of spiritual renewal, one similar to Momaday's *HOUSE MADE OF DAWN* or Silko's *CEREMONY*. *Going for the Rain* chronicles Ortiz's circular journey from the Acoma Pueblo, around the United States, and back to his home. In "Albuquerque Back Again 12/6/74," Ortiz as Coyote draws strength from his connection to the natural world as his survival is imperiled by a mechanical and hostile environment. Grounded in a profound sense of place and heritage, derived from Acoma, Ortiz returns to the restorative power of place through memory and connection. "Relocation" anatomizes the psychological trauma he experiences because of the mechanized harshness of the city and his separation from the land; and "Hunger in New York" marks his greatest separation from the pueblo, and contains a poignant appeal to mother earth to sustain him spiritually. Similarly, *A Good Journey* incorporates a travel cycle, narrating Ortiz's experiences on the road as well as including poems about his children. In "Canyon de Chelly," he contrasts his philosophical reflections on the eternal beauty of the canyon to his son's climbing or preoccupation with putting rocks in his mouth, resonant moments of childhood and potent symbols of connection to the land.

FIGHT BACK: FOR THE SAKE OF THE PEOPLE/ FOR THE SAKE OF THE LAND (1980) celebrates the 300th anniversary of the 1680 Pueblo Indian Revolt. In its consideration of the history of indigenous peoples in general, the work scrutinizes contemporary government and corporate exploitation, both of the people and of the land's resources such as water and uranium. In his call to resist the continued destruction of the land, and the spiritual and psychological destruction of its people, Ortiz also reaches out to the white people who suffer similar depredation from corporate exploitation and pollution of the land. *Woven Stone* (1992) in a sense weaves together the narrative and thematic strands of *Going for the Rain, A Good Journey,* and *Fight Back,* and Ortiz's new "Introduction" provides biographical background and discusses several historic and personal influences behind the volumes of poetry among his oeuvre.

From Sand Creek: Rising in This Heart Which Is Our America (1981) earned Ortiz the Pushcart Prize for poetry. The book memorializes John Chivington and the Colorado Territory Militia's massacre of peaceful Cheyenne and Arapaho families led by Black Kettle (Cheyenne) at Sand Creek in Southern Colorado on November 29, 1864 — a brutal massacre and mutilation, primarily of old men, women, and children. Treating the atrocity as a horrific example of the devastation of the people and the land by the dominant culture, Ortiz expresses an intense but controlled and articulate anger at such brutality. He also takes advantage of the military connection to explore the psychological and physical wounds that Indian military veterans have received during America's wars.

Ortiz shapes *After and Before the Lightning* (1994) around a seasonal calendar, after the late rain of the fall and before the first rain of the spring. Written while Ortiz lived on the Rosebud reservation, the work synthesizes diverse elements of people, location and history: the Lakota and Acoma, South Dakota and New Mexico, the past and present. Using Keres in the prayers of the Acoma Elder, and addressing the buffalo spirit, Muushaitrah, in connection with the return of the sun in spring ("February 14," 102), Ortiz unites his Southwestern identity with the Sioux of the northern plains.

In *Men on the Moon* (1998), Ortiz argues for environmental justice in a thoroughgoing indictment of white society, especially the government and corporate powers, for their historic and ongoing rapacity of the land and its resources. Ortiz also challenges his readers to comprehend the detrimental effect of such callous attitudes, and to work for beneficial change. In this collection, even the Apollo moon landing is enlisted as further evidence of white society's mistaken attempt to subdue all nature.

Out There Somewhere (2002) expands Ortiz's vision to include the plight of indigenous peoples worldwide, as a dominant capitalist culture exploits, represses and disproportionately imprisons those who have claim to the land; yet he tempers his often passionate criticism with a call to action that includes the dispossessed and the working classes of all races:

> How and what is it today we shall do?
> This is the way you must be thinking.
> We must continue to be.
> It is necessary [98].

And here, as in his earlier works such as *Fighting Back*, Ortiz equates the liberation of the people with the liberation of the land from those who would exploit it.— Thomas P. Fair

Bibliography

Blaeser, Kimberly M. "Sacred Journey Cycles: Pilgrimage as Re-Turning and Re-Telling in American Indigenous Literatures." *Religion & Literature* 35. 2–3 (2003): 83–104.

Cheyfitz, Eric. "Balancing the Earth: Native American Philosophies and the Environmental Crisis." *Arizona Quarterly* 65.3 (2009): 139–162.

Ortiz, Simon J. *After and Before the Lightning.* Tucson: University of Arizona Press, 1994.

_____. *Fight Back: For the Sake of the People for the Sake of the Land.* In *Woven Stone,* 286–365. Tucson: University of Arizona Press, 1992.

_____. *From Sand Creek.* Tucson: University of Arizona Press, 1981.

_____. *Going for the Rain.* In *Woven Stone,* 36–147. Tucson: University of Arizona Press, 1992.

_____. *A Good Journey.* In *Woven Stone,* 149–283. Tucson: University of Arizona Press, 1992.

_____. *Men on the Moon.* Tucson: University of Arizona Press, 1999.

_____. *Out There Somewhere.* Tucson: University of Arizona Press, 2002.

_____. *Woven Stone.* Tucson: University of Arizona Press, 1992.

Simon J. Ortiz: A Poetic Legacy of Indigenous Continuance. Ed. Susan Berry Brill de Ramirez and Evelina Zuni Lucero. Albuquerque: University of New Mexico Press, 2009.

Fight Back: For the Sake of the People for the Sake of the Land, Simon J. Ortiz (1980)

Commemorating the 1680 Pueblo Revolt, *Fight Back: For the Sake of the People for the Sake of the Land* is Simon Ortiz's third collection of poems, first published in 1980 and updated as the final section of *Woven Stone* in 1992. In the introduction to *Woven Stone,* Ortiz addresses *Fight Back:* "The American political-economic system was mainly interested in control and exploitation, and it didn't matter how it was achieved — just like the Spanish crown had been ignorant of people's concerns and welfare" (31). Ortiz links the 1680 revolt to his call for a continuing resistance, in 1980, to the government and corporate forces responsible for uranium mining on Pueblo lands, the consequent destruction and poisoning of the land, and the devastating effect on traditional culture.

An opening prayer links Ortiz to the historic past and asserts an eventual victory inextricably connecting the land and the people: "The land shall endure, / There will be victory," (287). The following section, "I. Too Many Sacrifices," brings together a series of poems that explore the development and management of the uranium mines near Grants and Milan, New Mexico, as extensions of historic and current government and corporate exploitation of the land and the people. Ortiz interweaves biographical and anecdotal material exploring the people's connection to the land. The powerful genocidal associations of the title "Final Solution: Jobs, Leaving" amplify the horrific despoliation and toxic pollution of the pueblo lands, as well as the attendant economic hardships of a people unable to support themselves. The railroad's promise of jobs elsewhere creates a diaspora of fathers and families, and destroys the extended family of tribal associations. The sequence of poems examines the political and quasi-legal maneuvering of the local politicians, business leaders and authorities to exploit the people and profit from the mines. Ironically noting the racist attitude of local authorities in "Indians Sure Come in Handy," Ortiz recounts how local authorities in Grants exploited Indian men to break strikes and unions; "Starting at the Bottom" reveals the falsehoods concerning job opportunities and prosperity for the people; "Affirmative Action" ironically addresses the affirmative action signs posted in Grants' "new and bigger city jail/ ... now filled/ with Cajuns, Okies, Mexicans, and Blacks/ as well as Indians" (303), suggesting that corporate exploitation affects everyone. Attaching emotional and spiritual significance to the physical and geographic reality of the land, "That's the Place Indians Talk About" recounts Ortiz's meeting with a Paiute man who kept repeating the phrase, "That's the place Indians talk about" in reference to sacred lands the government closed to the public.

In the significant pairing of "The First Hard Core" and "To Change in a Good Way," Ortiz contrasts a story of friendship and understanding against an established context of racist misperceptions and ignorance. "The First Hard Core" recounts an autobiographical moment when Ortiz worked the mines as a teenager and encountered in Herb, a fellow worker, the oblivious yet pervasive racism of the early 1960s. The distorted bigotry in Herb's questions puzzles the young Ortiz, who learns the pervasiveness of such demeaning distortions as part of the general American perception. However, the following poem, "To Change in a Good Way," suggests the possibility of honesty and friendship making connections through the land that transcend race and culture (308). The poem tells of two families, Pete and Mary, a Laguna couple, and Bill and Ida, a white couple from Oklahoma. The men work together in the mine, and the two families become close friends, a point Ortiz metaphorically enhances through connections to the land: successful with their own traditional plot, Pete and Mary help Bill and Ida improve their "stunted and wilty looking" garden. Using the garden as symbolic of the human connection to the land, Ortiz links improving the land's fertility to developing human friendship and the possibility of future growth. The death of Bill's brother Slick in Viet Nam, a parallel example of destruction and disruptive loss, expands the poem's application to the universal. Bill rejects the platitudes that attempt to rationalize his brother's death, especially those that connect the conflict in Viet Nam with the white settlers' conflicts with the Indian. Healing occurs when Bill turns to Pete's gifts of a traditional medicine bundle and corn, both connected to the land and growth: "You can plant it. / It's to know that life will keep on, / your life will keep on" (313).

Combining a prose narrative with occasional personal, poetic expressions in "II. No More Sacrifices," Ortiz provides a history and personal narrative to the poetic vignettes of the first section. His inclusion of Aacqumeh language and spelling, traditional religious figures, and sacred landscapes connects antecolonial pueblo life to the present and blurs temporal distinctions in a vision that encompasses history, his parents' memories, and his own experiences. In a series of paragraphs recounting loss and change, Ortiz connects people and events from THOMAS JEFFERSON to Crazy Horse, and MANIFEST DESTINY to the Sky City as a modern roadside attraction, and notes the disappearance of Indian names from the map, for Spanish and English ones. Recognizing the connections between history and the present, the shared fates of the indigenous people and the Anglo-population, Ortiz limns his fundamental conviction that healing of the land is finally synonymous with the healing of the people, culminating in a direct plea for cooperative action:

Only when we are not afraid to fight against the destroyers ... who profit handsomely off the land and people will we know what love and compassion are. Only when the people of this nation, not just Indian people, fight for what is just and good for all life, will we know life and its continuance. And when we fight, and fight back those who are bent on destruction of land and people, we will win. We will win [363].

Fight Back concludes characteristically, with a trenchant poetic statement in which Ortiz shapes an experience with ignorant racism into a repetition of history — to which he responds: "'No,' I said. No" (365). — Thomas P. Fair

BIBLIOGRAPHY

Cheyfitz, Eric. "Balancing the Earth: Native American Philosophies and the Environmental Crisis." *Arizona Quarterly* 65.3 (2009): 139–162.
Ortiz, Simon J. *Fight Back: For the Sake of the People for the Sake of the Land.* In *Woven Stone*, 286–365. Tucson: University of Arizona Press, 1992.
_____. "That's the Place Indians Talk about." *Wicazo Sa Review* 1.1 (1985): 45–49.
Simon J. Ortiz: A Poetic Legacy of Indigenous Continuance. Ed. Susan Berry Brill de Ramirez and Evelina Zuni Lucero. Albuquerque: University of New Mexico Press, 2009.

Parkman, Francis (1823–1893)

Francis Parkman, Jr. was born in 1823 to an established and financially secure Boston family. He was poor in health from childhood to death, but in youth developed, through adventures in local woods and reading JAMES FENIMORE COOPER's novels set on the American frontier, a lifelong fascination with the exploration and conquest of the North American continent. As a university student at Harvard, he resolved to transform this fascination into a life-long project, and continued to spend his summer vacations in forests of the Northeast. These trips did not improve his health, as he had hoped, but did lead to his first publication: a set of sketches based on his trips appeared in the *Knickerbocker Magazine* in 1845.

After graduating from Harvard Law School in the spring of 1846, Parkman traveled with a companion and guides along a stretch of the Oregon Trail and, as a highpoint of the trip, lived for several weeks with the Oglala Sioux. He returned from the trip in worse health than when he had left, but he also transformed his experiences, which he had chronicled in journals, into serialized form for the *Knickerbocker Magazine* and, later in 1849, into the book still widely known and read today, THE OREGON TRAIL.

In his search for a sympathetic style, Parkman often had others — including his wife Catherine Scollay Bigelow whom he married in 1850, and later his children — read aloud to him and transcribe his words, as in his creation of *The Conspiracy of Pontiac and the Indian War After the Conquest of Canada* (1851). Parkman explained that the purpose of this work was "to portray the American forest and the American Indian at the period when both received their final doom" (*The Dial* 452). Parkman continued to pursue this uniquely American side of the conflict between world powers in his seven-part study *France and England in North America*. Delayed again by health problem and by grief over the death of both his wife and son, he published the first volume in 1865. He worried that he might not complete the full project before his death, and indeed died in 1893, one year after the final volume saw print. Parkman's immense productivity while struggling with poor health, declining capacities, and personal grief have prompted a number of commentators to view him as "heroic." His early biographer, Mason Wade called him a "Heroic Historian," and permutations of the phrase (and the sentiments behind that phrase) reappear in more recent publications, both popular and academic.

Reevaluations of Parkman's works have demonstrated that he exercised some poetic license in the pursuit of his expository mission, altering some details of his experiences on the Oregon Trail, as well as details of the grand histories that he set out to record — his aim being primarily to improve the sense of unity, as well as the dramatic effect of his works. Current historical research tends to focus on economic, cultural, and social forces rather than on the actions of "great men," and ethnography today is marked by a heightened awareness of the researcher's innate cultural biases. Parkman's contributions to history are thus not without their share of criticism, and he has been sharply criticized for his portrayal of marginalized groups, including Native Americans, the working class, women, emigrant families, and French peoples in the United States. Nevertheless, Parkman's lifelong project has lasting significance. *The Oregon Trail* remains widely read today, and the multi-volume work *France and England in North America* was republished in 1983 by the Library of America. — James Bernard Kelley

BIBLIOGRAPHY

The Dial. Chicago: Dial, 1898.
Doughty, Howard. *Francis Parkman.* New York: Macmillan, 1962.
Gale, Robert L. *Francis Parkman.* New York: Twayne, 1973.
Jacobs, Wilbur R. *Francis Parkman, Historian as Hero: The Formative Years.* Austin: University of Texas Press, 1991.
Jennings, Francis. "Francis Parkman: A Brahmin Among Untouchables." *William and Mary Quarterly* 42 (July, 1985): 305–328.
Pease, Otis A. *Parkman's History: The Historian as Literary Artist.* New Haven: Yale University Press, 1953.
Van Tassel, David D. *Recording America's Past: An Interpretation of the Development of Historical Studies in America, 1607–1884.* Chicago: University of Chicago Press, 1960.
Wade, Mason, *Francis Parkman: Heroic Historian.* New York: Viking, 1942.

The Oregon Trail, Francis Parkman, Jr. (1849)

The Oregon Trail was the land route used extensively in the 1840s by settlers traveling from Missouri, across the Great Plains, to "Oregon country." Long stretches of the trail were also used by Mormons, as well as prospectors in their travels westward. Francis Parkman, Jr.'s well-known work, *The Oregon Trail,* describes his four- to five-month experience in the summer of 1846 (after graduating from Harvard Law School) traveling along the eastern part of the route with his cousin, trail guides and companions. They departed from St. Louis and traveled first by steamboat up the Missouri River into Kansas, and then by horseback as far west as Fort Laramie, Wyoming. Parkman kept a detailed journal and recorded, among other things, his participation in buffalo hunts and experiences in powerful thunderstorms, as well as his extended interactions with Native Americans, European American emigrants, and his guides.

Upon returning home, although in poorer health than before and with impaired vision, Parkman had the account serialized in *The Knickerbocker Magazine* (1847–49) and later published as the book *The California and Oregon Trail* (1849). At the author's request, subsequent editions bore the author's original title, *The Oregon Trail.* Wilbur R. Jacobs has examined in detail the many transformations (including the condensation of some material, exaggeration of other material, and deletion of many references to the author's physical ailments) in the transformation from the journal entries through the multiple editions of *The Oregon Trail.* In summarizing these changes, Jacobs writes that "Parkman's narrative gained greatly in continuity, clarity, and coherence," an improvement achieved "by manipulating time sequence, by exaggeration of certain details, and by enhancing his image as bold young traveler-explorer" (39). The various editions of *The Oregon Trail* may account at least in part for the differing opinions of its literary merit. *Masterplots* states that it "reflects the attempts of a literary apprentice" and is marred by Parkman's "self-conscious college writing techniques, such as the out-of-place Byronesque epigraphs." Later editions did not include the epigraphs, and Jacobs finds that Parkman's later editions can be "read for the story alone because, like the volumes of his *History*, it has the literary structure of a good novel, with plots and episodes yielding a maximum of suspense. Parkman wanted to be widely read, and he knew how to avoid dullness and tell a good story" (32).

The work has indeed been widely read, often serving as an early example of travel literature and nature writing, but it is also widely valued today for the glimpses that it provides into an educated and wealthy, east-coast American man's view of westward expansion, the vanishing frontier, and the diminishing presence of Native Americans. Readers recognize that Parkman was acutely aware that what he experienced while traveling — including the western "wilderness" and the Native Americans who inhabited it — was already beginning to disappear. This awareness of impending loss, however, is not easily equated with a desire to understand the ecological systems or to protect them. Wil Verhoeven writes: "One might even say that Parkman was fascinated with the western wilderness and Indian life *because* it was disappearing" (142).

Parkman's relation to the natural world is indeed interesting and complex. For example, he had intellectual connections to his contemporaries RALPH WALDO EMERSON and HENRY DAVID THOREAU, and Paul Giles views *The Oregon Trail* as illustrating an "Emersonian antithesis, defining a primal innocence against various 'perverse' forms of social corruption" (167). Parkman also exercised a strong influence on notable figures such as THEODORE ROOSEVELT and FREDERICK JACKSON TURNER, helping shape their views of the American landscape, as discussed by both David Scott Brown and Daniel G. Payne. In 1898, Turner praised Parkman's writings as chronicles of America's vanishing wilderness, Turner also cites *The Oregon Trail* in Chapter 4 of his highly influential study, THE FRONTIER IN AMERICAN HISTORY.

Recent critical statements are equally interesting and inconsistent. Smith believes that Parkman, with his privileged background, "could afford better than anyone else to indulge himself in the slightly decadent cult of wilderness and savagery" (52). Jacobs writes that Parkman "could never be accused of being an environmentalist as we now understand the term. Yet there are observable themes of environmentalism in his varied writings, in his experiments with plants, and in his lifelong fascination with natural history" (341). Other recent critics read Parkman's autobiographical and historical accounts as being less about the prairie, the forest, or even American history, as about the author himself. These critics frequently focus on Parkman's poor health, his social and economic class, and his ethnic and national loyalties as they are indirectly revealed through his overt discussions of nature and history. In *The American Adam*

(1955), R.W.B. Lewis observes of Parkman: "What interested him was the struggle, not its resolution; the quality and power of the assaults, not their conclusion. What interested him was the struggle in general — as the condition of life" (170). More recent critics are often less positive. Kim Townsend writes, for example, that Parkman's purpose in *The Oregon Trail* "was to establish his manhood and in his terms he did, and in the process, in those terms, all but destroyed himself.... As he created this manly self in his writings he deprived it of its humanity — and others of theirs. He is perhaps the first of all too many examples of the American male's destructive quest for manhood" (98). George M. Fredrickson similarly writes: "When he went West to explore *the Oregon Trail* in 1846, *Parkman* sought not only to slake his thirst for the strenuous life, but to look for models of manliness among the Indians and frontiersmen to hold up as examples for the effete Bostonians he had left behind" (33). Finally, Brian Roberts writes that Parkman "entered the vast solitude of the prairie seeking a cure for this illness of overcivilization, ... his narrative pictures the West as a place of rejuvenation, characterized by the freedom of buffalo hunts, wild and violent chases in which Parkman, despite his illness, somehow manages to take part" (59). Like Fredrickson, Roberts sees Parkman as seeking "alternatives to a bourgeois way of being" (59) and the opportunity, "for a few moments at least, to forget his illness and his overcivilized background" (59–60). According to such critics, the author's interest in experiencing and writing about the natural world might generally come from his personal desire to endure hardships and survive, to prove himself in an endlessly repeated struggle of man versus nature; yet the *anatomy* of this struggle is rich in broader significance, though Parkman himself may not have explored this element — as HEMINGWAY and others *would*.

Another factor complicating attempts to locate an ecological sensibility in Parkman's account is his participation in the buffalo hunts, particularly as recorded in the journals and in early editions of *The Oregon Trail*. Daniel G. Payne observes that, in general, "Although Roosevelt and Parkman considered the passing of the buffalo and the end to the frontier to be regrettable, in their linear view of history this was all part of the ineluctable progress of American civilization" (112). Jacobs explains, with closer attention to *The Oregon Trail*, that the later editions omit some of "the bloody accounts of buffalo killings, a few of them almost sadistic in tone," in which Parkman gladly participated as a young man. In these later editions, Wilbur further observes, a more mature Parkman "seems to have outgrown his youthful enthusiasm for shooting every wild animal that came within range of his beloved rifle, 'Satan,' and in his *History*, he protested against the senseless slaughter of the Canadian beaver" (37).

The Oregon Trail continues to be valued by scholars and teachers and scholars alike as an important, first-hand account of westward expansion in the early- to mid-nineteenth-century United States. In his scholarly work, Andrew C. Isenberg uses Parkman's journal entries to document the social organization of the Indian buffalo hunt or the inflated prices at Fort Laramie (86, 107). In the "Territorial Expansion" section of *Environmental Discourse and Practice: A Reader*, a resource that seems designed primarily for post-secondary instruction, Lisa M. Benton and John R. Short present the opening section of *The Oregon Trail* alongside works by Turner ("The Significance of the Frontier in American History," 1894) and Smith ("The Garden of the World and American Agrarianism," 1950), among others. Even as many readers' views of the environment today are radically different from what they would have been in the nineteenth century, Parkman's work thus continues to be of lasting interest and value.—James Bernard Kelley

BIBLIOGRAPHY

Benton, Lisa M., and John R. Short, eds. *Environmental Discourse and Practice: A Reader*, Malden, MA: Blackwell, 2000.

Brown, David Scott, *Beyond the Frontier: The Midwestern Voice in American Historical Writing*. Chicago: University of Chicago Press, 2009.

Fredrickson, George M. *The Inner Civil War: Northern Intellectuals and the Crisis of the Union*. Champaign: University of Illinois Press, 1993

Giles, Paul. *Transatlantic Insurrections: British Culture and the Formation of American Literature, 1730–1860*. Philadelphia: University of Pennsylvania Press, 2001.

Isenberg, Andrew C. *The Destruction of the Bison: An Environmental History, 1750–1920*. New York: Cambridge University Press, 2001

Jacobs, Wilbur R. *Francis Parkman, Historian as Hero: The Formative Years* Austin: University of Texas Press, 1991.

_____. "Francis Parkman–Naturalist–Environmental Savant," *The Pacific Historical Review* 61.3 (May 1992): 341–356.

Lewis, R.W.B. *The American Adam: Innocence, Tragedy, and Tradition in the Nineteenth Century*. Chicago: University of Chicago Press, 1955.

Parkman, Francis. "The Oregon Trail." *Masterplots, Definitive Revised Edition*. Salem Press, 1976. *eNotes.com*. 2006. 13 May, 2011 http://www.enotes.com/oregon-trail-francis-parkman-salem/oregon-trail.

Payne, Daniel G. *Voices in the Wilderness: American Nature Writing and Environmental Politics*. Hanover, NH: University Press of New England, 1996.

Roberts, Brian. *American Alchemy: The California Gold Rush and Middle-Class Culture*. Chapel Hill: University of North Carolina Press, 2000.

Smith, Henry Nash. *Virgin Land: The American West as Symbol and Myth*. Cambridge: Harvard University Press, 1970.

Townsend, Kim. "Francis Parkman and the Male Tradition." *American Quarterly* 38:1 (Spring 1986): 97–113.

Turner, Frederick Jackson. "Francis Parkman and His Work." *Dial* 300, no. 25 (16 December 1898): 451–453.

_____. *The Frontier in American History*. New York: Henry Holt, 1921.

Verhoeven, Wil, "Ecology as Requiem: Nature, Nationhood and History in Francis Parkman's 'History of the American Forest.'" *Configuring Romanticism*. Ed. Theodoor Liebregts D'Haen and Wim Peter Tigges. Amsterdam: Rodopi, 2003. 137–52.

Peyer, Bernd, ed. (1768–1931)

The Elders Wrote, Bernd Peyer, ed.

As Peyer's anthology suggests, the earliest Native American writers had largely become assimilated to the white culture by the time they began to write. In their remembered cultural heritage, however, many of them exhibited a continued sense of ecological awareness and responsibility that profoundly differentiated them from the dominant white culture. Their attitude toward the land often led Native Americans to approach the nonhuman environment as a dynamic force rather than a static collection of objects to be manipulated and possessed. The natural world was understood as a place of reciprocal — often mystical — relations between humans, the land, and plants and animals on earth, all ineluctably connected. While Native Americans generally viewed the land as a sacred site, the dominant white culture's rapacious desire for domination over the American 'wilderness' disrupted the intuitively ecological mode of life of the Native Americans. The writings in this anthology demonstrate the difficulties of maintaining the environmental ethos of the Native Americans in a world increasingly shaped by the exploitative lifestyles of the dominant culture.

Although most Native Americans hunted and participated in small-scale agricultural projects prior to the coming of the whites, their belief systems generally discouraged exploitation of their natural environment. The accounts in this anthology, however, lend credence to William Hagan's contention that, by the time of the nineteenth-century Indian removals, "[t]here was virtual unanimity of opinion that agriculture was superior to hunting as a way of life and was a necessary first step for the Indian" (77). While some Native American writers argue against the Indian removals by insisting that their tribes have been able to take up agriculture and forsake hunting, others regret that the Native American way of life has been drastically altered since the coming of the whites, who typically assaulted nature through massive deforestation or wide-scale slaughter of the wildlife. The Ojibwa George Copway and others, for example, argue that moving west will not shield the American Indians against the whites' rapacious attitude toward the nonhuman world: "The game is being killed more and more every year. It is computed by recent travelers, that one hundred thousand buffaloes are killed by trappers for their tongues and hides, which are sold to traders up the Missouri. Game of all kinds is fast disappearing from this side of the mountains" (82). While Native American writers had mixed attitudes toward farming, they all seemed to agree that the native way of life had been forever changed by white culture, which had destroyed the balance between nature and humans that had been achieved and actively practiced by the American Indians for centuries.

Native American writers became increasingly critical of forced assimilation practices after seeing the effects of destructive policies enforced by the United States government. In addition to their direct harm to nature and native culture, these policies exacerbated the imbalance between humans and the nonhuman world that had characterized Native American Indian life. Copway writes that the white man's "progress of aggression has gone on with its resistless force westward.... The rivers that once wound their silent and undisturbed course beneath the shades of the forest, are made to leave their natural ways..." (75–76). Such changes to the natural landscape had far-reaching consequences for the Native American and for the landscape; but the doctrine of MANIFEST DESTINY adopted by many in the dominant Eurocentric culture presupposed the superiority of whites and their culture, and predicted (and legitimized) the inevitable demise of the American Indians and their way of life.

A reverence for the nonhuman world as a sacred place pervades the writings of most of the Native American writers in this anthology. In an article entitled "Why I Am a Pagan," Gertrude Bonnin writes of ancient "pagan" American Indian values which she has adopted. Whether viewing the "green hills" and the "great blue overhead" or listening to the "soft cadences of the river's song," she experiences a oneness with nature and "the loving Mystery round about us" that is far removed from the exploitation of the natural environment that she has witnessed in the more recent years of Native American life on a reservation (138). In her mystical "excursions into the natural gardens where the voice of the Great Spirit is heard in the twittering of birds, the rippling of mighty waters, and the sweet breathing of flowers," she recovers a belief system that stands against exploitative practices (141). Even Christianized Native Americans often continued to hold to many of the ancient beliefs about the natural world; the Seneca Maris Bryant Pierce, for example, employs Christian language to suggest the desirability of a revitalized relation between humans and the nonhuman environment: "I ask then to let us live on, where our fathers have lived — let us enjoy the advantages which our location affords us ... so that the deserts and waste places may be made to blossom like the rose, and the inhabitants thereof utter forth the high praises of our God" (65). Writers like William Apess, an ordained Methodist of the Pequot tribe, consistently employ the very terms often used to demean Native Americans in their critique of the oppressive practices of the dominant white culture, leading critics like Cheryl Walker and Maureen Konkle to take note of Apess's rhetorical "reversals." Konkle identifies "savage for civilized" as Apess's "obvious favorite," adding that "the 'reversals' are ironic, and their effect is usually to show that whites and Native peoples are equals" (106). A life in tune with nature is not a sign of "savage" life in Apess's treatment; instead, a low regard for the natural environment indicates an essential misunderstanding of the world that is itself "savage." Thus, Apess undermines the assumed superiority of the dominant race and reclaims the Native Americans' traditional attitude of reverence for the natural world.

The informing mystery of harmony and wholeness with the natural world is also explored in the writings of Native Americans, such as Charles Eastman, who contrasts the white economic system with its American Indian counterpart in similar terms: "To the wild Indian, his worldly occupation is a sort of play. The thing which above all else occupies his mind is the Great Mystery. Him he never forgets. In civilization, as it appeared to me at first — 'Will it pay? Can I make anything on it?' seemed to be the 'Great Mystery' of the white people" (143). Rather than seeking to own and control land as property to be used and abused at will, the Native American plays *within* nature as well as partaking of its mystery. Carlos Montezuma also calls upon his fellow American Indians to remember this heritage of living harmoniously with and freely in nature: "We must free ourselves. Our peoples' heritage is freedom. Freedom reigned in their whole make-up. They harmonized with nature and lived accordingly" (163). Arthur Parker, of Seneca ancestry, bluntly indicts modern white civilization for undoing the American Indian people's way of life: "civilization has swept down upon groups of Indians and, by destroying their relationship to nature, blighted or banished their intellectual life, and left a group of people mentally confused" (174).

Parker mentions the destructive influence of trading and living on a small plot of land rather than ranging freely, as they had done in the past. Even more concerned to restore their traditional balance between nature and humanity, the Sioux Chief Luther Standing Bear claims, "The old life was attuned to nature's rhythm — bound in mystical ties to the sun, moon and stars; to the waving grasses, flowing streams and whispering winds.... The white race today is but half civilized and unable to order his life into ways of peace and righteousness" (189). A few decades after the Indian removals, an almost nostalgic reaction by a segment of the dominant culture reassessed the now-removed natives and took a view much closer to that of Apess. As Bernd Peyer notes in the introduction to his updated and expanded anthology of *American Indian Nonfiction*, "The back-to-nature movement, which began after the Civil War and culminated in a veritable national mania by the close of the century, proved to be highly receptive to expositions on the Indian's 'healthy' relationship with the environment" (26). This back-to-nature movement encouraged conservation practices that sought to actively restore healthy human interaction with the earth (THE CONSERVATION MOVEMENT).

With varied degrees of resistance, Native American writings before the Indian Reorganization Act of 1934 reflect the forced assimilation policies of the United States government. Whether advocating or opposing assimilation, however, most of the earliest Native American writers deplored the loss of ecological awareness and respect for the land of their ancestors. Whether Christianized like Pierce or pagan like Bonnin, many Native Americans continued to believe in the sanctity of the natural world despite varying degrees of assimilation. *The Elders Wrote* highlights and explores the profound difference between viewing the land as a sacred space, and considering the land as little more than a commodity; and offers hard-won, even tragic wisdom concerning humanity's place within the larger natural environment.— Steven Petersheim

BIBLIOGRAPHY

Hagan, William T. *American Indians.* 3rd ed. Chicago: University of Chicago Press, 1993.

Konkle, Maureen. *Writing Indian Nations: Native Intellectuals and the Politics of Historiography, 1827–1863.* Chapel Hill: University of North Carolina Press, 2004.

Peyer, Bernd C., ed. and Introduction. *American Indian Nonfiction: An Anthology of Writings, 1760s–1930s.* Norman: University of Oklahoma Press, 2007.

_____. *The Elders Wrote: An Anthology of Early Prose by North American Indians, 1768–1931.* Berlin: Dietrich Reimer Verlag, 1982.

Walker, Cheryl. *Indian Nation: Native American Literature and Nineteenth-Century Nationalisms.* Durham: Duke University Press, 1997.

"Pima Stories of the Beginning of the World"

Aw-Aw-Tam Indian Nights: The Myths and Legends of the Pimas provides English translations of "Pima Stories of the Beginning of the World" from the Pima Native American peoples. The narratives are divided into four categories, each representing a night following the creation of the world, and together chronicle the progression of humankind from newly created beings to individuals who hunt, farm and use fire. In particular, the narratives focus on the Pima people and the plants and animals essential to the sustenance of Pima life. The inclusion of countless stories concerning these essential plants and animals demonstrates the importance of the environment to the Pimas: for them, life essentials like corn and deer are as sacred as the creation of humankind and the Pima deities. The equal valorization of nature and humankind is a distinctive and recurrent motif in the collection, and the narratives clearly employ this motif to demonstrate how disrespect toward any human or natural form upsets the balance of life. In essence, the narratives portray a didactic message that respecting humankind and ensuring its continuation means respecting the plants and animals necessary for human sustenance — a message that took five hundred years and mounting global threats to humanity to penetrate the conquering European's collective psyche.

The anatomy of this critical insight, frequent in aboriginal narratives, is partially limned in "The Story of Hawawk," in which a tribeswoman is dishonest to a fellow tribesman and thus becomes bewitched for her actions. The consequence is that the woman bears a child named Hawawk who has "claws on its hands and feet like a wild animal" (75). When the child reaches maturity she terrorizes the people of the surrounding villages by eating their children. And, although a woman eventually kills Hawawk, her spirit lives on, bewitching these same villages. Only by throwing o-nook tree balls at the bears bewitched by Hawawk's spirit, allowing them to be shot, are the villagers able to end Hawawk's curse. The story demonstrates how disrespect for fellow humans results in a single but devastating imbalance in the world's natural order; and Hawawk, a telling fusion of girl and animal, is a living symbol of this fatal disruption.

The reliance on harmonic nature-human relations for world stability is also present in "The Story of Wayhohm, ToeHahvs and Tottai" and its focus on the creation of fire. In this instance it is reliance on the roadrunner to steal fire from Wayhohm, the personification of lightning, to save the city of Dthas

Seeven whose citizens are dying of cold. While the roadrunner completes the task, he also mistakenly ensures that sparks "got into all kinds of wood" so "there is fire in all kind of sticks even now, and the Indian can get it out by rubbing them together to this day" (73). While the reliance on nature is clear, there is also a critical human component to the narrative. The city people ask the roadrunner to steal the fire from Wayhohm, demonstrating that the roadrunner is himself an integral part of the Dthas Seeven community. Likewise, humans are the ones who must rub sticks together to create fire after the roadrunner steals from Wayhohm; again, the human and nonhuman are seen working in harmony to ensure the stability of both human and natural worlds.

This harmonic interrelation between humans and the environment is not, however, entirely symmetric, and the asymmetry too is telling. In "The Story of the Flood," for example, a great flood covers the Earth, killing all inhabitants except for three birds and the Pima deities. The flood recedes because of the birds' singing and, after ants have worked the land to make it dry (the ants were created by a deity after the flood), the Earth is once again able to sustain life. As Nina Baym notes, such a story "is important as a foundational narrative in that it tells not of creation but of re-creation, of the establishment or rebirth of the divine, natural and social orders" (Baym 24). But while Baym is surely right to highlight the story's overarching notion of nature's inherent capability to revitalize itself, equally important is what the story does *not* include: any need, or even role, for *humankind* in the Earth's revitalization; and this asymmetry is both central to and pervasive in the overall body of Pima creation literature. While all the other narratives emphasize the importance of humans working in conjunction with their surrounding environment to ensure stability and prosperity, "The Story of the Flood" offers the sterner warning that, ultimately, nature does not need man to sustain itself and thrive, but the reverse is not true — another hard-won and tenuous lesson being truly learned only of late. — Mitchell Grasser

BIBLIOGRAPHY

Baym, Nina. "Pima Stories of the Beginning of the World." *The Norton Anthology of American Literature*. New York: W. W. Norton, 2003. 23–33. Print.
Lloyd, John W., Comalk-Hawk-Kih, and Edward H. Wood. *Aw-Aw-Tam Indian Nights: The Myths and Legends of the Pimas*. [S.l.]: Forgotten, 2008.

Pirsig, Robert M. (1928–)

Robert M. Pirsig's "Metaphysics of Quality," a compelling fusion of Eastern philosophy and Native American ethos, is described in two semi-fictional works, ZEN AND THE ART OF MOTORCYCLE MAINTENANCE: AN INQUIRY INTO VALUES (1974) and *Lila: An Inquiry into Morals* (1991), which together reenvisage man's fundamental relation to the environment in a technological age.

Robert Maynard Pirsig was born in 1928, in Minneapolis Minnesota, the son of Maynard Pirsig, later a longstanding law professor and dean at the University of Minnesota, and Harriet Marie Sjobeck, of Swedish descent. After a brief stint in England, during which Pirsig recalls frequent family trips about England on a motorcycle with sidecar, the family returned to Minneapolis, and the boy was immediately advanced from kindergarten to Grade 2 on the strength of his extraordinary intellectual precocity, a destabilizing move that would be repeated in a number of contexts later in his education. After a successful relocation to the Blake school, devoted to gifted children of U of M professors, Pirsig scored 170 on the Stanford-Binet IQ test (a 1 in 50,000 result), and entered the U of M High School at age 11, where he was again accelerated by 2 years, entering U of M in biochemistry at 15. At 18, when most students are entering their freshman year, Pirsig was expelled from the university, for failing grades, immaturity and inattention to studies.

And thus begins one of the most fabled lives in modern American literary history, as Pirsig's relentless exploration of fissures in the essential architecture of Western thought led him first to the East and a seminal confrontation with Zen Buddhism, then to the Montana reservations of the Cheyenne, and finally to an attenuated and violent mental breakdown in 1961–3, after his failed attempt to integrate his personal inquiries into the academic strictures of the University of Chicago's Aristotelian-centred "Analysis of Ideas and Study of Methods" program. At this point, in the fall of 1963, his father committed him to incarceration at the Veterans' hospital in Minneapolis for EST (Electro-convulsive Shock Therapy), which effectively burned away the philosophical personality which in *Zen* he calls "Phaedrus" after a student in Plato's eponymous dialogue. The reappearance of this personality after five years of relative stability, during the long backcountry motorcycle trip that provides the novel's narrative skeleton, prompts the brilliant and haunting self-exploration at its core. Indeed, Pirsig incarnates in the fragmentary tale of this suddenly discovered "ghost" the central elements of the "Quality" philosophy which led to Phaedrus' destruction.

The apparent stakes, then, of serious engagement with this philosophy, with its Eastern questioning of Western modes of life and thought, are high indeed, and of existential as well as intellectual significance. Rooted equally in elements of American Pragmatism, Taoism and Zen Buddhism, and in Native American life and thought, the Metaphysics of Quality is governed above all by one of the Grand Pronouncements of Vedantic Hinduism: the *Tat tvam asi* ("Thou art that"). This asserts that the "subjective" world of individual experience and identity, and the "objective" world of nature and technology, are essentially undivided. Enlightenment consists precisely in realizing this lack of division. While at times metaphysically abstruse, the environmental implications of this link between Eastern philosophy and Western Native culture are both clear and far-reaching, challenging as it does the fundamental union that has dominated Western notions of progress since the Bible, between man's sacred "dominion" over the natural world and the dominance provided by his increasingly godlike technologies.

Pirsig followed the spectacular success of *Zen* with *Lila: An Inquiry into Morals* (1991), elaborating his philosophy of Quality; but the latter's sales and reception paled in comparison, partly owing to its overtly philosophical tenor, in contrast to the gripping narrative of self-discovery that frames the philosophy in *Zen*.— Doug Melrose

BIBLIOGRAPHY

Adams, Tim. "Zen and the Art of Robert Pirsig." *The Observer* interview. 19 Nov. 2006. Available online. URL: http://www.robertpirsig.org/Observer%20Interview.htm . Accessed February 8, 2009.

Glendinning, Ian. "Biographical Timeline of Robert Pirsig." Available online. URL: www.psybertron.org/ timeline.html. Accessed February 7, 2009.

"MOQ.org." Available online. URL: www.moq.org. Accessed February 7, 2009.

Pirsig, Robert M. *Lila: An Inquiry into Morals.* New York: Bantam, 1991.

_____. *Zen and the Art of Motorcycle Maintenance: An Inquiry into Values.* New York: Bantam, 1974.

Zen and the Art of Motorcycle Maintenance, Robert M. Pirsig (1974)

Robert M. Pirsig's *Zen and the Art of Motorcycle Maintenance* combines elements of autobiography, travelogue and philosophical treatise to create a work which evades easy categorisation or analysis. Profoundly idiosyncratic in its subject matter and execution, Pirsig's work advances a philosophical inquiry into what he terms "the metaphysics of quality." However, rather than presenting such a theory in a conventional academic context, Pirsig instead integrates this philosophical perspective within sections of personal recollections, descriptions of the natural world, and detailed procedures of motorcycle maintenance.

Yet in spite of this integration, academic criticism has tended to analyse the philosophical dimension of *Zen and the Art of Motorcycle Maintenance* in isolation, as if the work were a standard philosophical text. However, such an investigation overlooks the fundamental strength of Pirsig's non-conventional approach. Rather than the journey and its accompanying natural descriptions merely forming a backdrop to the discussion of the metaphysics of quality, or what has been termed as "a narrative structure that sweetens the blow of having to think" (Joicey), the other elements are central to the structure and evolution of Pirsig's thought.

By undertaking a motorcycle journey through the Great Plains to Montana, Pirsig, his son Chris, and Sylvia and John Sutherland are able to escape the fact that:

> In a car you're always in a compartment, and because you're used to it you don't realize that through that car window everything you see is just more TV. You're a passive observer and it is all moving by you boringly in a frame [*Zen* 12].

Through their choice of a motorcycle as transport, "the frame is gone" and they are "completely in contact with it all," "in the scene" (*Zen* 12). Such immersion means that they spend their "time being aware of things and meditating on them," "thinking about things at great leisure and length without being hurried and without feeling you're losing time" (*Zen* 15).

It is this immersion within the landscape, provided through the medium of their motorcycle journey, which is key to Pirsig's "narration" of his philosophy, providing a means of accessing his memories. As Pirsig's journey progresses through the emptiness of the Great Plains it is gradually revealed to the reader that he has undergone electroshock therapy, and that the self he was before the procedure is no longer fully accessible. Through a deft use of what might be termed metaphysical grammar, Pirsig is able to establish a division between his post-procedure self referred to as *I*, and a pre-procedure identity which Pirsig names "Phaedrus" after a dialogue by Plato, and which the writer refers to as *he*. It is not until the end of the work that this schism is bridged and Phaedrus is referred to as *I*, symbolizing the writer's reintegration of a lost past. While the grammar heightens the tension and pathos of separation in the novel, it is the openness of Pirsig's means of transportation through an increasingly familiar landscape which grounds and frames the process of reconciliation.

It is through the physical (and psychological) journey, with its recovery of the memories as Phaedrus, that Pirsig advances the philosophical dimension of his work. While his theory has a logical progression roughly analogous to that of a conventional philosophical treatise, its force and momentum are rooted in suffering and the medium of the journey — the journey of both Phaedrus and his post-procedure self. This process reflects the fundamental premise of Pirsig's philosophy, which ultimately aims to unify what he perceives as "*two* realities, one of immediate artistic appearance and one of underlying scientific explanation" (*Zen* 61). Characterizing the former as "romantic," and the latter as "classical" understanding of the world, Pirsig explores how an exclusive immersion within either perspective results in an impoverished and philosophically problematic experience of existence. Instead, by combining Greek thought, Kantian metaphysics, Eastern Philosophy and Native American spiritual practices, Pirsig attempts to integrate these two divergent perspectives within one unified theory, that of the metaphysics of quality.

Consequently, when *Zen* is subjected to a conventional philosophical analysis, such of that of Baggini, the stripping away of the context of the journey means that it is only an impoverished form of the metaphysics of quality which is analysed, an approach analogous to the reductive worldviews that Pirsig himself critiques. This phenomenon was noted by Pirsig himself, who stated that Baggini's approach was:

> typical of a lot of academic philosophers. They think: Here's this guy who doesn't even have an MA in philosophy, and he has written what they call a "New Age" book, and the bias comes [Adams].

Such a critical approach to Pirsig's work embodies the western, classical perspective to which he referred, excluding the romantic dimension which is provided by the aesthetic aspect of the narrative framing of his journey. In doing so, such an approach ignores the holistic dimension of *Zen and the Art of Motorcycle Maintenance* and its attempt to create a new way of viewing the world, in terms of quality.

It is precisely this holistic dimension of the metaphysics of quality, marginalized in philosophical criticism, which makes Zen and the Art of Motorcycle Maintenance such an interesting text for contemporary ecological thought. In its rejection of a purely classical or a purely romantic vision of human interaction with the natural world, it provides a potential method of escaping the separation from the environment, which Pirsig sees as endemic to modern life,

and destructive both to that life and to its environment. Yet, through the importance of the motorcycle and its nuts-and-bolts world in the novel, Zen avoids false oppositions between nature and technology. As he states:

> The Buddha, the Godhead, resides quite as comfortably in the circuits of a digital computer or the gears of a cycle transmission as he does at the top of a mountain or in the petals of a flower. To think otherwise is to demean the Buddha — which is to demean oneself [Zen 26].

This assault on the artificial divisions between self, technology and environment, grounds a holistic conception of ecology which is not solely dependent upon either arguments for the preservation of the aesthetic quality of the natural world, or upon scientific discourses of environmental impact. Instead, through the concept of quality as a means of exploring humanity's related interactions with the environment and technology, both arguments have the potential to be integrated into a rich and powerful synthesis.

Therefore, while the metaphysical basis of Pirsig's philosophy of quality may be open to question, his narrative strategy and his striving for a holistic view provides a useful model for environmental literature. In addition, *Zen and the Art of Motorcycle Maintenance* questions the primacy of conventional academic discourse in approaching the environment, suggesting instead that conceptual work is possible without limiting or artificially reducing the scope and range of human experience. — Phillip Pass

BIBLIOGRAPHY

Adams, Tim. "Zen and the Art of Robert Pirsig." The Observer *interview. 19 Nov. 2006.* Available online. URL: http://www.robertpirsig.org/Observer%20Interview.htm . Accessed: 8 February 2009.
Baggini, Julian. "An interview with Robert Pirsig." *The Philosophy Magazine.* Available online. URL: http://www.philosophersnet.com/magazine/pirsig_transcript.htm. Accessed: 23 April 2009.
Joicey, Ben, "Zen and the Art of Motorcycle Maintenance: An Unappreciation." *ForAgainst.* Available online. URL: http://sites.google.com/site/foragain/Home/zen-and-the-art-of-motorcycle-maintenance-an-unappreciation. Accessed: 22 April, 2009.
"MOQ.org." Available online. URL: www.moq.org. Accessed: 21 April, 2009.
Pirsig, Robert M. *Zen and the Art of Motorcycle Maintenance: An Inquiry into Values.* London: Vintage, 1974.

Poe, Edgar Allan (1809–1849)

Short story writer, poet, theorist, and critic, Edgar Allan Poe is one of the most important American writers of the 19th century. Although his impact on American literature was fairly limited during the 19th century, his distinctive brand of psychological fiction influenced many major European authors, including Dostoyevsky, Conrad, and Kafka, and his ideas about poetry permeated French literature for several generations. In addition, as a critic he was the first American author to compose a body of literary theory that achieved lasting significance. While his critical theories are less valued today, Poe is generally acknowledged to have been a master of the short-story form, and a highly original and influential force both in Europe and finally in his native country.

Poe was born in Boston, in 1809, to itinerant actors David and Eliza Poe. Not long after Edgar's birth, David abandoned the family, and the boy was soon orphaned when Eliza herself died of consumption in 1811. Poe was taken in by John and Frances Allan in Richmond, Virginia. John Allan was a merchant of considerable means, but Poe had a troubled relationship with his foster father, and as an adult neither benefited from Allan's wealth nor received any inheritance. At the age of 17, Poe enrolled at the University of Virginia, but was forced to leave the school after one year because of debts incurred through gambling. In May 1827, several months after leaving the university, Poe enlisted in the Army under the name of Edgar A. Perry, but eventually left the army to enroll in West Point. Again growing restless, and perhaps with the aim of spiting his foster father, Poe deliberately neglected his duties until he was dismissed from the military academy.

After leaving West Point, Poe embarked on a writing career, seeking to sustain himself entirely through his literary work. He had already published a slim volume of poetry entitled *Tamerlane and Other Poems,* and in 1829 he published a second volume, *Al Aaraaf, Tamerlane, and Minor Poems*, and a third, *Poems,* in 1831. All of these collections gave indications of what Thomas Ollive Mabbot calls the type of poem "Poe made peculiarly his own, the imaginary landscape" (189). Following this last volume, Poe turned his attention almost entirely to the more profitable pursuit of fiction writing. For the rest of his life he worked as editor for a number of journals, and steadily published his short stories, essays, and poems. Though Poe was well-known as a harsh reviewer of books, it was not until 1845 that he achieved fame (but not financial security) with the publication of "The Raven." In the fall of 1849, he was discovered in a state of delirium on a Baltimore street, after having gone missing during the week prior. After several days of half-consciousness under a doctor's care, Poe died on October 7, 1849, under mysterious circumstances.

Poe is remembered primarily for his tales of psychological terror, and for a handful of highly musical and evocative poems that express his philosophy that ultimately beauty, and not truth, should be the goal of poetry. His essays, "The Poetic Principle" and "The Philosophy of Composition," were highly influential to French writers for many years, and were especially important to the movement of "pure poetry."

Lesser known in Poe's oeuvre are the many tales and sketches that demonstrate Poe's fascination with environmental themes. Like most notable Romantic writers, Poe maintained a keen lifelong appreciation of the beauties of the natural world. The "imagined landscape" to which Mabbot refers — particularly evident in "The Valley of Unrest" — reappears in a number of Poe's poems, including the well-known "Fairyland," which is set in a realm of "Dim vales — and shadowy floods —/ and cloudy looking woods." In "Dream-Land" Poe envisions a world "Out of Space — Out of Time" that represents an environment unbound by natural laws. The poem invokes the concept of the "ultimate dim Thule," an emblem during Poe's time of an abstract and spectacular environment unreachable by humans, existing at the limits of the known world.

The imaginary landscape also plays a role in some of Poe's sketch pieces. "The Domain of Arnheim," and its companion piece "Landor's Cottage," illustrate Poe's interest in the art of landscape gardening, a practice firmly ensconced in that critical American environment of the "middle landscape," described by LEO MARX in his seminal *MACHINE IN THE GARDEN*; in these sketches, as Dawn B. Sova notes, Poe "expressed a rapturous appreciation of natural beauty" (116). In "The Domain of Arnheim," the protagonist, Ellison, has inherited "four hundred and fifty millions of dollars" (1269), and uses the money to fashion a piece of land into a personal paradise. The domain, called Arnheim by Ellison, exists as nature "in the sense of the handiwork of the angels that hover between man and God" (1276). "Landor's Cottage," similarly, is largely a descriptive piece in which a traveler wanders through a country environment in New York State, admiring the wonders of the natural world, when he encounters the residence of Landor, which lies on a peninsula stretching out into a river. The narrator emphasizes the harmony between Landor's home and the surrounding environment, likening the scene to a poem. These two works draw a connection between the human capacity for artistry and God's design of the natural world, a theme that Poe would greatly expand upon in his lengthy and ambitious cosmological treatise, *Eureka*.

Two similarly picturesque tales conceive of the idealized landscape as a symbolic setting. In the romantic story "Eleonora," a narrator resides with his cousin Eleonora and her mother in a secluded natural paradise called "the Valley of Many-Colored Grass." The idyllic valley grows even more beautiful and luxuriant as the narrator and Eleonora discover their love for one another. When the young Eleonora dies, however, the environment changes, shrinking from its former beauty, and the narrator is forced to leave the valley and live a more realistic existence. "The Island of the Fay" elaborates the theme of the impermanence of great beauty. Once again, a traveler describes at length the unreal and lush beauty of an island that he happens upon in the wilderness. The narrator encounters a Fay whom he follows to the east side of the island, which is, in contrast, gloomy and decaying. The Fay ultimately disappears, symbolizing the inevitable loss of ideal beauty.

While Poe's environmental themes are perhaps most explicitly evident in his minor works, some of his most famous tales rely on elements of the natural environment to evoke a mood of mystery or unreality—*the imaginary*. The dismal setting of "The Fall of the House of Usher" contributes to the isolation and mystical character of the house itself. Poe's striking first paragraph, a vivid and haunting description of what appears to be a stretch of Southern low country, is devoted to capturing the mysterious and ominous quality of the landscape, foreshadowing the supernatural events that follow. At times Poe's representation of the natural environment shares much with the traditional romantic vision of nature as a place where strange and inexplicable things frequently occur—where the supernatural, we might say, is natural. In "A Tale of the Ragged Mountains," for example, the protagonist, Augustus Bedloe, is transported back in time to a previous life during a walk through the woods near Charlottesville.

In addition, Poe contributed several important pieces to the tradition of sea fiction, including his only novel, the much-studied and influential *The Narrative of Arthur Gordon Pym of Nantucket*. Here, as often elsewhere, Poe uses natural environments as locales for sublime experience, combining the world's natural features with visions of supernal beauty or unsettling mystery. In "A Descent into the Maelstrom" a Norwegian fisherman and his brother are caught in a monstrous whirlpool on their return from fishing. The powerful tale captures the harrowing experience of the fisherman as he confronts, and ultimately reflects on, the awesome power of nature, being drawn down into the vortex but ultimately surviving by keeping his wits until the cataract subsides. The brother, contrariwise, panics and perishes in the depths of the whirlpool. The fisherman describes the experience as a sublime confrontation with the divine: "I began to reflect how magnificent a

thing it was to die in such a manner, and how foolish it was in me to think of so paltry a consideration of my own individual life, in view of so wonderful a manifestation of God's power" (588). Tracy Ware argues that this passage "affirms [the fisherman's] acceptance of divine ways" (77), and that traditional readings conceive of the story as involving "an archetypal descent and reascent and a successful quest for 'spiritual transcendence'" (77).

The image of the abyssal cataract also appears in Poe's early story "MS. Found in a Bottle," in which an unnamed narrator, adrift in the sea after a tempest strikes his ship, is picked up by another ship sailing for Antarctica. The narrator finds that the crew of this ship are all phantoms who seem not to notice him. When the ship reaches the South Pole, they encounter a raging whirlpool that presumably leads through the center of the earth (Poe incorporates here the theory of the hollow earth propounded by John Cleves Symmes, Jr. in 1818). As with "A Descent into the Maelstrom," the narrator is simultaneously thrilled and terrified by the sublime experience, ultimately submitting to the event as an opportunity for spiritual enlightenment: "It is evident that we are hurrying on to some exciting knowledge — some never-to-be imparted secret, whose attainment is destruction" (145).

The most important of Poe's sea fiction, *The Narrative of Arthur Gordon Pym*, is a vivid but enigmatic sea adventure that some critics suggest may have influenced HERMAN MELVILLE. The narrator, Pym, recounts his experiences after stowing away on board the whaling vessel Grampus. After Pym and two companions confront and defeat a group of mutineers, the ship is damaged by a hurricane, and the last four survivors are at the mercy of the sea. After beginning as a relatively typical sea narrative, the tale becomes increasingly bizarre as the environments which the characters encounter assume a mysterious, phantasmal quality. After resorting to cannibalism to survive, and after having spotted a derelict ghost ship populated with corpses, the final two survivors, Pym and crew member Dirk Peters, are rescued by another ship, the Jane Guy. Following an episode during which the crew of the Jane Guy are all killed by a group of savage island natives, Pym and Peters set out from the island in a canoe, having narrowly escaped the massacre. The story ends abruptly when, having reached the South Pole, Pym is confronted by a colossal white figure in the shape of a man that rises from yet another great cataract in the water, presumably the hole that, in Symmes's theory, was believed to exist at the pole. Nothing is said about what happens during or after the encounter. The progressive strangeness of the narrative and its inconclusive ending result in a work that has intrigued but puzzled most critics, leading J. Gerald Kennedy to refer to the study of the work as an "Abyss of Interpretation." The enduring intrigue and appeal of the work, as with much of Poe's oeuvre, stems largely from the way in which Poe represents his environments as radically beyond human experience, yet — partly owing to this very remoteness — as profoundly *influencing* human experience.

Thus, isolation and personal spiritual experience are common themes running through Poe's environmental imaginary. The narrator of "The Island of the Fay," for example, claims that "the man who would behold aright the glory of God upon earth must in solitude behold that glory" (600). Ultimately, Poe's strange and idealized landscapes represent glimpses of the divine, and such transcendent experience must necessarily be isolate and personal. Mark Canada, in fact, argues that the remote physical locations represent "remote mental regions" (66), and while traditional Romantic authors often saw nature as sublime in itself, Poe depicts landscapes and natural events that are infused with elements of the surreal, the supernatural, or the divine, making them emblems of both a physical, and spiritual realm unreachable by humans in the normal physical world — what Christopher Smith calls the "psychological exotic" (qtd by Canada). — Matthew S. Elder

BIBLIOGRAPHY

Canada, Mark. "Flight into Fancy: Poe's Discovery of the Right Brain." *Southern Literary Journal* 33.2 (2001): 62–79.

Kennedy, J. Gerald. The Narrative of Arthur Gordon Pym *and the Abyss of Interpretation.* New York: Twain, 1995.

Poe, Edgar Allan. *Edgar Allan Poe: Complete Poems.* Ed. Thomas Ollive Mabbot. Urbana: University of Illinois Press, 2000.

_____. *Edgar Allan Poe: Tales & Sketches.* Ed. Thomas Ollive Mabbot. 2 vols. Urbana: University of Illinois Press, 2000.

Quinn, Arthur Hobson. *Edgar Allan Poe: A Critical Biography.* Baltimore: Johns Hopkins University Press, 1998.

Silverman, Kenneth. *Edgar Allan Poe: Mournful and Never-Ending Remembrance.* New York: HarperPerennial, 1992.

Sova, Dawn B. *Edgar Allan Poe, A–Z.* New York: Checkmark Books, 2001.

Ware, Tracy. "'A Descent into the Maelstrom': The Status of Scientific Rhetoric in a Perverse Romance." *Studies in Short Fiction* 29.1 (1992): 77–74.

Pohl, Frederik G. (1919–)

Pohl was born in 1919 to Frederik George Pohl, Sr. and Anna Jane Pohl. While still a teenager Pohl helped found the Futurians, a science-fiction fan group based in New York City that included Damon Knight, Isaac Asimov and other writers. Pohl also joined the Youth Communist League in 1936, and though he left the organization in 1939 after the Stalin-Hitler pact, the ideas of socialism continued to influence his work, in particular his critique of capitalism as a political and ecological disaster.

Pohl's writing career began in the late 1930s, though for the first 15 years he wrote under a pseudonym. He was a prolific writer and important science fiction editor who helped shape the field as it emerged from the pulps. From 1959 to 1969 he edited *Galaxy* and *if* magazine. Apart from winning three Hugo Awards for his editorial skills, he also received three Hugos and multiple Nebula Awards for his writing.

Much has been made of Pohl's brief involvement after the war with the Madison Avenue agency Thwill and Altman, an involvement he describes negatively in *The Way the Future Was* (1978). Thomas Clareson, for example, argues that Pohl's experience in the firm gave him a lifelong distaste for contemporary management practices and business strategies (14). This distaste finds its most acute embodiment in *THE SPACE MERCHANTS* (1953), a dystopian satire about a world ruled by advertising agencies. Written collaboratively with C.M. Kornbluth, *The Space Merchants* represented the high point of what David Samuelson calls Pohl's "consumer cycle," (81) a series of disconnected stories and novels he wrote in the 1950s that examine American consumption patterns and their potentially negative impact on the environment. In *The Space Merchants* unfettered consumption has exhausted the Earth's resources, leading capitalists and conservationists alike to vie for Venus as a second chance. Other noted texts from the consumer cycle include "The Midas Plague" (1954) and "The Census Takers" (1956).

Even after the consumer cycle ended in the 1960s, however, Pohl's work continued to engage with questions of environmental degradation. Indeed, the theme of overpopulation and depleted resources reappears in many of Pohl's later works, for example *Jem* (1980), in which humans must again leave a ravaged Earth to seek out a new world for colonization.

While Pohl's primary outlet for environmental critique was fiction, he also co-wrote the non-fiction handbook *Our Angry Earth* (1991) with fellow science fiction writer Isaac Asimov. Discussing topics such as environmental homeostasis and the Gaia hypothesis, Pohl returns again and again to the idea that humans can save the environment only by "making considerable social, economic and political changes in the world. These changes go far beyond anything we can accomplish as individuals" (x). Both Pohl's fiction and non-fiction, while lauding individuals for making green choices at the personal level, ultimately emphasize transforming large-scale economic and political systems. For Pohl, science fiction, with its frequently inter-planetary perspective, proved the best method for teaching readers to both think and act globally.—James Landau

BIBLIOGRAPHY

Clareson, Thomas. *Frederik Pohl*. Starmont Reader's Guide 39. Mercer Island, WA: Starmont House, 1987.
Pohl, Frederik. *The Way the Future Was: A Memoir*. New York: Ballantine, 1978.
_____, and Isaac Asimov. *Our Angry Earth*. New York: Tor, 1991.
_____, and C.M. Kornbluth. *The Space Merchants*. New York: St. Martin's Press, 1987 (1952).
Samuelson, David. "Critical Mass: The SF of Frederik Pohl." *Science Fiction Studies*. 7: 1 (March 1980), 80–95.

The Space Merchants, Frederik Pohl and C.M. Kornbluth (1953)

First serialized in the journal *Galaxy* as "Gravy Planet," *The Space Merchants* represents Pohl's final version of his and Kornbluth's original text. Though published in 1953, the novel eschews typical Cold War anxieties about nuclear war or ideological hegemony to envisage, instead, massive ecological collapse linked to capitalist over-consumption. While some scholars argue that the text's critique actually centers on emerging management practices (Clareson 14), most critics see the dystopian satire as a straightforward attack on capitalism as a whole. And *The Space Merchants* would appear to support this, with its evocation of a future in which capitalism's economic need for consumers has inexorably led to over-population and the depletion of the earth's resources.

The novel's protagonist, Mitchell Courtenay, works at Fowler Schocken Associates, a multinational conglomerate that markets such consumer items as Coffiest, a beverage laced with an addictive chemical guaranteed to boost sales. As an executive, Courtenay begins the novel believing in advertising, consumption and materialism, but has a change of heart after coming face to face with their environmental and social consequences.

The plot divides into roughly three acts. In the first Courtenay becomes head of his company's Venus Section, a division tasked with colonizing Venus. In the second he is kidnapped by a rival and awakens in Costa Rica to find his identity erased. With no way home and the world believing him dead, he becomes a grunt worker in the Chlorella Corporation's food-production center, a facility built around Chicken Little, a warehouse-sized lump of undifferentiated and constantly growing flesh. Hoping to escape, he infiltrates the Conservationists, a conspiracy that, having failed to prevent environmental apoca-

lypse on earth, aims to co-opt the Venus colonization project. Finally, in the third section he returns to New York City, inheriting control of Fowler Schocken Associates after Schocken dies. Marked by Courtenay's political transformation, this section relates his usurpation of the Venus project for the Conservationist cause.

His transformation ultimately stems from Courtenay's exposure to the "real" world, one in which overpopulation and over-consumption have led to the near-exhaustion of natural resources. In this world America has become a crowded nation of 800 million people. Resources have grown so scarce that the vast majority of people must bathe in salt water rather than fresh; ride bicycles because of oil depletion; and sleep in stairwells or, if they are lucky, single-room quarters reminiscent of the Victorian tenements described in JACK LONDON'S *The People of the Abyss*. However, as in KURT VONNEGUT'S *Player Piano*, Kornbluth's story "The Marching Morons," and David Riesman's "Nylon Wars," *The Space Merchants* explores how advertising pacifies the masses, transforming them into passive, mindless consumers.

The novel generates its dystopia largely through an act of extrapolation, a grand *reduction ad absurdum* of our present practices and social structures, such that the reader may gain a better understanding of contemporary life and its potential consequences. As Frederic Jameson explains, the production of imaginary futures allows the reader to pierce the fugue of normality that masks the present (152). Apart from the detrimental effects of advertising, Pohl and Kornbluth take aim at technological optimism that supports the exploitation of nature. Early in the narrative, for example, Courtenay declares, "science is *always* a step ahead of the failure of natural resources. After all, when real meat got scarce, we had soyaburgers ready. When oil ran low, technology developed the pedicab" (14). Such optimism was standard fare among futurists of the period, and science fiction writers in particular. Pohl and Kornbluth, however, contested not merely the capacity of technology to solve environmental ills, but the whole notion of "technological" solutions *per se*. *The Space Merchants* critiques the entire corporate ideological position, siding with the Conservationists (aka the "Consies"), described initially as "those wild-eyed zealots who pretended modern civilization was in some way 'plundering' our planet" (14). As M. Keither Booker notes, the "Consies (although somewhat reminiscent of the modern Greenpeace organization) are rather transparent stand-ins for communists, and their role in the book serves as part of an effective satire of the anticommunist oppression of the McCarthy era" (40).

The Conservationist movement is primarily composed of society's lower classes, also known as "consumers" (as opposed to the "executives" and "producers"), and Courtenay's realization "that I'd never really known any consumers except during the brief periods when they were serving me" (64) makes explicit the society's class divisions. While the first portion of the book describes the opulence of the executives' world, the remainder reveals the misery that supports it and the environmental catastrophe that awaits it. More importantly, Pohl's satiric portrait reveals the crippling inertia of this economic structure. Courtenay, for example, suddenly living the life of the proletariat, realizes that the lower class "never got out of debt. Easy credit was part of the system, so were irritants that forced you to exercise it" (76). This state of indentured servitude, in turn, leads to a "hopeless, trapped feeling that things were this way, that they would always be this way" (78).

Nonetheless, this inequity motivates the conflict between the Conservationists and the capitalists for the Venus Flight, which the Consies win when Courtenay converts to their cause. A blank space for the mapping of different needs and desires, Venus represents a ready-made answer to the problems faced by both camps. For the capitalists it marks a new epoch in the history of capitalism; Fowler Shocken explains that "we've actually and literally conquered the world. Like Alexander, we weep for new worlds to conquer" (6). Having commodified the entire earth, the capitalist world-order must now look outward for more: more markets, more space, more resources. *The Space Merchants*, in turn, maps this classic theme of science fiction — space exploration — onto capitalism's constant need for more. In recalling Alexander the Great, Schocken inadvertently makes obvious the link between economic colonization and political imperialism. The novel, David Seed writes, "depicts a world and indeed a universe as empty space awaiting specifically America appropriation" (84).

Yet, while *The Space Merchants* clearly assails a specifically American form of big business capitalism, it ultimately emphasizes the environmental rather than politico-economic consequences of such malpractice. Not surprisingly then, Pohl and Kornbluth turn to a biological metaphor in describing this imperialism, offering Chicken Little, that rubbery slab of autogenetic synthetic protein, as an allegory both for ecological and economic disaster:

> Chicken Little grew and grew, as she had been growing for decades. Since she had started as a lump of heart tissue, she didn't know any better than to grow up against a foreign body and surround it. She didn't know any better than to grow

and fill her concrete vault and keep growing, compressing her cells and rupturing them. As long as she got nutrient, she grew [76].

Chicken Little grows blindly, blind not just to her environment, but also her own individual cells, which rupture as they press against one another. In a similar way, capitalism, *The Space Merchants* suggests, is itself a kind of cancerous growth, one that will continue dividing until it destroys itself.

On the other hand, the Conservationists, faced with overpopulation and the exhaustion of natural resources, imagine Venus as a genuine second chance: "think what Venus means to us — an unspoiled planet, all the wealth the race needs, all the fields and food and raw materials" (87). Yet, in their utopian conception of Venus as a *new* space, the Conservationists inadvertently acknowledge the failure of their revolutionary project on *earth*. And this suggests a pessimism on behalf of the authors, regarding both our environmental and economic future, deeper than the deepest irony. — James Landau

BIBLIOGRAPHY

Booker, M. Keith. *Monsters, mushroom clouds, and the Cold War: American science fiction and the roots of postmodernism, 1946–1964*. Westport, CT: Greenwood Press, 2001.
Clareson, Thomas. *Frederik Pohl*. Starmont Reader's Guide 39. Mercer Island, WA: Starmont House, 1987.
Jameson, Fredric. "Progress Versus Utopia; or, Can We Imagine the Future?" *Science-Fiction Studies*. 9:2 (July 1982), 147–158.
Pohl, Frederik, and C.M. Kornbluth. *The Space Merchants*. New York: St. Martin's Press, 1987 (1952).
Seed, David. *American Science Fiction and the Cold War: Literature and Film*. Chicago: Fitzroy Dearborn, 1999.

Pound, Ezra (1885–1972)

Ezra Loomis Pound was born in 1885 in the small frontier town of Hailey, Idaho, where his father, Homer Loomis Pound, ran a United States Land Office that served the local miners by filing their claims and assaying their ore. When his father was appointed as an assistant assayer at the U.S. Mint, Ezra Pound and his family moved to Philadelphia, finally settling north of the city, in Wyncote, where Pound played in still uncleared hill country as a boy. Pound attended the University of Pennsylvania and Hamilton College, and studied Anglo-Saxon and Romance languages, both of which were to be foundational as he began writing his own poetry. He later travelled to Europe, lived in London and Paris, worked with W.B. Yeats, married Dorothy Shakespear, and became instrumental in the publication of other modernist writers, including T.S. ELIOT, James Joyce, and ERNEST HEMINGWAY. Pound was central in the formation of the Imagist and Vorticist movements in poetry and art, both of which waned during and after World War I. He later produced liberal free verse translations of Chinese poetry and began his greatest work, *The Cantos*, which was published in sections from 1925 to 1969.

After World War I, Pound was drawn to political and economic subjects; he came to believe that the war had been caused and extended by the interests of finance capitalism, and adopted Major C.H. Douglas' social credit theories, which Pound further associated with the American populist ideal of THOMAS JEFFERSON's yeoman farmer (AMERICAN PASTORAL). From the early 1920s, Pound lived in Italy and eventually embraced the policies of Benito Mussolini as well as fascism and antisemitism. During World War II, Pound made a series of politically charged radio broadcasts that, following the entry of the United States into the war, led to charges of treason; Pound was held at a U.S. Army detention facility near Pisa but was deemed mentally unfit to stand trial when returned to America. He thereafter spent 12 years in a mental institution, and returned to Italy after his release in 1958, where he lived until his death in 1972.

Scholars of Pound typically emphasize his central role in the modernist era, his distinctive understanding of aesthetics, or his deep interest in economics, politics, and American history; for this reason, Pound is not frequently connected with environmental concerns, yet each aspect of his poetics was in fact deeply influenced by his views of nature and the place of the human community in relation to the earth. Unlike most other American writers of his generation, Pound cannot be said to write straightforward nature poetry; however, many of his verses are ecological, in that they focus on the interdependence of nature or on how humans act within that relationship, either by embracing nature (as did the ancient Greeks and Chinese who so influenced Pound), or by destroying nature though the greed of industry and capitalism. In his classic text, *The Pound Era*, Hugh Kenner identifies Pound closely with ecology as it was then understood, and argues that Pound saw the ecological unity between humans and nature as fractured and eroded due to the effects of modern industry, economics, politics, and religion (377). Yet Pound believed society could recover its connection to the world if it reactivated its ancestral knowledge, which Kenner illustrates through Pound's 1912 realization of "our kinship to the vital universe, to the tree and the living rock.... We have about us the universe of fluid force, and below us the germinal universe of wood alive, of stone alive" ("Psychology 92"). For Pound, those individuals who inherently comprehend their consciousness in a germinal sense, through which "Their thoughts are in them as the thought of the tree is in the seed, or in the grass, or the grain, or the blossom," are those whose "minds are the more poetic, and they affect mind about them, and transmute it as the seed of the earth. And this latter sort of mind is close on the vital universe" ("Psychology" 92–93).

One environmental thinker that significantly interested Pound in seeking this vital universe was W.H. Hudson (1841–1922), the noted naturalist, ornithologist, author, and novelist. In an essay on Hudson, Pound reacts to his warning of the coming extinction of plants, birds, and mammals. Hudson had urged that "the life of even a single species is of incalculably [great] value to mankind, for what it teaches and would continue to teach"; for which reason "we should protect and hold sacred ... Nature's masterpieces." Hudson compares the disinterest of the general public to this environmental destruction with the outcry he imagines would ensue were the great British museums to suffer a similar destruction (qtd, in Pound, "Hudson" 429–430). Pound agrees but responds with regret that the public actually cares little for the environment or for art; he construes these two aspects of disinterest as similar symptoms of a society that had strayed too far from its union with the natural world. Consequently, Pound looks back to the art of ancient Greece and China in order to explore that union and return to a poetics that better expresses the authentic voice of humanity. Pound clearly sees the hierarchy enshrined in industrial capitalism as the root problem that destroys art, the environment, and the human community: "A bloated usury, a cowardly and snivelling politics, a disgusting financial system, the sadistic curse of Christianity work together, not only that an hundred species of wild fowl and beast shall give way before the advance of industry ... in our alleged 'society' the same tendencies and the same urge that the bright plumed and the fine voiced species of the genus anthropos, the favoured of the gods, the only part of humanity worth saving, is attacked" ("Hudson" 430).

Another decisive influence on Pound was Ernest Fenollosa (1853–1908), the American Orientalist who lived in Japan during the Meiji period of modernization. Based on Fenollosa's writings on Chinese poetry and Japanese Noh drama, Pound wrote his own free verse translations and developed an argument about how poetic language could better reflect nature. In Fenollosa's study of Chinese ideograms as a medium for poetry, he writes that "Nature herself has no grammar," for "A true noun, an isolated thing, does not exist in nature.... Neither can a pure verb, an abstract motion, be possible in nature. The eye sees a noun and verb as one: things in motion, motion in things" (Fenollosa and Pound 90, 46). Kenner argues that, on this basis, Pound reasoned that the language of English modernist poetry must reject the wordy verbiage of earlier poets in favor of a new use of language that would seek the immediacy of Chinese poetics; for theirs was "a script that would let no man with an eye forget what energy it is that fills words: the energy of process in nature" (160).

In some of his best known texts, Pound adopts the ecological sentiments of Classical and Chinese literature by referring to the vitality of a natural world invested with divine life; these include references to the spirits of trees, the children of the grass, and even a translation of a Christian canticle by St. Francis of Assisi that identifies the Earth as our mother (*Poems* 127–28). Pound's translation of Rihaku's "The River-Merchant's Wife: A Letter" uses nature as a mirror of the young wife's longing for her husband through the "sorrowful noise" of monkeys, the mosses that overgrow their unused lane, the autumn wind that blows dead leaves, and the jealousy-inducing "paired butterflies ... already yellow with August" (*Poems* 251–52). In his translation of "Liu Ch'e," Pound again closely identifies human emotion with nature, by first translating the original Chinese poem's account of an emperor's sorrow over the death of a lover, and then inventing a new line drawn from a natural image that is not in the original to describe the still strong influence of the dead woman on the emperor's emotions—as "A wet leaf that clings to the threshold" (*Poems* 286). Pound's famous short poem "In a Station of the Metro" adopts a similar image: "The apparition of these faces in the crowd; / Petals in a wet black bough" (*Poems* 287). Despite the urban setting of the first line, the poem is profoundly ecological, both in its employment of the contained and natural style of a Japanese haiku, which omits unnecessary words and here radically superimposes two striking images upon one another; and in its use of the Classical Greek image of petals for the souls of the dead, in order to emphasize the brevity of human life, which must ultimately return to the earth in spite of the distancing strategies of modern urban life. The emphasis on the continued interconnectedness of humans and nature throughout time is later acknowledged by Pound in a translation of *The Confucian Analects* when he urges, "Observe the phenomena of nature as one in whom the ancestral voices speak" (*Poems* 681).

Pound's greatest work, the long poem *The Cantos,* shows the same attention to the human place in natural ecology, but his viewpoint expands to interrogate the human use of nature for agriculture and industry, and to express the spiritual aspects of humanity's vital connections to the natural world. He attacks the economic system of industrialized capitalism, and in particular rejects usury, which he defines as a "sin against nature" and "against Nature's increase" because commerce determines that agriculture be used to produce consumer goods for sale instead of for the consumption of those who farm the land (XLV, LI). He bemoans the use of human technologies to subjugate nature when, for instance, "the first thing Dave lit on when they got there / Was a buzz saw, / And he put it through an ebony log: whhsssh, t ttt, / Two days' work in three minutes" (XVIII). Pound shows concern that "the true base of credit" is really the "abundance of nature / with the whole folk behind it," at once categorizing the earth and human communities as commodities manipulated for the profit of the banking system (LII). Later cantos instead celebrate the ancient Chinese political leaders who affirm that the "Earth is the nurse of all men," or, again connecting the environment to economics, "I now cut off one half the taxes.... Let farm folk have tools for their labour it is / for this I reduce the said taxes" (LIV). Peter Liebregts demonstrates that these "China Cantos" name the religious rituals to be celebrated throughout the year in imperial China; these crucial rituals illustrate "the right principles from which all goodness springs," and Pound uses them to proclaim the human obligation to revere the rhythm of the seasons, in order to preserve both the link to the vital universe and an ordered society in balance with nature and itself (236–37). Throughout, Pound highlights ancient images of ecological balance in order to urge modern readers to acknowledge their increasing and increasingly destructive tension with the environment; for example, Canto XLVII expresses a Classical Greek view of farming by referring to Hesiod's *Works and Days*, which ritualizes the farmer's cyclical relationship to the land in a manner that ultimately approaches sexual and ecstatic union; and Canto XLIX returns to the Chinese setting by delivering a picturesque description of rural life that respects the environment to a degree that in fact approaches the earlier picture of Greek divinities in harmony with nature presented in Canto XVII (AMERICAN PASTORAL).

While held in an American military detention center near Pisa after Italy surrendered to the Allies, Pound began Cantos LXXIV to LXXXIV, which are known as the "Pisan Cantos." Isolated and kept in an outdoor maximum security wire cage, Pound described his environmental surroundings, including Italian peasants harvesting in nearby fields, birds sitting on wires, katydids and ants, mint and clover, a eucalyptus pip, the birth of a wasp, and, in Canto

LXXIX, an extended address to a lynx that directly alludes to W.H. Hudson. The best known of the *Pisan Cantos* is Canto LXXXI, which begins with the mythic-sounding, "Zeus lies in Ceres' bosom"; a phrase that actually describes a sunrise between two hills but further imagines the union of the divine with the natural environment. After an epiphany during which the eyes of a goddess appear in the narrator's tent, the text rejects human vanity in the presence of nature:

> What thou lovest well remains,
>   the rest is dross
> ....
> Whose world, or mine or theirs
>   or is it of none?
> ....
> The ant's a centaur in his dragon world.
> Pull down thy vanity, it is not man
> Made courage, or made order or made grace,
>   Pull down thy vanity, I say pull down.
> Learn of the green world what can be thy place
> In scaled invention or true artistry,
> Pull down thy vanity,
>   Paquin pull down!
> The green casque has outdone all your elegance
> [LXXXI].

As the American writer and farmer WENDELL BERRY observes, "In Canto LXXXI, Ezra Pound wrote, whether intentionally or not, some lines that could serve as the epigraph of the science of ecology. Again the message is to escape the abstractions; man will have to break out of the context of his own assumptions and measure himself by the truer measure of 'the green world'" (415). Though the exact meaning of this striking passage has been variously interpreted, Pound's words unquestionably and unforgettably call for humans to reassess their destructive treatment of the environment, and to exercise humility before nature by recognizing its sacredness and our dependence upon it.— Kelly C. MacPhail

BIBLIOGRAPHY

Berry, Wendell. "A Secular Pilgrimage." *The Hudson Review* 23.3 (1970): 401–424.
Fenollosa, Ernest, and Ezra Pound. *The Chinese Written Character as a Medium for Poetry: A Critical Edition.* 1936. Ed. Haun Saussy, Jonathan Stalling, and Lucas Klein. New York: Fordham University Press, 2008. Print.
Kenner, Hugh. *The Pound Era.* Berkeley and Los Angeles: University of California Press, 1971.
Liebregts, Peter. *Ezra Pound and Neoplatonism.* Madison and Teaneck: Fairleigh Dickinson University Press, 2004. Print.
Pound, Ezra. *The Cantos of Ezra Pound.* 1970. New York: New Directions, 1996.
_____. "Hudson: Poet Strayed into Science." *The Little Review* May-June 1920. Rpt. *Selected Prose: 1909–1965.* Ed. William Cookson. New York: New Directions, 1973. 429–432.
_____. *Poems and Translations.* New York: Library of America, 2003.
_____. "Psychology and Troubadours." *The Spirit of Romance.* 1910. Rev. ed 1952. London: Peter Owen, 1970. Print. 87–100.

Purdy, Jedediah (1974–   )

Jedediah Spenser Purdy was born in 1974 in rural Chloe, West Virginia, where his parents Wally and Deidre Purdy had moved "to live with few needs" (xvi). He and his younger sister Hannah were homeschooled. At 13 Purdy enrolled in Calhoun County High School but left at 16 to enroll in Phillips Exeter Academy in New Hampshire. After graduation he attended Harvard, where he received a B.A. in Social Studies and graduated *summa cum laude* in 1997. In 2001 he earned his J.D. from Yale Law School, and is currently an Associate Professor of Law at Duke University, where among his courses he teaches Sources in Environmental Law, and Climate Change and the Law.

Purdy's scholarship reveals a strong interest in politics, ethics, and the environment. He has written four books: FOR COMMON THINGS: IRONY, TRUST, AND COMMITMENT IN AMERICA TODAY (1999); *Being America: Liberty, Commerce, and Violence in an American World* (2003); *A Tolerable Anarchy: Rebels, Reactionaries, and the Making of American Freedom* (2009); and *Dominion: Property and the Legal Imagination* (forthcoming 2010). He served as editor for the book *Democratic Vistas: Reflections on the Life of American Democracy* (2004). In addition to his books, Purdy has written numerous articles on such topics as property law, globalization, and biopolitics. Three recent articles concentrate on environmental issues: "Climate Change and the Limits of the Possible" for *Duke Environmental Law and Policy Forum* (2008); "Corn Futures: Consumer Politics, Health, and Climate Change" with James Salzman for *Environmental Law Reporter* (2008); and "What Has to Change for Forests to be Saved?: A Precedent from U.S. History" *Duke Journal of Comparative and International Law* (2009).

Purdy is perhaps best known for his first book, *For Common Things: Irony, Trust, and Commitment in America Today.* While the work gained notoriety as an attack on Jerry Seinfeld and his show, *Seinfeld*, it reveals an almost metaphysical connection to the natural environment of West Virginia, as well as a fundamental conviction that excessive environmental damage is an unacceptable cost of economic growth. Although Purdy discusses a variety of geographic locales in *For Common Things*, a significant portion of the book focuses on the issue of coal mining in West Virginia, and the inexpensive but devastating method of mountain top removal. Purdy deems such mining techniques untenable. As he explains, the environmental destruction caused by such practices creates an uncertain future that carries potential risk: "Our destructive energy economy might be called a crisis of social ecology" (147). Analogously, Purdy contends that healthy social interactions take precedence over our need for cheap energy. His study of coal mining, emblematic of his broader thematic concerns, reveals the hidden costs, both environmental and social, in practices that place economic gain over vital social responsibilities. Ultimately, and throughout his work, he argues that members of a society have an ethical obligation to create sustainable political and economic networks that do not harm the natural environment, and insists we neglect our common interest in the environment at considerable hazard.—Arthur Rankin

BIBLIOGRAPHY

Purdy, Jedediah S. *For Common Things: Irony, Trust, and Commitment in America Today.* New York: Vintage Books, 2000.
School of Law. Dept. home page. Duke U. Available online. URL: http:www.law.duke.edu/fac/purdy/. Accessed 29 June 2009.
Sella, Marshall. "Against Irony." *The New York Times Magazine.* 5 Sept. 1999. Available online. URL: http://partners.nytimes.com/library/magazine/home/19990905mag-sincere-culture.html Accessed 25 June 2009.

For Common Things: Irony, Trust, Commitment in America Today, Jedediah Purdy (1999)

Jedediah Purdy's *For Common Things*, his first book, explores the need in modern America to resist the seductive, but ultimately fatal, ironic stance that pervades society. Purdy explores how the ironic attitude came to dominate modern society, while also calling for a renewed commitment to communal obligations that once were expressed through proper political action. Although a substantial portion of the book investigates the ironic stance as an escape from the modern world and its excessive media culture, Purdy, himself raised and home-schooled in a remote West Virginia locale, also probes the relationship between irony, detachment, and the environment. The ironist fears, as Purdy tells us, the possibility that valued ideas and issues "might be trivialized" (xv) and left gutted by "the harsh light of a reflexively skeptical time" (xv). Indeed, Purdy approaches the argument that an ironic stance allows environmental degradation to occur because the ironic pose lacks a sense of trust , thereby distancing people from the communal engagement needed to influence economic and environmental policy.

In his call for a renewal of community spirit, which he sees as the main function of politics, Purdy most closely approaches the work of BILL MCKIBBEN, particularly McKibben's ideas concerning community and the environment articulated in *Deep Economy: The Wealth of Communities and the Durable Future.* McKibben's argues that the economic policies related to "hyper-individualism" (97) in the modern era act as a driving force in the destruction of sound communal policies toward the environment. For McKibben, as for Purdy, an extreme focus on the self is destructive, most fundamentally and above all, to any healthy community spirit. Both McKibben and Purdy demonstrate that environmental problems occur when people forget their obligations to one another.

That same sense of hyper-individualism underscores the ironic pose that Purdy assails. Rather than be duped, ironists protect their ego from true engagement, and thereby create a barrier between their most intimate self and the world. With the connection to the world severed, it becomes much easier to allow practices to evolve that corrupt the environment. Consider Purdy's argument about farming. He contends that farming is done correctly when it allows for practices that sustain the environment rather than obliterate it. As he asserts, "farming done well and conscientiously is partly public work" (104), and this public aspect of farming connects the latter to other types of "public" employment, including work done by teachers, merchants, and artisans. All types of work potentially create sustainability, specifically when they are done meticulously and with an eye to the work's influence on society. For Purdy, then, a sense of sustainability supports a healthy environment by promoting thinking in terms of five thousand years (104), instead of the five years that may result in quick profits but an exhausted, ruined environment.

Moreover, in evoking this sense of a sustainable engagement with the landscape, Purdy suggests that sustainability also offers the potential for establishing a deep connection to place — the very connection that irony resists. For Purdy, this sense of connection is personified by his fellow Appalachian, the essayist and poet, WENDELL BERRY. Purdy argues that Berry represents "America's most articulate source of caution against heedless self-seeking" (109–10). By returning to his birthplace in Kentucky to farm, Berry demonstrates for Purdy the essential act of sane choice. This choice, to connect to the land and nurture it, offers a profound rejection of the ironic stance; and Purdy thus sees in Berry's choice to heal an exhausted farm, a profound ethical act.

The choice to connect also calls to mind three

essential common traits that make up Purdy's moral ecology: cultural practices, political institutions, and the natural world, which latter is set against the other two (99–101). These three traits weave themselves into a society's ethos. When the traits balance and sustain each other, the society remains healthy. However, when one or the other of the three fails, the social order faces the sort of stress that often results in negative environmental policies. Consider Purdy's birthplace of West Virginia. His parents migrated to West Virginia to find a life of "few needs" (xvi) and of community bonds. Unfortunately, much of the Appalachian area has faced an explosion of coal mining. In Chapter Four, Purdy analyzes the destruction wreaked by mining practices on the environment of West Virginia and Southern Appalachia. As he points out, some of the oldest existing mountains in the world are succumbing to such practices, specifically mountaintop removal. Though a cheap ("five year") method of mining coal, mountaintop removal is *environmentally* expensive, and he exposes some of the most significant environmental problems left in the aftermath of such drastic mining methods; among them, polluted water, loss of native plant life, and destruction of fragile ecological systems. The mining practices in Appalachia reveal that the relationship among the essential "common traits" of Purdy's moral ecology has become unbalanced, with a heavy cost to the natural world.

This environmental cost lies at the heart of Purdy's argument against the ironic stance. When cultural practices and political institutions devolve into organizations that serve the economic interests of a few at the expense of the many, and the power to change such actions seems impossible to achieve, it becomes much easier to hide behind a pose of ironic detachment. Such detachment, then, turns out to be a form of acquiescence to powerful forces; irony evolves into surrender. Nonetheless, Purdy maintains the importance of "the maintenance of a world, natural and social" (207), as well as its power to move communities to action. Purdy understands that environmental policy coexists with communal action. Hiding behind the ironic mask denies the fact that humans inhabit both communities and natural environments, and that the health of both is interdependent.

Ultimately, *For Common Things* makes a compelling and contemporary case for the mutual dependence of natural and human "cultures," reminding us, yet again and at the most fundamental level, that the natural world does not exist solely as a vehicle for human economic use. Abuse of the natural world reveals that common institutions have ceased to function properly; and an ethical approach toward the environment requires a commitment to

honest policies, both political and cultural, that value the natural world in its own right, while at the same time — and *in this way*— helping to create a sustainable community.— Arthur Rankin

BIBLIOGRAPHY

McKibben, Bill. *Deep Economy: The Wealth of Communities and the Durable Future*. New York: Henry Holt, 2007.
Purdy, Jedediah. *For Common Things: Irony, Trust, and Commitment in America Today*. New York: Vintage Books, 2000.

Pyle, Robert Michael (1947–   )

Looking back on his eventful, circuitous life in his memoir *Walking the High Ridge: Life as a Field Trip* (2000), distinguished lepidopterist, prominent conservationist, and award-winning environmental writer Robert Michael Pyle notes that the famous Russian-born novelist, poet, literary critic, and butterfly specialist Vladimir Nabokov decisively shaped his "outlook, both through his uncanny attention to the detail of the world, and by his reinforcing belief that there must 'exist a high ridge where the mountainside of "scientific" knowledge joins the opposite slope of "artistic" imagination'— where 'the Precision of Poetry and the Excitement of Science' can meet" (48). As Pyle demonstrates in his memoir and other writings, he has sauntered along this metaphorical ridgeline ever since his childhood in suburban Aurora, Colorado. Born in Denver in 1947, the third child of Robert Harold Pyle, a salesman for an office supply firm, and Helen Lee Lemmon Pyle, he early on developed a keen interest in the more-than-human world around his home near the High Line Canal, and became precociously preoccupied with seashells; and then, in fifth grade, with butterflies, his lifelong passion and the focus of his later academic career, conservation work, and many major publications. By the time Pyle completed his formal scientific training with a Ph.D. in ecology and environmental studies from Yale in 1976, he had founded, in 1971, the Xerces Society, a "nonprofit organization that protects wildlife through the conservation of invertebrate and their habitat," and already written prolifically on butterflies and various other ecological as well as environmental issues for both specialist and generalist publications.

While a student at Yale, Pyle also met Edwin Way Teale, at this time one of the best-known nature writers in the U.S., and Teale's example encouraged him to pursue a freelance existence that has since allowed him to pursue his vision of "ridgelines," and to integrate rigorous scientific research, a broad variety of writing projects, conservation work and environmental activism, as well as teaching for more than three decades now. This career move also gave Pyle the opportunity not merely to complete two comprehensive, beautifully written, and immensely popular field guides, *The Audubon Society Field Guide to North American Butterflies* (1981) and *The Audubon Society Handbook for Butterfly Watchers* (1984), but also to purchase Swede Park, an old farmstead in Gray's River in rural Wahkiakum County in southwestern Washington, where he has lived with this third wife, Thea, since the early 1980s.

Pyle has written extensively about his home in the Willapa Hills, most notably in *WINTERGREEN: RAMBLES IN A RAVAGED LAND* (1986), a text firmly located in the tradition of North American nature writing, but which also marks, as the title indicates, a departure from many of the generic conventions. In *Wintergreen*, Pyle perceptively and engagingly discusses the complex, intertwined natural and cultural histories of the area, but in contrast to many of his literary predecessors, he can only ramble through imperiled remnants of wild old-growth forests, as international logging companies have recklessly and repeatedly ravaged the Willapa Hills in their pursuit of rapidly diminishing profits. Pyle harshly criticizes past and present harvesting and business practices, but unlike many other texts about environmental degradation and exploitation, *Wintergreen* never wistfully or nostalgically evokes an idealized, quasi-Edenic past or impending doom. Instead, it celebrates the undiminished beauty, diversity, and resilience of the more than–human–world, a world that adapts and flourishes in the face of human carelessness and shortsighted greed, and that can and will be protected if it is only properly understood. Pyle has significantly contributed to our understanding of, and ethical regard for, the more–than–human world in general, and butterflies in particular, by successfully exploring the ridgeline between "the Precision of Poetry and the Excitement of Science," and by eloquently sharing his in-depth knowledge and irresistible enthusiasm with specialists and general audiences alike.— Micha Edlich

BIBLIOGRAPHY

Kuhlken, Robert. "Robert Michael Pyle." *Twentieth-Century American Nature Writers: Prose.* Ed. Roger Thompson and J. Scott Bryson. Detroit: Thomson-Gale, 2003. 261–70. Print. Dictionary of Literary Biography 275.

Pearson, Michael. "Robert Michael Pyle." *American Nature Writers.* Ed. John Elder. Vol. 2. New York: Scribner's, 1996. 733–39. Print.

Pyle, Robert Michael. *Walking the High Ridge: Life as a Field Trip.* Minneapolis: Milkweed, 2000. Print. Credo Ser.

_____. *Wintergreen: Rambles in a Ravaged Land.* 1986. Seattle: Sasquatch, 2001. Print. Library of the West.

Slovic, Scott. "Robert Michael Pyle: A Portrait." *Walking the High Ridge: Life as a Field Trip.* By Robert Michael Pyle. Minneapolis: Milkweed, 2000. 119–46. Print. Credo Ser.

Wintergreen, Robert Michael Pyle (1986)

In the early 1980s, the well-known lepidopterist, conservationist, and environmental writer Robert Michael Pyle permanently moved to Swede Park, an old farmstead in Gray's River in rural Wahkiakum County in southwestern Washington, and with his wife Thea, he began to explore the complex and closely connected natural and social histories of the surrounding Willapa Hills, "the clump of Coast Range mountains lying between the Cascades and the Pacific, the Olympic Mountains and Oregon" (*Wintergreen* 5). Pyle presented the results of his thorough, multilayered investigation of this bioregion a few years later in *Wintergreen: Rambles in a Ravaged Land*, an ambitious, award-winning collection of essays that has significantly affected his subsequent career as a writer. As he explains in his memoir *Walking the High Ridge: Life as a Field Trip* (2000), this project finally allowed him to achieve this artistic vision by "giving free rein to [his] scientific *and* poetic impulses" (69), and it "gave [him] the rationale and the vessel for a personal, perceptual entrée to the woods, the human and other-species culture of the woods, and the conservation politics of the woods" (68). His insights in these and numerous other respects remain, 25 years after the first publication of *Wintergreen*, timeless, profound, and provocative.

Wintergreen is, in part, a depressing assessment of the enormous environmental degradation and destruction resulting from the reckless harvesting and business practices employed by several elusive but politically powerful international logging corporations, which have ruthlessly and repeatedly exploited this part of Washington State and its inhabitants since the late nineteenth century. To Pyle, "these hills have been logged all to hell — positively butchered" (*Wintergreen* 17), and only huge stumps, a few "big old wolf trees" (*Wintergreen* 188), as well as tiny imperiled pockets of old growth attest to the former grandeur and complexity of the now greatly diminished local ecosystems. As Pyle points out in the afterword to the 2001 edition of *Wintergreen*, and in his 2007 nonfiction narrative *Sky Time in Gray's River: Living for Keeps in a Forgotten Place*, "the sack of the woods" in the Willapa Hills is far from over (*Wintergreen* 157), and environmental activism on behalf of a "seemingly dull and impoverished landscape" (*Wintergreen* 11) continues to be as important and frustrating as it was in the 1980s. His stance concerning environmental activism is nuanced and pragmatic: highly protective of the last wild stands of trees but not rigidly opposed to logging per se, Pyle persuasively lists both the devastating ecological effects and considerable social costs that the predominant business model, "cut and run" (*Wintergreen* 157), currently entails for the local human and more-than-human communities. He also emphasizes that the specific case presented in *Wintergreen* is, in several respects, exemplary and therefore highly instructive to outsiders as well: "Clearly Willapa is a metaphor for wasted lands everywhere. I hope that by framing some pictures of this green and damaged land, these essays will help a little in our efforts to coevolve with the rest of the living things of the planet" (xii). Pyle's work in general — and *Wintergreen* in particular — highlights, according to environmental critic Scott Slovic, "the value of learning from and celebrating even diminished landscapes and natural systems, and yet without calmly accepting gratuitous exploitation and degradation" (123).

In *Wintergreen*, this balanced stance is strengthened by Pyle's "cosmic optimism" (266), an evolutionary and non-anthropocentric perspective shaped by the work of Charles Darwin and premised on the related basic insight that "nature bats last" (261). Humanity has never been at the center of the universe, Pyle argues, and the more-than-human world will continue to evolve long after *Homo sapiens* has ceased to exist: "The land has been hurt. Misuse is not to be excused, and its ill effects will long be felt. But nature will not be eliminated, even here. Rain, moss, and time apply their healing bandage, and the injured land at last recovers. Nature is evergreen, after all" (269). Thus, "*Wintergreen* does tell a tale of resilience and a chronicle of toughness" in ecological as well as social terms (xii), as the local inhabitants of Gray's River likewise adapt to the precarious, constantly shifting socioeconomic conditions in the region. In this sense, the human community necessarily albeit unintentionally approaches what the Australian landscape ecologist Bill Mollison refers to as "permaculture" (290): "Peaceful, creative stability makes more sense than rapid growth that outstrips its resources and is bound to bust again and again. In this sense, Willapa makes a model for any crashed community in the postindustrial wasteland" (289).

Despite this refreshing emphasis on social concerns and his self-conscious break with the North American pastoral tradition of environmental writing at the beginning of the book (AMERICAN PASTORAL), Pyle is clearly indebted to his literary predecessors. In terms of genre, structure, and themes, *Wintergreen*, echoes the writings of HENRY DAVID THOREAU, JOHN BURROUGHS, and a host of other nature

writers past and present; not surprisingly, then, the book similarly often turns into a paean to the beauty of the more-than-human world. As Pyle demonstrates again and again in his essays, even the "devastated hills" (12) surrounding his home still yield new and highly enjoyable insights to those who are willing to pay attention. While the Willapa Hills are home to only a few species of butterflies — an obvious but acceptable disadvantage to a passionate lepidopterist like Pyle — the constantly evolving bioregion contains many other wonders great and small. Pyle covers the natural history of a hitherto neglected area systematically, comprehensively, and rigorously, but he never comes across as bookish or boring. Even scientific minutiae are usually presented with a poetic flourish, and his extended overview of the local flora, for instance, is stylistically somewhat reminiscent of WALT WHITMAN's catalogue verse (*Wintergreen* 66–75). Pyle thus gradually emerges as a "better, more rounded naturalist" (*Wintergreen* 112) and as the unofficial poet laureate of Gray's River, who, just like a logger, happens to make his living by exploring and exploiting the woods. "I came with the romantic yet semipractical notion of harvesting words grown out of the soil of the hills and the valleys," Pyle writes. "This book is a direct result; it is a kind of a crop, a new one for Willapa" (254). A quarter of a century after he published this sentence, Pyle, continues to live in, draw creative strength from, and write on behalf of the rainy, ravaged, but resilient bioregion surrounding Swede Park. — Micha Edlich

BIBLIOGRAPHY

Kuhlken, Robert. "Robert Michael Pyle." *Twentieth-Century American Nature Writers: Prose.* Ed. Roger Thompson and J. Scott Bryson. Detroit: Thomson-Gale, 2003. 261–70. Print. Dictionary of Literary Biography 275.

Pearson, Michael. "Robert Michael Pyle." *American Nature Writers.* Ed. John Elder. Vol. 2. New York: Scribner's, 1996. 733–39. Print.

Pyle, Robert Michael. *Sky Time in Gray's River: Living for Keeps in a Forgotten Place.* New York: Mariner-Houghton Mifflin, 2007. Print.

_____. *Walking the High Ridge: Life as a Field Trip.* Minneapolis: Milkweed, 2000. Print. Credo Ser.

_____. *Wintergreen: Rambles in a Ravaged Land.* 1986. Seattle: Sasquatch, 2001. Print. Library of the West.

Slovic, Scott. "Robert Michael Pyle: A Portrait." *Walking the High Ridge: Life as a Field Trip.* By Robert Michael Pyle. Minneapolis: Milkweed, 2000. 119–46. Print. Credo Ser.

Ricketts, Edward F. (1897–1948)

An iconoclastic marine biologist and pioneering ecologist, Ed Ricketts reinterpreted Pacific Coast intertidal marine life along ecological principles in his 1939 classic *BETWEEN PACIFIC TIDES*. Abandoning traditional taxonomic organization, Ricketts focused instead on a holistic study of habitats and intertidal zonation. He applied a similar ecological approach to produce important studies of sardine behavior and migration. Beyond biology, his wide-ranging intellectual explorations influenced writers as diverse as novelist JOHN STEINBECK and mythologist Joseph Campbell. Although Ricketts is perhaps best known as the inspiration for some of Steinbeck's most memorable characters — Doc in *Cannery Row* (1945) and *Sweet Thursday* (1954), Doc Burton in *In Dubious Battle* (1936), and Casy in THE GRAPES OF WRATH (1939) — scientists and environmentalists have increasingly looked beyond the Steinbeck myth to recognize in Ricketts's holistic approach a significant contribution to the study of Pacific Coast marine habitats in particular, and environmental ecology in general.

Edward Flanders Ricketts was born in Chicago in 1897, the son of an accountant. After military service as a clerk in the Army Medical Corps during World War I, he enrolled at the University of Chicago, where he studied zoology under W.C. Allee, an early ecologist whose work on cooperative group behavior among invertebrates left a lasting impression on the young scientist. In 1923, he left the university without a degree, moving to Pacific Grove, California to start Pacific Biological Laboratories, which supplied slides and prepared biological specimens for research institutions and schools. Ricketts's small lab, relocated in 1928 to Monterey's Cannery Row, soon became a magnet for artists, writers, scientists, and the area's bohemian population. Here Ricketts and his friends pursued their diverse intellectual passions, which extended beyond biology to early music, poetry, metaphysics, and Asian philosophy.

In 1930, he met John Steinbeck, beginning a close friendship and intellectual collaboration that would last until Ricketts's death in 1948. From March 14 to April 18, 1940, with Steinbeck's royalties from *The Grapes of Wrath*, the two organized and conducted a biological expedition to the Gulf of California to provide data for what they envisioned as a trilogy on Pacific Coast marine life: the already completed *Between Pacific Tides*, the *Sea of Cortez*, and *The Outer Shores*, the latter a study of the coasts of British Columbia and Alaska based on a 1932 Alaskan expedition Ricketts had undertaken with Joseph Campbell. The Steinbeck-Ricketts collaborative study, *The Sea of Cortez*, was published in 1941. Ten years later, Steinbeck published the narrative portion of the study, prefaced with a biographical portrait of Ricketts, as THE LOG FROM THE SEA OF CORTEZ. While Steinbeck made extensive use of Ricketts's notes and unpublished essays in preparing the text, Ricketts was given no authorial recognition on its publication. Nevertheless, the book is philosophically as much Ricketts's as Steinbeck's. Alternating between travelogue, scientific description, and metaphysical speculation, the *Log* represents an experiment in what Ricketts and Steinbeck call "non-teleological thinking" (*Log* 132), which replaces traditional cause/effect logic with a Zen-like acceptance of "is," anticipating ROBERT PIRSIG's conception of pure "Quality" in ZEN AND THE ART OF MOTORCYCLE MAINTENANCE. "Man," Steinbeck / Ricketts writes, "is related to the whole thing, related inextricably to all reality, known and unknowable" (*Log* 217).

In the spring of 1948, Ricketts and Steinbeck prepared for a collecting expedition north to the Queen Charlotte Islands to gather additional data for *The Outer Shores*. On May 8, while driving home from his lab, Ricketts's car was struck by a train. He died three days later. — Michael Zeitler

BIBLIOGRAPHY

Astro, Richard. *John Steinbeck and Edward F. Ricketts: The Shaping of a Novelist*. Minneapolis: University of Minnesota Press, 1973.
Hedgpeth, Joel W. (ed.) *The Outer Shores* (2 vols.) Eureka, CA: Mad River Press, 1978.
Ricketts, Edward F. *Breaking Through: Essays, Journals, and Travelogues of Edward F. Ricketts*. Editor, Katharine A. Rodger. Berkeley and Los Angeles: University of California Press, 2006.
_____, and Jack Calvin. *Between Pacific Tides*. 3rd Edition. Palo Alto: Stanford University Press, 1962.
Steinbeck, John. *The Log from the Sea of Cortez*. New York: Viking, 1962.
Tamm, Eric Enno. *Beyond the Outer Shores*. New York: Thunder's Mouth Press, 2004.

Between Pacific Tides, Edward F. Ricketts and Jack Calvin (1939)

Long before such terms as "wave shock," "competitive exclusion," "habitat," or "food chain" were in common scientific or popular usage, Edward F. Ricketts's 1939 text, *Between Pacific Tides*, co-authored with editorial assistance from Jack Calvin and illustrated with over 100 line drawings by Richie Lovejoy, sensitively and suggestively explored the natural history of Pacific Coast intertidal marine life within an ecological framework. Ricketts had studied animal ecology at the University of Chicago under Warder Clyde Allee, whose 1922 *Animal Aggregations* analyzed the effects of environmental stimuli on cooperative group behavior among invertebrates. Allee's ideas clearly influenced Ricketts's thinking. "In this book," Ricketts wrote in response to criticism of his iconoclastic approach, "there will be frequent considerations of an ecological and sociological nature, as contrasted to the usual systematic approach. Ecology will be defined, briefly, as that science that deals with the framework of relations between an animal or a society of animals and its environment, both biological and physical" (quoted in Hedgpeth, Vol. I, 33). Although not academically credentialed as a zoologist (he never completed his undergraduate degree), Ricketts nevertheless brought to his naturalist studies fifteen years of practical, hands-on collecting experience in tide pools ranging from Pacific Grove, California, south to the Baja peninsula and north to Alaska.

Eschewing traditional taxonomic organization, which typically involved specific chapters on the classification of sponges, snails, starfish, or crabs, Ricketts focused instead on the interactive, adaptive animal communities of the region's most common environmental habitats: rocky shores, open coasts, sandy beaches, bays, estuaries, and wharf pilings. He further subdivided these habitats into four zones based on the degree of tidal exposure (how often and for how long an organism was typically covered and uncovered). Despite initial skepticism from the academic community, Ricketts's holistic orientation, a philosophical approach he shared with his long-time friend, Pacific Grove neighbor, and sometimes collaborator JOHN STEINBECK, has been increasingly well received by marine biologists and lay readers; since its 1939 publication, *Between Pacific Tides* has gone through five editions, selling over 100,000 copies, and perennially placing among Stanford University Press's most popular books (Tamm 33).

Ricketts typically introduces a habitat by elaborating the survival problems it poses for an organism — the necessity of coping with wave shock or the need for strong methods of attachment on rocky shores, or the elaborate devices developed by sand and mud-flat animals to avoid suffocation or to retain orientation. He explains the adaptations necessary to survival for animals of the upper tide pools that are drenched with fresh water in the rainy season, and subject to wide and rapidly fluctuating changes in sunlight, temperature and salinity "in addition to the usual problems of wave shock, respiration, and drying" (*Tides* 27). Although, like other guides to Pacific coast marine life, *Between Pacific Tides* supplies keys to identification, life cycle, behavior, and reproductive patterns for over 500 distinct invertebrate species, Ricketts's frame of reference — and his broader significance to American environmental literature — emerges from his holistic understanding of tide pool economies, where "everything is accounted for" (41). A fish dies and the process is set in motion. Crabs dispose of large chunks of food, beach hoppers minute particles, and sea cucumbers, buried in the

substratum, sweep the bottom surface with their tentacles for adherent particles. Brittle stars pass the sand and dirt through their alimentary canals, extracting nourishment and further breaking down the organic debris, until, at last, bacteria attack what is left (*Tides* 41).

Throughout, Ricketts's tone is informative, yet informal; chatty, yet instructive; at one point reminding would-be collectors to bring a small, stout trowel or, later, to replace overturned rock exactly so as to do as little environmental harm as possible. He reacts to the tide pools with his whole person; with, for example, an eye for the inherent beauty and fragile delicacy of these creatures who nevertheless survive in such harsh environments. New-born jellyfish, he writes, "swim away with all the assurance in the world, propelling themselves with little jerks. It is a pity that they are so small, for they are delicate, diagrammatic, and beautiful.... If they were larger and correspondingly better known we should probably eat our outdoor summer luncheons against a background design of *Obelia* medusae on the paper napkins" (319). His interest extends even to the anthropological and culinary. "By Italians these snails [*Tegula*] are considered fine food. They are cooked in oil and served in the shell," he notes, in the hopes that his readers "may even develop an epicurean appreciation of many of the intertidal delicacies" (23).

The significance of *Between Pacific Tides*, however, goes beyond such "aesthetic and emotional delight" (405). From his earliest introduction to ecological thinking in W. C. Allee's University of Chicago seminars, Ricketts understood that the world of the tide pool and human culture were interconnected, and that recognition is central to his collaborations with John Steinbeck, and in their separate writings, as central to *The GRAPES OF WRATH* and *The Pearl* as to *Between Pacific Tides*. Allee's contention that "co-operation should rank as one of the major biological principles" (148) is evident in *Between Pacific Tides*, where observations on sea anemones lead Ricketts to speculations on "the evolutionary background behind the gregariousness of animals, even humans" (40). It is just as evident in Steinbeck's *The Pearl*, where the small Mexican fishing community is an organic whole, coexisting with other communities in the natural world and subject to the same natural laws, "a thing like a colonial animal," Steinbeck writes, with its own "pulse and vibrating nerves" (27).

Before his untimely death in 1948, Ricketts had completed work on the second edition of his book, and environmental concerns were even more at the forefront of his thinking. Commercial overfishing had destroyed the Monterey sardine industry, industrial pollution increasingly threatened marine life worldwide, and the potential effects of radioactivity were beginning to reach the popular press. "Nature," Ricketts emphasizes in conclusion, striking a keynote of environmental thinking, "is an interrelated system that should not be lightly tampered with.... As a species, we must not forget that our continued well-being is in turn dependent on the well-being of our ecosystem" (405).—Michael Zeitler

BIBLIOGRAPHY

Allee, Warder Clyde. *Animal Life and Social Growth.* Baltimore: Williams and Wilkins, 1932.

Astro, Richard. *John Steinbeck and Edward F. Ricketts: The Shaping of a Novelist.* Minneapolis: University of Minnesota Press, 1973.

Hedgpeth, Joel W. (ed.) *The Outer Shores* (2 vols.) Eureka, CA: Mad River Press, 1978.

Ricketts, Edward F., and Jack Calvin. *Between Pacific Tides.* 3rd Ed. Palo Alto: Stanford University Press, 1962.

_____. *Breaking Through: Essays, Journals, and Travelogues of Edward F. Ricketts.* Editor Katharine A. Rodger. Berkeley and Los Angeles: University of California Press, 2006.

Steinbeck, John. *The Log from the Sea of Cortez.* New York: Viking, 1962.

_____. *The Pearl.* New York: Viking Press/Bantam Paperback, 1956 (1947).

Tamm, Eric Enno. *Beyond the Outer Shores.* New York: Thunder's Mouth Press, 2004.

Roberts, Elizabeth Madox (1881–1941)

Elizabeth Madox Roberts is primarily remembered as a novelist, but as her readers know, and critics agree, she has the soul and voice of a poet—a poet of place, nature, and identity. Since most of her works center on the people and environment of Kentucky, she has been too easily dismissed in the past as a "regionalist." She may more accurately be called a literary *autochthon*, albeit one who brings to her native place a profound understanding and engagement with modern philosophy, high Modernism, and classical music, among other influences. She also demonstrated knowledge and interest in Daniel Boone and JOHN JAMES AUDUBON, figures present in her published and unpublished fiction. She in turn influenced many writers of the Southern Renascence, most notably ROBERT PENN WARREN.

Roberts was born in 1881 in Perryville, Kentucky. In 1884 her family moved to Springfield, which Roberts "would regard as home the rest of her life, despite temporary absences" (Ward 150). After High School, she enrolled in the University of Kentucky, but withdrew due to poor health. For the next 10 years she taught school in and around Springfield. In one journal she writes that her students' papers "had the marks of the soil upon them, marks of gen-

erations of soil, of closeness to the ground, or the struggle with clods and hard earth" (qtd. in Rovit 142). It is just such people and such affinity for the earth and environment that makes Roberts's novels and poetry so rich. As H.R. Stoneback remarks, Roberts has a "well-developed gift for evocation of the landscape, the telling creation of a sense of place through attention to luminous detail" ("Notes" 5).

In 1910 Roberts, now burdened with tuberculosis, moved to Colorado to live with her sister. It was not until the years 1917–1921, when she enrolled in the University of Chicago, that she really blossomed as a writer, even though at 36, as Robert Penn Warren observes, she was "a freshman old enough to be the mother of her classmates" (7). She was active in the University Poetry Club, serving as president her senior year, and became friends with Glenway Wescott, and Yvor Winters, as well as meeting Harriet Monroe, and the famous writers who populated her salon including Edgar Lee Masters and Carl Sandburg among others. Some of Roberts's poems from this era were published in the *Atlantic Monthly* and *Poetry*.

After publishing a collection of poems in 1922, *Under the Tree*, Roberts turned to writing novels typically centered on the lives and environment of the Kentucky mountain people. *The Time of Man* (1926), her most successful work, thrust her onto the literary stage. An international critical and popular success, it was chosen as a Book-of-the-Month selection and was translated into several languages. She followed this with two more novels which were not as well received, but her fourth novel, THE GREAT MEADOW (1930) was again hailed as a literary and popular success. She continued to write, despite poor health, and published a total of seven novels, two collections of short stories, and three collections of poetry. Roberts died in Florida in 1941 of Hodgkin's disease. She is buried in the Springfield cemetery, site of an annual graveside poetry reading in April associated with the Roberts Society Conference.—Michael J. Beilfuss

BIBLIOGRAPHY

Elizabeth Madox Roberts Society. The Elizabeth Madox Roberts Society, n.d. Web. May 21, 2011. www.emrsociety.com

Rovit, Earl H. *Herald to Chaos: The Novels of Elizabeth Madox Roberts.* Lexington: University Press of Kentucky. 1960.

Stoneback, H.R. "Notes on Roberts' Unpublished Fiction: With an Introduction to *Sallie May* and 'The Prophet.'" Stoneback, Camastra, and Florczyk. 3–6.

_____, Nicole Camastra, and Steven Florczyk, eds. *Elizabeth Madox Roberts: Essays of Discovery and Recovery.* New York: Quincy & Harrod Press, 2008.

_____, and Steve Florczyk, eds. *Elizabeth Madox Roberts:*

Essays of Reassessment & Reclamation. Eds. Nicholasville, KY: Wind, 2008.

Warren, Robert Penn. "Elizabeth Madox Roberts: Life Is from Within." *Saturday Review.* March 2, 1963: 20–21, 38. Rpt. Stoneback and Florcyzk. 5–13.

The Great Meadow, Elizabeth Madox Roberts (1930)

Part historical fiction, part mythmaking poetic narrative, *The Great Meadow* is set during the revolutionary war and the early settlement of the Kentucky frontier. The novel details the experiences of Diony Hall, beginning with her early maturation in rural Albemarle County, Virginia. After a brief courtship, she marries Berk Jarvis and joins him and his family as they travel over Boone's Trace to settle in the wilderness of Kentucky. To suggest that the settlers contend with nature on a daily basis is a misleading understatement. Roberts rather construes nature as constitutive of her characters' very being, as much as individual, family, and communal relationships.

Diony is an educated, self-aware character whose sensitivity to her environment is based on her ongoing struggle with the philosophy of Bishop Berkeley. Roberts quotes him throughout the novel, establishing one of the major themes early: "Not one of the heavenly bodies nor any part of the furniture of the earth can have being without mind to think it. Mind." (58) While Diony employs Berkelian ideals as a foundation for her developing identity, she avoids the solipsism which can result, by exploring and engaging the external environment. At times though, the philosophy fails her: "Over this lay another way of knowing, and she saw clearly how little she could comprehend of those powers on the other side" (274). The hardships of the frontier make evident "the hostility of the forest to her life," and she finds that "The indefiniteness of the outside earth, beyond herself, became a terror" (275). Despite this fear, she discovers both strength and love within herself, which ultimately help her sense an imminent, redemptive order in the universe.

Roberts's use of Berkeley's subjectivist philosophy enriches the novel on a number of levels. It provides her with the opportunity to describe and explore the natural world with impressionistic vivacity. *The Great Meadow*, like Roberts's other works, depicts a powerful sense of place, evocative of a deep understanding of the local landscapes. H.R. Stoneback explains that on a literary level, "The most extraordinary thing about her landscapes is the way they serve as objective correlatives for the inner states of being and feeling of her characters, usually young women with an intense sacramental sense of connection with

the land [...]. But there are moments in Roberts where the land stands for itself, where *terra* (the earth) [...] is simultaneously oracular and sufficient unto itself, beyond simile and metaphor, beyond symbol" (66). This dual function of landscape demonstrates Roberts's artistic aspirations and her ecological consciousness. The natural world and environment may serve as literary, cultural symbols, but they also have intrinsic value.

Diony's struggle with Berkeley's philosophy also reflects Roberts's own thoughts on her creative endeavors. In her journal, Roberts explains her efforts at "poetic realism": "Somewhere there is a connection between the world of the mind and the outer order — It is the secret of the contact that we are after, the point, the moment of union" (qtd. in Warren xxviii). When Diony and the weary travelers rest below the Cumberland Gap, she experiences just such a moment of contact between her inner world and the outer order. As Diony cools her feet in a mountain stream, she listens to another traveler explain the route ahead over the mountain. She feels the water become "a more intense reality, as if it were more of itself than formerly, as if the gateway to be seen from the south were related to the wimpling flow of the creek, as if they were the same in some breath-getting, leaping inner part of herself" (163). Scenes such as this occur throughout the novel, attesting to Roberts's sensitivity to intimate, personal human relationships with the environment, and her attempt to render such moments of communion for her readers.

Although the novel is full of idyllic scenes and romanticized landscapes, Roberts inscribes telling moments of tension into the narrative. The settlers decide to move to Kentucky for the promise of a new life, based on the reports they receive from explorers returning to Virginia from their surveys of the wilderness. Here Kentucky is described as an Edenic paradise, a "promised land" with "soil rich like cream." The land is so fertile, they are told, that they "wouldn't have to raise a hand to cultivate" (10) (THE BIBLE). They of course discover that the reality is not as paradisiacal as they imagined. The isolation of the settlement limits their supplies, and the long winters mean scant food for survival. They must also contend with recurring Indian raids, encouraged in part by the British. The simple acts of grazing cows and raising crops is fraught with peril.

Roberts introduces more subtle tensions in her story with the benefit of an ironic distance from the limited omniscient narrator, and suggests something of the ominous nature of the settler's incursion into the wilderness. On one hand, the reader is allowed into Diony's thought as she dreams about the development of the frontier, beginning modestly with plowed fields, flocks of sheep, stone walls and fences. Her dream grows to include farms and surplus crops, markets, bridges, and finally the leisure and infrastructure to allow for letters to pass from Kentucky to Virginia (207–212). On the other hand, Roberts moves well beyond the confines of the novel to suggest the rippling ramifications of the settlers' invasion of the frontier. Two separate passages provide pastoral depictions of birds, one of which, the Passenger Pigeon, was long extinct by the time Roberts wrote the book; the other, the Ivory-Billed Woodpecker, was well on its way to extinction. Such scenes can be read in a number of ways: on their surface they seem like romantic descriptions of wildlife; on another level they serve as nostalgic reveries for creatures that have been irrevocably lost; and finally they may be interpreted as subtle condemnations of the naïveté and hubris of a people who mindlessly destroyed the biological diversity of the very "promised land" they settled.

Ultimately, the novel provides three dialectical perspectives on the wilderness and frontier. In Robert's words, figures such as Daniel Boone represent "the indefinite earth, the outside of chaos, but he is an apostle to chaos to prepare it for man's order." Next come the settlers like Diony, who "represents ordered life." Finally there are those like Berk, who "represents art" through his power of storytelling, his ability to render the parts of experience into a recognizable story — a story that demonstrates humanity's connections to the earth, and the spirit's freedom from determinism (qtd. in Stoneback 70).— Michael J. Beilfuss

BIBLIOGRAPHY

Roberts, Elizabeth Madox. *The Great Meadow*. New York: Viking, 1930.

Stoneback, H.R. "'Strange Caterwauling': Singing in the Wilderness with Boone & Audubon, Elizabeth Madox Roberts & Robert Penn Warren." *Elizabeth Madox Roberts: Essays of Discovery and Recovery*. Eds. H.R. Stoneback, Nicole Camastra, and Steven Florczyk. New York: Quincy & Harrod Press, 2008. 64–76

Warren, Robert Penn. Introduction: "Elizabeth Madox Roberts: Life Is from Within." *The Time of Man*. By Elizabeth Madox Roberts. Lexington: University Press of Kentucky. xxi–xxxiii.

Roosevelt, Theodore "Teddy" (1858–1919)

As the twenty-sixth President of the United States of America, Republican Theodore Roosevelt is regarded as one of the most significant environmental Presidents in American history, as well as one of the most engaging writers ever to sit in the oval office.

Born the fourth of six children to the affluent Dutch-American Roosevelt family in 1858, "Teedie"— his childhood nickname — was a sickly child. Burdened with asthma, doctors cautioned Roosevelt to avoid strenuous activity, which indirectly fostered his lifelong appreciation for the literary arts. The young Roosevelt became an avid writer and reader, but refused to allow impediments to permanently dictate his lifestyle. Dynamic, dignified, and determined, the adult Roosevelt disregarded his childhood cautions to avoid "the strenuous life," and embraced precisely that, by becoming an avid hunter, fisherman and environmental enthusiast.

Roosevelt graduated magna cum laude from Harvard in 1880 with a Bachelor's Degree in Natural History. While at Harvard, Roosevelt continued to cultivate his passion for sports and literary composition, as a boxer, and member both of the rowing team and of the Alpha Delta Phi literary society, in addition to editing a student magazine. Afterward, he enrolled in Columbia Law School, leaving in 1881 to pursue a career as the youngest member of the New York assembly. An enthusiastic legislator, Roosevelt introduced one of the most significant bills passed in the New York Assembly, the 1884 Reform Charter Bill, which changed the political structure of New York City, ending much abuse and exploitation of power. Roosevelt relinquished his position as assemblymen in 1884 after the simultaneous deaths of his mother from typhoid fever, and first wife Alice Hathaway from Bright's Disease.

After these tragedies, Roosevelt sought refuge in the isolation and immensity of the Western landscape. Moving to North Dakota Roosevelt explored his profound and complementary interests in conservation, self-reliance and the proper role of governance in America. While there, Roosevelt combined his passions for the outdoors and literature by writing about the American frontier for Eastern magazines. His writings were infused with an optimistic interpretation of social Darwinism, echoing strong American values, such as ambition and strength, within the context of frontier expansion.

After a particularly harsh winter killed-off much of Roosevelt's cattle herd, he moved back to New York City to rekindle his political career. After failing to garner the Republican candidacy for mayor of New York City, he married his childhood sweetheart Edith Kermit Carow, and in 1888, successfully reentered the political realm as the United States Civil Service Commissioner under Presidents Benjamin Harrison and Grover Cleveland. In 1895, Roosevelt accepted the position as president of the board of New York City Police Commissioners, and during his two-year tenure he radically reformed what was once the most corrupt police department in the United States.

During the 1898 Spanish-American war, Roosevelt, as the Assistant Secretary of the Navy, was instrumental in establishing the first U.S. volunteer cavalry regiment, which consisted of citizens from throughout the United States, and thereby garnered a reputation as a national statesman. During the war, at the battle of Kettle Hill to take San Juan, Puerto Rico, Roosevelt courageously led his "Rough Rider" brigade to victory, resulting both in immediate celebrity acclaim, and much later in his posthumous reception, in 2001, of the Medal of Honor — America's highest military award.

Elected as the Republican Governor of New York in autumn 1898, Roosevelt continued his enthusiastic assault on political corruption and advocacy for social reform. Establishing himself as a popular and capable political force, Roosevelt was recommended as a running mate for William McKinley in the 1900 Presidential election, which the dynamic pair subsequently won. As Vice-President, Roosevelt created the Boone and Crockett club, an association "dedicated to preserving wild game by promoting a degree of restraint or so-called etiquette among sports hunters," a precursor to the enormously influential Ducks Unlimited conservation group (THE CONSERVATION MOVEMENT). Less than a year later, after the assassination of President McKinley on September 6th, 1901, Roosevelt was sworn in as America's twenty-sixth President. In 1904, Roosevelt secured his second term as President, receiving an overwhelming majority of the electoral votes; and over the combined seven years of his presidency, he worked tirelessly to enforce social and governmental reform.

As President, some of Roosevelt's most important contributions came in the area of conservation policy, and he devoted much time and effort to the preservation and protection of wildlife, establishing a vigorous foundation for the wildlife refuge system. Roosevelt established the Forest Reserves Act in 1891, which empowered the president to set aside public lands as national forests; and in 1905 the Forest Service, which encouraged the efficient use of natural resources while opposing exploitation and insensitive development. Roosevelt's support of the National Reclamation Act (or Newlands Act) in 1902 gave the federal government control over dam construction and irrigation projects, while the Reclamation Act brought scientific expertise to bear on the task. In 1906, Roosevelt extended federal control over the "wonders of the west" through the Antiquities Act, intended to preserve landmarks throughout America's western frontier. In all, Roosevelt created 16 na-

tional monuments, 51 wildlife refuges, and five National Parks, promoting the preservation of American flora and fauna.

In addition to justly acquiring a sterling reputation as President, Roosevelt was a prolific and popular American author who published 18 books, including his autobiography, and several articles, on an array of subjects ranging from foreign policy to ranching and wildlife, in poetry as well as prose. Perhaps his most ambitious narrative was a four-volume history entitled *The Winning of the West* (1889–1896), which connected present-day Americans and their way of life to that of their ancestors who endured the austere conditions of the frontier. One of the more significant periods in Roosevelt's literary career occurred just after his marriage to his second wife, Edith. During this period, in 1886, Roosevelt wrote a series of articles on western life for Century Magazine (later published as *Ranch Life and the Hunting Trail*), which were influenced by his experience as a rancher and sportsman in Dakota. Roosevelt's depiction of the West prompted many affluent Easterners to explore the plains and foothills as curious tourists, prompting the establishment of "Dude Ranches" (for urban "dudes"). Although Roosevelt's writings contributed to the growth of a new western industry, more significantly these narratives created a perception of Western life as one imbued with distinctive "American" virtues such as self-reliance, honor, loyalty, and determination, which made of the West a kind of proving ground for the quintessential "American" spirit.

Roosevelt's writings about the Western frontier at the turn of the century were complemented by the increasing popularity of nature writing in general, and Roosevelt's high-profile reputation at one point embroiled him in the "Nature Fakers Controversy," after a 1903 article by naturalist JOHN BURROUGHS lambasted some nature writers for their fantastical, often anthropomorphic depictions of wildlife. Roosevelt published articles in support of his friend Burroughs, claiming that authors who wrote fantastical nature writings were sensationalists and crude exaggerators, and in fact coining the term "Nature Fakers" in his 1907 article of the same name. Although Roosevelt adored the wilderness, like most "conservationists" he perceived it as ultimately serving the purpose of satisfying humans needs and advancing the Anglo-Saxon race, a theme prevalent throughout his life and writings.

While on an expedition into the Brazilian jungle in 1916, Roosevelt contracted malaria which weakened him and eventually lead to his death in 1919 at the age of 60. His profound influence on the American west, and on America's self-understanding —

both as a writer and a statesmen — earned him a Nobel Peace Prize in 1907, the title of Chief Scout Citizen (an honor bestowed onto him alone by The Boy Scouts of America), and a place among the illustrious presidential giants portrayed on Mount Rushmore. — Katrina Berry and Mitchell Grasser

BIBLIOGRAPHY

Stewart, Frank. *A Natural History of Nature Writing.* Washington, D.C.: Island Press, 1995.
"Theodore Roosevelt." *American Earth: Environmental Writing Since Thoreau.* Ed. Bill McKibben. New York: Literary Classics of the United States, 2008. 129–133.
"Theodore Roosevelt." *The Norton Anthology of American Literature: Seventh Edition, Volume C, 1865–1914.* Ed. Jeanna Campbell Reesman & Arnold Jurpat. New York: W.W Norton, 2001. 1153–1159.

Outdoor Pastimes of an American Hunter, Theodore Roosevelt (1908)

Outdoor Pastimes of an American Hunter chronicles many of Roosevelt's turn-of-the-century hunting trips, arguing throughout for game protection and wilderness preservation laws, especially in the American West. Parts of the book were originally published throughout the 1890's, in publications of the Boone and Crockett Club. They were initially copyrighted by the Forest and Stream Publishing Company, the company that published much popular writing about the outdoors and sport hunting. The selections chosen for *Outdoor Pastimes* were published in book form by Charles Scribner's Sons of New York in 1905, at the beginning of Roosevelt's second term as President of the United States. By this time, Roosevelt already had a well-established reputation as a sport hunter, naturalist, writer, progressive politician, and conservationist. These elements of his intellect and his era are showcased in *Outdoor Pastimes.*

Outdoor Pastimes is divided into 11 chapters and demonstrates the features typical of Roosevelt's writing, and of many hunting narratives at the time. Rather than organize his hunting stories chronologically, as one might expect, Roosevelt focuses each chapter on experiences about hunting a particular type of animal: cougars, bears, wolves, prongbucks, mountain sheep, whitetail deer, mule-deer, and round-horned elk. This organizational structure, which suggests a catalog, indicates that the author is composing a natural history as much as a hunting narrative. Indeed this catalog-style of organization characterized much of Roosevelt's other naturalist writing; his early *Hunting Trips of a Ranchman* (1885), for example, not only focuses each chapter on an animal, but arranges those chapters in a taxonomic hierarchy (Phillipon 48).

Another notable feature of the book's structure is an opening letter addressed to the renowned nature writer JOHN BURROUGHS. Dated October 2, 1905, the letter expresses Roosevelt's gratitude for Burroughs' contributions to literature of the outdoors. He especially praises Burroughs for writing nonfiction and presenting a realistic portrait of animals and nature in his work. Roosevelt frequently insisted on the realistic portrayal of nature in his own writing (Altherr 16), and this attitude shines through in his letter to Burroughs, where he argues that writing fiction about animals, anthropomorphizing them, or demonstrating any sentimentality towards them was "useful ... in the way of encouraging people to the right view of outdoor life and outdoor creatures," but was "unpardonable for any observer of nature." As a keen "observer of nature," Roosevelt heavily emphasizes the realistic depiction of animals in the wild, making Outdoor Pastimes also a natural history of big game animals in the West.

Another prominent feature of *Outdoor Pastimes* is the inclusion of more than four dozen photographs, inserted on separate pages throughout the text. These photographs show a variety of stages in the hunting process, such as wide-angle views of Roosevelt and his fellow hunters on the chase; a bobcat, alive, up in a tree; a bear, killed, on the ground between two rocks; Roosevelt and fellow hunters showing off the coyotes they have killed; and men standing outside tents and at campfires. Photographic images were novel to include in books at the time and added to the depiction of "the real" — Roosevelt's realistic version of the hunting process and of animals in their natural habitats.

The text of each chapter meets the expectations for realism established by the structure, the letter to Burroughs, and the photographic images. It blends a lively hunting narrative with detailed observations of big game animals. The hunting narratives are often a blow-by-blow account of a chase, and include details about Roosevelt's traveling companions, including his trip with John Burroughs, and a visit with JOHN MUIR. Meanwhile, the text's scientific disposition is evidenced in the inclusion of tables, such as the one in Chapter I, "With the Cougar Hounds," which records the weight, length, gender, and color of the cougars killed on a hunting expedition (31). The text also provides descriptions of big game animals and histories of each species. Chapter VIII, "The Wapiti, or Round-Horned Elk," for example, provides a lengthy account of this nearly-extinct animal, its lifecycle, mating habits, diet, and range. Importantly, Roosevelt accounts for changes in the wapiti's lifestyle, tracing those changes to over-hunting and the disruption of its natural habitat. He explains how settlement and eager hunting has limited the range of this type of elk, which he calls "the largest and stateliest deer in the world" to just a few areas of the West, where once it also roamed far East and North in the United States (256). In methodical and observant accounts like these, Roosevelt lays the empirical and authoritative foundations for wilderness conservation.

Perhaps the most important chapter of *Outdoor Pastimes* comes near the end, in Chapter IX, *"Wilderness Reserves; The Yellowstone Park."* In this chapter, Roosevelt argues that the disappearance of the big game animals can best be remedied by wilderness preservation on a national scale. He makes a direct plea to his readers to "strike hands with the far-sighted men who wish to preserve our material resources in the effort to keep our forests and our game beasts, game birds, and game fish ... from wanton destruction" (289). He argues that preservation as a national policy is "essentially a democratic movement," one that benefits "all lovers of nature," even those who do "not possess vast wealth" (289). It is important to note that Roosevelt argues here to preserve "large tracts of wilderness" which are "valueless for agricultural purposes and unfit for settlement" (289). Preservationists frequently argued that intended parklands were useless for any purpose other than recreation, and in the early progressive era, that recreation had to be couched in terms of its democratic reach.

While Americans still champion parklands and democratic recreation, there are undertones of elitism throughout *Outdoor Pastimes* that may trouble the contemporary reader. For example, the book furthers Roosevelt's view that hunting is a "manly sport," and preserving the Western land and big game animals was arguably about preserving the "manliness" of the propertied white American male — and all the privileges that came with it. Furthermore, Roosevelt's depiction of the violent slaughter of animals may disturb modern readers. Roosevelt and his hunting companions considered themselves "hunter-naturalists," which meant that they insisted on the relationship between hunting and scientific study, and abided by a code of sportsmanship (see Altherr). But despite this scientific disposition, and rules for "fair chase," it can be difficult to see how the hunting of the "hunter-naturalists" was any different from that of the "savage" Indians they so despised.

Contemporary readers and environmentalists might also criticize such "hunter-naturalists" by noting that they were motivated by the recreational interests of the upper-class, white, land-owning and often office-holding American men. But the influence of books like *Outdoor Pastimes* cannot be overlooked. The movement to preserve the rapidly decreasing big game animals in the western United States gave rise to early conservation laws and wilderness preserves, many under the purview of President Roosevelt himself (THE CONSERVATION MOVEMENT). And, it is important to remember that Roosevelt and other such hunters were, at heart, lovers of nature, keen observers of ecosystems, and truly far-sighted in their preservation policies — much like many members of the modern "Ducks Unlimited" conservation society. With this in mind, *Outdoor Pastimes* marks a significant turning point in American environmental consciousness. — R. Lindsay Dunne

BIBLIOGRAPHY

Altherr, Thomas L. "The American Hunter-Naturalist and the Development of a Code of Sportsmanship." *Journal of Sport History.* 5.1 (Spring 1978): 7–23.

DiSilvestro, Roger. *Theodore Roosevelt in the Badlands: A Young Politician's Quest for Recovery in the American West.* New York: Walter, 2010.

Phillipon, Daniel. *Conserving Words: How American Nature Writers Shaped the Environmental Movement.* Athens: University of Georgia Press, 2004.

Reiger, John F. *American Sportsmen and the Origins of Conservation* (Third Edition). Corvallis: Oregon State University Press, 2001.

Roosevelt, Theodore. *Outdoor Pastimes of an American Hunter.* New York: Scribner's, 1905.

Rowlandson, Mary (c. 1637–1711)

Born Mary White in Somersetshire, England, the Puritan Mary Rowlandson migrated to America with her family as a young woman, and eventually settled and married John Rowlandson in Lancaster, Massachusetts in 1656, on the frontier of that time. When Lancaster came under attack from neighboring Indians in 1675, Mary Rowlandson and her three children were among the hostages taken. For almost four months she was forced to follow the Indians as they fled the colony militia's pursuit, deep into the dreaded Puritan "wilderness" (THE BIBLE), until finally being ransomed, for 20 pounds raised by the women of Boston in a public subscription. Her detailed and searching account of her captivity was later published as the *Narrative of the Captivity and Restoration of Mrs. Mary Rowlandson* (1682), and offered her contemporaries (and us) a telling insight into America's "other" — and themselves.

Beyond its unique insights into the life and environment beyond the narrow confines of colonial existence, Rowlandson's narrative transforms the author's physical experience into a spiritual one that could be used for didactic purposes in the Puritan community, and employs Puritan rhetoric to develop a profoundly important American construct — that of the wilderness. The Puritan practice of typology, reading people and events from the Old Testament as prefiguring people and events in the New Testament, which in turn was read to prefigure people and events in New England, shaped Rowlandson's response to the forest through which she travelled. Everything she witnesses or experiences is a sign from God that she must "read." Rowlandson's text, organized in a series of twenty chapters chronicling what she calls "removes," is an example of a travel narrative; but more importantly, it is a tale of spiritual growth and faith couched in descriptions of her environment.

The focus of the narrative, then, is not just on Rowland's physical hardships in the natural environment (from which the Indians are, for Rowlandson, barely distinguishable), but on her being cast out of Eden into the wilderness as punishment for not leading a godly life. The wilderness becomes a metaphor for all the afflictions that come in a life that is empty of God's grace. The dark forests and deep rivers, sucking swamps and bogs, are all described in a way that reveals the darkness of life outside of the light. Rowlandson admits of occasional kindness from her captors, but never wavers in her conviction that the Indians are vastly inferior to the Puritans and behave monstrously.

There is a tension throughout the narrative between civilization, defined by life in the villages of the Englishmen, particularly of Lancaster, Massachusetts, which was on the western edge of the Puritan settlements; and barbarism, the life defined, effectively, by how the Indians lived. Of particular recollection in her narrative are the foods that she ate, or more often than not, that the Indians ate and would not share with her. Rowlandson's constant hunger leads her to comment frequently on the search for food, providing insight into how the Indians found sustenance in the wilderness. The Indians spend a large part of their day gathering food from the forest — game when they can get it, but more often ground nuts, acorns, even tree bark. The forest is generally described in vague terms: wilderness, dark, cold — and a few rivers and other geographical features that she can identify. In terms of food, however, Rowlandson provides great detail, particularly of items that formerly she would not have deigned to eat (horse liver, bear meat in broth, boiled horse hooves).

Rowlandson does her best to understand the seemingly erratic wandering of the Indians as they evade the English, and to adjust to life in the forest as she awaits deliverance. The importance of identifying places and features as she marches, however, is secondary to her desire to clothe her experience of the physical wilderness in terms of the allegorical spiritual wilderness that her Puritan readers would appreciate. "For virtually every [...] description of geography," David Mazel points out, Rowlandson evokes an accompanying "biblical landscape" (Mazel 52). In the Sixteenth Remove, Rowlandson recalls,

> We began this Remove with wading over *Baquaug* River. The water was up to the knee and the stream very swift, and so cold, that I thought it would have cut me in sunder. I was so weak and feeble, that I reeled as I went along, and thought there I must end my days at last, after my bearing and getting through so many difficulties.... The Lord gave me experience of the truth goodness of that promise, *Isa. 43. 2. When thou passest thorough the waters I will be with thee, and: thorough the rivers, they shall not overflow thee.*

Her relation of her time in the forest is thus colored significantly by the Puritan rhetoric of "wilderness," and what wilderness means in both spiritual and mundane parlance.

The term looms large in American literature. No matter that the land was cultivated by native peoples before the arrival of the Puritans; WILLIAM BRADFORD would set the precedence for viewing the landscape as a "hideous and desolate wilderness, full of wild beasts and wild men." In Rowlandson, as in other Puritan authors, the wilderness was more of a mere signifier for what was *absent*— civilization. The settlements strove to tame the wilderness, to cultivate civilization in the form of gardens and structures, supplying what the vast forests lacked. The wilderness was everything that was fearful for the early settlers: a lack of light, of amenities, of easily obtainable food. It was not celebrated for its beauty, but reviled for its impenetrable mysteries.

It is this impenetrable mystery that non–Puritan writers such as THOMAS MORTON, and later authors such as JAMES FENIMORE COOPER cherished. Unlike these authors, Rowlandson writes from the perspective and through the lense of Puritan spirituality. Thus, although the daily lives of her Indian captors and the Puritans themselves would have been predicated on the sustenance that the forests and fields offered them, Rowlandson was unable to shake the allegorical descriptions of her journey, to provide the modern reader with a real look at the New England wilderness; and her reader is ultimately left with a deeper (but no less valuable) understanding of *how* she saw, than *what* she saw.— Patricia Kennedy Bostian

BIBLIOGRAPHY

Derounian-Stodola, Kathryn Zabelle. *Women's Indian Captivity Narratives*. London: Penguin Books, 1998.

Mazel, David. *American Literary Environmentalism*. Athens: University of Georgia Press. 2000.

Wesley, Marilyn C. "Moving Targets: The Travel Text in a Narrative of the Captivity and Restauration of Mrs. Mary Rowlandson." *Essays in Literature* 23.1 (Spring 1996): 42–57.

Santayana, George (1863–1952)

George Santayana, a leading figure in classical American Philosophy, was born in 1863 in Madrid, Spain. His father studied law and eventually became governor of Batang Island in the Philippines, and his mother was the daughter of a Spanish diplomat. When Santayana was eight, his father sent him to live with his mother, who had relocated to Boston to raise children from a previous marriage. He entered Harvard College in 1882, and after completing his doctorate there, was appointed an instructor of philosophy at Harvard, a position he held until 1912. While at Harvard, the American philosopher William James was among his teachers, and his notable students included T.S. ELIOT, WALLACE STEVENS, ROBERT FROST, and Conrad Aiken, all of whose work reflects his influence. He was a popular teacher, yet resigned despite the protests of the college, feeling that American academia had become offensively business-oriented, and that philosophy as a discipline had lost its sense of the "good life" and the celebration that is the philosopher's essential task. After spending the years of the Great War in Oxford, he traveled extensively throughout Europe for the rest of his life, producing a voluminous oeuvre that includes poetry, essays, a best-selling novel and an autobiography.

In 1923, Santayana published *Skepticism and Animal Faith*, generally considered the inaugural work of his mature naturalist philosophy. In contrast to his earlier writing, this work represents an "ontological turn" toward materialism and away from the subjectivist, anthropocentric philosophy that dominated his previous period. This shift in Santayana's thinking was generally consistent with the broader modernist trend of rejecting the idealism of the nineteenth century. He believed that consciousness is a byproduct of nature, and took as the starting point of his philosophical system the simple fact that human beings are animals acting in the natural world. John Lachs, who has written extensively on Santayana, explains the work's central concept, "animal faith," as follows: "Although this environment is vast and sometimes treacherous, we approach it with 'animal faith,' an unreflective confidence in its basic structures. For a philosophy to have relevance to life it must be a discernment and critical articulation of the details of this trust" (Lachs 42).

This animal faith in certain features of the natural environment is not a matter of reason; it is simply expressed in an animal's observable interaction with its environment. Nor is such faith religious or spiritual, but more akin to "common sense," which may or may not reach the level of consciousness. For Santayana, the philosopher's task is to determine through observation what the tenets of this common faith are, as a means of understanding humanity's place in the world. This project represents a radical break with rationalist philosophy, whose criterion for knowledge is certainty. Santayana considers such a criterion laughably impractical, even dishonest, and routinely illustrates the dishonesty of the rationalist position with reference to the most basic natural behaviors, such as eating. For example, there is no use in theorizing that the bread in my pantry is nothing more than an effect of consciousness if, whenever I am hungry, I eat it without hesitation. In rejecting the idea that the world is determined by cognition, and claiming instead that the world is there to be encountered, often in a semi- or even unconscious manner, Santayana's thought shares something with the pragmatism of his teacher and colleague William James. One can detect this similarity in the preface to *Skepticism and Animal Faith*: "I think that common sense, in a rough dogged way, is technically sounder than the special schools of philosophy, each of which squints and overlooks half the facts and half the difficulties in its eagerness to find in some detail the key to the whole ... I stand in philosophy exactly where I stand in daily life; I should not be honest otherwise" (*Skepticism* 3–4).

While Santayana's starting point is the observable interaction between animals and the natural world, he leaves the empirical study of nature to science. "Speculations about the natural world, such as those of the Ionian philosophers, are not metaphysics, but simply cosmology or natural philosophy. Now in natural philosophy I am a decided materialist — apparently the only one living ... I do not profess to know what matter is in itself, and feel no confidence in the divination of those *esprits forts* who, leading a life of vice, thought the universe must be composed of nothing but dice and billiard-balls" (*Skepticism* 5). Thus, Santayana draws a clear line between metaphysics and his own interest in matter and nature, which is to identify the pervasive, often subterranean and automatic beliefs we have about them. Lachs argues that "his belief in the autonomy of science functioned like a double-edged sword. On the one hand, it served to control the excesses of philosophers in trying to compete with science on the basis of mere speculation or moral demands. On the other hand, however, it placed sharp limits on the scope of science, restricting its valid application to the sphere of nature alone" (Lachs 7). The metaphysical inadequacy of science is reflected in the fact that we never lose our sense of wonder at the sheer irrational facts of life and death, no matter how many "facts" we may learn about the composition of matter (Lachs 14).

Matter, Santayana famously said, is "the insane emphasis" of existence (Lachs 13). His radical materialism extends to the claim that matter is the basis for all thought; without matter, there would be no consciousness, no morality, and no spirit. The organism's expectations and fears vis-à-vis its environment determine the shape of its internal life, its views, and whatever may be called subjectivity. The "soul" too is material, arising out of organic experience. In Santayana's system, the "psyche" or animating force of an organism has nothing to do with cognition but rather with natural contingency: "The environment determines the occasions on which intuitions arise, the psyche — the inherited organization of the animal — determines their form, and ancient conditions of life on earth no doubt determined which psyches should arise and prosper; and probably many forms of intuition, unthinkable to man, express the facts and the rhythms of nature to other animal minds" (*Skepticism* 81–2). The idea that nature determines excellence is Aristotelian, and Santayana had, in addition to his American pragmatism, an avowed affinity for classical Greek philosophy (Hodges and Lachs 47).

The first section of *Skepticism and Animal Faith* establishes, in Cartesian fashion, a method of reasoning through doubt. But ultimately, Santayana's doubt is more total than Descartes', since he holds that nothing, not even the existence of the mind or the self, can be known with certainty. This conclusion, however, does not trouble him. Rather, he presents his philosophical system as an alternative to skepticism, to which he objects primarily because its practitioners contemplate thought without reference to embodied experience. Any product of such mediation will bear no resemblance to human behavior, as it ignores one of the basic tenets of animal faith: that a world of objects exists independently of the animal, and that he can affect and be affected by it. Among the other tenets of animal faith are a belief in memory and sensory information, and the organism's ability to respond to his environment on the basis of such information.

While the work of artists, in which Santayana had a lifelong interest, is not evidence of animal faith, he believed that art was a higher-order demonstration of the human animal's implicit belief in nature: "Art is the true discoverer, the unimpeachable witness to the reality of nature. The master of any art sees nature from the inside, and works with her, or she in him" (*Skepticism* 213). Santayana is himself often praised for the beauty of his prose, and while his poetry has a good many critics, the poet and social theorist John Ransom Crowe wrote in 1937 that Santayana's account of the realm of matter (developed at length in *The Realm of Matter* [1930]) is "a great literary achievement, and should be recommended equally to soft-hearted sentimentalists and hard-headed positivists. The account is more exciting than Milton's picture of Chaos, because nothing should have been expected of Chaos except the chaotic, but in nature we hope to find perfect animal fulfillments and rational processes; for, though we may often have been cheated, we have animal faith" (Ransom 411). This is an artist's eloquent articulation of the conviction, consistent throughout Santayana's works, that nature is where we will see ourselves most truly, with our hopes for fulfillment and our sense of what in life is good. — Katie Van Wert

BIBLIOGRAPHY

Hodges, Michael, and John Lachs, eds. *Thinking in Ruins: Wittgenstein and Santayana on Contingency.* Nashville: Vanderbilt University Press, 2000.
Lachs, John. *George Santayana.* Boston: G. K. Hall, 1988.
Ransom, John Crowe. "Art and Mr. Santayana." *Animal Faith and Spiritual Life.* Ed. John Lachs. New York: Meredith, 1967. 401–418.
Santayana, George. *The Realm of Matter: Book Second of Realms of Being.* New York: Scribner's, 1930.
_____. *Skepticism and Animal Faith.* New York: Scribner's, 1937.

Sierra Club *see* The Conservation Movement

Sigourney, Lydia Howard Huntley (1791–1865)

Lydia Sigourney (*nee* Lydia Howard Huntley), was perhaps the most famous American literary woman of the first half of the 19th century. Deemed "the sweet singer of Hartford," Sigourney was a prolific and multifaceted writer, a devout Christian and a dedicated educator. Sigourney's verse and prose were sentimental and often revolved around her principal thematic binary of life and death. Her celebration of religious and patriotic values, as well as her reputation for intense moral integrity, combined with her traditional poetic rhythms and her talent for writing commemorative poetry, strongly appealed to the antebellum audience, allowing Sigourney to become one of the first women in the United States to establish a successful career as a popular writer and educator.

Born in Norwich, Connecticut, the only child of Zerviah Wentworthy Huntley and Ezekiel Huntley, Sigourney was encouraged from an early age by her parents, and by her father's employer, Mrs. Daniel Lathrop, to read and write. Sigourney's life and work were committed to education, writing and charity. In 1811, after having pursued her own education, Sigourney opened a school for young ladies with her friend, Nancy Maria Hyde; and three years after this school closed due to Hyde's death, Sigourney, with the assistance of family friend Daniel Wadsworth, opened a second school for girls in Hartford. In addition to helping her establish an educational institution, Wadsworth was also instrumental in ensuring the publication of Sigourney's first book in 1815, a piece of conduct literature entitled: *Moral Pieces in Prose and Verse.*

Although Sigourney delayed marriage in favour of caring for her aging parents, in 1819 she married Charles Sigourney, a well-to-do widower 13 years her senior. Charles openly objected to Sigourney's writing career and preferred that she focus on her duties as a wife and mother to the couple's five children — three from Charles' previous marriage and two from their marriage. Concealing her activities from Charles, Sigourney continued to write and publish anonymously; however, when her husband's prosperity began to decline, and it became necessary to assist her parents financially, Sigourney, determined to integrate her authorial ambitions with her domestic duty, abandoned her anonymity and began to publish her writings under her own name — and at a remarkable pace.

Collectively, and interestingly, these events shaped Sigourney's perspective as a female nature writer, since her conviction that women could adhere to their pastoral/patriarchal duties while pursuing their personal and professional aspirations both provided a context for her educational and written works and illustrated her fundamental belief that all things in nature strive for balance and equality; one does not have supremacy over another. And this notion of the complementarity of the human and natural worlds is one that LAWRENCE BUELL deems a fundamental trait of environmental literature, "the need for the human order to accommodate itself to the natural [and] vice versa" (Buell 48). These experiences also contributed to Sigourney's extraordinary ability to perceive nature as both an insider and an outsider, thus enabling her to represent the often painful but always rewarding interdependence between humans and nature — much like that which exists between men and women — throughout her poetry.

While Sigourney began her writing career composing social and domestic manuals for young girls — *Letters to Young Ladies* (1833) is arguably her best known work — it is her poetry, Victorian both in convention and sentimentality, that established her as an influential nature writer. *Scenes in my Native Land* (1844), a collection of poems and essays on American subjects, is Sigourney's extended ode to the landscape that surrounded her, and succeeds in presenting a conservative, yet progressive vision of 19th-century American nature and culture. "Niagara," a poem from the compilation, evinces many of the characteristics common to her poetry — religious and naturalistic fervour, romanticism, and a fascination with the eternal and fecund cycle of life and death — while celebrating the scenic grandeur of an infant nation already teeming with notions of splendour, supremacy and strength.

> Flow on for ever, in thy glorious robe
> Of terror and of beauty. Yea, flow on
> Unfathom'd and resistless. God hath set
> His rainbow on thy forehead, and the cloud
> Mantled around thy feet. And he doth give
> Thy voice of thunder power to speak of Him
> Eternally — bidding the lip of man
> Keep silence — and upon thine alter pour
> Incense of awe-struck praise [ll. 1–9].

The first stanza of this well-known poem describes the vast, varied and unaffected scenery of early America using language that is representative of the dominant and perseverant culture that grew alongside, and increasingly encroached upon, that landscape. The blending of these two worlds — nature and culture — highlights Sigourney's view that harmony between the two is necessary for their *mutual* well-being. Since culture and nature, like men and women, must exist in the same sphere, they must do so in a way that conduces to the health of both as independent yet mutually implicated entities. The role of religion in the poem strongly supports this thesis, as both are regarded as integrated and unified creations of God.

Another typical characteristic of Sigourney's poetry is its welcoming of natural objects, such as insects and birds, to speak for the poet, in an interesting parallel to the work of her English contemporary, the Romantic poet, William Blake. *The Butterfly* is a prime example, not merely of this element of Sigourney's style, but of some of her central themes:

> A butterfly bask'd on a baby's grave,
>   Where a lily had chanced to grow:
> "Why art thou here, with thy gaudy die,

When she of the blue and sparkling eye,
   Must sleep in the churchyard low?"
Then it lightly soar'd through the sunny air,
   And spoke from its shining track:
"I was a worm till I won my wings,
   And she whom thou mourn'st like a seraph sings
   Woulds't thou call the bless'd one back?"

Sigourney's resistance to the anthropocentric tendencies of her age further illustrates her deep-seated conviction that all living things maintain harmony in flourishing nature — man holds no supremacy over the butterfly, and ultimately no supremacy over anything.

"The Dying Philosopher," in an alternate collection entitled *Poems* (1827), advances deeper into this conceptual landscape, and exemplifies Sigourney's preoccupation with death, decay and rebirth. The dying eye has an alternative outlook on life and death, and one that differs greatly from that of the living eye, since the former is able to see beyond the gap that seemingly exists between the two realms, and therefore recognizes the inviolable connection between the natural world and human culture. Sigourney's fascination with death highlights the fact that humanity and nature both possess a God-like invincibility — neither can be completely eradicated by the other since they are part of each other; half-created by each other, for each other, and utilized in the same manner. Nature dies to give back to humans; humans die to give back to nature. Offering a view from the philosopher's deathbed as he "crept forth to die among the trees" (1), the poet appeals to Nature to let him die alone, outside, under the "holy stars" (51), bringing him back to the earth, and illustrating the mutual interdependence of human self and nonhuman environment.

A devoted daughter, wife and mother, as well as a gifted writer who composed and published over 200 articles and 67 books, including autobiographies, educational manuals and travel narratives, as well as poetry, Sigourney died in 1865 at her home in Hartford. Although her educational manuals advance feminist views striking for her time, it is her deep admiration for nature that shines through her poetry, and the themes and aspirations that shaped her poetic oeuvre resonate as much or more today, when the *necessity* for establishing a mutually beneficial harmony between man and his natural environment is becoming ever more clear and pressing.— Katrina Berry

BIBLIOGRAPHY

Buell, Lawrence. *The Environmental Imagination: Thoreau, Nature Writing, and the Formation of the American Culture.* Cambridge, MA: Belknap, 1995.
De Jong, Mary G. "LEGACY Profile: Lydia Howard Huntley Sigourney (1791–1865)." *Legacy.* 5.2 (1988): 35.
Finch, Anne. "The Sentimental Poetess in the World: Metaphor and Subjectivity in Lydia Sigourney's Nature Poetry." *Legacy.* 5.2 (1998): 3.
"Lydia Huntley Sigourney." *American Earth: Environmental Writing Since Thoreau.* Ed. Bill McKibben. New York: Literary Classics of the United States, 2008. 46–47.

Silko, Leslie Marmon (1948–   )

Novelist, essayist, photographer and filmmaker, Leslie Marmon Silko is best known for CEREMONY (1977), the Native-American novel most assigned in college and university courses for the last 30 years. She is the recipient of many awards, including a 1980 National Endowment for the Humanities Grant to make the film, *Arrowboy and the Witches*, based on the traditional Pueblo story at the center of *Ceremony*. In 1981, she received a John D. and Catherine T. McArthur Foundation Fellowship.

Silko was born in 1948 in Albuquerque, New Mexico and grew up on the outskirts of the Laguna Pueblo in New Mexico. Her ancestry is mixed Laguna Pueblo, Mexican and Caucasian. In her collection of essays, *Yellow Woman and a Beauty of the Spirit,* she recalls that at five years old, when she entered a Bureau of Indian Affairs Day School at Laguna, she was forbidden to speak the ancient Keres language of her grandmothers, and this forced her to express her Pueblo worldview in English. She also instinctively knew that her mixed racial background made her different from her Pueblo schoolmates. She writes that life "at Laguna for me was a daily balancing act of Laguna beliefs and Laguna ways and the ways of outsiders" (Silko, *Yellow Woman* 17).

Silko received her Bachelor's degree at the University of New Mexico and then entered law school. However, after three semesters, she decided "the only way to seek justice was through the power of stories," so she dropped out to devote all her time to writing (Silko, *Yellow Woman* 20). Silko's creative endeavors since then have consistently and compelling articulated the connections between social and environmental justice. Indeed, the founding documents of both the environmental justice movement and the global indigenous rights movement read like anatomies of Silko's overarching themes. Like *The Seventeen Principles of Environmental Justice*, written at the First National People of Color Environmental Summit in 1991, Silko's work affirms the sacredness of Mother Earth and the ecological unity and interdependence of all species, asserts the right of people to be free from ecological destruction, and calls for universal protection from toxic wastes that threaten the fundamental right to clean air, land, water and food (Principles 1, 4). Like the *Declaration on the Rights of Indigenous Peoples*, adopted by the United

Nations General Assembly on September 13, 2007, Silko's work recognizes the right of indigenous peoples to maintain, control, protect and develop their cultural heritage, language, knowledge, lands and resources.

Silko's oeuvre has also helped to shape and challenge the expectations that readers bring to literary works by Native American authors. Like the protagonists of earlier ground-breaking Native American novels such as D'Arcy McNickle's *The Surrounded* and N. SCOTT MOMADAY's *HOUSE MADE OF DAWN*, the main protagonist of Silko's *Ceremony*, Tayo, must resist and survive oppressive practices both on and off the reservation, and find his way back to home and healing. After being captured by the Japanese and surviving the Bataan Death March in the Philippines, Tayo returns to the reservation still trying to make sense of the death and destruction he has witnessed. With the help of his grandmother and a half–Navajo medicine man, Tayo begins to gather fragments of his cultural and personal past, and piece them together in ways that have meaning in the present. This helps him to heal from both his cultural alienation and his post-traumatic stress syndrome. Silko clearly connects this personal quest for healing with a larger process of healing Mother Earth. After Betonie's ceremony, Tayo stands at the edge of a large uranium mine located outside Laguna Pueblo, and finally comprehends what he terms a "monstrous design" of death and destruction that has affected all life on the planet. He now sees the connections between the historical oppression of indigenous peoples all over the globe, the exploitation of their resources, the contamination of their lands, and the deadly World War in which the uranium extracted near his home was employed to kill non-indigenous people thousands of miles away.

Silko's highly anticipated second novel, *ALMANAC OF THE DEAD* (1991), ranges from Africa to Mexico to America, and tells the seemingly fragmented stories of a cast of over fifty characters, including slave traders, indigenous rebels, murderers, healers, and ecowarriors. What holds these stories together is the motif of a character returning to Laguna Pueblo. As she did in *Ceremony,* Silko again employs a return home to draw attention to the ways that powerful nations and multi-national corporations sacrifice marginalized peoples and their resources to profit in the global economy. Sterling, a Laguna Pueblo man, retires from his railway job in California and returns to New Mexico to spend his remaining days with his own people. He is compelled, as was Tayo, to crawl under the fence surrounding the now abandoned uranium mine. He remembers when the government first began sinking test holes in the fields

where the Laguna people were cultivating corn, squash, and chili. Despite his elders' opposition to these tests, U.S. scientists and officials assured the people that the mine would make the nation safe from its enemies and simultaneously strengthen the Pueblo economy. Unlike *Ceremony*, this novel does not end with the main character simply reflecting on a "monstrous design" of death and destruction. Instead, an indigenous Army of Retribution and Justice is marching from Central America towards the U.S.–Mexico border, and groups of non-indigenous and indigenous people are meeting together at a Holistic Healers Convention in Tucson, Arizona. Together, these people are working together for constructive change. Thus, *Almanac of the Dead* fictionally illustrates the stated goals of the UN Declaration on Indigenous Rights, to recognize the richness and diversity of all peoples, while at the same time affirming the right of indigenous peoples to organize for political, economic, social, cultural and environmental protection of their cultures, lands, and resources

In *Gardens in the Dunes* (2000), Silko explores in depth the assault on indigenous agricultural practices and foodways that has taken place since the beginning of the colonial era in the Americas. Once again, Silko employs the motif of an indigenous character being forced away from a beloved homeplace, then, after travel in distant lands, returning home to work for the healing and well-being of her community. The main protagonist, Indigo, is a small Native American girl being raised in the late 1800s by her grandmother and taught traditional subsistence farming in the desert American Southwest. Caught by U.S. government soldiers and sent to a boarding school in California, Indigo escapes and is later adopted by Hattie and Edward, a wealthy white American intellectual couple interested in botany. While Hattie seems genuinely interested in Indigo's welfare, and takes her on an extended educational tour through Europe, visiting the gardens of the wealthy, Edward is clearly more self-interested. He is engaged in what prominent environmental thinker and physicist, Vandana Shiva, has termed "biopiracy" or the unscrupulous appropriation of the "seeds, medicinal plants, and medical knowledge" of the "original owners and innovators" of indigenous flora and fauna (Shiva 4). By juxtaposing Edward's quest for bioprofits with Indigo's struggle for the continued practice of traditional indigenous agriculture, Silko's novel imaginatively anticipates (and illustrates) the rationale for the 2007 UN Declaration regarding the right of indigenous peoples to maintain and control their own "knowledge of the properties of fauna and flora" (Article 31).—Joni Adamson

BIBLIOGRAPHY

Adamson, Joni. "Reinventing Nature: Leslie Marmon Silko's Critique of Euro-American 'Nature Talk.'" *American Indian Literature, Environmental Justice, and Ecocriticism: The Middle Place*. Tucson: University of Arizona Press, 2001.

Barnett, Louise K., and James L. Thorson, eds. *Leslie Marmon Silko: A Collection of Critical Essays*. Preface by Franklin Gish. Albuquerque: University of New Mexico Press, 2001.

Environmental Justice/Environmental Racism. "The Seventeen Principles of Environmental Justice." Updated July 19, 2009. Downloadable PDF available online. http://www.ejnet.org/ej/index.html. Accessed August 11, 2009.

Shiva, Vandana. *Biopiracy: The Plunder of Nature and Knowledge*. Boston: South End Press, 1997.

Silko, Leslie Marmon. *Almanac of the Dead*. New York: Simon & Schuster, 1991.

_____. *Ceremony*. New York: Penguin, 1977.

_____. *Gardens in the Dunes*. New York: Simon and Schuster, 2000.

_____. *Yellow Woman and a Beauty of the Spirit: Essays on Native American Life Today*. New York: Touchstone, 1996.

The United Nations Permanent Forum on Indigenous Issues. "United Nations Declaration on the Rights of Indigenous Peoples." Available online. URL: http://www.un.org/esa/socdev/unpfii/en/declaration.html. Accessed August 11, 2009.

Almanac of the Dead, Leslie Marmon Silko (1991)

Early reviewers of Leslie Marmon Silko's *Almanac of the Dead* admitted their disappointment at finding the novel so different from Silko's previous works. *Almanac* lacked the focus on Native American storytelling and healing practices found in *Storyteller* and CEREMONY, and, instead, focused on an Army of Retribution and Justice marching from Mexico towards the U.S., along with other loosely linked stories about ecowarriors, politicians, biotechnologists, military generals, and murderers.

Nearly two decades later, critical appreciation of *Almanac of the Dead* has increased dramatically as the novel has taken a prominent place among works described as "literature of environmental justice" (Adamson 129). This genre recasts environmental issues as social and economic justice issues, in works such as SIMON ORTIZ's *FIGHT BACK*, Octavia Butler's *Xenogenesis* series, Ana Castillo's *So Far from God*, Jonathon Harr's *A Civil Action*, LINDA HOGAN's *Solar Storms*, and Karen Tei Yamashita's *Tropic of Orange*. These works differ from other American environmental literature written since the 1980's, which reflects what Cynthia Deitering terms a "toxic consciousness." Novels such as John Cheever's *Oh What a Paradise It Seems*, DON DELILLO's *WHITE NOISE*, and John Updike's *Rabbit at Rest* describe America not so much in terms of what it produces but what it wastes; and their typical protagonist, writes Deitering, struggles in some way with the imminence of ecological collapse while dreaming of a "pastoral homesite associated with innocence and harvest" (200).

In contrast, characters in the literature of environmental justice recognize that dreaming will not solve such complex problems. These characters actively resist state and corporate actions that put their cultures and environments at risk, and are often modeled on actual community or activist groups. For example, *Almanac of the Dead*'s ecowarriors respond to threats to the environment posed by the construction of dams by engaging in monkeywrenching tactics similar to those of the real-life environmentalist group EarthFirst! (CONSERVATION MOVEMENT). Silko's fictional Army of Retribution and Justice actively defend their community from corrupt military generals and greedy corporate schemers, and seem modeled on leaders of the "Zapatistas," an activist group working in Chiapas, Mexico, in the decade before Silko published *Almanac*. In 1994, the Zapatistas rebelled against the Mexican government for its signing of the North American Free Trade Agreement, or NAFTA. Zapatistas leaders stated that they would oppose implementation of NAFTA because it favored large, corporate agribusiness, and thus impoverished the indigenous farming communities they represented (Adamson 131–136). As T.V. Reed writes, *Almanac* was widely read in Chiapas in the years before the rebellion. But whether or not Silko was aware of the Zapatistas' activities and modeled her characters on them, or the rebels took inspiration from the novel, is less important than the obvious affinities between the imagined and real activism. There "is nothing accidental in this coalescence," Reed concludes, "around issues of social and environmental justice" (34).

Almanac has also garnered increasing respect among readers and critics interested in the new ground the novel claimed for both Native American fiction and environmental literature. Dismissing the boundaries some critics have drawn around "authentic" Native American literature, and others have drawn around "nature writing," Silko insists that she is not afraid to write about the survival of people and the Earth in ways that may not respect the supposed borders of these genres. As she told interviewer Laura Coltelli, those who would understand her project must put aside ambiguous notions of "novelist merit" and read her book — as the title clearly indicates — as an almanac (Coltelli 151). Silko's work was inspired by the ancient Mayan hieroglyphic almanacs, or codices, that priests once used to teach children about their culture, mathematics, history, royal lineages, rituals, and prayers (Adamson 136–140). By weaving elements of the Mayan almanacs into her novel, Silko dispels the notion that "Native American literature" and "nature writing" are new genres that first emerged in the 1960's, reminding her readers that indigenous American peoples have been orally recording and writing about their cultures and environments for hundreds, even thousands of years.

In the novel, a secret "almanac" is in the possession of Yoeme, a Yaqui Indian grandmother who survived the 1910 Mexican Revolution. Yoeme is the most recent "keeper of the almanac." For hundreds of years, the "keepers" have augmented the original Mayan texts with additional documents, including early colonial American "farmer's almanacs" (Silko 570). Yoeme knows that from the 1600's until the early 1800's, American farmers believed that the earth was alive and that the sun, moon, and stars influenced both the human body and the land. By following the advice in their almanacs (watching the seasons closely, observing changes in plants, dancing in the fields to encourage fertility, etc.), good colonial farmers hoped Mother Earth would provide them with a bounteous harvest (Adamson 143). Yoeme, a twentieth-century witness to the devastating damage being done to the earth, collects copies of these almanacs to document the fact that Euro-American peoples did not always believe that the Earth was inert matter that could be exploited for personal gain. She and other keepers also add their own personal histories and newspaper articles detailing crimes, atrocities, and indigenous uprisings to their collection of documents. Sensing she is nearing her death, Yoeme passes the collection down to her twin granddaughters, Lecha and Zeta Cazador, explaining that the book would tell them "who they were and where they had come from" (Silko 246). With these documents, Lecha, Zeta, and others who care about the Earth, will be able to see that the natural world has been interpreted differently by diverse groups of people throughout history. No one group should be allowed to impose their interpretation on others, especially if that interpretation might lead, as Yoeme puts it, to the end of all life on the Earth (Silko 719).

Leche asks her Anglo-American assistant, Seese, to type and save all the documents onto a computer so that they will be safe and increasingly useful to them in their work to support a growing transnational, multi-ethnic network of groups that includes the Army of Retribution and an army of the homeless. The implication of Lecha's and Seese's work is that saving humans and the Earth will require a deep understanding of the historical roots of ecological crisis, and thorough preparation to enter into dialogue with international politicians, bankers, corporate executives, and developers over what it will mean to protect the planet. The almanac offers indigenous people and their non-indigenous allies the information they will need to come to the negotiation table prepared for the discussions. Thus, Silko's action-oriented characters offer profound insight into the 80 years of dedicated work by actual indigenous leaders from all over the world who wrote and, along with their non-indigenous allies, organized the campaign for adoption of the United Nations Declaration on Indigenous Rights (see "About UNPFII and a Brief History"). Reading the 41 Articles of the Declaration offers insight into the reasons why Silko's indigenous activists travel to a Holistic Healer's Conference near the end of the novel, and illuminates the goals of their work. At the Conference, these characters insist that saving the Earth will require an end to murder, rape, discrimination, illegal appropriation of lands, and unethical exploitation of natural resources.

The novel ends before Silko's fictional army takes any action, and thus seems to some inconclusive. However, the work is clearly more concerned with the modest task of sowing, rather than hasty reaping, and the Holistic Healers Convention simply but profoundly suggests that those who care about the future need most of all to remember the past, form effective alliances, and engage in innovative actions that work towards social, economic and environmental justice.—Joni Adamson

Bibliography

Adamson, Joni. "A Place to See: Self-Representation and Resistance in Leslie Marmon Silko's *Almanac of the Dead*." *American Indian Literatures, Environmental Justice, and Ecocriticism: The Middle Place*. Tucson: University of Arizona Press, 2001.

Deitering, Cynthia. "The Postnatural Novel: Toxic Consciousness in Fiction of the 1980s." In *The Ecocriticism Reader: Landmarks in Literary Ecology*, Cheryll Glotfelty and Harold Fromm, eds. Athens and London: University of Georgia Press, 1996. 196–203.

O'Meara, Bridgit. "The Ecological Politics of Leslie Silko's *Almanac of the Dead*." *Wicazo Sa Review* 15.2 (2000): 63–73.

Reed, T.V. "Toxic Colonialism, Environmental Justice, and Native Resistance in Silko's *Almanac of the Dead*." *MELUS*. 34.2 (Summer 2009): 25–42.

Silko, Leslie Marmon. *Almanac of the Dead*. New York: Simon and Schuster, 1991.

The United Nations Permanent Forum on Indigenous Issues. "About UNPFII and a Brief History of Indigenous Peoples and the International System." Available online. URL: http://www.un.org/esa/socdev/unpfii/en/history.html. Accessed August 17. 2009.

The United Nations Permanent Forum on Indigenous Issues. "United Nations Declaration on the Rights of Indigenous Peoples." Available online. URL: http://www.un.org/esa/socdev/unpfii/en/declaration.html. Accessed August 11, 2009.

Ceremony,
Leslie Marmon Silko (1977)

Since the publication of *Ceremony*, the novel's highly favorable critical reception has extended through a host of varied disciplines, with literary, cultural, philosophical or historical emphases. What begins as the story of a young World War II veteran's struggle to confront his psychological trauma, compounded by the war and witnessing his cousin's death, evolves into an examination of the interconnected natural and social forces shaping an individual's life. Confronting the horrors of his war experience, Tayo also encounters elements of Pueblo Indian history and tradition, contends with his disjointed family and his racially and socially liminal experiences, and struggles with potentially crippling feelings of bafflement, loss and anger. The novel's nonlinear temporality adds psychological realism to Tayo's emotional disruption, as well as developing the Indian perception of the simultaneity of past and present, thereby connecting the mythic to the real. Through the guidance of several Pueblan "Yellow Woman" avatars, Tayo overcomes his spiritual morbidity (reflected in part by the pervasive drought dominating the narrative), recognizes the choices before him, and ultimately reconnects with both nature and life.

Building on Keresan (Pueblo) beliefs, Silko connects the negative and destructive forces, within individuals and society alike, to witchery and the efforts of "the destroyers," the personification of all things antithetical to life and happiness. The myth the shaman Betonie recounts to Tayo particularly emphasizes the destroyers' antipathy to the land: "They grow away from the earth.... The world is a dead thing for them.... They see no life" (125). Although witchery may often occur in a direct and deliberate form, such as in Emo's attempt to destroy Tayo, it also appears in a broader and analogous context as part of human selfishness, insensitivity, and cruelty to creatures, other men, and the land. Having established such a complex but integral basis for the psychic and social disjunction that Tayo and the others experience, Silko interweaves the historic confiscation and destruction of Indian homelands, the repression of native culture and its religious connection to nature, and the breakdown of familial and tribal social structure because of white cultural hegemony. His mother Laura's need for white acceptance, and her subsequent ruin and death, erode Tayo's emotional stability and identity. His Aunt Thelma's adoption of white social and religious values precludes her following traditional Laguna principles of accepting and nurturing family members. She dis-

dains Tayo for his illegitimacy and mixed ancestry, and turns her son Rocky away from Laguna traditions so that he might better succeed in the white world. Floyd Lee's proprietary fencing of the sacred mountain Tse-pi'na (Mt. Taylor) and the nearby uranium mines exemplify further the dominant culture's disregard for the land and its people. As an embodiment of such evil, Tayo's nemesis Emo reveals an intense self-hatred through his contempt for his own heritage and nature: "Look. Here's the Indians' mother earth! Old dried up thing!" (27). Emo desires power, and derives pleasure from killing and destruction; his bag of teeth taken from a Japanese colonel illustrates his connection to the destroyers and witchery. The intense enmity that Emo bears toward Tayo establishes them as opposing forces of death and life, and lays the groundwork for the novel's final confrontation, which Tayo must surmount to complete his healing.

Within the Keresan mythological subtext of tribal stories that parallel Tayo's struggle to overcome his alienation, Silko introduces different avatars of the Yellow Woman, who guide Tayo. This deity often accompanies the hunter figure, manages the game, and brings rain. Because Yellow Woman unites the agrarian dimension of Pueblo culture with the hunting elements, to create a productive environment, she becomes a goddess of fertility. Moreover, in a striking reversal of America's traditional lines of cultural influence, her activity has the power to restore missing or damaged components of society. Often perceived as an agent of transformation, she develops models necessary for adjustment or renewal, and reveals the importance of change to cultural strength and continuity.

Silko inscribes Betonie's grandmother, and by extension Betonie, Night Swan, and Ts'eh, as embodiments of different manifestations of Yellow Woman, who guide Tayo. In a distant past, Betonie's grandmother recognizes the growing power of the destroyers, and with her husband, the shaman Descheeny, constructs a strategy to counter their destructive threat. She trains Betonie from his childhood in the magic necessary to work against destroyers; consequently, Betonie's assistance in Tayo's healing and instruction originates with her. Night Swan, the first Yellow Woman manifestation Tayo encounters, sexually and emotionally initiates the adolescent Tayo to counter his alienation, to instruct him about the importance of change, and to prepare him for his future: "Indians or Mexicans or whites — most people are afraid of change.... They are fools.... But remember this day. You will recognize it later. You are part of it now" (92). Night Swan also prompts Josiah to purchase Ulibarri's Mexican cattle to liberate himself and Tayo from the frequently failed Indian attempts to raise the demanding Hereford breed. The Mexican cattle signify the necessary return to tradition, and emerge as a model for a sustainable human relationship to the land. Often described as deer-like, these cattle exist in the harsh conditions of the Southwest, eat the rough vegetation of the region, and survive on minimal water. Rather than require more than the land can provide, the cattle live a balanced existence within the parameters of their environment. The herd, free roaming since Josiah's death, becomes the focus of Tayo's quest, and symbolizes his struggle to confirm his connection to Nature and the land, as well as to heal psychologically. As Night Swan assists Josiah, Ts'eh Montaño aids Tayo in capturing the cattle, thereby uniting him with the symbolic benignity of the animals and establishing a spiritual connection to Yellow Woman. The eventual establishment of the herd, the addition of the healed, yellow bull, and the birth of new calves, parallel Tayo's own healing, rejuvenation, and reintegration into the tribe.

Tayo's relationship with Ts'eh, the most direct Yellow Woman manifestation, enables his regeneration and his completion of the "ceremony." Guided by Betonie's directions, Tayo initially encounters Ts'eh in his attempt to regain his cattle. Both symbols and colors attest to Ts'eh's Yellow Woman persona in their first meeting: a hunter is her companion, her blanket has a storm cloud pattern, her moccasins have silver rainbird buttons, and her features initially appear on the Ka't'sina antelope mask. Ts'eh's name suggests Ts'its'tsi'nako (see below) and the aforementioned sacred mountain Tse-pi'na, and Montaño explicitly connects her to the mountains, home to spirits like Yellow Woman. Tayo's subsequent meetings with Ts'eh teach him to recognize the forces and interconnectedness of nature, and to see himself again as part of the web of existence spun by Ts'its'tsi'nako, the Spider-Woman, a creative deity. In addition to personal fulfillment with Ts'eh, Tayo regains his awareness of, sensitivity to, and concern for nature: he spreads pollen, collects plants for propagation, and helps Ts'eh make offerings at the ancient she-elk petroglyph.

Ts'eh also shares her foreknowledge of the coming conflict, to prepare Tayo for the destroyers and Emo. Tayo must confront Emo alone: only he can choose to follow or to reject witchery. His ability to contain his anger and resist the temptation to kill Emo completes the story of the ceremony that now provides *others* with the means to overcome modern witchery. Tayo's realization that "she had always loved him, she had never left him; she had always been there" (237) connects him with the earth and the feminine eternal, through Yellow Woman and Ts'eh. Retelling

his story to the elders at the kiva integrates it into tribal history, and signals Tayo's successful healing and full incorporation into the tribe and life — the fulfillment of the "ceremony." — Thomas P. Fair

BIBLIOGRAPHY

Leslie Marmon Silko's Ceremony: *A Casebook.* Ed. Allan Chavkin. New York: Oxford University Press, 2002.

Silko, Leslie Marmon. *Ceremony: 30th Anniversary Edition.* New York: Penguin Books, 2006.

_____. "Landscape, History, and the Pueblo Imagination." *The Woman That I Am: The Literature and Culture of Southwestern Landscapes in Women's and Art.* Ed. Vera Norwood. New York: St. Martin's Press, 1987.

_____. *Yellow Woman.* Ed. Melody Graulich. New Brunswick, NJ: Rutgers University Press, 1995.

Smith, Patricia Clark, and Paula Gunn Allen. "Earthly Relations, Carnal Knowledge: Southwestern American Indian Women Writers and Landscape." *Yellow Woman.* Ed. Melody Graulich. New Brunswick, NJ: Rutgers University Press, 1995. 115–150.

Simms, William Gilmore (1806–1870)

William Gilmore Simms was a leading literary figure in the antebellum South. During his lifetime he achieved national fame, and his contemporary EDGAR ALLAN POE praised him as "The best novelist this country has, on the whole, produced." However, Simms's reputation declined quickly after his death, and critics have only recently begun to reevaluate the importance of his work. A reason for this may be, as John Caldwell Guilds asserts, that Simms has been "thought of primarily, and almost exclusively, as the most important literary representation of the mind of the Old South" (xiii); hence, after the civil war, he was considered by many as little more than a symbol of a vanquished culture, a stigma that Poe, the other major antebellum southern writer, managed to avoid. While Simms was an important and prolific poet, essayist, critic, short story writer, and historian during his lifetime, today he is remembered primarily for his Revolutionary War novels, especially *The Partisan*, and his border romances, such as *Border Beagles: A Tale of Mississippi.*

Although Simms achieved national fame for his writings, he largely stayed away from the major publishing centers in New England, instead spending his entire life in his beloved South Carolina. Simms harbored disdain for the Northern states, frequently condemning in his writings what he called in 1838 the "mercantile and money-loving condition of things" in the "Yankee" region of the country. Simms's two essays from 1841, "The Good Farmer" and "The Ages of Gold and Iron: From an Agricultural Oration," promote an agrarian lifestyle and, as James Everett Kibler, Jr., writes, "posit a Southern way against what was becoming an urban, Northern 'American' one" (Review). Simms was one of the chief critics of the northern mentality of mercantilism and utilitarianism. During and after the civil war, he was particularly horrified by the destruction of southern land by union troops, including the city of Columbia, which he bitterly documented in his journalistic work *A City Laid Waste: The Capture, Sack, and Destruction of the City of Columbia* (1865).

Despite the limited critical attention he has received, Simms is generally credited with at least one important literary accomplishment: his sensitive representation of Native Americans. Simms was among the first to present a realistic and balanced rather than romanticized picture of the American Indian. Unlike JAMES FENIMORE COOPER, who relied largely on secondary sources for his information about Native Americans, Simms drew from direct personal experience, having traveled extensively on the Southern American frontier as a young man with his father, and associated with various Indian tribes. In a letter to O.J. Victor, Simms writes, "I have traveled, in early years, greatly in the South and South West on horseback, seeing the whole region from Carolina to Mississippi personally, and as far back as 1825 when ⅔ was an Indian Country; ... I saw the red men in their own homes; could imitate them in speech; imitate the backwoodsmen, mountaineers, swamp suckers &c." (qtd. by Guilds xiv).

Simms connected his view of Native Americans to his concern over the natural environment. To him, industrialism threatened the survival of the American Indian as well as the unspoiled landscape, and he bemoaned the process of "the life of civilization usurping the domain of the savage" (qtd. by Guilds xxiv). As Guilds observes, "Simms recognized that the primeval forests were sacred to the Southeastern Indian's spirit and essential to his way of life. A recurring theme in his work is the conflict between the Indians' reverence for nature and the relentless encroachment on and exploitation of it by the European settler" (xxiii). In total, Simms composed over 100 literary works about Native Americans, the most important of which is probably his novel *The Yemassee* (1835).

Simms's other notable contribution to environmental literature is his sizeable body of poetry, which is charged with vivid and sometimes rhapsodic natural imagery. Like his fiction, the poetry of Simms has only recently garnered significant scholarly attention, but Kibler asserts that Simms "probably wrote more poems descriptive of nature than any American poet before or after him" ("Perceiver and Perceived" 106). Simms was an admirer of the great English nature poet William Wordsworth, and his poetry explores the spiritual qualities of the individual's relationship to nature, and reflects the author's belief in the proper stewardship of the Earth. Ever anxious about the encroachment of civilization on the natural environment, Simms captures his feelings in the long poem "The Traveller's Rest," (1853) lamenting the loss of forested land over which "hung the brooding countenance of God":

> Alas! the forward vision! A few years
> Will see these shafts o'erthrown. The profligate hands
> Of avarice and of ignorance will despoil
> The woods of their old glories; and the earth,
> Uncherish'd, will grow barren, [...] [157].

— Matthew S. Elder

BIBLIOGRAPHY

Guilds, John Caldwell. Introduction to *An Early and Strong Sympathy: The Indian Writings of William Gilmore Simms*. Columbia: University of South Carolina Press, 2003.

Kibler, James E. "Perceiver and Perceived: External Landscape as Mirror and Metaphor in Simms's Poetry." In *"Long Years of Neglect,"* edited by John Caldwell Guilds, 106–125. Fayetteville: University of Arkansas Press, 1988.

———. Rev. of *From Nationalism to Secessionism: The Changing Fiction of William Gilmore Simms*. Findarticles.com. Available online. Url: http://findarticles.com/p/articles/mi_hb3524/is_n1_v49/ai_n28669307/. Accessed June 23, 2009.

———. "Stewardship and *Patria* in Simms's Frontier Poetry." In *William Gilmore Simms and the American Frontier*, edited by John Caldwell Guilds and Caroline Collins, 209–220. Athens: University of Georgia Press, 1997.

Simms, William Gilmore. "The Traveller's Rest." In *Selected Poems of William Gilmore Simms*, edited by James Everett Kibler, Jr., 155–165. Athens: University of Georgia Press, 1990.

Smith, Henry Nash (1906–1980)

Henry Nash Smith was born in Dallas, Texas, and throughout his life identified strongly with Texas and the Southwest region of the United States. He graduated from Southern Methodist University in 1925 and then from Harvard with an M.A. in 1927. He returned to SMU in 1927 to begin his teaching career and remained there until 1937, when he returned to Harvard to pursue his Ph.D. He was the first to graduate from Harvard's American Civilization doctoral program in 1940, and his first book, VIRGIN LAND: THE AMERICAN WEST AS SYMBOL AND MYTH (1950), reflects his interdisciplinary background.

While at SMU Smith was a co-editor of the *Southwest Review*, which brought him into contact with various leading Texas intellectuals like John McGinnis and J. Frank Dobie who were committed to nurturing the development of Texan and Southwest culture. McGinnis, Smith's mentor and co-editor, was "passionately interested in the landscape, culture, and literature of the region" (May 7). Smith's effort on the *Southwest Review* led him to repeatedly comment on the cultural condition of the region. Richard Bridgman notes that "in his commitment to regionalism, Smith pointedly distinguished the Southwest from the South," and "although Smith criticized the primitive state of development in the Southwest [...] nonetheless, when the time came, he was confident that the region's literary results would differ from those produced in the South" (Bridgman 261). The specific and unique quality of the Southwest identified by Smith was "'a quality of experience of actual human beings in immediate contact with a semi-parched earth — its dust and heat and relentless distances, its austere plants and lean animals'" (Bridgman 261). This awareness of and devotion to the West and Southwest of the United States led to his most significant work, *Virgin Land*.

Throughout his long career in academia Smith published dozens of articles, and wrote or edited numerous books, including *Popular Culture and Industrialism 1865–1890* (1967), *Democracy and the Novel* (1978), and a number of works on MARK TWAIN. However, it is *Virgin Land* that led to his scholarly renown and his lasting influence on American studies and environmental literature. "Based upon years of study of attitudes to the West in the East, including such popular literature as dime novels" (Gossett), the work "traces the impact of the West, the vacant continent beyond the frontier, on the consciousness of Americans and follows the principal consequences of this impact in literature and social thought" (Smith 4). The seminal study brought serious attention to the role and influence of the natural environment in general on the lives, art, and culture of America. And in providing a thorough treatment of the influence of the natural landscape of the West in particular, it has come to be regarded as a landmark both in American studies and in environmental literature. — Conor Walsh

BIBLIOGRAPHY

Bridgman, Richard. "The American Studies of Henry Nash Smith." *American Scholar*, 56.2 (Spring 1987): 259–268.

Gossett, Thomas F. "Henry Nash Smith." *Handbook of Texas Online*. Available online. URL: http://www.tsha online.org/handbook/online/articles/SS/fsm76.html. Accessed 6 March, 2009.

May, Henry F. "The Rough Road to Virgin Land." *American Literature, Culture, and Ideology: Essays in Memory of Henry Nash Smith*. Ed. Beverly R. Voloshin. New York: Peter Lang, 1990. 1–23.

Smith, Henry Nash. *Virgin Land: The American West as Symbol and Myth*. New York: Vintage, 1950.

Virgin Land: The American West as Symbol and Myth, Henry Nash Smith (1950)

Winner of the Bancroft Prize from Columbia University in 1950 and the John H. Dunning Prize from the American Historical Association in 1951, Henry Nash Smith's *Virgin Land* made an instant impact in the academic world. Although focusing on the history of the American West, the work "promised to unite a fractured academy by crossing disciplines. It promised to open whole new areas for study, to invigorate literary criticism with history, and enrich economic and political history by attending to the symbolic aspects of the human imagination" (Fabian, 542–543). Lately, this once seminal work has drifted to the periphery of contemporary studies in American history and literature. However, despite changes in generational and academic perspectives, *Virgin Land* is still an important book, especially in light of the current emphasis on the natural environment in all areas of academic and popular culture. In 1950 Richard Hofstader ended his positive review of *Virgin Land* with the assertion that "it is one of those seminal books that grow more capacious the more the reader brings to them. There is hardly a phase of American thought about America that it does not directly or tangentially illuminate" (Hofstader 282). The current "environmental" phase in such "American thought" is particularly illuminated.

In the author's own words, *Virgin Land* "traces the impact of the West, the vacant continent beyond the frontier, on the consciousness of Americans and follows the principal consequences of this impact in literature and social thought" (Smith 4). The work employs multiple sources and academic disciplines to investigate how "nineteenth-century Americans view the huge blankness of the West, and in turn, how did their imaginative conceptions affect their behavior" (Bridgman 263). Smith divides his work into three sections. The first, "Passage to India," considers the conception of the American continent as a commercial empire possessing access to both the Atlantic and Pacific oceans, strategically located between Europe and Asia. As the push to the Pacific gained momentum, the second view of the West took shape. "Sons of Leatherstocking" explores the peopling of the continent between the coasts. Frontiersmen and mountain men became symbolic of the Western hero, and embodied a profound tension in relation to the environment they inhabited. Larger-than-life figures like Daniel Boone or DAVY CROCKETT came to be seen both as champions of frontier living in communion with nature, free of civilization and its ills, and as heralds and agents of this same civilization through their exploration and settling of that frontier. Smith's third section, "The Garden of the World," considers the final and perhaps most lasting view of the West:

> With each surge of westward movement a new community came into being. These communities devoted themselves not to marching onward but to cultivating the earth. They plowed the virgin land and put in crops, and the great Interior Valley was transformed into a garden: for the imagination, the Garden of the World. The image of this vast and constantly growing agricultural society in the interior continent became one of the dominant symbols of nineteenth-century American society [Smith 138].

However, over time and through the efforts of land speculators and railroad companies, "this symbol, like that of the Wild West, became in its turn a less and less accurate description of a society transformed by commerce and industry" (Smith 139). Smith stresses in the book's conclusion, however, the curious but compelling fact that such symbolism of the West remained strong even after the reality upon which it was based had effectively ceased to exist.

Smith's primary concern is with the human conceptions of the West, and thus he seldom addresses specific elements of the natural environment. Despite its backgrounded presence, however, the natural environment is shown — through the human reactions to it — to be immensely influential on American culture and history. Primarily, American society viewed the West in terms of attaining "free access to the bounty of nature — whether in the form of game or land" (Smith 68); yet despite this materialistic and ultimately rapacious view, the majority of society also held the Romantic view that the West offered a chance to "restore man's lost harmony with nature" (Smith 51); a contradiction explored critically in D.H. LAWRENCE's CLASSICS IN AMERICAN LITERATURE. The Americans of the East looked to the West and its popular images of wild animals and wild men as remedies to the ills of civilization in which they felt mired. "Men who felt themselves divorced from nature seemed to hope that by dwelling upon these symbols they might regain a lost imaginative contact with some secret source of virtue and power in the universe" (Smith 84). Though few could replicate HENRY DAVID THOREAU's wilderness excursions, they could in a sense restore themselves through the *image* of the West.

Moreover, the symbolism of the vast and bountiful natural environment held deep and lasting meaning for the American identity, beyond resources or spirituality. As Smith emphasizes, "from the perspective of the physical geographer the continents and oceans,

the mountain ranges and river systems group themselves into a system having a supreme and unbreakable order which is at the same time absolutely good. This order will ultimately determine the condition of the civilizations of the earth, elevating the United States above all other nations" (Smith 43). The awe-inspiring natural environment of the continent led to an optimistic nationalism that culminated in the dreams of MANIFEST DESTINY, inextricably linking the greatness of the country to the greatness of its environment:

> If the earth is the final arbiter of human destinies, then the student of society should direct his gaze toward nature rather than to history. The important thing about man is not his past, not a cultural tradition, but his biological adjustment to his milieu, which is a matter of the present and of the future [Smith 44].

Common perceptions of the natural environment, Smith notes, are divided between seeing it as a "thing" to be mastered and as a "living entity" to which one must adapt. But in either case, he argues, the fundamental importance of the environment must be acknowledged in any attempt to define or understand American culture and history.

> A century of speculation concerning the West and the destiny of America focused itself about Walt Whitman's question of what the Great Mother Continent meant with respect to the human race. The answer of the 1880's may likewise be expressed in Whitman's words: the continent, especially the developing West, was "a refuge strong and free for practical average use, for man and woman." [...] The character of the American empire was defined not by streams of influence out of the past, not by a cultural tradition, not by its place in a world community, but by a relation between man and nature — or rather, even more narrowly, between American man and the American West [Smith 217].

Thus, despite — or perhaps *because of*— the gap between the reality and images of the West, the environment and landscape of the continent remains an active and ever renewed force in the forging of America as a country and a culture. — Conor Walsh

BIBLIOGRAPHY

Bridgman, Richard. "The American Studies of Henry Nash Smith." *American Scholar*, 56.2 (Spring 1987): 259–268.

Fabian, Ann. "Back to *Virgin Land.*" *Reviews in American History*, 24.3 (Sep., 1996): 542–553.

Hofstader, Richard. Rev. of *Virgin Land: The American West as Symbol and Myth*. *American Quarterly*, 2.3 (Autumn, 1950): 279–282.

Smith, Henry Nash. *Virgin Land: The American West as Symbol and Myth*. New York: Vintage, 1950.

Smith, Captain John (1580–1631)

Few figures in American history have generated as much veneration or reproach as Captain John Smith. Some contend that he is America's first great author; others debate the veracity and integrity of his prolific writings. Biographer Bradford Smith writes that "No figure in American history has raised such a ruckus among scholars as Captain John Smith" (Smith 11). The central problem hinges on whether "Smith was (or was not) one of the world's most successful liars and braggarts" (12). Whatever the case, John Smith's several books stand as monuments of early American literature and nature writing, and the importance of his role — however it be judged — as an early American explorer, geographer, and colonizer cannot be understated or ignored.

Smith was born into a farmer's family in Lincolnshire, England, most likely in 1580 (the earliest record of his life is a baptism date of January 9 of that year). After his father's death in 1596, he abandoned his shopkeeper's apprenticeship to become a soldier, a move that marked the beginnings of his seafaring life. The exploits of these years in the military have become legendary, although the precise facts remain a source of critical contention. As Smith himself describes (and perhaps embellishes) in his 1630 *The True Travels, Adventures, and Observations of Captaine John Smith*, he fought for the Dutch in the Netherlands, and later battled against the Turks in the Austrian army, famously beheading three Turkish captains. While in Hungary, he was wounded, taken captive, and sold as a slave in Constantinople. After killing his master and escaping, Smith eventually made his way back to England in 1604.

Capitalizing on his reputation as a soldier, in December 1606 Smith sailed with the Virginia Company to help establish a colony at Jamestown (in present-day Virginia). During the voyage, however, Smith was accused of plotting to overthrow the leaders and subsequently jailed. Set to be executed, he instead found freedom when, upon landing in North America, the sealed instructions for the company were opened and Smith was named as one of the seven council members. Over the next year, he extensively explored coastal Virginia, searching for food, and mapping and recording his observations of the flora, fauna, and Native peoples he encountered. While out surveying he was taken captive and brought before Powhatan, chief of the Chesapeake Bay Indians. According to Smith he was about to be killed when the chief's daughter, Pocahontas, famously intervened, offering her own life in place of the white man's. The following summer, in 1608, he sent an account of Jamestown's brief but colorful history back to England, where it was published under the title *A True Relation of Such Occurrences and Accidents of Noate as Hath Hapned in Virginia*. Elected president of the council in 1608, Smith is credited with single-handedly ensuring the survival of the colony, his forceful command and strict work ethic enabling the settlement to survive sickness and starvation. As the number of his enemies mounted, however, Smith increasingly became a target, and after being wounded in a gunpowder explosion, following a failed assassination attempt, he finally returned to England in 1609. Over the next decades Smith reworked the material printed in *A True Relation* and published his story about the settlement in Virginia several times. The collaborative *A Map of Virginia* appeared in 1612, but Smith's reputation as a writer rests mainly on his vast and eclectic GENERALL HISTORIE OF VIRGINIA, NEW-ENGLAND, AND THE SOMER ISLES (1624). Together, his writings bear the mark of an uncommonly skillful and passionate reporter, historian, storyteller, and observer of natural history.

Despite the acclaim for his role in the Jamestown settlement and his work on Virginia's natural history, John Smith wrote most frequently about New England; in fact he was the first to call that region "New England." He sailed there from England in 1614, and published *A Description of New England* two years later — a book of immense importance to the Pilgrim and Puritan settlers who arrived in Massachusetts in 1620. Smith had become "the greatest living expert on America," and *A Description of New England* contained invaluable information about the landscape and resources to be found there, as well as the most detailed map available (Lemay 207). Smith himself wished to return to New England, and offered to lead the 1620 voyage on the Mayflower, but the Pilgrims opted instead for Captain Miles Standish. Even so, Smith's *Description of New England* served not only as the primary source of knowledge about the region for years, but also as an important promotional tract that established New England in the minds of the English populace.

John Smith never had ambitions to become a literary artist. Nearly all of his writings, like so many produced by early explorers, are utilitarian in nature and written with a specific agenda. Much of what he published reflects his entrepreneurial, propagandistic motives, and these inclinations color his descriptions of the natural environment in North America. His descriptions of commodities such as plants or minerals, for example, frequently lapse into advertisements of their value to potential colonizers, and he often exaggerates the abundance of resources that would appeal to his prospective English supporters. Sometimes his writing, much in the manner of modern advertising copy, becomes more creative, employing inventive and appealing metaphors. "And is it not pretty sport, to pull up two pence, six pence, and twelve pence, as fast as you can hale and veare a line?" he writes in *A Description of New England*, suggesting such a plenitude of valuable fish that one can simply go angling for money (347).

In the final years of his life, Smith continued to write, publishing *An Accidence or the Path-Way to Experience* (1626) and *A Sea Grammar* (1627), both seaman's manuals, and the promotional *Advertisements for the Unexperienced Planters of New England* (1631). By the time he died in 1631, Captain John Smith had already become a legendary soldier, explorer, and historian. And while he guaranteed his literary reputation by writing the first English book in America, his books have played an essential role in environmental literary history: more than anyone else in the seventeenth century, Smith planted and cultivated the American landscape in the popular European imagination. — Tom J. Hillard

BIBLIOGRAPHY

Lemay, J. A. Leo. *The American Dream of Captain John Smith*. Charlottesville: University of Virginia Press, 1991.
Price, David A. *Love and Hate in Jamestown: John Smith, Pocahontas, and the Heart of a New Nation*. New York: Knopf, 2003.
Smith, Bradford. *Captain John Smith: His Life and Legend*. Philadelphia: J. B. Lippincott, 1953.
Smith, John. *The Complete Works of Captain John Smith*. Ed. Philip L. Barbour. 3 vols. Chapel Hill: University of North Carolina Press, 1986.

A Description of New England, John Smith (1616)

Smith's text is a good example of early promotional literature, its principal aim being to attract colonial investors "to adventure their purses" (Dedicatory Epistle To the right Worshipfull Adventurers). Hence, the non-human environment is seen primarily in terms of what commodities can be exploited for profit, resulting in almost no physical description of New England that does not, at least overtly, serve that purpose. Yet promotional texts such as *A Description of New England*

> compel the attention of anyone interested in a general consideration of ecocritical and ecological issues, even though they are not what we would call "green" texts. They are not, for example, antigrowth. On the contrary, in a proto–Lockean recognition that wealth derives from the human transformation of the environment, [...] promoters articulated, arguably for the first time, the paradigm of growth that has since become naturalized in political and economic discourse [Sweet 401].

This is clear throughout Smith's text. Though self-interest is clearly a motivating factor, Smith broadens and deflects this into promoting the colonial venture as beneficial to the commonwealth. In the dedicatory epistle "To the right Worshipfull Adventurers for the Countrey of New England," for example, Smith writes, "I am perswaded that few do think there may be had from *New England* Staple commodities, well worth 3 or 400000 pound a yeare, with so small charge, and such facilitie, as this discourse will acquaint you."

Central to Smith's awareness "that wealth derives from the human transformation of the environment" is his binary of "industrie" and "idleness." He naturalizes this pursuit by employing a brief fable in the epistle to the Adventurers, comparing colonial exploitation to the "industrious" ant and bee. As this analogy clearly indicates, the resources gathered are taken back to the hive or hill, the metropolitan centre of the burgeoning British Empire. Not only is wealth generated in this way; there is also another benefit to the commonwealth. Colonialism draws off surplus labour — both "idle" labourers and "idle" gentlemen who unproductively consume resources in England — that does not contribute to the enrichment of the commonwealth. There is, however, a paradox at work here. In the land of plenty described by Smith, where the labour of "industrious men" will be their pleasure (31), "worthy is that person to starue that heere cannot liue; if he haue sense, strength and health: for, there is no such penury of these blessings in any place, but that a hundred men may, in one houre or two, make their prouisions for a day" (31). In addition, such ant- and bee-like industriousness furthers England's development through competition with other European colonial powers, especially Spain.

Much of Smith's text, however, is a justification for returning to England with "onely such fish as came to my net" ("To the right Worshipfull Adventurers"). As his narrative begins, he states, "our plot was there [New England] to take Whales and make tryalls of a Myne of Gold and Copper. If those failed, Fish and Furres was then our refuge [...]. For our Golde, it was rather the Masters deuice to get a voyage that proiected it, then any knowledge hee had at all of any such matter" (1). Smith turns this to his and the commonwealth's advantage. Although fish, "a mean and base commoditie" (10), may not be as appealing as the gold that drives the Spanish colonial enterprise, Smith recognizes that the fish trade is essential to another developing European empire. Fish is the "*Primum mobile* that turnes all their [the Dutch] *Spheres* to this height of plenty, strength, honour and admiration" (12). From this realization,

Smith sketches his model of a self-sustaining colony built on fishing, noting also that, unlike the Dutch who must trade their fish for the materials necessary to sustain their fleet, New England "has everything to outfit and maintain a large fishing fleet" (13). While this is a model of sustenance and development on a strictly material level, it is by no means "green." The abundance of fish is seen as infinite: "the Saluages compare their store in the Sea, to the haires on their heads" (Smith 17). The establishment of a fishing fleet will provide a firm base for the exploitation of other commodities both within the colony, in terms of trade with the Native peoples, and between the colony and England: "Europeans took hold of the traditional maize-fur trade network and transformed it from a system of binary village exchange to a link in the new Atlantic economy" (Cronon 94).

Incorporating the Native peoples into the developing Atlantic economy also points to another justification for Smith's industrious colonialism — religion. The conversion of the Natives furthers the economic and political stability of Smith's colonial model: "what can hee doe lesse hurtfull to any; or more agreeable to God, then to seeke to conuert those poore Saluages to know Christ, and humanitie, whose labors with direction will triple requite thy charge and paines?" (31). The theological justification for colonialism (THE BIBLE) is made explicitly clear in Smith's concluding comments, which can be usefully read through Lynn White, Jr.'s "The Historical Roots of Our Ecological Crisis"—"*Adam* and *Eve* did first beginne this innocent worke, To plant the earth to remaine to posteritie; but not without labour, trouble & industrie" (Smith 59). The nonhuman environment (like "Saluages") is ordained to be subdued, although the notion of this being an extension of Adam and Eve's "innocent worke" sits uncomfortably with "trouble," which only came about with the expulsion from the garden.— Jim Daems

BIBLIOGRAPHY

Cronon, William. *Changes in the Land: Indians, Colonists, and the Ecology of New England*. New York: Hill & Wang, 1983.

Smith, John. *A Description of New England: or The Observations, and discoueries, of Captain John Smith (Admirall of that Country) in the North of America, in the year of our Lord 1614: with the successe of sixe Ships, that went the next yeare 1615; and the accidents befell him among the French men of warre: With the proofe of the present benefit this Countrey affoords: wither this present yeare, 1616, eight voluntary Ships are gone to make further tryall*. London: 1616.

Sweet, Timothy. "Economy, Ecology, and Utopia in Early Colonial Promotional Literature." *American Literature* 71.3 (Sept. 1999): 399–427.

The Generall Historie of Virginia, New England, and the Summer Iles..., John Smith (1623)

The six books that comprise John Smith's *The Generall Historie of Virginia, New England, and the Summer Iles* are an eclectic mix of many genres (among them, ethnographic essays, accounts written by others, personal history, short descriptive passages of various land masses, timelines, lists of men and supplies, adventure stories) culled from Smith's earlier writings and outside sources, and including new writings intended to attract investment and laborers for the Virginia Company. It covers the exploration and settlement of early Virginia, Bermuda (also called the Summer Isles), and New England. First published in 1623, some fifteen years after Smith had returned to England, *The Generall Historie* is valued today as an indispensable record of the beginnings of one of the first permanent English efforts at colonization in America.

Book I consists mostly of accounts of the New World from what Smith terms the "Ancient Authors"—CHRISTOPHER COLUMBUS, John Cabot, Sir Walter Raleigh, Sir Francis Drake, and THOMAS HARRIOT, among others. Book II is substantially a reprint of Smith's *A Map of Virginia*, published in 1612. Books III and IV follow the founding and eventual flourishing of Jamestown, with detailed descriptions of flora and fauna, English settlers and native peoples, and various trials and tribulations (including Smith being removed from office and forced to return to England). Book V provides a record of life in the Summer Islands (Bermuda), and Book VI of New England, though Smith never visited either place.

Important to remember about the Jamestown effort is that it was above all an entrepreneurial venture, organized and financed by the members of the Virginia Company in London, with the goal of finding gold, silver, and other riches rumored to be in abundance in America. The conditions at the rustic settlement were harsh, and the earliest settlers (many descended from aristocracy and lacking skills to plant crops, build homes, and manage farms) were not prepared for the hard work required to survive in a colony far away from their more comfortable native land. Moreover, the Virginia settlement was not like its more famous relation in Massachusetts Bay, whose early inhabitants were united by their common Puritan faith; competing interests, profit seeking, and lack of preparedness plagued the early Jamestown colony through its tumultuous first years. Smith eventually unified the colonists when elected their leader; however, though his labor policies and negotiations with natives for food most likely saved the colonists' lives, his strict discipline and autocratic style made him increasingly unpopular.

Though the work is somewhat loose and unfocused in structure, beyond the seminal importance of its informing colonial *ethos* it is important to the history of environmental writing in America because of its record of all aspects of early English colonial life. Smith (whom Leo Lemay calls America's "original environmentalist" for encouraging the early settlers to make crop decisions based on the natural qualities of the landscape) presents Jamestown as a recreation of Eden (THE BIBLE), where fruits and vegetables flourished, abundant wild animals provided an endless food source, and natives, though often troublesome, could be contained and would support the colonists' mission (15). Book II, in a section called "The Commodities in Virginia, or That May be Had by Industrie," provides a good example of the rhetoric Smith used to create an image of Virginia that could potentially entice the English to relocate there: "The mildnesse of the ayre, the fertilitie of the soyle, and situation of the rivers are so propitious to the nature and use of man, as no place is more convenient for pleasure, profit, and mans sustenance, under that latitude or climat" (113). Local waterways and bays provide means to transport silk, gold, furs, and other treasures back to England, something Smith notes is already being done by France, Spain, and other European countries. Lacking only "industrious men to labour," Virginia is an ideal place for "soldiers, mariners, merchants," and laborers to make their fortunes (114). Through observation of native practices, Smith learns the importance of crop selection, rotation, and management. However, though this practice may argue for his proto-environmentalist tendencies, it is clear that the land (like other natural resources) is consistently perceived as serving man's needs, and not the other way around.

Book III contains adventurous tales of Smith's escapades, including the discovery and naming of rivers and land masses, conflicts with natives, sicknesses, and a fire that virtually destroyed the settlement. Smith also provides detailed information about Powhatan, chief of a conglomeration of Chesapeake Bay Indians, and the latter's system of governance. The Confederation, though initially persuaded by Smith to aid the struggling settlers with food and other necessities, eventually united in a determination to halt white encroachment on their lands, a decision which created numerous and violent encounters between the settlers and Indians. In late 1607, Smith and a few colleagues set out for talks with

Powhatan to resolve some of the tensions, were ambushed by Indians, and brought before Powhatan for execution. In what would become a popular myth re-told by contemporary and later authors, Powhatan's daughter Pocahontas begged for Smith's life to be spared and hers taken instead. This story, though a minor one told in a few short paragraphs, would become a legendary foundation for colonists' belief in the acceptance, on the part of natives, of white superiority. As many scholars have pointed out, Pocahontas's willingness to sacrifice herself may, in reality, have been just part of an elaborate Powhatan adoption ceremony, but came to symbolize and support the Europeans' colonial and imperial ambitions.

Despite his belief in the superiority of the English, it is clear that Smith wants to understand the natives on their own terms — their seasons, what they eat, how they plant, how they make things (baskets, bows and arrows, fish hooks, and so on). But he always does this with a purpose — to promote the potential of this new region for the glory of the King of England. The land here is meant to be used, as are the natives, to provide wealth and material goods for the homeland. Smith is clearly a proponent of colonization and therefore sees no inherent conflict in seizing lands inhabited for centuries by other people. He presents himself as an authoritative figure in all his encounters with native peoples, able to resolve disputes in his favor, either through a show of force or through his rhetoric (sometimes just by reminding the natives that the colonists had superior weapons).

The clearest example of Smith's personal impact on Virginia and its future may be seen in his decision to grow tobacco crops. He and his fellow colonists realized that the soil and weather conditions in Jamestown were near perfect for growing tobacco, at the precise moment when the demand for tobacco was growing exponentially in England and other parts of Europe (not to mention in America itself). If the colony's initial mission was to claim land for God and the English King, Smith and his Virginia Company acted as a catalyst to shift attention toward the secular concerns of trade and mercantilism, a shift that would become more explicit in the next century with the explosion of African slavery in British America.

Nonetheless, *The Generall Historie* marks a critical shift from earlier literature of exploration, such as Thomas Harriot's *A Brief and True Report of the New Found Land of Virginia*, which was mostly concerned with placing new experiences in the context of paradigms familiar to its British readers. Smith too analogizes the new in terms of the old (comparing fruits and vegetables in the New World to more familiar ones in England, for example), but he, more than others of his time, recognizes the impact that the land itself would have on its inhabitants and their way of life. As Larzer Ziff notes, Smith "is the first writer in English whose works embody a sense of America as a shaping force rather than merely a place to be shaped" (512). England will enjoy cultural and economic profits from America, but America will also impact those who explore and colonize it; and Smith goes beyond simple reporting to the English about his findings in America, to include what "America is doing to the consciousness of the English" (517).—Jacqueline Megow

BIBLIOGRAPHY

Boorstin, Daniel Joseph. *The Americans: The Colonial Experience*. 2nd ed. New York: Vintage, 1974.

Castillo, Susan, and Ivy Schweitzer, ed. *The Literatures of Colonial America*. Oxford: Blackwell, 2001.

Emerson, Everett. *Captain John Smith*. 2nd ed. New York: Twayne, 1993.

Lehman, Forrest K. "Settled Place, Contested Past: Reconciling George Percy's 'A Trewe Relacyon' with John Smith's *Generall Historie*." *Early American Literature* 42.2 (2007): 235–263.

Lemay, J. A. Leo. *The American Dream of John Smith*. Charlottesville: University Press of Virginia, 1991.

Ziff, Larzer. "Conquest and Recovery in Early Writings from America." *American Literature* 68.3 (1996): 509–525.

Snyder, Gary (1930–   )

Best known as the author of *TURTLE ISLAND*, which won the Pulitzer Prize for poetry in 1975, Gary Snyder typically strives to embrace and elucidate a practice wherein modern human cultures can begin "re-inhabiting" the planet in communities that accurately reflect biological regions and respect all living and non-living elements. This "bioregionalism" emerges naturally from Snyder's many years as a mountaineer, trail crew worker, logger, and lookout, in combination with his formal study of anthropology, Zen Buddhism, and aboriginal cultures.

Gary Snyder was born in 1930 in San Francisco, but when he was two his family moved to Lake City, Washington where they operated a small dairy farm, orchard, and cedar shingle operation. In the forest just beyond the pastures Snyder had his first encounter with the wild lands that would profoundly inform his later work. In 1942, he moved with his family to Portland, Oregon where he climbed and explored many of the Northwest's major peaks, and worked odd jobs. In 1951 he graduated from Reed College with a B.A. in anthropology and English. During college he hitchhiked across the country, joined the Merchant Marine, visited South America, and worked for the National Park Service. Snyder also published his first poems in the Reed College

Janus. After brief graduate study in anthropology at Indiana University, he moved to San Francisco and enrolled as a graduate student in East Asian Languages at UC Berkeley, where he would remain until 1955.

In the fateful year of 1955 Snyder met many of the figures who would influence his career, and became involved in two of the 20th century's major American literary movements, the "San Francisco Renaissance" and the "Beat Generation." On October 7, he read with ALLEN GINSBERG, Philip Lamantia, Michael McClure, and Philip Walen at the Six Gallery poetry reading, moderated by Kenneth Rexroth; and figures such as JACK KEROUAC, Lawrence Ferlinghetti, and Ann Charters were in the audience. In the fall of 1955, he lived with Jack Kerouac in a small cabin in Mill Valley, just outside San Francisco. The scene of the Six Gallery Reading and Jack Kerouac's time living with Snyder are loosely fictionalized in Kerouac's 1958 novel *THE DHARMA BUMS*, where Snyder is portrayed as Japhy Ryder, a Zen student, poet, and mountaineer. While he eventually split with Kerouac, Snyder and Ginsberg remained lifelong friends, and maintained a rich correspondence and a close personal and literary friendship until Ginsberg's death in 1997.

A practicing Zen Buddhist and Buddhist scholar since the 1950's, Snyder aided in the transmission of Buddhism to the United States, and is largely responsible for the presence of Buddhism in the works of Allen Ginsberg, Jack Kerouac and other Beat writers. Snyder left for Kyoto, Japan in 1956 to live in a monastery and study Zen Buddhism, and would remain in Japan until 1968 except for a few short trips to the United States for literary events and climbing and backpacking trips. He cites as critical to his interest in Buddhism its disciplined and effortful inclusion of all life, and its struggle against the typical dualisms that often render other religions and worldviews harmful to the non-human world.

While living abroad, Gary Snyder published his first collections of poetry, *Riprap and Cold Mountain Poems* (1959) and *Myths and Texts* (1960), both exploring the experiences and influences of Snyder's early years, and serving as milestones in his development as a poet, essayist, and environmental philosopher. The poems in *Riprap and Cold Mountain Poems* express Snyder's penchant for the wilderness and manual labor, and the typical interchange of the human and non-human when the former two elements are combined. Despite this characteristic material and the stylistic austerity of these poems, a Zen-like calm is evident throughout, with words chosen carefully, "deliberately," as the author of *WALDEN* would say, "like rocks./ placed solid, by hands/ In choice of place, set/ Before the body of the mind/ in space and time." The "Cold Mountain Poems" are translations of the Tang Dynasty Zen poet Han Shan, who was fabled to live in a cave high in the mountains. *Myths and Texts* is one long poem Snyder worked on for many years, from 1953. It is divided into three major sections: Hunting, Logging, and Burning; and these three themes, explored in tesselative detail in the verse, highlight the innate connection between the animistic beliefs and knowledge of primitive hunter-gather cultures, Buddhism, and human, animal, and inanimate relationships, ultimately as an antidote to the deleterious effects of modern material culture. After these two works came *A Range of Poems* (1966), *The Backcountry* (1968), and *Earth House Hold* (1969), comprising prose and poetry ranging in subjects from journals during his days as a fire lookout, tanker crew, and Zen student in Japan, to translations of Chinese Zen stories.

In 1970, Snyder moved back to the United States, purchased land near Nevada City, California, and began what he calls "the real work" of re-inhabiting the land. Upon arriving, Snyder along with friends and students hand-built his home and home base, *Kitkitdizze* (after a local plant), which remains his home to this day. At Kitkitdizze, he produced works that continued to demonstrate the environmental themes prevalent in his early work, but with the added idea of manifesting them in daily life as a path to a practice that would repair the rift between humans and the rest of the world. The first work toward that end was *Regarding Wave* (1970), followed by *Turtle Island* (1974), which he was awarded the 1975 Pulitzer Prize in poetry. Following *Turtle Island*, Snyder published three collections of prose, *The Old Ways* (1977), *He Who Hunted Birds in His Father's Village: The Dimensions of a Haida Myth* (1977), and *The Real Work: Interviews and Talks 1964–1979* (1980). These works, particularly *The Old Ways* and *The Real Work*, provide insight into Snyder's attitude toward poetry and the responsibilities of a poet, as well as the genesis of his ideas of bioregionalism and reinhabitation.

As Snyder's work matured around the conceptual triptych of wilderness, Buddhism, and reinhabitation, he continued to produce collections of verse, including *Axe Handles* (1983), and *Left Out in the Rain* (1986); the latter a collection of poems from 1945 to 1984, not included in other collections, but representing in one volume the full breadth of his work up to that time. In 1986 he began teaching at UC Davis in the English Department, developing a first of its kind Wilderness and Culture Program, aimed at formally teaching what he had spent his life writing about and practicing.

Snyder proposes, in the eight essays comprising his *The Practice of the Wild* (1990), to "investigate the meaning of wild and how it connects with free," and to take on "the basic conditions as they are — painful, impermanent, open, imperfect," as means to develop a way of life that takes account of every being's place and role in that environment. Snyder's later years have been no less searching or productive. In 1992, *No Nature: New and Selected Poems* was a finalist for the National Book Award. After *No Nature*, came another collection of essays *A Place in Space* (1995), and in 1996, *Mountain and Rivers Without End* was published — a book-length poem that he began in 1956. He published his collected works, *The Gary Snyder Reader*, in 1999.

Recent work includes a collection of poems, *Danger on Peaks* (2004), a collection of essays entitled *Back on the Fire* (2007), and *The Selected Letters of Allen Ginsberg and Gary Snyder* (2009). In addition to the Pulitzer Prize, Gary Snyder has been awarded the Bollingen Prize for Poetry (1997), the John Hay Award for Nature Writing (1997), and the Ruth Lilly Poetry Prize (2008). — Michael Sims

BIBLIOGRAPHY

Snyder, Gary. *The Gary Snyder Reader*. Washington, DC: Counterpoint, 1999.
_____. *The Practice of the Wild*. New York: North Point Press, 1990.
_____. *The Real Work: Interviews and Talks 1964–1979*, New York: New Directions, 1980.
_____. *Riprap and Cold Mountain Poems*. San Francisco: North Point Press, 1990.

Turtle Island,
Gary Snyder (1974)

Winner of the Pulitzer Prize for poetry in 1975, Gary Snyder's *Turtle Island* is a collection of poems written as early as 1956, which "speak of place, and the energy-pathways that sustain life"; it established Snyder as one of the preeminent environmental voices of the late 20th century. "Turtle Island" is the name given to the land that is now North America in the creation stories of several Northeastern Woodland Native American tribes such as the IROQUOIS, and it came into widespread use in the environmental movement of the late 1960's as a telling means to signify the North American continent in non-political and pre–European terms.

The collection emerged from, and was profoundly informed by, the swirl of events and works of the 1960's and early 1970's. One of the outcomes of the counter-culture movement and its radical antecedents was the realization that the increasingly tenuous survival of the natural environment was the linchpin for the survival of humans and other species hitherto thought invulnerable. In 1962 RACHEL CARSON published *SILENT SPRING* to wide acclaim and indignation, in 1964 Lyndon Johnson signed into law the Wilderness Act (THE CONSERVATION MOVEMENT), and in 1968 EDWARD ABBEY published his landmark work of bioregionalism, *DESERT SOLITAIRE*. Turtle Island sought to distill and integrate all the disparate energies and actions of this quiet revolution, and lay the mythopoeic foundations for a new way of seeing and being on the earth, one which, like the Buddhism that its author practiced, regarded all life with reverence.

At its core, *Turtle Island* encourages deep cultural and political change as a means to literally salvage the Earth, and generate some semblance of a human culture based on reverence for life. To some, however, it is seen primarily as an invective against the societal and governmental agents who were spearheading the destruction of the natural world and its human and nonhuman communities. Beyond these (complementary) attributes, the work was an eloquent herald and proponent of "bioregionalism," a term now in widespread use, which recognizes the innate value of all parts and aspects of a region, and seeks to look beyond politico-economic values in interactions with it. Snyder sees this "bioregional ethic" behind the poems as grounded above all in "a sense of place, of plants, soils, climactic cycles, community of beings, in one area [that] are all ancient ... necessary components of the information by which we actually live" (RW 139). The poems of *Turtle Island* anatomize, integrate and celebrate these "necessary components," as in the first stanza of "On San Gabriel Ridges"

> I dream of—
> soft, white, washable country
> clothes.
> woven zones.
> scats
> up here in the rocks;
> seeds, stickers, twigs, bits of grass
> on my belly, pressed designs — [*TI* 40].

or the compelling list in "Facts," which articulates with ruthless precision the fatal consumptiveness of modern American life in the 1970's, including:

> "The U.S. has 6 percent of the world's population; consumes the ⅓ energy annually consumed in the world. The U.S. consumes ⅓ of the world's annual meat" [*TI* 31].

Despite its seeming inescapability, Snyder never accepts the direness of his own anatomization, but restlessly and resourcefully strives for solutions, often found in THOREAUVIAN simplicity and engagement with the natural world, such as is evidenced in the deceptively simple observation that "Our primary source of food is the sun."

The collection also contains a host of well-known poems illustrating Snyder's earnest engagement with region, place, family, and daily life; among them, "The Bath," a celebration of bodies, life, and the "energy pathways that sustain life," and an acknowledgment of the power and necessity of the family — both the smaller family units that bring forth life and the greater family of beings that inform and sustain life. While bathing his son in their backwoods sauna, the poet reflects on the interconnectedness of the human body and the body of the earth:

> Washing Kai in the sauna,
> The kerosene lantern set on a box
>   outside the ground-level window
> Lights up the edge of the iron stove and the
>   washtub down on the slab
> Steaming air and crackle of waterdrops
>   brushed by on the pile of rocks on top
> He stands in warm water
>
> Is this our body?

Each stanza's common refrain, "Is this our body?," frames the speaker's search, not merely for the interconnections between our physical bodies as sexual, procreative beings, but for some understanding of the increasing troubled relationship between the ancient biological imperative of reproduction and the earth's ability to support the life that is created. After the bath, bodies washed, the interplay of the body of the family and the body of the earth, both life-giving mothers, begin to be personified as one:

> Clean, and rinsed, and sweating more, we stretch
>   out on the redwood benches hearts all beating
> Quiet to the simmer of the stove,
>   the scent of cedar
> And then turn over,
>   murmuring gossip of the grasses
>   talking firewood

The question echoing through the first half of the poem finally becomes an acknowledgment that the human body is inseparable from the body of the earth, and the question becomes a statement — a realization:

> This is our body. Drawn up crosslegged by the
>   flames
>   drinking icy water
>   hugging babies, kissing bellies,
> Laughing on the Great Earth
> Come out from the bath [*TI 12–14*].

True to its ultimately salvational and not merely diagnostic purpose, the collection concludes with a hard-won sense of hope in the face of the accelerating decline in the health of the earth and its communities. The penultimate poem of the collection, "For the Children" offers a fragile but enduring foundation for benignant change:

> The rising hills,
> the slopes,
> of statistics
> lie before us.
> The steep climb of everything, going up,
> up, as we all
> go down."

The foundation lies with the children, the future and the hope of all human communities, for a lasting conversion of our way of seeing and living on the earth:

> To climb these coming crests
> one word to you, to
> you and your children:
> *stay together*
> *learn the flowers*
> *go light.*

Turtle Island ends with the prose section "Plain Talk," which, as its title suggests, seeks to translate into easily accessible and discursive terms, the essential thrust of the verses preceding it. For example, its "Four Changes" outlines ways and means for human communities to improve in four major areas: population, pollution, consumption, and transformation. These four outlines, like "Plain Talk" as a whole — and indeed, the poetry that precedes it — seek to address, constructively and sustainably, the destruction and fragmentation that a rapidly maturing industrial economy typically has on ecosystems, human communities and entire regions of the earth. As a result, *Turtle Island*'s prose, although written in 1969, still stands as an inspiration and guide for coherent grassroots action to repair damage done to Earth's communities, and create a society based on compassion and respect. Snyder's masterpiece ultimately serves as a composite distillation of his mature life- and thought-practice, including his study of Zen Buddhism, and the Oriental and Occidental poetic traditions; it speaks from and *for* the often luminous places inhabited by — and at the same time inhabiting — its author. — Michael Sims

BIBLIOGRAPHY

Snyder, Gary. *The Real Work: Interviews and Talks 1964–1979*, New York: New Directions, 1980.
_____. *Turtle Island*, New York: New Directions, 1974.

Stegner, Wallace (1909–1993)

Referred to as the "reluctant conservationist" by one of his biographers (Fradkin), Wallace Stegner enjoyed a life and career that married his interests in writing, political action and the wilderness.

Stegner grew up in Saskatchewan, Canada, from 1914–1920, a period and a place that influenced his perspective on wilderness and land use. A graduate of the University of Iowa (M.A. 1932; Ph.D. 1935), he went on to teach English at Augustana College, the University of Utah, the University of Wisconsin, Harvard, and Stanford. Stegner, who taught at Stanford from 1945–1971, was founder and Director of its Creative Writing Program. There, his students included EDWARD ABBEY, Larry McMurtrey, WENDELL BERRY, and Ken Kesey.

Stegner's nonfiction work focused on Western figures such as John Wesley Powell, WILLA CATHER, Bret Harte, and Bernard DeVoto (who Stegner met at Harvard). His biography of John Wesley Powell, *Beyond the Hundredth Meridian* (1954), established him as a writer of environmental literature, alerting the public to the history of mistakes over western land use and water policy (Benson "Down" 36).

In his Pulitzer Prize–winning historical novel, *Angle of Repose* (1972), in which Easterners move West to make their fortune, the lack of water in the West is dramatized through the character Oliver Ward, a civil engineer whose task it is to build a canal to bring water to the high desert of Idaho. All three of his last books made the bestseller lists: *Crossing to Safety* (1987), *Collected Stories* (1990), and *WHERE THE BLUEBIRD SINGS TO THE LEMONADE SPRINGS: LIVING AND WRITING IN THE WEST* (1992).

According to his son Page, Stegner's "Wilderness Letter," addressed to the Wildland Research Center in 1960, has become "one of the central documents of the conservation movement" (30). The Letter makes an eloquent case for the "restorative value of wilderness," reminiscent of ALDO LEOPOLD's "The Land Ethic" and THOREAU's "Walking"; and it was instrumental in launching Stegner's public service career in 1961, as a special assistant to Stewart Udall, President Kennedy's Secretary of the Interior. From 1961–6, he served on the advisory board for the National Parks and Monuments, and from 1964–1968, he was on the governing board of the Sierra Club, serving at the same time as Ansel Adams. During the Reagan era, Stegner served on the Wilderness Society's Governing Council (1984).

Stegner wrote over 60 articles on conservation, and as a well-known author of fiction, he was able to get his conservation pieces published in more widespread publications. His essays appeared in such popular magazines as the *New Republic* ("Battle for the Wilderness," 1954) and *Sports Illustrated* ("We Are Destroying Our National Parks," 1955), which bridged the often damaging gap between academic and popular culture. In "We Are Destroying Our National Parks" (1955), he describes the paradox that exists in the very notion of a national park system: "The American people love their parks and threaten to trample them to death. The more successful the Park Service is in keeping a park wild and beautiful, the more people it will draw and the more it has to contend with a thundering herd." He argues that camping and other outdoor activities in the parks must be further regulated, and implores the average outdoor-loving citizen to understand that even though the kind of park preservation that he advocates will be expensive, the cost will be amply repaid in long-term conservationist benefits: "the money will produce returns of another kind: health and sanity and the profound and personal sense of belonging to something good and beautiful that cannot be measured in dollars. A primeval park offers values that are close to the values of religion." Stegner's influence endures, both in print and in the social imagination. At what would be his centennial, the *New York Times* published an article assessing his legacy and claiming that Stegner has "grown in stature" (Egan).— Sarah L. Dammeyer

BIBLIOGRAPHY

Egan, Timothy. "Stegner's Complaint." *New York Times*. 18 Feb 2009.
Steensma, Robert C. *Wallace Stegner's Salt Lake City*. Salt Lake City: University of Utah Press, 2007.
Stegner, Page (Ed.). *The Selected Letters of Wallace Stegner*. Berkeley, CA: Shoemaker Hoard, 2007.
Stegner, Wallace. "It All Began with Conservation," *Smithsonian* 21 (April 1990). 35–43.
_____. "We Are Destroying Our National Parks." *Sports Illustrated*. 13 June 1955. 28–9.

Where the Bluebird Sings to the Lemonade Springs: Living and Writing in the West, Wallace Stegner (1992)

Stegner's autobiographical collection speaks to the paradox that is the American spirit and its relationship to its land. The essays cover a vast and disparate array of topics and concerns, all broadly unified by Stegner's passionate and articulate sensibility; from the lasting impact that a landscape has on its inhabitants, and the effects of unsustainable uses of natural resources, especially water; to the need for sustainable healing of those overused resources; the power of human beings over the land and resources (both in the sense that knowledge may generate the power to combat abuse to the land, and in the sense that ignorance in the form of mythologies cause potentially irreparable destruction to a place); the aesthetics of landscape and the West's different approach to its resources, in response to the profound differences in its landscape; the effects of trying to fit nature into the rational agricultural model; the role of storytellers, mythologies, and dreams in the destruction of natural resources; and the special place that the dream of MANIFEST DESTINY has had in the destruction of the American West.

Despite his fears for the West he once knew, the West before dams and mass agriculture, in the "indigenous hopefulness" about which and with which he writes, Stegner believes that a few generations from now will witness means to both live on the land and restore it — a "compromise" (xxii). Even in this his last publication, Stegner himself represents the uninterrupted "western hope" that he has long chronicled (xxii).

In the introduction, Stegner brings his life and work full circle, back to his 1943 *Big Rock Candy Mountain*, whose title came from Harry McClintock's "The Big Rock Candy Mountain," a hobo ballad about the ever-giving West. Stegner's essays catalogue the riches of the American West and the lack of attention to sustainability that has characterized its use and settlement. He presents himself as one who knows well the "hope, energy, carelessness, and self-deception" about which he writes, because his father epitomized those qualities.

The essays of "Part I: Personal" focus on the way that he and his family have been shaped by place. These autobiographical sketches employ reflections on his growing up in the American West, to assess "borderland" life in general, with its often conflicting desires to control or destroy the wild, and to relish and revere it (8). Here he characterizes the "pillagers" and "settlers," and vividly recalls his own ambivalence toward the wild in a story about his trapped badger (9).

Reminiscent of the "hybrid" work of JOHN MUIR and JOHN BURROUGHS, as well as the later interdisciplinary writing of BARRY LOPEZ, "Part II: Habitat," the intellectual core of the book, approaches the land from both an aesthetic and scientific/biological perspective. In "Thoughts on a Dry Land," Stegner again differentiates, here between the land itself and the dream of what the land might be. He notes that *reports* of the West have profoundly influenced Americans' understanding — of the West and of itself— at least as much as firsthand seeing, and that people find it hard to change their ideas in light of new evidence. In "Variations on a Theme by Crèvecoeur," Stegner invokes ALDO LEOPOLD in discussing contrasting notions of "wilderness," distinguishing the West of the imagination from the reality of the West (101). He discusses cowboy mythology and other "folklore of the West" (103), decrying them but recognizing their great influence on the American imaginary.

He extends this examination to a broad critique of Eastern North Americans' "perceptual habit" (52), challenging them to develop new ways of knowing and seeing, finding a new aesthetic, partly in terms of scale, color, and form. Stegner quotes Clarence Dutton, stressing the "westernization of perceptions that has to happen before the West is beautiful to us" (53). Stegner explores a different but no less important fear in this section: that the adaptation will come too late. In "Living Dry," Stegner outlines a history of the West's rights and claims, chronicling land management practices and policy, including the role of the state and federal governments in water rights and the eventual involvement of the Supreme Court. He questions the mass movement westward to free land as a means of enhancing democracy (68) and introducing agriculture to the West in a direct challenge to the West's aridity.

Invoking authors as disparate as John Wesley Powell (66), Gertrude Stein (72) and William Least Heat Moon, he notes that aridity is anathema to Americans' search for plenty and impatience with restrictions, leaving but two options: adapt, or "engineer it [aridity] out of existence" (75). In "Striking the Rock," Stegner more specifically chronicles the history of water use and regulation in the West, critiquing the moral and aesthetic choices of settlers who treat the cultivation of the West as an ultimately "immoral" means of ownership and domination, even "an act of arrogance" (78)—a "sin of scale" (79). While not disparaging the notion of settlement completely, Stegner worries about the architectural incongruity of developments that demand massive qualities of water in the midst of the desert. In his criticism of dams, for example, Stegner assails the public's mistaken views, with a warning and call for the change in Americans' thoughts and behavior. At his most pessimistic, Stegner laments that the West is no longer a "geography of hope" (98).

In "Part III: Witnesses," Stegner's essays focus on writers and writing of the West, applying the intellectual critique of the second section to tease out salutary truth from deleterious falsehood.— Sarah L. Dammeyer

BIBLIOGRAPHY

Benson, Jackson J. "Evaluating the Environmentalist." *Down by the Lemonade Springs: Essays on Wallace Stegner.* Reno: University of Nevada Press, 2000.
_____. *Wallace Stegner: His Life and Work.* New York: Viking, 1996.
Fradkin, Philip L. *Wallace Stegner and the American West.* New York: Alfred A. Knopf, 2008.

Steinbeck, John (1902–1968)

Novelist, short story writer, journalist and Nobel Prize winner, John Steinbeck chronicled the struggles and aspirations of ordinary people with compassion and an abiding commitment to social justice. His subjects were migrant workers and striking fruit pickers, bus drivers, peasants, farmers, scientists and prostitutes, the homeless and dispossessed. Yet, although his 1939 masterpiece, THE GRAPES OF WRATH, would redefine the nation's moral and political compass as few works of fiction have, Steinbeck's novels are more than sociological studies or political tracts. Deeply ecological, his narratives seamlessly connect the social and biological landscapes of what has come to be called "Steinbeck Country," the hills, valleys, mountains, rivers, and coastlines of Central California. "Man," Steinbeck writes in THE LOG FROM THE SEA OF CORTEZ, "is related to the whole thing, related inextricably to all reality, known and unknowable" (217).

Born in Salinas, California, in 1902, the son of the County Treasurer and a former schoolteacher, Steinbeck rapidly developed an intimate knowledge of the coast and hill country of Central California. He supported himself from boyhood, working summers and weekends on nearby ranches. After graduating from Salinas High School in 1919, he attended Stanford University sporadically for six years, studying English, history, and biology, before leaving in 1925 to pursue a writing career in New York. Returning to California a year later, he struggled for a decade to master his craft with little artistic or financial recognition. *Tortilla Flat* (1935), a comic novel of life among the paisanos of Monterey, marked his first popular and critical success. It was rapidly followed, however, by *In Dubious Battle, Of Mice and Men, The Long Valley,* and *The Grapes of Wrath,* a series of powerful fictions drawn from his first hand experience of the lives and struggles of agricultural laborers in the fields and orchards of California. While these novels remain his greatest achievement, Steinbeck continued for another three decades to be one of the most important chroniclers of the American scene, writing fiction (*Cannery Row, The Pearl, East of Eden*), journalism (*Once There Was a War, A Russian Journal, Travels with Charley*), and natural history (*The Log from the Sea of Cortez*). He was awarded the Nobel Prize for Literature in 1962.

In 1930 Steinbeck met marine biologist Ed Ricketts, beginning a close friendship and intellectual collaboration that would last until Ricketts's death in 1948. Ricketts's biological laboratory, located on Monterey's Cannery Row, was a magnet for artists, writers, scientists, and the area's bohemian population, a place where friends gathered for food, drink, music, and the pursuit of intellectual passions that ranged from marine biology to poetry and Asian philosophy. Ricketts had done his undergraduate work at the University of Chicago under W. C. Allee, a pioneer ecologist who studied the effects of environmental stimuli on cooperative group behavior among invertebrates. As Steinbeck and Ricketts surveyed the tide pools of the California coast in the early 1930s, they theorized about similar socio-biological patterns in humans, and together explored what they came to call "non-teleological thinking," which replaces traditional cause-effect logic with a Zen-like acceptance of "is." Their wide-ranging discussions profoundly influenced the young novelist. In the spring of 1940, using royalties from the recently published *The Grapes of Wrath*, Steinbeck and Ricketts rented a boat, hired a crew, and explored the intertidal habitats of the Gulf of California, resulting in *The Log from the Sea of Cortez* (1951). Ricketts himself became the inspiration for some of Steinbeck's most memorable characters: Doc in *Cannery Row* (1945) and *Sweet Thursday* (1954), Doc Burton in *In Dubious Battle* (1936), and Casy in *The Grapes of Wrath* (1939), whose connection to nature is drawn heavily from Ricketts's holistic philosophy. "There was the hills, an' there was me, an we wasn't separate no more," Casy tells Tom Joad. "We was one thing. An' there was me an' the hills an' there was the stars an' the black sky, an we was all one thing. An' that one thing was holy" (*Grapes of Wrath* 83).

Throughout his career, Steinbeck's novels would examine the interconnectedness of human culture and the natural world. In *The Pearl* (1956) the small Mexican fishing community that serves as the novel's setting is an organic whole, coexisting with other communities in the natural world and subject to the same natural laws. It is "a thing like a colonial animal," with its own nervous system and its own emotional life (*Pearl* 27). Like any living organism, the town's "pulse and vibrating nerves" (27) react to external stimuli, and its interconnected ganglia transmit information. In *Cannery Row* (1945) the community of marginalized outcasts and eccentrics is introduced by a prayer to "Our Father who art in Nature" (15), and framed by a detailed description of life in the Great Tide Pool off Pacific Grove. In *The Grapes of Wrath* the Joad's westward journey is equally patterned on biological models.

Beyond their ecological emphasis on human communities as interconnected habitats, Steinbeck's narratives exhibit a strong land ethic and environmental awareness. *The Grapes of Wrath* chronicles an environmental disaster. It begins in drought and ends in flood, in between exploring the impact of a largely man-made catastrophe in ways that anticipate our current political and environmental concerns. *The Log from the Sea of Cortez* warned of the coming environmental impact of increased development and industrialized fishing practices on the Gulf of California; and in his last book, *America and Americans* (1966), Steinbeck decries how "our rivers are poisoned by reckless dumping of sewage and toxic wastes, the air of our cities is filthy and dangerous to breathe from the belching of coal, coke, oil, and gasoline" (144). He finds hope, nevertheless, in his sense of America's increased outrage over continued environmental mismanagement. By his death in December 1968, a new ecological and environmental consciousness was emerging in America, and few writers contributed more to that spiritual and scientific evolution than Steinbeck himself. — Michael Zeitler

BIBLIOGRAPHY

Astro, Richard. *John Steinbeck and Edward F. Ricketts: The Shaping of a Novelist*. Minneapolis: University of Minnesota Press, 1973.

Beegel, Susan F., Susan Shillinglaw, and Wesley N. Tiffany (Eds.) *Steinbeck and the Environment: Interdisciplinary Approaches*. Tuscaloosa: University of Alabama Press, 1997.

Benson, Jackson. *The Adventures of John Steinbeck, Writer*. New York: Penguin Books, 1990.

Owens, Louis. *America and Americans*. New York: Viking Press, 1966.

_____. *Cannery Row*. New York: Viking Press, 1945.

_____. *The Grapes of Wrath: Text and Criticism*. Peter Lisca and Kevin Hearle, Eds. New York: Penguin Books, 1997.

_____. *John Steinbeck's Re-Vision of America*. Athens: University of Georgia Press, 1985.

_____. *The Log from the Sea of Cortez*. New York: Viking Press, 1962.

_____. *The Pearl*. New York: Bantam, 1956.

The Grapes of Wrath, John Steinbeck (1939)

The Grapes of Wrath, John Steinbeck's epic Pulitzer Prize winning novel of the Great Depression, tells the story of the Joads, once independent farmers but now Dustbowl refugees, migrant laborers on the road to California after the bank forecloses on their Oklahoma farm. Their story translates the epic myth of the Western frontier, the settler's struggle for a piece of land and a share of the American Dream, into the harsh economic, social, and political realities of 1930s America. Controversial, even inflammatory, on its initial publication in 1939, *The Grapes of Wrath* was a monumental bestseller despite being banned in countless libraries, publically burned in Bakersfield, California, and denounced as communistic propaganda in the United States Senate. Seventy years later it continues to sell hundreds of thousands of copies a year in almost every major language in the world.

With its radically progressive social agenda *The Grapes of Wrath* permanently redefined the nation's moral and political center as few works of fiction ever have. It critiqued market capitalism, arguing that Americans should not go hungry when farms produce abundant food or live without homes when foreclosed houses stand vacant. It documented abuses of migrant workers in California's fields and orchards, and supported labor's right to organize for a fair, living wage. It showed the importance of humanitarian relief programs and safety nets for the old, the frail, children, the homeless, and the unemployed, and argued that the rule of law should give as fair a deal to the powerless as to the well to do.

In addition to its progressive social agenda, Steinbeck's novel is deeply ecological in its analysis, detailing the consequences of a largely man-made environmental disaster, and suggesting the then radical notion that government land-use policy should not be solely under the control of corporations. *The Grapes of Wrath* also prefigures by half a century many of today's most important ecological concepts. Like all of Steinbeck's books, it emphasizes the interdependence of all life; the idea, as he puts it in THE LOG FROM THE SEA OF CORTEZ, that "man is related to the whole thing, related inextricably to all reality, known and unknown" (*Log* 217). Steinbeck drew much of the novel's philosophical orientation from his long time friend and intellectual collaborator, the marine biologist Ed Ricketts, whose pioneering study of Pacific coast intertidal habitats, *Between Pacific Tides*, had just been published. Preacher Casy's emphasis on the interconnectedness of human culture and the natural world draws its inspiration from Ricketts's holistic philosophy. "There was the hills, an' there was me, an' we wasn't separate no more," Casy tells Tom. "We was one thing. An' there was me an' the hills an' there was the stars an' the black sky, an we was all one thing. An' that one thing was holy" (*Grapes of Wrath* 83).

The Grapes of Wrath also addresses what Harvard biologist EDWARD O. WILSON identifies in his 1984 memoir, *Biophilia*, as the human need to connect emotionally with other species, a need denied by science's long-standing taboo against "subjectivity" in its reporting. For Wilson the artist's narrative subjectivity can "re-enchant" the natural world — a necessary step toward changing human-environmental interactions. "It is time," he wrote, echoing not only Steinbeck, but ALDO LEOPOLD's Land Ethic, "to invent moral reasoning of a new and more powerful kind, to look at the very roots of motivation and understand why, in what circumstances and on which

occasions we cherish and protect life" (*Biophilia* 138–39). Steinbeck directly politicizes these scientific "objective" and personal "subjective" ways of seeing the environment. For the banks, the Oklahoma land is an economic investment, fueled by non-farming speculators and government wheat subsidies, causing a frenzy of plowing-under the grasslands until the price dropped out and the soil eroded:

> The bank — the monster has to have profits all the time. It can't wait. It'll die. No, taxes go on. When the monster stops growing, it dies. It can't stay one size.... The tenant system won't work any more. One man and a tractor can take the place of twelve or fourteen families. Pay him a wage and take all the crop. We have to do it.
> But you'll kill the land with cotton.
> We know. We've got to take cotton quick before the land dies [35].

Steinbeck contrasts this view of the land with how a farmer knows that same land: as memory, as narrative, as community. As farmer Muley tells Tom and Casy, "the place where folks live is them folks" (55). Humans are inseparable from the environment they inhabit because they have invested it with meaning, because their minds are filled with its stories. The land is enchanted, filled with our ghosts, our culture, our history, and to destroy it is to destroy something human about ourselves. The whole, Steinbeck reminds us, echoing Wilson, is more than the sum of the parts:

> ... nitrates are not the land, nor phosphate; and the length of fiber in the cotton is not the land. Carbon is not the man, nor salt nor water, nor calcium. He is all these, but he is much more; and the land is so much more than its analysis. The man who is more than his chemistry, walking on the earth, turning his plow point for a stone, dropping his handles to slide over an outcropping, kneeling in the earth to eat his lunch, that man who is more than his elements knows that the land is more than its analysis. But the machine man, driving a dead tractor on land he does not know or love, understands only chemistry, and he is contemptuous of the land and himself [117].

Another way this difference between dead objectivity and living subjectivity manifests itself is in relation to animals — the turtle Tom picks up for the kids and then lets go when they leave for California, the Joad dogs, the dog killed by the speeding car of a rich tourist, the rabbits and snakes that repopulate the abandoned farms, or the horses no longer needed behind the plows:

> And when a horse stops work and goes into the barn there is a life and a vitality left, there is a

breathing and a warmth, and the feet shift on the straw, and the jaws clamp on the hay, and the ears and the eyes are alive. There is a warmth of life in the barn, and the heat and smell of life. But when the motor of a tractor stops, it is as dead as the ore it came from. The heat goes out of it like the living heat that leaves a corpse [117].

Yet even as their houses and possessions are being tractored under, Steinbeck's migrants adapt and survive. Here, too, the novel's holistic and organic descriptions of communities interacting with and adapting to their immediate surroundings are patterned on biological models. Even before the Joads leave Oklahoma, Steinbeck metaphorically roots the coming diaspora in biology, the struggle for survival, and the reproduction of species:

The concrete highway was edged with a mat of tangled, broken dry grass, and the heads were heavy with oat beards to catch on a dog's coat, and foxtails to tangle in a horse's fetlocks, and clover burrs to fasten in sheep's wool; sleeping life waiting to be dispersed, every seed armed with an appliance of dispersal, twisting darts and parachutes for the wind, little spears and balls of tiny thorns, and all waiting for animals and for the wind, for a man's trouser cuff or the hem of a woman's skirt, all passive, but armed with the appliances of activity [18].

So, a pregnant Rose of Sharon climbs up on the old Hudson truck, attaching herself on top like the clover burrs and thistles to better the chances of her seed's survival.

As the migrants push westward along Route 66, the shift from the personal and individual "I" to the collective and communal "we" is also given a biological metaphor: "This is the zygote. For here 'I lost my land' is changed; a cell is split and from its splitting grows 'We lost our land'" (152). A similar metaphorical use of biology occurs in Chapter 17, again illustrating the collective response to a perceived threat: "In the daylight," Steinbeck writes, "they scuttled like bugs to the westward, and as the dark caught them, they clustered like bugs near to shelter and to water.... They huddled together, they talked together; they shared their lives, their food, and the things they hoped for in the new country" (194). This theme runs throughout Steinbeck's novel. "Every night a world created," described with the same sensitivity and reverence for detail that he and Ricketts had once brought to the Pacific tide pools — a habitat of water, a river bank, a spring, an unguarded faucet, some flat land to pitch tents, a little brush to build a fire, a garbage dump to scavenge supplies, but most importantly, the interconnected biological and human communities that bind us together.— Michael Zeitler

BIBLIOGRAPHY

Astro, Richard. *John Steinbeck and Edward F. Ricketts: The Shaping of a Novelist.* Minneapolis: University of Minnesota Press, 1973.
Beegel, Susan F., Susan Shillinglaw, and Wesley N. Tiffany (Eds.) *Steinbeck and the Environment: Interdisciplinary Approaches.* Tuscaloosa: University of Alabama Press, 1997.
Benson, Jackson. *The Adventures of John Steinbeck, Writer.* New York: Penguin Books, 1990.
Owens, Louis. *The Grapes of Wrath: Trouble in the Promised Land.* Boston: Twayne, 1989.
Steinbeck, John. *The Grapes of Wrath: Text and Criticism.* Peter Lisca and Kevin Hearle, Eds. New York: Penguin Books, 1997.
_____. *The Log from the Sea of Cortez.* New York, Viking Press, 1962.
_____. *Working Days: The Journals of The Grapes of Wrath.* Robert De Mott, Ed. New York: Viking Press, 1989.
Wilson, Edward O. *Biophilia.* Cambridge, MA: Harvard University Press, 1984.

The Log from the Sea of Cortez, John Steinbeck (1951)

Part travelogue, part scientific survey, and part metaphysical speculation, John Steinbeck's *The Log from the Sea of Cortez* recounts the author's 1940 scientific expedition to the Gulf of California with his friend, marine biologist Ed Ricketts. The resulting collaborative study, listing dual authorship, was first published in 1941 as *Sea of Cortez: A Leisurely Journal of Travel and Research.* A decade later, after Ricketts's death, Steinbeck republished the narrative portion of the text, together with a lengthy biographical portrait of Ricketts, under the current title. Although Steinbeck made extensive use of Ricketts's notes and unpublished essays in preparing the text, Ricketts was given no authorial recognition. Nevertheless, *The Log from the Sea of Cortez* is philosophically as much Ricketts's as Steinbeck's. A classic of ecological analysis, *The Log* represents an experiment in what Ricketts and Steinbeck call "non-teleological thinking" (*Log* 132), which replaces traditional cause-effect logic with a Zen-like acceptance of "is." "Man," Steinbeck writes, "is related to the whole thing, related inextricably to all reality, known and unknowable" (*Log* 217).

For Ricketts *The Sea of Cortez* represented the second volume in his projected three-part study of Pacific Coast marine life, along with the recently published *Between Pacific Tides* and his in-progress work on *The Outer Shores,* a study of the intertidal habitats of British Columbia and Alaska. For Steinbeck the six-week Gulf of California expedition was an escape from the sudden celebrity and political controversy surrounding the phenomenal success of THE GRAPES OF WRATH (1939). It was also an opportunity for him to continue the philosophical and biological speculations he and Ricketts had been discussing since their first meeting in 1930. Steinbeck had studied marine biology at Stanford University in the 1920s and Ricketts had done his undergraduate work at the University of Chicago under W.C. Allee, an early and seminal ecologist who studied the effects of environmental stimuli on cooperative group behavior among invertebrates. As Steinbeck and Ricketts explored the intertidal habitats of the California coast, the two friends theorized about similar ecological relationships in humans, ideas that profoundly influenced the young novelist. Throughout his early fiction, Steinbeck would explore a variety of ecological communities, from oyster beds to mountain streams, from the Great Plains to Mexican fishing villages, from orchards to ranches to migrant labor camps. Taken together, a pattern emerges that emphasizes the interconnectedness of all things; the significance of memory in binding us one to another, to nature and the past; and the evolutionary importance of human culture, the community without which we cannot survive. "The impulse which drives one man to poetry," he writes, "will send another man into the tide pools and force him to try to report what he finds there" (*Log* 1). For Steinbeck, both *The Grapes of Wrath* and *The Log from the Sea of Cortez* were holistic attempts to see the "ecological" interconnectedness of human culture and the natural world.

In March 1940 Steinbeck and Ricketts hired a 75-foot Monterey sardine purse seiner, *The Western Flyer*, and a four-person crew. Outfitted with collecting equipment, a makeshift lab, and a small library of scientific texts, *The Western Flyer* set sail for the Gulf of California. Their goal, Steinbeck writes, was "to observe the distribution of invertebrates, to see and to record their kinds and numbers, how they lived together, what they ate, and how they reproduced.... We wanted to see everything our eyes would accommodate, to think what we could, and, out of our seeing and thinking, to build some kind of structure in modeled imitation of the observed reality" (*Log* 2). Yet, to record the "observed reality," Steinbeck felt he must go beyond the objectivity of what passes professionally for scientific truth. To catalogue the Mexican Sierra fish's dorsal fin spikes according to the nomenclature of the classification charts, he notes, is to dissect a dead fish in a formalin solution. It is not, he writes, "the only, even the most important truth about the fish." A true knowledge of the fish must also be experiential and interactive:

> But if the sierra strikes hard on the line so that
> our hands are burned, if the fish sounds and
> nearly escapes and finally comes in over the rail,

his colors pulsing and his tail beating the air, a whole new relationship comes into being — an entity which is more than the sum of the fish plus the fisherman" [*Log* 2].

Any journey, like any book, Steinbeck observes, takes on a life of its own, a "characteristic design" (*Log* 84). During the day, the crew collected and catalogued specimens along the Gulf's rocky shores, open coasts, bays, estuaries, and reefs. They discovered snails, crabs, sea worms, sea hares, starfish, octopi, mussels, anemones, shrimp, sponges, limpets; in all, 550 species, of which about 10 percent proved to be new. They found an "exuberant fierceness" in the rocky shore littoral at Cabo San Lucas, where the "ferocious survival quotient excites us and makes us feel good" (*Log* 58). Between collecting excursions, they talked with harbor officials, native fishermen, farmers, and bar patrons in La Paz, Cabo San Lucas, and Guaymas. At night, they "talked and speculated, talked and drank beer" (*Log* 84). To Steinbeck, each venue, whether tide pool, harbor, bar, or boat, was a habitat, an ecosystem, a part of the mosaic. "Species," Steinbeck writes, "are only commas in a sentence ... one merges into another, groups melt into ecological groups until the time when what we think of as life meets and enters what we think of as non-life: barnacle and rock, rock and earth, earth and tree, tree and rain and air" (*Log* 216).

The concept of non-teleological thinking, originating first in Ricketts's unpublished essays (later published in Hedgpeth's *The Outer Shores*) and further developed in collaboration with Steinbeck, is at the philosophical center of *The Log from the Sea of Cortez*. Steinbeck's fullest discussion of the concept is contained in what has come to be called the *Log*'s "Easter Sunday Sermon." Aristotelian causality, he argues, is merely a label for our partial and biased mental reconstructions, a fragmentary part of the whole. "The whole picture is portrayed by *is*, the deepest word of deep ultimate reality, not shallow or partial as reasons are, but deeper and participating, possibly encompassing the Oriental concept of *being*" (*Log* 151). In the spirit of WHITMAN and EMERSON, Steinbeck ends his Easter sermon on the sandy beach at La Paz with a transcendent, even spiritual, connection to the natural world: "Quality of sunlight, blueness and smoothness of water, boat engines, and ourselves were all parts of a larger whole and we could begin to feel its nature but not its size" (*Log* 151).

Like many sermons, however, Steinbeck's meditation carries with it a warning. The "iron teleologies" of modern industrial society, he implies, separate us from the natural world and "twist the tide pools and the stars into the pattern" (*Log* 87). The world, psychologically disconnected, "is furrowed and cut, torn and blasted by man. Its flora has been stripped away and changed; its mountains torn down by man; its flat lands littered by the debris of his living" (*Log* 87). Across the harbor, new hotels are under construction (the result of a new airport), and a Japanese shrimp fishing vessel, a huge floating processing plant, is radically altering both the Gulf's ecology and the native fishing economy even before Ricketts and Steinbeck can record it.— Michael Zeitler

BIBLIOGRAPHY

Astro, Richard. *John Steinbeck and Edward F. Ricketts: The Shaping of a Novelist.* Minneapolis: University of Minnesota Press, 1973.
Beegel, Susan F., Susan Shillinglaw, and Wesley N. Tiffany (Eds.) *Steinbeck and the Environment: Interdisciplinary Approaches.* Tuscaloosa: University of Alabama Press, 1997.
Benson, Jackson. *The Adventures of John Steinbeck, Writer.* New York: Penguin Books, 1990.
Hedgpeth, Joel W. ed. *The Outer Shores* (2 vols.) Eureka, California: Mad River Press, 1978.
Parini, Jay. *John Steinbeck: A Biography.* New York: Random House, 1997.
Steinbeck, John. *The Log from the Sea of Cortez.* New York: Viking, 1962.

Stevens, Wallace (1879–1955)

Wallace Stevens was born in Reading, Pennsylvania in 1879. After studying at Harvard from 1987 to 1900, and briefly pursuing journalism in Manhattan, he chose an unorthodox career for a poet: insurance law. By 1934 he would be a vice-president at the Hartford Accident and Indemnity Corporation, and the income from this job allowed him to settle in the wealthy suburb of West Hartford, Connecticut, where he lived until his death in 1955. Stevens' writing garnered attention slowly, beginning in 1914 when the journal *Poetry* published a few pieces; his first book, *Harmonium*, appeared in 1923, received mixed reviews, and sold poorly, although Marianne Moore was an early supporter. Throughout the 1930s and 1940s, Stevens published increasing quantities of work in both short and long form (especially his acclaimed 1942 *Notes Toward a Supreme Fiction*), and his reputation blossomed. *Auroras of Autumn* won the National Book Award in 1951, as did his *Collected Poems* in 1954 (the latter also received a Pulitzer). In addition to his poetry, Stevens published a collection of critical essays, *The Necessary Angel* (1951), and in 1966 a large posthumous selection of his fascinating *Letters* appeared.

For several decades after his death, most critics and readers assumed Stevens' writing was primarily devoted to abstract philosophical speculation, rather than contemporary history or day-to-day experience.

More recently, however, scholars such as James Longenbach and Gyorgyi Voros have demonstrated that, for all its density and difficulty, his poetry is informed by the events of his lifetime, including World War II and the spread of technology-intensive industrial capitalism. In her pioneering work, Voros argues that ecology provides a framework for understanding his poetics, both as a literal point of reference (given his passionate interest in natural phenomena such as weather, plants, and animals) and as an analogue to his fundamental belief that texts, selves, and the encompassing physical world are dynamic, interconnected webs of phenomena: he "offered an affirmative, frequently joyful vision as an alternative to the twentieth century's increasing objectification of Nature and alienation from it" (Voros 3). Or as Stevens himself puts it, he aimed to create his version of "the great poem of the earth [that] remains to be written" ("Imagination as Value," *NA* 142).

Like the work of "inhumanist," ROBINSON JEFFERS, Stevens' poetry rejects the idea that humans, and the human, are the most important elements in the universe, a misconception that Stevens traces to both Judeo-Christian religion and Enlightenment humanism. While he associates the latter with "the gaunt world of the reason" ("The Figure of the Youth as Virile Poet," *NA* 58), the former receives still more of his disdain. In the early poem "Sunday Morning," for example, a woman plays hooky from church and decides that "Divinity must live within herself" rather than in some transcendent realm; she chooses instead to savor immediate events and sensual objects such as fruit, weather cycles, birds, and sunlight. At the same time, however, Stevens highlights the natural environment's amorality and fundamental indifference to humanity: as the speaker of "The Snow Man" observes, "One must have a mind of winter" in order to see "Nothing that is not there and the nothing that is" (*CP* 9–10). In a world of great beauty but no gods, poetry serves as a "supreme fiction," a comforting spiritual resource for human beings faced with existential loneliness. Constructing this fiction entails sensitivity toward one's physical environment. Perhaps Stevens' finest formulation of this idea comes in *Notes Toward a Supreme Fiction*: "From this the poem springs: that we live in a place / That is not our own and, much more, not ourselves / And hard it is in spite of blazoned days" (*CP* 383). Anticipating what LAWRENCE BUELL argues is a fundamental trait of environmentally oriented literature (Buell 7–8), Stevens treats the nonhuman world as valuable in its own right, not simply a resource for humans to consume. That said, however, human happiness requires us to make imaginative use of nature as we encounter it. Only by forming what "An Ordinary Evening in

New Haven" calls "imaginative transcripts" (*CP* 479) of the world can we dwell contentedly in it. These guiding texts mark "The difference that we make in what we see / And our memorials of that difference" ("Description Without Place," *CP* 344).

Critics such as Angus Fletcher and Dorothy Nielsen contend that a truly "ecologized" poetics would frame both human selves and literary texts as entities open to the dynamics of nature, rather than closed systems detachedly observing the world. Stevens endorses this kind of interconnectivity. In "The Planet on the Table," a poem is an environmental conduit: the poet's "self and the sun were one / And his poems, although makings of his self, / Were no less makings of the sun" (*CP* 532). Likewise, the speaker of "Yellow Afternoon" declares, "It was in the earth only / That he was at the bottom of things / And of himself," and realizes that "one loves that / Of which one is a part as in a unity" (*CP* 236)

Further, in his essays Stevens theorizes *poesis* itself as an interchange between the "imagination" and "reality." As he uses these terms, the former denotes the inherent human impulse, exemplified by poetry, to rearrange the world we experience according to our visions of what is necessary for a good life, while the latter is that world itself, indifferent but still captivating. There is a "universal interdependence" between the two, not a stark divide, he writes in the essay "The Noble Rider and the Sound of Words" (*NA* 24). Stevens contends that as a poet, "nature [is that] which I desire to reduce: master, subjugate, acquire complete control over and use freely for my own purpose, as poet" (*L* 790), but nonetheless imagination literally cannot function without the surrounding world — it "loses vitality as it ceases to adhere to what is real" and "has the strength of reality or none at all" ("Noble Rider," *NA* 6–7). This is the crux of the meditation in "Study of Two Pears": "The pears are not seen / As the observer wills" (*CP* 197). By striking a balance between the two forces, a writer creates what "The Bouquet" (*CP* 448) calls "medium nature," a text composed of equal parts human meditation and environmental input.

"Medium nature" is also a good way to describe the domesticated, cultivated environments Stevens frequently depicts. Unlike many canonical environmental poets, such as GARY SNYDER and Robinson Jeffers, he almost never writes about wilderness, and when he does, as in "Anecdote of the Jar" (*CP* 76), it is something that is fading: the jar "made the slovenly wilderness / Surround that hill. / / The wilderness rose up to it, / And sprawled around, no longer wild." He instead portrays the kinds of spaces and phenomena a prosperous suburbanite who liked horticulture, collected art, and took vacations in Key West would be familiar with: parks, still-life botanical paintings, gardens, the local climate and weather of Connecticut, fruit, tropical beaches, and common animals like those that inhabit his famous "Thirteen Ways of Looking at a Blackbird" (*CP* 92–95). Nor is he a didactic writer; Stevens' sensitivity toward nature did not engender what we would now call "environmentalist" claims, because he was writing before modern American eco-activism became a political force in the 1960s. Nevertheless, he offers a way of looking at the world — with wonder and humility — that accords with the spiritual attachments and policy priorities of environmentalists, even though it does not anticipate their public rhetoric.

As Stevens sees it, life without divine certainties is often lonely, but it is not necessarily unpleasant, thanks in large part to the relationships with our surroundings that poetry helps us form. The poet's "role, in short, is to help people live their lives" by capturing their attention until "his imagination become[s] the light in the minds of others," Stevens argues in "The Noble Rider and the Sound of Words" (*NA* 29). He has faith in what the philosopher Edmund Husserl calls the *lebenswelt* ('life-world'), which is the shared physical space of all subjective experience — in other words, this felt earth. "On the Road Home" (*CP* 203) stages this idea, asserting that although people construct their own forms of meaning ("There are many truths / But they are not parts of a truth"), all construction takes place on public ground: "It was at that time, that the silence was largest / And longest, the night was roundest, / The fragrance of the autumn warmest, / Closest and strongest." While we must survive without the supernatural, and accept that full knowledge of other human minds will always elude us, there still remains "the honey of the common summer" ("Esthétique du Mal," *CP* 316). — Ryan Boyd

BIBLIOGRAPHY

Buell, Lawrence. *The Environmental Imagination: Thoreau, Nature Writing, and the Formation of American Culture.* Cambridge, MA: Belknap, 1995.

Fletcher, Angus. *A New Theory for American Poetry: Democracy, the Environment, and the Future of Imagination.* Cambridge, MA: Harvard University Press, 2004.

Longenbach, James. *Wallace Stevens: The Plain Sense of Things.* Oxford and New York: Oxford University Press, 1991.

Nielsen, Dorothy M. "Ecology, Feminism, and Postmodern Lyric Subjects." *New Definitions of Lyric: Theory, Technology, and Culture.* Ed. Mark Jeffreys. New York and London: Garland, 1998. 127–149.

Stevens, Wallace. *The Collected Poems of Wallace Stevens* [*CP*]. New York: Alfred A. Knopf, 1954.

_____. "The Figure of the Youth as Virile Poet." *Necessary Angel.* 39–67.

_____. "Imagination as Value." *Necessary Angel.* 130–156.

_____. *Letters of Wallace Stevens* [*L*]. Ed. Holly Stevens. Berkeley, Los Angeles, and London: University of California Press, 1966.

_____. "The Noble Rider and the Sound of Words." *The Necessary Angel: Essays on Reality and the Imagination* [*NA*]. New York: Vintage, 1951. 3–36.

Voros, Gyorgyi. *Notations of the Wild: Ecology in the Poetry of Wallace Stevens.* Iowa City: University of Iowa Press, 1997.

Stratton-Porter, Gene (1863–1924)

Gene Stratton-Porter is Indiana's most famous nature photographer, environmentalist, and novelist. She worked to preserve and protect the Limberlost swamp, a rainforest of more than 25,000 acres that once covered Northeast Indiana (Finney). Before the swamp dried up due to logging, oil drilling, and corn monoculture, Stratton-Porter recorded its flora and fauna in photographs, in novels, and by transplanting thousands of plant species facing extinction to land she bought and deeded to the state in Rome City, Indiana.

Stratton-Porter grew up on an Indiana farm, where she embraced the spirit and freedom of pioneer life. This gave her a comfort and confidence in the outdoors possessed by decreasing numbers of women in her day. Stratton-Porter wanted to share her love of nature, plants, animals, and vigorous activity with other women, and with the increasingly urbanized world around her. Photography provided her first means to do so.

In 1895, Stratton-Porter received a new camera. Since she loved to wander into the nearby Limberlost swamp, she began to take photographs there. JOHN JAMES AUDUBON, the most prominent name in bird-species cataloging to this point, killed his specimens and drew them stuffed. Stratton-Porter wanted to document animal behavior and surroundings, and felt live images conveyed a more accurate and realistic portrait than did paintings. Therefore, Stratton-Porter lugged her heavy camera and equipment far into the swamp, to spots where she had seen birds or moths, and waited patiently (Long, 144). Often she waited for days, in buggy, muddy and hot conditions, to get the perfect print. Many of these prints survive, and they are remarkable both for their artistry and naturalism. As a result of these strengths, Stratton-Porter sold many photographs to nature magazines, and became a regular photographer for *Outing* and *Recreation* (Long 148, 162).

While in the swamp for these extended periods, Stratton-Porter noticed how vulnerable the swamp was, and how quickly it was being destroyed. She sought attention and protection for this environment, and realized that photos and factual articles were not reaching a wide enough audience to achieve this. In the media culture of her day, the way to generate an audience was through novels, so Stratton-Porter began producing them, and between 1909 and 1924, she sold a book a minute; at the time of her death, between eight and nine million copies of her books had been sold (Mott 219).

Representative of both her style and thematic inclinations, *Freckles*, published in 1904, tells the story of the swamp from the perspective of a boy who works there. Hired to patrol the logging roads to protect them from poachers, Freckles falls in love with the environment, and describes it in vivid, naturalistic detail, humanizing the ecosystem by presenting it through a child's eyes. Freckles befriends a black vulture "family," and comes to love each tree, moaning in pain as it is cut down. The novel thus blends scientific information with a preservationist message and a sentimental, intimate story. This novelistic strategy of Stratton-Porter's ultimately brought worldwide attention to the Limberlost area and its needs.

Stratton-Porter then published *A Girl of the Limberlost* in 1909, which tells the coming-of-age story of Elnora Comstock, who was raised in the swamp and is in love with its beauties. Elnora wanders the swamp constantly, learning about moths and collecting rare specimens. Again, intriguing information about moth and bird behavior, and an understanding of the environment as a system which must remain intact if it is to survive at all, are deftly interwoven with an unfolding human drama, which makes them more compelling still. Stratton-Porter's outreach strategy worked almost too well, since her reading public swarmed to the swamp to see and admire it for themselves, and these crowds ironically increased the pressure on this dying ecosystem. Ultimately, Stratton-Porter could not compete with industrialization, and the swamp was virtually eliminated by 1913 (Weinhardt).

Nevertheless, and emblematic of the best regional environmental literature, Stratton-Porter's work had increased consciousness about this area, about the individual's role in preserving it, and about the environmental price of "progress." A very large reading public had learned extensively about birds, moths, trees, and herbs, almost without knowing they were learning. Stratton-Porter's books are still in print, and still popular, though with a smaller audience. With the profit from her book sales, Stratton-Porter brought property in Rome City, Indiana, and single-handedly transplanted 3,000 species there (Finney). Many of these survive exclusively because of her efforts. Two State Historic Sites in Indiana commemorate her life and work.

Stratton-Porter was a bold and iconoclastic woman, who continued to be a pioneer throughout her life. After her move to Rome City, she again transplanted herself to Southern California, where she was becoming as enthusiastically acquainted with its wild desert ecosystem when she was killed in a car crash. She had already begun the process of turning her most popular books into movies, again adapting to new opportunities for spreading her preservationist message. Ultimately, she is perhaps most worth remembering both as an environmental advocate, and as an innovator in communicating environmental messages to a wide audience.—Anne Balay

BIBLIOGRAPHY

Finney, Jan Dearmin. *Gene Stratton-Porter The Natural Wonder; Surviving Photographs of The Great Limberlost Swamp by Gene Stratton-Porter*. Mattituck, NY: Amereon, 1983.

Long, Judith Reick. *Gene Stratton-Porter: Novelist and Naturalist*. Indianapolis: Indiana State Historical Society, 1990.

Stratton-Porter, Gene. *Freckles*. New York: Grosset, 1904.

_____. *A Girl of the Limberlost*. New York: Grosset, 1909.

Thaxter, Celia Laighton (1835–1894)

In her late teens Celia Laighton Thaxter was dubbed a "pretty little Miranda" by NATHANIEL HAWTHORNE for her close association with the Isles of Shoals, a small group of islands off the coast of Maine and New Hampshire. Her devotion to these islands indeed motivated virtually all of her literary work, including two collections of poems and two works of nonfiction, AMONG THE ISLES OF SHOALS (1873) and *An Island Garden* (1894).

Thaxter lived on the Isles of Shoals for most of her childhood. Her parents' successful inn-keeping ventures led to early interactions with famous guests, including John Greenleaf Whittier (who would in later life become her close friend), Richard Dana, Jr., then–Senator Franklin Pierce, and NATHANIEL HAWTHORNE. At the age of 16 she married Levi Thaxter, who had been her tutor and her father's business partner; but this marriage would prove an unhappy one, as Levi's health and temperament rejected the climate and isolation of the Isles while Thaxter's devotion to her family and childhood home kept her wedded to them. In later years the couple would live apart—Thaxter on Appledore, Levi in Massachusetts or Maine—but their divergent convictions about where to live plagued them from the beginning of their relationship.

Thaxter's first published poem, "Land-locked," depicts her anguish at living away from the Isles, yet it launched her into New England literary culture:

James and Annie Fields became good friends, and through their connections and her own charm she met several of the period's most well-known and respected writers, including Charles Dickens and Sarah Orne Jewett. Thaxter gained considerable fame as a poet and was able to support her family on the income earned from her writing. In 1869 she began submitting nonfiction sketches about her island home to the *Atlantic*, and in 1873 she collected the sketches in book form as *Among the Isles of Shoals*. A collection of her poems appeared in 1871 (*Poems*), an expanded version of this text came out in 1874, and a new book of poems appeared in 1878 (*Driftwood*).

In addition to her poetry and nonfiction Thaxter delighted in other art forms, especially painting. She adorned hundreds of pieces of china with intricate floral details, and throughout the 1880s and until her death in 1894 she nurtured nineteenth-century artists and musicians at her salon on Appledore, including Norwegian violinist Ole Bull and American impressionist painter Childe Hassam, with whom she would collaborate on her final published work, *An Island Garden* (1894).

The Isles of Shoals, and particularly her cottage and garden on Appledore, remain central to almost all of Thaxter's literary productions. Her attention to the details of her home place—revealing a deep familiarity with the flora and fauna, the tides and currents, the peculiarities of local language—situates her work in the tradition of American regionalism, and in this way her work resembles that of her friend Sarah Jewett. While not a public preservationist in the manner of her contemporary JOHN MUIR, Thaxter nevertheless expressed such an environmentalist impulse in her personal protest of the use of bird feathers in women's clothing, and in her literary work's celebration of the isolation and distinctiveness of the islands' environment. In 1890 she began a correspondence with the naturalist Bradford Torrey about this topic, and specifically about birdlife on the Isles of Shoals, which Torrey had never visited. Her legacy of environmental stewardship to her beloved Isles continues today, with the restoration of her garden on Appledore and the marine science research conducted by students and faculty at Shoals Marine Laboratory.—Lauren E. LaFauci

BIBLIOGRAPHY

Cornell University and University of New Hampshire. "Shoals Marine Laboratory." Available online. URL: http://www.sml.cornell.edu/index.html. Accessed June 14, 2009.

Mandel, Norma H. *Beyond the Garden Gate: The Life of Celia Laighton Thaxter*. Hanover: University Press of New England, 2004.

_____. "Celia Thaxter Timeline." Seacoast New Hamp-

shire. Available online. URL: http://www.seacoastnh.
com/celia/life.html. Accessed June 15, 2009.

Thaxter, Rosamund. *Sandpiper: The Life and Letters of Celia
Thaxter and Her Home on the Isles of Shoals.* Francestown,
NH: Marshall Jones, 1963.

Among the Isles of Shoals, Celia Thaxter (1873)

Celia Thaxter's *Among the Isles of Shoals* (1873)
lyrically portrays the archipelago of rocky islands off
the coast of Maine and New Hampshire where Thaxter spent the majority of her childhood and the happiest years of her adult life. Published simultaneously
in two formats — in hardcover by J.R. Osgood and
Co. and in cheap paperback designed for sale in railroad stations for 50 cents (Mandel 71) — the text was
an expansion of four serial articles about the islands
that Thaxter had written for the *Atlantic Monthly* in
1869–70. In *Shoals* Thaxter creates a vivid portrait
of the Isles alongside a relation of their social, political, and natural history, and of her own experiences
there. Today, *Among the Isles of Shoals* is not only
Thaxter's best-known work but also a defining text
of American regionalist writing of the late 19th century.

Thaxter addresses her readers directly in the work,
often in a conversational style, and speaks in the first
person about her experiences on the islands, exhibit-
ing a deep knowledge of their natural history. She
notes details about the islands' flora and fauna with
vivid precision, and mingles these observations with
lyrical figurative language. Her description of an im-
mature sculpin is representative: "Sometimes in a
pool of crystal water one comes upon him un-
awares, — a fairy creature, the color of a blush-rose,
striped and freaked and pied with silver and gleaming
green, hanging in the almost invisible water as a bird
in air, with broad, transparent fins suffused with a
faint pink color, stretched wide like wings to upbear
the supple form" (86). She also records with reverential exactness the timing of natural events, such as
the arrival "[b]y the 23d of April" of "the first swallow
and flocks of martins, golden-winged and downy
woodpeckers, the tiny, ruby-crowned wren, and [...]
kingfishers [... and] little nuthatches" (158). Such descriptions reveal the dominant mode of narration in
Shoals, where Thaxter's lyrical poetic voice unites
with an authoritative knowledge gained from a lifetime of curious exploration and observation of the
islands' every nook and cranny.

Complementing such poetic observation is Thaxter's holistic view of her home's natural ecosystem.
She expresses this environmental consciousness in
three principle ways: through her relation of the timing of natural occurrences and her appeals to an in-

herent "order of nature," through her gentle critique
of certain forms of environmental destruction, and
through her imagination of certain plants and animals as possessing agency and a status equal or near-
equal to that of humankind. In the first instance she
highlights, for example, the ways in which Appledore's rich plant diversity flouts the usual "order of
nature" in its bountiful wildflower displays, where
the iris, wild rose, goldenrod, and aster all bloom simultaneously, despite their "normal" disparate flowering times (27). And while she acknowledges the
importance of the White Island light to seafarers, she
mourns its complicity in the death of thousands of
birds: "The lighthouse, so beneficent to mankind, is
the destroyer of birds, — of land birds particularly"
(110); and reveals that a lighthouse keeper "picked up
three hundred and seventy-five [dead birds] *in one
morning* at the foot of the lighthouse" (111, emphasis
added). Her gentle critique also implies that the sea-
birds "natural" to the place suffered less from this
form of destruction than did the "land birds" unfamiliar with the lighthouse, suggesting once again her
sense of the proper "order of nature" and its ecological niches, while reminding us of the great and subtle
difficulties in managing human-nature relationships.
Finally, she treats many of the islands' creatures as
companions, if not friends. In one compelling passage, she tells of learning the "loon language" so well
that she could "almost always summon a considerable
flock by going down to the water and assuming the
neighborly and conversational tone which they generally use" (112). Taken together, these examples illustrate not only Thaxter's deep familiarity with the
flora and fauna of her home place, but also her sense
of its fragility, distinctiveness, and ecological wholeness.

Alongside these glowing descriptions of the islands' natural communities are depictions of the dangers that island life presents to humans. She does not
romanticize her home but instead draws attention to
the grisly events in the islands' history and to the desolation and isolation of the winter months especially.
She describes men driven to cannibalism upon being
shipwrecked at Boone Island; the skeletons of sailors
found a year after their deaths on Smutty-nose
Island; and, in one particularly gruesome account,
the discovery of two boots, "not mates, [...] each contain[ing] a human foot" (23–24). Indeed, the text is
replete with images of ruin, desolation, and death as
much as with descriptions of the islands' beautiful
and diverse flora and fauna — a balance reflecting that
of nature itself.

Among the Isles of Shoals was Thaxter's first book-
length work of nonfiction, though she had gained
considerable fame as a poet by the time of its publi-

cation. Her poems often describe the landscapes and natural elements of the Isles, and her first published poem, "Land-locked," portrays the distress of her separation when forced to live on the mainland early in her marriage. In her final published work, *An Island Garden* (1894), Thaxter returned to nonfiction, celebrating her life-long love of flowers; instructing her readers on the basics of cultivation, from seed germination to the application of manure; and, with paintings by Childe Hassam, beautifully illustrating her garden on Appledore. Today, Thaxter is most often associated with the work of late 19th-century American regionalism, particularly with Sarah Orne Jewett, who, along with Annie Fields, was a dear friend. Among literary scholars, *An Island Garden* and *Among the Isles of Shoals* remain her most well-known and studied works, as they reveal her deep knowledge of and devotion to her home region.— Lauren E. LaFauci

BIBLIOGRAPHY

Fetterley, Judith, and Marjorie Pryse. *Writing Out of Place: Regionalism, Women, and American Literary Culture*. Urbana: University of Illinois Press, 2003.
Mandel, Norma H. *Beyond the Garden Gate: The Life of Celia Laighton Thaxter*. Hanover, NH: University Press of New England, 2004.
Thaxter, Celia. *Among the Isles of Shoals*. 1873. Hanover, NH: University Press of New England, 2003.

Thoreau, Henry David (1817–1862)

Resting mostly on the basis of his foundational environmentalist text WALDEN, Henry David Thoreau's reputation has transcended the literary and registered amongst pop-culture iconography. He is the original American literary hermit, the Socratic *idiotes* ("private man") who rejected human society for the society of nature, and established a rich and enduring legacy of protest, one cited by Gandhi and Martin Luther King, Jr. And although he composed millions of words — now *read* by millions — over his brief lifetime, his corpus argues consistently and eloquently for simplicity (for what we can "do *without*") over prodigality, individuality over conformity, and, ultimately, a return to nature as the living anchor of any righteous and decent life.

Thoreau was born in 1817, in the town that would become synonymous with American intellectualism: Concord, Massachusetts. This proved fitting, as Thoreau would join a locus of great thinkers (RALPH WALDO EMERSON, MARGARET FULLER, and NATHANIEL HAWTHORNE would also call Concord home) intent upon writing distinctly "American" literature. He was the third of four children, and the youngest son. While his older brother John was more outgoing, Henry was a serious young man who enjoyed the New England countryside. Because of his solemn demeanor, he was chosen, as the Thoreau's had only enough money for one of their sons to go to college, to attend Harvard, where he matriculated in 1833. John, it was reasoned, possessed ample social intelligence to flourish without higher education — Henry was a different story. Although not an exceptional student, Thoreau was a good one, preferring language courses. He spent a summer teaching under the instruction of Orestes Brownson — a significant event not only for its anticipation of Thoreau's postgraduate vocation, but also for its exposure of the young Thoreau to the evolving philosophy of TRANSCENDENTALISM.

In 1837, Thoreau graduated from Harvard and returned home; but just as his formal education finished, another more liberal schooling commenced. Thoreau spent considerable time with Emerson, 14 years his elder, a neighbor and philosopher, writer, speaker, and transcendentalist thinker who had achieved intellectual fame and notoriety. The latter had just been banned from Harvard for a controversial address he had delivered at the Divinity School ("THE DIVINITY SCHOOL ADDRESS"). Emerson encouraged Thoreau to question — and challenge — the status quo. As a means of harnessing and developing the latter's thoughts, he also advised the 20-year-old Thoreau to keep a journal, from which many of his later works would evolve; moreover, through it he found that writing suited him as a trade.

Yet Thoreau began his professional career as a schoolteacher. In the first of many life-altering applications of Emersonian thought, Thoreau took issue with the school's policy of corporal punishment, and was dispatched. Yet he continued teaching, collaborating with his brother to form a private school, one geared more toward experiential learning (as opposed to the regurgitation favored at the time, even at Harvard) and rooted in hands-on experience. Their sessions regularly took place outdoors, utilizing nature as a classroom — a move that would anticipate Thoreau's biocentric literary "teaching." Working with John, his brother and best friend, encouraging young minds to think for themselves, and doing both outside — Thoreau was at peace. In 1839 the two embarked on a two-week canoe trip that would serve as the inspiration for Thoreau's first book. They even fell in love with the same girl, each having their marriage proposals refused.

On the first day of 1842, John cut himself shaving, and little more than a week later, a calm and resigned John succumbed to lockjaw, passing in Henry's arms.

Thoreau was devastated, even manifesting sympathetic symptoms of lockjaw himself for some time. In addition, in the same month, Emerson's only son, Waldo, to whom Thoreau was quite close, died suddenly of scarlet fever.

Emerson was at the heart of Thoreau's eventual recovery. "Sharing and articulating his loss in ways Thoreau did not or could not," Emerson bounced back relatively quickly after his son's demise (Richardson 114). In the subsequent months, he put Thoreau to work — both physically and intellectually. Living with the Emersons, Thoreau received a steady stream of fix-it requests; Emerson was often away, and even when present, was not very handy (unlike Thoreau, the accomplished boat-maker and celebrated melon grower). And Emerson continued to encourage Thoreau to write, eliciting essays for the transcendentalist journal *The Dial*, including Thoreau's initial foray into nature writing, his "Natural History of Massachusetts," which helped in reconnecting the still emotionally frail Thoreau to the natural world — one he had learned could be quite harsh, but which now healed and comforted.

The following year saw still another change for Thoreau. He embarked for Staten Island, where he would serve as a tutor for relatives of Emerson. He also hoped to secure access, for future publications, to the literary spheres of New York City. Neither endeavor proved successful. Missing the forests and streams of Concord, he languished in the city, and returned to Concord — although his sights were truly set on the *outskirts* of the town.

Eager for a chance to experience life at its most elemental — as well as to work his many notes regarding his canoe trip with John into a book-length manuscript, Thoreau secured a patch of land along the shores of Walden Pond for the purposes of his experiment in living. Just as he and John had taught, his would be an endeavor in immersion learning (in fact, one of his favorite pastimes was bathing in Walden Pond). He moved into his small cabin on Independence Day, July 4, 1845 (a date sometimes cited as the beginning of the environmental movement), and would remain there for just over two years. While it was most certainly not the wilderness excursion some mistake it for (he was only about a mile from town, which he frequented), he was afforded the opportunity, "to live deliberately, to front only the essential facts of life, and see if I could not learn what it had to teach" (*Walden* 394). Thus he read not only Homer but also weather patterns, laboring over his manuscripts and his garden while probing the depths both of the pond and human experience. Like his Socratic precursor Thoreau concerned himself, ultimately and almost exclusively, with how we live — and how we should live. Hence, while writing *A WEEK ON THE CONCORD AND MERRIMACK RIVERS*, he also produced the first draft of *Walden*.

Thoreau explained that he left Walden, in part, because he felt he had "several more lives to live" (579). The most immediate to him, at that point, involved publishing *A Week*, which he finally did in 1849, at his own expense. The move, however, proved financially unwise. The book found neither critical acclaim nor a popular audience, and Thoreau wound up buying back from the publisher over 700 of the 1,000 copies printed.

This failure spurred Thoreau to meticulously revise his *Walden* manuscript over the following years, eventually working the text through seven revisions before its successful publication in 1854. His dedication to formulating the right text for reform — and revolution — was paralleled by his progressive social agenda, as his writings began to include political as well as natural subjects. The 1850 Fugitive Slave Act enraged Thoreau, who fervently embraced the abolitionist movement, producing notable essays like "Resistance to Civil Government" (posthumously retitled "Civil Disobedience"), "Slavery in Massachusetts," and "Life without Principle." An agent of the Underground Railroad and a staunch admirer of John Brown, he famously spent a night in jail for refusing to pay a tax he saw as financing a slaveholding nation in fighting an imperialistic war with Mexico.

Throughout the 1850s, Thoreau's disillusionment with society was reflected in his frequent natural and literary digressions, continually eschewing any romantic ties and seeking ever greater freedom in nature; thus, fittingly, his later texts often take the form of literal or figurative excursions. Texts like *Cape Cod* and *The Maine Woods* demonstrate Thoreau's increased penchant, in his later years, for arriving at well-founded conclusions by way of intense observation, be it of a region's plant, animal, or human inhabitants: his "Kalendar" project sought a comprehensive synthesis of natural facts in an attempt to arrive at higher "Truth." His "excursive" activities finally and naturally included a deep fascination with and respect for the ways of the American Indians; and as he continued to trend toward deeper ecologies, life, in its many varied and variegated forms, at last became Thoreau's true field of study. Thus, his later work is characterized by meticulous investigations of nature, such as "The Dispersion of Seeds" and "The Succession of Forest Trees," his "major contribution to scientific knowledge" (Harding 439). Works like these, along with most of Thoreau's more scientific essays were, for decades, dismissed as "minor Thoreau," mere post–*Walden* cataloguing, but this view is increasingly under attack, as readers schooled in broader environmental hermeneutics sense the subtle but unmistakable lines of analogy and affinity between Thoreau's "natural" and "philosophical" works — lines that were perfectly obvious to and constantly articulated by Thoreau himself.

Thoreau had previously battled tuberculosis, but after becoming ill while remaining outside in the rain to count tree rings in 1860, the disease took on a fatal shape. After a trip to Minnesota proved unsuccessful in tempering his illness, Thoreau resigned himself to preparing his final manuscripts; his sister helped him, and was at his side when he passed away — peacefully, as his brother had — on May 6, 1862, at the age of 44. "One world at a time," he said on his deathbed, when asked about life after death. Humble as his words may seem, they are equally befitting of a man whose life was continually re-dedicated to envisioning new worlds.— David Visser

BIBLIOGRAPHY

Harding, Walter. *The Days of Henry Thoreau: A Biography.* Princeton: Princeton University Press, 1962.
Richardson, Robert D., Jr. *Henry Thoreau: A Life of the Mind.* Berkeley: University of California Press, 1986.
Thoreau, Henry David. *A Week on the Concord and Merrimack Rivers; Walden; or, Life in the Woods; The Maine Woods; Cape Cod.* 1849. Ed. Robert F. Sayre. New York: Library of America, 1985.

Cape Cod,
Henry David Thoreau (1865)

Published posthumously, Henry David Thoreau's *Cape Cod* records his expeditions undertaken between 1849 and 1855 from Concord, Massachusetts, through the Cape Cod peninsula. While better known for his novel *WALDEN,* or his writings on political philosophy, *Cape Cod* was one of a number of accounts of Thoreau's travels which included *An Excursion to Canada* (1853) and *THE MAINE WOODS* (1864). Part travelogue, part meditation upon the natural and cultural history of the region, Thoreau's work provides a valuable record of Cape Cod's environment and society in the mid-nineteenth century.

However, this contemplative and observational turn in Thoreau's thought met with a degree of criticism amongst his contemporaries. As RALPH WALDO EMERSON stated in his often quoted eulogy for Thoreau, "I cannot help counting it a fault in him that he had no ambition," for "[h]ad his genius been only contemplative, he had been fitted to his life, but with his energy and practical ability he seemed born for great enterprise and for command" (*Thoreau* 248). Yet, as John S. Pipkin notes, "Twentieth-cen-

tury literary and environmental scholarship worked to rescue Thoreau from the judgments of his neighbors and his mentor" (Pipkin 527). Central to this was an appreciation of the subtlety and importance of works of natural and social observation such as *Cape Cod,* which explored, early and eloquently, a number of issues which have concerned modern ecology and environmental writing.

Divided into ten sections, beginning with the journey from Concord to Cohasset, and ending with the arrival at Provincetown, Thoreau's *Cape Cod* provides a detailed description and evocation of the natural world through which he passes, yet also a cultural history of the inhabitant's attempts at control and exploitation of their environment. Like the sea which forms a constant backdrop for Thoreau's journey, *Cape Cod*'s prose is in a state of constant pulse and tide, alternating between descriptions of the effect which the "sublimely dreary" (*Cape Cod* 18) coastline has had upon him as an individual, juxtaposed against his attempt at providing an erudite account of the cultural forces which attempt to contain and dominate the natural world. This tide-like quality to his writing is further augmented through Thoreau's extensive reference to other texts such as the *Collections of the Massachusetts Historical Society,* and *Barber's Historical Collections.* Like the driftwood Thoreau describes at length, these intertexts break up the often near-rhapsodic surface of his own description, providing dryer, denser fragments of prose to intersperse with his moments of TRANSCENDENTALISM, or of detailed cultural and philosophical reflection.

It is this complex, tripartite narrative structure, which, while alienating for a number of his contemporaries, makes *Cape Cod* of such interest and importance for twentieth century and contemporary ecological thought. Unlike the exclusively individual-centred doctrine of Emerson's transcendentalism, in which "[t]he greatest delight which the fields and woods minister, is the suggestion of an occult relation between man and the vegetable" (*Nature* 16), Thoreau's immersion within the natural world is more ambiguous and complex. Emerson, for example, stated that:

> When we speak of nature in this manner, we [...] mean the integrity of impression made by manifold natural objects. It is this which distinguishes the stick of timber of the wood-cutter, from the tree of the poet. The charming landscape which I saw this morning is indubitably made up of some twenty or thirty farms. Miller owns this field, Locke that, and Manning the woodland beyond. But none of them owns the landscape. There is a property in the horizon which no man has but he whose eye can integrate all the parts, that is, the

poet. This is the best part of these men's farms, yet to this their warranty-deeds give no title [Nature 14].

Yet, while Thoreau is also able to view landscape in this poetical manner and to describe it accordingly, he does so with an equal focus upon the cultural world of production which Emerson disparages. By combining such transcendentalism with practical concern within a single narrative, Thoreau is able to explore issues of sustainability and interconnection which have since become of decisive importance in modern ecological thought.

This concern with issues of unsustainable exploitation receives its fullest exploration in the third section, entitled "The Plains of Nauset." By describing the current activities of The Cape Cod community, and using intertexts to provide a historical context, Thoreau is able to show how the commonly held belief that the supply of clams "was thought to be inexhaustible" (Cape Cod 23) is in fact erroneous. As Thoreau references:

> "For," runs the history, "after a portion of the shore has been dug over, and almost all the clams taken up, at the end of two years," it is said, "they are as plenty there as ever" [*Cape Cod* 23].

However, by describing the current state of the fishing communities, and of the individuals who live within them, Thoreau is able to show how, while the supplies of giant clams may have withstood exploitation, the harvest of small clams, or *Mya arenaria*, had declined by the 1850s. Such a development was attributed by Thoreau to overexploitation and the fact that "the clam ground has been stirred too frequently" (*Cape Cod* 23). If such a fate could occur with small clams, then the implication is that it could also happen with the giant variety. Rather than the false certainties of the source he cites, or those of contemporary residents, Thoreau thus provides an early exploration of the concepts of sustainability and the responsible management of resources which have come to be central to modern environmental discourse.

Thoreau's depiction of the effect of unsustainable exploitation is not limited to the fishing industry; in "The Wellfleet Oysterman" section he also describes the hunting of sea birds. As with the clams, Thoreau reports that "the large gulls were now very scarce, for, as he said, the English robbed their nests far in the north, where they breed" (*Cape Cod* 62). Similar to his earlier description, Thoreau is able to use the harvesting of the gulls not merely as an example of local issues of sustainability, but also as a means of exploring the environmental interconnection of ecosystems. This allows him to demonstrate how un-

sustainable local exploitation can have wider global consequences, a theme which has again come to dominate subsequent ecological debate.

Therefore, while Thoreau's engagement with the natural world in *Cape Cod* demonstrates elements of transcendental thought, it also remains rooted in the historical and cultural impact which humanity has had upon its environment. This is achieved through the tide-like quality of Thoreau prose, which can switch between rhapsodic, poetical descriptions of the "sea, vast and wild as it is, [which] bears thus the waste and wrecks of human art to its remotest shore" (*Cape Cod* 80), and detailed cultural descriptions and historical intertexts. This allows for both an appreciation of the beauty of the natural world and the interconnection of its ecosystems, and an exploration of sustainability, in the same work, and in a complementary and convergent fashion.— Phillip Pass

BIBLIOGRAPHY

Emerson, Ralph Waldo. *Nature, Addresses, and Lectures.* New York: George Routledge, 1849.
_____. "Thoreau." *The Atlantic Monthly*, Volume X. Boston: Ticknor and Fields, 1862.
Pipkin, John S. "Hiding Places: Thoreau's Geographies." *Annals of the Association of American Geographers*, Vol. 91, No. 3. Oxford: Blackwells, 2001, pp. 527–545
Thoreau, Henry David. *Cape Cod.* Mineola, NY: Dover, 2004.

Excursions, Henry David Thoreau (1863)

Published posthumously, *Excursions* contains nine of Thoreau's essays, from his early and late periods, overarching his most successful, middle period during which he wrote WALDEN. Though a number of the essays were written as Thoreau was dying, the collection betrays none of the despair and decay of death, but is an unmitigated celebration of nature in all its seasons; for Thoreau saw winter, not as an old man, but as a time to live a more "inward life" (133), when "the heavens seem nearer to earth" (117). All the essays are united by a fascination with and reverence for nature, inspiring readers to open themselves up to the heartbeat of nature through which, the transcendentalists believed, we could reach the divine. Thoreau employs all his senses, and his reflective mind, in observing, admiring, and cataloguing all aspects of nature, both organic and inorganic, from the tinniest spawn to the largest mountain, ultimately in order to enrich and discipline his philosophy.

Excursions begins with RALPH WALDO EMERSON's biographical sketch of Thoreau as the quintessential woodsman who lived a simple, solitary life; perfectly satisfied with minimal comforts, beholden to no one, working as a carpenter and a laborer when necessary, in order to walk in the woods and experience nature; not that Thoreau rejected human company, he simply (but religiously) enjoyed his minimum of four hours of walk each day in nature. In the course of these excursions he catalogues the flora and fauna of Massachusetts, building on the knowledge of those who have preceded him. He knows when leaves change color, what color they change into, and the exact date each species of apple ripens. He knows of every foothill, path, and gully, the texture of the snow in winter; and speaks of every biped, quadruped, and limbless creature of the woods as a member of his family. He camps on mountaintops to experience the light, wind, cold and color of nature, distant and near. All his notes are taken during his daily walks, and no less than three essays specifically focus on walking, for like Socrates he is a peripatetic teacher.

In "A Walk to Wachusett," Thoreau walks to Wachusett Mountain and climbs it, nourished by the raspberries and clean water of the brook on the way, in order to survey from the mountaintop all of the natural perspective. He reads Virgil on the way, and is disconcerted at being offered a newspaper by country folk who see communication with the town as highly desirable. He camps on the mountaintop and is amazed by the adequate light offered by the stars in the dark of the night. The walk ends with the philosophical observation that irrespective of one's location, the heavens and skies are always within human reach, and "so is each one's world but a clearing in the forest, so much open and closed space" (83).

In "A Winter Walk," Thoreau walks at dawn, unaffected by the cold, observing that, "if our lives were more conformed to nature, we should not need to defend ourselves against heat and cold" (114). "There is a slumbering subterranean fire in nature which never goes out, and which no cold can chill," and this self-same fire also lights the human heart (115). He describes the landscape in the changing light of dawn, as he breathes in the air "purified by the cold" (113), marveling at the "wondrous purity of nature" when all decay is concealed by snow, and "all things noxious die, or withdraw into warm spaces" (114).

"Walking" crystallizes Thoreau's philosophy, and he begins the essay by expounding on the art of walking or sauntering, a word that he claims was most likely derived from the Middle Ages, when pilgrims begged for alms to visit Sainte Terre and were thus called Sainte Terrers that later evolved into saunterer. He walks not to exercise but to contemplate nature, and notes that, although "half the walk is but the retracing of our steps" (162), the hardest part of walking is deciding the direction; but if we pay attention

to the subtle magnetism in nature we will find our way. This force directs Thoreau westward, for in the West lies the wild, where nature is most free and alive. This observation prompts him to surmise that in literature too, we are drawn to the wild, for "dullness is yet anther name for tameness. It is the uncivilized free and wild thinking in 'Hamlet' and the 'Iliad,' in all the Scriptures and the Mythologies ... that delight us" (193). He prefers walking above all else, even more than acquiring knowledge, for "the highest that we can attain to is not knowledge but Sympathy with Intelligence" (204). The contemplation ends with a quote from the Vishnu Purana clarifying the concepts of knowledge and freedom: "That is active duty which is not for our bondage; that is knowledge which is for our liberation" (205).

The walker inevitably needs an innkeeper, and in "The Landlord," Thoreau describes the perfect innkeeper, who is open and charitable, loves all people equally, and is willing to listen to their tales with no heed to his privacy and no desire to be alone at any time. Thoreau concludes by comparing the church with the tavern, "for the church is a place where prayer and sermons are delivered, but the tavern is where they are to take effect, and if the former are good, the latter cannot be bad" (108). The landlord is thus a representation of moral humanity.

"The Succession of Forest Trees" is a speech Thoreau delivered to the Middlesex Agricultural Society in 1860. In it he marvels at the magical power of seeds to travel long distances and grow into trees, noting that the seed is the cause of pine trees growing out of hewn oak trees, not pine trees miraculously growing out of oaks, and adds that in our agricultural practices of mixing tress and hewing them at different times we are imitating nature's "silent economy and tidiness" (124).

In "Autumnal Tints," Thoreau celebrates the changing colors of nature, from the purple grass, to the red maple and the yellow elm, that shed leaves at different times in autumn and carpet the ground with wild colors that delight our eyes. The beautiful, bright colors a leaf shows just before it dies makes him wish that human death was as beautiful as the death of a leaf. Physiologists claim that leaves change colors because they absorb more oxygen, but Thoreau believes that leaves change color through the same process of ripening and maturing as in fruits.

In "Wild Apples," Thoreau recounts the intertwined history of humans and the apple tree, which apparently came into existence shortly before humans appeared on the planet. Apples, he claims, emanate an essence that is ambrosial, and hence were known as the antidote for aging amongst the gods. This quality of the apple leads him to philosophize that "nectar and ambrosia are only those fine flavors of every earthly fruit which our coarse palates fail to perceive, — just as we occupy the heavens of the gods without knowing it" (273). Yet, we harvest fruits without showing our gratitude or appreciation; but all natural products, he claims, have this same "volatile and ethereal quality which represents their highest value ... and cannot be vulgarized or bought and sold" (273). The collection ends with a short essay extolling the pleasures of walking at night, and the lunar influence on the poet, who at night depends less on the sense of sight, and thus opens up her/his other senses to the natural world. Ultimately, the collection offers a vivid illustration of Thoreau's informing belief that humans should live close to nature, move with its rhythms, and appreciate its beauty and gifts, in order to sense, and even participate, in the divine. — Sukanya B. Senapati

BIBLIOGRAPHY

Adams, Stephens, and Donald Ross. *The Composition of Thoreau's Major Works*. Charlottesville: University Press of Virginia, 1987.

Buell, Lawrence. *The Environmental Imagination: Thoreau, Nature Writing and the Formation of American Culture*. Cambridge, MA: Harvard University Press, 1995.

Harding, Walter. *The Days of Henry David Thoreau: A Biography*. Princeton, NJ: Princeton University Press, 1962.

Schneider, Richard J. *Henry David Thoreau*. Boston: Twayne, 1987.

Thoreau, Henry David. *Excursions*. 1863. Ed. & Intro. by Leo Marx. New York: Corinth Books, 1962.

The Maine Woods,
Henry David Thoreau (1864)

Published posthumously, and often neglected in the college classroom, Thoreau's travelogue *The Maine Woods* chronicles his three visits to a wilderness area that to this day remains the nation's most expansive east of the Mississippi. The excursions, made in the summers of 1846, 1853, and 1857, are depicted in three separate sections entitled, respectively, "Ktaadn," "Chesuncook," and "The Allegash and East Branch," and are followed by an extensive Appendix. These excursions begin, fittingly, while Thoreau is living at Walden; and just as he goes to the pond to attempt a new way of life, so he explores the Maine wilderness in an attempt to conceive of a truly new mode of living, an alternative to the "bald, staring town-house, or meeting-house, and a bare liberty-pole, as leafless as it is fruitless" (*Maine* 710). That is, Maine functions as both concrete and symbolic frontier, and Thoreau displays an intense proclivity for both, asserting that "everything may serve a lower as well as a higher use" (*Maine* 685). *The Maine Woods* thus demonstrates the duality of both

ideal *and* material, which Thoreau increasingly embraced as his interest in natural science grew, transcending the more anthropocentric and exclusive Emersonian emphasis on the former. He strives here for synthesis, overcoming doubt and fear, and ultimately finding solace in the realization that "the country is virtually unmapped and unexplored, and there still waves the virgin forest of the new world" (*Maine* 655).

The Maine woods function for Thoreau as an ultimately promising space, an uncompromised frontier, aligned with the essence of Spirit, capable of affording him the opportunity to envision new means of existence — finally, to "begin life as Adam did" (*Maine* 602). In his essay "Walking," Thoreau famously wrote, "in Wildness is the preservation of the World" ("Walking" 75). Hence, in a world threatened by encroaching industrialization he turns to the wilderness and its past occupants — the American Indians — for answers and alternatives. Robert Sattelmeyer, discussing Thoreau's reading habits, notes that "This sentiment suggests the role — as an antidote to the burgeoning material culture of nineteenth-century America — that the classics played in Thoreau's Transcendentalism" (8). The same premise applies to his adventures in Maine; only here, "classic" refers to aboriginal modes of life instead of works by Homer and Virgil. His ventures into Maine are pilgrimages "to drink at some new and more bracing fountain of the Muses, far in the recesses of the wilderness" (*Maine* 712).

But the knowledge Thoreau seeks cannot, ultimately, be culled from any text, as he insists that "the possession and exercise of practical talent merely are a sure and rapid means of intellectual culture and independence" (*Maine* 602). Thus, similar to his endeavor in WALDEN, Thoreau rejects any relative cabin passage in favor of actual concrete experience, a seeming echo of his "Spartan-like" pledge "to put to rout all that was not life, to cut a broad swath and shave close, to drive life into a corner, and reduce it to its lowest terms, and, if it proved to be mean, why then to get the whole and genuine meanness of it, and publish its meanness to the world" (87). Having lost his brother and closest friend, John, to an infection suffered shaving, Thoreau cannot possibly be said to employ this metaphor lightly.

Thus, his foray into the Maine interior is no pedestrian enterprise. He is confident, however, that "the deeper you penetrate into the woods, the more intelligent, and, in one sense, less countrified do you find the inhabitants; for always has the pioneer been a traveller, and, to some extent, a man of the world; and, as the distances with which he is familiar are greater, so is his information more general and far reaching than the villager's" (*Maine* 608). Thoreau endeavors to explore the truly wild, essentially transcending the pastoral existence he has fashioned in Concord, be it on the shores of Walden Pond, bunking at Emerson's, or sequestered in his attic room at home. He has tinkered with modification and re-thinking in *Walden*, but this is his opportunity to observe, practically, how another entire society, a vast neglected citizenry, the Indians, go about living.

So Thoreau, a traveling companion (cousin George Thatcher in 1846 and 1853 and friend Edward Hoar in 1857), and various Indian guides, hike, canoe, fish, hunt, and sleep under the stars, engagements Thoreau deems "next to living like a philosopher on the fruits of the earth which you had raised," and consequently "perfectly sweet and innocent and en-nobling" (*Maine* 683–684). In this way, Maine re-turns Thoreau to "the creations of the old epic and dramatic poets" (*Maine* 640).

Inherent in investigating this new world is, naturally, the consideration of the Indian language, communicated to Thoreau primarily by his final guide, Joe Polis, whom EMERSON would later place in Thoreau's pantheon of most-admired men, along with John Brown and WALT WHITMAN (Harding 426). As Polis guided Thoreau into the physical wilderness, he served as his conduit to a new (albeit ancient) lifestyle: that of the American Indian. Confronting a foreign existence in an unsettled land required of Thoreau the essential, foundational work of acquiring the Indian language (many words of which are catalogued in the Appendix). His fondness for the Indian tongue prompts him to proclaim, in fact, "I felt that I stood, or rather lay, as near to the primitive man of America, that night, as any of its discoverers ever did" (*Maine* 697). *Walden* and *The Maine Woods*, therefore, share a common innovative foundation: whereas the former entailed inventing a previously unused (and still unnamed) hybrid genre, the latter calls for Thoreau's inculcating of a language previously marginalized, one characterized by Thoreau as "a purely wild and primitive American sound" (*Maine* 696).

Along the way, Thoreau encounters new challenges presented by the acute harshness of the wilderness, indicative of the supreme challenge of deviating from the established convenience of the ever-industrializing West. This wilderness immersion (climbing Mount Ktaadn and losing his companion overnight are two of the more intriguing cases) illuminates, as never before, his transcendental aims, as he asserts that "we have not seen pure Nature, unless we have seen her thus vast and drear and inhuman.... Nature was here something savage and awful, though beautiful" (*Maine* 645). The untamed sublimity of

the landscape, although daunting, inspires him to confront existence at the most fundamental level: "Think of our life in nature,—daily to be shown matter, to come in contact with it,—rocks, trees, wind on our cheeks! the *solid* earth! the *natural* world! the *common sense! Contact! Contact! Who* are we? *where* are we?" (*Maine* 646). He is struck by ontological questions, interrogating his very essence and relation to the universe. Ultimately, the Maine frontier has shown him a new intellectual frontier, has proposed to him, in fact, a new mode of being, which he acknowledges as he writes,

Thus a man shall lead his life away here on the edge of the wilderness, on Indian Millinocket stream, in a new world, far in the dark of a continent, and have a flute to play at evening here, while his strains echo to the stars, amid the howling of wolves; shall live, as it were, in the primitive age of the world, a primitive man [*Maine* 652].

Thoreau's Maine excursions thus demonstrate his transcendentalist belief that every moment is, indeed, one of creation, of possibility, of hope. What is needed to re-educate a man—ultimately, to re-invent him—is within the reach of anyone who would endeavor to seek it. His optimistic flourish in the final line of *Walden*—that "The sun is but a morning star"—would seem equally at home, then, in *The Maine Woods* (324).—David Visser

BIBLIOGRAPHY

Harding, Walter. *The Days of Henry Thoreau: A Biography.* Princeton: Princeton University Press, 1992.
Sattelmeyer, Robert. *Thoreau's Reading: A Study in Intellectual History.* Princeton: Princeton University Press, 1988.
Thoreau, Henry David. *The Maine Woods.* 1863. Ed. Robert F. Sayre. New York: Library of America, 1985.
_____. *Walden: An Annotated Edition.* 1854. Ed. Walter Harding. New York: Houghton Mifflin, 1995.
_____. "Walking." 1862. Ed. William Rossi. Athens: University of Georgia Press, 2002.

Walden, Henry David Thoreau (1854)

Henry David Thoreau's *Walden,* tellingly if temporarily subtitled "Life in the Woods," is a cornerstone of American ecological literature, indeed perhaps the text appearing most frequently on environmental reading-lists and syllabi. The book—equal parts converted journal, seasonal calendar, figurative slave narrative and anti-social harangue—is an account of two years (1845–1846) spent in a Massachusetts wood situated on EMERSON's estate.

Thoreau's cabin on Wyman Meadow is by now one of American literature's sacred sites. His "rude hut" was not, however, as is widely believed, a remote haven but instead an in-between place, close to his hometown and his literary comrades. This hand-made home was a kind of self-made purgatory from which to view nature's Heaven and society's small-scale Inferno. While the second version of the work was actually dedicated "To My Townsmen," the TRANSCENDENTAL gospel of self-reliance is given its most famous test in Thoreau's pages.

Despite its praise for wild and free living, *Walden* (initially published in 1854) is a product of several rewritings. The book underwent seven revisions as Thoreau furrowed, planted, nurtured and harvested his own text. The book's narrative contour is telling; it traces a seasonal circuit but allows for several de-tours and doublings-back, its "annual" shape com-plicated by frequent cross-reference.

Indeed a quick survey of several of *Walden's* chapter titles reveals much. The chapters "Reading" and "Sounds" form a dialectic of sorts, in which our "rational" eye's reading of human documents is con-trasted with our "intuitive" ear's learning by at-tending to elemental sounds. The chapters "Solitude" and "Visitors" can also be paired off as a drama in which solitude is impossible in ever-buzzing, ever-blooming Nature. The chapter "Visitors" can simi-larly be contrasted with "Brute Neighbors" — Walden is as attentive to peers and proximities as it is to iso-lation.

Thoreau's guiding "book-as-house" metaphor foreshadows what the German philosopher Martin Heidegger would call "writing-as-dwelling." In *Walden* the process of writing a book parallels the act of building a cabin. In this view (and example) one should treat all of nature as an extended inhabitance. Thoreau aspires to write an "unroofed book" taking in the "slanted rays" of the sun. Moreover, the fre-quent pun on Walden as "Walled-in," suggests a kind of cellular dwelling, with Thoreau cell-bound as a self-made hermit and cell-studying as an amateur botanist.

Thoreau's abode, composed mainly of cast-off planks, was deliberately completed on July 4, 1845, a mere two miles away from Concord Battle Field. While comparing his personal liberation to our na-tional independence, Thoreau is keenly alert to the paradoxes of being a "Native New Englander." Thoreau the semi-recluse is surrounded by the very material (tree fiber) used to make the books that would eventually publish his conservationist views. This irony intensifies when we realize that Walden Pond is now a tourist spot littered with beer cans: Thoreau's attempts at conservation have turned it into a commodity.

"Walden" itself means "wooded" in German; the phrase "Walden Woods" doubly emphasizes its status as uncut wilderness. The chapter title "*Where* I Lived, What I Lived *For*" promotes Place ahead of Purpose, and initiates the American literature of *locale* so im-portant to contemporary ecocriticism. Thoreau reads Walden Pond itself as a page in the Book of Nature. The pond is a figurative field, its ripples furrows of a "lower heaven," alternately "crystalline" and "green-ish-blue," a surface by which to read divine signals. During the spring thaw, cleavages of cracking ice are like "characters of some oriental language," as Thoreau reads an etched writing in elemental textures and contours.

The motives behind Thoreau's vigil at his pond were complex. Mocked for several years following his accidental burning down of several hundred acres of woodland during a cooking mishap, Thoreau's writing frequently bears a tone of self-defense. *Walden's* most quoted line, "I went to the woods be-cause I wanted to live *deliberately*" (from the Latin *librare*, "to balance") literally expresses a desire to *weigh* his anti-social options and alternatives.

Despite such separatism, *Walden* is composed out of a series of iconic scenarios all commenting on our elemental *entwinement*. Thoreau in his canoe playing hide-and-seek with a loon is a lesson in interspecies recognition. Comparing a battle between red ants and black ants to a Trojan combat is an example of mock-heroic, but also suggests an epic importance to nature's small, under-noticed layers. Eric Sund-quist suggests that Thoreau's digging spade clinking on buried Indian arrowheads is a microcosmic drama in which Euro-American and Native American tools of livelihood clash point-to-point. Thoreau's fre-quent reference to Aurora (the Goddess of Dawn) is clearly bred by his troubled conscience over Indian genocide and African slavery, his keen awareness of America's "New Garden" as a primeval place.

Such awareness breeds skepticism. "Simplify, sim-plify" is Thoreau's main mantra, expressing his wari-ness of America's coming Age of Progress. Thoreau is a paragon of self-denial; his imperatives include commands to eat one meal a day and to have a per-sonal menu of five different dishes. "Man is rich in proportion to the number of things he can do *with-out*" in Thoreau's Spartan credo. "Our fingers are burned by our possessions," he writes on a site not far from Salem, where a century before (during its witch trials) people were burned for a different kind of "possession."

Lambasting fiscal hoarding and excessive (or at least misdirected) labor, Thoreau finds infinite riches in small natural details. *Walden's* much-examined sandbank is an eco-poetic primal scene. The shapes and figures revealed on a slowly unfreezing sand-

and-clay railroad embankment reveal an organic riot of resemblances, in which soil breaks and crumbles into shapes resembling leaves and lungs and lobes. Robert E. Abrams observes a kind of grotesque holism in Thoreau's writing, where natural objects are "lifelike, dead, mammalian, reptilian, vegetative, and excremental all at once," in a "collapse of primary categories and visual boundaries." (142)

Located a small distance from his sandbank Thoreau's bean patch is a formative site for American eco-literature as well. The word "legend" grows from a similar root as "legume," and *Walden* is insistent on finding its fables in natural items like foodstuffs. The hoe-wielder teaching his field to "say 'beans'" is a grammar-tutor to his native ground. In Thoreau's claim, a metaphor is not only a figure of speech but a literal "turning"—a writer is a farmer turning over a cliché to find fresh loam. Writing is frequently compared to plowing in *Walden*: a furrow is at once a seedbed and a printer's line. To compose is to compost as Thoreau fertilizes his page, turning words over to examine their "root" meanings.

Walden approaches such metaphor as an engine of metamorphosis, insistently claiming that our language is a primary aid in viewing nature in an always-unstable, ever-teasing flux. Michael T. Gilmore (in a well-regarded article on "The Curse of Trade") examines Thoreau's hostile views toward commercial transaction, but *Walden* is also a book rejoicing in changeovers and conversions. Metaphor itself is a prime mode of such transfer—mountains are likened to coins from heaven's mint, butterflies are compared to advertisements—our very language is dependent on figures of commerce of a figurative nature.

Reports of Thoreau's self-denying nature tend to be exaggerated; *Walden* is as much a study in sensuality as it is an experiment in voluntary poverty. Thoreau compares himself to a "vegetable mould" and likens his blood to an ascending "sap." He refers to his own "appetite for sound," his eyes whetted by a cricket's call, his "oracular" sense of smell, and his admiration of children because "Their whole body is one sense." In *Walden* "lipped words" give a reader/taster objects to "chew upon." Thoreau's own clucking, scolding tongue is a wind-propelled leaf, a parcel of human flesh reveling in its kinship to vegetable life. In Thoreau's nomenclature, our cheek is a fertile valley, our jaw is a winnowing harvester, our gullet is a grain elevator, our viscera is a furnace—indeed, our human body is a farming plot, a "few cubic feet of flesh" on which to plant.

Walden is in fact a study of language as living matter. Thoreau aspires to a "spheral speech" as active as a yeast molecule, even as he prides himself on baking "Indian meal" requiring no such leaven. Thoreau dreamed of eventually transcending words and letters and dealing in traced leaf-outlines, a tender language still showing "angles of [its] rugged bark," its leaves marked by "sinuses" and "scallops," its scooped contours taking the place of consonants and vowels. Thoreau toted bark samples and vegetable spores alongside his sheaves of writings, and Bronson Alcott indeed tasted "the sod and sap and flavor of New England" in Thoreau's work, as if *Walden*'s pages were slices of turf raked from its local soil or petrified plates of Massachusetts pine resin.

Walden's fertile play of language has created its own bio-region of wide-ranging critiques and supports. John Greenleaf Whittier regarded *Walden* as "wicked" for advocating a human being live like a woodchuck; Robert Louis Stevenson regarded its basic stance as a "womanish" retreat. Philip F. Gura examines Thoreau's philological side, his obsessive digging toward a word's dangling roots. Victor Carl Friesen portrays Thoreau as an only-partial ascetic (a vegan longing to suck life's marrow) and suggests such a paradoxical regard of our human body (a mingling of distaste and revelry) is a key to *Walden*'s drama. Gordon V. Boudreau makes much of Thoreau's "Tree of Life" metaphor and how *Walden*'s organic metaphors form a self-examining circuit. Henry Golbemba similarly suggests a battle between "willed" literature and a more "wild" rhetoric, waged across *Walden*'s pages.

Thoreau's writer-as-natural-worker is a precursor to such wide-ranging voices as GARY SNYDER and WENDELL BERRY, A.R. Ammons and ROBINSON JEFFERS. *Walden* continues to impress in part because of its famed, echoing phrases, from its "different drummer" to "The mass of men lead lives of quiet desperation." "There is more day to dawn" at *Walden*'s final moment: it is fitting that Thoreau's text and its emphasis on renewal has maintained its freshness and relevance for generations of inheritors—as a hectoring literary conscience, a freely offered map, and a still-revealing critique.—Mariquit S. Reder and John P. Reder

BIBLIOGRAPHY

Abrams, Robert E. *Landscape and Ideology in the American Renaissance: Topographies of Skepticism.* Cambridge: Cambridge University Press, 2003.

Boudreau, Gordon V. *The Roots of Walden and the Tree of Life.* Nashville: Vanderbilt University Press, 1990.

Friesen, Victor Carl. *The Spirit of the Huckleberry: Sensuousness in Henry Thoreau.* Edmonton: University of Alberta Press, 1984.

Gilmore, Michael T. "*Walden* and 'The Curse of Trade.'" In *Ideology and Classic American Literature.* Cambridge: Cambridge University Press, 1986.

Gura, Philip F. *The Wisdom of Words: Language, Theology and Literature in the New England Renaissance.* Middletown, CT: Wesleyan University Press, 1981.

McKusick, James C. *Green Writing: Romanticism and Ecology.* New York: St. Martin's Press, 2000.

Sundquist, Eric J. "Plowing Homeward." In *Henry David Thoreau* (ed. Harold Bloom). New York: Chelsea, 1987.

A Week on the Concord and Merrimack Rivers, Henry David Thoreau (1849)

Thoreau's first book-length publication, *A Week on the Concord and Merrimack Rivers*, emerged from a trip taken by Thoreau and his brother John, in 1839. John's sudden death a few years later affected Thoreau profoundly, and its significance is partly demonstrated by Thoreau's decision to detail their shared experience. Thoreau's principle literary reason for removing to Walden Pond in 1845, in fact, was to write the book that would become *A Week*. John's significance to the text is apparent in its first lines, as he is invoked by the author: "Be thou my Muse, my Brother —" (2).

Coping with John's death requires Thoreau to acknowledge the passage of time that brings us all closer to death. *A Week* confronts this temporal dilemma directly, and not surprisingly, in natural terms. Rivers in particular serve as potent symbols for Thoreau (just as, in *Walden*, he is "thankful that this pond was made deep and pure for a symbol" [279]). As H. Daniel Peck contends, "an immersion in the flow of time was necessary to overcome time" (35). Furthermore, Lawrence Buell maintains that addressing the "paradox of timelessness versus time" speaks to "Thoreau's apparent literary objective in the book as a whole: to immortalize the excursion by raising it, in all its detail, to the level of mythology" (209). Transcendence, therefore — of time, and of the temporal and mundane — is at the core of *A Week*.

Popular institutions, including even the church, are not spared. Thoreau creates space for his own conceptualization of time and mythologizing by dismissing organized religion. His "Sunday" chapter functions as an extended diatribe against the complacency fostered, and obedience required, by the church, leaving him to opine, "Men reverence one another, not yet God" (53); and this aphorism expresses, at the same time, a key Thoreauvian inclination: searching for Spirit in nature, not in the village. For, much as in *Walden*, transcending common thought requires Thoreau to transcend common space.

Yet this is not solely a leisurely endeavor. The speaker and his traveling companion (never explicitly depicted as John) can only escape quotidian views by paddling "upstream," against the tide of both current and popular opinion. Laboring in the face of adversity typifies Thoreau's challenge in *A Week*, as

he attempts to capture, via natural description, digression, and travelogue, a piece of eternity made manifest by the Concord and Merrimack; all the while acknowledging the cathartic benefits the journey affords: "It is worth the while to make a voyage up this stream, if you go no farther than Sudbury, only to see how much country there is in the rear of us; ... such healthy natural tumult as proves the last day is not yet at hand" (8–9).

Thoreau ultimately requires this tumultuous test because of what it requires of *him*; nothing less than the attitude and endurance of an epic hero. The voyage situated as the principle engagement of the text is much more than a canoe and hiking trip. Thoreau, for example, offers the following verse:

> Some hero of the ancient mould,
> Some arm of knightly worth,
> Of strength unbought, and faith unsold,
> Honored this spot of earth;
>
> Who sought the prize his heart described,
> And did not ask release,
> Whose free-born valor was not bribed
> By prospect of a peace [16].

In *A Week* Thoreau dons the epic garb of Odysseus and Lancelot, substituting for their mythic realms his own backdrop of rural New England, since "The characteristics and pursuits of various ages and races of men are always existing in epitome in every neighborhood" (21). His own version of the knight's quest, in "There and Back Again," concerns neither war nor romance, but rather an intimate search to come to terms with his brother's death; and his charge is that of the eternal transcendental poet, "he who can write some pure mythology to-day without the aid of posterity.... The matutine intellect of the poet, keeping in advance of the glare of philosophy, always dwells in this auroral atmosphere" (49–50).

His poetic endeavor outlined, the succeeding chapters, named for the days of the week so as to keep time foremost in the reader's mind, chronicle the brothers' travel northward; but Thoreau's striving for the transcending quality of the mythic is never far beneath the surface:

> When the first light dawned on the earth, and the birds awoke, and the brave river was heard rippling confidently seaward, and the nimble early rising wind rustled the oak leaves about our tent, all men, having reinforced their bodies and their souls with sleep, and cast aside doubt and fear, were invited to unattempted adventures [95].

So begins the "Monday" chapter of *A Week*. Thoreau derives consolation from the dead waters of the Concord giving way to the "living stream" of the Merrimack (72). The river inspires his temporal quest, as he resolves, "A man's life should be constantly as fresh as this river. It should be the same channel, but a new water every instant," effectively aligning past and present (107). He questions, "Where is the spirit of that time but in / This present day, perchance the present line?" (205) An extended flashback in the "Tuesday" chapter reinforces the idea that "then" and "now" can exist concurrently. The "Wednesday" chapter contains a lengthy contemplation of friendship, during which Thoreau finally arrives at the peace he has sought, stipulating, "my Friend shall forever be my Friend, ... and time shall foster and adorn and consecrate our Friendship" (232). By "Thursday" he surmises, "The life of a wise man is most of all extemporaneous, for he lives out of an eternity which includes all time" (255). "The poet," Thoreau proclaims in his concluding chapter, "Friday," "leads us through a varied scenery, ... to meet with a fine thought in its natural setting" (304). This "fine thought" is ultimately the text of *A Week on the Concord and Merrimack Rivers* itself, as Thoreau asserts that "poetry, though the last and finest result, is a natural fruit." Borne of nature, Thoreau's elegy to the memory of his brother is an important reconciliation with time and nature that would endure for the rest of his days, and inform the rest of his work.

Although a commercial failure, *A Week* nevertheless served several important functions for Thoreau. First, it provided a literary space in which Thoreau was able to let go of his brother, ultimately arriving at the stalwart optimism that pervades his oeuvre, from *Walden's* sun as the morning star, to the "faith in a seed" that he maintains in his later ecological writings. Second, that very failure motivated Thoreau to set about a meticulous revision of *Walden*, eventually producing the classic that it finally became. Third, and perhaps most importantly, *A Week* served as a kind of rough road map for the rest of Thoreau's career — and life. Fittingly meandering and, at times, seemingly unpredictable, *A Week* is a snapshot of the heroic, epic, even mythic life of the Poet to which Thoreau aspired, of one who eschews societal convention and expectation in favor his own intuitions, ultimately transcending both temporal and spatial constraints along the way. — David Visser

BIBLIOGRAPHY

Buell, Lawrence. *Literary Transcendentalism: Style and Vision in the American Renaissance.* Ithaca: Cornell University Press, 1973.
Peck, H. Daniel. *Thoreau's Morning Work: Memory and Perception in a Week on the Concord and Merrimack Rivers, the Journal, and Walden.* New Haven: Yale University Press, 1990.
Thoreau, Henry David. *Walden.* 1854. Ed. Walter Harding. New York: Houghton Mifflin, 1995.
_____. *A Week on the Concord and Merrimack Rivers.* 1849. Ed. Robert F. Sayre. New York: Library of America, 1985.

Toomer, Jean (1894–1967)

Best known for CANE, Jean Toomer's other work includes poetry, essays and other fiction manuscripts, and a large correspondence that has become of interest as Toomer has gained critical prominence. Toomer's early work interrogates a central problem of modernity: how to understand race, identity, and otherness as rural, pastoral America becomes increasingly urbanized. Influenced by religious experiences, Toomer eventually rejected the pastoral lyric in favor of broader reflections on the human condition, but his work continued to reveal a fundamental place-awareness.

Nathan Pinchback Toomer was born in 1894 in Washington, D.C., to Nathan Toomer, a Georgian planter, and Nina Pinchback Toomer, the daughter of Pinkney Benton Stewart Pinchback, a prominent politician in Louisiana during Reconstruction. At the age of four, after his parents' divorce, he and his mother moved to P.B.S. Pinchback's house in Washington, where the boy was renamed Eugene Pinchback. His childhood was marked by profound change, from his mother's remarriage and death, and the family's financial struggles, to subsequent moves from upper-middle-class, mostly white neighborhoods to lower-income, interracial neighborhoods. In 1914 Eugene Pinchback enrolled at the University of Wisconsin, but left only a few months later; and over the next five years would attend five other schools, never receiving a degree.

In 1919 he changed his name to Jean Toomer and began to write, mostly unsuccessfully, until his acceptance of a teaching position at a rural black school in Sparta, Georgia. Here his first successful poems, two plays, and *Cane* were completed, and his friendship with Waldo Frank began. Toomer was disappointed with *Cane's* pastoral aesthetic soon after its completion, explaining that due to modernization, "'Back to nature,' even if desirable, was no longer possible, because industry had taken nature unto itself.... Those who sought to cure themselves by a return to more primitive conditions were either romantics or escapists" (qtd. in Ford 145). In his letters to Frank in this period, Toomer also complains of being classified as "a Negro writer" (Byrd 49), which he found a facile, restrictive understanding of race. This led him to reject the pastoral lyric, which he felt was too strongly associated with African-American history and poetics, and set out on a search for spiritual wholeness and universal identity. His search led to Eugene Gurdjieff, then scientology, and eventually the Society of Friends.

Though Toomer rejected traditional pastoral nature experience, nature continued to permeate his writing, and he was deeply aware of the role physical environment plays in constructing the individual — an effect he considered detrimental. In "New Mexico," Toomer writes "One place gives you what others can't. You give to one place what you cannot give to others.... Do all you can, it is sufficiently difficult to become a citizen of the world. You may overcome prejudices and move towards universality; but preferences linger, and preferences tend to localize you" (Rusch 252). Yet despite his own rejection of pastoral place and aesthetics, Toomer's unpublished writing reveals his continued awareness of place as fundamental to identity.

After a long illness in the 1950s and 60s, Toomer died in 1967 in Doylestown. — Amber Pearson

BIBLIOGRAPHY

Byrd, Rudolph P. *Jean Toomer's Years with Gurdjieff: Portrait of an Artist 1923–1936*. Athens: University of Georgia Press, 1990.

Fabre, Geneviève, and Michel Feith, eds. *Jean Toomer and the Harlem Renaissance*. New Brunswick, NJ: Rutgers University Press, 2001.

Ford, Karen Jackson. *Split-Gut Song: Jean Toomer and the Poetics of Modernity*. Tuscaloosa: University of Alabama Press, 2005.

McKay, Nellie Y. *Jean Toomer, Artist: A Study of His Literary Life and Work, 1894–1936*. Chapel Hill: University of North Carolina Press, 1984.

Rusch, Frederik L., ed. *A Jean Toomer Reader: Selected Unpublished Writings*. New York: Oxford University Press, 1993.

Cane,
Jean Toomer (1923)

Jean Toomer's *Cane* is a problematic and complicated environmental text, partly owing to its unusual and experimental hybrid form: a mix of poetry, vignettes, short story, and a drama/story. In addition, the content of the work addresses a dizzying array of themes and lends itself to manifold interpretations; it is at once lyrical, historical, and spiritual. Through its links to a violent past the environment is at times viewed as suspect, while at other times it seems to provide respite and the possibility for redemption. In either case, Toomer appears to suggest that any connection to the natural environment, once severed, may be difficult if not impossible to reestablish.

Cane is comprised of three sections: the first includes stories and poems set in the rural Georgia town of "Sempter," modelled partly on the town of Sparta where Toomer briefly lived in 1921; the second also includes a number of stories and poems, but the

setting shifts north to the urban environments of Washington, D.C. and Chicago; the last section returns to Sempter with the single, long drama/story "Kabnis." The book is structured largely on juxtapositions: rural vs. urban, nature vs. technology, and the past vs. the present. While it seems to celebrate a folk tradition and a rootedness in the earth, it also ties that rootedness and tradition to the bloody history of slavery and the troubling conditions of African Americans living in both the rural South and the urban North.

As a result, though the work is often lyrical, its descriptions of the landscape as often contain underlying tensions. "Karintha," for example, the first story of the book, features a strikingly beautiful young woman whom the text inextricably links to her natural surroundings: "Her skin is like dusk on the eastern horizon," and "she was as innocently lovely as a November cotton flower" (Toomer 1). The former image generates tension through the space created between the dusk on the western horizon, and the gathering darkness on that "eastern horizon" which represents Karintha's skin-tone. And the "innocence" of the latter image is replete with irony when viewed in light of cotton's connection to the slave past and the contemporaneous context of a boll-weevil epidemic, a crashed cotton market, and African-American peonage (Foley 183).

Cane does not, however, focus exclusively on such problematic representations of mankind's relationship with the environment. It also offers multi-dimensional images that draw the reader into the landscape created by the text. The short poem "Nullo" offers a case in point, providing striking tactile images of nature (Toomer 18) while simultaneously transporting the reader through "five levels of space in nature" (Bush and Mitchell 106). The depth and breadth of space and nature are compressed into seven lines, providing the reader with what Bush and Mitchell call a "conceptual compound image of the subject in its totality and in its essence" (108).

These compound conceptual images extend into the urban environments of the book as well. In the poem "Her Lips Are Copper Wires" the reader is presented with an unnatural, constructed landscape that is juxtaposed with sensual expression. We are led through a "gleaming" and "incandescent" maze of billboards, telephone and electrical wires, and street lamps. The delicate presence of breath, lips, and a tongue attempts to communicate something human, and by extension natural, in this mechanical environment, but it hardly succeeds. In the vignette "Seventh Street" Washington is depicted as "white and whitewashed." The whispering sound of the pines in Sempter are replaced by the mechanical whine of engines: "zooming Cadillacs, / Whizzing, whizzing down the street-car tracks" (Toomer 39). While the first third of the book is set largely outside in the natural environment, the second part of the book is set in the often chaotic and dispiriting indoor environments of the city, be it an automobile, house, gymnasium, or jazz club.

The book ends with a return to the rural landscape of Sempter in the long drama/story "Kabnis." But the corrupting influences of the city follow the lead character back to the small town. Rather than depicting the relief of open places and the natural world, this story too is set mostly in cramped, claustrophobic interiors, this time in shacks and basements, suggesting that once we abandon our ties to the rural and natural world, they cannot be retrieved. The whispering pines that were drowned out by the whine of engines are replaced here with the sound of "vagrant poets," which is created by the wind moving between the cracks in the walls of a cabin. Although the story ends with a traditional symbol of hope, in a sunrise, the image is juxtaposed with the lead character carrying a bucket of spent coal, and an old man languishing in the darkness of the basement.

In discussing canonical authors like FAULKNER, FROST, and HEMINGWAY in his seminal work THE MACHINE IN THE GARDEN, LEO MARX notes that they "invoke the image of a green landscape — a terrain either wild or, if cultivated, rural — as a symbolic repository of meaning and value. But at the same time they acknowledge the power of a counterforce [...] which has stripped the old ideal of most, if not all, of its meaning. Complex pastoralism, to put it another way, acknowledges the reality of history" (Marx 362–63). Although Marx never directly addresses *Cane*, Toomer's book represents an excellent example of the "complex pastoral." The hand of human history, both in sociological and technological terms, can be seen weighing on and shaping the environment throughout the book. In a posthumously published autobiographical selection Toomer explains that he felt the modern "trend was toward the small town and then towards the city — and industry and commerce and machines. The folk-spirit was walking in to die on the modern desert. That spirit was so beautiful. Its death was so tragic [...]. *Cane* was a swan-song. It was a song of an end" (Toomer and Turner 142). Much of what Toomer wrote about has indeed faded; yet some remains, and if we are careful we may yet hear his "swan-song" as much as a warning as a eulogy. — Michael Beilfuss

BIBLIOGRAPHY

Bush, Ann Marie, and Louis D. Mitchell. "Jean Toomer: A Cubist Poet." *Black American Literature Forum* 17.3 (1983): 106–08.

Foley, Barbara. "'In the Land of Cotton': Economics and Violence in Jean Toomer's Cane." *African American Review* 32.2 (1998): 181–98.

Ford, Karen Jackson. *Split-Gut Song: Jean Toomer and the Poetics of Modernity*. Tuscaloosa: University of Alabama Press, 2005.

Marx, Leo. *The Machine in the Garden: Technology and the Pastoral Ideal in America*. New York: Oxford University Press, 2000.

O'Daniel, Therman B. *Jean Toomer : A Critical Evaluation*. Washington, D.C.: Howard University Press, 1988.

Scruggs, Charles. "Jean Toomer and Kenneth Burke and the Persistence of the Past." *American Literary History* 13.1 (2001): 41–66.

Toomer, Jean. *Cane*. Ed. (1923). New York: Liveright, 1975.

_____, and Darwin T. Turner. *Cane : An Authoritative Text, Backgrounds, Criticism*. A Norton Critical Edition. New York: Norton, 1988.

_____, and Mark Whalan. *The Letters of Jean Toomer, 1919–1924*. 1st ed. Knoxville: University of Tennessee Press, 2006.

Turner, Darwin T. "Introduction." *Cane*. New York: Liveright, 1975. ix–xxv.

Transcendentalism

New England Transcendentalism was an intellectual movement born in the early 1830's and centered in Boston, Concord, and Harvard. Its importance as an American version of literary Romanticism, a network of influential parlors and lecture halls, and a skeptical debunking of the Puritan inheritance has been exhaustively discussed, but its status as an early environmental movement has been considerably less explored.

The best-known representatives of Transcendentalism are EMERSON and THOREAU, but its roster of major figures is deep and diverse, from visionary eccentrics like Jones Very and Bronson Alcott to socially committed voices like Orestes Brownson and Theodore Parker. Many formative Transcendentalists were disaffected Unitarian clerics; Philip Gura refers to "Come-Outers" who abandoned conventional church membership to attend to a deeper, more "inner" sense of Spirit. As a product of disillusioned preachers and academic rebels Transcendentalism (during its major phase) was empirical and intuitive at once, divided between progressive science and more personal "influxes" of revelation. This sense of divinity as an inner, sensual quality is key to understanding Transcendentalism's treatment of Nature as an illuminating and allegorical "impress" upon our human senses.

"Transcendentalist" actually began as a pejorative term, but has since accrued a broader range of meanings; Joel Myerson claims that "Defining Transcendentalism is a lot like grasping mercury" (xxv). "Concord" suggests a place of harmony, but Concord-bred Transcendentalism was composed of a discordant and even contradictory mix of influences — Alan Hodder accuses its writers of a kind of "intellectual colonialism" (201). A blend of post–Puritan, Neo-Platonic, Hindu, Gnostic, and Kantian sources, Transcendentalism was an intensely eclectic movement. Its Neoplatonism suggests that Nature is a low rung on a ladder leading up to Divinity; its Hinduism sees Nature as *maya,* a frolicsome but potentially misleading illusion; its Gnosticism portrays reality as a piece of mischief conjured up by a malevolent Deity. To this rich stew of influences, Transcendentalism adds a dash of Yankee optimism and pragmatism — Emerson's foundational essay "NATURE" views all of reality as a commodity and a utility as well as a soul-stimulating set of metaphors.

Despite the wide-ranging list of influences discussed above, a brief survey of canonical Transcendental writings suggests some degree of shared environmental vision. William Ellery Channings' "Likeness to God" denounces all "distanced" notions of Deity in favor of a Divinity "immanent" in Nature itself. Christopher Pearse Cranch's poem "Correspondences," with its portrayal of Nature as a textual array of elemental metaphors, comes close to serving as a position-poem or a capsule summary of a shared Transcendental outlook. Sampson Reed's essay "Genius" portrays our blossoming brain as the product of an implanted "germ" related to the fellow germs that cause a landscape to blossom. This vision anticipates deep ecology's sense of the human form as but one organic ingredient in Nature's recipe. Thoreau's "Autumn Tints" locates Nature's glory in its tendency toward decay and circular self-feeding; in the way that all objects collapse into their own compost and so Death is a vitalizing precondition of Life.

"Transcendentalism" means "a little beyond" (in Emerson's phrase), and in one sense Nature is always "beyond" any comprehensive grasp. In Emerson's "Compensation" Nature "is made of one hidden stuff," a kind of universal matter stirred into human and tree and pond alike. However, this sense of organic continuum is no guarantee of "belongingness"; Richard Francis refers to the frequently found word "almost" as Transcendentalism's "poignant adverb," and Thoreau constantly strives for a sense of true "contact" which is never fully attained.

Barbara Packer locates a large part of Transcendentalism's force in its "refutation of Locke" and his *tabula rasa*— his notion that the human mind begins as a "blank slate" to be written upon by experience. Transcendentalists instead tended to affirm a Kantian belief in innate faculties and capacities lending our human senses certain primeval (indeed timeless) bonds to Nature and the Godhead. Transcendental Nature-worship thus represents a critical challenge

to the fundamental Puritan belief in human dominion *over* Nature. In Emerson's "The American Scholar," for example, the American landscape is less confined by human planning, and our elemental habitat more robust and sublime in comparison to England's more humanly tamed environments. The Transcendental writers indeed treated their local landscapes (particularly Massachusetts' cranberry bogs and kettle-ponds, storm-lashed sandbars and cordillera mountains) as a sacred and symbolically beckoning Book of Nature.

The Swedish visionary Swedenborg provided Transcendentalism with a quasi-science of "correspondences" between natural objects and "spiritual facts." Nature here is viewed as an inspired volume to be read, a Third Testament of sorts. The most important influence on Man Thinking (according to Emerson's "American Scholar" address) is Nature itself. The argument for God's existence from Nature's complex symmetry had long made Nature-study a Christian pursuit, and Emerson's "We should read God [and by implication, Nature] instead of books" is a very Protestant view, a search for unmediated vision. The Godhead is inherent in Nature in early Transcendentalism, but in a second-wave figure like Thoreau nature study is its own reward, no longer merely a proof of divine abundance and symmetry.

Ultimately, Transcendentalism may be seen as a by-product of Christianity's liberalization into "natural religion," but also an effect of the rising interest in empirical science. By the 19th century, geologists were overturning Biblical estimates of our planet's age; Nature's own fossil "testimony" was finally read; Darwin repositioned our sense of humanity's proper placement by locating our species along evolution's horizontal chain of being. Equally radically, Brownian motion (initially detected in 1827) had exposed matter's random, ever-shifting foundation, while Louis Agassiz (for whom Thoreau worked as a specimen-collector) lent Nature a more gradual and epochal sense of time and scale through his studies on glacial motion, shrinking human history into a mere nanosecond of geologic "deep time."

In historical terms, Transcendentalism dominated the intellectual landscape of America in the antebellum era, from 1830 to 1850, a period marked by a questioning of what had previously been regarded as "naturally" self-evident in human conduct and society. MARGARET FULLER's "The Great Lawsuit," initially appearing in Transcendentalism's quarterly journal *The Dial* in July 1843, is a trenchant critique of "every arbitrary barrier" between Man and Woman, in an early effort to separate "social" forces that shape our sense of gender from "natural" ones.

As a social movement Transcendentalism weakened

in a number of telling ways. Its utopian Brook Farm community languished and finally burned down due to a lack of pragmatic will and expertise; Bronson Alcott's Fruitlands "anti-society" was an ironic victim of its own land's relative barrenness; Orestes Brownson converted to Roman Catholicism, emblematic of a more general return to institutions.

Theodore Parker once worried whether Transcendentalism's impact would be "transient" or "permanent"; ironically, its continued relevance is partly owing to its emphasis on natural flux and transience. Harold Bloom attempts to trace a Transcendental continuum through figures ranging from WALT WHITMAN to WALLACE STEVENS, by locating the conflict between alienated self and indifferent Nature (but also the harmony between human and host) as a prime theme of American writing. While Transcendentalism has been assailed by current ecocritics as egocentrically hostile toward the very Nature it claims to revere, works like Emerson's "Nature" and Thoreau's WALDEN (alongside the experiments in rural, communal living at Brook Farm and Fruitlands) provide American environmental writing with a large part of its literary foundations.— John P. Reder

BIBLIOGRAPHY

Bloom, Harold. *The Poems of Our Climate*. Ithaca: Cornell University Press, 1977.

Francis, Richard. *Transcendental Utopias: Individual and Community at Brook Farm, Fruitlands, and Walden*. Ithaca: Cornell University Press, 1997.

Gura, Philip F. *American Transcendentalism: A History*. New York: Hill & Wang, 2007.

Hodder, Alan D. "Concord Orientalism, Thoreauvian Autobiography, and the Artist of Kouroo." In *Transient and Permanent: The Transcendental Movement and Its Contexts*. (Charles Capper and Conrad E. Wright, eds.) Boston: Northeastern University Press, 1999.

Howe, Susan. *The Birth-Mark: Unsettling the Wilderness in American Literary History*. Middletown, CT: Wesleyan University Press, 1993.

Myerson, Joel. *Transcendentalism: A Reader*. Oxford: Oxford University Press, 2000.

Packer, Barbara L. *The Transcendentalists*. Athens: University of Georgia Press, 2007.

Turner, Frederick Jackson (1861–1932)

Frederick Jackson Turner was a son of Middle America, fitting for a scholar who promulgated the notion of the heartland's crucial role in determining American culture. Born in Portage, Wisconsin in 1861, his early journalistic career was also marked by stints in Chicago and Milwaukee. But instead of continuing to follow his father into the newspaper business, Turner instead embraced his father's favorite hobby: history. Earning his Ph.D. at Johns Hopkins University, Turner returned home and accepted an assistant professorship at his undergraduate alma mater, the University of Wisconsin at Madison, in 1889.

Four years later Turner delivered the lecture for which he is still best known: "THE SIGNIFICANCE OF THE FRONTIER IN AMERICAN HISTORY." Delivered at the now infamous Chicago World Columbian Exposition, the talk included Turner's "frontier thesis," which maintained that the westward expansion of the nation fostered cultural characteristics that had since become synonymous with America, among them individualism, egalitarianism, and democracy. In his own words: "The existence of an area of free land, its continuous recession, and the advance of American settlement westward explain American development." This claim drew immediate and hostile responses for its challenge to conventional wisdom: Turner effectively unseated New England as the cradle of Americana, instead bestowing this title on the continent's vast internal prairies and rugged western spaces. Moreover, rather than accepting America as the hybrid product of (mostly) English, French, and even German forbears, Turner's thesis holds that the challenging countryside itself dictated the institutions — and culture — that had evolved in America.

Influential as they undoubtedly were, and critical to our understanding of the fundamental importance of landscape to American identity, Turner's conclusions themselves have since come under serious attack, being cited as Romantic and naïve at best, and ethno- and androcentric at worst. His thesis elicits scorn, in particular, from those who cite its neglect of minorities and women. The landscape he envisions resembles more the widely discredited conception of MANIFEST DESTINY that emphasized America's inherent right to what was essentially seen as empty, "free land," regardless of existing occupancy (a rather surprising oversight on Turner's part, given that his doctoral dissertation focused on the Indian trade in Wisconsin).

Yet even if they are assailed today as exclusionary, Turner's ideas marked an epochal moment in the evolution of America's environmental understanding and imagination, and laid the heuristic foundation for more sensitive and inclusive approaches to the natural world. JACK LONDON's characters, for example, both human and nonhuman, are continuously formed and reformed by their experience of the frontier. WILLA CATHER's Nebraskan families' very lives revolve around the rhythms of planting and harvesting, and her *O Pioneers!* heroine Alexandra Bergson even fantasizes of a corn-scented "land man," the embodiment of her desire for a harmonious relationship with the world around her. Many of JOHN STEINBECK's characters serve as twentieth-century pioneers, continually moving in search of that more hospitable, nurturing landscape.

Turner's career was as academically impressive as it was environmentally significant. He published on a wide range of subjects, including THEODORE ROOSEVELT, the Louisiana Purchase, the West, and his native Wisconsin. After receiving job offers from Princeton, the University of Chicago, and Stanford, he left the heartland for the coasts. He taught at Harvard from 1910–1924 and finally made his way west, retracing the migration so important to his frontier thesis. He died in Pasadena, California in 1932 while a researcher at the Huntington Library.— David Visser

BIBLIOGRAPHY

Billington, Ray Allen. *Frederick Jackson Turner: Historian, Scholar, Teacher.* New York: Oxford University Press, 1973.

Edwards, Everett E. *The Early Writings of Frederick Jackson Turner.* Madison: University of Wisconsin Press, 1938.

Flagg, Jeffrey B. *Frederick Jackson Turner: 1861–1932.* Spring 1997. Bowling Green State University. 1 September 2011. http://www.bgsu.edu/departments/acs/1890s/turner/turner.html.

"Frederick Jackson Turner." *New Perspectives on the West.* 2001. PBS. 1 September 2011. http://www.pbs.org/weta/thewest/people/s_z/turner.htm.

Jacobs, Wilbur R. *The Historical World of Frederick Jackson Turner.* New Haven: Yale University Press, 1968.

"The Significance of the Frontier in American History," Frederick Jackson Turner (1893)

Delivered at Chicago's World Columbian Exposition in 1893, Frederick Jackson Turner's essay "The Significance of the Frontier in American History" is a foundational text for both American history and literature, as well the burgeoning field of ecocriticism. In response to the 1890 census that declared the frontier "closed," Turner, a professor of history at the University of Wisconsin and ultimately Harvard, asserted that American institutions, and therefore cultural consciousness itself, is directly and profoundly linked to the landscape.

Turner's approach is, first, postcolonial: he examines how the North American wilderness precipitated the fundamental shift of the U.S. from a European to a truly distinctive American culture. "The wilderness," he asserts, "masters the colonist" (4); but "Little by little he transforms the wilderness" (4). Turner holds the inverse true also. Continually creating frontiers spawns a recurrent American renaissance. And the principle formative element determining these rebirths is nature. Turner elaborates:

The buffalo trail became the Indian trail, and this became the trader's "trace"; the trails widened into roads, and the roads into turnpikes, and these in turn were transformed into railroads.... The trading posts reached by these trails were on the sites of Indian villages which had been placed in positions suggested by nature; and these trading posts, situated so as to command the water systems of the country, have grown into such cities as Albany, Pittsburgh, Detroit, Chicago, St. Louis, Council Bluffs, and Kansas City [14].

The development of the country as a whole can be witnessed in the transformation from Indian camps to the aforementioned cities. Turner explains that first on the scene are pioneers, who occupy the frontier until it is "somewhat subdued" (20). Next come purchasers of the land, who ready the area for "civilized life" by the establishment of a basic infrastructure (20). Finally, the capitalists arrive, and their lucrative offers to the foregoing groups pull many of them into their class, while others search for a new place to begin, effectively restarting the process.

The landscape, according to Turner, affected not only the location of population and cultural centers, but also the ideology that would flourish therein, while "the demand for land and the love of wilderness freedom drew the frontier ever onward" (22). And just as the settler and frontier affected each other, so did the developments in the West influence mindsets on the East coast and even Europe. The frontier, for example, fostered "the formation of a composite nationality for the American people" (22). Turner claims that "In the crucible of the frontier the immigrants were Americanized, liberated, and fused into a mixed race, English in neither nationality nor characteristics" (23). The distance between this new "race" and the port cities where European influence still loomed large, in turn decreased dependence on Great Britain, and the manner by which these new lands were to be governed became a primary topic in U.S. politics. The rapid advance to the Pacific, primarily through the mid-nineteenth century gold rush, left as "the frontier" an entirely internal space, a central void left spanning the Midwest, Great Plains, and Rocky Mountains. This "Middle region," according to Turner, "mediated between East and West as well as between North and South. Thus it became the typically American region" (28), a literal crossroads populated heavily by waves of immigrants seeking cheap land (the Homestead Act of 1862 even provided for free land). Innovations in transportation spurred a unifying nationalism, as "Nothing works for nationalism like intercourse within the nation. Mobility of population is death to localism, and the western frontier worked irresistibly in unsettling population" (30). Finally, and most important for Turner, is the role the frontier has played in "the promotion of democracy here and in Europe," an influence he attributes primarily to the individualism and self-reliance cultivated in the wilderness (30).

The timing of Turner's essay was crucial to its reception. According to Ray Allen Billington, "Turner's thesis appealed to a people suddenly aware that their efforts to build a powerful nation had not been in vain; it was equally alluring to all who believed that their revered democratic institutions had wrought this miracle" (x). For a nation on the verge of becoming a superpower, Turner's thesis provided a sort of natural legitimacy to the American endeavor, attributing American achievement to its taming of vast unforgiving spaces and unruly indigenous peoples, and engendering a sense that, for better or worse, whatever America had become had been earned (MANIFEST DESTINY). But after "dominating the teaching of American history for a generation," the popularity of his frontier thesis waned in the 1930s (Billington xiii). Moreover, although Turner was "in no sense a mono-causationist," critics took issue with his "reliance on a single force to explain American development" (xii, xvii). He sought not, however, to posit the frontier as "*the* explanation of American society," but rather to situate it as "one of numerous forces contributing to its social evolution" (xviii).

Ultimately, Turner's work takes an "earth-centered approach" to American history, just as ecocritics do with literature (Glotfelty xviii). The western environment functions as more than setting, more than a stage upon which the affairs of men are played out. Turner latently acknowledges Marxist claims that institutions determine consciousness, but argues that these institutions were themselves shaped and molded by the frontier. The ultimate result is the aligning of Americana with the North American landscape itself. Specific traits, such as American "rugged individualism," are rooted in the interaction between settler and the West, qualities forged rather than prepossessed.—David Visser

BIBLIOGRAPHY

Billington, Ray Allen. "Foreword." *The Frontier in American History.* Frederick Jackson Turner. New York: Robert E. Krieger, 1976. Vii–xviii.
Glotfelty, Cheryl. "Introduction." *The Ecocriticism Reader.* Ed. Cheryl Glotfelty and Harold Fromm. Athens: University of Georgia Press, 1996.
Turner, Frederick Jackson. "The Significance of the Frontier in American History." 1893. *The Frontier in American History.* For. Ray Allen Billington. New York: Robert E. Krieger, 1976.

Twain, Mark (Samuel Clemens) (1835–1910)

In "A Day at Niagara," a tale he wrote about Niagara Falls, Mark Twain admits, "There is no actual harm in making Niagara a background whereon to display one's marvelous insignificance in a good strong light, but it requires a sort of superhuman self-complacency to enable one to do it" ("A Day" 18). He mocks the tourist's thirst for photographs in the face of the falls' overwhelming permanence, naturalness, and reality. Twain instead strays from the falls and tries, but fails, to find and greet authentic Native Americans (there is the allure of impermanence about this quest). Ultimately, the "Day" offers a superbly uneasy introduction to Twain's relationship with the environment: his awareness of civilization's degradation of land and people goes hand in hand with his urge to witness these degradations for himself.

Mark Twain is rarely successful at self-complacency. During the Civil War, he spent one fortnight in a militia of the Confederate army before deserting, and then accepting his brother Orion's offer to join in the pursuits of greedy thrill-seekers in the Wild West, which he chronicles in *ROUGHING IT* (1872). In one ambiguous scene, Twain accidentally sets fire to a section of forest and has a good laugh over his power for destruction and showmanship. The book ends with Twain becoming a writer and lecturer, and concludes with a moral dichotomy: "stay at home" or be of "no account" (960)—the latter, according to Neil Schmitz, defined by being "not bound to home and hearth, to cultural ideals, to a single belief system" (30). Twain is popularly known as a tramp, traveler, and tourist, because of his choice, but it is also crucial to see him as intellectually on the move. Great humor and satire are commissioned by the thoughtful traveler's willingness to compare and contrast what is thought to be incomparable (such as one's home). He is a shrewder tourist on the lookout for more challenging vistas: *The Innocents Abroad* (1869) lampoons the assumptions of Americans on pilgrimage in Europe, *Following the Equator* (1897) records the effects of European imperialism he witnessed while on a lecture tour of the globe, and the classic HUCKLEBERRY FINN (1885) ruthlessly critiques the settled attitudes of those who live along the Mississippi River.

Ron Powers claims that Twain's "steamboat years remained the most hallowed period of his life" (77), and that what is miraculous about steamboats is that "they subjugated the natural world under a spreading curtain of smoke, sparks, sound, and light" (77). Twain can be quite sensitive to the cruelty of man-made endeavors, as he is at Niagara Falls, but he also expresses delight in man-made creations. Larzer Ziff asserts that Twain's "achievement and his fame [grew] in step with the fast-flying industrial development that enthralled him with its inventiveness, technical efficiency, and quickening accumulation of riches" (3). In short, Twain learned a forceful "sense of style" from these beautiful, commercial vessels (Ziff 90); he even invented himself as "Mark Twain" (after the depth-sounding of a Mississippi ferry), stylishly and forcefully, as man-made as they come.

In the 1880's, Twain stopped writing about his latest travels, in order to revisit his Mississippi past, and he ventured even further back in time in two medieval fantasies, *The Prince and the Pauper* (1882) and *A Connecticut Yankee in King Arthur's Court* (1889). This new concern for travelling across time instead of across space centers on the idea that man-made things like ships, names, or ideas have lasting and potentially permanent consequences. These later writings explore what Ziff calls "the debilitating persistence of the past" in the forms of racism, provincialism, and environmental exploitation (44). In *Life on the Mississippi* (1883), published two decades after his experiences as a cub pilot on Mississippi steamboats, what lingers is the memory of Twain's youthful relationship with nature. Because Twain is older and wiser, *Life on the Mississippi* registers, in the words of LEO MARX, "the passing of a way of life, a mode of apprehending nature, and by inference, a literary style" (54). As steamboats were becoming outmoded by the speed and breadth of railroads, Twain's relationship with the natural world was shifting from surface rapture to deeper knowledge and *sympathy*. As a pilot, he had to sense the capricious whims of the river so as to anticipate and avoid snags and perils. He boasts, "The face of the water, in time, became a wonderful book—a book that was a dead language to the uneducated passenger, but which told its mind to me without reserve..." (283). However, his knowledge was not solely positive: "But I had lost something, too.... All the grace, the beauty, the poetry, had gone out of the majestic river!" (284). Only in the uniquely rough voice of Huck Finn will the passenger's lovely river and the pilot's menacing river become "one" again (Marx 57).

Twain's mastery over the natural world as a pilot is no longer the pure whim of watching the flames in *Roughing It*; now he is responsible for every move he makes. Both are examples of what Joseph Coulombe sees as Twain's "adversarial relationship" with nature (121). In *Tom Sawyer*, Tom muddles his geography lesson and "turned lakes into mountains, mountains into rivers, and rivers into continents, till chaos was come again" (52). Geography may get the better of Tom, but Tom winds up warping geography. "Which is best?" Twain asks, and asks well, but never answers.— Jonathan Gaboury

BIBLIOGRAPHY

Coulombe, Joseph L. *Mark Twain and the American West*. Columbia: University of Missouri Press, 2003.

Marx, Leo. "The Passenger and the Pilot: Landscape Conventions and the Style of *Huckleberry Finn*." *Mark Twain: A Collection of Critical Essays*. Ed. Henry Nash Smith. Englewood Cliffs, NJ: Prentice-Hall, 1963. 47–63.

Powers, Ron. *Mark Twain: A Life*. New York: Free Press, 2005.

Schmitz, Neil. "Mark Twain, Traitor." *Arizona Quarterly* 63 (2007): 25–37.

Twain, Mark. *Adventures of Huckleberry Finn*. *Mississippi Writings*. New York: Library of America, 1982. 617–912.

_____. *The Adventures of Tom Sawyer*. *Mississippi Writings*. New York: Library of America, 1982. 1–215.

_____. "A Day at Niagara." *The Complete Short Stories of Mark Twain*. Garden City, NY: Doubleday, 1957. 16–22.

_____. *Life on the Mississippi*. *Mississippi Writings*. New York: Library of America, 1982. 217–616.

_____. *Roughing It*. *The Innocents Abroad* and *Roughing It*. New York: Library of America, 1984. 525–986.

Ziff, Larzer. *Mark Twain*. Oxford: Oxford University Press, 2004.

The Adventures of Huckleberry Finn, Mark Twain (1884)

Published in 1884, but set during the pre–Civil War 1840s, Samuel Clemens' *The Adventures of Huckleberry Finn* invokes and complicates 19th-century literary conventions and cultural assumptions about nature and societal norms. Clemens, writing for a popular audience in what many authors and critics—including ERNEST HEMINGWAY—have claimed is the most important American novel ever written, begins his famous work with a warning to readers: "Persons attempting to find a motive in this narrative will be prosecuted; persons attempting to find a moral in it will be banished; persons attempting to find a plot in it will be shot" (2). It proves to be an ironic admonition for a text that has cultivated a cottage industry of criticism, much of which wrestles with the role that nature plays in this semi-fictive world set on and near the Mississippi River and the western frontier. In this regard, *The Adventures of Huckleberry Finn* seems to insist that those interested in the relationship between the natural and constructed worlds avoid tempting interpretations regarding the role of the landscape in the novel and its relationship to the society tied to it.

The novel's first section focuses primarily on Huck Finn's adventures in and around St. Petersburg, Missouri, a small town on the Mississippi River, home to Huck's childhood friends, Judge Thatcher, Huck's abusive father, and the Widow Douglas, who adopts

Huck and attempts to "sivilize" him. Huck's views, as expressed in what Twain describes as an "ordinary 'Pike County' dialect" (2), have for over a century led readers and critics alike to view the opening section as proof that this fictive but familiar world near the edge of the frontier broke neatly along a singular line, one half belonging to the wild, free realm of the wilderness area specific to the river and the frontier beyond its western shore, and the other to that of the cramped confines of the civilized towns, with their rules, schools, adults, and duties. In his groundbreaking study of 19th-century, land-based American literature, VIRGIN LAND, HENRY NASH SMITH argued the following: "Natural man beleaguered by society, but able to gain happiness by escaping to the forest and the river: this is undoubtedly an important aspect of the meaning that thousands of readers have found in the novel" (95). Smith's interpretation, presented in an axiomatic manner that does not invite a rejoinder, harmonizes with countless others, but fails to account for what occurs in the novel, or how, more importantly, Clemens constructed the text. Though Huck repeatedly complains about the disadvantages associated with being civilized, his outlook remains equally grim while he is in the woods and on the Mississippi.

The second section of the novel features Huck and Jim's "adventures" as they make their way down the river. Commencing when Huck fakes his own murder while his father is away in St. Petersburg, the section is replete with accounts of death, deceit, cowardice, and cruelty, all of which conclude in the section of the book that has, until relatively recently, left many readers confused and frustrated, especially those who subscribe to the nature/culture dichotomy when attempting to interpret the text. On the river, while Huck escapes his dead father and Jim flees for his life in a society built by and around slavery, the two encounter in succession a half-sunken house of thieves, slave catchers, swindlers, "a steamboat that had killed herself on a rock" (65), and another one that tore the raft in half—a boat that, as Huck states, "all of a sudden [...] bulged out, big and scary, with a long row of wide-open furnace doors shining like red-hot teeth, and her monstrous bows and guards hanging right over us" (91). These run-ins with the worst elements of society underscore how the novel blurs the distinction between the natural and unnatural, and between the ostensibly free frontier associated with the river and the West, and the cultural clutter common to that place at that time.

Two passages, in particular, have defined the orthodox, first-order understanding of the novel's environmental binary; the first describes Huck's idyllic existence in the bosom of the river: "Two or three days, and nights went by; I reckon I might say they swum by, they slid along so quiet and smooth and lovely. Here is the way we put in the time. It was a monstrous big river down there—sometimes a mile and a half wide; we run nights, and laid up and hid daytimes; soon as night was most gone we stopped navigating and tied up [...]. Then we set out the lines. Next we slid into the river and had a swim, so as to freshen up and cool off; then we set down on the sandy bottom where the water was about knee deep, and watched the daylight come" (113); the second model is the oft-quoted excerpt from the final scene, wherein Huck famously claims, "But I got to light out for the territory ahead of the rest, because Aunt Sally she's going to adopt me and sivilize me, and I can't stand it. I been there before" (281). Fittingly, the novel ends with Huck revealing his inability to learn from experience, having apparently not noticed throughout his harrowing adventures how thoroughly society had spread, like smallpox, along the length of the Mississippi and soon the width of the rest of the continent.

Still, just as the myth of the untamed river and the related idea of open land to its West seem to inoculate the often somber but resilient protagonist against the downsides of the industrial revolution, European culture, and urban life in the Gilded Age, the novel would in turn, and for centuries to come, debunk quixotic ideals while reifying faith in the land and the literature it inspires.—Colin Irvine

BIBLIOGRAPHY

Bercovitch, Sacvan. "Deadpan Huck," *Kenyon Review* 24.3/4 (2002): 90. *Academic Search Premier*. EBSCO. Web. 14 April, 2010.
Fishkin, Shelley Fisher (ed. and introd.). *The Mark Twain Anthology: Great Writers on His Life and Works*. New York: Library of America, 2010.
Smith, Henry Nash. *Virgin Land: The American West as Symbol and Myth*. Cambridge, MA: Harvard University Press, 1978.
Twain, Mark. *Adventures of Huckleberry Finn*. New York: Bantam Books, 1981.

Roughing It, Mark Twain (1872)

In Mark Twain's book about his youthful travels to the rough-and-tumble West it is nature's extremes that draw the protagonist's attention and provoke his response. Throughout his descriptions of the many natural wonders he encountered, Twain repeatedly portrays his younger self as awestruck by the Western environment's extremity: the land is more austere, rich, beautiful, and various than he had ever imagined. However, the real tale, with its subtle depiction of man's relation to the wilderness, is more complex.

In his preface Twain describes *Roughing It* as a "personal narrative" in which he, the now experienced narrator, records his youthful "vagabondizing." The young Samuel Clemens travels via stagecoach from St. Joseph, Missouri, to Carson City, Nevada, with his brother, who had been appointed the Secretary of Nevada Territory. After an arduous and adventurous journey, they arrive in the crude city. From there Clemens sets off on two failed ventures to make the land yield him a fortune: he establishes a timber ranch at Lake Tahoe, but accidentally burns down the whole hillside; then catches mining fever and claims several mines, but through a series of accidents fails to work his one profitable mine and so loses his claim. After these setbacks he becomes a newspaper reporter in Virginia City, finally finding a way to earn a living, and coining the pseudonym under which he will become famous. Eventually he moves to San Francisco where he works sporadically for various newspapers; and then, bored with this life, lands a contract with the Sacramento *Union* to travel to the Sandwich Islands and send back letters for publication.

Because of the great variety of experience described in *Roughing It*, the book is episodic and can seem unstructured. HENRY NASH SMITH, however, identifies the narrative strategy Twain uses to connect his sprawling plot: "the pronoun 'I' links two quite different personae: that of a tenderfoot setting out across the plains, and that of an old-timer, a veteran, who ... now looks back upon his own callow days of inexperience" (53). By satirizing his own youthful misconceptions, Twain links his motley adventures thematically, portraying himself as holding clichéd notions of Western life, which when he actually experiences that life, inevitably turn out to be (often comically) wrong.

Initially Twain views his trip West as a lark on which he is bound to become rich and have grand adventures (2). During his stagecoach journey, however, he repeatedly confronts the harsh realities of the Western environment. When they approach the desert, for example, he is initially excited with the thrilling adventure:

> This was fine — novel — romantic — dramatically adventurous —*this*, indeed, was worth living for, worth traveling for! We would write home all about it.

Yet,

> This enthusiasm, this stern thirst for adventure, wilted under the sultry August sun and did not last above one hour. The poetry was all in the anticipation — there is none in the reality. Imagine a vast, waveless ocean stricken dead and turned to ashes [123].

His description of the desert's desolation continues for the rest of the chapter. And when he arrives in Carson City he finds no respite from the harsh elements: "Visibly our new home was a desert, walled in by barren, snow-clad mountains" (137). This barren place was subject to a daily battering by the "Washoe Zephyr," a gale that tears through town bringing a "dust-drift about the size of the United States" (138). As Joseph Coulombe states, "Twain ... saw the natural elements as an array of overwhelmingly dangerous forces pitted against relatively helpless humans" (116). While the young Twain expected the West to contain benignant marvels and adventures, he found that more often the reality was, though marvelous, brutally harsh.

Twain experiences a similarly rude awakening when he attempts to extract his fortune from the earth. When he begins prospecting, he is elated: "Of all the experiences of my life, this secret search among the hidden treasures of silver-land was the nearest to unmarred ecstasy. It was a delirious revel. By and by, in the bed of a shallow rivulet, I found a deposit of shining yellow scales, and my breath almost forsook me! A gold mine" (185). Unfortunately, he has found only glittering mica; and when he tries his hand at actual mining, he declares it "the weariest work!" (192). Instead of being ripe for the picking, his "fortune seemed a century away!" (191). The earth held great wealth, but would not easily yield it; or as Coulombe puts it, "Mining was all-out war with nature" (120), and Twain loses by underestimating the unyielding character of the land.

These novice experiences with the harsh Western environment finally lead (the veteran) Twain to burlesque the romantic notions of the landscape that he had initially maintained. For instance, though originally a "disciple of Cooper and a worshipper of the Red Man," when the young Twain actually sees American Indians he finds them to be "treacherous, filthy and repulsive," utterly dismantling his "mellow moonshine of romance" (128–29). Such a derogatory view of Indians may be just as wrong as FENIMORE COOPER's, but Twain is clearly intent most of all on overturning naïve (and ultimately damaging) Eastern attitudes toward the Western environment. Gary Henrickson describes this as a general theme in *Roughing It* and throughout Twain's work: "Time and again, Twain notes the falsity of the sublime, whether the sublime Romantic landscape or the sublime of nostalgia" (47). And as Henrickson points out, when Twain comes to the "Big Trees" of Yosemite, he refrains from depicting them, refusing to repeat clichéd, touristy descriptions (42).

Yet, and here the tale reveals its deeper meaning, even though Twain continually depicts the Western environment as surprisingly severe and inhospitable, his experiences do not cause him to completely reject his naïve notions of the West as a place of natural marvels. As Michael Hobbs explains, "The tenderfoot's encounter with nature, which begins as a quite Emersonian or Thoreauvian transcendental experience, becomes an infernal inversion of the reverential moment. But far from being negative, this inversion seems to afford the veteran's imagination a deeper comprehension of nature and the world" (17). Hobbs claims particularly that Twain's experiences at Lake Tahoe, Lake Mono, and Kilauea Volcano reveal nature to be not merely harsh, but also "terribly beautiful" (23). In describing the volcano, for example, Twain marvels at its phenomenally destructive power and its "unapproachable splendor" (515)—both unmistakably sublime. Thus, while his discovery of nature's severe, Western reality might appear to threaten his ability to appreciate its attraction, Twain in fact ends up only more profoundly awestruck by nature's "fascinating, bewitching, entrancing" beauty (152).—Jeffrey Bilbro

BIBLIOGRAPHY

Coulombe, Joseph L. *Mark Twain and the American West.* Mark Twain and his Circle Ser. Columbia: University of Missouri Press, 2003.

Henrickson, Gary P. "The Missing Landscapes of Mark Twain." *Mark Twain Annual* 2 (2004): 41–9.

Hobbs, Michael. "Transcendentalism: The Lake Episodes in Roughing It." *American Literary Realism* 26.1 (1993): 13–25.

Smith, Henry Nash. *Mark Twain: The Development of a Writer.* Cambridge: Belknap Press of Harvard University Press, 1962.

Twain, Mark. *Roughing It.* Ed. Harriet Elinor Smith and Edgar Marquess Branch. Berkeley: University of California Press, 1997.

Utopian Communities

This brief survey of America's Utopian communities will not focus on such groups as pure and pristine alternatives to our more commercial society's environmental compromises. Instead, such communities are perhaps more productively viewed as illustrations of the key problems and paradoxes entailed in any effort to "live green." These groups, holding diverse ideas on the goal of social perfection, were essentially efforts to radically overhaul our human interaction with the environment; and their failures, as much as their successes, illuminate many key issues in current ecological debates.

The double meaning of utopia, initially exploited by Sir Thomas More in his *Utopia* (1516), implies both *eutopos* ("good place") and *outopos* ("no place"). This contradiction in the word's root meaning is quite appropriate, since it underscores the longstanding paradox that has challenged most efforts at communal living. Many critics and reviewers have pointed out how "utopia" seems by definition to refer to a project impossible to achieve but noble to attempt. Indeed, groups founded on Utopian objectives who *do* succeed (Mormons, Mennonites, Quakers, etc.) tend to cease being referred to *as* Utopias, even when clear Utopian principles informed such groups' beginnings.

Utopian ventures in colonial America include Roger Williams and Anne Hutchinson's respective spiritual communities in 1630's Rhode Island, the products of two well-known religious extremists driven out of Puritan society. These ventures were hardly environmental in motive, but did establish an early version of radical (literally "root-grasping") groups seeking out alternative environments in which to pursue communal values. Several early would-be Utopias were composed of dissidents who fled from Germany to avoid persecution; some groups were descended from millennial sects bred during a large outbreak of dissenting Puritanism during England's Civil War. Some were based on a Rousseau-derived belief in private property's inherent evils, in early contrast to THOMAS JEFFERSON's notion of government as mainly a protector of such property.

"Nature is static, history is progressive" says an old cliché, but many early American Utopian groups were efforts to escape some of the traps of unchecked commercial progress. The so-called Market Revolution, a rapid economic expansion during America's post–Revolutionary years, was counteracted by a kind of agoraphobic Counter-Revolution. As New England's factories treated workers as faceless components and prized mass manufacture over handiwork, many groups turned to more modestly agrarian scenarios. These American *communards* were driven by Yankee pragmatism as much as Utopianism—their environmentalism was mainly a belief in smallness of scale and self-sufficiency, 200 years before the counter-culture revolution of the *WHOLE EARTH CATALOGUE* "discovered" these virtues.

Unitarian preacher George Ripley's Brook Farm was directly inspired by 1837's Financial Panic, and was conceived as a means to sidestep capitalism's tendency toward excess and exploitation. Ripley sought to establish a small-scale "city of God" on a "sweet spot" near West Roxbury, Massachusetts. The farm lasted six years despite problems ranging from poor soil to class feuds, but EMERSON accused Brook Farm of a "perpetual picnic," and Richard Francis similarly refers to an "if-only dimension" of wild-eyed daydreaming. Still, Barbara Packer notes "Brook Farm was not a commune but a joint-stock company" populated by shareholders and showing a clear-eyed awareness of the challenges to its survival. In a November 9, 1840 letter to Emerson, Ripley suggests that his farm was not an insular retreat but an opportunity "to insure a more natural union between intellectual and manual labor," an attempt to resolve the severe separation between Mind and Body that has haunted much Christian enterprise.

Bronson Alcott's Fruitlands was similarly an attempt at a "consociate family," but was hobbled by poor planning and lasted only half a year (1843–1844). Fruitlands (located at Harvard, Massachusetts) was financed by Charles Lane, a Utopian advocate who denounced the nuclear family as unnatural and urged marital reform. Lane referred to a "Third Dispensation," an era following our "tribal" and "national" ages and destined to realize a "Universal" project in which all interests are shared and non-competitive. Fruitlanders were absolute vegans, abstained from alcohol and caffeine, and enlisted in a regimen of cold showers to insure a near-sexless lifestyle. In Alcott's view, a meat-eater is a "replenisher of graveyards" whose "carnal code" is repellent to any civilized outlook. The Fruitland creed was based on negation and renunciation, refusing to use traps (seen as an unfair advantage over fellow animals) and believing that manure-use was a cheating of soil's more "natural" tendencies. Fruitlanders likewise avoided cotton, silk and wool (as unfair to slaves, worms and sheep) in favor of brown linen tunics and trousers. In Alcott's journals, our bodies are as "farmable" as a turf—indeed "soul" and "soil" provide frequent puns in Alcott's writing.

Many TRANSCENDENTAL Age communes were based on principles derived from the French utopian planner Charles Fourier, a Pre-Marxian Socialist whose family had lost its fortune during France's Revolution. Fourier proposed an eradication of all revolution and unrest by a "Harmonian" treatment of human talents and tendencies. There is an ecological vision of the human body in his work, a holistic sense of our laboring mortal body as a microcosm of all reality. Fourier referred to a "harmonian man" whose urges could be satisfied and whose alienation from labor could be cured. "Attractive industry" depends on a rotation of tasks, aimed at producing new harmonies in human behavior, circulating between chores and pastimes like segments on a color-wheel.

Albert Brisbane's 1840 *Social Destiny of Man* (which popularized Fourier's beliefs for American audiences) was read by most of the major Transcendentalists. Brisbane referred to a kind of alternating division of labor as "parceled exercise." In Fourier's vision of a social "phalanx," a group of devoted individuals swap tasks and develop a broad range of faculties. "The body is a bio-region" according to latter-day commentator Deborah Slicer; in American communes our human body resonates and reflects ecological laws. Emerson in "The American Scholar" had lamented Man in his "divided or social state," a division these Utopias tried to remedy. According to Fourier, by alternating tasks we move "serially" across Nature's many demands. This notion of social holism was an effort to reform (a Transcendental keyword) each participant into an "original unity," but such an endeavor had a wearying impact on many practitioners.

There are indeed certain comic side-effects engendered by such generally noble enterprises. Emerson mocked Fourierism for its anticipation of a coming age when all humans would speak in blank verse and for its belief in Mesmer's vision of a race of more "natural" humans eventually regrowing tails. The eating of raw foods was believed to conduct living force directly into its eater, but Fruitlands' soil was not especially amenable to fruit-growing. Fruitlanders only consumed "aspiring" vegetables whose consumable portion grew above-ground, and avoided root vegetables (carrots, beets) that pointed Hellward. Annie Russell Marble, a one-time member of Brook Farm, claimed such groups "dove into the infinite, soared into the illimitable, and never paid cash." (xiii) This was a time of quackery and pseudoscience, of wet sheets wrapped around bodies to draw out disease, of coarse towels deployed in "flesh-brushing" exercises, and of "environmental engineering" plans to tugboat icebergs to relieve overheated New England summers.

A Romantic bias against practical science rendered many communes ill-outfitted to grow food and materials. These groups tended to underestimate nature's darker, more stubborn and literally *intractable* aspects. These small-scale societies also underrated Emerson's notion of "self-reliance"—anarchist Josiah Warren was briefly a Harmonist but believed a lack of individual voice endangered any group. Warren refers to "nature's own inherent law of diversity," a law neglected by Utopians in general.

Some early Utopians (like R.D. Owens) eventually turned to spiritualism (an even less pragmatic, more meditative approach to human harmony). Others followed Charles Lane and became Shakers, a group whose insistence on celibacy would eventually spell its own demise. George Ripley became a book reviewer in New York City's teeming anti–Utopia, Bronson Alcott became a pioneer of what is now referred to as "continuing education," limiting his Orphic, Utopian effusions to classroom-scaled lessons.

Despite so many large-scale and well-noted failures, some Harmonite groups lasted over a century—

New Harmony still survives in rural Indiana. B.F. Skinner's utopian novel *Walden Two* inspired Twin Oaks, a group founded in 1967, clearly showing an ongoing tie between environmental literature and utopian applications. In 1980, the U.S. Census began including communes in its records, and today estimates over 3,000 nationwide. Some groups are by now showing more practical valences: Oneida Community of Mohawk Valley, New York is a manufacturing corporation listed on New York's Stock Exchange, while Iowa's Amana group specializes in microwave ovens (Moment 47).

Some believe a more radical smallness of scale will be necessary for any degree of future success in Utopian projects. Thoreau's experiment at Walden Pond was a kind of "community of one" according to Richard Francis, and still serves as an ongoing template for smaller ventures. Eco-poet GARY SNYDER's Kitkitdizze in California's Sierra Nevada range may well be regarded as a family-scale Utopian community. Ironically, many Utopian principles have grown fragmented, narcissistic and self-serving in certain New Age movements, in which tribal traditions are retrofitted to serve as "self-improvement" trends. Still, several latter-day pundits have predicted our pending oil crisis will lead to a less meat-intensive diet and a more localized and communally interdependent sense of habitat, a kind of Utopia-by-necessity forced by a less easily-traversed globe.—John P. Reder

BIBLIOGRAPHY

Alcott, Louisa May. *Transcendental Wild Oats and Excerpts from the Fruitlands Diary.* Boston: Harvard Common Press, 1981.
Brisbane, Arnold, and Redelia Brisbane. *A Mental Biography.* Boston: Arena, 1893.
_____. *The Social Destiny of Man: or, Theory of the Four Movements.* New York: R.M. DeWitt, 1857.
Francis, Richard. *Transcendental Utopias: Individual and Community at Brook Farm, Fruitlands, and Walden.* Ithaca: Cornell University Press, 1997.
Gura, Philip F. *American Transcendentalism — A History.* New York: Hill & Wang, 2007. (Annie Lee Marble quotes.)
Hill, Christopher. *The World Turned Upside Down: Radical Ideas During the English Revolution.* New York: Viking Press, 1972.
Moment, Gairdner B. "Man the Maker." In *Utopias: The American Experience* (eds. Gairdner B. Moment and Otto F. Kraushaar). Metuchen, NJ and London: Scarecrow Press, 1980.
Packer, Barbara L. *The Transcendentalists.* Athens: University of Georgia Press, 2007.
Skinner, B.F. *Walden Two.* New York: Macmillan, 1976.
Slicer, Deborah. "The Body as Bio-Region." In *Reading the Earth* (ed. Michael P. Branch). Moscow: University of Idaho Press, 1998. pp. 107–116.

Vonnegut, Kurt (1922–2007)

Initially a science fiction writer, Kurt Vonnegut challenged the limits of fiction, often incorporating black humor, illustrations, and metafictive techniques. Throughout his 14 novels, a play, and numerous short stories and essays, Vonnegut lamented (often bitingly) the state of the planet and its inhabitants, while remaining optimistic regarding the potential for humanity to improve its lot, in a fashion reminiscent of MARK TWAIN.

Kurt Vonnegut, Jr. was born in 1922, to Kurt, Sr. and Edith in Indianapolis, Indiana. His father was an architect and his mother came from a brewing fortune that was later lost in the Great Depression. Vonnegut studied chemistry at Cornell before leaving to enlist in the U.S. Army. On Mother's Day, 1944, his mother committed suicide and her death haunted him, especially as he feared at times that he too might commit suicide. The next year, Vonnegut was captured near Dresden by Nazis and imprisoned in a slaughterhouse, which ironically protected him from the Allied firebombing that destroyed the city. Vonnegut later noted, "Dresden had no tactical value; it was a city of civilians. Yet the Allies bombed it until it burned and melted. And then they lied about it. All that was startling to us" ("*Playboy*," 95). Vonnegut's disillusionment led to *Slaughterhouse-Five* (1969), a book that took over 20 years to write. Combining science fiction, black humor, and metafiction, the novel not only wrestles with the events of Dresden, but how one even tells such a story.

Vonnegut tackled environmental issues in several novels with his trademark scathing satire, including *Breakfast of Champions* (1973), where Vonnegut's alter ego Kilgore Trout ironically rants, "I used to be a conservationist. I used to weep and wail about people shooting bald eagles with automatic shotguns from helicopters and all that, but I gave it up" (86). Trout's defeatism displays Vonnegut's fear that humanity has surrendered, and is in need of stiff tonics in order to reverse this trend. His most notable work of environmental literature was *GALÁPAGOS* (1984), in which a small group of people become shipwrecked. The novel explores the negative aspects of evolution — particularly the "big brain" — while addressing how Darwin's ideas affect society's understanding of itself. In 1973 Vonnegut told an interviewer, "I'm not very grateful for Darwin, although I suspect he was right. His ideas make people crueler" ("*Playboy*" 76). A million years from 1986, when the novel is written, brains are smaller and society is better off.

Vonnegut's style avoids lyricism in favor of direct, concise sentences, fueled by an inveterate cynicism toward his times. However, he remains confident in humanity's ability to right itself. "God damn it, you've got to be kind" (129), Eliot Rosewater advises newly baptized babies in *God Bless You, Mr. Rosewater*, and for Vonnegut, this call for kindness and cooperation can heal an ailing society (and planet) ravaged by greedy, power-hungry people. Vonnegut's anti-authoritarianism and humanism made him a counterculture hero, and he remains the most vocal moralist in contemporary American literature. — Peter C. Kunze

BIBLIOGRAPHY

Allen, William Rodney, ed. *Conversations with Kurt Vonnegut*. Jackson: University Press of Mississippi, 1988.

Vonnegut, Kurt. *Breakfast of Champions*. 1973. New York: Dial Press, 2006.

_____. *Galápagos*. 1985. New York: Dial Press, 2006.

_____. *God Bless You, Mr. Rosewater*. 1965. New York: Dial Press, 2006.

"*Playboy* Interview." Interview. Conducted by David Standish. *Playboy* 20 (July, 1973): 57+. Rpt. in Allen 76–110.

Galápagos, Kurt Vonnegut (1985)

In this his eleventh novel, Kurt Vonnegut examines Charles Darwin's theory of natural selection and the implications of evolution, characteristically blending humanistic philosophy with dark humor and biting cynicism. Vonnegut destabilizes the notion of progress achieved by evolution, arguing that large brains are the source of mankind's troubles and "the only villain in my story" (167). In doing so, he offers a counterexample to authors associated with naturalism — most famously, STEPHEN CRANE, Frank Norris and Theodore Dreiser — whose fictional worlds show the influence of Darwin (AMERICAN NATURALISM).

Leon Trotsky Trout, son of Vonnegut alter ego Kilgore Trout, narrates the apocalyptic story one million years after 1986, when humans have (d)evolved into small-brained creatures with flippers. However, this condition has made life considerably easier now that humans cannot overthink their existence. Using evolution and the environment as twin focuses for his inquiry, Vonnegut elaborates a philosophy, consistent throughout his work, which is ultimately confident in the potential of humanity, despite disappointment in their progress thus far. Although Vonnegut commented on mankind's treatment of the environment earlier in novels like *Breakfast of Champions*, *Galápagos* is the most complete articulation of his concerns for humans as a species and their destructive role within nature.

The novel opens at the Hotel El Dorado in Guayaquil, Ecuador, where six people have assembled for the launching of the *Bahía de Darwin*: James Wait, a conman; Mary Hepburn, a biology teacher and recent widow; Zenji Hiroguchi, the inventor of Mandarax, an electronic translator; Hisako Hiroguchi, his pregnant wife; Andrew MacIntosh, a millionaire hoping to recruit Zenji; and Selena MacIntosh, his blind daughter. Advertised as "the Nature Cruise of the Century," the *Bahía de Darwin* will tour the Galápagos Islands, where Darwin famously made the observations that led to the theory of natural selection. The cruise had attracted worldwide attention and guests like Jacqueline Kennedy Onassis were scheduled to attend; however, growing worldwide panic combined with an aerial attack by Peru lead to the cruise's cancellation and the subsequent looting of the ship. In the resulting chaos, Zenji and Andrew are murdered while James, Mary, Hisako, and Selena manage to escape onto the ship. The ship — "the new Noah's Ark" (132) — lands on Santa Rosalia in the Galápagos Islands, where the survivors begin repopulating the earth through Mary's experiments in artificial insemination.

Vonnegut employs various stylistic techniques to explore and examine the concept of evolution, including his characteristic fragmented style. The narrator Leon Trotsky Trout was killed in the construction of the *Bahía de Darwin* and tells the reader that, as a ghost, he has "access to all human knowledge" (155). The narrative treats time relatively, moving from 1986 to the "present" (one million years later), and lighting down, with little or no introduction or context, on a host of varied incidents in the lives of the characters. These passages are intermingled with information about wildlife, Charles Darwin, and quotations from Mandarax. This fusion of fiction and nonfiction calls attention to Vonnegut's role as both an artist and an investigator of the human condition, hoping to better understand the humanity he both adores and chastises. As a graduate student, Vonnegut had studied anthropology at the University of Chicago (*Cat's Cradle* was later accepted as his master's thesis).

Written after a visit to the eponymous islands, *Galápagos* combines a retrospective of Darwin's work in the Galápagos, and scientific information about the wildlife there, with a fictional narrative that playfully explores both, blurring the line between fact and fiction. "I've tried to make the book as responsible as possible scientifically," Vonnegut said at the time (qtd in Moore). He challenges the notion of "survival of the fittest," showing how accidents and dumb luck can have profound consequences for years to come, and how those humans who survive are not necessarily those who were best suited to do so. True to his postmodern proclivities, Vonnegut is skeptical about how knowledge (in this case, scientific knowledge) is acquired, and how it attempts to explain the world. The supposed order brought to people's understanding of themselves and their relationship with the environment through the theory of natural selection troubles Vonnegut, who feels the application of logic to an illogical world is futile and ultimately dangerous. In writing *Galápagos*, a novel which itself attempts to understand the relationship between nature and its (arguably) most advanced creature, Vonnegut places himself in the company of Darwin, but the former refuses to privilege the analysis of a scientist like Darwin over the interpretations offered by novelists such as himself; both are seekers of truth, but with different methods of exploration. Vonnegut's solution — "abdicating the irritating abilities of man's troublesome brain," as Peter Freese describes it — reveals an artist and examiner who is deeply concerned about the state of humanity, but who ultimately accepts his powerlessness to assuage the situation, by approaching the subject with humor and bemused resignation. — Peter C. Kunze

BIBLIOGRAPHY

Freese, Peter. "Surviving the end: apocalypse, evolution, and entropy in Bernard Malamud, Kurt Vonnegut, and Thomas Pynchon." *CRITIQUE: Studies in Contemporary Fiction* 36.n3 (Spring 1995): 163(14). *Expanded Academic ASAP*. Gale. Florida State University. 14 June 2009 http://find.galegroup.com/itx/start.do?prodId=EAIM.

Moore, Lorrie. "How Humans Got Flippers and Beaks." Rev. of *Galápagos*. *The New York Times* 6 Oct. 1985. *The New York Times Online*. 15 June 2009 http://www.nytimes.com/1985/10/06/books/how-humans-got-flippers-and-beaks.html?&pagewanted=1.

Vonnegut, Kurt. *Galápagos*. New York: Delacorte, 1985.

War on the Environment

As the environmental historian Alfred Crosby has demonstrated in such works as *Ecological Imperialism* (1993) and *The Columbian Exchange* (1972), from the 14th-century catapulting of plague-ridden corpses as a form of biological warfare, to the U.S. Army's destruction of the American bison herds to conquer the indigenous nations of the Great Plains, human conquest has inevitably been accompanied by ecological conquest. Perhaps the most telling example, however, comes from the American War in Vietnam, where, as former Operation Ranch Hand pilot Paul Cecil notes in *Herbicidal Warfare* (1986), the United States actually declared "war upon the environment." It is not a coincidence that the term "ecocidal" was coined during the war in Vietnam, when a significant portion of the world's chemical industry was harnessed to produce the defoliants sprayed over 10 percent of the south of Vietnam, wiping out whole ecosystems and poisoning multiple generations of

enemies and allies alike with the defoliants' deadly byproduct, 2,3,7,8 tetrachlorodibenzo-p-dioxin, dioxin's most toxic form. Both in the U.S. and in Vietnam, many have taken the dioxin poisoning from Agent Orange and other defoliants as their starting point, including such writers as Stephen Wright in *Meditations in Green* (1983), Bobbie Ann Mason in *In Country* (1985), and Duong Thu Huong in *No Man's Land* (2005). These works, like all of the literature of war on the environment, detail the many varied ways in which human violence toward one another also produces violence against the environment, and vice versa.

Not surprisingly, American and Vietnamese writers have treated the defoliation in Vietnam and its consequences in substantially different ways. On the one hand, just as the spraying program was ending in 1971, American ecologists such as Thomas Whiteside and John Lewallen wrote extensively about the impact on the land and land systems in books such as *Defoliation* (1970) and *Ecology of Devastation* (1971). More technical than scientific, writers in the 1980s such as John Buckingham and Paul Cecil detailed the spray program itself, chronicling its strengths, weaknesses, and overall success or failure as an instance of military problem solving. At the opposite end of the spectrum, fiction writers such as Wright and Mason abstracted the defoliation into larger, overarching metaphors. For Wright, the defoliation was like the United States itself; the chemical reaction forced the vegetation to grow so rapidly that it outconsumed its own ability to sustain itself. For Mason, the mysterious and poorly understood illnesses attributed to Agent Orange exposure that American veterans suffered were emblems of the larger problems they faced in rejoining American society, being accepted, and being understood.

Vietnamese writers, on the other hand, could not afford such metaphorical distance. For them, the damage done by exposure was real, pervasive, and devastating. When the country initiated a replanting program, the human cost of the defoliation began to become clear. Tens of thousands of exposed veterans began to suffer from fatal illnesses such as diabetes, lymphatic leukemia, and Hodgkin's disease, and miserably debilitating skin disorders such as chloracne and porphyria cutanea tarda. Writers such as Ma Van Khang, Nguyen Quang Lap, and Minh Chuyen began to tell the stories of this suffering in fiction and nonfiction published in daily newspapers and weekly literature magazines. In 1984, Khang's "A Child, a Man" told the story of a small boy abused by a stepmother who suffered from an exposure-related illness. The story ends with the protagonist asking, "How could that woman ever recover from such an illness?" in a moment of empathy that typified the Vietnamese literary response to Agent Orange for the next 25 years, when writers explored the vastly different ways that defoliation had impacted the lives of the Vietnamese.

Unfortunately, the literature of war on the environment does not end with the American War in Vietnam. The burning of the oil fields and the unmonitored use and incineration of chemical weapons during the first Persian Gulf War created human and environmental damage that has yet to be fully comprehended. More than 200,000 American veterans of that war believe they suffer from what has become known as Persian Gulf War Syndrome, which a report by the U.S. National Academy of Sciences suggests is caused by their exposure to acetylcholinesterase inhibitors, a component of nerve agents. Veteran writer Gabe Hudson has pioneered the American literary response to this environmental damage in his collection of stories, *Dear Mr. President* (2002). — Charles Waugh

BIBLIOGRAPHY

Cecil, Paul Frederick. *Herbicidal Warfare: The Ranch Hand Project in Vietnam.* New York: Praeger, 1986.

Crosby, Alfred W. *The Columbian Exchange: Biological and Cultural Consequences of 1492.* Westport, CT: Greenwood Press, 1972.

_____. *Ecological Imperialism: The Biological Expansion of Europe, 900–1900.* Cambridge: Cambridge University Press, 1987.

Duong Thu Huong. *No Man's Land.* Trans. Nina McPherson and Phan Huy Duong. New York: Hyperion East, 2005.

Hudson, Gabe. *Dear Mr. President.* New York: Knopf, 2002.

Lewallen, John. *Ecology of Devastation.* Baltimore: Penguin, 1971.

Mason, Bobbie Ann. *In Country.* New York: Harper & Row, 1985.

Whiteside, Thomas. *Defoliation.* New York: Dutton, 1970.

Wright, Stephen. *Meditations in Green.* New York: Scribner's, 1983.

Warren, Robert Penn (1905–1989)

Robert Penn Warren is best known as the author of *All the Kings Men*, and perhaps as America's most famous New Critic. A prolific writer, he authored some 17 books of poetry, 10 novels, six historical and biographical works, five book-length works of criticism, three children's books, a collection of short stories, and a play. He began his career as a Rhodes Scholar (1928–1930), and in 1943 received the Shelly Memorial Award, followed by an appointment as the Chair of Poetry at the Library of Congress in 1944 — a position that was later renamed Poet Laureate, and which was again awarded to Warren in 1986. He is the only American author to have received the Pulitzer Prize in both fiction (1947) and poetry (1958 & 1979). He was granted the National Book Award (1958), a National Arts Foundation Award (1969), a Bolligen Prize in Poetry (1967), the Presidential Medal of Freedom (1980), and a MacArthur Prize fellowship in 1981 (the so-called "genius grant"), among other awards, honorary doctorates, and appointments (Frey). As this record suggests, he is more commonly thought of as a traditional man of letters than as an environmental writer, but his poetry often reflects his deep and abiding concern for nature and humanity's relationship to the natural world.

Warren was born and raised in rural Kentucky. His father, Robert Franklin Warren, aspired to be a poet but had to work as a banker and proprietor to support his wife Anna Ruth Penn and his three children. Warren's biographer, Joseph Blotner, notes that while he was growing up, Warren often found time "to play amateur naturalist in the woods" (30). His childhood friend Kent Greenfield, "a self-taught naturalist," tutored Warren in everything out-of-doors, from bird calling and sketching, to making bows and arrows with which they hunted small game. Additionally, Warren wandered in the woods and sketched birds during his summer visits to his grandfather's farm (17–18). These early, formative experiences would become sustained and sustaining habits of the mature writer, right up until his death in 1989; in an interview he once confirmed that, "I can't work very long in cities [...] I just have to be able to walk in the woods, to be outdoors, to be alone" (331 *Talking*).

After graduating from Vanderbilt in 1925, where he roomed with Allen Tate, he lived a transient life for the next quarter century, traveling back and forth across the United States and often spending time abroad, particularly in Italy. He received an M.A. from UC Berkeley, during which time he explored the Sierra Nevada, and in 1931 he returned to Vanderbilt to teach for three years, before being appointed assistant professor at LSU. After teaching there for six years, he was unsatisfied with the contract LSU offered him, and secured a position at the University of Minnesota in 1942. He would never live in the South again, although he often returned to visit family and friends, and for research. Warren's friend, the historian C. Vann Woodward, remarked that, "the South furnished the setting for virtually all of Warren's fiction and much of his poetry as well as the subject of his nonfictional prose" (283). Warren's keen sense of place, particularly of the South, remained a prominent feature of his writings, as did the other four famous "senses" of the Southern Renascence: a sense of the past, the community, family,

· and religion. These senses were viewed as interrelated and indispensable for an authentic rootedness in a place or region. For Warren, one of the Nashville Agrarians, knowledge of the natural landscape and environment was an integral aspect of a sense of place, and his poetry and fiction often reflects his acute observation of the environments he inhabited during his journeys. However, his early immersion in the Southern landscape and culture left an indelible and unequalled imprint on his work.

Shortly after leaving Minnesota to teach at Yale University, Warren settled in New England, where he remained for much of the latter half of his life. After his first marriage with Cinina Brescia dissolved, he married the novelist Eleanor Clark. Together they had two children, Rosanna Phelps Warren and Gabriel Penn Warren. After more than a decade without publishing any new collections of poetry, Warren returned to the commanding form that would dominate his later years. A number of his poems from this period are set in rural Vermont, where he built a cabin and constructed trails on his property. He continued to travel, often spending months in the Italian countryside, particularly at La Rocca, a sixteenth-century fortress near Porto Ercole. Warren's 1957 collection of poems, *Promises*, features scenes set in both Vermont and Italy, and vividly evokes the environment, both natural and personal, of these two starkly different places.

In *Audubon: A Vision*, published in 1969, Warren chronicles a number of emotionally charged incidences in the life of the great bird authority JOHN JAMES AUDUBON. The short sequence of poems evoke a strange American wilderness and the dangers of frontier travel, as well as the incongruity of a wandering frontiersman finding himself mimicking birdcalls in the "silken salons" of Europe. Always searching for a personal connection to his subjects, near the close of the sequence Warren writes:

Long ago, in Kentucky, I, a boy, stood
By a dirt road, in first dark, and heard
The great geese hoot northward.

I could not see them, there being no moon
And the stars sparse. I heard them.

I did not know what was happening in my heart
[*Collected Poems* 266].

This lyrical moment not only demonstrates Warren's sensitivity to the natural world, but also exhibits an almost mystical convergence, here between the poet, his subject (Audubon), and intense intimacy with the environment. In a parallel moment earlier in the poem, he describes Audubon observing a bear and a bumblebee in a blueberry patch; Audubon is moved to consider "how thin is the membrane between himself and the world" (255). Such convergence of place, personal past, historical past, and the communion of humanity, sparked in part by an intimate connection with the environment, is typical in Warren's writings.

All of Warren's work — his poetry, fiction, non-fiction, and criticism — argues for specificity, concreteness, and the importance of "environment," whether in the form of con-text or natural surroundings, integrated with personal experience, in dealing with even the most abstruse and refractory questions of human existence. In many ways, Warren adhered to EZRA POUND's dictum to "go in fear of abstractions." This commitment to inscribing and universalizing actual experience in his writing, led Warren to assail the work of some of America's most influential writers and thinkers, among them RALPH WALDO EMERSON and THOMAS JEFFERSON, whom he felt were unduly influenced by Enlightenment values and a belief in the perfectibility of humanity. Although Warren was not religious in the traditional sense, he often addressed broadly Christian themes, particularly original sin, and the doctrine of the fall, convinced that an acknowledgment of these doctrines was necessary for an understanding of human nature and for the possibility of hope in an often acutely dispiriting world (THE BIBLE).

Warren's sharpest critique of Jefferson comes in his book-length poem *Brother to Dragons*, which is primarily concerned with reconciling Jefferson's optimistic dreams for the country and mankind, as laid out in the Declaration of Independence, with the brutal murder of a slave in the Kentucky frontier committed by Jefferson's nephews. Warren also addresses Meriwether Lewis's life and travels during the LEWIS AND CLARK expedition. Nature and the environment factor into *Brother to Dragons* as an important subtext, especially as a critique of the exploitive tendencies at work in America's self-perceived MANIFEST DESTINY. One of the great ironies of Warren's critique of Jefferson is that in many ways Jefferson is the father of the kind of Southern Agrarianism that Warren and the Nashville Agrarians later professed, albeit with important differences, in their collection of essays *I'll Take My Stand*.

Warren's criticism of Emerson is perhaps most evident in his poem "Homage to Emerson," where Warren employs strikingly original imagery in his critique of Emersonian idealism, especially as it conceives of nature and the natural in Emerson's seminal essay "NATURE." Warren recognized the importance of the writers of the American Renaissance, but his criticisms of Emerson extended to Thoreau; on the other hand, he praised the less heralded work of HAWTHORNE and MELVILLE, and helped to revive interest in Melville's poetry when he edited a collection of his poems, complete with an introduction that reexamined Melville's place in American letters as a poet, and not merely the author of *MOBY DICK*.

Among the many writers who impacted Warren's thought and writing, Dante Alighieri, S.T. Coleridge, T.S. ELIOT, and WILLIAM FAULKNER stand out most prominently, and all share his keen sense both of the absolute importance of place and concrete experience, and of their universal implications. Warren in turn had a profound influence not only on other writers in the twentieth century, but also countless students and scholars, as his widely influential college textbook *Understanding Poetry*, edited with Cleanth Brooks, served as a hallmark of New Criticism. He died in Vermont, in 1989, of complications from bone cancer.— Michael Beilfuss

BIBLIOGRAPHY

Beck, Charlotte H. *Robert Penn Warren, Critic.* Knoxville: University of Tennessee Press, 2006.
Blotner, Joseph. *Robert Penn Warren: A Biography.* New York: Random, 1997.
Burt, John. *Robert Penn Warren and American Idealism.* New Haven: Yale University Press, 1988.
Clark, William Bedford. *The American Vision of Robert Penn Warren.* Lexington: University of Kentucky Press, 1991.
_____. *Critical Essays on Robert Penn Warren.* Boston: G.K. Hall, 1981.
Corrigan, Lesa Carnes. *Poems of Pure Imagination: Robert Penn Warren and the Romantic Tradition.* Baton Rouge: Louisiana State University Press, 1999.
Grimshaw, James A, Jr. *Understanding Robert Penn Warren.* Columbia: University of South Carolina Pres, 2001.
Runyon, Randolph Paul. *Ghostly Parallels: Robert Penn Warren and the Lyric Sequence.* Knoxville: University of Tennessee Press, 2006.
Strandberg, Victor. *The Poetic Vision of Robert Penn Warren.* Lexington: University of Kentucky Press, 1977.
Warren, Robert Penn. *Brother to Dragons: A Tale in Verse and Voices.* Baton Rouge: Louisiana State University Press, 1996.
_____. *The Collected Poems of Robert Penn Warren.* Ed. John Burt. Baton Rouge: Louisiana State University Press, 1998.
_____. *Talking with Robert Penn Warren.* Eds. Floyd C. Watkins, John T. Hiers, and Mary Louise Weaks. Athens: University of Georgia Press, 1990.
Woodward, C. Vann. *The Burden of Southern History.* 3rd Edition. Baton Rouge: Louisiana State University Press, 1993.

Whitman, Walt (1819–1892)

Walt Whitman published work in a number of different genres, but is most noted for his mythopoeic evocation of American Being in LEAVES OF GRASS (1855–1891), a collection of poetry that he edited and expanded throughout his lifetime. His project, as he defined it in 1888, was "an attempt, from first to last, to put a Person, a human being (myself, in the latter half of the Nineteenth Century, in America,) fully and truly on record" (Whitman 671). By grounding his poetry in an embodied self, he explored the interconnections of human and environment in startling new ways. His frank depictions of the body earned harsh criticism but were integrally related to his attempt to be the poet who "incarnates" America's "geography and natural life and rivers and lakes" (7). The first, self-published edition's physical design featured tendrils emerging from the title on a green background, illustrating his recurrent metaphor of words as growing plants. For Whitman, the poet's voice was always emerging from the natural world, so the poet's role was to speak for the earth, reconciling "the round impassive globe," with the "Soul of man," by standing between the two and "wholly and joyously blend[ing] them" (648). Gazing with an inclusive and empathetic eye on the continents, countries, peoples, animals and plants of the earth, he named them all, like Adam in Paradise, in long inventories scattered throughout his poetry. Montages of disparate items reflected his sense of his country's geographic and demographic diversity. Long lines extending beyond the margins of the page mirrored his vision of the continent's vastness, as he first imagined it from the shores of Long Island, New York. Ultimately, his vision of the poet as "uniter" (648) of Nature and the human soul produced both a bold new style of poetry and a new conception of man's relationship to the environment.

Born Walter Whitman in West Hills, Long Island, in 1819, he spent most of his life in New York and New Jersey, dying in Camden, N.J., in 1892. When Whitman was four his family moved to Brooklyn, a bustling city in its own right. Surrounded by water, he rode the ferries that ran across the river to Manhattan, and returned often to Long Island, visiting his Quaker grandparents. In 1846 Whitman made his first excursion into the continent he would claim (in the 1855 Preface) to embody, heading by train and steamboat to Louisiana to work for the New Orleans *Crescent*. Within a year, however, he resigned and returned to Brooklyn. Back in New York he began publishing his own newspaper and continued to write, cultivating both a self, and a style of verse that would proclaim this self "Walt Whitman, a kosmos" (52), as "Song of Myself" announced to the world when, in 1855, he first published *Leaves of Grass*. Without any of the section numbers later added, "Song of Myself," its focal work, was one long poem, running 1346 lines. In it the reader confronts a persona earnestly striving for connection, and leaving readers with a promise that his presence will, through the earth we tread in common, remain with us.

Though Whitman's expressions of joy in nature and calls to rely on one's own perceptions displayed the influence of EMERSON's TRANSCENDENTALISM, as well as the Quakerism he was exposed to as a child, he went beyond their emphasis on the visual to embrace the whole body as a vehicle of perception. Moreover, Whitman viewed his own being as enmeshed in, even one with, the environment, as he sings in "Song of the Open Road" (1856):

I inhale great draughts of space
The east and the west are mine, and the north and
  the south are mine.
I am larger, better than I thought,
I did not know I held so much goodness [300].

In countless poems the speaker walks the continent, and this is how the body of man and the body of the land meet and discover their "free range and diversity" ("Our Old Feuillage," 319). Written in 1860, "Our Old Feuillage" (French for foliage) explores the implications of union and disunion that emerge from the juxtaposition of body and continent, and its impassioned plea for the former was, among other things, an attempt to avoid the disaster that nonetheless arrived — the conflict he called the Secession War.

Whitman published a third, expanded edition of *Leaves of Grass* before the war broke out, and this 1860 edition included a "cluster" (his name for groupings of poems) called *Calamus*. Named after the calamus plant, also called sweet flag, a reed with a phallic shape, the poems extol "manly love" for other men. In his 1876 Preface to *Two Rivulets*, he claimed these poems were actually political, that "sane affection of man for man" was necessary for the country to become a "living union" (1011). These quasi-erotic nature poems thus suggest that the human body is not only that which apprehends nature, but also that which propels America, the democratic nation he loved.

Despite what later readers saw as homoeroticism in the *Calamus* poems, at the time the *Enfans d'Adam* poems (the cluster later renamed *Children of Adam)* most shocked his audience. "I Sing the Body Electric" proclaimed "limitless limpid jets of love hot and enormous, quivering jelly of love, white-blow and delirious juice" (253). The sexuality praised in the poems was, however, hard to pin down. When English critic John Addington Symonds tried to press Whitman into an explicit acknowledgment of the homosexuality implicit in so many of his poems, Whitman denied it, claiming to have himself sired flocks of illegitimate children. Although this biographical detail has never been proven, the concept of procreation is undeniably and absolutely fundamental to his unifying vision of the natural and human world.

Though the rupture between the States struck a blow to his ideal of diverse peoples and places held together in unity, Whitman found solace in his admiration for the soldier. When his brother George enlisted and was injured, Whitman went to Fredericksburg to find him. He then settled in Washington, D.C., in order to minister to the wounded; he read to them, wrote their letters and generally brought comfort, supporting himself with clerical government work. *Drum-Taps*, a collection of poems on the war, was first published as a separate book in 1865 and later included in *Leaves of Grass*. The poems mingle grief at the loss of life, admiration for the exhibition of masculinity, and excitement at the movement of peoples. He was enamored, as well, of President Lincoln, whom he passed occasionally on the streets of Washington, and whose second inauguration he attended. His two elegies, "When Lilacs Last in the Dooryard Bloom'd" and "O Captain! My Captain!" were added to the ever-expanding *Leaves of Grass*.

As Whitman's reputation grew, fame was mixed with outrage at the sexuality expressed in many of his poems, and he was eventually fired from his government position. His friend William O'Connor's passionate defense of Whitman coined the term "The Good Gray Poet" to describe him, a phrase that stuck, as it described both Whitman's physical appearance of long, gray beard and hair, and his idealistic sensibility. After the outcry, Whitman was hired to a new position in the Attorney General's office in Washington, where he worked until 1874. During this time he published three essays, collected as *Democratic Vistas*, which begin by proclaiming that "the greatest lessons of Nature through the universe are perhaps the lessons of variety and freedom, the same present the greatest lessons also in New World politics and progress." (929). He turns, as always, to the natural realm, for healing of the political system. This same year of 1871 saw the publication of "Passage to India," which celebrates human interaction across natural boundaries. The poem honors the recent opening of the Suez Canal, the joining of the Union Pacific and the Central Pacific railroads and the successful completion of the laying of the Transatlantic cable.

In 1873 Whitman suffered a stroke and moved in with his brother George in Camden, New Jersey, where, despite failing health, Whitman continued to write and lecture. He made a journey to Boston in 1881, visiting Emerson in Concord, Massachusetts. In 1882, he published *Specimen Days*, a volume of prose drawn from the notes he had kept through his life, as well as "A Backward Glance O'er Travel'd Roads." Whitman purchased a house at 328 Mickle Street, Camden, New Jersey in 1884. He published the so-called "death-bed edition" of *Leaves of Grass* in 1891. A year later, he died at the Mickle Street house and was buried in Harleigh Cemetery, Camden, New Jersey. His reputation and influence mounted steadily after his death, and he has indeed come to be considered the "Good Gray Poet," the father of modern American poetry and a towering figure in environmental literature. — Robin Morris

BIBLIOGRAPHY

Belasco, Susan, Ed Folsom, and Kenneth M. Price. *Leaves of Grass: The Sesquicentennial Essays*. Lincoln: University of Nebraska Press, 2007.
Folsom, Ed, and Kenneth M. Price. "Walt Whitman." The Walt Whitman Archive. Available online. URL: http://www.whitmanarchive.org. 1995–2009. Accessed June 2009.
Mickle Street Review. "Walt Whitman and Place." Issue 17/18. Ed. Tyler Hoffman. 2005. Available online. URL: http://micklestreet.rutgers.edu/archives/Issue%201718/index.html. Accessed June 2009.
Reynolds, David S. *Walt Whitman*. New York: Oxford University Press, 2004.
Whitman, Walt. *Whitman Complete Poetry and Collected Prose*. Ed. Justin Kaplan. New York: Library of America, 1982.

Leaves of Grass, Walt Whitman (1892)

Walt Whitman's *Leaves of Grass* was first published in 1855 as a sequence of 12 poems. The much revised and extended final edition of 1891–92 includes most of his literary production. Its many interwoven themes, including individuality, democracy, and comradeship; engagement in natural and urban environments; love, longing, and loss; are permeated by Whitman's ecological concerns. In *What Is Nature?* Kate Soper discusses three usages of the term "nature": the visible landscape, underlying natural forces or principles, and the unconstructed environment (or nature as opposed to culture). Whitman's writing encompasses all three. His regional landscapes, influenced by his childhood experience on Long Island and excursions in his beloved island city of "Manhatta," emphasize coastlines, while his panoramic lists depict the great variety of ecosystems throughout North America. He reveals a deep and sensitive interest in natural principles through references to scientific advances in fields such as evolution, hygiene, and recycling. For Whitman, as for the TRANSCENDENTALISTs EMERSON and THOREAU, nature represents the realm of the authentic, as well as a gateway to the spiritual. Yet his dynamic representation of the environment and his emphasis on cor-

poreality and mobility support a view of nature and culture as convergent.

The radical newness of Whitman's poetics hinges on his perception of a dynamic, animating energy within all natural processes. While Thoreau structured WALDEN around diurnal and seasonal cycles, much of Whitman's poetry reflects ongoing, pulsating rhythms such as those of waves and breath. For critic Angus Fletcher, Whitman is the innovator of the "environment poem." By manipulating phrases to reflect the rhythm of waveforms, both ocean waves and those described by particle physics, he invites readers into, and surrounds them by, a highly charged and resonant environment; while, by shifting focus from the underlying energy to the visible landscape and cityscape, he implies an interconnectedness across scale. Ultimately, nature is the text Whitman asks his readers to study, and its message is consistent, but never static:

> If you would understand me go to the heights or water-shore,
> The nearest gnat is an explanation, and a drop or motion of waves a key
> ["Song of Myself" 47.1252–1253].

Into this dynamic territory Whitman introduces a vigorously corporeal and perceptually acute persona. Often this persona appears as a traveling commentator for whom nature is a field for experience, comradeship, and exchange; and he freely shifts his position from participant to observer, one "Both in and out of the game and watching and wondering at it" ("Song of Myself" 4.79). This technique of flexible engagement allows Whitman's persona to be a reflective speaker without dissociating himself from embodied context. Moreover, he can shift from a robust individual to the spokesperson for a new American "everyman." The continuity of the persona's characterization as he passes through both natural and urban spaces implies a comfortable relation between nature and culture, although nature remains the touchstone of authenticity.

Whitman's delight in the variety of the natural world parallels EMILY DICKINSON's assertion that "My splendors are menagerie" (Fr. 319). In sharp contrast to her condensed stanzas, however, are Whitman's long lines of free verse, and the catalogue technique in which he rolls out long lists in parallel syntax, encapsulating features of a national landscape perceived as fecund and teaming with life. Such environmental sensitivity intersects with Whitman's praise of democracy in passages depicting a respect for the many life forms he has "studied":

> Aware of the buffalo herds...
> Of earth, rocks, Fifth-month flowers experienced, stars, rain, snow, my amaze,

Having studied the mocking-bird's tones and the
    flight of the mountain-hawk
["Starting" 1.9–12].

His attitude combines wonder, "amaze," and at-
tentiveness. He hears "chants" (3.4–7) of various regions and plans to "make a song" (6.7). He claims
to be neither pure inventor nor scribe of nature's
sounds; rather, his verse represents "the One form'd
out of all" (6.13), an integration of multiple impressions. He acknowledges nature as a source of sustenance and inspiration, while also affirming his own
creative capacity.

Like Emerson, Whitman urges his readers to explore their own direct perceptions of nature. In "Song
of Myself," one of the best-known sections of *Leaves*,
he stages a movement from visual to tactile impressions in order to guide readers toward embodied participation. His persona wants to become "undisguised
and naked," lose his cultured adornments and touch
raw life: "I am mad for it to be in contact with me"
("Song of Myself" 2.20). He is immersed down to
the level at which "every atom belonging to me as
good belongs to you" (1.3), and affirms a shared humanity deeper than allegiances to "creeds and schools,"
which he associates with a cultural veneer (1.10). As
translator of nature's energies, claims Whitman,

I harbor for good or bad, I permit to speak at every
    hazard,
nature without check with original energy ["Song"
1.11–12].

He defines this energy as "the procreant urge of
the world" (3.45), a leap that allows him to present
poetic creation as parallel to biological reproduction.
While human creativity augments nature's voices,
the two zones remain convergent. And by suggesting
that human expression is an extension of the expres-
siveness of the natural world, Whitman avoids any
damaging nature/culture disjunction.

Such an optimistic viewpoint must nonetheless
confront two challenges in defining humanity's relation to the rest of the natural world, namely language and death. Section 6 of "Song of Myself" addresses both issues through the metaphor of grass.
The grass is a truly democratic plant, "sprouting"
broadly without discrimination (6.107–108). Further,
he compares its tapering shape to mouths, with the
earth's voice composed of the "many uttering tongues"
(6.129) of the departed, whose "hints" the poet can
try to translate (6.121). Maria Farland cites a Biblical
passage in which human frailty is compared to grass
that dies after a season, and points out how Whitman
converts this analogy into a testament that the grass's
seasonal recurrence proves "there is really no death"

(6.126) (Farland 813–14). Thus, the recurring natural
cycles structure Whitman's worldview as well as contributing to the pulsating rhythms of his verse.

Whitman also stages the acceptance of death in
"Out of the Cradle Endlessly Rocking." With memorable pathos, the poem describes a boy observing a
mockingbird grieving for its lost mate. As he struggles with his sense of loss, the sea "whisper'd" him
the "low and delicious word death" (166). The waves,
"endlessly" replacing one another, allow him to
accept death as a balance for life. As Jimmie Killingsworth notes, Whitman enriches nature's evocations;
from the bird's song and the ocean's bare reminder
of death's inevitability, the poet develops a nuanced
affirmation of ongoing life cycles.

In "This Compost," Whitman confronts death as
a problem of hygiene. Maria Farland discusses the
growing awareness in Whitman's epoch that decaying
matter was unhealthy, leading to a concern about
contact with the earth where the dead are buried.
Soon after the poem's composition, however, scientists discovered how composting converts decay into
nourishment for new life; and Whitman incorporates
the new scientific developments into his optimistic
framework, to indicate how the earth can purify
itself. Again natural cycles assist in his acceptance of
death as part of the life cycle.

In addition to his regionalist, experiential, and scientific interests in the environment, Whitman is considered America's first urban poet. His focus on embodiment and mobility continue in his city views.
He shifts from a focus on individuals or "types," people representing professions, ethnicities, etc., to a
view of crowds where individuality blends into the
ensemble. Such shifts in scale suggest, even in the
densest urban context, a fundamental relatedness between the individuals and their environments. An
extension of this technique is seen in "Crossing
Brooklyn Ferry," where Whitman envisions people
in future times arriving in his beloved environment
like a succession of waves. The ferry, on which passengers are both moving and standing still, enables
Whitman to depict time as both ongoing and endlessly present. In an unusually transcendent passage,
he declares that "you furnish your parts toward eternity" (131), suggesting that life energy, though immanent, transcends temporal appearances. This creative dynamism in Whitman's narrative viewpoint
and in his portrayal of the environment encourages
an optimism that incorporates scientific advances,
converts loss to hope, and allows him to depict interactive vitality in both natural and cultural settings;
an optimism ensuring that his contribution to environmental writing will remain a major component
of his lasting influence. — Mary Newell

BIBLIOGRAPHY

Farland, Maria. "Decomposing City: Walt Whitman's New York and the Science of Life and Death." *ELH* 74.4 (2007): 799–827.

Fletcher, Angus. *A New Theory for American Poetry: Democracy, the Environment, and the Future of Imagination.* Cambridge: Harvard University Press, 2004.

Handley, George B. *New World Poetics: Nature and the Adamic Imagination of Whitman, Neruda, and Walcott.* Athens: University of Georgia Press, 2007.

Killingsworth, M. Jimmie. *Walt Whitman and the Earth: A Study in Ecopoetics.* Iowa City: University of Iowa Press, 2004. Available online. URL: http://www.whitmanarchive.org/criticism/current/anc.00162.html#n72. Accessed June 24, 2009.

Outka, Paul. "(De)composing Whitman." *ISLE* 12.1 (2005): 56.

Whitman, Walt. *Leaves of Grass, a Norton Critical Edition.* Ed. Michael Mood. New York: W. W. Norton, 2002.

Williams, Terry Tempest (1959–   )

Terry Tempest Williams was born in 1959 and raised in Utah, a fifth-generation member of the LDS church whose writing is highly inflected by her spiritual experiences of the Western landscape. Unlike many environmental writers, however, Williams does not seek to channel a "wild" landscape, or a landscape "purified" of the influences of humanity. Rather, her works tend to rest at the unstable juncture where civilization *meets* and interacts with wilderness, a juncture whose instability is a product of its artificiality. Her oeuvre highlights the *inter*relationships between human and animal, constructed place and natural place, in a way that ultimately points to the falseness of these dichotomies.

Williams is most famous for REFUGE: AN UNNATURAL HISTORY OF FAMILY AND PLACE (1991), which has been canonized both within the corpus of environmental literature and within a smaller body of literature about Utah. The book presents alternating vignettes about Williams' family as her mother — a breast-cancer survivor — battles ovarian cancer, with narratives of Williams' visits to the Bear River Migratory Bird Refuge, which is threatened by the rising Great Salt Lake. The work artfully interweaves the public and private, the global politics of environmentalism and the personal politics of life and death.

Refuge is most famous, perhaps, for Williams' linking of her mother's cancer to nuclear testing in the Nevada desert during the '50s and '60s. However, it is important to note that this argument is *not* the major thrust of the work, which is much more a personal account of coping with death — with tolerating change while remaining rooted in a place — than it is a political polemic about nuclear testing. William's herself claims that its fundamental premise is "that an intimacy with the natural world initiates an inti-

macy with death, because life and death are engaged in an endless, inseparable dance" (qtd. in *Contemporary Authors*).

Williams has also written and co-written children's books dealing with natural themes, and earned acclaim for her 1994 volume of essays *An Unspoken Hunger: Stories from the Field.* She has written other volumes on the American Southwest, including *Pieces of White Shell: A Journey to Navajo Land* and *Coyote's Canyon.* In 2000 she published *Leap,* a study of Hieronymous Bosch's painting "Garden of Earthly Delights."

Williams' environmental writing is most noted for its intense focus on *place* and human relationships with and within those places. She constructs what she calls "an erotics of place" (qtd. in *Contemporary Authors*), an intense expression of the sensibilities and sensitivities of environment — place as poetry. And her poetic animation of place is finally as unique and expressive as the Utah desert itself, explaining perhaps why her words are so often chosen to represent that landscape. — Laura Boynton Johnson

BIBLIOGRAPHY

"Terry Tempest Williams." *Contemporary Authors Online* (2002). Reproduced in *Biography Resource Center.* Gale Group. Available online. URL: http://galenet.galegroup.com/servlet/BioRC. 30 June, 2009.

Refuge: An Unnatural History of Family and Place,
Terry Tempest Williams (1991)

Williams' *Refuge: An Unnatural History of Family and Place* combines memoir, nature writing, and political commentary; in effect, it "crystallizes what is the general though perhaps unstated aim of most nature writing: to write about the natural world and about oneself simultaneously, to look mutually outward and inward" (qtd. in Riley 600). In its departures from more classic works of nature writing, *Refuge* finds its success *as* nature writing.

Refuge is the most famous work of a rich and varied oeuvre whose highlights include a number of other volumes on the West and the Southwest, including *An Unspoken Hunger: Stories from the Field* (1994), *Pieces of White Shell: A Journey to Navajo Land* (1995), and *Coyote's Canyon* (2001). *Refuge* earned Williams universal acclaim, establishing her reputation as a seminal voice in American literature on the environment.

The book's primary narrative follows the fate of Williams and her family after her mother's diagnosis with ovarian cancer. Interspersed with the family narratives are those describing Williams' visits to the rising Great Salt Lake, where she meditates on subjects ranging from nature, to loss, and history both collective and personal. Clearly, the menace of the rising lake, especially its threat to Bear River Migratory Bird Refuge, is meant to be symbolic of the menace of cancer, yet the connection is subtler and less didactic than this would suggest. Each of the book's 37 essays moves more intimately between family and lake than the last, such that the stories gradually merge.

Accordingly, the book's major environmental themes focus on the interconnections between civilization and nature, especially amidst opposing forces of stability and change. Throughout, Williams struggles with her own sense of rootedness — expressed through family relationships, Mormon genealogy, and the cycles of Great Salt Lake that had previously seemed predictable — amidst the violence and pain of change. In the words of Williams scholar, Charles Mitchell, "How can we feel at home on a landscape that is always in flux? How do we belong to something — a family, a place — that refuses to stay put?" (169); in Williams' own words, the novel is a story about "begin[ning] to find a refuge in change" (178).

Unlike some nature writing, *Refuge* does not present "wilderness" in conceptual or historical isolation, or highlight the hostilities between the human and nonhuman. Instead, the experience of nature — in contrast to the rugged masculine ideal we have inherited — is presented as a shared, communal experience (see Riley 590; Mitchell). Williams frequently goes to the lake with friends or family members, at which point her musings become conversation, in contrast to silent, solitary figures like MUIR or THOREAU. Thus the distinction between human and environment — on which so much environmental writing and cultural supposition rests — is finally a false binary for Williams, a product of "a cultural framework that fosters fragmentation" (Chandler 655).

Under the narrative and meditative surface of the book, Williams argues that her mother's ovarian cancer — along with the cancers of other women in her family — is likely a result of government nuclear testing in Nevada during the 1950s and 1960s. These tests may account for higher levels of cancer in populations downwind from the test sites. Although this claim is arguably the element for which *Refuge* is most widely remembered — and may therefore be its greatest environmental legacy — the book is far richer and more personal than such a cause–effect argument would suggest. Indeed, Williams discusses nuclear testing only in the final essay, "The Clan of One-Breasted Women," the only essay of the 37 *not* named for a bird species. Although this essay obviously stands out from the others, its message must

not be allowed to overshadow theirs, or much of the work's hard-won insight and wisdom will be forsaken.

Katherine Chandler argues that *Refuge* is essentially a study in the interplay of tensions: "[Williams] is torn by what she perceives as oppositions, incompatibilities that mark the years surrounding her mother's contraction of cancer" (658). These oppositions include "cultural dichotomies like those of objectivity and subjectivity, science and religion, body and spirit" (656), and nature and civilization. Even when Williams leaves the ostensibly predictable world of science, family and faith, for the bird refuge, she confronts the uncertain reality of a menacing flood. Peaceful resolution of the oppositions Williams presents is ultimately impossible, and the writing process proves to be one of *negotiating* reciprocal tensions rather than arrogantly resolving them.

Other tensions are more personal: *Refuge* evokes the complicated identity politics of Williams' position as woman, naturalist, member of the LDS church, activist, and daughter, again revealing the poverty of standard cultural wisdom that pits such positions against one another. Perhaps this evocative examination of identity is what leads Jeanette Riley to argue that *Refuge* "examine[s] our politics of identity" *through* the natural environment (Riley 586).

Cassandra Kircher offers a more nuanced reading of the dichotomies in *Refuge*, acknowledging the complexity of Williams' relationship to stereotypical cultural tensions such as those of masculinity and femininity, and nature and culture. On the one hand, Kircher argues, Williams upholds these distinctions. She reinforces the overdetermined association of woman with nature, and man with culture, especially in her narrative of the Canadian Goose Gun Club's members' celebration over the removal of the burrowing owls, or in her opposition of the "Tree of Utah" — presented as a garish, phallic, unnatural contrivance by a male artist — with the Sun Tunnels, constructed by a female artist in careful coordination with the surrounding desert and the movements of the stars. In such passages, Williams seems to imply that women have a privileged understanding of nature, one from which men are excluded. "Williams sees women's connection to nature as virtuous, empowering, comforting, and good, while portraying the institutions she identifies with the patriarchy as harmful or, at least, problematic" (Kircher 97).

And yet, Kircher argues that *Refuge's* position on such dichotomies is more complex: even as Williams seems to reiterate the tired oppositions to patriarchy, she subtly questions the totality of such divisions. For example, she narrates "inappropriate" female behaviors on her part — like performing Mormon blessings traditionally reserved for men, "flipping off" the gun club members, and telling jokes that critique masculinity to her mother and grandmother. Such episodes reveal her misgivings about patriarchal systems, particularly the LDS church, but do not seek to divorce her from those structures. Interestingly, in such situations, Williams' mother always reacts with tolerant surprise at her daughter's audacity, as if she functions on some level to mediate, or even to corral female behavior back into "proper" roles. And yet her more-or-less authoritative position hardly inspires rebellion or resentment from Williams, and the fact that the book narrates the process of her death quietly suggests the passing of this era of femininity.

More significantly, Williams does not seek to *reject* the institutions she critiques; she remains faithful to the Church, for example, even while recognizing its limitations. And her portrayal of masculinity, as Kircher argues, is not simply dismissive, as her male family members and her husband perform nuanced roles that leave masculinity open to question and evolution. Ultimately, Kircher claims that *Refuge* narrates a complex negotiation of cultural tensions that are neither fully upheld nor rejected, leaving room for readers to understand, debate, and conclude as they see fit. In contrast to much nature writing that simplistically pits human against nature, profane against pristine, *Refuge*'s openness to piercing, upholding, or quietly challenging cultural binaries constitutes its most distinctive environmental contribution.— Laura Boynton Johnson

BIBLIOGRAPHY

Chandler, Katherine R. "Whale Song from the Desert: Refuge Without Resolution and Community Without Homogeneity in Terry Tempest Williams's *Refuge*." *Women's Studies* 34 (2005): 655–670.

Kircher, Cassandra. "Rethinking Dichotomies in Terry Tempest Williams's *Refuge*." *ISLE: Interdisciplinary Studies in Literature and Environment* 3.1 (1996): 97–113.

Mitchell, Charles. "Reclaiming the Sacred Landscape: Terry Tempest Williams, Kathleen Norris, and the Other Nature Writing." *Women's Studies* 32 (2003): 165–182.

Riley, Jeannette E. "Finding One's Place in the 'Family of Things': Terry Tempest Williams and a Geography of Self." *Women's Studies* 32 (2003): 585–602.

Williams, Terry Tempest. *Refuge: An Unnatural History of Family and Place.* 1991. New York: Vintage Books, 2001.

Wilson, Edward Osborne (1929–   )

Edward O. Wilson is an expert on ants and a leading evolutionary biologist whose research on habitat ecology, population studies and biodiversity has significantly changed strategies for world conservation. He was born in 1929, in Birmingham, Alabama, and was blinded in one eye as a child, through a fishing accident, which limited his visibility to close-range; yet this very limitation, he maintains, only enhanced his passionate investigation of ants and other small insects. In 1955, after receiving his doctorate in Biology from Harvard, he joined Harvard's faculty, and until 1997 held many prestigious positions, including the Frank B. Baird Professor of Science, the Mellon Professor of Science, and the Pellegrino University Professorship. He has won numerous, international, scientific and conservation awards, chief amongst which is the Royal Swedish Academy's Crafoord Prize which he shared with Paul Ehrlich; he won two Pulitzer Prizes in non-fiction, one for *On Human Nature* (1978) and the other for *The Ants* (1990) which was written in collaboration with Bert Holldobler.

Wilson made a series of important discoveries that significantly expanded the lagging knowledge-base of the biological sciences. Through his study of ants in New Guinea and other islands, he made important discoveries on species equilibrium, and along with ecologist Robert H. McArthur, theorized about biogeography in *The Theory of Island Biogeography* (1967), which is now a standard reference book on ecology. During this time he also made the important discovery that ants and subsequently all insects communicate through pheromones or chemicals.

In 1971, he published *The Insect Societies*, a comprehensive work on social insects. From observing the social behavior of ants, he began theorizing about higher order social species including Homo sapiens, and here his narrower interests attained far more than merely analogical importance to broader environmental questions. Through his 1975 publication, *Sociobiology: The New Synthesis*, he virtually created the new field of sociobiology, wherein he made the controversial claim that the social behavior of humans is also predicated on gene expression. He argued that even what many hold to be the pinnacle of uniquely human goodness, altruism, may also be explained through evolutionary biology: in altruism preservation of the gene pool supersedes the preservation of the individual.

By the late 1970s, Wilson was completely focused on global conservation and in 1984 published *Biophilia*, in which he explored the psychological and evolutionary features of humans' love of nature. In 1992, he published THE DIVERSITY OF LIFE, a seminal primer on the principles of biodiversity and our obligation to conserve Earth's ecosystems. In *Consilience: The Unity of Knowledge* (1998), *The Future of Life* (2002) and *Creation: An Appeal to Save Life on Earth* (2006), he argues for the convergence of all fields of sciences and humanities to meet the urgent challenge of preserving our planet. His autobiography *Naturalist* (2006), and his novel *Anthill* (2010), further evidence Wilson's passionate and skilful commitment to raising consciousness and appreciation of the natural world. Finally, as a naturalist, conservationist and founder of the Biodiversity Foundation, he makes the novel and critical suggestion that instead of expending our energies in the conservation of lone large (and "photogenic") species such as the panda or polar bear, we should focus on preserving complete ecosystems, specifically 20 fragile and vulnerable ecosystems all over the world, whose preservation will maintain minimal levels of biodiversity—with a more lasting effect on our own and the planet's survival.— Sukanya B. Senapati

BIBLIOGRAPHY

"Wilson's Life & Works." *EO Wilson Biodiversity Foundation*. 2011. Available online. Accessed: May 28, 2011. URL: http://www.eowilson.org.

The Diversity of Life, Edward O. Wilson (1992)

The last decade of the twentieth century saw a paradigm shift in conservation discourse through the introduction of the concept of biological diversity or "biodiversity" (THE CONSERVATION MOVEMENT). Edward Wilson, the pioneer in this field, declared that although biodiversity is our most valuable resource, it is the least appreciated and most neglected (281). He claims that biodiversity is absolutely essential for the sustenance of life on earth because when a natural disaster like a storm, earthquake or meteorite collision wipes out life in a local site, enough diversity exists for other similar species to rush in and fill the empty site. These opportunistic species, he claims, evolved against just such calamities, but took millions of years to evolve and thus "have eaten these ... [natural disasters]— folded them into [their] genes — and created the world that created us" (15). Furthermore, he adds, "Millions of years of testing by natural selection have made organisms chemists of superhuman skill, champions at defeating most of the kinds of biological problems that undermine human health" (320).

Wilson notes that to comprehend the impact of biodiversity we have to remember that it happened over vast lengths of geological time, and understand the Energy-Stability-Area Theory of Biodiversity, which posits that diversity is significantly enhanced by solar energy, area and climate stability (199). So the general rule of thumb used in assessing biodiversity extinction is that a 90 percent loss in the area of a habitat causes a 50 percent reduction in the number of species (xviii). Biologists divide biodiversity into

a three-tiered hierarchy: ecosystem, gene and species. An ecosystem is a community of different species of plants, animals and microbes and the habitat they occupy; a gene is a basic unit of heredity; and a species is "a closed gene pool that perpetuates itself in nature" (xii) and "does not exchange genes with other species" (42). However, since the boundaries of ecosystems overlap and genes are hard to identify or count, the species became the unit of measure. Perhaps this hierarchal categorization is the problem, because it focused attention on the species, not on the ecosystem, for to save the species the ecosystem itself must be protected. Nonetheless, 1.5–1.7 million species have been identified, but the total number of species is far from having been identified and counted.

Wilson points out that five major spasms of extinction have occurred naturally during Earth's history, and humans are poised to cause the sixth. Extinction is caused not by just one factor but a combination of many factors, and in the 3.5 billion years of Earth's biological history, 98 percent of the species that once existed have become extinct. Hence, one of the arguments set forth by some policy makers is that we should do nothing and let nature take care of itself. Wilson counters this argument by arguing that we must remember that evolution requires at least 10 million years to restore pre-disaster levels of diversity, and in the meantime if we ourselves wish to survive, we have to preserve the various ecosystems we depend on to clean our water and air, and enrich our soil (xxii).

The major cause of habitat extinction is the explosion of human population, which will peak at 8– 10 billion in the mid-twenty-first century before it stabilizes. This staggering population in turn requires sufficient quantities of food, water, shelter, energy, etc; and the human impact of population on the planet is measured by the "ecological footprint" which determines the amount of land needed to supply each person with this minimal standard of living. While the ecological footprint of a person in a developing nation is half a hectare, that of a U.S. citizen is five hectares, and if all people were to have the same standard of living as those in the U.S., two more entire earths would be required (xi). This problem is further exacerbated by the fact that the stewards of the most diverse and vulnerable ecosystems, like the Amazonian rainforests, are unfortunately among the world's poorest (partly through the colonial rapacity of the rich countries in the past), and hence cannot easily afford to think in terms of long-term effects, goals, or plans.

Wilson says the first thing we have do to address the problem of the rapid loss of biodiversity is to define, accurately and realistically, the environmental problems. According to Wilson there are ultimately only two categories of environmental problems. The first is the alteration of the environment, making it unsupportive to life. This category, which includes pollution, ozone depletion, climate change, etc, can be reversed with collective will. The second, however, is the loss of biodiversity, which cannot be reversed and hence needs top prioritization. The old approach to biodiversity conservation was to close off and guard large stretches of pristine land, which worked to some degree in the U.S., but not in the developing countries. Hence, Wilson exhorts scientists, economists and policy makers to join forces in developing sustainable policies for biodiversity that will help the poor and at the same time save the worlds' remaining ecosystems, for "in a world created by natural selection, homogeneity means vulnerability" (301).

Secondly, to save and sustainably use the biodiversity of the earth, Wilson has come up with four simple steps: (i) survey the world's fauna and flora; (ii) create biological wealth through bio-economic analysis of ecosystems; (iii) promote sustainable development in developing countries through debt forgiveness in exchange for conservation; (iv) save remaining ecosystems rich in biodiversity. To meet the needs of the first step, Wilson calls on scientists to identify, catalogue and classify all organisms in all habitats through a central platform that will speed things up and give us a far more accurate picture of Earth's biodiversity. The second step is for economists to factor in wilderness and living species into financial equations and economic policies. The third step is the most complex, requiring cooperation amongst scientists, economists and policymakers in coming up with population policies, and educating stewards of vulnerable ecosystems to carefully and sustainably mine and preserve the wild lands for nutritional and pharmaceutical products. The last step also demands much cooperation, for it requires the preservation of what still remains. Wilson has identified 18–20 hotspot ecosystems around the world that are rich in biodiversity, and if preserved may save what biodiversity still remains on earth. These hotspots range from whole islands, like Madagascar, Sri Lanka and Philippines, to whole mountain ranges, like the Usambara mountain forests of Tanzania, and the San Bruno Mountains of California, to mere slopes of mountains, like the lower slopes of the Himalayas, and the Western Ghats of India, and other similarly endangered habitats, both underwater and on land.

Finally, Wilson declares that with the creation of the new discipline of biodiversity studies, which is defined as "The systematic study of the full array of organic diversity and the origin of that diversity, to-gether with the methods by which it can be maintained and used for the benefit of humanity," we will be able to educate — and thereby save — ourselves, by properly valuing and protecting the immense contributions of biodiversity to life on Earth (312). — Sukanya B. Senapati

BIBLIOGRAPHY

Wilson, Edward O. *The Diversity of Life.* New York, London: Norton, 1992.

Winthrop, John (1588–1649)

John Winthrop was born in Groton, England in 1588. In contrast to John Bradford's meager beginnings, Winthrop was raised on a prosperous farm. His father bought the land from Henry VIII, which allowed Winthrop to grow up in relative economic advantage. He was educated at Cambridge University and later studied to become a lawyer instead of managing his family's estate. During his time at Cambridge, Winthrop was heavily influenced by the Puritan beliefs held by many students. Unlike the Pilgrims who sailed to America in 1620, however, Winthrop was not a separatist, and sought reform within, rather than without the church. Nonetheless, political pressures influenced Winthrop to seek new opportunities elsewhere. After school, and through the privilege of his upbringing, Winthrop joined the Massachusetts Bay Company, which in 1629 obtained a charter that would allow it to establish a colony in America based on Puritan ideals and theology. According to Puritan scholar Perry Miller, "These Puritans did not flee to America; they went in order to work out that complete reformation which was not yet accomplished in England..." (11). Winthrop was elected governor in the same year, and along with 700 others, sailed to for New England in 1630. Over the span of his life, Winthrop served as Governor or deputy Governor of the Massachusetts Bay Colony on numerous occasions, often in the midst of controversy and political struggle.

Along with his *JOURNAL*, Winthrop's most anthologized work is "A Model of Christian Charity." Scholars disagree as to exactly when Winthrop delivered this his most famous "sermon." It is popularly believed that Winthrop addressed the passengers on the flagship *Arbella* during the voyage west; however, recent scholarship argues that it more likely occurred just before the ship left England's harbors. Regardless, this famous address proposed the religious ideals that would ground and frame this new colony in America — and in many ways, to this day, its vast continental descendant. The organization of the address shows Winthrop's lawyerly training as well as his religious education. Parts of the sermon resemble sixteenth-century catechisms like the Scots Confession (1560), the Heidelberg Catechism (1563), and the Second Helvetic Confession (1566). In this way, Winthrop hoped to teach these Puritans the foundations of the faith and practices that would secure their success in America.

The primary theme of the sermon is Christian charity. Although it is said that Winthrop could be overzealous at times, it is clear that he was committed to teaching the importance of community, selfless living, and harmony. At the beginning of the address, he remarks that "there are two rules whereby wee are to walke one towards another: justice and mercy." Again, he states that "wee must be knit together in this work as one man." Ultimately, he believed ardently that the world would be watching, and ultimately judging, this American "experiment." Readers get the feeling that there was great urgency in Winthrop's sermon, that his hearers would understand the great burdens of establishing a Christian colony in New England. This idea is evident in Winthrop's most famous and widely quoted passage: "For wee must Consider that wee shall be as a Citty upon a hill. The eies of all people are upon Us, so that if wee shall deale falsely with our god in this worke wee have undertaken, and soe cause him to withdrawe his present help from us, wee shall be made a story and a by-word through the world."

Ultimately, these Puritans believed that their migration was divinely inspired; therefore, their new land must be devoted to living out God's mission and acting in Godly ways toward one another: "This duty of mercy is exercised in the kinds, Giving, lending, and forgiving." Not only did Winthrop use this sermon to prepare the hearts and minds of these immigrants, but it also played a significant role in preparing the Puritans for a physical life in the rugged wilderness of the New World. According to J. Baird Callicot and Pricilla S. Ybarra, "The Puritan settlers of New England, steeped in the Old Testament biblical worldview, believed they found themselves in such a 'wilderness condition' of continental proportions. It was their God-ordained destiny to transform the dismal American wilderness into an earthly paradise, governed according to the Word of God" (THE BIBLE). Although scholars usually point to the pejorative descriptors given to the land and the wilderness by Puritan writers, Winthrop's sermon continually calls the "land whither we are going" as good. At one point, he mentions that the wilderness was the place where God chose to speak to David, and not the palaces; suggesting, correctly and significantly, that their "errand into the wilderness" would be as much a physical exodus and trial as spiritual. Winthrop died in Boston in 1649.— Jacob Stratman

BIBLIOGRAPHY

Bremmer, Francis J. *John Winthrop: America's Forgotten Founding Founder*. New York: Oxford University Press, 2005.

Callicott, J. Baird and Priscilla Solis Ybarra. "The Puritan Origins of the American Wilderness Movement." *Wilderness and American Identity* essays. National Humanities Center. http://nationalhumanitiescenter.org/tserve/nattrans/ntwilderness/essays/puritan.htm. July 2001.

Miller, Perry. *Errand into the Wilderness*. New York: Harper Torchbooks, 1956.

Morgan, Edmund. *The Puritan Dilemma: The Story of John Winthrop*. New York: Little, Brown, 1958.

The Journal of John Winthrop 1630–1649, John Winthrop

John Winthrop's *Journal* recounts the beginnings of the Massachusetts Bay Colony up until a short time before the author's death. As Daniel Phillippon states in his survey of pre-twentieth century American environmental literature, colonial authors, in contrast to promotional writers like THOMAS HARRIOT, "show a much greater interest in and sensitivity to the nonhuman environment, both because their survival depended on it and because they hoped their detailed descriptions would encourage more Europeans to emigrate" (129). Winthrop's attention to the environment, much like WILLIAM BRADFORD's in OF PLYMOUTH PLANTATION, is focused primarily on issues of survival and, ultimately, the fledgling colony's sustenance and growth. There is, however, very little direct naturalistic description of the environment. Winthrop only notes extreme weather, storms, and earthquakes almost solely in relation to their effect on crops. Richard S. Dunn argues that, due to the fact that the servants sent ahead in 1628–9 failed to sufficiently prepare for the arrival of the colonists, Winthrop had little leisure to record the initial struggle to establish a foothold in America. Yet, as Dunn states, Winthrop,

> would never have described the physical process of settlement [...] for he always excluded such mundane matters from his personal correspondence and his journal. And he had his reasons for silence on many other issues. The journal was a semipublic statement by the leader of the colony, and in the crisis months of 1630 he reported nothing that might get him in trouble with his fellow colonists or with the company at home or with Charles I's government [194].

While we certainly lament the lack of "mundane" detail in the first year of the *Journal*, the second reason Dunn provides is evident throughout the work. The colony consistently punished anyone sending back adverse reports to England regarding either the colony's difficulties or for the land's inability to sustain such an enterprise. But the colony did survive, by exploiting the natural resources for its sustenance and in order to pay off the debts it incurred, ultimately establishing an agrarian settlement that allowed the colonists to practice their religion, as well as maintain and expand their colony. This had much broader economic and environmental consequences.

In terms of agrarianism, the landscape itself was significantly altered. We should note, however, that the environment in which the colony was established was not untouched nature. What they met with had already been transformed by centuries of Native habitation. The most obvious of these transformations was corn, which quickly became a key component of the English colonists' survival in an unfamiliar environment, providing both sustenance and a tradable commodity. Incorporating corn into the English agrarian settlement brought about much more significant environmental markers of human habitation than that of Native corn production, particularly when coupled with the other crops that were introduced and, especially, domestic livestock. As William Cronon states,

> Domesticated grazing mammals — and the tool which they made possible, the plow — were arguably the single most distinguishing characteristic of European agricultural practices [...]. The effects of that control ramified through most aspects of New England's rural economy, and by the end of the colonial period were responsible for a host of changes in the New England landscape: the seemingly endless miles of fences, the silenced voices of wolves, the system of country roads, and the new fields filled with clover, grass, and buttercups [128].

Ploughs, fences, and domestic animals are only the most obvious physical manifestations of how the landscape was transformed by the colonists. While these innovations had the obvious effect of displacing the Native peoples of Massachusetts Bay and introduced the mostly (and critically) alien notion of private property, the possession implied by fencing fields, for example, is also evident in the renaming of the landscape by the English settlers. While the English "most frequently created arbitrary place-names which either recalled localities in their homeland or gave a place the name of its owner, the Indians used ecological labels to describe how the land might be used" (Cronon 66). Cronon recognizes that there are exceptions that suggest a form of possession in Native place names, but his point is valid. In Winthrop's *Journal* the switch from a Native ecological place-name to an entirely arbitrary one is ap-

parent. For example, "Agawam" — "fish curing place" (Dunn and Yeandle 28) — was renamed for an English city, Ipswich. On a trip along the Charles River in 1632, the names given to places reveal both an ecological and a possessive purpose: a brook with a lot of beaver dams is named Beaver Brook, while a rock formation is named Adam's Chair for Winthrop's young son; a second rock formation is named Mount Feake for "one Robert Feake who had married the governor's daughter-in-law" (Winthrop 43). Not only did settlers replace Native geographical names, but they also renamed sites to distinguish them from other Europeans. The one curious example of this in the *Journal* is "Hues Crosse," which seemed too Catholic to the Puritans, as such a place name "might hereafter give the papists occasion to say that their religion was first planted in these parts." Hence, the name is appropriately, from a Puritan perspective, changed to "Hues Follye" (Winthrop 52) — all evidence of the earth's fundamental (and female) "impressibility" in the face of man's Biblically inspired "dominion" (THE BIBLE).

Though "Hues Follye" is a rather ridiculous example of colonial competition (and a profound example of colonial inscription), the colony faced more serious challenges from other European colonial powers, as well as other English colonies. In 1633, for example, both the Dutch West Indies Company and the Massachusetts Bay Colony charters claimed the Connecticut River. The English, Dutch, and French competed for beaver furs, often entering into shifting alliances with various Native groups. Economic need drove the colonists: "the need to find commodities that would repay debts to European merchants. In this sense, Europeans took hold of the traditional maize-fur trade network and transformed it from a system of binary village exchange to a link in the new Atlantic economy" (Cronon 94), a transformation whose considerable extent is evidenced by a 1634 entry claiming that the Dutch are getting about nine or ten thousand beaver skins a year at the Hudson River (Winthrop 69). Clearly, this moved the fur trade far beyond the Native people's need into the rapacious demands of the larger Atlantic economy. This included not only trade between the colony and England, but also between the New England colonies and the West Indies for corn, livestock, and African slaves, who are first noted in Winthrop's *Journal* in the 1630s.

The introduction of European diseases also furthered the colonists' appropriation of both Native trade networks and land. Much like the war with the Pequots in 1636–7, the decimation of Native social structures by disease easily allowed the Europeans to step into the broken links of the trade system and vacated lands. While European diseases had already affected the Native population in New England since first contact, the high mortality from smallpox that Winthrop recorded in the winter of 1633–4 was so extensive that it negatively impacted trade: some Natives, Winthrop writes, "informed us that the smallpox was gone as far as any Indian plantation was known to the W[est], and much people dead of it, by reason whereof they could have no trade" (63). This outbreak of smallpox ironically coincided with pressures within the colony for more land from the people of Newtown, Ipswich, Watertown, and Roxbury: "The occasion of their desire to remove was for that all towns in the Bay began to be much straitened by their o'er nearness one to another, and their cattle being so much increased" (Winthrop 81). Like Bradford, Winthrop lamented the separation that would result from expansion, but it was, in both the case of the Plymouth and Massachusetts Bay Colony, a result of their successful adaptation to and exploitation of a radically a new environment.— Jim Daems

BIBLIOGRAPHY

Cronon, William. *Changes in the Land: Indians, Colonists, and the Ecology of New England.* New York: Hill & Wang, 1983.

Dunn, Richard S. "John Winthrop Writes His Journal." *The William and Mary Quarterly* 41.2 (Apr. 1984). 185–212.

_____, and Laetitia Yeandle, eds. *The Journal of John Winthrop, 1630–1649.* Abridged edition. Cambridge, MA: Belknap Press, 1996.

Phillippon, Daniel. "United States Environmental Literature before the Twentieth Century." *Teaching North American Environmental Literature.* Ed. Laird Christensen, Mark C. Long, and Fred Waage. New York: Modern Language Association of America, 2008. 126–38.

Winthrop, John. *The Journal of John Winthrop, 1630–1649.* Abridged edition. Eds. Richard S. Dunn and Laetitia Yeandle. Cambridge, MA: Belknap Press, 1996.

Wright, Richard (1908–1960)

As a leading practitioner of literary naturalism, Richard Wright was deeply concerned with the shaping role of the physical environment. Though Wright is not typically classified as a "nature writer," his work displays a striking awareness of human/nonhuman relationships and is now becoming recognized as a cornerstone of African-American environmental justice literature.

Due to the popularity of his great Chicago novel, *Native Son* (1940), Wright may be considered a primarily urban writer. However, his origins were thoroughly rural. He was born on Rucker's Plantation, near the hamlet of Roxie, Mississippi, in a log cabin that he described as "too far back in the woods to hear the train whistle" (Wallach 9). His grandparents had been field slaves on the plantation, and his parents struggled as sharecroppers in the post–Reconstruction South. Though Wright's family left the countryside when he was only a few years old, the influence of the southern landscape and rural culture can be overtly seen in his short story collection, *Uncle Tom's Children* (1938), in his autobiographical novel of childhood, *Black Boy* (1945), and in his nonfiction study *12 Million Black Voices* (1941).

In the opening pages of *Black Boy*, Wright describes the beauty and fertility of the farm in lyrical, almost romantic, terms. However, as Scott Hicks argues, Wright goes on to "denaturalize" and "defamiliarize" this optimistic pastoral, as he links southern agrarian life to the bare facts of racist violence and economic exploitation (213). In the stories of *Uncle Tom's Children*, for example, the wilderness is a space where lynchings occur, where floods destroy the houses of the poor, and where vicious dogs hunt runaways. By blending these two impulses — a sensitivity toward nature, with an awareness that nature imagery is itself implicated in oppression — Wright's work exemplifies what LEO MARX called the "complex pastoral," an ambivalent and multidimensional portrait of agricultural society (Hicks 214) (American Pastoral).

In the 1930s Wright moved to Chicago, where he became involved in leftist politics, read widely, and worked various jobs, including a stint as a city guidebook editor for Works Progress Administration, a position which brought him into contact with environmental justice struggles over housing and sanitation. During this period Wright was also influenced by, and in turn influenced, the Chicago School sociologists, who used biological metaphors to describe urban social organization. While not "ecological" in a contemporary sense, these thinkers induced Wright to consider the role of physical space as an active, determining agent in his fiction. Urban environmental justice themes come to the fore in Wright's best-known work, *Native Son*, particularly in the depiction of the dangerous, unsanitary, and famously rat-infested tenement building that shelters the protagonist's family.

Wright lived the final years of his life as an expatriate in France, where he spent time at a farmhouse in the village of Ailly, enjoyed tending a garden, and turned to composing the haiku, later published as *HAIKU: THIS OTHER WORLD* (1998), which weaves together a lifetime of environmental awareness and reflection. It is in these seventeen-syllable poems, suggests Lisa Woolley, that Wright achieved his most sophisticated treatment of the nonhuman world, moving from a depiction of animals as mere symbols and plot devices, to a grasp of individual animal life

in all its concrete and compelling particularity.—
Tristan Sipley

BIBLIOGRAPHY

Buell, Lawrence. *Writing for an Endangered World: Litera-
ture, Culture, and Environment in the U.S. and Beyond.*
Cambridge, MA: Belknap Press of Harvard University
Press, 2001.

Dixon, Melvin. *Ride out the Wilderness: Geography and
Identity in Afro-American Literature.* Urbana: University
of Illinois Press, 1987: 56–82.

Geilern, Monika. "Of Parasites and Humans: Encounters
with Nature in Richard Wright's *Native Son* and Charles
Johnson's *Dreamer*." *Restoring the Connection to the Natural World: Essays on the African American Environmental
Imagination.* Ed. Sylvia Mayer. New Brunswick: Transaction, 2003: 97–115.

Hicks, Scott. "W. E. B. Du Bois, Booker T. Washington,
and Richard Wright: Toward an Ecocriticism of Color."
Callaloo 29.1 (Winter 2006): 202–222.

Taylor, David A. *Soul of a People: The WPA Writers' Project
Uncovers Depression America.* Hoboken: Wiley, 2009.

Wallach, Jennifer Jensen. *Richard Wright: From Black Boy
to World Citizen.* Library of African-American Biography. Chicago: Ivan R. Dee, 2010.

Woolley, Lisa. "Richard Wright's Dogged Pursuit of His
Place in the Natural World." *Interdisciplinary Studies in
Literature and Environment* 15.1 (Winter 2008): 175–188.

Wright, Richard. *Black Boy.* 1945. Perennial Classics. New
York: HarperCollins, 1998.

_____. *Haiku: This Other World.* Ed. Yoshinobu Hakutani
and Robert L. Tener. New York: Arcade, 1998.

_____. *Native Son.* 1940. Perennial Classics. New York:
HarperCollins, 1998.

_____. *12 Million Black Voices: A Folk History of the Negro
in the United States.* New York: Viking Press, 1941. Rpt.
in *Richard Wright Reader.* Ed. Ellen Wright and Michael
Fabre. New York: Harper & Row, 1978: 144–241.

_____. *Uncle Tom's Children.* 1938. New York: Harper-
Collins, 1993.

Haiku: This Other World,
Richard Wright (1998)

In their poetry, ancient haiku masters expressed
reverence for nature and the need for humans to live
in harmony with the natural world to achieve an understanding of their rightful place in the universal
order. During the last 18 months of his life, Richard
Wright wrote more than 4,000 traditional haiku, and
Julia Wright suggests that these poems kept her father
"spiritually afloat" because they operated as "self-de-
veloped antidotes against illness," provided closure
as he mourned the death of his mother and several
friends, and "enabled him to reach out to the black
boy part of himself still stranded in a South that continued to live in his dreams" (viii–xi). *Haiku: This
Other World,* published in 1998, is a collection of 817
of these haiku that Wright himself selected and
arranged, and in this collection Wright repeatedly
engages nature as a source of expression, identity,
and spirituality.

Wright's haiku illustrates the vital and irreplaceable power of nature as a medium to express feeling
and thought. In their afterword to *Haiku: This Other
World,* Yoshinobu Hakutani and Robert L. Tener explain that although many of the classic Zen haiku
masters attempted to avoid the expression of emotion
and intellect in their poetry, "haiku is nonetheless
concerned with one's feeling and thought" and that
"[i]f haiku conveys the poet's feeling, that feeling
must have been aroused by nature" (265). They add
that to express emotion and thought "the poet needs
to look straight at things and to transform the perception into words that do not depend upon metaphors or symbols" (276). An example of Wright's objective representation of perception is in haiku 64 as
he juxtaposes contrasting details from nature to express the complexities of the joy and grief created by
living and dying:

> The harbor at dawn:
> The faint scent of oranges
> On gusts of March wind.

At the surface level this haiku might be read as an
optimistic forecast of oncoming spring or a praise of
absent beauty, but such cheerful interpretations are
complicated by nature's ambivalent imagery. Dawn
implies a new beginning, but this new reality might
be loneliness, poverty, or death. The scent of oranges
suggests beauty, warmth, and life, but the speaker is
far moved from the oranges' place of origin. The
March wind carries a sweet aroma, but these are the
gusts of an often cruel and bitter month tottering
between winter and spring. As narrator, Wright may
sense a new beginning, but in real life he was
suffering in self-exile from his native land, mourning
recent deaths of several people who were emotionally
close to him, and suffering from an illness that would
soon take his life; he had little reason to believe he
would experience the happiness implied by the
images of distant joy and beauty.

Imagery drawn from the natural world consistently
teaches that humans are merely sojourners in this
world, fated to experience loss, sorrow, and death.
This version of human identity is evidenced by nature's infinite reminders of time's passage and death's
inevitability, such as the setting sun, melting snow,
clouds blown before the wind, a rotting log, fallen
leaves, and a frozen lake. Wright's observation of a
snowflake in haiku 37 brilliantly summarizes the brief
and vain struggles of human life:

> Past the window pane
> A solitary snowflake
> Spins furiously.

The window pane suggests the time frame of
human life on earth, the lone, spinning snowflake

suggests human attempts to embrace this fleeting life, and the accumulated snow suggests the whole of humanity that came before this flake, and the mysterious and continuous cycle of being.

Haiku 39 expresses some of the same sentiments:

> A soft wind at dawn
> Lifts one dry leaf and lays it
> Upon another.

In this poem the final page of earthly existence is turned by a soft wind at the dawn of a new life, and the dry leaf of the spent life is cast among the hordes of dry leaves.

Wright's haiku also demonstrate that as nature reveals the temporal nature of human life, it also offers meaning and comfort. Hakutani and Tener state that as the 1950s came to a close, Wright was "in an ambivalent mood, ready for union with that which lies beyond the artist" (269). The nature with which Wright sought union was an immortal force that, as is shown in haiku 764, welcomed and embraced humans at the conclusion of their worldly trials:

> The oaken coffin,
> Between the porch and the car,
> Was christened by snow.

This haiku depicts the mortal human body encased in an oaken vessel wrought from nature, and this vessel and its contents are welcomed and blessed by immortal and omniscient nature, as is implied by the sprinkling of the white, pure snow. Haiku 733 provides an image of the continuance of life following death and burial:

> In a dank basement
> A rotting sack of barley
> Swells with sprouting grain.

In its dank grave the old self is generating new life, and soul or spirit is blossoming out of the ruined body.

Hakutani and Tener point out that Wright engaged the motifs of nature throughout his writings (266), and that his "haiku reveal more clearly than his great novels or polemical tracts his sympathetic awareness of the complex relationship between people and nature — that a person needs to know *where* he or she is going, *when* one will reach the destination, and *what* one will be when that happens" (294). The dependency upon nature expressed in these haiku implies that the human species, which is gaining ever more power to destroy its environment, must realize that any diminishment of nature is a diminishment of human expression, identity, and spirituality, and that if a healthy environment is not allowed to exist there will be no future *where* or *when* humans can choose *what* they wish to become. — Phillip Howerton

BIBLIOGRAPHY

Hakutani, Yoshinobu, and Robert L. Tener. "Afterword." *Haiku: This Other World*. New York: Anchor Books, 1998. 245–300.

Wright, Julia. "Introduction." *Haiku: This Other World*. Ed. Yoshinobu Hakutani and Robert L. Tener. New York: Anchor Books, 1998, vii–xiv.

Wright, Richard. *Haiku: This Other World*. Ed. Yoshinobu Hakutani and Robert L. Tener. New York: Anchor Books, 1998

Index